Christian Ethics

Christian Ethics

Problems and Prospects

EDITED BY

Lisa Sowle Cahill
and James F. Childress

The Pilgrim Press
Cleveland, Ohio

The Pilgrim Press, Cleveland, Ohio 44115

© 1996 by Lisa Sowle Cahill and James F. Childress

Printed in the United States of America on acid-free paper

01 00 99 98 97 96   5 4 3 2 1

Library of Congress Cataloging-in-Publication Data

Christian ethics : problems and prospects / edited by Lisa Sowle
    Cahill and James F. Childress.
        p.   cm.
    Includes bibliographical references and index.
    ISBN 0-8298-1136-2 (alk. paper)
    1. Christian ethics.   2. Religious ethics.   3. Social ethics.
BJ1251.C498   1996
241—dc21   96-39058
                                                       CIP

Contents

Preface

These essays have been collected in honor of James Gustafson, who taught all of the authors, and directed most of their dissertations, either at Yale (1955–1972) or Chicago (1972–1988). The reader will note immediately that the essays are not focused on Gustafson's own writings, though references to him occur throughout the volume at a rate commensurate with his stature in the field of twentieth-century theological ethics. That fact reflects Gustafson's own skill and style as a mentor and teacher. It was always a matter of principle to him to refrain from assigning his own writings to students in courses; much less would he ever have demanded that we fit into a theological mold that would mark us as his intellectual progeny. One of Jim Gustafson's greatest talents as a teacher is his ability to project sympathetically the worldviews of theological "greats" as different as Aquinas and Calvin, Rahner and Barth, the Niebuhrs and Yoder. He taught each of us to appreciate the best our own traditions have to offer, while accepting criticism and enlargement from a variety of other Christian standpoints. He prepared us to engage a plurality of voices within our ancient, common heritage, while never giving up either on the idea that some expressions of Christianity are more authentic than others or on dialectical engagement with philosophy and science in a common search for truth.

Currently the Henry Luce Professor of Humanities and Comparative Studies at Emory University, James Moody Gustafson was born in 1925, and raised in the Swedish immigrant community of an iron-ore mining town in Michigan's Upper Peninsula, to which his father referred as "God's Country." Gustafson's boyhood left lasting impressions both of the cultural particularity of the Christian churches and of the magnificence of nature, through which may be perceived something of the divine. After a tour of duty in India and Burma during the Second World War, he married Louise Roos, graduated from Northwestern University, and pursued ministerial studies and ordination in the Congregational Church. He holds a B.D. from the Federated Theological Faculty of the University of Chicago and Chicago Theological Seminary, and a Ph.D. from Yale University. He is an ordained minister in the United Church of Christ.

His war experiences and his years as a young pastor heightened Gustafson's sensitivity to human suffering and confirmed the depth of cultural differences. His convictions that religion is a dimension of human experience, occasioned by nature and not limited to institutional channels, and that it is deeply affective and not wholly amenable to rationalistic explanation, found theological resonance in the Reformed tradition. John Calvin, Jonathan Edwards, and his own mentor at Yale, H. Richard Niebuhr, remain among the important benchmarks for James Gustafson's work, even as he has drawn increasingly on the social and natural sciences to offer strong critiques of traditional Christianity (as in *Ethics from a Theocentric Perspective*, 2 vols., 1981–1984).

The structure of this collection reflects Gustafson's consistent concern in writing and teaching with a critical interaction at the foundational level among scripture, tradition, philosophy, human experience, and the natural and social sciences, and well as with the importance of making method cash out in the practical moral life. At both of these levels, and as demonstrated particularly in the work he has done over the years in bioethics, his ecumenical interests have always been prominent.

The contributors to this volume differ widely in their theological perspectives. We represent Roman Catholicism and Protestantism about as evenly as we represent Yale and Chicago, and while some of us are interested in establishing common ground among religious traditions and various realms of secular discourse, others are more concerned to express clearly the distinctive differences that religious commitment makes.

When most of us studied with Gustafson two or three decades ago, the burning methodological question which he significantly clarified was the nature and function of moral norms. U.S. theologians and colleagues of Gustafson, including Paul Ramsey, Richard McCormick, Charles Curran, and John Howard Yoder, debated whether scripture provides norms; whether Christian moral norms are unique or, more cautiously, "distinctive"; and how biblical, religious, and theological norms may move, if at all, into the public realm. In bioethics, sexual ethics, economic and political ethics, it could be difficult to see how specifically religious contributions could be brought to bear in a way helpful and convincing to those debating "secular" ethics and policy. Conversely, it was easy to see how norms could be developed without any specifically religious content or backing at all. Thus, theological ethicists faced not only the task of showing in public how and why they made sense, but also of convincing their interlocutors that they had something to say that was theologically important as well as relevant.

Now the regnant "postmodern" mood in philosophy and theology has undermined the traditional truth claims of theological ethics, as well as its confidence that reasonable social consensus can be reached among traditions and even across cultures. Theologians' interest in distinctive Christian identity, particularity, and community has been heightened. On the one hand, many have rediscovered a certain culturally relative streak in theological ethics, evident even in Gustafson's early book, *Treasure in Earthen Vessels* (1961). On the other hand, many have renewed their commitment to the discovery of a common morality, able to sponsor practical action on global problems such as international conflicts, human rights, and the environment. The latter may take their lead from Gustafson's own appeals to common human experiences of God and nature, scientific interpretations of the human and natural worlds, and environmental responsibility, which he rendered so engagingly in *A Sense of the Divine: The Natural Environment from a Theocentric Perspective* (1994). The tension between particularity and universality in ethics, expressed in attempts to balance the irreducibility of Christian commitment and the importance.of public discourse yielding joint moral ventures, is a key and pervasive theme of this collection.

We asked contributors to set out the "state of the question" on a given topic in religious ethics, identifying the current issues and positions they consider to be most significant or problematic, and then developing a constructive argument or answer. Hence, the volume as a whole provides an overview of major contested areas in Christian ethics, while indicating some possible ways out of each impasse.

Beyond our theological and ecclesial diversity, we Gustafson students are, above all, imbued with a personal loyalty to our mentor exceeded only by what we have experienced as his paternal and professional loyalty to us. Jim's combination of unyielding theological integrity and personal and pastoral humility make him a critic and a defender of Christianity whom we do well to emulate, as well as a teacher with whom we can only hope to compare. We offer the following chapters as a fulfillment of the theological trajectory on which he set us: Critically appropriate Christian traditions; be theologically rigorous and intellectually courageous; take the challenges of the modern world and its knowledge seriously; and be responsible to the human experiences of God in the midst of sinfulness, suffering, compassion, friendship, and hope.

Lisa Sowle Cahill
James F. Childress

Part 1

Shaping Theological Ethics

Chapter 1

The Bible and Christian Moral Practices

LISA SOWLE CAHILL

Scripture is most relevant to the Christian life at the level of establishing basic communal practices, instead of in formulating specific rules for action. Historical information about early Christianity is valuable in defining an analogous shape for Christian communities today. In contrast to some current uses of historical Jesus research, however, I understand Jesus' expectation of the transcendent reign of God to be integral to the moral meaning of his teaching and life, and an important premise of theological ethics. And yet, the first Christians carved out their moral identity in an interactive and symbiotic relation with cultural wisdom, not in communitarian insulation from non-Christian values. Use of the Bible in ethics today may likewise profit from sensitive and nuanced incorporation of insights from philosophy, the sciences, other religious traditions, and common human experience.

How Is Scripture a Moral Guide?

The Bible is a diverse collection of works by different authors, spanning centuries, and written in many historical settings for different immediate purposes. There are gaps, repetitions, changes, inconsistencies, and even immoralities in the biblical narratives. Yet the faith communities that have collected and passed on these traditions see the narratives as mediating the self-revelation of a God to whom believers are invited to respond. People of faith have always reinterpreted the Bible in reappropriating it. Its diversity offers a richness of models for faith and practice. Biblical interpretation is crucial for Christian ethics, as Christians discern what the Bible means morally in their own lives, in their own cultural settings, and in relation to their own special circumstances, especially their experience of God as handed on in the community of faith itself and as renewed or tested in light of present events.[1]

This historical process has important consequences for ethics. First, the Bible is authoritative for churches whose members have a number of overlapping identities (cultural, political, familial), providing multiple understandings of themselves and their world. Reading the Bible is thus an activity that relies on interdependent resources, such as Christian traditions, various philosophical influences, one's own personal or cultural experience, and understandings of human experience and the world in general, as made available by the physical and social sciences.[2]

Second, the Bible cannot be treated as a direct source of timeless moral rules. Biblical authors were interested in the virtues or conduct that would best express fidelity to God for their own communities; our circumstances may be different and may demand different responses. General biblical directives like the ten commandments ("Thou shalt not kill"), or Jesus' instruction to love both our neighbors and enemies, are of perennial relevance, but they must be applied anew in every age. More specific instructions, like Jesus' prohibition of divorce (Matt. 5:31–32, 19:9; Mark 10:11–12; Luke 16:18) or Paul's qualified permission of it (1 Cor. 7:10–11, 12–16), are relevant to the degree that the circumstances Jesus or Paul addressed are comparable to ours.[3] Moreover, later Christians confront moral quandaries never envisioned by the biblical authors, and must develop the implications of biblical faith and community for those problems.

A third, more critical, consequence of the Bible's internal pluralism and historical development is the possibility that some teachings, themes, or texts simply cannot be reappropriated constructively, in any form, by the believing community today. Perhaps they must be rejected as nonrevelatory, nonauthoritative, and even destructive of an authentic relationship to God or to Jesus' fundamental message. Some of the Bible's moral teachings are offensive to the Christian view of a compassionate, redeeming God. Examples are biblical acceptance of slavery, in both the Old and New Testaments; violence, wars, and genocide commanded by God; and the patriarchal organization of family, society, and church.

The question whether everything in the canon must retained as scripture for the church is complicated. Some authors highlight certain biblical themes as most central to the gospel to develop a line of criticism internal to the canon itself.[4] They may also acknowledge that while one meaning or effect of the text which has prevailed in Christian interpretation cannot be accepted as authoritative, the text taken at some other level can still be instructive. For example, Sandra Schneiders, a feminist biblical scholar, rejects the idea that texts commanding submission of women are authoritative as such.[5] Yet she draws on more egalitarian or liberating texts to reconform Christian conceptions of gender roles.[6] She also points out that even texts that fail to embody Jesus' message of inclusion and equality can teach us that either the biblical communities or we ourselves may have a valid insight about the nature of faith and yet come up with a wrong application which needs to be revised. For instance, Paul proclaimed that baptism overcomes differences of race, gender, and social status (Gal. 3:27–29), and addressed women leaders in the churches he founded (e.g., Prisca [Rom. 16] and Chloe [1 Cor. 1]). Yet he still tried to limit women's participation in worship, and acceded to cultural ideas that women should be submissive to their husbands.[7] Paul's fallibility on the roles of women and other specifics can be understood in relation to his cultural circumstances and his limitations as a human apostle and author. Yet his basic message of faith and of unity in the Christian life is a trustworthy rendition of the gospel. At the moral level, Paul teaches us that Christian community must try to engage with culture, whatever the difficulties and dangers of so doing; and that weakness and wrongness in the results we produce must not discourage commitment in a context of ongoing self-criticism and reform.

These introductory remarks have been intended to show that relating scripture to ethics is a complex interpretive process. Biblical texts as literary units, their place in the entire Bible or "canon," our own situation, and the situations of the authors and communities that adapted biblical accounts over time, are all relevant.

Although each of the many aspects and multiple theories of biblical interpretation is deserving of further development, I want to concentrate on one type of biblical criticism which has gained considerable prominence in the past few decades, and which seems especially pertinent to Christian ethics. I refer to the use of social history and sociology. Interpretation using these methods seeks to understand the communities that produced the Bible and to clarify what impact biblical portrayals of God might have had in their original settings. On the one hand, this is a descriptive task. But descriptions of the first Christians can contribute to normative ethics by allowing us to see what their interpretation of discipleship in light of the gospel meant in practice. Even if not every moral command in the New Testament is relevant today, we can still aim to form communities whose moral practices, though different in some aspects, embody the "reign of God" in recognizably similar ways.

The Bible illustrates specific ways in which the first Christians embodied a transformed way of life. The basic contours of the gospel—the kingdom or reign of God as preached by Jesus, and the presence of the risen Jesus to the community of faith—have fundamental and radical moral implications. It is true that specific rules concerning sex, gender, violence, government, or economics may have been aimed at extinct cultural settings, thereby rendering the rules not directly applicable today. Yet such rules may also represent challenges to the social order and its standard ways of structuring human relationships according to status hierarchies and dominance. The basic social stance they illustrate is relevant to and authoritative for all Christian communities. Christian ethics seeks contemporary practices whose function is *analogous* to the destabilizing effect of early Christianity on patterns of social relationship.[8] Sociology and social history can shed light on the moral and social effects of Christian conversion in the first century. (Although the present essay will treat the New Testament, similar research has also been done on the Old Testament.)[9]

The remainder of this essay will address three questions: What are the methods or tools scholars use to study the Bible? (The emphasis here will be on new types of historical research on the first Christians.) What do we know when we study the Bible—how do we come to know God in and through the Bible? (The emphasis will be on Jesus' preaching of the reign of God, his ministry in first-century context, and inferences about the experience of God in Jesus as disclosed by New Testament depictions of Jesus' teaching and actions.) How does what we know about God through the Bible shape Christian identity and community? (The emphasis will be on the correlation of traditions about Jesus, cultural practices and moral understandings, and concrete moral dilemmas, with a focus on the Pauline churches.)

What Are Methods of Biblical Interpretation?

The late nineteenth and early twentieth centuries saw the rise of a historical-critical approach to the Bible, inspired by modern scientific method, the derivative goal of "objective historiography," and historical and archeological discoveries, which allowed comparison of Israel with other ancient cultures.[10] Historical critical research has an affinity with traditional interest in the "literal" sense of the Bible, in that it investigates the original meaning of the biblical texts to their creators, and functions as a brake on theological interpretation—whether traditionalist or novel—that bears little resemblance to that meaning.[11] Some of the concerns of historical criticism are the authorship of and process of editing behind texts; the occasions of and purposes behind texts; their literary style or form, which is dependent on and revealing of their audiences and purposes (e.g., prayer, liturgical formula, aphorism or saying, letter); and the influences of other cultural traditions with which the authors of texts might have been familiar.[12] The sometimes "deconstructive" tone and connotations of both historical-critical and social research on the Bible are due not so much to the methods themselves as to modern infatuation with "objective" science, the modern (and postmodern) mistrust of transcendence and of all authorities, and the valuing of active, constructive approaches to human knowledge and to reality itself.[13]

Social history and sociology, which gained prominence in the 1970s, likewise investigate the social settings of biblical authors and communities, how texts emerged out of and functioned within those settings, and how and why different authors and communities may have adapted similar materials differently for distinct purposes.[14] Social history describes the specific social conditions, organization, history, or worldview of given communities in antiquity,[15] while sociology and anthropology provide models to understand how human societies are organized or function in general. These models enable scholars to make hypotheses about the dynamics of ancient Israelite, Greco-Roman, or early Christian societies.[16] These two methods can be used in combination.

Social description of early Christianity, interpreted partly with the use of sociological models, has concentrated on several factors which are extremely pertinent to ethics.

These include its *Jewish* background: purity observance; the relation between the religious leadership and ordinary Jews, both peasant and urban; Jewish political movements under Roman rule; wisdom traditions; apocalyptic traditions; and traditions of care for the poor. They also include factors in the *Greco-Roman* milieu: the dynamics of honor-shame societies; patron-client relations in the "embedded" economy of the ancient world; the social function of the patriarchal family; and the ways in which Hellenistic philosophy criticized the culture of its day, and presented alternate moral ideals or virtues.[17]

What Do We Know When We Study the Bible?

One of the most important themes of historical research on the Bible—one reemphasized by social history—is that the center of Jesus' ministry was the imminent reign or "kingdom" of God.[18] Mark's Gospel portrays Jesus' ministry as beginning when he "came to Galilee proclaiming the gospel of God: 'This is the time of fulfillment. The reign of God is at hand. Repent, and believe in the gospel'" (1:14). Jesus not only preached about the approaching reign of God. He also demonstrated its power and presence by his healings, exorcisms, and association with "sinners" and other social outcasts.

Jesus' Jewish identity is important background to his announcement of God's reign. The prophets and psalms had referred to God as king and to God's kingly rule. Sometimes the dominion of God was associated with the Israelite kingdom or the Davidic monarchy (1 Chron. 28:5), but it usually had a broader sense in which the whole history of Israel was recapitulated: God's creation of the universe, liberation of God's chosen people from slavery in Egypt, the reign of David, Israel's sin and eventual fall despite the prophets' warnings, Israel's exile into Babylon, the destruction of Jerusalem, the promise of a future restoration of Jerusalem and the temple, the conquest of the gentiles, and the reestablishment among human beings of God's eternal rule, manifest in mighty deeds (Ps. 145:11–13; Ps. 17:32–38). Sometimes a human agent or intermediary was envisioned as instrumental in the culmination of this process (e.g., the "Son of Man" [Dan. 7; Enoch 46, 48]). Eschatological and apocalyptic interpretations of the kingdom became more influential after the Romans gained control over Palestine around 60 B.C.E. Under foreign domination, it was difficult for Jews to see God's reign directly reflected in their present circumstances, and difficult to expect that an independent Jewish line of monarchs, Jerusalem, or the temple could be reestablished by political or revolutionary means. It became easier to anticipate that God would intervene directly in history in some dramatic and definitive way, even bringing the end of history as we know it.[19] Jesus made the reign of God much more central in his ministry than it had been in Jewish tradition; in fact, he used this image as a symbolic nexus for his most important and transformative insights.

It is widely accepted that God's reign for Jesus entailed a reversal of worldly values, including an upset of standard social and religious criteria of worthiness and acceptability. "Jesus proclaimed the loving forgiveness of God the Father, a prodigal [parent] who freely bestows . . . forgiveness on sinners who have no strict claim on God's mercy (see, e.g., the parables of the prodigal son, the lost coin, the lost sheep, the unmerciful servant, the great supper, the two debtors, the rich man and Lazarus, and the Pharisee and the publican.)"[20] God cares for those who are in need, whether or not they are especially deserving or virtuous. Disciples are to imitate God's mercy and compassion, to forgive enemies, and to give freely to others, even at disproportionate personal cost. (See the Sermon on the Mount in Matthew 5–7, the Sermon on the Plain in Luke 6, and the parable of the Good Samaritan in Luke 10.) God's reign is entered by those who see and live in a new way. This has profound immediate consequences for personal relationships, and correspondingly profound implications for the social practices in which such relationships are set: economy, family, politics, and religious observance.

During his lifetime, Jesus had a well-attested reputation for associating and sharing meals, not only with the poor and the social underclass, but with "toll collectors"[21] and "sinners" (Matt. 11:18–19, cf. Luke 13:28–29, 14:12–14), who in Jewish eyes were not living according to God's law (i.e., nonobservant Jews). He was not hesitant to suggest that followers might have to choose between God and family loyalties (Mark 3:35, Matt. 23:8–9). He challenged male authority over wives by forbidding divorce (Mark 10:2–9, 10–12; Luke 16:18; Matt. 5:31–32), and by approaching women directly, not through the usual male intermediary. Feminist New Testament scholar Elisabeth Schüssler Fiorenza interprets Jesus as a wisdom prophet, the spokesperson of the divine Sophia or wisdom. Jesus establishes a "discipleship of equals," breaking down social barriers and including society's rejected, whether by class, gender, family status, or religious standing.[22]

John Dominic Crossan presents Jesus as an itinerant Jewish teacher, who challenged convention in much the way as the Hellenistic Cynic philosophers. He projected an alternative social vision embodied in his "magical" healings outside accepted channels of religious authority, and his open table fellowship outside the bounds of religious and social respectability.[23] Even if the picture of Jesus as a Cynic is overdrawn and suggests unwarrantedly that Jesus' frame of reference was thoroughly temporal rather than eschatological,[24] the point that his teaching had immediate and iconoclastic social effects still stands. Rather than observing the status differences customary at feasts and banquets, Jesus is remembered as exhorting guests to refrain from assuming a place of honor, and hosts to invite their social inferiors on an equal or preferential basis with their peers (Luke 14:7–14). John Meier, Crossan, Marcus Borg, and E. P. Sanders[25] all put a great deal of emphasis on Jesus' miracles as the practical demonstration of the power of God's reign inaugurated in Jesus' ministry. Jesus demanded no reward, repudiated the idea current that sickness was divine punishment for sin, and iconoclastically restored contact with persons like lepers who had been cast out of the social order. Biblical portrayals of Jesus, as well as recent social scientific research (to be developed in the next section) support the conclusion that his ministry, death, and resurrection subvert a whole array of institutionalized power relationships.

Jesus, however, neither planned nor initiated any specific social reforms, nor (unlike the prophets) directly addressed systemic evils like economic exploitation, political oppression (both of which the Jews were then experiencing), slavery, patriarchy, or war. It is true that Jesus did embody what Crossan and Borg refer to as an "alternative social vision"; yet, as Sanders maintains, Jesus did not "urge the creation of a new social entity."[26] Neither Jesus nor his first followers enjoyed social positions that would have offered much advantage in instigating reforms; more importantly, Jesus proclaimed the end of this age and the decisive rule of God in a new one.

Some authors today, including Crossan and Borg, stress the social, political, and ethical ramifications of Jesus' ministry, while downplaying its relation to the inbreaking power of a transcendent God on whom present discipleship action ultimately depends.[27] Yet the image of God's reign would have carried with it in first-century Palestine the connotation of Israel's eschatological hopes for the future, which Jesus did nothing to dispel (in contrast to the anticipated subjection of gentiles).[28] In E. P. Sanders's words, "If we calmly survey the kingdom sayings, we shall see that most of them place the kingdom *up there*, in heaven, where people will enter after death, and *in the future*, when God brings the kingdom to earth and separates the sheep from the goats."[29] At the same time, part of Jesus' distinctive usage of this symbol is the immediacy and presence of God's reign during his own lifetime, and specifically in his own ministry (Luke 11:20, 17:20–21; Matt. 11:12). The two senses are not incompatible. God's rule is present in eternity and in history now; people can enter God's reign now by seeing and living in a new way; the fullness of the reign, which depends on God's decisive action, is a future reality which our present action anticipates. "What gives the reign of God its character as 'eschatological consummation' is its *energy out of the reach of observation*."[30] In other words, the morality of the gospel has a divine and transcendent basis which allows reconformation of human relationships to be radical and sustained, and to survive despite suffering, failure, and contradiction.

What Kind of Community?

Although space constraints prohibit a thorough survey, the social implications of early Christian conduct, as illumined by social scientific investigation, can be briefly indicated along the axes of honor-shame, economy, family, and purity. These axes intersect. Perhaps the most important reason why they do so is that in ancient Mediterranean societies one's access to the whole array of material and social goods was defined by one's place in a highly stratified system of hierarchy and dependence. In this system, the sum total of goods available (both material and social or political) was assumed to be limited. Moreover, the different types of goods, as well as the institutions by which they were allocated, were intermeshed.[31] Religion, economics, education, politics, and family were not differentiated and relatively independent social spheres, as they are in modern industrialized societies. High or low status in one was much more likely to be correlated with high or low status in the others (though not absolutely so). Persons of lower standing had to rely on patronage by superiors, on whom they were often dependent for even the basic necessities of life. An enormous degree of envy, anxiety, and competition was endemic in social relations among those vying for status by means of patron-client relationships. Even among the relatively small elite, relations termed friendship depended on a delicate balance of reciprocal favors and gifts. Among the numerous poorer classes, good relations with wealthier patrons were critical, especially during times of agrarian hardship or high taxes, when debt could overwhelm a family's survival.

In both Jewish and Greco-Roman culture, the family was a means of consolidating and passing on assets through advantageous marriages and inheritance (especially favoring firstborn sons). Although women were gaining legal rights under Roman rule, their key roles were obedient wife, organizer of household affairs, and producer of sons. In Greco-Roman culture, the family was subject to social and philosophical norms, as well as to civil legislation prescribing family order and mandating procreation as a duty to the state. Even allowing for a gap between such norms and practice, the family was less a nexus of close emotional ties and fulfillment than a means of social control, especially of the upper classes.

Honor was a core concern of people in Mediterranean society, determining relations and prerogatives in marriage, business, and politics. Honor referred not to one's personal integrity, but to social recognition of worth and value, as determined by one's status in the community. Cultivation and maintenance of honor required both a positive sensitivity to how one was perceived in the eyes of others, and an abhorrence of any situation or action which would diminish one's own status or that of one's family. Honor and shame were ascribed to entire families or kin groups. It was incumbent on the family as a whole to meet challenges to its honor, and the most important duty of an individual was to behave honorably on behalf of the family.[32] Status could accrue from birth into a high-status family, but it could also be acquired or earned. It could be lost by "dishonorable" behavior, including loss of control over one's social subordinates. Control over women was important to male honor, especially control by fathers, brothers, and husbands of women's sexual conduct.

Purity observance under Jewish law developed significantly during the exile, and centered on dietary laws and ritual purification. Purity was originally a way of maintaining Jewish identity even without a land or the temple, as well as of dedicating every moment of ordinary life to God. Purity still had this function in Jesus' day, and there is no reason to think that Jesus abandoned purity observance. What he did challenge was the co-optation of purity by a social system in which cleanness or uncleanness (according to regulations based on the laws of Leviticus) was used to demarcate social status. Although not all priests were rich, the high priestly families owned land and exacted taxes from the Jewish population for upkeep of the temple and the temple cult. Under Herod (one of the client Jewish kings installed by the Romans), taxes increased exorbitantly to support expenditures for cultural and building projects and to cultivate political allies. The priestly class defined interpretations of purity requirements. Cleanness or uncleanness could result from birth or physical condition (disease, disfigurement, menstruation, and childbirth), or it could result from nonobservance of dietary laws and ritual washing. Since purity was associated mostly with Jerusalem and the temple, it did not affect all Jews equally or at all times. However, purity functioned to some extent as a symbol of social hierarchy and set boundaries of inclusion and exclusion. Anthropologist Mary Douglas theorizes that controlling what passes in (food) and out (emissions of bodily fluids and the birth process) of the orifices of the body symbolizes and maintains the order of society and its egress and access routes.[33]

Scholars have also drawn out the concrete socioeconomic implications of Jesus' inclusive practices.[34] In a zero-sum society, where goods were tightly channeled, sharing with the needy without respect to desert or to expectation of return was a revolutionary act. Moreover, sharing in communities under duress could reduce insecurity and mutual competition, thus resocializing members away from dependency on the patriarchal family, the social patronage system, and religious leadership that cultivated its own position or collaborated with an oppressor state. Although Jesus' disciples and first followers did not establish a sectarian way of life completely outside these axes of social organization, "relations were supposed to be egalitarian in the community, which was conceived of as an extended nonpatriarchal 'family' of 'siblings.' The movement resisted rank, power, and prestige, valuing instead service to the community (e.g., Mark 10:25–45; Luke 11:42, 44, 46)."[35]

Early Churches and Their Memories of Jesus

Writing in the fifties, Paul antedates the final composition of the gospels, and states more directly the dynamic relation of the early churches to the ministry and teaching of Jesus, seen in the light of their post-Easter faith. The basic unit of his communities was the housechurch, in dialectic with itinerant evangelists. Paul's pastoral missives illustrate the challenges of community formation in a plurality of new situations, especially the movement from Jewish sect to gentile culture. The Jewish symbol "kingdom of God" hardly figures in Paul's teaching; claiming credibility as an apostle on the basis of his encounter with the risen Savior, he makes few allusions to the historical Jesus and his recollected words.[36] The consistent thread in Paul's message is the continuing and integral presence of Christ Jesus in the community as Christ's body. Believers are incorporated into Christ as, in baptism, they share in his dying and rising, and in the eucharist, partake of his body and blood. Practices like hospitality to traveling preachers and giving to those in need in their own or other communities built up a concrete sense of unity among churches.[37] (Paul understood Christian community both in terms of local churches [1 Thess. 1:1] and in terms of their unity in one God and one faith [Rom. 16:16].)

Paul's moral exhortations reflect the same sense of transformed relations that Jesus communicated in preaching and acting out the inclusive reign of God. With resurrection faith, Paul sees communal solidarity as dependent on the person of Jesus, crucified, raised, and present in Spirit. Conversion "resocializes" members with layers of religious, cultural, political, and kinship identities into a "family" of believers where unity in Christ is their shared and most important concern.[38] This unity, of course, has consequences for the texture of their other identities, though tensions and ambiguities remain. The baptismal formula of Galatians 3:28 is emblematic of the boundaries which would be overcome in churches genuinely conformed to God's rule, "For through faith you are all children of God in Christ Jesus" (3:26). "There is neither Jew nor Greek, there is neither slave nor free person, there is not male and female; for you are all one in Christ Jesus" (3:28).

Both Paul's own Jewish background and his Hellenistic context are important to the way he shapes the church in a new moral pattern. Cohesion as a people was critical to Israelite identity. It was reinforced by daily practices, and oriented by a strong theocentrism. Morally reformative strands included the prophets with their concern for the poor, and sapiential traditions about conventional and wise behavior. Later, more-sectarian and apocalyptic groups like the Qumran community urged withdrawal from a world caught in the grip of evil forces, focused in the Roman empire. Yet Philo of Alexandria engaged a conversation with Hellenistic culture and philosophy, emphasizing moral education while still seeing Israel as the chosen people of God and Moses as God's spokesman.[39]

In the highly stratified cities of ancient Greece and Rome, one's identity depended heavily on one's social role. By Paul's time, several philosophical schools had already protested many of the attendant conventions, and urged their pupils to transcend the foolish standards by which most of their contemporaries measured success. Yet the social criticism of schools such as the Cynics, Epicureans, and Stoics was not for the most part directed to communal reformation, but to individuals with enough self-control and perspicacity to raise themselves, not only above the masses, but above the so-called social elites. The key was to master the emotions and passions that drive the actions of most men, thus to enjoy the sort of satisfaction and security attainable only in an austere life strictly governed by reason and self-control. (Only the Epicureans seem to have included women as equals in their philosophical communities.)[40]

From Judaism, Paul brought a strong concern with communal identity and attentiveness to care of members for one another, not only for family members and friends. The prophets of Israel and its sages, as well as Hellenistic philosophers who challenged their followers to see through the customary to the real, could all serve as models for Paul; borrowing philosophical wisdom had precedents in Judaism, too.

Providing a model for Christian ethics today, Paul appropriates cultural virtues and certain assumptions about morally upright behavior but takes care to renovate them in the shape of communal solidarity, inclusiveness across status boundaries, and compassion and forbearance in mutual relationship. Pauline morality is communal, not individualistic. Asceticism, whether of the apostle himself, his traveling associates, or Christians deciding about celibacy or marriage, is a means to communal service, not an end in itself or a tool of self-improvement. Almost equally fundamental is the egalitarian impulse in community. Paul adopts Hellenistic social forms such as friendship and family but reinterprets them counterculturally. Christian identity begins to resist the elitist bonding of aristocrats, patronage, and pay-backs, and the firmly patriarchal structures governing subordinates under senior men.

For example, in a culture of honor and shame, Paul claimed weakness and vulnerability and loathed boasting. Not self-mastery but reliance on Christ was the foundation of the moral life. Stanley Stowers employs social history to access the audience to which Paul might plausibly have addressed himself in Romans: gentiles attracted to Jewish morality on account of the self-restraint for which it was respected among Greek writers.[41] Paul argues that the law does not guarantee self-mastery, and that identification with Jesus' faithfulness is a more secure way to righteousness before God. The alternative Paul holds up is identification with the crucified Christ, who, submitting to the suffering and death of the body, won justification for all by faith, apart from the works of the law (Rom. 2:17–29, 3:21–31).[42]

The gentiles cultivate self-mastery in a quest for honor, respect or reputation. Christians find peace not through the esteem of others, but through service and cooperation. Christians boast only in Christ, not in their own accomplishments (Rom. 5–6). Paul's practical concern is with social cohesion and fellowship, enabled by a spirit of love.[43] He does not posit an essential opposition either between the law and righteousness, or between reason and faith, but criticizes misuse of law and reason to assert independence, strength, or honor.

Similar concerns appear in his letters to the Corinthian Christians, who had broken into factions celebrating their own superiority (1 Cor. 1:10–12). An appalling symptom is division at the Lord's supper, where the rich provide sumptuous food and drink for themselves, while letting the poor leave hungry (1 Cor. 11:17–34). Some seem to have been priding themselves on a higher way of life entailing strict asceticism, including celibate marriage (1 Cor. 7:1–7). Paul extols neither moral perfectionism nor invulnerability to life's vicissitudes, as did the Stoics, but accepts sickness, death, conflict, and his own weakness. It is better to accept weakness in Christ than to boast, seeking strength and honor (1 Cor. 4:6–19; 9:15–23). Cooperative, compassionate virtues and a spirit of love and humility must be enjoyed before reasonable discernment of the right course in practical matters will even be possible (1 Cor.

10:23–33; 1 Cor. 13). Factiousness and pride prevent sensitive, faithful moral deliberation and responsible choice favoring the community's weak or needy.[44]

Paul, among New Testament authors, devotes the most attention to specific moral problems—including virginity, marriage and divorce, homosexuality, prostitution, roles of women (all mentioned in 1 Cor.), and obedience to government (Rom. 13:1–7).[45] Yet his message is not focused in a set of rules or principles, but in a mode of life characterized by love and service, centered on the cross as a contradiction of moral "success," and confident in the risen Savior as enlivening and enabling Christian moral agency through God's Spirit.[46] Paul's flexibility in adapting to the pluralistic cultures of Greek cities broadened his audience, for gentiles could often admire the moral ideals he propounded. It also permitted Christians to rely on and be educated by layers of moral wisdom furnished in multiple traditions, practices, and communities. This openness did create inevitable tensions with Christianity's strong Jewish roots (as in the debates over food laws and circumcision). Moreover, it risked cultural accommodations that undermined the radicality of the Christian transformation of life (e.g., acceptance of slavery and ambivalence on gender hierarchy). Paul himself is acutely sensitive to the dangers as well as the wisdom of the surrounding world, and establishes community boundaries marked by Christian virtues. Nevertheless, his legacy is not a sectarian but a dialogical ethic.[47]

As sociology and social history demonstrate, early Christian community and moral behavior tended to undermine institutions and relationships that permitted powerful elites, both religious and political, to exploit the large majority of people. For instance, Paul's advice to the widowed or unmarried to remain virgin or celibate was in effect a challenge to the patriarchal household, a key unit of social organization by which the Roman imperial state kept control over the lives and bodies of citizens.[48] A more direct and obvious example is the early Christian practice of communal sharing and forgiveness, which undermined the control that the social and economic elites had over the dependent masses. These instances do not necessarily mean that Christians should always prefer virginity to marriage, or socialist to capitalist economic systems. They do require that the central concern of Christian ethics be to identify and realize moral practices that embody the compassion, mercy, solidarity and inclusiveness of God's reign. The social history of early Christianity can illumine many practical ramifications of the moral exhortations and guidance we encounter in scripture. Thus moral ideals like forgiveness and love move from seeming abstract, impracticable, or irrelevant, and become more concrete, compelling, and possible for communities of faith today.

Notes

1. Since early Christianity, literal and spiritual or allegorical interpretations of the Bible have competed, although they are not fundamentally opposed to one another. Medieval inter-

preters developed four levels of biblical meaning, which could all be sought in the same text: the literal (the historical events); allegorical (a theological or spiritual meaning); anagogical (a reference to our future in heaven or to heavenly realities); and moral (morality and Christian practice). Both Thomas Aquinas and the Reformers emphasized the literal sense as the most foundational and important, because allegorizing interpretations could be extravagant and idiosyncratic. See Robert M. Grant with David Tracy, *A Short History of the Interpretation of the Bible*, 2d ed. (Philadelphia: Fortress Press, 1984).

2. James M. Gustafson, "The Place of Scripture in Christian Ethics: A Methodological Study," *Interpretation* 24, no. 4 (1970): 430–55.

3. See Raymond F. Collins, *Divorce in the New Testament* (Collegeville, Minn.: Liturgical Press, 1992).

4. Elisabeth Schüssler Fiorenza, *In Memory of Her: A Feminist Theological Reconstruction of Christian Origins* (New York: Crossroad, 1983).

5. Sandra M. Schneiders, *The Revelatory Text: Interpreting the New Testament as Sacred Scripture* (New York: HarperCollins, 1991), 3.

6. She uses the Samaritan woman who meets Jesus at the well (John 4:1–42) as an example of leadership in mission and evangelization (ibid., 181–99).

7. Sandra M. Schneiders, "Living Word or Dead(ly) Letter: The Encounter between the New Testament and Contemporary Experience," Catholic Theological Society of America *Proceedings* 47 (1992): 59.

8. William Spohn speaks of Jesus as a "concrete universal"—a particular life with universal implications for the Christian life, discerned by an analogical imagination ("Jesus and Ethics," *Catholic Theological Society of America Proceedings* 49 [1994]: 40–57; "Jesus and Christian Ethics," *Theological Studies* 56, no. 1 [1995]: 101–7).

9. See, for instance, Walter Brueggemann, "Trajectories in Old Testament Literature and the Sociology of Ancient Israel," *Journal of Biblical Literature* 98 (1979): 161–85; Norman K. Gottwald, *The Tribes of Yahweh: A Sociology of the Religion of Liberated Israel, 1250–1000 B.C.E.* (Maryknoll, N.Y.: Orbis Books, 1979); and "Sociological Method in the Study of Ancient Israel," in *The Bible and Liberation,* rev. ed., ed. Norman K. Gottwald (Maryknoll, N.Y.: Orbis Books, 1983); Robert K. Wilson, *Sociological Approaches to the Old Testament* (Philadelphia: Fortress, 1984); and Leo G. Purdue, ed., *The Family in Ancient Israel* (Louisville: Westminster John Knox, forthcoming).

10. Joseph A. Fitzmyer, S.J., "Historical Criticism: Its Role in Biblical Interpretation and Church Life," *Theological Studies* 50, no. 2 (1989): 246–47.

11. See Pheme Perkins, "The New Testament—The Church's Book?!," in *Catholic Theological Society of America Proceedings* 40 (1985): 39.

12. See Fitzmyer, "Historical Criticism," 249.

13. Darrell Jodock, *The Church's Bible: Its Contemporary Authority* (Minneapolis: Fortress Press, 1989), 17, 76, 86. See also Fitzmyer, "Historical Criticism," 252–55.

14. Important early works were John Gager, *Kingdom and Community: The Social World of Early Christianity* (Englewood Cliffs, N.J.: Prentice-Hall, 1975); and Abraham J. Malherbe, *Social Aspects of Early Christianity* (Baton Rouge: Louisiana State University, 1977). See Carolyn Osiek, R.S.C.J., "The New Handmaid: The Bible and the Social Sciences," *Theological Studies* 50, no. 2 (1989): 260–78; and Bruce J. Malina, "The Social Sciences and Biblical Interpretation," *Interpretation* 37, no. 3 (1982): 229–42.

15. See Jonathan Z. Smith, "The Social Description of Early Christianity," *Religious Studies Review* 1 (1975): 19–25.

16. Bruce Malina describes the three main social science models as the structural functionalist, the conflict, and the symbolic models ("Social Sciences," 233–37.) See also Bruce J. Malina, *Christian Origins and Cultural Anthropology: Practical Models for Biblical Interpretation* (Atlanta: John Knox Press, 1986).

17. As general resources, see Wayne A. Meeks, *The Moral World of the First Christians* (Philadelphia: Westminster, 1986); Carolyn Osiek, R.S.C.J., *What Are They Saying about the Social Setting of the New Testament?* (New York/Ramsey: Paulist, 1984); and Bruce J. Malina and Richard L. Rohrbaugh, *Social-Science Commentary on the Synoptic Gospels* (Minneapolis: Fortress Press, 1992).

18. The Greek New Testament word is *basileia*, traditionally translated "kingdom," but better understood as "the dynamic notion of God powerfully ruling over" creation, the people of God, and history (John P. Meier, *A Marginal Jew: Rethinking the Historical Jesus* [New York: Doubleday, 1994], vol. 2, *Mentor, Message, and Miracles*.)

19. Ibid., 241.

20. Ibid., 331 (cf. n. 155, p. 385). The essential message here is God's gratuitous mercy, a core that goes back to the historical Jesus.

21. The exact identity and the reason for the poor reputation of the tax collectors or toll collectors is unclear. Meier speculates that they were "minor functionaries who collected the payment of tolls or customs (indirect taxes) on goods being transported across borders" (Ibid., 1037). They may have been reviled simply because they were thought to take advantage of their frequent opportunities for graft.

22. Elisabeth Schüssler Fiorenza, *Jesus: Miriam's Child, Sophia's Prophet* (New York: Crossroad, 1994).

23. John Dominic Crossan, *The Historical Jesus: The Life of a Mediterranean Jewish Peasant* (New York: HarperCollins, 1991); and *Jesus: A Revolutionary Biography* (New York: HarperCollins, 1993).

24. As in the opinion of Hans Dieter Betz, "Jesus and the Cynics: Survey and Analysis of a Hypothesis," *Journal of Religion* 74, no. 4 (1994): 453–75.

25. As well as Crossan, Meier, and Sanders, see Marcus J. Borg, *Jesus in Contemporary Scholarship* (Valley Forge, Pa.: Trinity Press International, 1994).

26. E. P. Sanders, *The Historical Figure of Jesus* (London: Penguin Books, 1993), 179.

27. The apocalyptic nature of Jesus' message has been debated since the turn of the century. Some of the earlier historical critics, preeminently Johannes Weiss and Albert Schweitzer, stressed apocalyptic and portrayed Jesus as expecting during his own lifetime a cataclysmic event that would bring the end of the world. The failure of this expectation then seemed to discredit his authority and his relevance to modern Christians. In different ways, scholars such as Rudolf Bultmann, C. H. Dodd, and, in the 1960s, Norman Perrin tried to restore the present significance of Jesus' vision of God's reign by showing how it can and should affect the faith and actions of later Christians. But these attempts were generally premised on the assumption that the supernatural aspects of the biblical notion of reign had to be translated into this-worldly terms for modern people. Following this trajectory, some scholars have minimized both the apocalyptic (cataclysmic end of history) and eschatological (the end time has begun and will be completed by God) elements in Jesus' view of God's reign. See Borg, *Jesus*, 57, 69, 151–55.

28. Ibid., 269–70.

29. Sanders, *Historical Figure of Jesus*, 176.

30. Roy A. Harrisville, "In Search of the Meaning of the 'Reign of God,'" *Interpretation* 47, no. 2 (1993): 149.

31. See, for instance, Meeks, *Moral World*, 32–38; Halvor Moxnes, *The Economy of the Kingdom: Social Conflict and Economic Relations in Luke's Gospel* (Philadelphia: Fortress, 1948); and Richard A. Horsley, *Sociology and the Jesus Movement* (New York: Crossroad, 1989), 83–90.

32. Malina and Rohrbaugh, *Social-Science Commentary*, 42, 76–77; Wayne A. Meeks, *The Origins of Christian Morality: The First Two Centuries* (New Haven and London: Yale University Press, 1993).

33. Mary Douglas, *Purity and Danger: An Analysis of Concepts of Pollution and Taboo* (London and Henley: Routledge & Kegan Paul, 1966); and *Natural Symbols: Explorations in Cosmology*, rev. ed. (London: Barrie and Jenkins, 1973, orig. publ. 1971).

34. Moxnes, *The Economy of the Kingdom*; Horsley, *Sociology* .

35. Horsley, *Sociology*, 123.

36. Joseph A. Fitzmyer, S.J., *Paul and His Theology: A Brief Sketch* (Englewood Cliffs, N.J.: Prentice-Hall, 1989), 33, 101. Paul uses "kingdom of God" primarily as a contrast point to vice lists he has inherited from pre-Pauline catechetical instruction or preaching (e.g., Gal. 5:21, 1 Cor. 6:9–10).

37. Meeks, *Origins*, 104–8.

38. Meeks, *Moral World*, 126; *Origins,* 45–51; *The First Urban Christians: the Social World of the Apostle Paul* (New Haven and London: Yale University Press, 1983), 84.

39. Meeks, *Moral World*, 68–85.

40. Ibid., 40–62.

41. Stanley K. Stowers, "Readers in Romans and the Meaning of Self-Mastery," in *A Rereading of Romans* (New Haven and London: Yale University Press, 1994), 42–82.

42. James M. Gustafson proposes that elements of human experience like radical suffering prompt a deep reexamination of Christian beliefs such as providence and resurrection, and a refocusing on the cross (*Ethics from a Theocentric Perspective,* 2 vols.[Chicago: University of Chicago Press, 1981–1984], vol. 1, *Theology and Ethics,* 260–79). For a consideration of this proposal in light of social research on Paul's theology, see Lisa Sowle Cahill, "Kingdom and Cross: Christian Moral Community and the Problem of Suffering," *Interpretation* 50 (1995): 156–68.

43. Ibid., 73.

44. Stanley K. Stowers, "Paul on the Use and Abuse of Reason," in David L. Balch, Everett Ferguson, and Wayne A. Meeks, *Greeks, Romans, and Christians: Essays in Honor of Abraham J. Malherbe* (Minneapolis: Fortress Press, 1990), 266.

45. For a discussion of such texts in historical context, see Victor Paul Furnish, *The Moral Teaching of Paul: Selected Issues*, rev. ed. (Nashville: Abingdon Press, 1985).

46. See Pheme Perkins, "Paul and Ethics," *Interpretation* 38 (1984): 268–80; and Bernard C. Lategan, "Is Paul Developing a Specifically Christian Ethics in Galatians?," in Balch et al., *Greeks,* 318–28.

47. On the importance of such a model today, see James M. Gustafson, "The Sectarian Temptation: Reflections on Theology, the Church and the University," *Catholic Theological Society of America Proceedings* (1985): 83–94.

48. Peter Brown, *The Body and Society: Men, Women and Sexual Renunciation in Early Christianity* (New York: Columbia University Press, 1988).

Chapter 2

Scripture and Ethics:
Practices, Performances,
and Prescriptions

ALLEN VERHEY

Thirty years ago, in an essay that reported and interpreted developments in Christian ethics during the previous thirty years, James M. Gustafson drew attention to the relation of Christian ethics to biblical studies and lamented "a paucity of material that relates the two areas in a scholarly way."[1] Many cited[2] or echoed Gustafson's complaint, and many undertook to relate Christian ethics and biblical studies "in a scholarly way"—so many, in fact, that whatever else may be lamented about the relation of scripture and Christian ethics, it is now implausible to lament the lack of attention to their relationship.[3]

Gustafson's complaint prompted a considerable literature—and his methodological essay on "The Place of Scripture in Christian Ethics,"[4] which surveyed and classified appeals to scripture, "framed the question"[5] for much of it. Indeed, it can be said to have helped form a consensus concerning the relevance of scripture to Christian ethics. The consensus, however, has recently been criticized as holding the church's canon captive to historical criticism of the text and as abstracted from the "performances" of scripture within particular ecclesial communities.

This article begins with an account of Gustafson's survey and of the consensus it helped form; it continues with a consideration of recent critics of that consensus; and finally, by retrieving elements from Gustafson's work on the church, it suggests an agenda which takes seriously both the accomplishments of the consensus and the concerns of its critics.

I.   Gustafson's Survey

Gustafson's methodological study of "The Place of Scripture in Christian Ethics" brought some order to the diverse ways in which scripture was used within Christian reflection on the moral life. The essay began by distinguishing Christian ethics (and its use of scripture) from "biblical ethics" and by underscoring the general point that how a moral theologian uses scripture is correlated "to a considerable extent" with that moral theologian's account of the task of Christian ethics. Gustafson developed that general point by providing a typology of "ways of using scripture" in Christian ethics. He distinguished, first, between using scripture as "a revealed reality" and as "a revealed morality."

To use scripture as a "revealed reality" is to use it as an account of God and of the cause(s) of God that guide(s) human response and responsibility, informing the interpretations and assessments of historical processes and events, of the motives and intentions of human agents, and/or of the circumstances and consequences of human action.

To use scripture as a "revealed morality" is to use it as an account of a morality that is more directly authoritative for moral discernment and judgment. Here Gustafson refined the classification by distinguishing four models for the use of scripture as a "revealed morality": scripture is used either as a revealed law, or as a revealed set of ideals, or as a revealed set of judgments in historical circumstances analogous to contemporary circumstances, or as a witness "to a great variety of moral values, moral norms and principles through many different kinds of biblical literature."[6]

These diverse ways of using scripture had their roots in the history of biblical interpretation following the Protestant Reformation, and it will be helpful (if audacious) to survey that history briefly.[7] When the Reformers wrested control over scripture away from the ecclesial hierarchy, they had insisted that the "literal meaning" (or the "historical meaning" or the "plain meaning") be found and followed. They were confident that the historical meaning of the text would be of contemporary significance, and they were suspicious of any readings of scripture that were not disciplined by the grammatical and historical methods current in the "humanistic" study of classical literature in the universities of the day.

The social location for disciplined interpretation shifted to the university, and when the universities were "enlightened," the interpretation of scripture was assigned to a "scientific" reading of texts. A scientific reading required objectivity and neutrality; it required that scripture be treated like any other text. The historian's inquiry was limited to the historical situation about which (or in which) the text was written. The historian's methods provided results, to be sure, in the reconstruction of the history of Israel and Jesus and the early church, in the reconstruction of the historical situation of each text, and in the recognition of the diversity and distinctiveness of the texts. However, the historical meaning no longer could be identified quite so confidently with

the continuing significance of the text. The methods and results of post-Enlightenment historians fragmented the canon and drove a wedge between the historical meaning and the continuing significance of scripture.

Some Christian communities, to be sure, refused to surrender their canon to the
disinterested historians who conscientiously refused to judge the religious significance
of those texts. These communities—sometimes deeply suspicious of the university and
its scientific interpretation or "higher criticism" (and sometimes, frankly, obscuran-
tist)—frequently insisted that the texts revealed an objective moral order, a law, the
truth of which no "enlightened" historian or philosopher could test or prove.

Liberal Protestants, however, attempted to find the continuing significance of the
text by engaging it with the tools of historical criticism in an effort to discern the "eternal values" within it. The strategy was to rely on a historical reconstruction of "what
really happened" in order to disclose the progress of history and the presence and power
of certain eternal ideals. Scripture provided—and reason confirmed—a set of ideals.
This strategy lost some of its power when philosophical idealism stumbled and when
the historical critics discovered apocalypticism and were unable to reconcile it to notions of historical progress.

A different strategy called attention to relevant similarities between the historical
situations described by a scientific reading of scripture and some contemporary circumstances, relying on analogies to bridge the historical gulf and to license the use of
scripture in moral reflection on contemporary events and circumstances. Another strategy shifted attention from the objective history of the text to the text's expression of
an internal and spiritual sensibility—a mode of subjectivity that might still be won-
drously and warmly shared. Form critics like Bultmann, for example, attended to literary units and their expression of an existential and authentic mode of subjectivity
called "faith." "Faith" was always active as "love," but little more than that general principle traversed the historical gulf from scripture to contemporary moral reflection.[8]
Karl Barth's deliberate nonchalance about the historical-critical method shifted attention from the historical context to the narrative which characterizes God, which renders the agent who also creates and commands in the present moment.[9] Similarly, while
the "biblical theology" movement attended to history, it attended to history as "recital"
of God's work and way. (Dissimilarly, it found in the narrative recitals of history certain theological-moral concepts which gave unity to the canon and which made the
narrative itself expendable.)[10] Such positions understood scripture to provide for
Christian moral reflection a "revealed reality" to which Christians respond in all their
responsibilities rather than a "revealed morality," whether laws (or principles) or ideals
or historically analogous judgments.

Gustafson's essay brought a clarifying order to this diversity; moreover, by its advo-
cacy of the "great variety" model, it helped to form a consensus concerning the relevance of scripture to Christian ethics. In that model, scripture—as noted above—is a
witness "to a great variety of moral values, moral norms and principles through many

different kinds of biblical literature." This "great variety" of morally relevant materials is "not in any simple way reducible to a single theme"; the "different kinds of litera-ture" within which they are found are "directed to particular historical contexts"; and so, scripture is important but "not sufficient" to require any particular moral judgment in contemporary historical circumstances. To be sure, although the article advocated this "great variety" model, it would join it to and discipline it by a "revealed reality" model. Scripture testifies to God and to the cause of God, but there is no simple uni-tive understanding of God and the cause of God in scripture either. Moreover, it is noteworthy that the article set this use of scripture in the context of "the vocation of the Christian community . . . to discern what God is enabling and requiring [persons] to be and to do in particular natural, historical, and social circumstances."[11]

II. The Consensus

Following Gustafson's lament and methodological essay, many scholars (e.g., Birch and Rasmussen, Furnish, Hays, Ogletree, Sleeper, Spohn, and Verhey) attempted to relate scripture to Christian ethics and, in the attempt, accepted and affirmed elements of Gustafson's proposal. To be sure, there are important differences among these scholars and their works, but there was also a consensus among them. This consensus included several elements: a recognition of the great diversity within scripture, an acknowledg-ment that judgments about the unity or "wholeness" of scripture are not simply given with the text, an affirmation of attention to the particular historical contexts of par-ticular texts, an appreciation of the necessity of other sources in addition to scripture for reflection about the moral life and for contemporary moral judgments, a refusal to authorize a "prescriptive" use of scripture (that is, appeals to scriptural rules to settle directly a concrete question of what should be done today), and a recognition that the Christian community provides the context for reading and using scripture.

The consensus, of course, can also be explained historically. Michael Cartwright was among the first to identify and to criticize this consensus. He situated it histori-cally in the crisis of interpretation created by post-Enlightenment New Testament scholarship and its attention to "the gap between the first century and the twentieth century," in the failure of liberalism's attention to "eternal values" or ideals to resolve that crisis, and in the "demise of the biblical theology movement" and its confidence that the unity of the canon could be located in theological-moral concepts.[12]

III. Criticisms and Counterproposals

The consensus has not been without its critics, and the other models identified by Gustafson continue to be represented. Two new intellectual movements, however, seem to some to require a reformulation of the question of the use of scripture in Christian ethics, a revision of the consensus, and a different agenda for future work in this area.

The first of these is a turn toward literary criticism in reading scripture and, within literary criticism, a turn from the text to the reader. There had long been, of course, a "literary criticism" within historical-critical biblical scholarship. It was concerned with questions of authorship and sources, and it contributed to the effort of biblical scholarship to determine objectively "what the text meant then." The recent turn toward literary criticism, however, has been an appropriation of secular literary-critical theories, ranging from structuralism, with its focus on the text in itself and for itself (identifying its formal structure, inattentive to either author or reader), to deconstructionism, with its theory that there are no meanings in texts (and no limits on the meanings readers can construct in using texts for their own purposes). The turn to the reader within literary criticism sometimes has seemed to warrant simple subjectivism in the interpretation and use of scripture; but, more modestly and helpfully, it has provided backing for the claim that there are no self-interpreting texts and no totally objective methods of interpretation. This turn to the reader challenges the claims of historical-critical biblical scholarship both to objectivity and to hegemony over interpretation. It also challenges the assumption of the consensus that efforts to describe what the texts "meant then" (or "biblical ethics") can tidily be marked off from the interpretation of what the texts mean now for Christian ethics. The turn to the reader surely raises as methodologically significant the question, "Which reader?"

Stanley Hauerwas's provocative book on *Unleashing the Scriptures* represents this turn to the reader not only by invoking the literary-critical work of Stanley Fish but also by its resistance to the historical-critical method, by its rejection of the distinction between "meaning then" and "meaning now," and indeed, by its rejection of attention to the texts as if they were independent of readers. The book addresses the question, "Which reader?" by denying the "right of private interpretation," rejecting the "right" of individuals to read scripture "on their own." The reader of scripture is the church; members of churches read it not "on their own" but as instructed by that community of readers.[13]

In this turn to the community, *Unleashing the Scriptures* also represents a second important intellectual movement. There is a new appreciation of the importance of the social location of both text and reader. Consider, first, the social location of the text. Attention to the embeddedness of biblical texts in the practices and politics of ancient religious communities and to the social locations of those communities themselves (and the use of social-scientific methods in the service of such attention) has prompted a rich new set of studies concerning the social world of scripture. The social historians, however, are typically quite confident about the distinction between what a text "meant then" and what it "means now" and quite self-conscious about bracketing the question of the use of scripture in contemporary Christian ethics.[14] A quite different social location is given to the text when it is regarded—as in *Unleashing the Scriptures*—

as "canon." Then the social location of the text is the continuing church, and social-historical inquiry into the culture or community in which a text was first written and historical-critical inquiry into the "meaning then" may be regarded as fundamentally irrelevant.[15]

The turn to community has also invited attention to the social location of the reader and to the reader's community (or to the community of readers) when addressing the question, "Which reader?" When these texts are regarded as "canon," after all, the readers—as well as the texts themselves—are located within the church. "Canon" is the correlative of "church" rather than "university," and to read it as "canon" means to read it within an ecclesial community. Readers, then, are properly formed not by the habits and practices of "objective" biblical scholars in "enlightened" universities, nor by ideological commitments to rational individualism in "enlightened" cultures, but by the habits and practices of faithful ecclesial communities. The point is central to *Unleashing the Scriptures*.

Liberation theologians and feminist theologians have also attended to the social location of the reader and challenged conventional academic modes of interpretation as ideologically biased. They have underscored the point that there are no self-interpreting texts and no "objective" methods of interpretation. They are suspicious, however, not only of readers (and readings) located in the "enlightened" universities; they are no less suspicious of readers (and readings) located in those churches enmeshed in particular cultures—in capitalist and patriarchal cultures, for example.[16] They self-consciously identify with communities of the poor and oppressed in reading (and retrieving) scripture, but in the service of those communities they retrieve not only scripture but social-scientific and historical studies in reading it. Sometimes an overlooked text is read. Sometimes a familiar text is reread against its conventional interpretation. Sometimes a historical reconstruction is used against a reading—or against a text.[17] And always there is some revisioning of the story around themes of liberation and justice.

This turn toward the community surely raises as methodologically significant the question, "Which community?" The consensus had answered that question, of course. In Gustafson's essay, and again and again, the issue was framed in terms of the use of scripture in the Christian community. Ironically, the provocative and compelling criticism of the consensus by Stanley Hauerwas comes from one who answers that question the same way. The criticism, in effect, is that, while the consensus pays lip service to the church, it is not sufficiently attentive to the church as an interpretive community. If that is so, then it may be possible to regard the criticism and the counterproposals of such critics as friendly amendments rather than as alternatives to the consensus. It may be possible to suggest an agenda for future work that retrieves elements of the consensus while it honors the concerns of the critics. Before turning to that agenda, it will be useful to give a fuller account of the criticism and the counterproposals by attending to the works of Michael Cartwright and of Stephen E. Fowl and L. Gregory Jones.[18]

Cartwright complained that the consensus was "flawed by an oversimple conception of use," as if scripture and its texts were simply objects awaiting either the moralistic application that the consensus agrees is bad or manipulation by means of a method that some representative of the consensus thinks is good. He criticized the proposals for the "use" of scripture for being abstract and vague, remote from the real life of particular communities. Scripture, Cartwright insisted, is not simply object; it is always already interpreted—and enacted socially—in particular ecclesial communities. The effort to read scripture as if the churches (with their histories, politics, and practices) are not already there is shaped by the Enlightenment desire to transcend the partiality of particular communities and histories. Thus, ironically, it cloaks and perpetuates an individualistic ideology.[19]

Cartwright's proposal for a richer and more concrete account of the uses of scripture makes considerable use of the Russian literary critic Mikhail Bakhtin and especially of his claim that "[a]ny *utterance*, no matter how weighty and complete in and of itself, *is only a moment in the continuous process of verbal communication*."[20] Scripture may not be abstracted from the particular "chains of utterance" within which it is significant in particular ecclesial communities and traditions. History and community are always already there, and uses of scripture are always already there in the concrete practices and politics of ecclesial communities. Cartwright cites Nicholas Lash's observation that "the fundamental form of the *Christian* interpretation of scripture is the life, activity and organization of the believing community," and he claims that such "uses" of scripture "defy the current formalist consensus" by being "too rich and too diverse to be categorized according to 'levels of moral discourse,' 'modes of argument,' and other meta-ethical constructs."[21] Cartwright wants to hold us close to particular communities and their concrete practices. Because mainline Protestantism has been deeply affected by Enlightenment liberalism (it is hardly accidental, Cartwright observes, that many representatives of the consensus belong to that tradition), Cartwright looks elsewhere for examples of a "communal hermeneutic" and "interpretative performance." He looks, for example, to Orthodox worship, to the Anabaptist practice of church discipline, and to the ways that African American practices of singing the spirituals and "preaching the Word" mediated a "'chain of utterances' that constitute the core of the African American Christian *tradition* of biblical interpretation."[22]

It is characteristic of the "consensus" that it rejects "prescriptive uses" of scripture, and it is characteristic of Cartwright that he wants to retrieve a "prescriptive use" of scripture in Christian ethics, "not by returning to a deontological model but by locating usage in the practices and in the 'living dialogue' of those communities which lay claim to being churches." Any use of scripture, including a prescriptive use, involves "resourceful selectivity."[23] Such selectivity—including prescriptive uses of scripture—is always situated within competing "chains of signification" and within "particular communities of faith living in particular conditions of history in relation to particular ecclesial traditions in the midst of various ideological struggles." A "great variety" marks Cartwright's proposal, too, but at the point of performances of scripture rather than at the point of describing the morality of scripture itself. The possibility of distinguishing "superior and inferior performances" is asserted, but such assessments can only be made relative to particular communities and traditions, never independently of the continuing conversation of a particular community and scripture.[24]

The consensus was also criticized by Stephen E. Fowl and L. Gregory Jones in *Reading in Communion: Scripture and Ethics in Christian Life.* Like Cartwright, they object to the term "use" because it "suggests that Scripture is something out there waiting to be 'used.' All that is needed is the proper method. . . ." They complain that "the methods and presumptions upon which much current work on the use of Scripture in Christian ethics rests" have been shaped by "the dominant modern conceptions of the scope of ethics," and they charge that those "modern conceptions" surface in the effort to provide a method for anonymous individuals, in the lack of attention to character and community, in the false assumption that the Bible is addressed to independent individuals, and in a reliance on critical (and universal) reason to transcend and govern particular communities and their use of texts. An adequate conception of ethics requires attention to character and community, and not just as one component of a "comprehensive pluralism" in ethics but as "a different perspective on the shape of ethics itself."[25]

Fowl and Jones insist that hermeneutics is a "political" discipline. Interpretation is "a social activity," and the particular community within which interpretation takes place will make a difference to the "interpretive interest" and to the resources to perform and assess interpretation. They use this point, first, to contrast the modern university and the church as contexts for interpretation[26] and, second, to call attention to particular ecclesial communities and their "politics" and practices as contexts for interpretation.

For Christian communities the Bible is scripture, or canon. The intimate relationship of church and scripture entails both that the life (the politics) of Christian communities is to be "formed and regulated by the interpretation of Scripture" and that the Christian interpretation of scripture is rightly formed and assessed within communities whose politics and practices are already—if inadequately—performances of scripture. "Communities of committed disciples" are both the goal and the presupposition of interpretation.[27]

An implication of acknowledging that such communities are the presupposition of interpretation—an implication central to their counterproposal for the "use" of scripture—is that the politics of Christian communities needs to be "significantly rehabilitated if we are to enable wise reading and performance of Scripture." That rehabilitation will only take place in the readiness to "read the Scriptures 'over-against ourselves' rather than simply 'for ourselves.'"[28] There is no method to assure that we will learn to read scripture "over-against ourselves."[29] It can happen, however, in communities that perform baptism and practice the "transition from friendship with the 'world' into friendship with God" which baptism signifies. It can happen in communities that celebrate eucharist and practice the fellowship and the hospitality to strangers required by the eucharist. It can happen in communities that remember "the saints" whose lives and service to the world are "wise performances of Scripture" and "paradigmatic" for others in the community; we can learn to read and perform scripture well when we read "in communion" with the saints whose lives have been transformed by the witness of scripture.[30] The rehabilitation of Christian community and of its readings of scripture is not simply a matter of affirming the authority of scripture, developing a cadre of experts on what the text originally meant, or relying on another cadre of experts to bridge the gulf that separates past from present by determining what the text means today. It requires, rather, attention to the ways scripture has been and is "performed" in the rituals of the community, gathered, and in the service to the world by the community, sent.

It can also happen, however, that "[w]hen distortions of character enter and deeply penetrate the life of any Christian community, that community loses its ability to read Scripture in ways that would challenge and correct its character. Scripture simply becomes a mirror reflecting a community's self-deceptions back to itself disguised as the word of God." "Methodological sophistication" is helpless against the "vicious circle in which corrupt character and distorted interpretation mutually reinforce each other"; it cannot rehabilitate such a community or its readings of scripture.[31]

Communities can avoid interpretive self-deception and arrogance by cultivating an "openness to outsiders." Fowl and Jones identify scripture as an "outsider" in order to underscore once again that it is to be read "over-against" ourselves and not simply as "us in disguise." In this way the community can sustain an "interpretive humility" and an "openness to hearing the voice of scripture afresh." The other "outsiders" include those "in our midst" who are estranged from the life of the community and from its readings of scripture (e.g., homosexual persons), those "bearing a family resemblance" (e.g., the Jewish community), and "complete strangers" who both question our integrity and hold us to it.[32]

In the context of their treatment of "the outsiders in our midst," Fowl and Jones call for a conversation—for moral discourse in the community seeking to interpret and perform scripture—in which the voice of the outsider is not muted by the power or interpretive arrogance of the majority (and in which the "outsider" is not "unwilling to be reconciled to the body's reading and performance of scripture"). In this conversation, moreover, they recommend that we remember that "all of Scripture is canonical," that we acknowledge its "diversity," that we not "presume *a priori* that any particular text or texts must be determinative," that we recognize the historical distance between biblical terminology and practices and our own terminology and practices, and that we integrate the contributions "from other fields of inquiry" into our readings of scripture.[33] They do not cite here the consensus that they were at pains earlier to discredit, but important elements of it are surely here retrieved, if set in the context of their attention to character and community.

IV. A Communal Hermeneutic

The critics of the consensus are right to call attention to the ecclesial context for the reading and "use" of scripture, but the consensus accepts that point. They are right to insist on the "performance" of scripture, on *praxis*, but the consensus would share such an interpretive interest. Representatives of the consensus and its critics might profitably retrieve Gustafson's account of the church as a community of interpretation and action in *Treasure in Earthen Vessels,*[34] a work too much neglected. There Gustafson, like the later critics, described the church as a "political" community dialectically related to scripture, inviting attention to the ecclesial context for the interpretation and performance of scripture.

The church, according to Gustafson, has a social identity and remains faithful to it through history by "the internalization of meanings represented objectively in certain documents, symbols, and rites."[35] These documents exist, then, in some sense as "objects," independent of the church's continuing appropriation. Nevertheless, the intimate relation of church and scripture, so important to his critics, is no less important for Gustafson. On the one hand, without these documents, the church would not continue to be the church. Within the continuing church, however, these documents *are* appropriated, "internalized" and performed, to create and sustain the life and politics of the community. That is the process that enables integrity through time. On the other hand, without the continuing church, without the continuing "use" of these documents to form and reform the community's speech and memory, belief and action, the documents would not be "scripture."[36]

Because the Bible is "object," Gustafson can (and must) appreciate efforts to understand what the texts "originally meant." Because scripture is "internalized" and appropriated in the continuing church to form and reform the life and politics of particular communities, Gustafson does not (and cannot) reduce the hermeneutical problem to specialized study of what the texts "originally meant." To utilize a distinction made by Nicholas Wolterstorff, the texts are both "objects" and "instruments"; they are the effect of the actions of writing texts and the instruments that we use to perform certain other actions.[37] Such an approach to hermeneutics will not regard the "meaning" of a text as wholly contained within the language of the text nor as totally dissociated from the actions of writing a text.[38] Hermeneutics, then, is a communal undertaking within historically situated communities that use these "objects" as "instruments" and that continue (and continually assess) existing traditions of performance of the works created by authors and recognized as canon. Because the church is a community of interpretation, moreover, Gustafson (like his critics) refused to assign the task of interpretation, even the task of interpreting scripture, to the biblical scholars (who, nevertheless, "have a proper role").[39]

Gustafson identifies four "aspects" of the process he calls "internalization." The first aspect of internalization is "communication." The church is a community of language, and the Bible is "the principal source of the Church's language."[40] The second aspect of internalization is "interpretation," and the Christian churches are communities of interpretation. It is not enough simply to utter some biblical words; internalization requires that scripture (and liturgy and creeds) be interpreted in relation to changing historical contexts, and that such interpretations be used "to interpret the world."[41] It is important to note that for Gustafson, as for Royce—and in contrast to much hermeneutical theory on the Continent which stressed the finite *self* in relation to a text—interpretation is a communal task. For Gustafson, as for the critics of the consensus he helped form, the church is a community of interpretation; interpretation is not simply the province of the individual, not simply a matter of the "right of private judgment"; interpretation takes place in the context of the community and looks for communal validation. Interpretation has its proper location within the continuing church, and it sustains community. For Gustafson, no less than for Fowl and Jones, a faithful "politics" is both the presupposition and the goal for good interpretation.

The third aspect of internalization is "memory," and Christian churches are communities of memory. The Bible tells the story of Israel, Christ, and the church, and that story is internalized, owned as "our" story, in the continuing church. That past is not simply a series of events that can be described objectively but rather events to be celebrated in repentance and jubilee, to be rehearsed in ritual and festival. The Bible, then, is not the only "object" to bear the possibilities of a common memory in the Christian community, and it does not bear the possibilities alone, but it is surely the critical document for church's remembering.[42] The past, moreover, is not simply gone; we do not live in the past, but it lives in us. Against Kant and Kierkegaard, Gustafson does not understand the self as transcending temporality in some radical freedom as a noumenal self, undetermined by its historical and social existence; rather, following Augustine, he understands the self to be deeply conditioned by its past and its community.[43] For Gustafson, freedom is made possible, as well as limited, by our pasts and by our communities; agency marshals memories and relates to others. That past also nurtures certain expectations, or at least a sense of possibilities. Because the church is a community of memory, it is also a community of hope. As in Passover Haggadah, acts of remembering in Christian community at once own a past, reconstitute the community by the renewal of covenant, and point toward a future.

The fourth aspect of internalization is "action," and Christian churches are communities of belief and action. The memory and hope of the community have relevance for present action. The common "objects" of the Christian community are finally "internalized" only when they are "bound up with the deeds of the community."[44] They are "internalized" only when they are enacted, or "performed," to use Nicholas Lash's apt phrase, so central to Cartwright and Fowl and Jones. Worship, of course, is such an action, such a "performance," but so is moral action, and the church is not only a community of worship but also a community of moral decision and action. Moral decision and action express faith, and they also provide an occasion for memory and hope, for interpretation, and for communication. Decisions and actions do not internalize (or embody) the meanings borne by the documents and rituals of the church when they are made simply on the basis of, for example, a utilitarian calculus. They internalize (and embody) those meanings when, loyal to God, "Christians self-consciously seek in [Christ], and in the life of the Church, the basis for their lives."[45]

It is important to observe that these are "aspects," not "stages," of the process of "internalization." They are a heuristic division of integrated judgments when scripture is "used" to form and reform the life of Christian community, not a simple set of sequential steps. The church, in its dialectical relation with scripture, is a community of moral decision and action precisely by also being a community of communication, where scripture provides the common language; a community of interpretation, both of scripture and of all things in the light of scripture; and a community of memory and hope formed and informed by scripture. These four are aspects, not stages; even so, there is an important priority to the "objects" that bear the meanings internalized by the Christian community and an important finality to the praxis of the internalized meanings in worship and moral action.

V. Practices, Performances, and Prescriptions

Given the "communal hermeneutic" of *Treasure in Earthen Vessels,* the counterproposals of the critics of the consensus perhaps may be regarded as friendly amendments, and suggestive and instructive by their attention to particular practices and performances of scripture. Indeed, I intend in this section to follow them into a description of certain practices and performances[46]—and to raise once again the issue of the "prescriptive use" of scripture in the moral discourse of churches. I hope to honor both the accomplishments of the consensus and the concerns of its critics.

Consider, first, the practice of prayer. To pray, after all, is a performance of scripture and intimately associated with reading scripture in Christian community (signaled by prayers for illumination and of response in Christian liturgy). Perhaps we need to learn to read scripture prayerfully. Prayer is a practice.[47] It is learned in Christian community, and it is learned not only as an idea but as a human activity that engages one's body as well as one's mind, one's affections and passions and loyalties as well as one's rationality, and which focuses one's whole self on God. In learning to pray, one learns the good that is "internal to that form of activity"; one learns, that is, to attend to God, to look to God.[48] To attend to God is not easy to learn—or painless. Given our inveterate attention to ourselves and to our own needs and wants, we frequently corrupt the practice. We corrupt prayer whenever we turn it to a means to accomplish some other good than the good of prayer, whenever we make of it an instrument to achieve wealth, happiness, health, or moral improvement. In learning to pray, we learn to look to God; and after the blinding vision, begin to look at all else in a new light.

In learning to pray, we learn as well certain standards of excellence[49] that belong to prayer and its attention to God, standards of excellence that are "appropriate to" prayer and "partially definitive" of prayer. We learn *reverence*, the readiness to attend to God as God and to all else in relation to God. We learn *humility*, the readiness to acknowledge that we are not gods, but the creatures of God, cherished by God but finite and mortal and, yes, sinful creatures in need finally of God's grace and God's future. We learn *gratitude*, the disposition of thankfulness for the opportunities within the limits of our finiteness and mortality to delight in God and in the gifts of God. We learn *hope*, a disposition of confidence and courage that comes not from trusting oneself and the little truth one knows well or the little good one does well, but from trusting the grace and power of God. And we learn *care*; attentive to God, we grow attentive to the neighbor as related to God. These standards of excellence form virtues not only for prayer but for daily life—and for the reading of scripture. Prayer-formed persons and the prayer-formed communities—in the whole of their being and in the whole of their living—will be reverent, humble, grateful, hopeful, and caring. One does not pray *in order to* achieve these virtues. They are not formed when we use prayer as a technique. They are formed in simple attentiveness to God, and they spill over into new virtues for daily life and discernment.

What would a prayer-formed reading of scripture look like? There are some hints, I think, in these standards of excellence, but consider also the forms such attention to God takes. Prayer attends to God in the form of invocation and adoration, confession, thanksgiving, and petition. Invocation is remembrance.[50] We invoke (and revere) not just any old god, not some nameless god of philosophical theism, not some idolatrous object of somebody's "ultimate concern." We invoke the God "rendered" in scripture, and a prayer-formed reading of scripture will serve remembrance and invocation. So the practice of prayer both performs scripture and forms the practice of reading scripture in Christian community. We remember God; and, as we do, we are reoriented to God and to all things in relation to that God. This reorientation to all things is called *metanoia,* repentance. Invocation evokes repentance; attention to God in prayer, therefore, also takes the form of (humble) confession. Prayerful readings of scripture will serve confession, will form a readiness to read scripture "over-against ourselves" and not just "for ourselves"; "over-against" our lives and our common life and not simply in self-serving defense of them; "over-against" even our conventional readings of scripture, subverting our efforts to use the texts to boast about our own righteousness or to protect our own status and power. Confession is good for the soul, but it is also good for hermeneutics; it can form a hermeneutic humility. Such humility will attend carefully but without anxiety to the readings of saints and strangers (especially to the readings of the poor and the powerless and those whom it has been too much our impulse to shun and neglect), and it will attend to the whole church attending to the whole scripture.

Attention to God also takes the form of (grateful) thanksgiving. Gratitude to God can form in readers the readiness not to count what is given as "ours to dispose of as if we created it nor ours to serve only our own interests."[51] It can train readers to stewardship of their gifts, including scripture and the skills to read it. It trains readers to share their gifts, to use them in service to the community, without the conceit of philanthropy. The conceit of philanthropy divides the community of readers into two groups, the relatively self-sufficient benefactors (or scholars) and the needy beneficiaries of their interpretative skill. Gratitude trains readers to share their gifts (including the scholarly gifts of some readers) and to serve the community in the context of the acknowledgment that we are each and all recipient of God's gifts. Service is no less a response to gift than the prayers of thanksgiving themselves. Gratitude, moreover, trains readers to gladness, to delight in the gifts of God, including scripture. It forms an attitude toward scripture that is itself a "performance" of the psalmists' delight in Torah. Moreover, as prayers of thanksgiving are a form of attention to God, the gifts are celebrated not so much because they serve our interests but because they manifest God's grace and glory and serve God's cause. Prayers of thanksgiving, then, this form of attention to God, form in the community of readers a readiness to reform their reading habits and their "performances" that God may be manifest and God's cause served.

Finally, simple attentiveness to God takes the form of (hopeful and caring) petition. It is easy, of course, in petition to attend to ourselves rather than to God, to our wishes rather than to God's cause. The practice of prayer is corrupted when we use it as a kind of magic to get what we want, whether a fortune, or four more healthy years, or a resolution to an interpretative or moral dispute. When petition is a form of attention to God, however, then we pray—and pray boldly—that God's cause will be displayed, that God's good future will be present. We pray—and pray boldly—as Jesus taught us, for a taste of that future, for a taste of it not so much in an ecstatic spiritual experience but in such ordinary things as everyday bread and everyday forgiveness, in such mundane realities as tonight's rest and tomorrow's work, in such earthy stuff as the health of mortal flesh and the peace and justice of our communities. We govern our petitions—and our deeds, including the acts of reading and interpreting scripture—by a vision of God's good future and by the aching acknowledgment that it is not yet. That vision is evoked by remembrance and formed by reading scripture. A prayer-formed reading of scripture attends to God and to the cause of God, and it forms in turn both our words in petition and our works in everyday attention to God. So, the practice of prayer may form both the practice of reading scripture and the Christian life.

Consider, also, reading scripture itself as a practice.[52] Christians learn to read scripture (and to read scripture as important to the moral life) by being initiated into the practice of reading scripture in Christian community, not by being taught that a creed calls scripture an "infallible rule," nor by being taught by a biblical scholar that the Bible is a little library of ancient near eastern literature. The creed and the scholar may both be right, but Christians learn to read scripture in a community that affirms the creed and is hospitable to scholars. Moreover, in learning to read scripture, Christians learn as well the good that belongs to reading scripture, the "good internal to that form of

activity." They learn, that is, to remember.[53] They learn to remember not only intellectually, not just as a mental process of recollection, not just as disinterested recall of
historical facts; they learn to own a past as their own, and to own it as constitutive of
identity and determinative for discernment. Without remembering, there is no identity. In amnesia, one loses oneself; in memory, one finds an identity. And without common remembering, there is no community. It is little wonder that the church sustains
this practice and is herself sustained by it.

There are temptations to forgetfulness in public life, when Enlightenment assumptions demand generic principles and "scientific" knowledge, pushing "God" to the
margins. And there are temptations to forgetfulness in personal life, when the private
realm is construed as a space for the self-centered quest to satisfy desire. Forgetfulness
threatens a loss of identity, but the remedy for forgetfulness is remembrance, and remembrance is served by reading scripture.

Moreover, in learning to read scripture and to remember, Christians learn as well
certain standards of excellence "appropriate to" and "partially definitive" of this practice—three pairs of virtues for reading scripture: holiness and sanctification, fidelity
and creativity, discipline and discernment. Holiness is the standard of excellence for
reading scripture in Christian community that sets these writings apart from others,
and also sets apart a time and a place to read them and to remember.[54] The church sets
these writings apart as "holy" Bible, sets them apart as a whole as canon. To read any
text as canonical is to read it in Christian community and in the light of that "whole."
The canon itself, however, reminds its readers that texts have genre, authors, audience,
that they involve a process of tradition, that they have social and historical location. To
read any text as canonical, therefore, does not license reading it as if it stood in timeless transcendence over its own time and place. On the contrary, holiness invites and
welcomes attention to the textual, grammatical, literary, historical, and social investigations.

Sanctification is the standard of excellence in reading scripture that is ready to set
this canon (set aside) alongside our lives and our common life as their rule and guide.
It is the readiness to set the remembered story alongside all the stories of our lives—
stories of sexual desire, stories of sickness and healing, stories of wealth and poverty,
stories of our politics—until our conduct and character and communities are judged
and made new by the power of God, are formed in remembrance and hope, and render the story rendered by scripture. Sanctification invites and welcomes attention to
the saints as the best interpreters and to the skills and dispositions important to "performance interpretation."

Remembrance provides identity, and fidelity is simply the standard of excellence in
reading and performing scripture that is ready to live with integrity, ready to live faithfully in the memory that the church has owned as her own and in the hope that memory endues. Fidelity, however, requires a process of continual change, of creativity; for
the past is past and we do not live in it, even if we remember it. We do not live in

David's Jerusalem or in Pontius Pilate's, and an effort to "preserve" the past is doomed to the failure of anachronistic eccentricity.[55] Moreover, God's good future is not yet, still sadly not yet. We do not live in John's "new" Jerusalem either, and an effort to read scripture that neglects the continuing power of sin is condemned to the failure of utopian idealism. Creativity is the standard of excellence (nurtured in and limited by particular communities and traditions) that is ready to find words and deeds fitting both to scripture and to our own time and place, in order to live in the present with memory and hope and fidelity.

Discipline is the standard of excellence for reading scripture that marks one as ready to be a disciple in a community of disciples, ready to submit to and to contribute to the mutual admonition and encouragement of Christian community, to its interpretive and moral discourse. Discipline is the humility not to insist that scripture be read "for ourselves," either by insisting on a "right to private judgment" in interpretation or by demanding that any interpretation serve our interests. It is the humility to read scripture "over-against" ourselves and our communities. Discipline holds both individuals and their ecclesial communities to their responsibilities to read and to perform scripture, to form their lives and their common life by the truth of the story they love to tell.

Yet, the shape of that story and of lives formed to it requires discernment, the ability to recognize "fittingness."[56] In reading scripture, discernment is the ability to recognize the plot of the story, to see the wholeness of scripture, and to order the interpretation of any part toward that whole. It is to recognize how a statute, proverb, or story "fits" the whole. And in reading scripture as "profitable . . . for training in righteousness" (2 Tim. 3:16), discernment is the ability to plot our lives to "fit" the whole of scripture, to order our lives toward that whole. Discernment is a complex but practical wisdom. It does not rely on the simple application of general principles (whether of hermeneutics or of ethics) to particular cases by neutral and rational agents. Discernment is learned and exercised in the community gathered around the scripture, and it involves the diversity of gifts present in the congregation. Some are gifted with the scholarly tools of historical, literary, and social investigation. Some are gifted with moral imagination and religious sensitivity. Some are gifted with a passion for justice; some, with sweet reasonableness. Some are gifted with intellectual clarity; some, with simple piety. But all are gifted with their own experience, and each is gifted with the Spirit that brings remembrance (John 14:26).

To be sure, in the community some are blinded by fear, and some are blinded by duty, and the perception of each is abridged by investments in their culture or in their class. To be sure, sometimes whole communities are blinded by idolatrous loyalties to their race, their social standing, or their power. And to be sure, the practice of reading scripture is corrupted then. Frequently the habits of reading scripture do not measure up to the standards of excellence given with the practice, and communities can stand at risk of forgetfulness even when they have a creed that calls scripture an "infallible rule."

The remedy for forgetfulness is still to hear and to tell the old, old story, and to hear it now and then from saints and now and then from strangers.[57] Remembrance is served in a community of discernment, reading scripture with those whose experience is different from one's own and whose experience of the authority of scripture is different from one's own. In that dialogue, people must listen to scripture and to one another, muting neither scripture nor one another. In that dialogue, we may not demand that people violate what they know that they know in other ways; we may not use the slogan *"sola scriptura"* to silence other voices and other sources, to discount the experience of oppression or natural science or "natural" morality; we may not use the "authority of scripture" to put a stop to conversation, to beat those who speak from some other experience or for some other source into silence and submission. Of course, in the hermeneutical community gathered around scripture it will always be appropriate to invite each and all to the reconsideration of what we know that we know, to exhort each other to interpret our experience, or the "assured results" of science, or some minimal notion of morality in the light of scripture. In that dialogue, the authority of scripture is "nonviolent."[58] The moment of recognition of scripture's wholeness and truthfulness comes before the moment of submission to any part of it and prepares the way for it. We may learn in such discourse with saints and strangers that our reading of scripture does not yet "fit" scripture itself, and that our lives and our communities do not yet "fit" the story we love to tell and long to live.

Such a practice is certainly intimately related to another practice of the continuing church, the practice of moral discourse.[59] The practices of prayer and reading scripture—and the discipline of Christian ethics—are not to substitute for this practice but to serve and sustain it as another aspect of the integrated common life of Christian community. The practice of moral discourse is evidently nearly as old as the church itself. Paul described the Christian church(es) at Rome as "full of goodness, filled with all knowledge, and able to instruct one another" (Rom. 15:14). Nevertheless, he wrote "very boldly" to the congregations he praised "by way of reminder" (Rom. 15:15), reminding them of the "gospel of God" in order to encourage "the obedience of faith" (Rom. 1:5, 16:26). The reading of scripture in the context of moral discourse will also proceed "by way of reminder"; its good is remembrance, and its form is evangelical, remembering and telling "the gospel of God."

The early churches were (and contemporary churches are) communities of moral discourse by being communities of moral deliberation. They talked not only about *what* they ought to do but *why*. The concrete advice of discourse led inevitably to reason giving and reason hearing. Reason giving and reason hearing nurture personal responsibility without either surrendering it to the group or reducing it to secret and private preferences. To be sure, the answer to the question about what one should do might be provided by a charismatic prophet in the community or by an official leader of the community. However, the charismatic advice and the official's pronouncement required (and requires) testing by the whole community in deliberation, giving and hearing reasons. There was no one in the community authorized to say, "Do as I say because I say it." Reason giving and reason hearing sustain communal responsibility without either surrendering it to the leadership or reducing it to the public standards of other communities. The church as a community of moral deliberation can and must protect the *unity* of human life when the cleavage into a secret private life and an anonymous public life threatens to break it.

Sometimes the reasons given in the early church were simply the moral common-places of a Jewish or Hellenistic culture. Sometimes the reasons involved an appeal to the law or the prophets or the writings. Sometimes the reasons were simply an appeal to what nature teaches or what convention requires. There was no wooden scheme for deliberation, no simple checklist for determining what should be done, no fixed set of free-standing principles to be applied deductively to questions of conduct. Reasons were given and heard in the community, and any and all reasons had finally to be tested in the community and defended, discarded, or qualified by their coherence with the gospel. The churches were communities of moral discourse and moral deliberation, "able to instruct one another," because they were communities of moral discernment. Every judgment and every reason—even when they involved the citation of scrip-ture—were to be tested and qualified by a communal discernment of the shape and style of life "worthy of the gospel of Christ" (Phil. 1:27).

Discernment, or the perception of what is "fitting" or "worthy," is—as already noted—a complex human enterprise, and there is no recipe for it in scripture or in the community. Discernment in the community of Matthew almost certainly gave greater place and priority to the interpretation and application of the law of Moses than moral discernment in Mark's community (and discernment in any community is both lim-ited and enabled by the community's particular tradition and social location). Dis-cernment is clearly not simply reliance on an intuition or simply the deductive appli-cation of general principles. Communal discernment is not just a matter of sharing the little moral wisdom each member knows well or of compensating for the abridgments (major or minor) of each one's moral vision. Discernment, or the perception of what is fitting, was always in the church to be the discernment of what is fitting or worthy of the story Christians love to tell and long to live. It was that story which made them a community, and it was that story which called them to a discernment not conformed to this age, but transformed by the renewal of their mind (Rom. 12:1–2).[60] The churches were—and are—communities of discourse and deliberation and discernment by being communities of memory.

In this communal practice of moral discourse, prayer can play an important role—but not simply by making petition for an answer to a moral question. Prayer is not a technique to get what we want, whether what we want is four more healthy years or an answer to a hard moral question. It does not rescue us from ambiguity or free us from the necessity of thinking hard about cases, sorting out various principles, identi-fying the various goods at stake, and listening carefully to different accounts of the situation. Prayer does not rescue us from all that, but it does permit us to do all that while attentive to God and to be attentive to all that as related to God. Moreover, the standards of excellence for prayer—reverence, humility, gratitude, hope, and care—may spill over into communal discourse, deliberation, and discernment when we remember and call on God.

And in this practice of moral discourse, reading scripture can and does play an important role. To be sure, scripture can be cited (and frequently is cited) as part of the process of deliberation in Christian communities. It is "used" to defend a particular admonition or rule. And, of course, among the passages of scripture which can be cited (and frequently are) there are rules and "prescriptions." However, when scripture is used "prescriptively," appeals to scripture remain subject to the communal process of discernment. The church is a community of moral discourse and deliberation by being a community of moral discernment and memory. A prescription lifted from scripture may be and must be tested and accepted or qualified or rejected by the community's discernment. In that process of discernment, of course, scripture functions again, and most significantly, now to form community and character, identity and perspective, fundamental values and commitments, into something coherent with the story and capable of testing reasons, even "scriptural" ones.

The consensus, as Cartwright complained, rejected the "prescriptive use" of scripture. That complaint and this account of the practice of moral discourse can help to clarify the consensus and its rejection of the "prescriptive use"—and to demonstrate that Cartwright and Fowl and Jones share in it. The consensus did not deny the presence of prescriptions in scripture, nor did it propose that they be torn from the canon, from that collection of writings (in all their "great variety") which (as a whole) can and should rule the churches' life and speech. The consensus did not deny that citations of scriptural prescriptions *could be* appropriate in the deliberative process of giving reasons for specific moral judgments and rules. It denied that the fact that one could cite a scriptural prescription or prohibition was *sufficient* for the justification of a contemporary judgment or rule. It denied that one (or a community) could simply and definitively answer the question "What ought I do?" (the moral-rule level question) by citing a scriptural prescription or prohibition. The consensus insisted that the Christian community be a community of discernment and of memory by testing rules— even rules that are formally identical to scriptural prescriptions—by their creative fidelity to the whole story, by their ability to nurture and sustain a contemporary "performance" not of a little piece of the canon but of scripture as a whole. As we have already observed, when Fowl and Jones attended to moral conversation, they retrieved important features of the consensus that they were otherwise at pains to discredit, including the suspicion of a "prescriptive use" of scripture: "[W]e should not presume *a priori* that any particular text or texts must be determinative."[61] Cartwright objected to my discussion of Matthew 18:15–22 as an example of the dismissal of a "prescriptive use" of scripture.[62] He does not, however, propose that communities should "perform" Matthew's text by permitting divorce only for those *men* whose wives have committed adultery. He proposes, instead, following James W. McClendon Jr., an "ongoing community conversation" that exercises discernment in the reiterating and revising the rules.[63] Representatives of the consensus wanted to serve (not substitute for) such a conversation, such discernment, enabling Christian communities, for example, to use Matthew as Matthew had used the tradition of Jesus' words, "creatively and faithfully," "neither simply repeat[ing] his words as a rule for all Christian communities for all times nor disown[ing] them."[64]

We are indebted to the critics of the consensus for their many contributions to the ongoing scholarly and ecclesial conversation about the relation of Christian ethics to scripture. We have much to learn from their attention to the practices of particular communities, to the politics of communities of interpretation, to "performances" of scripture. Cartwright's call to be attentive to the "chains of signification" in particular ecclesial traditions and Fowl and Jones's call to be attentive to saints and strangers in reading scripture identify important research agendas. Their summons to develop characters and communities capable of reading scripture and of performing it well and wisely is a useful ecclesiastical admonition. Even so, their proposals are best seen as developments of, rather than as alternatives to, the consensus they were at pains to criticize, the consensus formed in large part—and still instructed—by Jim Gustafson's early work.

Notes

1. "Christian Ethics," in *Religion,* ed. Paul Ramsey (Englewood Cliffs, N.J.: Prentice-Hall, 1965), 285–354, 337; reprinted as "Christian Ethics in America," in James M. Gustafson, *Christian Ethics and the Community* (Philadelphia: Pilgrim Press, 1971), 23–82; and (in an abridged form) as "The Changing Use of the Bible in Christian Ethics," in *Readings in Moral Theology, No. 4: The Use of Scripture in Moral Theology,* ed. Charles E. Curran and Richard A. McCormick (New York: Paulist Press, 1984), 133–50.

2. Notably Bruce C. Birch and Larry L. Rasmussen, *Bible and Ethics in the Christian Life* (Minneapolis: Augsburg, 1976), 15–16; and Victor Paul Furnish, *Theology and Ethics in Paul* (Nashville: Abingdon, 1968), 7.

3. Only a sampling of the noteworthy literature can be indicated here: Birch and Rasmussen, *Bible and Ethics in the Christian Life,* rev. ed. (Minneapolis: Augsburg, 1989); Elisabeth Schüssler Fiorenza, *But She Said: Feminist Practices of Biblical Interpretation* (Boston: Beacon Press, 1992); Stephen E. Fowl and L. Gregory Jones, *Reading in Communion: Scripture and Ethics in Christian Life* (Grand Rapids, Mich.: Eerdmans, 1991); Victor Paul Furnish, *The Moral Teaching of Paul,* rev. ed. (Nashville: Abingdon, 1984); Stanley Hauerwas, *Unleashing the Scripture: Freeing the Bible from Captivity to America* (Nashville: Abingdon, 1993); Richard B. Hays, *The Moral Vision of the New Testament: A Contemporary Introduction to New Testament Ethics* (New York: HarperCollins, 1996); J. I. H. McDonald, *Biblical Interpretation and Christian Ethics* (Cambridge: Cambridge Uni-

versity Press, 1993); Wayne A. Meeks, *The Origins of Christian Morality: The First Two Centuries* (New Haven: Yale University Press, 1993); Stephen C. Mott, *Biblical Ethics and Social Change* (New York: Oxford University Press, 1983); Thomas Ogletree, *The Use of the Bible in Christian Ethics* (Philadelphia: Fortress, 1983); Letty M. Russell, ed., *Feminist Interpretation of the Bible* (Philadelphia: Westminster, 1985); Wolfgang Schrage, *The Ethics of the New Testament*, trans. David E. Green (Philadelphia: Fortress, 1988); William Schweiker, *Mimetic Reflections: A Study in Hermeneutics, Theology, and Ethics* (New York: Fordham University Press, 1990); C. Freeman Sleeper, *The Bible and the Moral Life* (Louisville, Ky.: Westminster John Knox, 1992); William C. Spohn, *What Are They Saying about Scripture and Ethics* (New York: Paulist, 1984); Allen Verhey, *The Great Reversal: Ethics and the New Testament* (Grand Rapids, Mich.: Eerdmans, 1984); Sondra Ely Wheeler, *Wealth as Peril and Obligation: The New Testament on Possessions* (Grand Rapids, Mich.: Eerdmans, 1995); John H. Yoder, *The Politics of Jesus* (Grand Rapids, Mich.: Eerdmans, 1972; rev. ed. 1994).

4. James M. Gustafson, "The Place of Scripture in Christian Ethics," *Theology and Christian Ethics* (Philadelphia: Pilgrim Press, 1974), 121–45; the article was first published in *Interpretation* 24 (1970): 430–55 and subsequently reprinted in Curran and McCormick, 151–77.

5. As observed, for example, most recently in Wheeler, *Wealth as Peril and Obligation*, 2–4.

6. Gustafson, "The Place of Scripture," 134.

7. See further David Kelsey, "Protestant Attitudes Regarding Methods of Biblical Interpretation," in *Scripture in the Jewish and Christian Traditions: Authority, Interpretation, Relevance*, ed. Frederick E. Greenspahn (Nashville: Abingdon Press, 1982); and J. I. H. McDonald, *Biblical Interpretation and Christian Ethics*.

8. Willi Marxsen, *New Testament Foundations for Christian Ethics* (Philadelphia: Fortress Press, 1993), continues this tradition.

9. See further Hans Frei, *The Eclipse of Biblical Narrative* (New Haven: Yale University Press, 1974), and David Kelsey, *The Uses of Scripture in Recent Theology* (Philadelphia: Fortress Press, 1975), 39–50.

10. See further David Kelsey, *The Uses of Scripture*, 33–38.

11. Gustafson, "The Place of Scripture," 134, 145.

12. Michael G. Cartwright, "The Uses of Scripture in Christian Ethics—After Bakhtin," in *The Annual of the Society of Christian Ethics: 1992*, ed. Harlan Beckley, 263–76; see also Cartwright, "The Practice and Performance of Scripture: Grounding Christian Ethics in a Communal Hermeneutic," in *The Annual of the Society of Christian Ethics: 1988*, ed. D. M. Yeager, 31–54; and "Practices, Politics, and Performance: Toward a Communal Hermeneutic for Christian Ethics" (Ph.D. diss., Duke University, 1988). Cartwright identified the essay by Gustafson, along with essays by Edward LeRoy Long Jr. and David Kelsey as formative for this consensus, and numbered Bruce Birch and Larry Rasmussen, Allen Verhey, Thomas Ogletree, and William Spohn as among its representatives.

13. Hauerwas, *Unleashing the Scriptures*, 19, 7, 34, 20, 27, 15.

14. Most notable of these studies is Meeks, *The Origins of Christian Morality*, 4. Meeks does, however, provide in the "postscript" to his book a tantalizing set of theses drawn from his social historical account of the early church that are relevant to "the lives of Christians and their neighbors today" (213).

15. See, for example, Hauerwas, *Unleashing the Scriptures*, 20: "If Paul could appear among us today to tell us what he 'really meant' when he wrote, for example, 1 Corinthians 13, his view

would not necessarily count more than Gregory's or Luther's account of Corinthians. There simply is no 'real meaning' of Paul's letters to the Corinthians once we understand that they are no longer Paul's letters but rather the church's Scripture."

16. Of much noteworthy literature here see, for example, Juan Luis Segundo, *The Liberation of Theology* (Maryknoll, N.Y.: Orbis Press, 1984), and Fiorenza, *But She Said.* It may be observed, however, that Hauerwas is also suspicious of readers in those North American churches deeply enmeshed in a culture of democratic liberalism, Enlightenment rationality, and Constantinian Christianity (e.g., *Unleashing the Scriptures,* 29–38).

17. Feminist biblical scholarship is sometimes suspicious not only of readers but of the text itself, of the canon, as deeply embedded in patriarchy; and it reaches sometimes behind the text to a historical reconstruction that allows contemporary women to reclaim the story and to criticize the canonical representation of it.

18. Stanley Hauerwas acknowledges the importance of their work to *Unleashing the Scriptures* (e.g., 39, 152, n. 15).

19. Cartwright, "The Practice and Performance of Scripture," 36. It is not that Cartwright holds that interpretation should be free of ideology; on the contrary, following Fredric Jameson (e.g., *The Political Unconscious: Narrative as a Socially Symbolic Act* [Ithaca, N.Y.: Cornell University Press, 1981]), he holds that no interpretative method is free of ideology, whether conscious of it or not (32–34).

Without minimizing the significance of Cartwright's denial of the ideological innocence of interpretation, it may be observed that one of the problems with Cartwright's argument is that he reads Jameson's argument that Northrup Frye's "formalist criticism" dismisses images of community and history in the service of an ideology of the individual as if it were immediately relevant to the consensus and its use of "formal" categories like modes and levels of moral discourse.

20. Cited in Cartwright, "The Uses of Scripture in Christian Ethics," 270. Cf. Hauerwas, *Unleashing the Scriptures,* 20.

21. Cartwright, "The Practice and Performance of Scripture," 40. Nicholas Lash, "Performing the Scriptures," *Theology on the Way to Emmaus* (London: SCM Press, 1986), 37–46, does, as Cartwright says, underscore the significance of particular Christian communities as communities of interpretation and the importance of "performance" of scripture. Moreover, Lash's account "has the further advantage of keeping the experts firmly in their place" (42). However, Lash also acknowledges the "indispensable contribution" of biblical scholarship and critical reflection to the "performative interpretation of scripture" (42–43). For Lash there is no "performative interpretation," no set of practices in particular communities, in which the "meaning" of scripture is definitively captured, and, because this is so, "the range of appropriate interpretations . . . is constrained by what the text 'originally meant'" (44). The performative interpretation that "*is* the life of the church" (43) must also always, therefore, be open to reform and renewal by the effort to understand what the text "originally meant" and by reflection about the relation of such interpretation to performative interpretation. That (I take it) is what the consensus was about. That there are different traditions of interpretive performance of, for example, *Hamlet,* does not mean that there is no text or that an assessment of a performance has no text to which it can appeal or that skills in trying to understand what Shakespeare was trying to do with the text are irrelevant to that assessment.

22. Cartwright, "The Practice and Performance of Scripture," 36, 37–41, 47–48; "The Uses of Scripture in Christian Ethics," 272. See also Vigen Guroian, "The Bible in Orthodox Ethics: A Liturgical Reading," *Ethics after Christendom: Toward an Ecclesial Christian Ethic* (Grand Rapids, Mich.: Eerdmans, 1994), 53–80; John H. Yoder, "Binding and Loosing," *The Royal Priesthood*, ed. Michael G. Cartwright (Grand Rapids, Mich.: Eerdmans, 1994), 323–58; and Cain Hope Felder, ed., *Stony the Road We Trod: African American Biblical Interpretation* (Minneapolis: Fortress, 1991).

23. Cartwright, "The Practice and Performance of Scripture," 32. Cartwright takes this phrase from John Howard Yoder, "The Hermeneutics of Peoplehood: A Protestant Perspective," *The Priestly Kingdom: Social Ethics as Gospel* (Notre Dame, Ind.: University of Notre Dame Press, 1984), 15–45, 31. Yoder uses Jesus' image of the householder (Matt. 13:52) to describe those in Christian community who remind us of scripture, that "collective scribal memory, the store *par excellence* of treasures old and new." It is, indeed, an "apt description," but the "resourceful selectivity" of a householder (or a scribe) can itself be more or less apt. The judgment about aptness belongs to the community in discourse and discernment, but such judgments will be necessary— and the discourse and discernment to make them will be helped by attention both to the text and to the methodological issues raised by selection and interpretation. Yoder condemns any usurpation of the place of the community by literary or historical critics, by theorists about authority, or by sociopolitical analysts, but he nevertheless regards such considerations as "worthy of attention" (31) and presumably helpful to the community's conversation and discernment.

24. Cartwright, "The Uses of Scripture in Christian Ethics," 276.

25. Fowl and Jones, *Reading in Communion*, 4–10. Attributing to Gustafson's essay an important role in "framing the question," they read it curiously as an instance of "the common presumption that the Bible's role is located in relation to particular decisions made by isolated individuals" (5). They acknowledge that some representatives of the consensus they criticize, notably Bruce Birch and Larry Rasmussen and Thomas Ogletree, do attend to character and community, but they object to the fact that such attention is simply "put alongside" other elements of the moral life (10). They call attention to the rejection of a prescriptive use of scripture by the consensus, and like Cartwright they propose a retrieval of moral rules; moral rules (including the moral rules of scripture) are not, however, to be regarded as "*independent* of the formation of character in socially embodied traditions." Rules are open to revision by people of practical wisdom, but certain rules are "partially constitutive of the tradition's identity" and, so, also "relatively stable and authoritative" (10–11).

26. In this context they assert that not only discussions of biblical interpretation but also discussions of the place of the Bible in Christian ethics have been carried on "primarily within the presumptions and ideologies of liberal thought and practice" (18), i.e., in the university. They later will acknowledge the important contributions of "biblical scholarship as it is carried out in the academy" (39–41) to the tasks of interpretation within the Christian community, but they do not similarly acknowledge the contribution of the methodological studies to the tasks of communal discourse and discernment of a life appropriate to scripture.

27. Fowl and Jones, *Reading in Communion*, 19, 64.

28. Ibid., 28 (see also 65–81 and Hauerwas, *Unleashing the Scriptures*, 8) and 42, citing Dietrich Bonhoeffer, "The Presentation of New Testament Texts," in *No Rusty Swords*, trans. E. H. Robertson et al. (London: Collins, 1970), 302–20. The final chapter of *Reading in Communion* discusses Bonhoeffer as an exemplary interpreter and "performer" of scripture.

29. Fowl and Jones, *Reading in Communion,* 42. Indeed, in their discussion of Bonhoeffer there is the suggestion that attention to method allows readers to evade the content of scripture, to discard what they do not want or do not like, to read the Bible *for* themselves, like the German Christians did (145). However, a "garage sale" method of reading scripture, which selects texts that the consumer-reader likes and do not cost too much, is only one possible method. To claim that it is a bad method will invoke methodological arguments, not dismiss attention to method. On the suspicion of "method" see also Hauerwas, *Unleashing the Scriptures,* 42.

30. Fowl and Jones, *Reading in Communion,* 70, 71, 63–64, 78–80. Hauerwas, *Unleashing the Scriptures,* also recommends attention to "the saints" (37). Hauerwas attends especially, however, to the practice of preaching. Indeed, his book, is not simply a discursive theological essay; he "exhibits" his use of scripture in sermons. The practice of preaching is taken as a performative interpretation of scripture itself "meant to help us live more faithfully as Christians who are part of the community called Church" (8). The exhibits are wonderfully challenging and edifying. Preaching itself, however, accepts responsibility to the church even as it exercises authority over the church. The practice of preaching involves an ecclesial responsibility to assess the preaching as well as to submit to it. In a curious inconsistency with the discursive essay (but consistent with the practice) Hauerwas introduces his "sermonic exhibits" with a note to the reader, "Before reading the following sermons, it is necessary to read the scriptures appointed. Part of the practice is the interaction between your reading and my sermons" (45). Readers—and hearers—of sermons are obliged to read scripture "on their own"; they are certainly not exercising some "right to privacy" when they do. They are surrounded by a community of interpreters, situated (consciously or unconsciously) in a tradition or traditions of interpretation, indebted to "chains of signification" when they do. However, they are personally responsible for reading and interpretation, and they may not surrender that personal responsibility to the group or to the preacher any more than they may exercise it "privately."

31. Fowl and Jones, *Reading in Communion,* 99, 104.

32. Ibid., 110, 112, 113–22.

33. Ibid., 113, 114, 115.

34. James M. Gustafson, *Treasure in Earthen Vessels: The Church as a Human Community* (New York: Harper & Brothers, 1961).

35. Gustafson, *Treasure,* 43. He acknowledges the influence of Josiah Royce, *The Problem of Christianity* (New York: Macmillan, 1913), II, 1–65.

36. Cf. Kelsey, *The Uses of Scripture,* 90–97. It seems to me that Gustafson anticipated the work of Kelsey in certain respects, and at least in this respect, that "'scripture' is used to name, not something the church is, but something she must use . . . to preserve her self-identity" (Kelsey, *The Uses of Scripture,* 96). Michael Cartwright objects to Kelsey's "focus on the 'interpreter' as the subject who carries out the imaginative construal of scripture" and calls attention to "the ecclesial context in which the interpreter stands" ("The Practice and Performance of Scripture," 43). The complaint about individualism, however, is mistaken. Kelsey himself objects to the arbitrary individualism that treats scripture as "'the weathercock in the church tower' which is turned hither and thither by every theologian's imaginative brainstorms" (170). The imaginative act of the interpreter "has its ground in features of the common life of the church as [the interpreter] knows it by participating in it" (170). The community enables and limits the proposals concerning an imaginative construal of scripture, first, by being "a community of discourse,"

requiring that the proposals be "capable of consistent formulation" and "patient of reasoned elaboration" (171); second, by being "culturally conditioned" (171–73); and third, by being situated in a particular ecclesiastical tradition with what Cartwright would call "chains of signification" (174–75).

37. Nicholas Wolterstorff, *Art in Action* (Grand Rapids, Mich.: Eerdmans, 1980), 80. In his *Divine Discourse: Philosophical Reflections on the Claim That God Speaks* (Cambridge: Cambridge University Press, 1995), Wolterstorff defends what he calls "authorial-discourse interpretation" against the attacks of both Ricoeur and Derrida, and distinguishes it from "performance interpretation" (130–82). Nicholas Lash may also be cited here; see n. 21.

38. I would no longer (as in *The Great Reversal*, 172–74) make knowledge of the "author's intention" necessary for interpretation. I accept the criticism that my talk of an "author's intention" there sounded like an invitation to a futile (and psychologizing) effort to examine the state of mind of the dead. I would, however, still argue that attention to an author's actions in forming a text can make us more aware that it remains the author's text and willing to recognize the potential value to interpretation of what can be known about the author's intention. Moreover, even if we are not able to know confidently an author's subjective intention, consideration of what an author *did* in forming a text can make a modest but important contribution to interpretation and to the assessment of performance. (See Wolterstorff, *Divine Discourse*, 183–201.)

39. Gustafson, *Treasure*, 59. Lash makes a similar point (see n. 21). And so do Fowl and Jones! After dismissing the presumption of some critical biblical scholarship that it "can deliver to us *the* meaning of the text apart from and despite thousands of years of interpretation and embodiment" (40), they nevertheless express their appreciation of the contributions of critical biblical scholarship to Christian communities engaged in interpretive practice, not least by withstanding the presumption of some particular communities that they are *the* tradition of scriptural interpretation and that the tradition is pure (39–44).

40. Gustafson, *Treasure*, 46.

41. Ibid., 56.

42. Note the similar claim by Stanley Hauerwas in "The Moral Authority of Scripture: The Politics and Ethics of Remembering," *A Community of Character* (Notre Dame, Ind.: University of Notre Dame Press, 1981), and in *Unleashing the Scriptures*, 36.

43. Gustafson, *Treasure*, 113–37. To read Gustafson as presupposing or invoking an Enlightenment individualism is simply a "bad reading."

44. Gustafson, *Treasure*, 131, citing Royce, *The Problem of Christianity* II, 65.

45. Gustafson, *Treasure*, 99.

46. Indeed, in *Ethics from a Theocentric Perspective,* 2 vols. (Chicago: University of Chicago Press, 1981–1984), vol. *1. Theology and Ethics,* 317 Gustafson observes that "one of the themes" of that book "is that visions, ways of life, and intellectual activities take place in particular historical and communal contexts," and that theological interpretation "must take place in the context of a religious community, with its first-order religious language, its liturgies and symbols, and its procedures for transmitting a heritage" (p. 318). He then turns to a consideration of prayer, among other things (pp. 318–25). The turn, then, to the practices of piety could be understood as following Gustafson as well as the critics.

47. Alasdair MacIntyre, *After Virtue: A Study in Moral Theory* (Notre Dame, Ind.: University of Notre Dame Press, 1981), 175, defined a practice as a "form of socially established cooperative human activity through which goods internal to that form of activity are realized in the

course of trying to achieve those standards of excellence which are appropriate to, and partially definitive of, that form of activity with the result that human powers to achieve excellence and human conceptions of the ends and goods involved are systematically extended." On prayer as a practice, see further Allen Verhey, *The Practices of Piety and the Practice of Medicine: Prayer, Scripture, and Medical Ethics* (Grand Rapids, Mich.: Calvin College and Seminary, The Stob Lectures Endowment, 1992), 15–28.

48. On prayer as attention see especially Iris Murdoch, "On 'God' and 'Good,'" in Stanley Hauerwas and Alasdair MacIntyre, eds., *Revisions: Changing Perspectives in Moral Philosophy* (Notre Dame, Ind.: University of Notre Dame Press, 1983), 68–91; Craig Dykstra, *Vision and Character* (New York: Paulist Press, 1981), 45–98; and Simone Weil, *Waiting on God*, trans. E. Craufurd (London: Routledge & Kegan Paul, 1951), 51.

49. Consider, for example, John Calvin's attention to the "rules" of prayer in *Institutes*, III. xx. 4–16. Calvin's "rules" are reverence, a sincere sense of want (that is, to pray earnestly), humility, and confident hope.

50. On prayer as an act of remembrance see Nicholas Wolterstorff, *Until Justice and Peace Embrace* (Grand Rapids, Mich.: Eerdmans, 1983), 152–56. Donald Saliers, "Liturgy and Ethics: Some New Beginnings," *Journal of Religious Ethics* 7 (fall 1979): 173–89, also emphasizes that "the shape and substance of prayer is *anamnetic*" (178).

51. James M. Gustafson, "Spiritual Life and Moral Life," *Theology and Christian Ethics* (Philadelphia: Pilgrim Press, 1974), 170.

52. On reading scripture as a practice, see further Verhey, *The Practices of Piety*, 41–51, and "The Holy Bible and Sanctified Sexuality," *Interpretation* 49, no. 1 (1995): 41–45.

53. For the notion of remembrance as the "good" of reading scripture, I am indebted to Hauerwas, "The Moral Authority of Scripture," 53–71. See also, of course, Gustafson, *Treasure*, 71–78.

54. See Fowl and Jones, *Reading in Communion*, 31–33.

55. Lash, *Theology on the Way to Emmaus*, 54, makes the point quite nicely with respect to the traditions and ecclesiastical dress of the Franciscans: "If, in thirteenth-century Italy, you wandered around in a course brown gown, . . . your dress said you were one of the poor. If, in twentieth-century Cambridge, you wander around in a course brown gown, . . . your dress now says, not that you are one of the poor, but that you are some kind of oddity in the business of 'religion.'" Fidelity to a tradition of solidarity with the poor requires creativity and change.

56. On discernment see especially James M. Gustafson, "Moral Discernment in the Christian Life," in *Norm and Context in the Christian Life*, ed. Gene H. Outka and Paul Ramsey (New York: Charles Scribner's Sons, 1968), 17–36.

57. Fowl and Jones, *Reading in Communion*, 62–64, 111–30.

58. Margaret Farley, "Feminist Consciousness and the Interpretation of Scripture," in *Feminist Interpretation of the Bible*, ed. Letty M. Russell, 41–51; see esp. 42–44. She cites Paul Ricoeur, *Essays in Biblical Interpretation*, ed. L. S. Mudge (Philadelphia: Fortress Press, 1980), 95.

59. James M. Gustafson, "The Church: A Community of Moral Discourse," *The Church as Moral Decision-Maker* (Philadelphia: Pilgrim Press, 1970), 83–95.

60. Meeks, *The Origins of Christian Morality*, 17:

> The moral life has a plot, and it is a plot that implicates not merely each individual, but humankind and the cosmos. It may be that what most clearly sets Christian ethics apart from all the other ethical discourse of late antiquity, with which it otherwise shares so much, is

just the creation of this peculiar story in which each of us is called on to be a character, and from which character itself and virtue take their meaning.

See further 189–210.

61. Fowl and Jones, *Reading in Communion*, 116.

62. Cartwright, "Practices, Politics, and Performance," 47.

62. Cartwright, "The Practice and Performance of Scripture," 47. He cites James W. McClendon Jr., *Systematic Theology: Ethics* (Nashville: Abingdon, 1986), 223–24.

63. Verhey, *The Great Reversal*, 173.

Chapter 3

The Reformed Tradition
in Theological Ethics

DOUGLAS F. OTTATI

Theologies are shaped and sustained by specific communities that bear particular heritages. This does not distinguish theology from other intellectual enterprises. The patterns of reason and scientific method also are traditional in the sense that they are handed down in communities of inquirers.[1] Inescapably, we are historical and social beings, and our knowledge is always knowledge-from-some-particular-point-of-view. Traditions constitute perspectives on the world. Traditions give rise to thought, and that is why we need to interpret them.

Theology and Theological Ethics

My interpretation of the Reformed tradition in theological ethics presupposes some broad judgments about theology and theological ethics. To recall the opening sentence of John Calvin's *Institutes of the Christian Religion*, theology is a convictional wisdom that has to do with matters of meaning and purpose. Theology is a reflective enterprise that addresses our practical orientation in the world, a knowledge of God and of ourselves that supports a way of negotiating life or of coming to terms with it.[2] As such, theology touches on many things. It interprets nature, history, human agency, civil government, family, religious community, technology, and more. There are also distinguishable dimensions of theological wisdom. For example, knowledge of God and of ourselves becomes biblical theology as it intertwines with the interpretation of scripture. As it bears upon and is borne upon by the worshipful assemblies and practices of congregations, it becomes liturgical theology. As it influences and is influenced by the practice of ministry, it becomes pastoral theology.

Theological ethics is knowledge of God and ourselves as it connects with the wellsprings, contexts, and guides for human action. It is a convictional wisdom that influences and is influenced by the ways we understand our human predicament, the causes to which we are loyal, the norms that guide our behavior, and the circumstances calling for action. Like theology, theological ethics is a reflective enterprise supported and transmitted by religious communities; its forms are particular rather than generic. Thus, Christian communities and their traditions bear Christian theological ethics, Islamic communities and their traditions bear Muslim theological ethics, and so on. Within each broad religious movement, there also are subcommunities and subtraditions (e.g., Shi'ite and Sunni, Greek Orthodox and Methodist).

Reformed theology is a specific sort of Christian theology. It is a distinctive pattern of Christian convictional wisdom about God and ourselves that is borne by Reformed Christian communities and their particular Christian subtradition. The Reformed tradition in theological ethics is a particular pattern of sapiential reflection with reference to the wellsprings, contexts, and guides of human action. It helps Reformed Christians to construe our human predicament, the fundamental causes to which we are loyal, the norms that guide our behavior, and the circumstances calling for action.

A Preliminary Account

The leading affirmation of Reformed theological ethics is that, first and foremost, we belong to God. By this principle, Reformed convictional wisdom points to *metanoia*: not thinking first about our loyalties to ourselves and our isolated groups, but being caught up into the messianic event of Jesus Christ, the person-for-others who embodies a way in life oriented by radical devotion to God. It indicates that the earth is God's and that we are not our own. It insists that genuine faithfulness is a life reordered and reformed by devotion to God and God's all-inclusive reign.

This insistence connects with further convictions. Reformed wisdom affirms that we are created good, equipped and sustained for responsible relations with God and others. Caught in the grips of sin, however, we become unresponsive and irresponsible. Sin is therefore a fundamental corruption of what we are equipped and sustained to be. Where this goes unrecognized, so do the persistently destructive tendencies of every person, community, and institution. At the same time, Reformed theological wisdom affirms that grace abounds. Grace means regeneration: the renewal, conversion, restoration, and rehabilitation of persons and communities. Where this goes unrecognized, so do the promising possibilities of every person, community, and institution.

Within the frame of Reformed theological ethics, then, all are subject to criticism even as all are affirmed. All are summoned to repentance and new life. Indeed, the faithful are called to reform all persons, communities, and institutions, to denounce and restrain corruption, and to announce and pursue possibilities for renewal. They are called to a life of participating faithfully within God's inclusive commonwealth.

Some History

This preliminary account emerges from a reading of the history of Reformed Christianity, but it needs to be further developed in the light of that history. The story of the Reformed movement is a dynamic tale of multiple contexts, institutions, and theological expressions. Indeed, the differently situated and articulated Reformed theologies and ethics constitute rich and varied storehouses of reflection concerning our knowledge of God and ourselves.

Classical Beginnings

Although Calvin's work at Geneva was decisive, the origins of the Reformed movement were multiple and intertwined with diverse linguistic, cultural, and political contexts. From the first, there were Ulrich Zwingli and Heinrich Bullinger in Zurich, John Oecolampadius at Basel, Martin Bucer at Strassburg and at Cambridge, Zacharias Ursinus and Caspar Olevianus in the Palatinate, and many more. Before the end of the sixteenth century, Reformed churches were present in Switzerland, Germany, France, Holland, Scotland, Hungary, and Poland.

Unity was strengthened by institutions of higher learning at Cambridge, Heidelberg, Leiden, St. Andrews, Ghent, Montaubon, Hanau, and elsewhere.[3] At the academy of Geneva, Calvin himself helped to train ministers who were active throughout Europe. Even so, multiple figures operating at multiple centers and in varied contexts produced multiple theological treatises, confessional documents, liturgies, and polities.

These exhibited important commonalities, such as theological emphases on the priority of God's Word over inherited church teaching, God's sovereign rule in nature and history, the radicality of sin, the sufficiency of grace in Jesus Christ, and the importance of sanctification or the regenerate life. There were also significant differences. For example, Zwingli and his followers at Zurich understood the Lord's Supper as a memorial, while Calvin insisted on a spiritual or mystical presence of Christ in the sacrament. The exiled English and Scottish reformers, Christopher Goodman and John Knox, studied at Geneva, but they differed from Calvin on the question of revolution. Like Huguenots in France, such as Phillippe du Plessis Mornay, they issued explicit calls for rebellion against illicit tyrants.[4] Diversity extended even to fundamental matters of polity; most frameworks of Reformed church government featured consistories, colloquies, or presbyteries, but the Reformed Church of Hungary retained bishops.

Subsequent Developments

By the beginning of the seventeenth century, Reformed Protestantism in the Netherlands spawned what proved to be a recurrent and typically Calvinist controversy over the teachings of Arminius concerning salvation, grace, and human agency. In response, the Synod of Dort (1618–1619) adopted the so-called Five Points of Calvinism (TULIP): total depravity, unconditional election, limited atonement, irresistible grace, and perseverance of the saints. Meanwhile, Reformed sympathizers in England became the driving force behind a wide-ranging Puritan movement both within and without established Anglicanism. A highly developed casuistry and literature of "practical divinity" emerged in works by William Ames, William Perkins, Richard Baxter, and others. In both old and New England, Puritanism's free-church wing mixed with Levellers, General Baptists, and other sects of the Radical Reformation. Its writers, such as John Lilburne, Richard Overton, and Roger Williams, developed egalitarian theories of political rights and responsibilities. They also tended to reject the idea that civil authority has any role to play in the restriction of religious belief and practice except to prevent outward harm.[5] More moderate English Puritans, assisted by Scottish commissioners, produced the influential (and magisterial) text of the Westminster Confession of Faith in 1647 in the midst of civil war.

These developments made for growing diversity. If the Calvinism of the Synod of Dort was not precisely Calvin's, then neither was the Puritanism of Westminster. Moreover, Arminian objections to schemes of strictly predestinate grace often received positive hearings among Reform-minded Christians in England. And, while Free Church Puritans were influenced by Swiss and Dutch social covenants, their willingness to relinquish the theocratic ideal introduced a new and creative element.

American Debates

One result of plurality within the Puritan movement was that Reformed Christians in America were Congregational, Separatist, Presbyterian, Baptist, Quaker, and even Episcopalian (as distinct from Anglicans in the Church of England). From the first, we must therefore speak of a Reformed *family of churches* in America, some of which shared detailed resemblances, and others of which were more distant relations. Nevertheless, all developed more or less free-church, denominational polities that affirmed the independence of the churches from state authority, the voluntary participation of laypeople in church government, and the relative independence of particular congregations from outside manipulation and control. This meant that Reformed communities tended to favor a broad separation of powers (which became characteristic of the new republic), that there would never be a single Reformed church in America whose institutional structures and doctrinal teachings might define the movement as a whole, and that there were significant variations of faith and practice among congregations within the same denominations. In consequence, a relatively free, somewhat laissez faire religious expectation emerged which routinely encouraged diversity in decisive beliefs and practices.

Consider early American controversies over orthodoxy and religious freedom, Arminianism, and the place of awakening experiences and emotions in the Christian life. Recall the heated debates about slavery and abolition, leadership roles for women, the rise of modern industry and ministries of economic justice, fundamentalism and modernism, and participation in ecumenical associations. In each instance, basic questions emerged. How shall we understand the principle of a free conscience in matters of religion, church, and state? Are Reformed churches best understood as gathered communities of explicit religious experience and commitment? Does Reformed theology preclude Arminianism? Does it require double predestination? Is slavery compatible with Reformed theology and ethics? Should women participate in all ministries of the church? Should our understandings of social justice be revised to take into account the increased interdependencies of industrial economies? Is the inerrancy of scripture an essential point of Reformed doctrine? Are the findings of modern sciences significant for theology and ethics? Should Reformed theology be revised in response to ecumenical ventures and discussions?

Although different answers to these questions often implied different interpretations of the central beliefs and appropriate limits of Reformed theology and ethics, none was simply and decisively answered once and for all. Different churches and theologians handled them differently. The same denominations sometimes answered one or more of these questions differently at different times, and different camps sometimes managed to coexist within the same denominations. Where there were especially sharp disagreements, however, Reformed communities did a voluntary and characteristically American thing—they split.[6]

A Worldwide Movement

This, of course, is not all. Even the briefest sketch of the Reformed movement should mention the immigration of Dutch Reformed and French Huguenot settlers to South Africa late in the seventeenth century, the subsequent development of Africaner Calvinism and Free Church strands there, and the more recent emergence of the Alliance of Black Reformed Christians in Southern Africa (1981).[7] Indeed, Reformed Christianity is genuinely global, and its churches confront a dizzying variety of issues and contexts. Thus, Reformed ministers in Pacific countries—such as the Cook Islands, Marshall Islands, Papua New Guinea, Kiribati, and Samoa—face questions about appropriate hymns, dancing, and architecture, as they encourage more indigenous and open styles of worship. Others ponder questions concerning the family and the individual in Nigeria, an ecumenical Christian witness in the Middle East, and the importance of secular values in India.[8] There are more Presbyterians in Korea today than in Scotland, and Korean Presbyterian churches are active in both the United States and Brazil. Reformed Christians in Canada, Zambia, Australia, and elsewhere have united with Methodists, thus prompting the World Alliance of Reformed Churches and the World Methodist Council jointly to declare that classical doctrinal differences concerning grace and salvation should not be seen as obstacles to unity.

In short, the Reformed movement seems comparatively loosely wound. It has not been as concentrated—either in its origins or its subsequent developments—as another great Protestant tradition, Lutheranism. Its theology and ethics have not been as dependent on a single towering figure. Neither have they been as tied to confessional documents written in the same region over a brief period of time.[9] Reformed Christianity has no tradition of a single hierarchical institution and its universal teaching authority, as does Roman Catholicism. To the contrary, it has a strong free-church tradition with an aversion to centralized structures. Finally, it is increasingly difficult to generalize about the ethnic backgrounds and cultural circumstances of Reformed Christians; the World Alliance of Reformed Churches now includes 193 churches in ninety-nine countries.

The Reformed Tradition in Theological Ethics

This foray into the history of the Reformed movement indicates that it is not easy to generalize about the Reformed tradition in theological ethics. For one thing, there are many ways in which this dynamic tradition may be understood. For another, the Reformed movement continues to develop, and so all interpretations must remain provisional.

Considerations such as these prevent us from claiming final authority for our reflections. Nonetheless, we fail to examine important dimensions of our own thinking if we do not develop our own understandings of the traditions to which we assent and in which we stand. With this in mind, I shall outline the pattern of Reformed theological wisdom as it influences and is influenced by understandings of our human predicament, the causes to which we are loyal, the norms that guide our behavior, and the circumstances that call for action. My approach is to plot Reformed interpretations of four motifs. These motifs are illustrative rather than exhaustive; others might be added helpfully. My intention is to suggest a pattern of sapiential reflection that accommodates a variety of constructive positions.

Sources of Insight

One motif is epistemological. What are the appropriate sources for our knowledge of God and ourselves? In general, theological ethics in the Reformed tradition emphasizes the priority of revelation or the Word of God even as it remains open to wisdom and insight wherever they are found.

Bullinger held that "the church is not built by [human] decrees, but founded, planted, assembled and built only by the Word of Christ."[10] Calvin claimed that scripture is a necessary guide and teacher for our knowledge of God as Creator and Redeemer, and Westminster affirmed the decisive importance of scripture or "the Word of God written" as "the rule of faith and practice." Even so, both Zwingli and Calvin made significant use of tradition in the form of early creeds and writings by church founders. The Scots Confession notes that, while some councils have erred "in matters of great importance," they serve to refute heresies and give public confession of the faith to generations following, as well as to maintain good order in the church.[11]

Calvin also appealed to classical philosophy and standards of "natural equity" as he preached on the Ten Commandments. Indeed, he could write that "the law of God which we call moral law is nothing else than a testimony of natural law and of that conscience which God has engraved upon the minds of [humans]."[12] Williams claimed that "conscience is found in all [hu]mankind, more or less, in Jews, Turks, Papists, Protestants, pagans, etc.," and that basic virtue and fair dealing are universally and naturally available.[13] Jonathan Edwards once jotted down in his notebook on "The Mind" a point supported by his understanding of God's universal and sovereign reign: "to find out the reasons of things in natural philosophy is only to find out the proportion of God's acting."[14] Recently, James M. Gustafson has argued that scientific explanations can alter some traditional religious claims, and that the substantial content of theology must be congruent in some way with what we know through the sciences.[15] Thus, Reformed ethicists have been willing to appeal to sources of insight well beyond the confines of historic Christian tradition. The reason, as Calvin himself insisted, is that "all truth is of God."[16]

There have also been heated debates. For example, the fundamentalist-modernist controversy was partly a conflict over more- and less-restrictive interpretations of the appropriate sources of insight for theology and ethics. In Europe, Karl Barth and Emil Brunner disagreed over our ability to know God's will. Brunner claimed that revelation furnishes us with knowledge of the good—of personal freedom, responsibility, and community—which, in turn, forms a basis for generalizations about created orders (e.g., family, labor, the state). Barth, who lamented the vestiges of a natural theology in the classical Reformers, complained that Brunner embraced a theology of compromise which threatened the independence of revelation from alien sources of insight.[17] He maintained that God commands in sovereign freedom and that the concrete and specific divine commands that come to us cannot be bound by generalizations. H. Richard Niebuhr tried to hold together concerns such as these by arguing that revelation in Jesus Christ precipitates a continuing revolution in our understandings of unity, power, and goodness.[18]

Sin and Good

A second matter concerns sin and good. Calvin thought that human beings are mirrors of God's wisdom, goodness, and power. Indeed, we are endowed with wondrous capacities, and God's image originally shone in their upright arrangement.[19] Like Augustine, however, he also believed that sin means radical and universal derangement. Sin infects all of our capacities as well as every aspect and institution of society (including the church), and it continues to produce a train of evil consequences. Similarly, Edwards held that sin is an active and persistent tendency, an orienting impulsion, or a disposing alignment of our powers.[20] The human project is therefore unavoidably skewed, and yet the pessimism engendered by the conviction of sin is not unmitigated. According to Calvin, Edwards, and others, God continues to uphold in fallen persons impressive abilities in the arts and sciences, as well as certain basic social affections and a rudimentary sense of justice or fairness.[21]

Regenerating grace brings a new tendency. For Calvin, our capacity for well-doing is restored by grace and the Spirit, and the basic fruits are piety toward God and charity toward neighbor.[22] Edwards thought that grace supports true virtue or a disposition of benevolence to being-in-general. Horace Bushnell claimed that persons in Christ are brought to a new reigning love, so that "life proceeds from a new center."[23] However, a further Augustinian conviction bridles inordinate optimism. As the Scots Confession, the Second Helvetic Confession, and Westminster put it, corruption continues even among the regenerate.[24]

The tension between pessimism and optimism was expressed by Puritan social conceptions. For example, the conviction of sin led John Cotton to insist that "It is necessary . . . that all power . . . on earth be limited."[25] On the other hand, the Mayflower Compact is one of many Puritan mutual agreements, covenants, and constitutions that were intended not only to restrain corruption but also to guide persons and groups toward the good.

Nicholas Wolterstorff, Allan Boesak, and John de Gruchy point to a prophetic dimension of the insistence that all social structures are corrupted: All therefore are deserving of ongoing critique.[26] Indeed, Reinhold Niebuhr's Christian realism may be understood in part as a creative retrieval of the Reformed doctrine of sin in the midst of economic depression, totalitarianism, and war. Feminists such as Valerie Saiving and Judith Plaskow claim that Niebuhr's emphasis on sin as pride both obscures and exacerbates the experiences of persons in dependent and oppressed positions, whose problem is the opposite of inordinate self-assertion.[27] Perhaps these criticisms will encourage us to reconsider the understanding of sin as contraction and grace as enlargement as found in Augustine, Edwards, and Gustafson. The human fault, says Gustafson, represents a contraction of our trusts and loyalties, our loves and desires, our rational construing of the world, and our moral interest. This narrowing of the human spirit may be corrected by an enlargement of soul and of interests that supports a more genuinely participatory posture in the world that is neither inordinately nor deficiently assertive.[28]

Law and Gospel

A third motif concerns the moral guidance that coheres with or comes from our knowledge of God and of ourselves. In general, Reformed theological ethics emphasizes the reordering of both inward disposition and outward action in thankful response to the gifts and grace of God.

Somewhat like Luther, Calvin was concerned about the proper motive for morality. We should not be moral because we believe that we merit salvation by our moral commitment and performance. We do not. Forgiveness is free; election is by the grace of God alone. Thus, our typically prudential reasons for being moral need reordering. True moral interest and good works proceed from thankfulness for God's goodness and grace.

To this, however, Calvin joined a distinctive understanding of moral law. Like Luther, he affirmed that law in its civil use restrains evil, and that it shows how far short we fall of true righteousness in its accusatory use. But Calvin added a "third and principal use which pertains more closely to the proper purpose of the law," namely, to guide and exhort the faithful in their efforts to do good.[29] Thus, gospel and free forgiveness are not simply the end of the law, and love is not all one needs. Law follows gospel, and it remains an essential ingredient of the Christian life.

This is why Calvin's Strassburg Liturgy directed the congregation to sing the Ten Commandments following a prayer of confession and assurance of pardon. It is also why the authors of the *Heidelberg Catechism* were at one with the Genevan reformer when they placed their discussion of good works and the law under the rubric of thankfulness. Because he refused to reduce the Christian life to inward disposition alone, the Puritan casuist, Richard Baxter, instructed husbands and wives in their mutual duties, and soldiers on the importance of having a just cause. He also exhorted physicians to help the poor as well as those who are able to pay.[30]

Nevertheless, if love alone was deemed insufficient, it was also understood to be entirely necessary. Thus, Edwards maintained that regenerating grace does not simply oppose our natural loves for ourselves and our own groups; it extends these affections and turns them away from what is merely partial and toward what is more truly general or universal. Lesser loves are reordered within the wider frame of love to God and to all things under God.[31] H. Richard Niebuhr claimed that radical faith transforms all of our lesser devotions to self, nation, race, and so on, by devotion to God's universal community of being.[32]

Barth's Calvinist understanding of gospel and law and his rejection of Lutheran attempts to separate them were near the center of his controversy with German Christians. "What these good folk obviously want," he wrote, "—a Church that is only inward and not at all outward—is identical with what National Socialism wants of the Church."[33] Even so, important Reformed theologians have departed from the insistence on both disposition and prescription for the Christian life. Emphasizing an ethic of character and virtue, Friedrich Schleiermacher wrote that "the two commandments cited by Christ as containing the whole law are not really commands"; they actually contrast love of God and neighbor with the whole law. He also claimed that Christian ethics will better fit dogmatics and its own purpose "if it drops the imperative mood altogether, and simply gives an all-round description of how [humans] live within the [dominion] of God."[34] Brunner held that the law accuses and reveals sin, and that "The life of the Christian stands under the leading of the Spirit, not of the law." He believed that the gospel is personal, while law is impersonal. In fact, Brunner wrote, "among the Reformers it was Luther alone who . . . clearly recognized the spontaneously individualizing nature of *agape*, its origin, its oneness with faith and its antagonism to all law."[35]

God and World

This brings us to the chief issue for Reformed theological ethics: the relationship of God and world. The way in which this motif is understood shapes all others. One may argue that justification is decisive for much Lutheran theological ethics, and that discipleship lies at the heart of theological ethics in radical Protestantism. But the decisive emphasis in Reformed theological ethics is on God's sovereign reign.[36]

Reformed theologians affirm that all things in nature and history are caught up into an intricate web of divine power, presence, and purpose. This is what renders the many a *universe*. Thus, Schleiermacher believed that all things are bound up in a single system of divine causality.[37] Abraham Kuyper claimed that the "root principle" of Calvinism is "*the Sovereignty of the Triune God over the whole Cosmos*, in all of its spheres and [dominions], visible and invisible."[38] No area of life, no corner of creation lies beyond the creating, sustaining, judging, and redeeming activity of God.

A corollary of this affirmation, for Calvin, was that we belong to God and ought to employ the full force of our ability in the service of the God.[39] He therefore began his *Geneva Catechism* by stating that the chief end and supreme good of human life is to know God. Humans are created to glorify God, and so it is proper that human life should be directed toward God's glory.[40] Edwards elaborated the point by arguing that God's chief end in creating the world, including humans, is God's own glory.[41] The Puritan, William Ames, regarded theology itself as "the doctrine or teaching of living to God."[42] Barth emphasized the centrality of God's command, insisting that God wills to rule over human beings, to take them into God's service, and to make them witnesses of God's glory.[43] H. Richard Niebuhr held that human life is response or reply to the prior action of God.[44]

With respect to the epistemological question, these convictions support the affirmation that God is the source of all truth. That human action responds to God's prior action supports the priority of revelation or the Word of God over church teaching. That God's reign is universal, that no corner of nature or history lies beyond God's creating, sustaining, and redeeming activity encourages Reformed communities to be open to genuine wisdom and insight wherever (in God's world) they may be found.

With respect to sin and goodness, the conviction of God's sovereign reign means that God alone creates and that therefore human beings cannot be essentially evil. They

can only be limited, good, and corrupted creatures of the one most powerful and excellent God. Moreover, that sin's corruption is not the only or the last word follows
from the affirmation that the great God who creates is the good God who redeems.
Grace abounds because God is faithful and refuses to abandon even wayward creatures
to derangement and destruction. Finally, that the Christian life is more than a matter
of advancing our own interests—that it is a matter of inward love, disposition, and motive, but also of outward actions, laws, practices, and institutions—follows from the affirmation that *all* of life belongs to God. Every dimension of living, both inward and
outward, should be reordered and redirected toward God and God's glory.

Reformed theological ethics is theocentric in the sense that it tries to put God's
reign and God's glory at the center of faithful living rather than our needs, wants, desires, or interests. This prophetic insight has been powerfully restated and developed by
Gustafson.[45] In Reformed theological ethics, we come across a convictional wisdom
that encourages people to reorder all of life in accord with the purposes of the God
decisively disclosed in Israel and in Jesus Christ. We come across a convictional wisdom that encourages us to take up a life of faithful participation that never merely endorses people and things as they are.

Traditionally, however, this stance reflects an important tension. On the one hand,
God is other and independent. God's reign cannot be equated with the way things are.
God's purposes do not simply ratify our cherished projects and commitments. On the
other hand, God is not loveless, thoughtless power. God is faithful. Human life is not
separate from God; it is life in the arena of God's presence and purpose.

The tension emerges in Calvin, who believed that God's nature is immeasurable,
that God's will and power are unlike any other, and that God's governance cannot be
enclosed within the stream of nature. For Calvin, God's ways are not our ways, and we
often fail to apprehend the reason and the goodness of God's acting. At the same time,
however, Calvin built his doctrine of providence largely on sustaining regularities of
order in the natural world. And he maintained that, in Jesus Christ, we come to know
God as our benevolent parent, the fountain and spring of all good, in whom we appropriately place our ultimate confidence and trust.[46]

Somewhat similarly, Barth emphasized the singularity and freedom of God's act,
claiming that God is "event, act and life in [God's] own way," and therefore distinct
from everything. However, he also insisted that God is "the source, reconciliation, and
goal" of all things.[47] Indeed, as Barth came to put it later in his life, Jesus Christ reveals
the humanity of God. God is for us.[48] Again, for H. Richard Niebuhr, God is "the
One beyond the many" whose purposes require a continuing transformation of all our
relative evaluations. Moreover, Niebuhr could refer to God as "the Determiner of Destiny," the "great void," and the "enemy of all our causes." Nonetheless, he also claimed
that in Jesus Christ "a strange thing has happened in our history and our personal life."
We have been enabled to call this reality God. We have been assured that God is faithful. "Redemption appears as the liberty to interpret in trust all that happens as con-

tained within an intention and total activity that includes death within the domain of life, that destroys only to reestablish and renew."[49]

Within the frame of Reformed theological ethics, Gustafson's position becomes most controversial at this point. Gustafson maintains the otherness or independence of God from human needs, wants, and desires by insisting that God's purposes do not guarantee the human good. Like Calvin and others, he also associates God with interdependent processes of nature and history that sustain human beings and that continue to create new possibilities. So understood, the divine governance furnishes us with grounds for appropriately measured confidence in the dependability of things as well as for senses of gratitude, possibilities, and direction. But there is no equivalent in Gustafson's position to Calvin's benevolent parent, Barth's humanity of God, or Niebuhr's christologically founded assurance that God destroys only to reestablish and renew.[50]

A Basic Pattern

The Reformed tradition in theology and ethics is a pattern of sapiential reflection that centers on an apprehension of God and God's glory. This decisive apprehension influences the ways that other important aspects of knowledge of God and ourselves are understood. The result is a convictional wisdom that combines an evangelical respect for God's Word with an openness to all truth, a pessimism about human corruption with an optimism born of grace, an attention to inward dispositions with an insistence on outward standards and practices. The result is a manner of living that encourages us to reorder all of life in response to God.

Understood in this way, the tradition is not without significant tensions. It has precipitated heated debates and it will continue to precipitate them. It will continue to develop in Lagos and in Geneva, in Capetown and in Belem, in Philadelphia, Seoul, Glasgow, Cairo, Amsterdam, and Sydney. But it should also continue to insist that all of life be reordered in response to the living God, whose sovereign reign bears all things in nature and in history. To do otherwise would be *un*Reformed.

Notes

1. Edward Shils, *Tradition* (Chicago: University of Chicago Press, 1981), 21–23.

2. John Calvin, *Institutes of the Christian Religion*, ed. John T. McNeill (Philadelphia: Westminster Press, 1960), I, i, 1.

3. Menna Prestwich, "The Changing Face of Calvinism," in *International Calvinism, 1541–1715*, ed. Menna Prestwich (Oxford: Clarendon Press, 1985), 4.

4. David Little, "A Christian Perspective on Human Rights," in *Human Rights in Africa*, ed. Abdullahi Ahmed An-Nuim and Francis M. Deng (Washington, D.C.: Brookings Institution, 1990), 91–97.

5. Max L. Stackhouse, *Creeds, Society, and Human Rights: A Study in Three Cultures* (Grand Rapids, Mich.: Eerdmans, 1984), 57–58; Little, "A Christian Perspective on Human Rights," 97–102.

6. I am reminded of what Felix Gear, former Moderator of the Presbyterian Church in the United States and professor at Columbia Theological Seminary, once said in conversation. "Presbyterians are like hickory. They're tough but they split easily."

7. John W. de Gruchy, *Liberating Reformed Theology: A South African Contribution to an Ecumenical Debate* (Grand Rapids, Mich.: Eerdmans, 1991), 8–13, 45; Allan Boesak, *Black and Reformed: Apartheid, Liberation, and the Calvinist Tradition* (Maryknoll, N.Y.: Orbis Books, 1990), 83–99.

8. Baranitre Kirata, "Report from the Pacific," *Reformed Liturgy and Music* (special issue, 1995): 38–40. Enyi B. Udoh, "The Reformed Family and Self Understanding Today: A Nigerian Portrait"; George Sabra, "Protestantism in the Middle East: Colonial Phenomenon? Western Transplant? or Something Else?"; Franklyn J. Balasundaram, "Reformed to Usher in Reformation: A Reformed Understanding of Indian Christian Identity Today," *The Reformed World* 43, nos. 1 and 2 (March and June 1993): 34–39, 40–52, 53–63.

9. John H. Leith, ed., *Creeds of the Churches: A Reader in Christian Doctrine from the Bible to the Present*, rev. ed. (Richmond, Va.: John Knox Press, 1973), 62.

10. Heinrich Bullinger, "Of the Holy Catholic Church," in *Zwingli and Bullinger*, introduction and notes by G. W. Bromiley (Philadelphia: Westminster Press, 1953), 308.

11. Calvin, *Institutes*, I, vi; *The Constitution of the Presbyterian Church (USA), Part I—Book of Confessions* (Louisville: Office of the General Assembly, 1991), 3.20, 6.002. Hereafter cited as BOC 3.20, 6.002. The point was partly polemical: All believed that the Roman Catholic Church had inappropriately elevated its own teaching authority and traditions. (See also BOC 5.001–5.005.)

There is no simple identification of the Word of God with the text of the Bible. Karl Barth thought this very important. He claimed that proclamation is the Word of God preached; that scripture, which points beyond itself to revelation, is written proclamation or the Word of God written; and that the Word of God revealed is Jesus Christ, the event of God with us in human history. Revelation thus engenders scripture, and scripture bears witness and attests to revelation. See Karl Barth, *Church Dogmatics*, trans. G. W. Bromiley (Edinburgh: T. & T. Clark, 1975), 1/1: 88–124.

12. Benjamin W. Farley, ed., *John Calvin's Sermons on the Ten Commandments* (Grand Rapids, Mich.: Baker Book House, 1980), 151–66. Calvin *Institutes*, II, viii, 1; IV, xx, 16.

13. David Little, "The Reformed Tradition and the First Amendment," *Affirmation* 2, no. 2 (fall 1989): 13–14.

14. Jonathan Edwards, *Scientific and Philosophical Writings*, ed. Wallace E. Anderson (New Haven: Yale University Press, 1980), 353. Edwards also had high regard for "natural conscience and the moral sense." See *The Works of Jonathan Edwards*, ed. Sereno E. Dwight (Edinburgh: Banner of Truth Trust, 1974), 1: 133–35.

15. James M. Gustafson, *Ethics from a Theocentric Perspective*, 2 vols. (Chicago: University of Chicago Press, 1981–1984), vol. 1, *Theology and Ethics*, 251–52.

16. John Calvin, *The Second Epistle of Paul the Apostle to the Corinthians and the Epistles to Timothy, Titus, and Philemon*, trans. T. A. Small (Grand Rapids, Mich.: Eerdmans, 1964), 363–64. Calvin makes this statement in commentary on Titus 1:12. "From this passage we may gather

that it is superstitious to refuse to make any use of secular authors. For since all truth is of God, if any ungodly [person] has said anything true, we should not reject it, for it also has come from God. Besides, since all things are from God, what could be wrong with employing to [God's] glory everything that can be rightly used in that way?"

17. Emil Brunner, *The Divine Imperative*, trans. Olive Wyon (Philadelphia: Westminster Press, 1937), 51–60, 291 ff. *Natural Theology*, ed. John Baillie (London: Geoffrey Bles, 1946), 71–72; Barth, *Church Dogmatics*, 1/1: 6, 72. At points, Barth seems confused over the status of appeals to "the law of nature inborn in [humans]" in Luther and Calvin. He is concerned to point out that they do not ground an "independent ethics" (*Church Dogmatics*, 1/2: 783).

18. H. Richard Niebuhr, *The Meaning of Revelation* (New York: Macmillan, 1941), 133–39.

19. Calvin, *Institutes*, I, xiv, 21; xv, 4.

20. Edwards, "Original Sin," *Works*, 1: 149–151.

21. Calvin, *Institutes*, II, ii, 12–18. Edwards, *Works*, 1: 122–139. BOC 5.046. This is evidence of God's mercy and continuing care, or "the common grace of God" in distinction from saving grace. See Heinrich Heppe, *Reformed Dogmatics Set Out and Illustrated from the Sources*, rev. and ed. Ernst Bizer, trans. G. T. Thompson (Grand Rapids, Mich.: Baker Book House, 1978), 363.

22. Calvin, *Institutes*, III, iii, 16; xiv, 5. Barth says that the emphasis on sanctification is characteristic of Calvin in distinction from Luther. See Barth, *Church Dogmatics*, 4/1: 524–525.

23. Horace Bushnell, *The New Life* (London: Richard D. Dickinson, 1885), 69.

24. BOC 3.15, 5.049, 6.035, 6.076.

25. Perry Miller and Thomas H. Johnson, eds., *The Puritans: A Sourcebook of Their Writings*, rev. ed. (New York: Harper & Row, 1963), 213.

26. Nicholas Wolterstorff, *Until Justice and Peace Embrace* (Grand Rapids, Mich.: Eerdmans, 1983), 16; Boesak, *Black and Reformed*, 86, 90–94; de Gruchy, *Liberating Reformed Theology*, 260.

27. Valerie Saiving, "The Human Situation: A Feminine View," in *Womanspirit Rising: A Feminist Reader in Religion*, ed. Carol P. Christ and Judith Plaskow (New York: Harper & Row, 1979), 25–42. Judith Plaskow, *Sex, Sin, and Grace: Women's Experience and the Theologies of Reinhold Niebuhr and Paul Tillich* (Washington, D.C.: University Press of America, 1980), 151. See also Robin W. Lovin, *Reinhold Niebuhr and Christian Realism* (New York: Cambridge University Press, 1995), 131–57.

28. Gustafson, *Ethics*, 1:293–317.

29. Calvin, *Institutes*, II, vii, 12.

30. BOC 4.086–115. *The Practical Works of Richard Baxter* (Ligonier, Pa.: Soli Deo Gloria, 1990), 1:431–38, 740, 743, 771–72, 775.

31. Edwards, *Works*, 1:130–133, 137–139.

32. H. Richard Niebuhr, *Radical Monotheism and Western Culture, with Supplementary Essays* (Louisville, Ky.: Westminster John Knox Press, 1993), 31–37, 49–77.

33. Karl Barth, *The German Church Conflict* (Richmond, Va.: John Knox Press, 1965), 72. See also Eberhard Busch, *Karl Barth: His Life from Letters and Autobiographical Texts*, trans. John Bowden (Philadelphia: Fortress Press, 1976), 266.

34. Friedrich Schleiermacher, *The Christian Faith* (Philadelphia: Fortress Press, 1976), 523–24.

35. Emil Brunner, *Dogmatics,* trans. David Cairns and T. H. L. Parker (Philadelphia: Westminster Press, 1962), vol. 3, *The Christian Doctrine of the Church, Faith, and the Consummation*, 307, 310.

36. Gustafson, *Ethics*, 1:160–2.

37. Schleiermacher, *The Christian Faith*, 200–219.

38. Abraham Kuyper, *Calvinism* (New York: Fleming H. Revell Company, n.d.), 99.

39. Calvin, *Institutes*, III, vii, 1. See also BOC 10.1.

40. *Calvin: Theological Treatises*, trans. J. K. D. Reid (Philadelphia: Westminster Press, 1956), 91. Barth rightly emphasizes the importance of the opening questions of this catechism. "In [humans], God is to be glorified." Thus humans owe their lives "to God, and to this particular purpose of God." This is the goal and the end of human life, "so that it is incumbent on us . . . to orientate our lives wholly to this end." Barth, *Church Dogmatics*, 3/2: 183. The opening question of *The Westminster Shorter Catechism* is similar. See BOC 7.001.

41. Edwards, *Works*, 1: 94–121.

42. William Ames, *The Marrow of Theology*, trans. John Dykstra Eusden (Boston: Pilgrim Press, 1968), 77.

43. Barth, *Church Dogmatics*, 2/2: 510.

44. H. Richard Niebuhr, *The Responsible Self: An Essay in Christian Moral Philosophy* (New York: Harper & Row, 1963), 108–26.

45. Gustafson, *Ethics*, vols. 1 and 2; James M. Gustafson, *A Sense of the Divine: The Natural Environment in a Theocentric Perspective* (Cleveland: Pilgrim Press, 1994).

46. Calvin, *Institutes*, I, v, 5; xiii, 1; xvi, 1–7. On Calvin's understanding of God's benevolence, see B. A. Gerrish, *Grace and Gratitude: The Eucharistic Theology of John Calvin* (Minneapolis: Fortress Press, 1993), 26–29, 38–41, 66–67.

47. Barth, *Church Dogmatics*, 2/1: 264.

48. Karl Barth, *The Humanity of God* (Richmond, Va.: John Knox Press, 1970), 37–65.

49. Niebuhr, *The Responsible Self*, 125, 140, 142, 175. See also H. Richard Niebuhr, *Faith on Earth*, ed. Richard R. Niebuhr (New Haven: Yale University Press, 1989), 97.

50. James M. Gustafson, *Can Ethics Be Christian?* (Chicago: University of Chicago Press, 1975), 100–103, 110–12; James M. Gustafson, "Preface" in *Radical Monotheism and Western Culture with Supplementary Essays*, H. Richard Niebuhr, 6–7; Gustafson, *Sense of the Divine*, 47–48.

Chapter 4

Tradition, Historicity, and Truth in Theological Ethics

DAVID HOLLENBACH, S.J.

In 1972 James Gustafson published an essay titled "The Relevance of Historical Understanding," which addressed the importance of such understanding in the work of theological ethics.[1] It is fitting to recall this essay in a volume in Gustafson's honor, for the issue it raised is even more pointed today. Gustafson argued that one of the central problems for religious ethics in a historically conscious intellectual milieu is how to negotiate the tricky waters between an absolutism regarding moral norms that is historically naive and a historical relativism that makes normative claims impossible. Today awareness of the historical, cultural, and communal embeddedness of all human thought, affection, and judgment is felt well beyond the intellectual spheres where it first hit home. It is particularly acute in the domains of ethics and religion, though it touches many other fields as well. It also reaches beyond the academic sphere to the larger culture, leading to a prevalent mood that Albert Borgmann has called the "sullenness" of the postmodern mentality. Borgmann hears this mood voiced in contemporary emphases on autonomy or freedom of choice as the preeminent, or even only, value that can be defended in public. There are surely good reasons for this emphasis in the face of the enslavements humans have attempted to impose on one another in the twentieth century. But Borgmann suggests that "What sounds like the assumption of ultimate responsibility is usually the flourish of moral retreat, the refusal to discuss, explain, and justify a decision."[2] If the historicity of values is pushed to its limit, no discussion, explanation, or justification of a decision is possible, for value commitments come to be seen as those of the self alone. Autonomy can thus serve as a screen for sullen disengagement.

Gustafson's 1972 essay did not predict that we were moving toward this outcome. But he was clearly concerned that historical consciousness raised challenges for theological ethics that would not be easy to meet. He pointed out how Ernst Troeltsch's intellectual biography had traversed a course from a stress on "the relativity of all historical movements in relation to the Absolute" to a stance at the end of Troeltsch's life in which he "was almost plaintively seeking a framework for greater universality."[3] There is a similar plea in Gustafson's own statement that

> The task of theological and ethical work becomes that of finding justification both for religious belief and for moral decisions which do not deny the relativities of history, but which provide an objectivity short of absolute claims. In ethics the task is to find some degree of order, continuity, and structure within historical change. If the absolutist has morality conforming to an immutable order and thus has difficulty in coping with historical change, the relativist has an openness to change but a difficulty in developing the criteria of purpose and action to guide choices and give direction to moral activities.[4]

The pull toward each of these clear-cut options and the difficulties with them remain evident today. In particular, Gustafson was not at all confident that developments in Roman Catholic moral theology toward a more historically conscious, less absolutist approach were sufficiently aware of the disorientation that could follow in the wake of such a move. The historical turn could liberate from false absolutes. But to at least some Protestants who had appropriated this historical awareness generations ago, the challenge was that of overcoming what Paul Ramsey called the "wastelands of relativism."[5]

Gustafson saw the problem as a continuation of debates between nominalists and realists: Is it possible to retain some universal judgments in the context of historicity and, if so, how? Do human beings have a nature or only an open and ever-malleable history? Are there abiding, unexceptionable moral principles and rules or only individual intuitions that are bound to particular circumstances?[6] In what turns out to have been an understatement, Gustafson predicted that the debates about these questions would continue for the foreseeable future. Today the advantage in the realist/nominalist argument seems to have tilted strongly to the nominalist side. But there have also been strong rejoinders reaffirming the reality of moral absolutes, particularly by Pope John Paul II and, in a very different way, by evangelical and fundamentalist Christians. In what follows I want to sketch some of the issues that are shaping this current debate. I will concentrate on some of the arguments advanced in the Roman Catholic ethical tradition. I will not attempt to deal with other traditions in Christian ethics or an empirical description of the manifestations of this tension in contemporary culture.[7]

Reaffirmation of Moral Absolutes Today

One of the strongest recent affirmations that there are binding principles or rules in Christian ethics that transcend the relativities of history is contained in Pope John Paul

II's 1993 encyclical, *Veritatis Splendor*. Much of the technical discussion of the encyclical has focused on the pope's rejection of "proportionalism" and "fundamental option," both of which are aspects of Roman Catholic moral theory that have developed in the years since the Second Vatican Council. It appears, however, that the encyclical's rejection of these theories is based on a conviction that they will lead to a loss of the moral compass that can be provided only by absolute, timeless moral norms. Further, the pope suggests that such a loss of moral bearings is directly linked with a loss of religious conviction and even faith in a transcendent, provident God.

John Paul II is clearly distressed by recent developments in Catholic moral theology as he interprets them. It is well known that there has been widespread disagreement with aspects of church moral teaching on sexual ethics. Contraception was the initial flash point, followed by further disagreement regarding traditional norms on homosexual expression, remarriage after divorce, and broader issues connected with gender roles. These matters are surely important concerns in the encyclical and provide part of the explanation for why it was written. The central issue for the pope, however, goes deeper than dissent from traditional Catholic teachings on sexual ethics. As the pope sees it, moral and ultimately religious relativism have reached crisis proportions both within the Catholic community and in the larger culture as well.[8]

Thus the pope states that his goal is to recall "certain fundamental truths" that are at the basis of "the whole of the Church's moral teaching," particularly those "regarding the natural law, and the universality and permanent validity of its precepts." This is necessary because within the church itself dissent is no longer "limited and occasional" but has become "an overall and systematic calling into question of traditional moral doctrine." In what I take to be the central motivation of the encyclical, John Paul II states that this crisis has been brought about by "certain anthropological presuppositions. At the root of these presuppositions is the more or less obvious influence of currents of thought which end by detaching human freedom from its essential and constitutive relationship to truth."[9]

The essential link between freedom and truth has been a major theme in much of the pope's teaching. It provides a key for interpreting his critique both of current Catholic moral theology and of important elements in its cultural context. For example, he argues that only commitment to the truth about the dignity and rights of the human person, the visible image of the invisible God, was capable of resisting the oppressive forces of totalitarian regimes in his native Poland and the former Soviet bloc generally. "Only upon this truth is it possible to construct a renewed society and to solve the complex and weighty problems affecting it, above all the problem of overcoming the various forms of totalitarianism, so as to make way for the authentic *freedom* of the person."[10] Historical relativism, the pope suggests, is powerless in the face of systems that would subordinate the dignity of the person to an ideology or, more relevant to the last days of the Soviet system, to the self-interest of ruling bureaucrats. He lists the following political conditions as dependent on commitment to the transcendent and permanent truth of human dignity: "truthfulness in the relations between those governing and those governed, openness in public administration, impartiality in the service of the body politic, respect for the rights of political adversaries, safeguarding the rights of the accused against summary trials and convictions, the just and honest use of public funds, the rejection of illicit means in order to gain, preserve or increase power at any cost." These social norms "are primarily rooted in, and in fact derive their singular urgency from the transcendent value of the person and the objective moral demands of functioning states."[11] Freedom that is not anchored in such truths about the person is not freedom at all. Here the pope goes beyond a facile distinction between freedom and license that is often heard in jeremiads directed by older generations at those who are younger. His point concerns the social and political consequences that in fact came to prevail in Eastern Europe under the ideology of historical materialism. This ideology produced cynicism, indifference, and (to use Borgmann's term), sullenness, all leading to acquiescence in unfreedom.

The pope's analysis not surprisingly converges with that of other leaders in the revolutions that toppled the regimes of the former Soviet bloc. The theme of "living in the truth," as opposed to coping with the lies of bureaucratic communism, appears repeatedly in Vaclav Havel's writings. Havel saw "living in the truth" as the power that enabled otherwise powerless people to bring about the "velvet revolutions" of 1989.[12] Similarly, the Czech philosopher Erazim Kohak, who now teaches at Boston University, wrote that the "the entire tenor of Czech dissent, whose most prominent figures are playwright-philosopher Vaclav Havel and priest-theologian Vaclav Maly, has been on *life in the truth*. . . . In word and deed, Czech dissidents have demonstrated their conviction that there is truth, that there is good and evil—and that the difference is not reducible to cultural preference."[13] Nor, they would suggest, is it merely historically relative.

Both the pope and Havel also have doubts about whether the West presently possesses the moral purpose and commitment necessary to sustain its own freedom. To Havel it appears "that the traditional parliamentary democracies can offer no fundamental opposition to the automatism of technological civilization and the industrial-consumer society."[14] More than the procedures of parliamentary democracy are needed to secure and sustain freedom. The pope's reading of the West is similar. The fall of Marxism has not solved the problem of freedom. He maintains that in the post-1989 world there is a genuine "risk of an alliance between democracy and ethical relativism."[15] As he observed in his encyclical letter *Centesimus Annus*,

> Nowadays there is a tendency to claim that agnosticism and skeptical relativism are the philosophy and the basic attitude which correspond to democratic forms of political life. Those who are convinced that they know the truth and firmly adhere to it are considered unreliable from a democratic point of view, since they do not accept that the truth is determined by the majority, or that it is subject to variation according to different political trends.[16]

Truth, then, is the basis of freedom, not the other way around.

Both John Paul II and Vaclav Havel go so far as to make genuinely ontological claims about the basis of the moral consciousness needed in both East and West today. These claims are sure to offend many Americans today, especially American intellectuals. John Paul II: "It is by responding to the call of God contained in the *being of things* that man becomes aware of his transcendent dignity. Every individual must give this response, which constitutes the apex of his humanity, and no social mechanism or collective subject can substitute for it."[17] Vaclav Havel: "The only genuine backbone of all our actions—if they are to be moral—is responsibility. Responsibility to something higher than my family, my country, my company, my success. Responsibility to *the order of Being*, where all our actions are indelibly recorded and where, and only where, they will be properly judged."[18]

For the pope then, with echoes in the writings of Vaclav Havel, there is considerable danger in the moral relativism that can be detected in contemporary culture and intellectual life. It can be doubted whether the pope is right in claiming that such relativism is to be found in the writings of the Catholic moral theologians against whom *Veritatis Splendor* is directed. Others have explored that matter elsewhere, and I will not review the discussion here.[19] It is clear, however, that he intends to challenge such relativism wherever it appears and especially to reject claims that it is an approach to ethics "having a basis in theory and claiming full cultural and social legitimacy."[20] In a way that leaves little doubt about what he intends, John Paul states that "the central theme of this encyclical" is the "*reaffirmation of the universality and immutability of the moral commandments*, particularly those which prohibit always and without exception *intrinsically evil acts*."[21]

What are these immutable norms, asserted to be always and everywhere binding? The encyclical does not attempt to give a systematic or exhaustive list. The enumeration it does provide is contained primarily in a passage quoted from the Second Vatican Council. This includes:

> whatever is hostile to life itself, such as any kind of homicide [perhaps better translated "murder"], genocide, abortion, euthanasia and voluntary suicide; whatever violates the integrity of the human person, such as mutilation, physical and mental torture and attempts to coerce the spirit; whatever is offensive to human dignity, such as subhuman living conditions, arbitrary imprisonment, deportation, slavery, prostitution and trafficking in women and children, degrading conditions of work which treat labourers as mere instruments of profit, and not as free responsible persons.[22]

And in the subsequent paragraph, which has led a number of commentators rightly to conclude that reproductive and sexual ethics were very much in the John Paul II's mind despite the wider agenda I am suggesting here, Paul VI's condemnation of contraception in *Humanae Vitae* is repeated. Further, the encyclical states that "from a theological viewpoint, moral principles are not dependent upon the historical moment in which they are discovered."[23] This suggests that the immorality of these practices is not only exceptionless but immutable. In other words, there exist standards of morality that are above the flow of history in the mind of God. Failure to apprehend these standards is explained in light of human finitude and sin. For the pope, however, the gospel of Jesus Christ, as this is interpreted and taught by the magisterium of the church, provides guidance in the midst of these weaknesses. It would not be claiming too much, therefore, to read *Veritatis Splendor* as asserting that the immutable moral teaching of the church is the bulwark needed to stem the tide of relativism John Paul sees lapping at the shores of civilization and culture throughout the world today.

A Look at Actual History

Is this claim to knowledge of moral norms that transcend history plausible? A recent and important essay by John Noonan on "Development in Moral Doctrine" suggests that it is not. Noonan's many books concerning the development of Christian thought on specific areas of moral life surely have been among the most important contributions to the study of the history of Christian ethics in our time.[24] Noonan's goal in this essay is to draw some general conclusions about how we might sustain a sense of moral direction today in the light of what the study of history reveals about the variations that have occurred in the past.

Noonan indicates the nature of the problem by sketching how the Christian tradition has changed its teachings on several questions of practical morality.

On usury: "Once upon a time, certainly from at least 1150 to 1550, seeking, receiving, or hoping for anything beyond one's principal—in other words, looking for profit—on a loan constituted the mortal sin of usury." Today, however, "the just title to profit is assumed to exist." Noonan states that the change can be exaggerated, for the taking of profit without just title continues to be rejected. But in practices such as taking interest on bank accounts and in the institutions of the entire financial world, the earlier rule against usury has disappeared in Catholic moral teaching. Ideas once unanimously taught by the church "are now so obsolete that one incites incredulity by reciting them."[25]

On slavery: "Once upon a time, certainly as late as 1860, the church taught that it was no sin for a Catholic to own another human being." Slaves should be treated humanely, and manumission was regarded as good. But from St. Paul, through St. Augustine, Henry de Bracton, and Juan de Lugo, down to the American Bishop Francis Kenrick in 1841, many of the practices associated with chattel slavery went unchallenged by ecclesiastical authority. But "again, all that has changed. . . . In the light of the teachings of modern popes and the Second Vatican Council on the dignity of the human person, it is morally unthinkable that one person be allowed to buy, sell, hypothecate, or lease another or dispose of that person's children."[26] It should be noted that John Paul II reiterates this condemnation of slavery, citing the Second Vatican Council, as does Noonan. The pope, however, makes no mention of the eighteen centuries during which it was tolerated if not endorsed.

On religious freedom: "Once upon a time, no later than the time of St. Augustine, it was considered virtuous for bishops to invoke imperial force to compel heretics to return to the Church." For a period of over twelve hundred years "the vast institutional apparatus of the Church was put at the service of detecting heretics, who, if they persevered in their heresy or relapsed into it, would be executed at the stake. Hand in glove, Church and State collaborated in the terror by which heretics were purged."[27] Gradually, however, the religious wars in post-Reformation Europe, and, definitively, the persecution of Christians by fascist and communist regimes in the twentieth century led to another shift in positions. In 1832, for example, Pope Gregory XVI had declared that the right to freedom of conscience is an "insanity (*dileramentum*)."[28] The dramatic change is evident if one juxtaposes this condemnation with the Second Vatican Council's declaration that "the right to religious freedom has its foundation in the very dignity of the human person, as this dignity is known through the revealed word of God and by reason itself."[29] Indeed Vatican II linked its support for human rights with the very core of Christian faith when it declared that "by virtue of the gospel committed to it, the Church proclaims the rights of the human person."[30] The affirmation of these rights is at the center of John Paul II's critique of relativism. Indeed he has called the right to religious freedom the "foundation" of all human rights.[31] That the church has denied this right through much of its history, in both solemn teaching and institutional practice, is passed over in silence.

The purpose of Noonan's rehearsal of these dramatic shifts is to provide a basis for developing a theoretical perspective on the conditions and limits of change within the Catholic moral tradition. What he says is also relevant, I think, to other religious-moral traditions as well. Noonan's perspective on change in moral teaching borrows from theories of development in more-directly doctrinal areas such as Trinitarian theology and Christology.

Theories of the Role of Tradition

Noonan rejects accounts according to which change has been simply a matter of the expression given to moral principles rather than a change in their substance. He also finds it implausible to claim that real advances occur only as the result of gradually working out the logical implications of the normative stances of scripture. More plausible is John Henry Newman's understanding of the development of moral understanding by analogy to the development of organic life or of personal identity as a child becomes an adult, and the Second Vatican Council's view that new moral understandings can arise through deepening insight into the reality of Jesus Christ. The explanation by analogy to organic growth, however, must be able to distinguish when new organic growth is appropriate and when it is more like the growth of a cancer. And, as Noonan observes, the claim that new insight into the reality of Christ has arisen must face the question of whether one is merely looking in a mirror and projecting one's own experience onto an image of Christ.[32] The issue then is how to distinguish between "true and false reform in the church" (to borrow the title of an influential book by Yves Congar).[33]

One response to this question is that advanced by the ecumenically influential Lutheran theologian George Lindbeck. Lindbeck's approach has notable parallels in the writings of Stanley Hauerwas, which themselves have had significant impact in the Catholic community. Lindbeck has proposed a "cultural-linguistic" theory of religion. This theory compares religion to a language or cultural system. Like language and culture, a religious tradition provides a framework that shapes the way those who have learned it perceive reality, speak about reality, and order their lives in action. For Christians, the canonical Bible as a whole, understood as if it were a "vast, loosely structured, non-fictional novel," tells the overarching story of the interaction of God with creation, especially with human beings. This biblical story is the normative standard in light of which the adequacy and fidelity of all subsequent developments of the tradition are to be judged. Since this story is centrally a rendering of who Jesus Christ is, the meaning of Jesus Christ as he is portrayed in the Bible is the norm that distinguishes "true and false" reforms in subsequent tradition. The practical task of the Christian community, which is at once religious and ethical, is "to be conformed to the Jesus Christ depicted in the narrative."[34]

Noonan, I think, would agree with Lindbeck up to this point. He would not, however, fully accept Lindbeck's description of how the Christian community goes about relating the biblical portrayal of Jesus Christ to changing patterns of society and culture, in the process reaching novel ethical standards like those that Noonan's historical work has identified. For Lindbeck, the portrayal of Jesus in the biblical story is a given, self-contained structure of meaning. It defines a world of meaning in light of which Christians are to shape their lives and form their way of acting. The relation between the biblical story and the form of life of postbiblical Christians is a one-way street: from the Bible to the ways of life of the later Christian community in different historical periods. As Lindbeck explains, "Scripture creates its own domain of meaning and the task of interpretation is to extend this over the whole of reality." Thus the task of the postbiblical community is to redescribe "reality within the scriptural framework rather than translating Scripture into extrascriptural categories. It is the text, so to speak, which absorbs the world, rather than the world the text."[35] The religious concern here is to avoid theories of interpretation that grant a normative role to contemporary experience, for such theories run the risk of losing touch altogether with the central realities of the Christian story. In Noonan's terms, they risk projecting contemporary needs and experience onto the mirror in which one claims to be seeing

Christ. As a language that one has already learned enables one to articulate and thus make sense of experience, so the Christian story enables one to interpret experience in a Christian way and to live in a Christian manner.

In Lindbeck's theory, therefore, the scriptural story is *applied* to the novel social and cultural realities encountered by the postbiblical church. These realities do not, in themselves, contribute to the meaning of Christian faith. Such applications may differ as historical circumstances change. To use an example treated by Noonan, the Christian tradition shifted its understanding of the morality of slavery from acceptance in New Testament times and through most of the postbiblical tradition to rejection in more-recent centuries. Lindbeck argues that this shift occurred because Christians had come to recognize through their historical experience that a stable social order without the institution of slavery was in fact possible. Thus the Christian story could be practically applied to practice in a new way. The meaning of story itself remained as it had always been. The newness comes from the fact that the "self-identical story" has been fused with "new worlds within which it is told and retold."[36] Novelty arises in the use to which the tradition is put, not in the tradition itself. Thus Christian norms remain self-identical through time; only their use develops. The development that occurs, therefore, is extrinsic to the meaning of the norms themselves.

Noonan thinks that the process by which such shifts occur is more complex, involving a *mutual* interaction between postbiblical experience and the biblical story. New experience, such as the possibility of a society without slavery, not only leads to a new application of the biblical story but also to new insight into the meaning of the story of Jesus Christ. Noonan notes, for example, that the impulse toward the abolition of slavery arose among individuals who "were ahead of the theologians and the Church." In Catholic France, Montesquieu, Rousseau, and the revolutionaries of 1789 brought about the new social and cultural framework that made possible Pope Leo XIII's condemnation of the institution of slavery. Lindbeck's description of the process as one in which the story of Christ has been "applied" to new circumstances fails to capture the fact that new insight into the meaning of the story itself has occurred in this process. Only after much argument and social upheaval did the requirement of Christ become clear. So though Noonan agrees with Lindbeck that the story of Christ in the New Testament is definitively normative for Christian ethics, "it is evident from the case of slavery alone that it has taken time to ascertain what the demands of the New [Testament] really are."[37] The meaning of both poles in the interaction of biblical story and postbiblical society and culture are clarified by each other in an ongoing way. Not only does the givenness of biblical story illuminate the meaning of experience, but new experience evokes new insight into the meaning of the biblical story itself. This two-way interaction generates the dynamism of tradition, leading to the sort of changes that Noonan points out.

Alasdair MacIntyre's recent work is quite helpful in showing how this dynamism is possible within a framework that sees continuity with the biblical story of Jesus Christ as essential to the identity of the Christian community. Like Noonan, MacIntyre has been influenced by John Henry Newman on this matter. Indeed MacIntyre acknowledges that his understanding of the functioning of a tradition owes a "massive debt" to Newman, even though he has judged it better for his philosophical purposes not to say much about what he has derived from Newman the theologian.[38] MacIntyre's theory, like Lindbeck's, can be called postliberal or postmodern in arguing that human experience and thought are thoroughly embedded in historical traditions. In *After Virtue*, MacIntyre argued that both virtuous living and philosophical theorizing about the moral life are impossible unless those who engage in them have been educated in the stories and ways of acting and thinking of a particular historical tradition. He wrote that "I can only answer the question 'what am I to do?' if I can answer the prior question 'Of what story or stories do I find myself a part?'"[39] His more recent work is directed at showing that the fact that moral virtue and reflection are rooted in historically contingent events, texts, and communities need not undercut the possibility of assessing the adequacy and truth of competing traditions. The historicity of moral thought and practice need not lead to relativism.

His argument rests on a recovery of the understanding of a tradition as a tradition of "enquiry." In a mature tradition, the process of "traditioning" is not simply a matter of retelling stories, citing and applying classic texts and authorities, and socializing young people into preexisting roles, as Lindbeck implies. These surely have an important place in any tradition that expects to remain intact. "Conservative action upon its past" was one of the criteria that Newman used to distinguish authentic developments of the Christian tradition from corruptions of it.[40] But a living tradition is also marked by its power to assimilate ideas originally discovered elsewhere. In Newman's words, ideas about human existence "are not placed in a void, but in the crowded world, and make way for themselves by interpenetration, and develop by absorption."[41]

In line with these ideas from Newman, MacIntyre understands a working tradition as dynamic, self-critical, and open to knowledge gained from outside itself. His understanding of a mature tradition as a tradition of inquiry demands this. Such inquiry begins with the stories, authorities, practices, and canons of rationality that have been handed on to one from the past. From this received starting point, critical reasoning can become necessary for a number of reasons: The received tradition finds itself internally subject to a number of interpretations by its adherents that require adjudication; the tradition encounters new questions that its mode of inquiry up to now has not prepared it to handle; or the tradition meets an alternative tradition that confronts it with an alternative account of how things are or ought to be.

An Illustration: Religious Freedom

The hero of MacIntyre's account of this process is Thomas Aquinas, whose great achievement was overcoming the conflict between Augustinian and Aristotelian traditions in the thirteenth century. Another, more recent, example is that noted by Noo-

nan: John Courtney Murray's successful effort to incorporate religious freedom as a demand of the dignity of the human person into the Roman Catholic tradition. The insight into the importance of religious freedom was discovered by the liberal tradition,
which gave it individualistic and sometimes skeptical overtones. Initially the Roman
Catholic tradition's commitment to the truth of biblical faith and its strong sense of
solidarity and the common good led to a straightforward rejection of the modern assertion of individual rights, especially the rights of conscience. It was Murray's genius
to have discovered intellectually compelling arguments that could incorporate the insights contained within the traditions of both Catholicism and liberalism, and to do so
on terms that could enable both traditions to hold to their valid insights while learning from each other. The incorporation of the liberal defense of religious freedom into
the Catholic tradition at the Second Vatican Council is well known. The possible contribution to liberal understandings of society by the continuing Catholic insistence that
fundamental truth claims about human dignity make sense only in the context of
equally fundamental commitments to social solidarity remains an ongoing project. But
the existence of such a possibility is due to the fact that Murray's argument for religious liberty was not simply a concession that the liberal tradition had it right and the
past Catholic tradition had it wrong. Murray *developed* the Catholic tradition; he did
not surrender it. Indeed he claimed (persuasively, I am convinced) that his interpretation of religious freedom not only solved problems that the encounter with liberalism
had revealed within the Catholic tradition, but that it could solve problems internal to
liberalism that liberalism was incapable of solving itself (chiefly its individualism and
tendency toward skepticism).[42]

Thus Murray's approach to development of the Catholic moral tradition on religious freedom exemplified the criteria that MacIntyre, following Newman, set forth
for a tradition's advance through inquiry. Murray's approach solved problems internal
to both Catholicism and liberalism; it could explain why these problems had arisen in
the first place; and it advanced an interpretation of religious freedom that could claim
continuity with core elements of the biblical story of Israel and of Jesus Christ. This
achievement should give scant comfort to those in Christian ethics who adopt a purely
narrative-based approach to their work or to theologians like Lindbeck who urge a cultural-linguistic theory of religion as backing for purely narrative-based Christian ethics.
The novelty in Murray's contribution to the development of Catholic moral teaching
was not simply a new application of the permanent legacy of an already-told story; it
achieved new insight into the meaning of this story in light of novel patterns of social
and political experience. In this sense, it added a new chapter to the story itself.

At the same time, the achievements of Aquinas and Murray, viewed in light of this
understanding of how Christian moral tradition develops, will give equally little comfort to those like John Paul II who stake so much on immutable norms in their case
against historical relativism. This understanding of development makes claims in the
face of the relativist mentality that are simultaneously concessionary and oppositional.

It concedes that there are few, if any, practical moral rules that are in principle un-revisable. Fundamental Christian stances, such as love toward God and neighbor and discipleship to Jesus Christ, are, of course, permanent norms for Christian behavior. There can be no Christianity where they are absent. They play a role in the Christian religion much like the principle of noncontradiction in the domain of thought or the imperative to "do good and avoid evil" in the moral life. There can be no rationality where a person finds self-contradiction acceptable, and there can be no moral life if one knowingly chooses to do evil. Similarly, there can be no Christianity without love of God and neighbor and an effort to know and follow Jesus Christ. These fundamental orientations can be specified further by what Thomas Aquinas has called the most ba-sic principles of the natural law and by very general orientations that follow from the gospel. What these principles and orientations actually mean in the conduct of life at a particular moment in history or in a particular culture, however, must be discerned historically and is subject to development and change. This is not merely a matter of "application" of principles whose meaning is already clear. I think it makes little sense to say, for example, that the identical Christian imperative to love one's neighbor has been applied in one way by a slaveholder in one society and in another way by an abo-litionist in a different time and place. Rather, it is the understanding of the meaning of Christian love itself that has shifted. Concrete action-guides such as "treat slaves kindly" or "never enslave a human being" are not simply diverse applications of a sin-gle general principle of love of neighbor. They represent differing understandings of the principle itself. Similarly, an action-guide that calls for the burning of heretics and one that affirms the human and civil right to religious freedom are not diverse con-cretizations of a constant understanding of the meaning of the creation of human be-ings in the image of God but represent genuine changes in that understanding itself.[43]

This understanding of the development of tradition, however, stands in clear op-position to a crude historical relativism. Crude relativism is itself incompatible with genuine inquiry. It has no reason to investigate the truth or falsity of interpretations of morality offered within a given tradition such as Christianity or in competing tradi-tions such as Catholicism and liberalism in the days before Murray made his arguments. Inquiry is based on the supposition that intellectual investigation can actually get some-where, including inquiry into diverse claims about the right way to live and the ulti-mate meaning of human life. As MacIntyre points out, a relativist would never have any reason to revise his or her beliefs, for in strict relativism there are no grounds to prefer one belief over another. The very possibility of revision depends on recogniz-ing that there is a truth that can cause such a revision to be necessary.[44] Relativists do not have any reason to argue at all; the best they can do is agree to coexist or cooper-ate. But what shape such coexistence and cooperation should take then reemerges as a matter demanding inquiry. At some point the choice becomes one between willing-ness to make a claim to truth and an acquiescence in some form of nihilism. John Paul II is right to fear the latter, which lurks beneath the surface of some postmodern "sullenness." In light of what is argued here, however, he need not make appeals to the timelessness of moral absolutes to provide an alternative to this danger.

Ethics *in Via*

John Finnis, one of the strongest supporters of the line of argument contained in the pope's *Veritatis Splendor*, maintains that the encyclical is not primarily about sexual ethics. In Finnis's words, "Faith, not sex, is the theme of *Veritatis Splendor*."[45] I think this is quite right. However, I also think that the faith at issue concerns quite a different matter than Finnis does. For Finnis, the issue is whether contemporary men and women have the capacity to accept that God, not they, are ultimately in charge of the universe. For Finnis, acceptance of this means willingness to obey God's absolute moral proscriptions even when the consequences are a deeply countercultural form of life or even martyrdom.[46] I agree that, *in extremis*, no other stance is compatible with Christian faith. I disagree, however, that the demands of God and the meaning of fidelity to Jesus Christ are given once and for all in the way Finnis believes to be clear. One of the dimensions of Christian faith is a trust that God is involved in history in a way that makes the process of inquiry-guided development itself worth trusting, at least to the extent of being willing to undertake such inquiry. As Avery Dulles has written:

> The Christian is defined as a person on the way to discovery, on the way to a revelation not yet given, or at least not yet given in final form. . . . The Christian trusts that, in following the crucified and risen Christ, he [or she] is on the route to the one disclosure that will fully satisfy the yearning of the human spirit. This confidence is sustained by a series of lesser disclosures which occur on the way, and are tokens or promises of the revelation yet to come.[47]

Christian ethics, both as a form of life and as an intellectual discipline, is rooted in a trust that the God who transcends all history is also present in and with these quests of the human spirit. Indeed it is the Wisdom and Spirit of God who makes human discovery possible. Thus all attempts to understand how to live this life are themselves on pilgrimage, *in via*. The efforts of Christian ethics must therefore be always ready to welcome fresh discoveries of God's gifts of freedom and reconciliation. We will be able to recognize new ideas and forms of life as coming from the hand of the God of Jesus Christ only if we have been schooled in the story of God told in the Bible, as Lindbeck and Noonan agree. However, being schooled in the biblical story and simply repeating what we have already learned of the Bible's meaning are two different things. Rather, the pilgrim nature of Christian life has an intellectual counterpart. Having learned from both Bible and past tradition, we then will be ready to recognize new moral insights though inquiry into new dimensions of experience and from traditions outside that of the Christian community. These new moral insights, in turn, can lead to new understanding of the meaning of the biblical story itself. Such an intellectual pilgrimage will continue until we have been given the final and full gift of God—God's own self.

Notes

1. James M. Gustafson, "The Relevance of Historical Understanding," in *Theology and Christian Ethics* (Philadelphia: Pilgrim Press, 1974), 177–95. This essay was originally published in Paul Deats Jr., ed. *Toward a Discipline of Social Ethics* (Boston: Boston University Press, 1972), 49–70. Further references here are to text in *Theology and Christian Ethics*.

2. Albert Borgmann, *Crossing the Postmodern Divide* (Chicago: University of Chicago Press, 1992), 10.

3. Gustafson, "Historical Understanding," 188, 194. Gustafson cites Troeltsch's essay "The Ideas of Natural Law and Humanity in World Politics," app. 1, in Otto Gierke, *Natural Law and the Theory of Society* (Boston: Beacon Press, 1957), 201–22.

4. Gustafson, "Historical Understanding," 194.

5. Ibid., 191–92. The reference is to Ramsey's *War and Christian Conscience* (Durham, N.C.: Duke University Press, 1961), chap. 1.

6. Gustafson, "Historical Understanding," 195.

7. For description and interpretation of a sociological sort, see, for the U.S. context, Robert Wuthnow, *The Restructuring of American Religion: Society and Faith since World War II* (Princeton, N.J.: Princeton University Press, 1988); for the global picture, José Casanova, *Public Religions in the Modern World* (Chicago: University of Chicago Press, 1994), and (somewhat tendentiously) Gilles Kepel, *The Revenge of God: The Resurgence of Islam, Christianity and Judaism in the Modern World*, trans. Alan Braley (University Park: Pennsylvania State University Press, 1994).

8. John Paul II, *Veritatis Splendor* (Vatican City: Libreria Editrice Vaticana, 1993), no. 5: 10.

9. Ibid., no. 4: 8.

10. Ibid., no. 99: 148.

11. Ibid., no. 101: 151.

12. See, for example, an essay that had wide influence in Czechoslovakia and beyond in the years before the revolutions of 1989, "The Power of the Powerless," in Vaclav Havel, *Open Letters: Selected Writings 1965–1990*, selected and ed. by Paul Wilson (New York: Vintage Books, 1992), 125–214.

13. Erazim Kohak, "Can There Be a Central Europe?" *Dissent* (spring 1990): 195–96.

14. Havel, "The Power of the Powerless," 208.

15. John Paul II, *Veritatis Splendor*, no. 101: 151.

16. John Paul II, *Centesimus Annus*, no. 46, translation in *Catholic Social Thought: The Documentary Heritage*, ed. David J. O'Brien and Thomas Shannon (Maryknoll, N.Y.: Orbis Books, 1992).

17. Ibid., no. 13, emphasis added. Throughout the English translation of the encyclical, the male gender is used to refer to all human beings. I have refrained from retranslating the Latin

into English in a way that uses gender-inclusive language because of the Vatican's indefensible insistence in other contexts, against criticism, on the exclusive use of masculine pronouns.

18. Havel, Address to a Joint Meeting of the House and Senate of the U.S. Congress, 21 February 1990, *Congressional Record* 136, H395, emphasis added. For one indication of the offense taken to Havel's language of "Being," see Richard Rorty, "The Seer of Prague," *New Republic*, 1 July 1991, 35–39.

19. For disagreement with the pope on this point, see, for example, the essays by Richard McCormick, Josef Fuchs, Nicholas Lash, Lisa Sowle Cahill, and Herbert McCabe in *Considering Veritatis Splendor*, ed. John Wilkins (Cleveland: Pilgrim Press, 1994), and Richard McCormick, "Some Early Reactions to *Veritatis Splendor*," *Theological Studies* 55 (1994): 481–506.

20. John Paul II, *Veritatis Splendor*, no. 106: 158.

21. Ibid., no. 115: 172, emphasis in original.

22. Ibid., no. 80: 123. The citation of Vatican II is from the Pastoral Constitution on the Church in the Modern World, *Gaudium et Spes*, no. 27. All references to Vatican II are from Walter M. Abbot and Joseph Gallagher, eds., *The Documents of Vatican II* (New York: America Press, 1966).

23. John Paul II, *Veritatis Splendor*, no. 112: 167.

24. John T. Noonan Jr., "Development in Moral Doctrine," *Theological Studies* 54 (1993): 662–77. Noonan's studies include: *The Believer and the Powers That Are: Cases, History, and Other Data Bearing on the Relation of Religion and Government* (New York: Macmillan, 1987); *Bribes* (New York: Macmillan, 1984); *Power to Dissolve: Lawyers and Marriages in the Courts of the Roman Curia* (Cambridge: Belknap Press of Harvard University Press, 1972); *Contraception: A History of Its Treatment by the Catholic Theologians and Canonists* (Cambridge: Belknap Press of Harvard University Press, 1965); *The Scholastic Analysis of Usury* (Cambridge: Harvard University Press, 1957). Also, Noonan et al., eds. *The Morality of Abortion: Legal and Historical Perspectives* (Cambridge: Harvard University Press, 1970).

25. Noonan, "Development in Moral Doctrine," 662–63.

26. Ibid., 664–67.

27. Ibid., 667.

28. Gregory XVI, *Mirari Vos Arbitramur*, translation in J. Neuner and J. Dupuis, *The Christian Faith in the Doctrinal Documents of the Catholic Church*, rev. ed. (Staten Island, N.Y.: Alba House, 1982), no. 1007.

29. Vatican Council II, *Dignitatis Humanae* (Declaration on Religious Freedom), no. 2.

30. *Gaudium et Spes*, no. 41.

31. John Paul II, *Veritatis Splendor*, no. 31: 52. There is an unfortunate ambiguity in John Paul II's discussion of religious freedom. Most of the time it is interpreted in a way that is compatible with Vatican II's statement that this right "continues to exist even in those who do not live up to their obligation of seeking the truth and adhering to it" (i.e., the right exists for believers and unbelievers alike). See *Dignitatis Humanae*, no. 2. At other times, the pope suggests that religious freedom means the right to hold the truth, as when he says "In a certain sense, the source and synthesis of these rights [all human rights] is religious freedom, understood as the right to live in the truth of one's faith and in conformity with one's transcendent dignity as a person" (*Centesimus Annus*, no. 47). I think the ambiguity here is a studied one. I have discussed it in relation to the clear positions of Vatican II and of John Courtney Murray in my "Freedom and

Truth: Religious Liberty as Immunity and Empowerment," in *The Growing End: John Courtney Murray and the Shape of Murray Studies,* ed. J. Leon Hooper and Todd Whitmore (Kansas City, Mo.: Sheed & Ward, forthcoming).

32. Noonan, "Development in Moral Doctrine," 669–73.

33. Yves Congar, *Vraie et fausse réforme dans l'église,* 2d ed., rev. and corr. (Paris: Éditions du Cerf, 1968).

34. George Lindbeck, *The Nature of Doctrine: Religion and Theology in a Postliberal Age* (Philadelphia: Westminster Press, 1984), 120–21. The characterization of the Bible as a loosely structured novel is borrowed by Lindbeck from David Kelsey, *The Uses of Scripture in Recent Theology* (Philadelphia: Fortress Press, 1975), 48.

35. Lindbeck, *The Nature of Doctrine,* 117–18.

36. Ibid., 83.

37. Noonan, "Development in Moral Doctrine," 674–76.

38. Alasdair MacIntyre, *Whose Justice? Which Rationality?* (Notre Dame, Ind.: University of Notre Dame Press, 1988), 353–54.

39. Alasdair MacIntyre, *After Virtue* (Notre Dame, Ind.: University of Notre Dame Press, 1981), 201.

40. John Henry Newman, *An Essay on the Development of Christian Doctrine* (Garden City, N.Y.: Doubleday Image Books, 1960), 200–204.

41. Ibid., 189.

42. On this reading of Murray and Vatican II, see R. Bruce Douglass and David Hollenbach, eds. *Catholicism and Liberalism: Contributions to American Public Philosophy* (Cambridge/New York: Cambridge University Press, 1994), esp. my own essay and Afterword in this volume.

43. This understanding of the relation between principles and applications reflects the discussion of *applicatio* in the hermeneutics of Hans-Georg Gadamer, without claiming to follow him in detail. See Hans-Georg Gadamer, *Truth and Method,* trans. and ed. Garrett Barden and John Cumming (New York: Continuum, 1975), 289–305.

44. MacIntyre, *Whose Justice?,* chap. 18. See also Alasdair MacIntyre, *Three Rival Versions of Moral Enquiry: Encyclopaedia, Genealogy, and Tradition* (Notre Dame, Ind.: University of Notre Dame Press, 1990), chap. 10, which relates this treatment of how traditions develop to the task of the university.

45. John Finnis, "Beyond the Encyclical," in *Considering Veritatis Splendor,* 69.

46. Finnis, *Moral Absolutes: Tradition, Revision, and Truth* (Washington, D.C.: Catholic University of America Press, 1991), 12–16, 105–6, and *passim.* See also John Finnis, Joseph M. Boyle Jr., and Germain Grisez, *Nuclear Deterrence, Morality and Realism* (Oxford: Clarendon Press, 1987), 371–88. One is led to wonder whether Finnis's discussion of martyrdom has had a direct influence on the treatment of the same matter in John Paul II, *Veritatis Splendor,* nos. 90–94.

47. Avery Dulles, "Revelation and Discovery," in *Theology and Discovery: Essays in Honor of Karl Rahner,* ed. William J. Kelly (Milwaukee: Marquette University Press, 1980), 27.

Chapter 5

Understanding Moral Meanings: On Philosophical Hermeneutics and Theological Ethics

WILLIAM SCHWEIKER

In the hands of a theologian, is philosophy only a tool—say, a hammer or scalpel, magnifying glass or map, scale or gauge—used to understand, guide, and judge the moral life? Is there, conversely, strife over the place of faith and reason in apprehending the human good, so that Christians must see philosophy as an instrument of war wielded to destructive ends? Perhaps faith is, as Friedrich Nietzsche suspected, a nihilistic denial of life before the infinite, nonreal God. Maybe faith exceeds moral reason because the logic of Christian love (if one can call it a "logic") overturns moral reciprocity, strict justice, with the superabundance of radical love. Must then one limit, chastise, or destroy reason in order to acknowledge faith (as, in different ways, Immanuel Kant, the philosopher, and Tertullian, the theologian, insisted)? And whose interests—the powerful, the suffering—are served in how these questions are posed and answered? The clash over the use of philosophy in theological ethics is so heated because it concerns the value and direction of our life as moral beings. It is about the subject of this essay: How are we properly to understand moral meanings?

The Aim of This Inquiry

In one sense, the question of the use of philosophy in theological ethics is unremarkable. Anyone thinking about the moral life analyzes concepts, charts arguments, and assesses judgments. These are philosophical tasks, and so every moralist uses philosophical resources in thinking about life and its problems. A theological ethicist wields philosophical scalpels, maps, and gauges. This has always been the case. Who could dispute this point?

Given that everyone uses these tools, the question of the place of philosophy in theological ethics traditionally has centered on three distinct but related topics: (1) the nature of moral knowledge, (2) the source of moral value, and (3) how one defines the moral agent. In order to demonstrate the importance of these matters, consider these questions present throughout the history of Christian moral reflection: Does Christian revelation supply moral knowledge unaccessible to fallible human reason, lost in sin? Does revelation, in fact, perfect reason? Are the Christian claims that human beings are created in the image of God, redeemed in Christ, and also sanctified by grace philosophically intelligible and morally relevant? Is moral value grounded in God, nature, or human communities? The real debate about the use of philosophy transpires around matters epistemological, axiological, and anthropological.

My aim in this essay is to make the case for a hermeneutical approach in theological ethics. Hermeneutics claims that human beings are self-interpreting animals, and, further, that human life transpires within a space of meaning and distinctions of worth.[1] Such claims seem consistent with the deepest impulses of theological ethics. After all, Christian faith conceives of human life set within a reality, a space, created and sustained by God which manifests the divine goodness, and yet this same faith acknowledges that persons also confront and reason about the perplexities of life. However, noting the formal similarity between a Christian outlook and hermeneutical reflection is not enough to warrant the use of hermeneutics in theological ethics. A theologian must provide distinctly theological reasons for the use of philosophical resources in moral inquiry. A theological ethics, in other words, begins and ends with claims about God; it does not move from moral theory to postulate beliefs about the deity.

In order to make a case for a hermeneutical turn in theological ethics, the present inquiry progresses through interrelated layers of reflection. I begin with the purpose of current hermeneutics. At issue here are matters broadly epistemological: the relation of self and other in an account of human understanding and meaning. Next, I examine a core axiological question in moral theory: how to account for the source of moral value. We will see that the current dispute over realism in moral theory is the ethical parallel to the relation of self/other in hermeneutics. Finally, I make the turn to anthropological and theological matters. This step in the argument entails drawing the connection between the question of value and the self/other relation with respect to the surprising return of God-talk within postmodern hermeneutics. And making this connection opens a distinctive space for theological ethical reflection in our time; it helps to warrant the use of hermeneutics in theological ethics.

This progression of thought from meaning through value to anthropological and theological claims per se is itself the journey of hermeneutical inquiry within theological ethics. However, I undertake this inquiry not simply to offer a distinctive "method" for theological ethics. I am trying to rehabilitate a venerable but now much maligned strand in Christian thought. This mode of reflection—evident in thinkers as diverse as Augustine, Calvin, John Wesley and many others—holds it important to discover *within* the dynamics of experience or consciousness the connection between knowledge of self and knowledge of God. The worth of human life and all creation is irreducible in relation to God, and for this strand of Christian faith there is testimony to this worth and relation in every human heart. Developing these claims means that consciousness and its forms once again become central in ethics despite the interest of hermeneutics in language. This signals that theological ethics is not developed solely from the dictates of the Bible, church dogma, or the commands of God. Theological ethics brings to articulation the fact that we always and already exist in relation to God in the depths of our self-relation; it provides an interpretation of our relation to the divine as this bears on the moral life.

A caveat is in order, however. I do not imagine, nor did previous theologians believe, that we simply *find* this testimony of heart. After Nietzsche, Freud, Marx, and other critics, reflection on self-consciousness does not reveal an obvious connection to God! Theologically stated, the reality of sin is such that a direct move from the human heart to God is not possible. Hermeneutics has grasped this point. It insists on exploring the social, psychological, and historical forces that shape and distort human life. There is no simple way into and yet through the human to the divine or to anything else for that matter. The difficult task for ethics, therefore, is to draw the connection between the social and linguistic power to make meaning and the source of value which constitutes moral consciousness while also recognizing the distortions that infest human life, language, and society.

Providing an account of human meaning-making along with isolating distortions in understanding and culture is the role hermeneutics must play in ethics. Theological reflection, I contend, transforms hermeneutical inquiry. It presents the radical claim that at the core of moral self-awareness we are enlivened from a higher source, we contend with powers not our own, we owe our existence to something other than ourselves, worthy of reverence, awe, trust, and, perhaps, love. But this insight and grace is only apprehended *within* our all-too-human acts of meaning-making, our struggles as persons and communities to make cogent sense of the value and tragedy of our lives and our world. The aim of the remainder of this essay is to present and defend these claims.

A final introductory note is in order. In his works, James M. Gustafson has had a constant concern with moral meanings—that is, meanings about values and our lives as moral agents. He has resisted the reduction of moral inquiry simply to matters of public action or social life. Gustafson argues that persons have senses of dependence, gratitude, obligation, remorse and repentance, possibility, and direction. These senses and their objects must be construed in order for them to be morally meaningful. Gustafson links this act of construal to "consciousness" without thereby limiting consciousness to cognition.[2] In piety, consciousness is construed theocentrically; we have a sense of the divine. I contend that the best resource for exploring the act of construal and moral consciousness is hermeneutical inquiry undertaken within the more comprehensive task of theological ethics. In this way, the essay witnesses to Gustafson's influence on the field of theological ethics, and, moreover, my own thinking as well.

Hermeneutics: Practical Philosophy and Reflexive Thinking

Over the last two centuries there has been a widespread debate in the West about how to picture the human. This debate is manifest in art and literature, competing political ideologies, disputes between atheist and religious existentialists, and, recently, the question of the "postmodern" and the place of tradition in the moral life. The crux of the matter can be put thus: Are human beings creators of meaning, or, conversely, do we always struggle to discover the meaning of our lot and life? The stakes are high in this dispute. If we create meaning, then, while we are alone in a morally vacant universe, we at least have the power to fashion a world we desire. We are trapped only in prisons of our making, whether these are linguistic, political, or economic. Conversely, if we discover morality, we inhabit a world permeated with value. This world confronts us with difficult and even tragic choices between goods. Yet we are primordially at home in the world. This dispute about human worth burns in contemporary culture; it is a clash about how we exist in a morally meaningful world. Philosophical hermeneutics purports to offer a way beyond this ongoing cultural battle. In order to see this, we need a clearer grasp of hermeneutics itself.

In the ancient world, hermeneutics was the art of interpretation, especially the interpretation of written texts. From the Greek God "Hermes," the messenger, the interpreter traverses boundaries bearing the meaning of encoded messages. The interpreter carries meanings from one realm (the text) to the world of human life traversing the ambiguous and wily realm of symbol, metaphor, discourse, and narrative. Yet this would, in fact, seem to be true of all human understanding and not simply the act of reading texts. In every act of understanding, human beings are in some profound way crossing experiential, linguistic, cultural, or psychic boundaries bearing messages. Seeing this point has meant over the last centuries that hermeneutics widened in scope to encompass inquiry into historical and linguistic consciousness and the entire domain of meaning.

There is something of grave importance in the expansion of hermeneutics beyond textual interpretation into a philosophy of understanding and human being. Contemporary hermeneutics holds, in Paul Ricoeur's words, that we invent in order to discover; we exert creative energy in making meanings so as to apprehend the character of our existence and our world.[3] Human beings make moral, religious, cultural, scientific, and poetic meanings in order to grasp the truth of their world and lives. This picture of human beings as meaning makers seeking to discover the truth of our existence is the route hermeneutics takes beyond the clash between construing the human as creating or discovering values.

Hermeneutical inquiry develops its claim about human existence in a distinctive way. On my account, it connects insights from classical practical philosophy with those of reflexive thinking found in ancient and modern thought. As a form of reflexive thinking, hermeneutics explicates the truth of consciousness becoming aware of itself; we are *self*-interpreting animals. As a type of practical philosophy, hermeneutics insists that understanding and meaning are bound to action and practice. Yet my insistence on this connection between practical and reflexive philosophy in hermeneutics is a strongly disputed point. I must, therefore, clarify it in order to specify the purpose of this form of philosophy.

Human beings exist knowingly in our world. One can easily distinguish different forms of human knowing. First, empirical knowledge is rooted in our capacity for perception: We sense, feel, taste, smell "things." I know things by encountering them in a sensible way—say, the scent of new-mown grass outside of my window. We validate empirical claims by testing them—that is, by seeing (sensing) what is the case. I stand and gaze out the window at my neighbor mowing his lawn. Second, theoretical knowledge is the capacity to think in terms of concepts that designate some shared nature among perceptible or logical things. I have the idea of "roses"; I always smell a rose. We can also develop theories or models about things. Botany entails theories of life. One might also develop a theory of pure ideas—say about unicorns or ideal numbers. The truth of a theory is its capacity to systematize and clarify phenomena as well as its own logical coherence. The question then is: Do perception and conception provide a complete picture of the way we exist knowingly in the world? If so, then we must either discover truth or invent conceptual schemes to endow our world with intelligibility.

Hermeneutics insists that human understanding is not reducible to perception or conception and their forms of truth. The object of understanding—that is, "meaning"—is neither perceived as a "thing" nor grasped only as an idea. I do not sense the meaning of a text; the meaning of an embrace is not exhausted by our concept "embrace." Meaning is also not defined solely in terms of the ability to learn how to use certain words in a coherent and grammatically consistent way. To be sure, a moral idea—say, justice—is grasped in this way. All of us must learn to speak a moral language and to speak it cogently; we must know how to use the word in order to communicate with others. Moral reason is always dependent on some community and its moral discourse. But this obvious fact does not exhaust an account of "meaning."

The hermeneutical definition of "meaning" is not limited to cognitive or empirical "sense" and how this "sense" is learned. Meaning as the object of understanding is the *connecting* of general thought and particular experience. For instance, I understand the meaning of an embrace by connecting in my very being a distinct sensible experience with an entire set of ideas and beliefs about human interaction. The embrace's meaning is this event of connection. And since my beliefs and experiences are uniquely mine, meaning will always be *in some sense* deeply personal. Linguistically, the event character of meaning is found most basically in the connecting of subject and predicate in a sentence. The meaning of the sentence is the *event* of connecting an idea (say, justice) and experience (our present social life) not reducible to perception or concept. Language is the power to present or articulate this connective space worked in a human life; it is the power to manifest meaning. Language is not simply a system of signs to depict the world and ourselves, a mirror of perceptions, or a storehouse of concepts. Language makes things manifest and thus helps to form life. As Ricoeur puts this about texts, we are interested in the "world in front of the text" as a disclosure of a possible way of life.[4] That "world" is neither sensed nor reducible to a concept; the text presents something rather than merely depicting the world. Thus, most profoundly, meaning designates a space of significance and import in which human existence can transpire knowingly and in which we must orient ourselves.

For example, in one of Jesus' parables, I do not "sense" the dominion of God as a mustard seed; the parable also does not purport to offer a concept for that reality. By presenting possibilities for life, the text discloses human freedom and God's grace. And freedom—let alone grace—is not a sensible thing or an "idea." Freedom is the inner meaning of our being agents; it is how we exist knowingly and personally as agents in the space called the "world." One can also speak of the "life-world," which is the domain of meaning manifest not in discourse but in a culture and its specific institutions and practices. The "life-world" is not a thing or a concept; it is a space within which agents must orient themselves. Meaning (life-world or textual world) comes to presentation through some medium of communication, some actual, natural language. And since we are partially constituted by our self-understandings, the language used to articulate this space of worth, our "world," helps to constitute that world and us. So, "meaning" has evaluative and cognitive components (it includes import *and* significance) because it concerns how we reflectively orient ourselves as persons and communities in some real or imaginary space of distinctions of worth (i.e., a world). "Meanings" are synthetic or connective *events*: Perceptible thing, idea, and the one thinking and perceiving are related in an event of import and significance that defines an arena of life in which persons must orient themselves practically.

This is why, as Hans-Georg Gadamer notes, hermeneutics is heir to classical practical philosophy.[5] The understanding of "meaning" is practical—and not just empirical or theoretical—because it always involves the one understanding trying to grasp the import of what is other than oneself for the sake of guiding further action in a shared space of life. This is sometimes put rather cryptically by theorists: Understanding is dialogical. Understanding involves an interaction through language between oneself and another in a mutually constituted arena of "reading" some message. The validation of an interpretation is an ongoing process, always open to counterargument, and is less strict than "scientific" verification. As Aristotle knew, in the domain of practical reason we ought not to expect the degree of precision—the same form of truth—as empirical and theoretic sciences.

Hermeneutical inquiry examines within the act of interpretation the relation between understanding and meaning that constitutes consciousness of self, world, and other. The complexity of this point is in realizing that one of the media of communication is our historically and linguistically funded experience, our own consciousness. Hermeneutical inquiry must then interpret the interpreter as an encoded message. And that is what I mean by insisting that hermeneutics is heir to reflexive thinking. Stretching from Plato and Augustine to twentieth-century thinkers like Martin Heidegger, Karl Rahner, Paul Tillich, H. Richard Niebuhr, Iris Murdoch, Paul Ricoeur, and Charles Taylor (to name but a few), reflexive philosophy explicates personal self-awareness. What this means is actually quite simple. Consider some rather ordinary activities. Individuals can reflect on things and persons. We can, for instance, ponder and wonder about the meaning of a loved one's embrace. But more than that, persons can also reflect on their acts of reflection, wonder about their wondering. In doing so, one reaches a new level of self-awareness and consciousness. We grasp ourselves in our most basic actions of feeling, thinking, willing, and valuing. As H. Richard Niebuhr put this, "It is only by looking within and catching as it were the reflection of ourselves in act that we are able to achieve some degree of critical self-awareness."[6] Reflexive thinking aims at this kind of self-knowledge. Hermeneutical philosophy holds that the most basic human act we must explore in order to reach valid self-awareness is the act of understanding a world of meanings. In understanding, knowing and valuing interact for the sake of orienting human life; exploring the act of understanding is then the crucial clue for grasping our distinctively human way of existing in the world.

Reflexive inquiry into human understanding does not necessarily mean that the self is trapped within itself in an endless circle of self-reflection. It need not lead to radical subjectivism. Reflexive thinkers also hold that when undertaken honestly and with rigor such inquiry demonstrates that in trying to understand oneself, one also grasps a relation to what is other than self but inscribed in the self. This inscription of other in self is found most obviously in historical consciousness. The past impresses itself on current awareness. To know self requires knowing the past which has funded experience. More radically, there may be an inscription of other persons, the good, or even God in the self, precisely as a prereflective, inarticulate openness to the other. In the act of understanding, I am always trying to apprehend what is not myself in relation to myself.

This radical reflexive kind of inquiry into self/other began in Christian thought with St. Augustine's claim that in reflecting on his thinking, feeling, and willing, he was directed beyond himself to God, a direction manifest prereflectively in his spiritual restlessness and desire for peace. Modern theologians in this tradition struggled to make the same point against the critics of religion. As Søren Kierkegaard put it, in relating itself to itself the self relates itself amid the feeling of anxiety to the power which establishes the self. This power is God. And Friedrich Schleiermacher, father of modern hermeneutics, says that the feeling of immediate self-consciousness is also a feeling of absolute dependence on a "whence," the divine. Still other thinkers could be noted. The point is the same. In coming to self-awareness, the self in its most basic activities is a testimony to itself and to another. The human *is* an act of self-transcendence to its other; this defines the self as primordially in a world, a shared space of distinctions of worth.

The claim of reflexive thinking about the connection of self/other has been challenged in the modern world. Its denial might even define modernity. This is because "modern" thinkers no longer hold, as the ancients did, that our relation to the good is objective to the self. The modern claim is that the self directed inward is not directed beyond itself (to God or to the idea of the Good) or to another *in* the self, but to itself (Descartes), to the "nature" in which it participates (Nietzsche), to the chaos and energy of the unconscious (Freud), or to a system of signs productive of meaning. This is why, as noted above, there is no easy way into and yet through the human to the divine. For many modern thinkers, self-reflection never seems to escape the inner-worldly and inner-psychic forces undergirding the self and its actions. Language seems to express, depict, or conceal only our meaning-making power. Subjectivism seems to rule.

This brings us to the root issue in current thought. The deepest impulse in postmodern hermeneutics is to respond to these criticisms by reclaiming the "other" in relation to the understanding self. Contemporary theorists insist that human consciousness, informed as it is by language, social life, and the natural conditions of existence, is the inescapable *medium* through which we apprehend the meaning of our world and ourselves. Yet while this is true, the question becomes whether our desires, aspirations, and understandings are utterly self-referential in terms of their *meaning* or content. Is consciousness open to and defined by its relation to an "other?" Hermeneutical philosophy, in the strict sense in which I intend the term, is that mode of inquiry fundamentally committed to answering this question in the affirmative.

The self/other relation is developed in hermeneutics with respect to the dynamics of understanding, language, and meaning. Now we see why this is the case. "Meaning" is the self-transcendence of the linguistic code. To understand something as meaningful is to grasp how a medium of communication (paradigmatically, language) intends what is other than itself and to understand oneself *in* that domain of otherness. To recall our earlier discussion, the parables of Jesus disclose the dominion of God and call for a response from the hearer. But this fact about meaning actually raises anew the question formulated earlier. In what does the value of human beings consist? Is our worth seen in the capacity to recognize, wonder about, and respond to a world beyond us manifest in discourse? Or is human value rooted in our power to create meanings which language expresses? In facing this question, hermeneutical inquiry must connect self/other with the question of value. This brings us to the second, axiological layer of our inquiry.

Moral Meaning: Created or Discovered?

The problem that contemporary hermeneutics seeks to address about self/other finds expression in debates about "moral realism" within ethics. We can further our reflection, then, by exploring this debate in order to see what moral reflection contributes to a hermeneutical theory of meaning and understanding. We will see, surprisingly enough, that this contribution centers on the question of the *value* of power.

By "moral realism" is meant the claim, or a theory developed to sustain the claim, that moral ideas and beliefs have truth value; they can be true or false.[7] A moral realist believes that in some final and irreducible way we discover morality; it is not a human invention. Morality is not only a matter of group consensus, personal preference, or calculations of social utility. It dips into the nature of things. The morally good and right life is a matter of conforming one's existence to the real. Clarity of thought and veracity of moral perception are crucial to the moral life. Moral discourse strives to be faithful to something beyond itself.

Strict moral realism takes two forms in Christian ethics: divine command ethics and natural law ethics. Traditionally, divine command ethics holds that what God commands is morally right and thus the moral life is about obedience to those commands. In this century, theologians like Karl Barth and even some philosophers have tried to rehabilitate divine command ethics. Yet problems continue to dog this form of moral theory. Assuming that God does command persons, on what grounds ought we to believe that they rightly hear—perceive—those commands? Further, in order to think that God's commands must be obeyed, one must have some idea of what is worthy of human worship. How are we to account for that scale of values which itself is not a divine command? One cannot avoid the problem of interpretation unless one wants to reduce divine commands and the source of value to consciousness itself, or to hold that the command is as obvious as other perceptible things in the world. Both answers are unacceptable to divine command ethics.

Traditional natural law ethics faces similar problems. Natural law classically linked an account of human reason with a claim about how nature indicates directions for action. This requires discerning the nature of the being in question and then deriving from that some claim about what ought to be done. For example, human beings are social animals, and, accordingly, the demands of social life are morally necessary. We can make the transition from *is* to *ought* because human reason participates in the divine mind, or what Thomas Aquinas calls eternal law, governing the world. This participation (natural law) is not known through perception—as divine command theory has it—but is known because consciousness bears within the precepts of the moral law.

Not only are these claims about human reason difficult to sustain, but, once again, problems of interpretation abound. How are we to understand the meaning of moral precepts in specific cases? How is it that we can know the ends and purposes nature indicates? Once we grant that human understanding is historically and socially embedded, what becomes of the claim of traditional natural law ethics to articulate universal precepts?

Revisions have been made in moral realism in order to take seriously the dynamics of historical understanding. A thinker can be a realist about a community's whole cognitive scheme, since it is this scheme, not specific ideas or experiences, that is about the world. Internal realism, as it is called, holds that people with different moral languages live in different moral worlds.[8] This follows from the fact that to understand any specific moral concept (say, justice) requires facility with the entire set of beliefs about reality in which that concept makes sense. For this kind of realism, moral reason is blind without some framework within which to understand and articulate our lives. One insists on realism in ethics with respect to a whole set of moral beliefs.

Narrative theologians like Stanley Hauerwas, John Howard Yoder, and James McClendon hold this kind of internal realism.[9] By insisting that Christian moral identity and understanding of the world are functions of the Christian narrative, they mean to say that Christian beliefs are not definable in the terms of other forms of moral understanding. This saves Christian moral meanings from being reduced to claims about natural morality or the moral beliefs of the wider public. The truth of Christian moral claims can only be established internal to those beliefs; one cannot refer to the world "out there" or to natural moral reason to validate or to refute Christian moral beliefs. Those beliefs are validated with respect to communities whose life and "world" they help to constitute. Other theologians use phenomenological methods to modify moral realism. Thomas Ogletree, for instance, draws on the work of the Jewish philosopher Emmanuel Levinas to center his ethics on the experience of the claim of other.[10] The other is not reducible to a conceptual scheme; we encounter the other in the sheer fact of his or her existence. The Roman Catholic moral theologian Josef Fuchs specifies the experience of obligation in conscience as definitive for the meaning of being a person.[11] These forms of modified realism ground morality in experience or self-understanding, rather than, as internal realists argue, the coherence and comprehensiveness of evolving moral traditions.

The difficulty with these various positions for hermeneutics is that they can devolve into defining moral meanings in terms of perception or conception. The narrative theologian thinks that experience is the product of the stories we tell, our conceptual scheme. Some thinkers who insist on encounters with "the other" as morally basic believe that the other breaks through our systems of ideas. The encounter is simply a brute fact. In each case, what is threatened with loss is the self-referential and deeply personal structure of the act of understanding meanings. This loss of the role subjectivity plays in valuing has fueled antirealism in ethics.

Antirealists hold that values are not ontologically grounded; morality is what we invent, not discover. As J. L. Mackie has put it, "values are not objective, are not part of the fabric of the world."[12] Morality strikes no deeper than social convention and rules of convenience aimed at social cohesion. Moral goodness and moral obligation are a function of how we (whoever this "we" is) choose to think about them. While persons often believe that moral values are part of the fabric of the world, the "world" is actually a function of language and social practices. Stripped of that discourse, we would not have any way to know what reality is like and we would not have any idea of who "we" are as persons and communities. Communities and traditions see and experience the world differently because of their moral outlooks, and so we ought to explore those outlooks rather than try to peer through them to "reality."

Some contemporary theologians talk as if they are antirealists. The feminist ethicist Sharon Welch, for instance, argues that moral claims have no status beyond the linguistic and power relations of communities.[13] Her concern is to expose the pretense to universality in all realistic forms of Christian ethics. A commitment to a feminist ethics of risk is grounded in nothing other than the sheer choice so to commit oneself. Yet while thinkers like Welch talk as antirealists, they merely have rejected traditional realism. Were that not the case, then, these thinkers would hold that not only our words about "God" but also the divine—or sacred—is a human invention. Yet Welch speaks of the power of relation as divine; others realize that the divine is transcendent, not reducible to the ongoing life of the community. Insofar as this is the case, few theologians are actually antirealists.

Other theologians insist on the constructed character of all belief systems but temper antirealism. They argue that human beings are always making meanings, but we construct them for the purpose of coping with a world we confront. Gordon Kaufman, for one, insists that theology is an act of imaginative construction where the theologian formulates an image/concept of "God" in order to relativize human pretense and to orient human action for the purpose of humanizing the world.[14] The fact that "God" is an "image/concept" shows that Kaufman does not believe that the word "God" is reducible to only a concept or to an object of perception. If it were, we could provide a sensible image for the divine (God is "mother," for example)—or a conception, like, say, God is "being itself." Kaufman is interested in how the theologian's construct *functions* to guide *meaningful* action. Moral reflection must take account of reality as we best know it. In recent work Kaufman seeks to provide a theistic construct to account for the surprising creativity of the universe. Values might not be written into the fabric of the world, but morality must account for the world as we find it.

Christian feminist ethicists often speak in this way. Sallie McFague and Lisa Sowle Cahill draw on different sides of the Western Christian tradition (Protestant and Roman Catholic respectively).[15] Each thinker has modified the moral claims of her tradition (sovereignty of God; natural law ethics) in the direction of acknowledging the historical and shifting shape of moral discourse. McFague explores the role of metaphors and models in theological discourse; Cahill is attentive to the variety of sources in moral theology. Yet each also insists that moral meanings are not invented; they are developed in response to a world in which we exist and which we must respect and enhance. We test moral and theological claims, Cahill and McFague insist, by the capacity of these claims to orient life. In moral reflection we do not simply discover or discern anything *moral* about the world, rather we try to orient ourselves in the world.

The debate in ethics about moral meaning ranges from positions which hold that it is discovered to those which insist on human creativity. The realist holds to a basic otherness in moral consciousness not reducible to human creativity. Moral discourse and good people strive to be faithful to something beyond themselves—the command of God, natural law, the reality of other persons. Antirealists ground human dignity in the power to create value; moral discourse manifests our response to our condition. For hermeneutics, problems arise in these moral theories either because moral knowing is defined in terms of perception or conception or because a moral theory tries to bypass consciousness and reduce the origin of value to the media of understanding (i.e., language). However, this debate in moral theory does expose the axiological dimension to the self/other question. And it exposes it in terms of power—the power to create or discover meanings. At root, the question of realism is whether the human power to create meanings is morally basic or whether there is some reality that thwarts human power. This poses one of the most fundamental of all moral questions: What is the value of power? In other words, is the capacity to respond to, influence, and create reality—that is, power—alone constitutive of value? How, if at all, does hermeneutics deal with this basic question? This brings us to the third and final layer of our inquiry, and, surprisingly, to the reality of God in current hermeneutics.

Hermeneutics and Theological Ethics

A hermeneutical approach to theological ethics must acknowledge that Christian faith entails some form of moral realism. This is because the source of morality (God) is not reducible to consensus, preferences, social utility, or the imagination. Christian consciousness—maybe all theistic consciousness—is defined by an irreducible otherness at the very heart of self-understanding. One should expect traces, signs, of this otherness in the dynamics of consciousness. Theologically, the problem is to show that these traces and signs testify to the God of all reality. But showing this means that we need an approach to ethics that takes seriously the self/other constitution of consciousness while acknowledging the mediation of all meaning and value through historical and linguistic understanding. If we can develop this approach in moral theory, we could call it "hermeneutical realism."[16]

In order to outline this hermeneutical realist position we must return to basic anthropological matters and link them to ones about language and meaning. Recall that the basic claim of hermeneutics is that human beings exist understandingly in a space of significance and import and thus one of distinctions of worth. The human agent lives in a moral universe manifest in the apprehension of meanings. Language, as noted before, is not simply a tool we invent or learn to use for certain purposes, although it is also that. As Charles Taylor notes, "What comes about through the development of language in the broadest sense is the coming to be of expressive power, the power to make things manifest. . . . What is made manifest is not exclusively, or even mainly, a self, but a world."[17] Language is expressive power; it is the capacity to manifest a world. For ethics, this claim about language means that every moral tradition presents an axiology of power (i.e., some evaluation of power with respect to human life in the world), insofar as its moral discourse presents a background of possibilities and values within which to orient life. What then are we to make of the insight that meaning rests on expressive power? Does this show, as critics hold, that a hermeneutical theory of meaning is a form of moral antirealism, and, thus, is incompatible with the deepest impulses of theological ethics?

The relation of language and power warrants a *critical* stance toward claims to meaning; it requires an eye for the distortions that infest all human meaning-making. Specifically, it demands attention to how the value or worth of persons and the world is too often defined exclusively by what or who exercises power in the making or ranking of values. In fact, this concern to counter the reduction of value to power is the reason for insistence on the "other" in so much contemporary thought. The "other" is taken to be the manifestation of a value beyond the range of subjective and linguistic power, whether that "other" is the past, a human face and its moral appeal, or the divine. This manifestation indicates that respect for others is basic to a meaningful human world; it founds the world morally. The will-to-power, even in the form of meaning creation, is not the basic truth of life. The desire to avoid reducing the other to some social system is the reason to insist on a hermeneutical account of "meaning" and, also, to continue and yet revise the tradition of reflexive philosophy. If it can be shown that the self/other relation is constitutive of consciousness and that language intends something beyond itself as a semiotic code, then the "other" cannot be reduced to our meaning-making power.

In my judgment, it is in this context of thinking about power/value in relation to self/other that we find the surprising return of God-talk in postmodern hermeneutics, precisely because God is the limit-case of otherness manifest in language. Some hermeneutical philosophers affirm the reality of God in order to endorse the value of the world on grounds other than strict utility. Other thinkers insist that the being of God is manifest with the noninstrumental worth of others. Taylor argues, for instance, that our perception of value is not devoid of our own creative meaning-making, but he also seeks something to thwart the triumph of power. "Put in yet other terms," he writes, "the world's being good may now be seen as not entirely independent of our seeing it and showing it as good, at least as far as the world of humans is concerned."[18] In this, Taylor finds an analogy to divine *agape*—a seeing good which also helps effect what it sees. Otherwise the world is devoid of value, a simple object to be used as we wish. Other philosophers, notably Ricoeur, argue that the self is constituted through its encounter with the "other."[19] Meaningful identity, the endowing of self with import and significance, transpires within our encounters with what is not self and also not reducible to our construals of life. For Ricoeur, the many ways of naming God in Christian faith are symbolic articulations of a primary affirmation of being against its negation. This affirmation is also manifest in the claim of the other not to be violated. Theological discourse provides the linguistic means to talk about the manifestation of worth not reducible to human power.

What are we to make of this return in postmodern hermeneutics to the classic, reflexive claim that self-consciousness is constituted by its other, even a divine other? Does this warrant the use of philosophical hermeneutics in theological ethics, or is it, once again, simply an example of the god of the philosopher? Can a theologian really accept what appears to be an anthropocentric endorsement of God by hermeneutical thinkers simply for the purpose of backing human values? I have been arguing that hermeneutics enables us to examine the domain of meaning and human understanding in ways consonant with deep impulses in Christian thought. It pictures the human existing in a space of value which finds expression in human consciousness. Yet properly speaking, a theologian ought to demand theological reasons for the use of a philosophical position. Christian claims about God must come first in a theological ethics. This is to preserve the freedom and integrity of theological reflection. So we must ask: Are there theological reasons for endorsing the religious turn in hermeneutics?

Christian faith, like all moral traditions, is an axiology of power. The diverse ways of naming God in Christian thought—from sovereign lord to suffering servant—manifest the divine being as value creating power, but a power that respects and enhances finite reality as its other. The symbol "God" as the way Christians speak about ultimate reality presents a claim to transvalue power in understanding self, world, and others by connecting the idea of ultimate power with an endorsement of finite worth. This "transvaluation" is the radical overturning of how power is valued in the creation of a meaningful world.[20] To believe that God creates, redeems, judges, and sustains the world is to insist that power is indeed axiologically basic but yet not exhaustive of value. Religiously and morally this means that one's faith, one's identity-conferring commitment, affirms that the ultimate power of reality is good. Yet that faith also dethrones the works of sheer power as the substance of all value. A theological construal of the world thus demarcates a space of action defined by this affirmation and also the dethronement of power. Such an outlook on the meaning of existence warrants a critical stance in ethics; it demands attention to the deceptions of power in all human activities. Yet this also signals that theologians must make the radical claim that the being of God is the ground of moral meaning. Can this claim be made?

Insofar as meaning is the manifestation of a world of significance and import expressed through but not reducible to the power of language, then the transvaluation of power—what Christians designate morally by their God-talk—is basic to understanding meaning and the human world. That is, the power of language to manifest a world amid the complexity of personal life is seen theologically as a sign or trace of the divine. Language testifies to the being of God insofar as persons create a meaningful and distinctive world through understandable discursive acts, but a world whose meaning is not reducible to that act of human power. In a word, language and human understanding are signs of the transvaluation of power which Christians believe defines the very being of God.[21] And insofar as language helps to constitute our self-understanding, then consciousness shaped by this radical claim of Christian discourse about the divine apprehends the worth of reality enlivened by a higher source. Christian consciousness senses that we owe the meaning of our existence to something other than our power yet discoverable within our acts of meaning-making. The moral space of life from this perspective has its condition beyond itself even as it also bears the marks—tragically, comically—of human struggles with power and meaning. At issue morally is how we—we who wield and suffer power in the search for meaning—will orient ourselves in a world whose condition of moral viability and survival demands the transvaluation of power. The moral requirement is that we, too, must transvalue our power to act in order to respect and enhance the integrity of life.

It is not possible in this short essay to trace the practical implications of these admittedly radical claims, nor even to elaborate them further. It is also not necessary to do so. My point has been to give the theological reason why hermeneutical inquiry is an important resource for theologians. That reason is that God is the source of moral meaning and so we ought to find some testimony to or denial of the divine in all apprehensions of meaning. Current hermeneutics and moral theory, I have shown, can be seen as addressing the question of the relation of human power to the source of value, and, thus, posing the question of God as it is presented in Christian thought. Theologians have the symbolic resources needed in current ethics to think and speak about the connection of power and value in human existence. Under these rubrics, it might be possible to undertake anew what H. Richard Niebuhr called Christian moral philosophy.[22] A hermeneutical form of theological ethics articulates and analyzes our self-understanding as agents and shows that in all meaning-making actions, all works of power, the divine is also encountered. This encounter with otherness can, may, and must transvalue how one understands and exercises power.

Conclusion

The purpose of this essay has been to outline the possibility and also importance of a hermeneutical approach in theological ethics. My deepest concern has been to show *within* the dynamics of understanding—thus, meaning and language—the connection between knowledge of self and the source of value, the divine. The loss of this form of thinking, I believe, would herald the triumph of power and technical reason over all values. It would condemn Christians to an insufferable silence about their most basic convictions concerning human life and the divine. Thus, I have drawn on hermeneutics to aid in articulating and analyzing the testimony to the divine within our moral meanings. In so doing, we have found the theological reason for the use of philosophical hermeneutics in ethics.

Notes

1. See Richard E. Palmer, *Hermeneutics* (Evanston, Ill.: Northwestern University Press, 1969); David E. Klemm, *Hermeneutics Inquiry*, 2 vols. (Atlanta: Scholar's Press, 1986); and William Schweiker, *Mimetic Reflections: A Study in Hermeneutics, Theology, and Ethics* (New York: Fordham University Press, 1990).

2. James M. Gustafson, *Ethics from a Theocentric Perspective*, 2 vols. (Chicago: University of Chicago Press, 1981–1984).

3. Paul Ricoeur, *Interpretation Theory: Discourse and the Surplus of Meaning* (Fort Worth: Texas Christian University Press, 1976).

4. Paul Ricoeur, *Hermeneutics and the Human Sciences: Essays on Language, Action, and Interpretation*, ed., trans., and introduction by John B. Thompson (Cambridge: Cambridge University Press, 1981). Also see Charles Taylor, *Philosophy and the Human Sciences*, Philosophical Papers 2 (Cambridge: Cambridge University Press, 1985); Irving Singer, *Meaning in Life: The Creation of Value* (New York: The Free Press, 1992); and David E. Klemm and William Schweiker, eds., *Meanings in Texts and Actions: Questioning Paul Ricoeur* (Charlottesville: University of Virginia Press, 1993).

5. Hans-Georg Gadamer, *Reason in the Age of Science*, trans. F. Lawrence (Cambridge, Mass.: MIT Press, 1981). Also see Hans-Georg Gadamer, *Truth and Method*, rev. translation by J. Weinsheimer and D. Marshall (New York: Continuum, 1989).

6. H. Richard Niebuhr, *Faith on Earth: An Inquiry into the Structure of Human Faith*, ed. Richard R. Niebuhr (New Haven: Yale University Press, 1989), 23.

7. See David Brink, *Moral Realism and the Foundation of Ethics* (Cambridge: Cambridge University Press, 1989), and *Essays in Moral Realism*, ed. Geoffrey Sayre-McCord (Ithaca, N.Y.: Cornell University Press, 1988).

8. See Hilary Putnam, *The Many Faces of Realism* (LaSalle, Ill.: Open Court, 1987).

9. See Stanley Hauerwas, *Christian Existence Today: Essays on Church, World, and Living In-Between* (Durham, N.C.: Labyrinth Press, 1988); John Howard Yoder, *The Priestly Kingdom: Social Ethics as Gospel* (Notre Dame, Ind.: University of Notre Dame Press, 1984); and James Wm. McClendon Jr., *Ethics: Systematic Theology* (Nashville: Abingdon Press, 1986).

10. Thomas Ogletree, *Hospitality to the Stranger: Dimensions of Moral Understanding* (Philadelphia: Fortress Press, 1985).

11. Josef Fuchs, *Christian Morality: The Word Became Flesh*, trans. B. McNeil (Washington, D.C.: Georgetown University Press, 1981).

12. J. L. Mackie, *Ethics: Inventing Right and Wrong* (Harmondsworth, Eng.: Penguin Books, 1977), 15.

13. Sharon Welch, *A Feminist Ethics of Risk* (Minneapolis: Fortress Press, 1990).

14. Gordon Kaufman, *Theology for a Nuclear Age* (Philadelphia: Westminster Press, 1985).

15. Sallie McFague, *Models of God: A Theology for an Ecological, Nuclear Age* (Philadelphia: Fortress Press, 1987); and Lisa Sowle Cahill, *Between the Sexes: Foundations for a Christian Ethics of Sexuality* (Philadelphia: Fortress, 1985), and also her *Woman and Sexuality* (New York: Paulist Press, 1992).

16. See William Schweiker, *Responsibility and Christian Ethics* (Cambridge: Cambridge University Press, 1995).

17. Charles Taylor, *Human Agency and Language*, Philosophical Papers I (Cambridge: Cambridge University Press, 1985), 238.

18. Charles Taylor, *Sources of the Self: The Making of Modern Identity* (Cambridge: Harvard University Press, 1989), 448.

19. Paul Ricoeur, *Soi-meme comme un autre* (Paris: Éditions du Seuil, 1990), and also his "Naming God" in *Union Seminary Quarterly Review* 34 (1979): 215–28.

20. The term "transvaluation" is first found in the work of Friedrich Nietzsche. He rightly realized that what is morally basic is how a culture develops a table of values with respect to the reality of power. I am arguing that the transvaluation of power entailed in Christian faith negates the centrality of the will-to-power in Nietzsche's thought and a world bent on the celebration of power. This is, in my judgment, the properly radical claim of Christian faith. See Friedrich Nietzsche, *Beyond Good and Evil: Prelude to a Philosophy of the Future*, trans. R. J. Hollingdale (New York: Penguin Books, 1973); see also William Schweiker, "Power and the Agency of God," in *Theology Today* 52, no. 2 (1995): 204–24.

21. In making this claim, I mean to recast in hermeneutical terms Saint Augustine's argument, in *De Trinitate*, about the *vestigium Trinitatis* etched on the human soul. On this see Saint Augustine, "On the Holy Trinity," in *Nicene and Post-Nicene Fathers*, first series, vol. 3 (Grand Rapids, Mich.: Eerdmans, 1980), and Karl Barth, *Church Dogmatics*, vol. 1, part 1 (Edinburgh: T. &. T. Clark, 1975).

22. H. Richard Niebuhr, *The Responsible Self: An Essay in Christian Moral Philosophy* (New York: Harper & Row, 1963).

Chapter 6

The Particularist Turn in Theological and Philosophical Ethics

GENE OUTKA

> Stand firm then, my friends, and hold fast to the traditions which you have learned
> from us, either by word or by letter.
>
> —2 Thess. 2:15, REB

Those of us who work in theological ethics draw on multiple "sources," and find ourselves stretched in many directions. The sources that refer to God and mandate the adjective "theological" present their own daunting requirements. In the case of Christian ethics, we must know the Bible and the Christian tradition, including Christian theology. If we evaluate and construct as well as describe and comment, we must determine what authority the Bible has for us and how we honor it; which figures and institutional movements in the history of the church matter most, positively and negatively; and which beliefs about God and the world shape and are shaped by the normative judgments we make. The nontheological sources, such as philosophy, experience, and human learning (in the natural and social sciences and in the humanities), complicate matters further. We must not only acquire suitable kinds of competence in these sources, too, but must indicate how we employ them and what weight we give them if our ethics is to remain recognizably theological.

How we employ and what weight we give "philosophy" is my subject. One religious assumption and one cultural location frame the approach I take. I assume that we violate the commandment to love God with our minds when we fail to esteem truth for its own sake and to employ our arguments responsibly. So we should rank cogency higher than rhetorical effectiveness. And so we should be open to philosophizing as an activity that strives to disentangle good and bad arguments and privileges high levels of rigor in elucidating concepts. To the extent that philosophy as practiced nowadays in college and university departments impels us to argue more clearly and think more rigorously, we should draw on its labors without ceasing to keep our own substantive counsels. Furthermore, my cultural location is Western as a matter of fate. Thus by "philosophy" I refer to its figures and movements (e.g., Aristotelian, Kantian, Hegelian, analytic) against the backdrop of traditional spheres of inquiry (e.g., logic, metaphysics, epistemology, philosophy of nature, philosophy of mind, and ethics).

Within this frame, I will concentrate on one movement in ethics that in the last fifteen to twenty years enters fully into mainstream Western thought. The movement I call "the particularist turn." It heeds Stoicism and Kant less and Aristotle and Hegel more; it turns away from formalist and universalist ethical theories and toward some particular historical-ethical community.

Three reasons lead me to impose so severe a restriction. First, I think that in a limited space we improve our chances of throwing light on the general question of "philosophy as a source" when we attend to an identifiable movement. Indeed, unless we do attend, the general question remains unacceptably indeterminate. My frame orients us somewhat, but it nevertheless affords enormous leeway for heterogeneous movements, some of which appraise the tasks of philosophy very differently. Moreover, for the movement I want to scrutinize, it is not that "philosophy" as a source happens in this instance to teach "particularism." Rather, particularists tend to assign a certain role to philosophy, one that brings it into close proximity with inquiries such as history. Even here, this tendency by no means yields full agreement. In brief, we do best to work from within one definite philosophical movement and the reference points that distinguish it. The second reason concerns sheer influence. I select this movement also because it has become a tide in the culture at large. It generates and epitomizes controversies that now cut across academic specialties, though many of its leading exponents are philosophers by training. It is so much a cultural datum that to decline to engage it carries the burden of proof.

My third reason is internal to Christian theology and ethics. I wish to secure room to consider two commitments and two corresponding fears we characteristically evidence, and to view the particularist turn as providing fresh impetus to think carefully about them. James Gustafson identifies the two commitments in this way: "Christianity has always claimed its historical particularity—the biblical events and their records—to have universal significance and import. Certainly a substantive enterprise in theology from the biblical times forward has been to overcome and sustain that particularity at one and the same time, to stand with and for that historic particularity while insisting that its significance is universal."[1] Many contend that in the late twentieth century Christians should more than anything else stand with and for historic particularity and that recent philosophical attacks on Enlightenment universalism equip them more effectively to do so. Again, this is our special line of country here. The fear that corresponds to the commitment to particularity I call *the fear of redundancy*. I take it to be an estimable not a bogus fear. If all that Christian beliefs and practices accomplish is to tell us in a loud voice what we otherwise may know and do (e.g., by independently founded philosophical schemes), then we trivialize commitment to historic particularity.

Still, commitment to universal significance is likewise something that Christians evidence through the centuries. To be sure, they must think from the vantage point of their particularity to arrive at their understanding of such significance. But their confession includes truth claims about God and God's relation to the world. It is not only about meanings for them or views they happen to hold within communities sharing such views. The fear corresponding to this second commitment I call *the fear of esotericism*. I take it to be an estimable fear as well. If all that Christian beliefs and practices accomplish is to tell believers that *they* are made in the image of God, for example, rather than that all people are thus made, whether or not they know it, then we trivialize commitment to universal significance.

In what follows, I propose to identify three major sites where the particularist turn provides an impetus to reflect on these commitments and fears. First, there is a site, familiar by now, where we canvass universalist claims about morality that come under attack and particularist claims that are advanced in their stead. I hardly can do detailed justice to criticisms of universalist claims, though I will try to be somewhat more nuanced than those who, without undertaking historical or philosophical inquiry of their own, merely adopt Alasdair MacIntyre's appraisals and condemn, mantralike, "the Enlightenment project."[2] I will conclude at this first site that the turn, in promoting awareness of the historical and social dimensions of moral thought, can aid and abet attention to Christianity's own historic particularity.

Second, there is a less familiar site where we distinguish *among* the particularist claims advanced. These claims prove to be distinct and sometimes rivalrous. They are often defended in terms of one or more of various "postisms" that circulate (e.g., postmodernism, postliberalism, posthumanism, and postenlightenment). I will focus on two such influential claims, referring to them simply as tradition-dependence and cultural contingency. That these claims differ, and differ in ways that may either harmonize or clash with positions held in theological ethics, are matters insufficiently explored. Such differences suggest that we worrisomely exaggerate when we take the quest for some "ahistorical" or "foundationalist" standpoint as the key to all of the difficulties we face in theological ethics. What sort of staying power traditions actually have and should seek to maintain, for example, is a subject fraught with difficulties of its own that the claims about tradition-dependence and cultural contingency goad us to confront. I will conclude at this second site that we need to disentangle and assess representative answers given to the question about the *historical* staying power of the Christian tradition.

Third, there is a site where we ask what lessons the turn may have to teach as we attempt to specify the meaning that universal significance carries for us. On this immense subject, I can only indicate here several possibilities that our study of the turn brings into clearer relief. I will conclude at this third site that we do well to revisit certain features of the distinctive view of human nature and the human good that the tradition presents as true, to see how they fare in light of the turn.

Site One: Fallibilism, History, and Social Identity

"Particularism" contrasts with "universalism," yet each word covers a multitude of claims. For our purposes, the key universalist claims about morality that come under particularist attack are these.[3] First, basic moral beliefs are known or apprehended through "reason" rather than "revelation"; they are available across cultures and historical periods, at least implicitly, in the conscience that is common to all human beings, to believers, agnostics, and atheists. Second, these moral beliefs are entirely or sufficiently justified without recourse to particular beliefs and practices that distinguish certain communities, including religious ones. Third, the class of those to whom basic moral beliefs apply is coterminous with the human race, and the moral obligations that trump are ones that as far as possible disengage from, and are comprehensible independently of, particular cultural contexts. So long as we accept these three claims, we may compatibly endorse political arrangements for which Jefferson rather than Robespierre sets the tone as we safeguard religious and other liberties within the civic order. Religious communities may present wider interpretations of human nature and destiny to their adherents and any others who take an interest, although they may never force outsiders to join or once inside to stay; nor may they impose their interpretations on the society at large. Religious communities may also valuably contribute to moral nurture.

Not all Christians reject these claims and the terms of civic peace that accompany them. Some, for instance those who think that apprehensions of natural law are not illusory, may draw on beliefs that antedate the Enlightenment according to which awareness of certain basic moral considerations is independent of membership in any particular community.[4] I will return to such beliefs at the site where I focus on universal significance. For the moment, I introduce senses of particularism that contrast with the universalist ones so far mentioned.

One sense of "particularism" is epistemic fallibilism. Here critics recoil from the epistemic hubris they discern in universalist claims. The hubris shows most obviously when we consider that what the claims lead us reasonably to expect collide with what we actually find. We expect broad moral agreement from the deliverances of a conscience common to all human beings. We find rampant diversity and disagreement. The extent of de facto disagreement stands then as an immanent critique of the claims themselves. We are sent back to our limits and feel the force of the case for epistemic humility. The hubris shows as well in certain quests associated with Enlightenment figures. For instance, the quest for comprehensive knowledge that would finally settle ethical questions appears overweening. Hegel, many of whose writings support the particularist turn, is viewed in this respect as the culminating figure of an Enlightenment ideal that strives to bring together everything knowable, about science, art, religion, philosophy, and history, under a single comprehensive rational system that constitutes an absolute standpoint.[5] Kierkegaard's objection, that such a standpoint is a reality only for God and not for any existing individual, because only for God do knowing and doing precisely coincide, evokes widespread sympathy.[6]

Another sense of "particularism" resides in the insistence that moral beliefs and concepts must be studied historically and contextually. Here critics turn away from epistemologically oriented and toward historically oriented philosophy.[7] A governing particularist claim is that we understand philosophical questions properly only when we understand their historical genesis. Unless and until we examine moral beliefs and concepts in light of their past vicissitudes and the resolutions they now reflect, we fail to grasp how and why we have come to hold the beliefs we do. This claim means, as MacIntyre was already contending in 1966, that moral concepts are not "a timeless, limited, unchanging, determinate species of concept, necessarily having the same features throughout their history, so that there is a part of language waiting to be philosophically investigated which deserves the title '*the* language of morals' (with a definite article and a singular noun)."[8] Two examples show insights we gain when we understand our present situation by narrating how it has emerged and what changes have occurred.

To be prepared to reexamine matters that have been represented as timeless truths yields insights into our own legacies in theological ethics when we track particular constellations of moral beliefs, some of which are intelligible only as we reckon with specifically Christian contributions. For instance, when Charles Taylor revisits the fact-value dichotomy, he judges its origins to be theological, as a thesis propounded in the first instance to vindicate God's sovereignty. Occam and others rebelled against the assumption that God is bound by creation, that God *must* will the goods internal to it. They preferred mechanism to a fixed and ordered cosmos with its principles of justification built into it, for a neutral universe waited to have purposes bestowed upon it by God's free actions. Later something of this conception of freedom was transferred to human beings:

> As against seeing our paradigm purposes as given to us by the nature of the cosmic order in which we are set, we find them rather in the nature of our own reasoning powers. These demand that we take control by objectifying the world, submitting it to the demands of instrumental reason. The purposes to which the surrounding world is instrumentalized are found within us.[9]

In short, to narrate how this new outlook emerges and what changes occur gives us insight into the fact-value split that we acquire in no other way.

To refuse to marginalize historical inquiry also alerts us to the importance of distinguishing traditions that develop over time in order to explain moral disagreement.

Consider, for instance, the tension some readers detect in Alan Donagan's writings.[10] He thinks on the one hand that morality as Kant conceives it amounts to "traditional Christian morality demystified and universalized," and that such morality "does not presuppose the truth of the Christian faith, but is presupposed by it."[11] And what is presupposed is a common morality that in the West is linked to the Jewish and Christian religions. Adherents of these religions not only agree in the main about it, but have specified many of its key features. Kant's second formulation of the categorical imperative perspicuously captures rather than jeopardizes its normative force.[12] Yet on the other hand, Donagan explicitly admits that such morality presupposes a view of human beings as autonomous and responsible and as living in a natural world governed by morally neutral laws—presuppositions that are at odds, he grants, with those found in other "venerable cultures" (e.g., Hinduism, and in some post-Christian theories of human nature, such as B. F. Skinner's radical behaviorism).[13] But then the crux lies in our recognizing how these latter presuppositions are tied to distinctive moralities. So we can explain the disagreements only when we see that the kind of common morality that Donagan defends emerges within a certain part of Western history.

A final sense of "particularism" is captured in the dictum that our sociality goes all the way down, that as Richard Rorty says, "there is nothing 'beneath' socialization or prior to history which is definatory of the human."[14] Under attack here are Enlightenment-inspired forms of atomistic individualism that radically separate the self from particular circumstances. Critics allege that such separation goes wrong descriptively and normatively. Hegel describes what obtains for all of us, as soon as we amend his statement to include both genders and various communities: "Each individual is the son of his own nation at a specific stage in this nation's development. No one can escape from the spirit of his nation, any more than he can escape from this earth itself."[15] As individuals, we depend on given social relations for the appearance of features that mark us as human, our acquisition of language, our mores, our activities spanning work and play. That we belong to a certain religious community, class, and culture is never incidental to our self-understanding. That we find it impossible to distinguish clearly the traditions and practices and familial and other social circumstances bequeathed to us from the decisions we make and the virtues and vices we display means that the most fitting way to view our individual human lives is to narrate our histories. Normatively, too, membership in our communities should count morally with us. We should seek to comprehend given practices of which we are a part rather than privilege considerations that are affiliation-free. We should develop accounts of justice relative to our particular culture and history and not ones perpetually revisionist and disengaged from our own socially constituted moral identities. We should view our traditions not as mere milieus but as repositories, not accidental but essential to the moral knowledge on whose basis we ought to order our lives.

These senses of particularism must suffice to convey the timbre of claims advanced. Taken cumulatively, I think that the claims may serve to promote attention to Christianity's own historic particularity. To the extent that doubts are successfully cast on Enlightenment moral claims, certain controversies about Christianity's own focus on paradigmatic historical events lose their point, and the fear of redundancy recedes. We may thereby accord greater prominence to two elementary features of that particularity: a normative feature to the effect that, *pace* the Enlightenment, Christianity tells us things religiously and morally that we cannot tell to ourselves, and an institutional feature to the effect that what Christianity tells us demands distinctive communal transmission. Let me comment on each feature.

To think from the vantage point of historic particularity to arrive at an understanding of universal significance does not require that we cease to esteem good arguments or that we resist every sort of generally negotiable moral appeal. But it does require that we resist Enlightenment-inspired accounts that leave commitment to historic particularity only accidental moral work to do, a mere matrix for moral reflection. For matrix theories tend to affirm that everything religiously and morally significant is available in principle to the unassisted reason. Basil Mitchell sounds here a fitting combination of notes. He ascribes a central role to rational acceptance of religious and moral beliefs. But he finds it nonetheless preposterous for Kant to demand that "the Holy One of the Gospels must first be compared with our ideal of moral perfection before we can recognize him as such." Mitchell observes:

> It is absurd to suppose that the fisherman of Galilee—when he made the confession: "Thou art Christ, the Son of the Living God"—had compared Jesus with his ideal of moral perfection (just as it was before any encounter took place) and had satisfied himself that he had, so to speak, achieved the required standard. He had, of course, judged for himself, and in judging he exercised moral insight, but he could not himself have preached the Sermon on the Mount.
>
> It is indeed, often misleading to talk . . . about choosing a model for imitation; what more often happens is that the model, by its sheer impressiveness, demands our imitation and in so doing not merely develops, but radically revises, our previous notions about what is worth imitating. If such acceptance is not to be uncritical fanaticism it must be possible for us to justify it, although it is evidently not necessary, or possible, for us to justify it wholly in terms that were available to us before we encountered the new paradigm.[16]

This statement suggests how commitment to historic particularity may require us to rethink the three universalist claims about morality. If "reason" is available across cultures and historical periods and "revelation" is not, then a new paradigm we did not anticipate may look more akin to something revelatory, so that not everything that matters morally is available to the unassisted reason. If a new paradigm brings its own credentials that we cannot justify entirely or sufficiently without recourse to the terms the paradigm itself discloses to us, then we must allow these terms to form and transform us, though not to take away our own critical judgment in the process. If a new paradigm depends on certain texts and a certain tradition and community, and if it carries distinctive injunctions, then we cannot seek to disengage ourselves from these texts and this tradition, or view the injunctions as comprehensible independently of the paradigm. Instead, we endorse a claim that these credentials or criteria are internal to this tradition.

If all of these things follow, and if we are willing to grant priority and even finality to the paradigm, then we see more clearly why we must confront directly Kant's confidence in what the unassisted reason delivers. Once more, we should keep our own substantive counsels and not repeat an old mistake—namely, to allow ourselves to be dominated by any independently founded philosophical scheme. We also see why the need for distinctive communal transmission assumes new urgency. For paradigmatic events to have ongoing sway in the lives of adherents, we must retain unbroken continuity with them. Such continuity depends on certain texts and a certain tradition and community where these texts occupy the center of gravity, where they are studied repeatedly, where the events to which they point are celebrated, and where their implications for allegiance and piety are specified. The case for this dependence allies itself naturally with sociological realism about what institutional arrangements are required for a tradition and community to survive over time, sending us back to works such as Gustafson's *Treasure in Earthen Vessels*.[17] Traditions are not interchangeable. Quite simply, if Christianity as our historical tradition is to perdure, the church is essential. To care about Christianity leads us to marshal our practical energies on the church's behalf. Especially when pluralism increases in surrounding social worlds, these requirements include particularist education, nurture, catechetics, formation, and the like, no less than evangelism and social action.[18]

Site Two: Tradition-Dependence and Cultural Contingency

So far, so good, or so I would argue. What receives less notice are the fuller accounts of particularist perspectives that critics of universalist claims about morality themselves go on to offer. Yet we can also learn much from such accounts, though we must then address further complexities which they introduce. I will distinguish two influential accounts whose potential lessons diverge in ways that we do well to consider.

The first account, tradition-dependence, is most importantly defended by MacIntyre. Stephen Mulhall and Adam Swift summarize his idea of tradition as follows:

A tradition is constituted by a set of practices and is a mode of understanding their importance and worth; it is the medium by which such practices are shaped and transmitted across generations. Traditions may be primarily religious or moral (for example Catholicism or humanism), economic (for example a particular craft or profession, trade union or manufacturer), aesthetic (for example modes of literature or painting), or geographical (for example crystallising around the history and culture of a particular house, village or region).[19]

Thomist Christianity is the tradition on behalf of which MacIntyre is an engaged partisan. Four features of his account show something of what tradition-dependence means for him. First, rational argument is possible and fruitful within this tradition, and between this tradition and others. But what is possible and fruitful is neither as ahistorical as Enlightenment figures maintain nor as devoid of methods and principles to which appeal can be made as Nietzsche and his followers suppose. Conceptions of rationality are internal to traditions. The hope that we will reach moral agreement only when, and as soon as, we free ourselves from "external constraints" is chimerical. "To be outside all traditions is to be a stranger to enquiry; it is to be in a state of intellectual and moral destitution."[20] Yet there can be genuinely rational inquiry within a tradition. To ask which party wins in rational argument never reduces to asking which group attains political and social hegemony. Rational appeals within a tradition, and rational debates between adherents of different traditions, are more than pretensions to be unmasked or strategies to be subverted. Second, a tradition like Thomist Christianity is dynamic rather than static in its operations, yet shows staying power and continuity. Aquinas himself had to appropriate and integrate both the Augustinian and the Aristotelian traditions, by a method and toward a conclusion that represented "the best answer reached so far."[21] His own method requires that his work remain essentially incomplete. And it bears "the mark of all worthwhile theorizing" in that it exhibits intellectual vulnerability, indeed, it renders itself "maximally vulnerable," "by setting out on any particular issue the strongest arguments yet advanced from any rival point of view against his own positions."[22] Still, its staying power is shown in that through successive stages "a certain continuity of directedness" emerges.[23]

Third, to be an engaged partisan means that one is a *member* of a tradition, not only that one knows about it. What conduces to the tradition's own well-being matters, including efforts to promote coherent communal self-understanding. More controversial possibilities—that give defining social shape and personal importance to membership in a religious tradition—also suggest themselves: To reflect adequately for and by oneself yet in the company of others may not be at odds with according to certain adherents the role of teaching authorities; for genuinely moral and theological inquiry to proceed, religious tests may have to be imposed and basic dissent excluded; to read a book correctly, one may have to be morally and theologically a certain kind of person, and to be such a person is not simply resident in one's generic humanity but requires a certain training and nurture.[24]

Fourth, commitment to tradition-dependence is compatible with an antirelativist commitment to truth.

There is nothing paradoxical at all in asserting that from within particular traditions assertions of universal import may be and are made, assertions formulated within the limits set by the conceptual, linguistic and argumentative possibilities of that tradition, but assertions which involve the explicit rejection of any incompatible claim, advanced in any terms whatsoever from any rival standpoint. So within every major cultural and social tradition we find some distinctive view of human nature and some distinctive conception of the human good presented as—*true*.[25]

Only spectators are permanently tempted to embrace relativism; participants in traditions are not. Participants in Thomist Christianity assert that however incomplete Aquinas' method is, nothing overturns "the finality of Scripture and dogmatic tradition"[26] as sources of its own truth claims. In relation to this finality, one discovers sin which disorders the will, allows passion to distract, and disorients the reason. One discovers as well the virtues of faith, hope, and love. From here one comes retrospectively to vindicate apprehensions of the natural law and the virtues of prudence, justice, temperateness, and courage, which provide an initial understanding of the core of the moral life, a core that may be corrected and completed but not displaced.[27] Added to this core are the precepts of justice that prohibit certain kinds of actions, such as the taking of innocent life, theft, perjury, and betrayal. These prohibitions are not restricted to any particular practice because the actions prove universally destructive of the bonds of any community.[28]

The other influential account of a particularist perspective, cultural contingency, centers on the ethos of a culture and how it pervades even the traditions that appear to have staying power. Here it is claimed that we deceive ourselves when we compartmentalize traditions and suppose that cultural changes do not affect all who live in a given epoch. Precisely because we are creatures of time and chance, we cannot escape such changes. For within a culture everything is in circuit with everything else. Shifts can discredit certain beliefs that traditions may carry from the past. While adherents of traditions may not renounce such beliefs officially, they mirror the larger cultural ethos in the issues they actually care about and those they effectively disregard. A culture does not "decide" to accept certain idioms and discard others, as an act of will or the conclusion of argument. Such changes within occur gradually, as part of complex webbed interactions, typically without attempts at centralized supervision. We cannot doubt all of the major elements in our inherited traditions in an instant. Still, a culture alters these traditions when certain earlier beliefs now fall outside the pale of what those in the culture can seriously entertain.

Rorty takes the particularist turn in this sort of direction when he describes the ethos of the culture that characterizes much of Europe and North America in the late twentieth century. Let us see what cultural contingency means for us as he views it.

Rorty's own defense of epistemic fallibilism is rooted in his assault on epistemological theory that goes back to Descartes.[29] And his critique of foundationalism is allied to conclusions that Charles Sanders Pierce, John Dewey, Ludwig Wittgenstein in his later work, Wilfrid Sellars, and Willard Van Orman Quine also reach. Rorty turns from epistemology to hermeneutics, where conversation rather than discovery properly describes philosophical inquiry. In ethics, no Enlightenment rationalist claims like the three I rehearsed will do. While such rationalism may have been essential initially to liberal democratic societies, it now impedes them, because its epistemic commitments cannot be sustained. We must turn to "something relatively local and ethnocentric—the tradition of a particular community, the consensus of a particular culture. According to this view, what counts as rational or fanatical is relative to the group to which we think it necessary to justify ourselves—to the body of shared belief that determines the reference of the word 'we.'"[30] Although he attaches quintessential importance to conversation within this particular culture, he ties more closely together than MacIntyre does the chronology of intellectual and wider cultural developments.

Rorty assuredly thinks that moral beliefs and concepts must be studied historically and contextually. This includes tracking moral beliefs, some of which are indeed intelligible only as we reckon with specifically Christian contributions. Rorty shares none of the hostility that Nietzsche displays toward Christianity. On the contrary, he cites Christianity as one of the "great intellectual and moral advances of European intellectual history," along with Galilean science, the Enlightenment, and Romanticism.[31] The result of "Saint Paul's metaphorical use of *agape*," of Christianity's influence overall, has been the alleviation of cruelty, something we should prize. Liberals themselves are "the people who think that cruelty is the worst thing we do."[32] But again, these contributions that have made us possible must be employed now in a world that is not only postreligious but increasingly postmetaphysical.

Finally, he thinks our sociality goes all the way down so that it is more accurate to say that selves are "networks of beliefs and desires" rather than "beings which *have* those beliefs and desires."[33] So our moral consciousness is historically conditioned through and through, a product as well of time and chance. Moreover, our liberal societies are contingent all the way down. We cannot justify them in universally compelling ways; they are historical accidents. They could easily have been otherwise. And one day they may be otherwise.

That particularist claims about fallibilism, history, and social identity allow for MacIntyre's and for Rorty's distinct elaborations indicate some of the possibilities that lie open. To turn away from Enlightenment claims about morality is not to turn toward any simple or single alternative. I find generally that a host of writers betray uncertainty about how much interplay there is between tradition-dependence and cultural contingency, and so what sort of staying power traditions actually have and should seek to maintain.

This uncertainty is shared by many in theology and theological ethics, and here the stakes arguably increase, for theological judgments are also at issue about the status of *this* tradition. I think that questions surrounding the interplay between tradition-dependence and cultural contingency, such as those we have uncovered, should goad us into extended debate about staying power. All I will attempt now in encouraging such debate is to offer four large theses. The latter two involve my own evaluation and construction and not only description and commentary.

Staying Power and an Ahistorical Standpoint

Once more, we should not run together questions about staying power with questions about whether we are historical or ahistorical. Consider the two criteria that Gustafson employs when he endorses shifts within a tradition: "Where historic particularity is adduced as support for ideas which are no longer viable or are marginal to the importance of what the tradition stands for, it can be eliminated."[34] Those who emphasize that certain traditions possess staying power can employ the second criterion (though often intense debate accompanies specific proposals about what is marginal) and still plausibly claim continuous identity over time. But for them to employ the first criterion gives greater trouble, for two reasons. First, the claim of continuous identity may then look less plausible, for shifts occur partly because the tradition is exposed, as Gustafson says, "to lights which come from relevant knowledge and to ideas from other movements of thought."[35] Second, Enlightenment claims about morality no longer occupy the center of attention that particularists can join ranks to oppose. If my findings about cultural contingency are at all accurate, we may reach a verdict of "no longer viable," without having to appeal to an ahistorical standpoint that we progressively approximate. We may reach such a verdict by appealing to other beliefs we hold, after we make the particularist turn. In Gustafson's own case, Stanley Hauerwas takes him to appeal increasingly to an ahistorical standpoint, while John Reeder takes him to be from first to last a certain kind of pragmatist.[36] However we decide this, we should note that Gustafson *need not* assume such an ahistorical standpoint in order to employ the first criterion.

Five Assessments of Staying Power

We should identify a spectrum of positions taken that provide different answers to questions about staying power.[37] I will allude to five here.

ONE: CONFESSIONAL OBEDIENCE REMAINS IN PLACE

The Christian community *has* staying power, intellectually and socially, as it adheres to the canonical texts and avoids Constantinian arrangements. Confessional obedience marks not only its internal life, but its relations to any larger society. It seeks to minimize susceptibility to outside cultural influences. The stress goes more to imitation and keeping faith than to development and making explicit what is implicit. When the Bible is read by the discerning community it can, John Howard Yoder holds, "by God's grace lead to a morally adequate knowledge of what God enables and requires believers to be and to do. Morally adequate means good enough to work with, sufficient to enable the community process of discernment. It does not mean absolutely clear, immutable, or without exceptions."[38] Yoder also contends that theologians and theological ethicists should approach their tradition respectfully, and this means both that they should be loyal to the principal claims that the tradition has made in the past and that their responsibility includes articulating those claims.[39]

Two: The Canonical Narrative Shapes Mainstream Identity

Christianity has an *abiding aspect* in the form of a comprehensive scheme or story, internalized as a set of skills by training and practice within the community. George Lindbeck articulates a "cultural-linguistic" and "postliberal" defense of this claim, employing Wittgenstein's case against private language. The canonical narrative tells us that "God is appropriately depicted in stories about a being who created the cosmos without any humanly fathomable reason . . . , appointed *Homo sapiens* stewards of one minuscule part of this cosmos, permitted appalling evils, chose Israel and the church as witnessing peoples, and sent Jesus as Messiah and Immanuel, God with us."[40] Such a common intratextual description persists, fusing itself with changing cultures and varying affective states. Lindbeck offers a regulative interpretation of the ancient creeds that likewise abides, and where at least three rules are at work: monotheism ("there is only one God, the God of Abraham, Isaac, Jacob, and Jesus"), historical specificity ("the stories of Jesus refer to a genuine human being who was born, lived, and died in a particular time and place"), and Christological maximalism ("every possible importance is to be ascribed to Jesus that is not inconsistent with the first two rules"). These rules, together with the commandments to love God and neighbor as an "unconditionally necessary practical doctrine," are permanently important "in forming mainstream Christian identity."[41] Lindbeck is prepared to confront the differences between traditional and modern thought and to explore the current "psychosocial" situation that he thinks favors theological liberalism. Yet it remains possible to specify continuities with the earlier comprehensive scheme, and those in the tradition should attempt to sustain them.

Three: Development and Elaboration Show Directional Continuity

A tradition such as Thomist Christianity has staying power along the lines we noticed in MacIntyre, where development, elaboration, and responses to new epistemological crises all occur, yet where again, *a certain continuity in directedness* persists. Some interpret him to say that membership in this tradition is rooted in and limited by the values that people in the tradition actually share and live out as a common manner of life. There are affinities to natural law in the commitment to rationality that opposes subjectivism and noncognitivism. Still, those who do not share in the life of the tradition lack access to the tradition's grounds for moral judgment. Views like MacIntyre's "provide an alternative to the universalism of natural law theory by holding that the actuality of a set of values is a necessary condition for moral knowledge. Moral norms . . . will be intelligible not to humans as such, but only to those for whom the relevant values are actual."[42] It is those who do share in the life of the tradition who can maintain the continuity in directedness.

FOUR: SELECTIVE RETRIEVAL CANNOT BE AVOIDED

Christianity in its present forms bears *no essential continuity in content* to its earlier forms. The earlier forms may serve as progenitors. Gustafson, referring approvingly to Ernst Troeltsch, claims that "Christianity is an historical movement, and thus is in interaction with other aspects of culture and society. It has changed, it will continue to change, and it may well disappear in some distant future."[43] Whether being a Christian now is harder than it was in the thirteenth century, it is surely different—so much so that we cannot assert with confidence any necessary continuity. Those in theology and theological ethics cannot avoid variation, selectivity, and retrieval in their work, and for them to suppose otherwise shows invincible or culpable ignorance. Moreover, they should not be limited or bound by historic creedal formulations. That our task "is to work out of tradition and to hand on tradition" Gordon Kaufman similarly regards as "authoritarian" and for us unjustifiable.[44]

FIVE: THE PAST HAS BEEN IRRECOVERABLY LOST

Traditions not only lack staying power, but contemporary philosophers and theologians who try to retain continuities with the past fail to see that the past has *decisively gone* and that their attempts are vain and indefensible. In addition to the pressures in this direction that Rorty exerts, Mark C. Taylor believes we must start "with the sense of *irrecoverable* loss."[45] Nietzsche depicts what is lost when he proclaims the death of God. I cannot consider Taylor's astute use of deconstruction as the "hermeneutic" of the death of God, and how he thinks this death reverberates in the loss of self, history, and book. I simply observe that Taylor represents what Edward Farley calls "theological epochalism."[46] Here two senses of "no longer viable" coexist. Sometimes cultural change occurs because inherited beliefs fall victim to good arguments. Sometimes cultural change itself discredits, so that a cultural ending is itself a refutation. Epochalism in the second sense constitutes a way to understand cultural contingency that supplants rather than stays in interplay with tradition-dependence.

A Proposed Place on the Spectrum

Let me next indicate, with desperate brevity, what point I think we should occupy on this spectrum. I reject the fifth assessment outright. I find it hard to see how, in relation to the key event, the death of God, "no longer viable" requisitely qualifies in either sense I mentioned. The *possibility* that God lives and dies as one epoch succeeds another assumes a projectionist account of religious belief, and such an account remains too controversial for us to conclude that good arguments have established it as *the* entrenched view in our culture.[47] The possibility that "God" has ceased to have meaning for us, and that as meaning fades, the thing fades, goes against the proclaimed convictions of millions. Then the description is elitist and/or patronizing, and those who want this are welcome to it.

I accept and reject parts of the first four positions, and occupy territory in the middle of this remaining spectrum. I want to adhere to the canonical texts, but not to be precritical or unhistorical in the ways I employ tradition. I agree with Robert Merrihew Adams that the conversion of Constantine is not a development merely to be deplored ("it is hardly thinkable that the church that had survived the rigors of the persecution of Diocletian would have declined Constantine's offer of imperial favor"), that the Christianization of the empire and subsequent arrangements had both advantages and disadvantages, but that nonetheless our present circumstances are likewise not merely to be deplored, for "Christianity is intrinsically adapted to existence in a pluralistic environment."[48] I want to approach the tradition always respectfully, holding that one should, as far as possible, not only give a faithful account of it but take it with governing seriousness when one assimilates new insights. The notion of a comprehensive scheme or story internalized within a community should constitute the permanent point of departure, though I want also to stress the importance of elaboration and development and responses to new crises, intellectual and social. I do not see how we avoid selective retrieval, and we should be forthright about our selection. Such selection is not, however, to be executed from some superior vantage point in principle, that itself determines what is tolerated, jettisoned, or reaffirmed, in the fashion of Kant or Hegel in different ways.[49] And assuming that the notion of a comprehensive story has validity, we need not and should not acquiesce to unaccountable eclecticism or welcome a sheer mélange of standpoints. Sometimes selectivity will involve critical revision—for example, in condemning slavery and misogyny. But we should also resist uncritical accommodation to whatever movements happen to be influential. To conflate becoming unfashionable with disproving begs too many questions in any case. That we can retain our own criteria for evaluating modernity and postmodernity means that we are not exhaustively the products of time and chance *qua* epochalism.

The Final Status This Tradition Has

Finally, sooner or later we should specify what status this tradition has for us. To honor the two commitments I identified at the start, I offer the following. Christianity denies universal epistemic access to the content of its own comprehensive convictions. The Bible and the history of the tradition remain indispensable for such convictions. Without these sources, the convictions are unavailable. Thus, the sources to which we are always called back are constant. Christianity's account of epistemic fallibilism appears to be that for it, we cannot sunder God, the Bible, and the tradition. Yet it claims that its convictions have universal significance. For the tradition to be truth-oriented and to avoid esotericism, it seems to assert a cognitive status: *It* "illumines and mediates the way things are."[50] It opens something of the character of divine and human reality. Although we live in multiple traditions, we accord priority to this tradition, not only relative authority. In brief, I take this status to mean that for those who stand within the tradition, the tradition is never ultimately dispensable. It has lasting value for which there is no substitute. But I do not take this status to mean supersessionism, or the refusal of interreligious dialogue; I repudiate both. God is neither governed nor circumscribed by the tradition, and the tradition itself must depend finally on God's prevenient grace. But those in the tradition rely on what we see as God's self-disclosure in this particular history. Our epistemic fallibilism does not prevent such reliance, but in our case it does require it.

Site Three: From Particularity to Universal Significance

When we move from Christianity's first commitment to its second, we move from particularist disclosure and justification to universal relevance and applicability. We stay with the first commitment as we offer a theistic account of true discoveries or recognitions about the character of divine and human reality, and as we tether this account to data internal to the tradition and the community. And we look for confirmations, and we test the spirits in our personal and communal lives. We refuse to reverse this order of knowledge and we see its circularity as virtuous.[51] We move to the second commitment by refusing to speak only esoterically. These discoveries and recognitions prove relevant in a world whose inhabitants are not exclusively adherents of the tradition.

MacIntyre's version of the turn affords an understanding of the second commitment. He thinks not merely that a case for tradition-dependence allows for an antirelativist commitment to truth. He contends, as we have seen, that every major tradition presents as true some distinctive view of human nature and some distinctive conception of the human good. What will concern me now are the instances he cites of Christianity's own views and conceptions. We recall that in relation to the finality of scripture and dogmatic tradition, he claims that one discovers sin and the theological virtues. He also claims that we see the retrospective vindication of elements of the natural law and the cardinal virtues. And he alludes to the prohibitions of actions found to be universally destructive of the bonds of any community. The discoveries of sin and the theological virtues warrant large generalizations about us, in the case of sin about human nature, and in the case of the virtues about human good. The remaining instances alter the focus from discoveries we make in dependence on the Bible and tradition, to recognitions that originate outside the tradition which become part of a core of the moral life that the tradition presents as true. I wish to locate certain issues which surround the several instances he cites that the turn again goads us to confront.

Sin and Sociality

The discovery of sin warrants a large generalization to the effect that no one entirely escapes, by dint of his or her own effort, the condition of being a sinner. We depend on our tradition for this discovery. (Kant's profound account of radical evil relies on so much substantial assistance from the Christian tradition that the latter proves to be, in this case even for him, more of a repository than a mere milieu.[52]) Yet this discovery has relevance and applicability across space and time and qualifies as universally significant. For sin is thought also to be more than part of a picture that happened to capture the mind of the West for a span of centuries but that no longer illuminates. This "more" makes sin an overlying notion. It does not simply describe specific space-time events or hold only in certain epochs.[53] Emphatically, it is not the only such generalization. Indeed, it is traditionally thought to be parasitic on a good creation and our being made in the image of God. We do not accomplish a new creation by sinning. We disorder and deform features that are good in themselves, for example, that we stand related to God; that we live in community; that in our own narrative history we bring together our agency, our reason, our needs and desires.

We must ascertain how we propose to relate the discovery of sin to the claim that our sociality goes all the way down. On the one side, if sin is truly an overlying notion, then we cannot reduce our depiction of human beings to a view that the only enduring propensity human beings possess (or at least that has moral standing) is shared susceptibility to cultural change. That our sociality goes all the way down may sometimes imply for Rorty that our malleability to social and historical context has no limits, and I respect his willingness to announce a possibility that many defenders of the claim likewise approach, without saying so. For example, he lauds "what political utopians since the French Revolution have sensed," namely, "that changing languages and other social practices may produce human beings of a sort that never existed before."[54] But again, to hold that the discovery of sin has ongoing relevance means that all such changes will not produce human beings of a sort who are totally innocent from the beginning to the end of their lives. And the conception of "innocent" at issue points to something in human beings that is not exhaustively defined by or utterly unique to our own cultural context. Sin sets certain limits to our social malleability in this respect, limits that lead utopians *everywhere* to eventual frustration. On the other side, to continue to take sin seriously as an overlying notion, we need not deny that many of its traditional accounts are underdetermined by social and historical ingredients. Moreover, to realize that there is no one-to-one correspondence between the primal tendency to sin and the given power deformations in our particular historical situation should prompt us to attend to the peculiar features that mark the deformations at hand. We should seek to demonstrate how the prime articulations of sin occur in the messy details of the actual social sphere in which we find ourselves.[55] Although we should explore both of these sides and try to attain a kind of "reflective equilibrium," any such equilibrium should show that we take the discovery of sin seriously, and that we thereby stand willing critically to assess and to nuance the claim that our sociality goes all the way down. Otherwise, once more, we trivialize our commitment to universal significance.

The Theological Virtues and Sociality

The discovery of the theological virtues of faith, hope, and love leads us to identify what kind of persons we need to become, even if perfection or utopian expectations exceed our grasp. The virtues also warrant large generalizations: here, to identify what shape our dispositions, attachments, attitudes, and actions need to assume when we trust God above everything else; to look to a final state when God's purposes are fulfilled; and to refer all things to God as our supreme good, a good incommensurable with any other.

How are these virtues universally significant? I find two senses. First, the virtues point to patterns of life that have their own sort of staying power. They not only can govern in the set of a person's own life and pervade the ethos of a local community, but they can recur, in the lives of persons and communities across stretches of space and even centuries of time. Second, the virtues accord with a true conception of the human good. I want to examine each of these two senses.

The first sense bears similarities to what I said about sin as an overlying notion. Despite the differences in what we learn (from the virtues, that we enjoy ongoing constructive possibilities of the most important kind, and from sin, that we stand under ongoing siege), the matters about which we are alternately assured and warned remain ongoing. So in the case of the virtues, too, we must ascertain how we propose to relate their discovery to the claim that our sociality goes all the way down. Those who think that the turn brings to the fore too many historical shifts and cultural differences to permit us to generalize with confidence about recurrent patterns, *inside or outside* the tradition, will draw back to local patterns and determine that this tradition or any other lacks the requisite staying power to avoid such an outcome. Those of us who decline to draw back altogether confront in the case of the virtues a task of attaining reflective equilibrium analogous to the one I indicated in the case of sin. And this requires us to assess and nuance still further the claim about sociality. As before, there is much work to be done in order to attain equilibrium that we cannot attempt now.

The second sense of universal significance expressly connects recurrent patterns that the virtues identify to the conception of the human good with which the virtues are in accord. This conception directs us quite simply to God and God's relation to the world. For we saw that the theological virtues accord with a conception of the good that is theocentric. God is our supreme good and incommensurable with any other. But incommensurability here means that God is the subject of unique veneration. It does not mean that the supreme good has no relevance for and applicability to the workaday relations and types of interaction in which we are immersed. Indeed, "relevance" and "applicability" are too weak; "governance" catches better the sense of universal significance at issue. The virtues enable us to correspond and attest to such governance. They dispose us explicitly to revere God as the center of value, and rightly to order and integrate these relations and interactions.

For all of the scope and detail such governance is thought itself to have, our accounts of it never float free of other beliefs we hold and assumptions that remain in place. Here we apply a general lesson that the turn has to teach. We view faith, hope, and love as essentially rather than accidentally linked to other convictions we share and practices we extol within the tradition. Often our deliberations and debates stay intramural much of the way—for example, how we take the virtues to remain distinct from yet to influence one another, and how we understand the normative content and dynamics of love in its several dimensions: love for God, love of neighbor, love of self, and various kinds of reciprocal love.[56]

On the Possibility That the Tradition Can Vindicate Moral Insights That Originate Outside

Many in the tradition, however, are prepared to ask whether we can rightly order and integrate our workaday relations and interactions unless we extend and supplement more than we have done so far. To pose this question leads us sooner or later to consider the possibility that the tradition may vindicate moral insights that originate outside. We go accordingly to the remaining instances: the elements of the natural law; the cardinal virtues of prudence, justice, temperateness, and courage; and the prohibitions of actions found to be universally destructive of the bonds of any community. These instances provide us greater moral specificity as we evaluate our relations and interactions. Yet the specificity sought is not of a local kind relative to historical shifts and cultural changes to which the turn sensitizes us. Rather what is sought is a thicker sense of universal moral significance, a more determinate way to depict the theocentrically governed moral life. This search is authorized by a traditional dictum: The theological virtues complete and fulfill rather than negate and displace features we apprehend as morally important in recurrent patterns of social exchange.

I offer a concluding speculation about the possibility of extending this sense of universal significance to recognitions originating outside the tradition that become part of a core of the moral life that the tradition presents as true. For here I think those in the tradition are divided, sometimes deeply, about whether (and, if so, how) we can extend this sense in a way that does not jeopardize the commitment to historic particularity. Let us return to our early example of what the commitment to historic particularity encompasses, namely, to Mitchell's case on behalf of a new paradigm that develops and revises our previous notions of what manner of life is worth following. While the paradigm discloses *more* than any recognitions originating outside (or else we reactivate the fear of redundancy), much depends on whether we emphasize development, revision, or other effects. There are many appraisals within the tradition of what the Christological paradigm implies for the possibility of extension. I will identify four that have special contemporary significance. How closely we correlate these appraisals with Roman Catholic and Protestant legacies is a matter I cannot take up now.[57] I want only to show that each appraisal, as it moves from particularist disclosure and justification to universal relevance and applicability, blends its own distinctive answers to questions like the following (which themselves overlap):

1. What ontomoral status, if any, do we ascribe to the recognitions outside?
2. Do we see more continuity or discontinuity overall between what the paradigm discloses and what we discover outside?
3. Do we distinguish between basic matters of faith such as soteriology and the Trinity, and our morality, or do they *all* form part of the comprehensive convictions to which there is no universal epistemic access?

Consider, then, this speculative sketch.

FIRST APPRAISAL OF THE THREE QUESTIONS:
DEVELOPMENT AND CONTINUITY

1. What the paradigm discloses is never, *pace* cultural contingency, imposed on a protean or morally structureless human world. What is disclosed tends rather to clarify, correct, and complete but not to displace a moral order that is thought to be permanently there, and which *anyone* who bears the human countenance violates at his or her peril. Completion instead of displacement may mean that our commitment to universal significance, including our refusal to speak only esoterically, is undergirded theologically by a doctrine of creation and philosophically by a realist concept of truth that is more or other than warranted assertibility. The moral order that the paradigm develops and completes is not true from this or that cultural standpoint. It is simply true.

2. So when we extend this sense of universal significance to recognitions originating outside the tradition that become part of a core of the moral life that the tradition presents as true, we cross no Rubicon. On the contrary, we come to see that what the Christological paradigm discloses to us is by no means at odds with what we apprehend morally as rational persons, when our own practical reasoning is in good order.

3. To be sure, the paradigm discloses far more than this, about our salvation, in-

cluding the forgiveness of sin, and the hope of glory. And about these matters, it is the case that the tradition denies universal epistemic access to the content of its own comprehensive convictions. But about moral matters, commitment to historic particularity requires no such strict denial. So we construe in a certain way any moral "revision" that the paradigm brings. What it discloses morally is again continuous with what we are in a position to apprehend—for example, about the natural law and the cardinal virtues—when we do not fail as practical reasoners. When the paradigm tells us something morally that we do not tell ourselves, this is because we have in fact *failed* as reasoners, or have allowed ourselves to be *corrupted* by erroneous moral theories and practices that deform our own cultural circumstances.

SECOND APPRAISAL OF THE THREE QUESTIONS: COMBINE DEVELOPMENT AND REVISION, CONTINUITY AND DISCONTINUITY

1. The paradigm does not confront a structureless moral world where every normative appeal we make is exhaustively subject to historical variation and cultural change. The paradigm and the surrounding tradition themselves point us decisively to the Decalogue and the Golden Rule, for example. We may well describe the second table of the former as prohibiting actions found to be universally destructive of the bonds of any community, and the latter as authorizing appeals for which we enjoy some natural affinity. Here the paradigm ratifies and reinforces and amplifies more than it revises. What is ratified never passes out of fashion or ceases to be relevant. It lacks the provisional status that we ascribe to appeals we see as altogether socially constructed. In our elucidations of the Decalogue and the Golden Rule, we do better to deploy a doctrine of creation than to appeal just to personal commitments, founded on sheer autonomous choice. Moreover, we should appropriate moral wisdom and good ideas wherever we find them. We are not so fully equipped that we can ignore serious moral reflection from any quarter.

2. Still, our appropriations should always bear the marks of our particularist beliefs, marks that clarify, correct, supplement, revise, modify, and transform, and not only develop and complete. Even our account of the Decalogue and the Golden Rule should remain in circuit with and be affected by other convictions about the paradigm we hold. We should not merely "vindicate" the natural law and the cardinal virtues, if this means they arrive before us self-contained, waiting to be certified. Our depiction of the natural law should never be entirely detheologized. Our account of justice should be influenced by our account of love. How we construe courage should differ from how a warrior culture construes it. And so on.

3. The yeas and nays of this second appraisal extend to the question of whether we should distinguish between basic matters of faith such as the forgiveness of sin and the hope of glory, and our morality. Yes, we should distinguish to this extent: We lack uni-

versal epistemic access to the regulative rules for example to which we referred earlier—monotheism, historical specificity about the person of Jesus, and Christological
maximalism. Yet in the instances of the second table of the Decalogue and the Golden
Rule, we can envisage a case for tradition-dependence that encompasses a mixture of
moral appeals, the intelligibility of some of which does not require membership in the
tradition. But no, our morality should form part of the comprehensive convictions resident in the tradition to this extent: We should finally keep our own counsels about
everything and not commit ourselves in principle to justifying any part of our morality in terms that are wholly available to us before we encounter in our case the Christological paradigm.

THIRD APPRAISAL OF THE THREE QUESTIONS: COMPREHENSIVENESS AND ANNEXATION

1. We see surrounding social worlds as characterized by contending moral schemes,
some of which come and go. Yet we can refer to "the ethical question" at least in the
singular. It concerns our common efforts to articulate criteria for the guidance of life.
We cannot reduce these efforts to custom, politics, or the social-scientific explanation
of institutional developments. The question recurs in every time and place. Those in
theological ethics should annex this question and take over the sense in which they
pose it as well as answer it.

2. Strict discontinuity holds respecting the terms of disclosure and justification, yet
there is "the widest possible referential expanse within the narrowest epistemological
brackets."[58] This expanse means that those in theological ethics assume a comprehensive standpoint toward moral insights originating outside the tradition rather than
merely a negative one. Such a standpoint makes criticism of insights originating outside possible but not necessary. We should make the most of whatever normative overlaps we find.[59] We are free to consider various ad hoc alliances.

3. Our ethics is viewed as a constitutive part of dogmatics, and so depends finally
on staying within the brackets. But the comprehensiveness prevents our being content
with a normative dualism in which we dwell solely on mutually incompatible features
between morality inside and outside the tradition.

FOURTH APPRAISAL OF THE THREE QUESTIONS: REVISION AND DISCONTINUITY

1. We confine ourselves to generalizing about recurrent patterns that the paradigm
discloses which consistently form and transform those within our own community
across space and time. We affirm sociality, and in the case of moralities outside, we see
little uniformity or constancy, beyond local agreements that make particular communities viable. In our case, however, we construe sociality chiefly in terms of tradition-
dependence rather than cultural contingency. The tradition has continuous staying
power. Often we explicitly insist that it is those who share in the life of the tradition

who can live out the manner of life that the paradigm discloses. Others lack access to the convictions that give this manner of life its intelligibility and point. Membership in the tradition is accordingly *required*.

2. Our commitment to historic particularity demands something other than the specificity that vindication of moral insights originating outside the tradition brings. Our commitment demands the sort of specificity that is *not generalizable* to those outside. Such specificity consists in behavioral thickness peculiar to membership. It thus stays internal to the history, culture, and social identity that distinguish this tradition. We go on to emphasize normative discontinuities between patterns inside and outside.

3. And we decline to distinguish between basic matters of faith such as the forgiveness of sin and the hope of glory, and our morality. They *all* form part of the comprehensive convictions to which there is no universal epistemic access. We are truth-oriented and refuse to speak esoterically only in the sense that we take what the paradigm discloses to form part of a true conception of the human good. Only members of the tradition are prepared to see that the paradigm has this universal significance. Yet what we see is really the case.

To combine elements of the second and third appraisals seems to me to hold the greatest promise when we engage wider social worlds. The detailed arguments require, of course, their own space. My concern here is with the theological appraisals that inform our reflection about the possibility of extension. This too conduces, I hope, to communal self-understanding. All four appraisals that I have identified demonstrate that it is accurate (if a platitude) to say that the task in Christian theology and ethics is to take historic particularity and universal significance to heart without becoming theologically or philosophically undiscriminating in our account of each, or in our attempt to hold them together.[60]

Notes

1. James M. Gustafson, *Ethics from a Theocentric Perspective*, 2 vols. (Chicago: University of Chicago Press, 1981–1984), vol. 1, *Theology and Ethics*, 68.

2. Robert Wokler questions the accuracy of MacIntyre's own account of the Enlightenment in "Projecting the Enlightenment," *After MacIntyre*, ed. John Horton and Susan Mendus (Notre Dame, Ind.: University of Notre Dame Press, 1994), 108–26. MacIntyre replies to him in the same volume, "A Partial Response to My Critics," 298–99. Samuel Fleischacker agrees with MacIntyre on the importance of tradition, but finds more support for such importance in certain strands of the Enlightenment than MacIntyre does, in *The Ethics of Culture* (Ithaca, N.Y.: Cornell University Press, 1994).

3. See also Gene Outka and John P. Reeder Jr., Introduction to *Prospects for a Common Morality*, ed. Gene Outka and John P. Reeder Jr. (Princeton, N.J.: Princeton University Press, 1993), esp. 3–5; John P. Reeder Jr., "Three Moral Traditions," *Journal of Religious Ethics* 22, no. 1 (spring 1994): 75–92.

4. For a careful statement on natural-law commitments, and the senses in which they are and are not tradition-dependent, see Joseph Boyle, "Natural Law and the Ethics of Traditions," *Natural Law Theory: Contemporary Essays*, ed. Robert P. George (Oxford: Clarendon Press, 1994), 3–30.

5. Fleischacker, *The Ethics of Culture*, 27–34.

6. From Søren Kierkegaard, *Concluding Unscientific Postscript to Philosophical Fragments*, ed. and trans. Howard V. Hong and Edna H. Hong (Princeton, N.J.: Princeton University Press, 1992), 1: 118–19:

> When an existence is a thing of the past, it is indeed finished, it is indeed concluded, and to that extent it is turned over to the systematic view. Quite so—but for whom? Whoever is himself existing cannot gain this conclusiveness outside existence, a conclusiveness that corresponds to the eternity into which the past has entered. . . . Who then is this systematic thinker? Well, it is he who himself is outside existence and yet in existence, who in his eternity is forever concluded, and yet includes existence within himself—it is God.

See also Fleischacker's discussion of this passage, *The Ethics of Culture*, 27–31.

7. For effects of this turn on various topics in religious studies, see Jeffrey Stout, *The Flight from Authority: Religion, Morality and the Quest for Autonomy* (Notre Dame, Ind.: University of Notre Dame Press, 1981).

8. Alasdair MacIntyre, *A Short History of Ethics* (New York: Macmillan, 1966), 1.

9. Charles Taylor, "Justice after Virtue," *After MacIntyre*, 18.

10. Jeffrey Stout, *Ethics after Babel: The Languages of Morals and Their Discontents* (Boston: Beacon Press, 1988), 124–44.

11. Alan Donagan, "Common Morality and Kant's Enlightenment Project," *Prospects for a Common Morality*, 54.

12. Alan Donagan, *Theory of Morality* (Chicago: University of Chicago Press, 1977).

13. Gene Outka, "Respect for Persons," *The Westminster Dictionary of Christian Ethics*, ed. James F. Childress and John Macquarrie (Philadelphia: Westminster Press, 1986), 541–45.

14. Richard Rorty, *Contingency, Irony, and Solidarity* (Cambridge: Cambridge University Press, 1989), xiii.

15. G. W. F. Hegel, *Lectures on the Philosophy of World History: Introduction*, cited in Robert Stern, "MacIntyre and Historicism," *After MacIntyre*, 148.

16. Basil Mitchell, *Morality: Religious and Secular* (Oxford: Clarendon Press, 1980), 152–53.

17. James M. Gustafson, *Treasure in Earthen Vessels: The Church as a Human Community* (New York: Harper, 1961).

18. Gilbert Meilaender, "The Singularity of Christian Ethics," *Journal of Religious Ethics* 17, no. 2 (fall 1989): 100.

19. Stephen Mulhall and Adam Swift, *Liberals and Communitarians* (Oxford: Blackwell, 1992), 90.

20. Alasdair MacIntyre, *Whose Justice? Which Rationality?* (Notre Dame, Ind.: University of Notre Dame Press, 1988), 367.

21. Alasdair MacIntyre, *Three Rival Versions of Moral Enquiry: Encyclopaedia, Genealogy, and Tradition* (Notre Dame, Ind.: University of Notre Dame Press, 1990), 124.

22. Ibid., 181.

23. Ibid., 116.

24. Ibid., 17, 60, 64, 133.

25. MacIntyre, "A Partial Response to My Critics," 295.

26. MacIntyre, *Three Rival Versions of Moral Enquiry*, 125.

27. Ibid., 140–41.

28. Alasdair MacIntyre, *After Virtue* (Notre Dame, Ind.: University of Notre Dame Press, 1981), 141–42.

29. Richard Rorty, *Philosophy and the Mirror of Nature* (Princeton, N.J.: Princeton University Press, 1979).

30. Richard Rorty, "The Priority of Democracy to Philosophy," *Prospects for a Common Morality*, 255–56.

31. Rorty, *Contingency, Irony, and Solidarity*, 48, 55, 184.

32. Ibid., xv, 17, 74. He borrows his definition of "liberal" from Judith Shklar.

33. Ibid., 10.

34. Gustafson, *Ethics,* 1:151.

35. Ibid.

36. Stanley Hauerwas, "Time and History in Theological Ethics: The Work of James Gustafson," *Journal of Religious Ethics* 13, no. 1 (spring 1985): 3–21; John P. Reeder Jr., "The Dependence of Ethics," in *James M. Gustafson's Theocentric Ethics: Interpretations and Assessments*, ed. Harlan R. Beckley and Charles M. Swezey (Macon, Ga.: Mercer University Press, 1988), 119–41. Hauerwas usefully surveys Gustafson's corpus, but I find Reeder persuasive when he characterizes Gustafson as a certain sort of pragmatist. For Reeder's own awareness of how many substantive issues remain to be settled after one rejects an ahistorical starting point for justification, understanding, and agreement, and takes the neopragmatist turn, see his "Foundations without Foundationalism," *Prospects for a Common Morality*, 191–214.

37. For these and other examples, see also Gene Outka, "Equality and the Fate of Theism in Modern Culture," *Journal of Religion* 67, no. 3 (July 1987): 275–88. Further relevant discussions include Stephen Sykes, *The Identity of Christianity* (London: SPCK Press, 1984); Maurice Wiles, *The Remaking of Christian Doctrine* (London: SCM Press, 1974); Basil Mitchell, "Traditionaliste malgré lui," *Theology* 82 (January 1979): 31–38; Mitchell, *Faith and Criticism* (Oxford: Clarendon Press, 1994).

38. John Howard Yoder, "Theological Revision and the Burden of Particular Identity," in *James M. Gustafson's Theocentric Ethics*, ed. Beckley and Swezey, 77.

39. Ibid., 80–81, 89–91.

40. George A. Lindbeck, *The Nature of Doctrine* (Philadelphia: Westminster Press, 1984), 121. For relations between Lindbeck's cultural-linguistic approach and certain "aftermath Jewish philosophers," see Peter Ochs, "A Rabbinic Pragmatism," *Theology and Dialogue: Essays in Conversation with George Lindbeck*, ed. Bruce D. Marshall (Notre Dame, Ind.: University of Notre Dame Press, 1993), 213–48. For remarks on Lindbeck and Troeltsch on Christianity and cultural change, see Hans W. Frei, "Epilogue: George Lindbeck and *The Nature of Doctrine*," in *Theology and Dialogue*, 280–82.

41. Lindbeck, *The Nature of Doctrine*, 85, 94.

42. Boyle, "Natural Law and the Ethics of Traditions," 16.

43. Gustafson, *Ethics*, 1:324.

44. Gordon D. Kaufman, *Theology for a Nuclear Age* (Philadelphia: Westminster Press, 1985), 17–18.

45. Mark C. Taylor, *Erring: A Postmodern A/theology* (Chicago: University of Chicago Press, 1984), 6.

46. Edward Farley, *Good and Evil: Interpreting a Human Condition* (Minneapolis: Fortress Press, 1990), 18–22.

47. For one example from a large literature, see William Alston, "Psychoanalytic Theory and Theistic Belief," *Faith and the Philosophers*, ed. John Hick (London: Macmillan, 1964), 63–102.

48. Robert Merrihew Adams, "Religious Ethics in a Pluralistic Society," *Prospects for a Common Morality*, 109–10.

49. In Hegel's case, see Cyril O'Regan, *The Heterodox Hegel* (Albany: State University of New York Press, 1994).

50. Edward Farley, "Theocentric Ethics as a Genetic Argument," *James M. Gustafson's Theocentric Ethics*, ed. Beckley and Swezey, 56.

51. For elaboration, see Gene Outka, "Augustinianism and Common Morality," *Prospects for a Common Morality*, 114–48.

52. Immanuel Kant, *Religion Within the Limits of Reason Alone*, trans. Theodore M. Greene and Hoyt H. Hudson (New York: Harper, 1960), bk. I, 15–49.

53. Farley, "Theocentric Ethics as a Genetic Argument," 57.

54. Rorty, *Contingency, Irony, and Solidarity*, 7.

55. For one such attempt, see Gene Outka, "The Ethics of Love and the Problem of Abortion," forthcoming.

56. For recent accounts of love, see, for example, Edmund N. Santurri and William Werpehowski, eds. *The Love Commandments: Essays in Christian Ethics and Moral Philosophy* (Washington, D.C.: Georgetown University Press, 1992), 1–103; Edward Collins Vacek, S.J., *Love, Human and Divine: The Heart of Christian Ethics* (Washington, D.C.: Georgetown University Press, 1994); Gene Outka, "Agapeistic Ethics," *A Companion to the Philosophy of Religion*, ed. Philip L. Quinn and Charles Taliaferro (Oxford: Blackwell), in press.

57. Without the nuancing that is vital, I associate the first appraisal with a Roman Catholic legacy that Pope John Paul II reaffirms in *The Splendor of Truth*, Vatican trans. (Boston: St. Paul Books & Media, 1993), and which Alasdair MacIntyre interprets in "How Can We Learn What *Veritatis Splendor* Has to Teach?" *The Thomist* 58, no. 2 (April 1994): 171–95; the second appraisal with the legacy of the "magisterial" reformers and a twentieth-century figure like Paul Ramsey; the third appraisal with the legacy of Karl Barth; and the fourth appraisal with the legacy of the "radical" reformers and a twentieth-century figure like Jacques Ellul. For elaboration of my understanding of the last three appraisals, see Gene Outka, "Discontinuity in the Ethics of Jacques Ellul," in *Jacques Ellul: Interpretive Essays*, ed. Clifford G. Christians and Jay M. Van Hook (Urbana: University of Illinois Press, 1981), 177–228, and "The Protestant Tradition and Moral Absolutes," forthcoming.

58. Gene Outka, *Agape: An Ethical Analysis* (New Haven: Yale University Press, 1972), 246. This characterizes Barth's views expressly; see, for example, Karl Barth, *Church Dogmatics*, II/2, trans. G. W. Bromiley et al. (Edinburgh: T. & T. Clark, 1957), 509–781.

59. The interpretation I give relies on past conversations with Paul Nelson, Edmund Santurri, and William Werpehowski.

60. For their perceptive counsel on this essay, I owe a debt to Lisa Cahill, James Childress, Richard Fern, Cyril O'Regan, John Reeder, and Philip Turner.

Chapter 7

Knowledge of Self and Knowledge of God: A Reconstructed Empiricist Interpretation

WILLIAM C. SPOHN AND THOMAS A. BYRNES

John Calvin opened his *Institutes of the Christian Religion* with the following thesis:

> Nearly all the wisdom we possess, that is to say, true and sound wisdom, consists in two parts: the knowledge of God and of ourselves. . . . For quite clearly, the mighty gifts with which we are endowed are hardly from ourselves; indeed our very being is nothing but subsistence in the one God. . . . Accordingly, the knowledge of ourselves not only arouses us to seek God, but also as it were, leads us by the hand to [God].[1]

In the present essay we will reflect on Calvin's thesis within the context of contemporary philosophical understandings of the nature of self-knowledge. The issue of practical self-knowledge is central to contemporary philosophy and the American empiricist tradition. Ernst Tugendhat recently explored the critical awareness of ourselves as moral agents in Martin Heidegger's existentialism and George Herbert Mead's pragmatic social phenomenology. We will relate the resulting account of self-knowledge to an American empiricist account of the knowledge of God. We propose that an adequate account of self-knowledge cannot be framed in terms of society and nature, but must include the religious dimension of experience. The affections of trust and loyalty, which are ingredients of natural piety, point beyond social norms and individual decision to an ultimate object of intention, which with Calvin we will recognize as nature in its fullest sense and acknowledge as God.[2]

Knowledge of Self

In *Self-Consciousness and Self-Determination,* Ernst Tugendhat has scrutinized modern philosophy's preoccupation with the special nature of self-consciousness and self-knowledge.[3] He argues that the accounts of self-knowledge originating with Descartes, Locke, and Kant are radically misconceived because they rely on two misleading models of knowing: the subject-object model and the observer model. In the subject-object model, the subject turns in on itself and takes its own consciousness as the object of its awareness. In the observer model, that act is likened to inner visual perception, which occurs when the subject turns its knowing gaze to this inner object, variously called the self, the ego, or consciousness. Tugendhat demonstrates the conceptual absurdities into which these models lead us.[4]

Heidegger and Mead offer constructive alternatives to this dead end of modern philosophy since they understand the self as a process of practical engagement in the world. They address the problem of self-knowledge in the practical form posed by the Delphic motto "Know thyself." The person who truly knows herself knows who she wants to be and what she wants to do with her life. Tugendhat believes that a fully adequate account of self-knowledge must incorporate the complementary insights of Heidegger and Mead.

For Heidegger, the self (*Dasein*) knows itself only as it relates itself to its very act of existence. In the affective mode of "care," the self chooses its own existence by freely and authentically deciding who it wants to be and what it wants to do. The self becomes authentic by setting itself over against others and asserting its independence of the social and even rational norms that others would use to constrain its decisions. The self defines itself in autonomous solitude, always retaining the freedom to step beyond social and rational norms.

Tugendhat credits Heidegger with finding an essential aspect of the self in this mode of authentic decision whereby it relates to itself in terms of what it is to be. However, Heidegger disregards questions of truth and the process of reasoning that evaluates and justifies options. Authenticity divorced from normative rational processes of reflection will be either vacuous or arbitrary. A necessary corrective to Heidegger is found in Mead's account of the self, in which society plays a constructive role.

Mead describes the emergence of the self as a social and moral construction. The self is an internalized conversation in which one takes toward oneself the attitudes taken by others. Choices of what to be or to do can be evaluated by comparing the various perspectives that would be taken on the options. Society presents different social roles to the self, which enable its deliberations to be guided by the norms of the community. The identity of the self, its choice of what sort of person it intends to be, is not determined in existential isolation but by deliberating on what is presented by society. The self accepts or rejects the descriptions and norms of the community of which it is a member. While Heidegger is correct that the self must finally take responsibility for its decisions and choices, Mead is also correct that those choices must take place within social and rational processes to which the self is responsible.

Unfortunately, Mead's account falters at this point. On what grounds will the self critique the set of its community's roles, its norms and descriptions? Mead can only suggest that one can take the perspective of another community to acquire critical distance. Can the self find within its own individual being a standard by which to make decisions about what is morally better with respect to the communities in which it lives? Authentic participation in a community structured by norms and roles requires just such a standard.

We propose that such a standard can be found within the individual, and that the tradition of American empiricist moral philosophy has developed a way to identify that standard. The standard is found in what Aristotle called the character of the individual, the set of behavioral dispositions that organize, orient, and motivate the self. We propose that a sense of piety toward nature as a whole, God, provides the means to overcome both subservient compliance to social roles and arbitrary willfulness in defying them. Character guided by natural piety, particularly by trust and loyalty, can enable one to be a critical participant in communal life. We now turn to thinkers in this American empiricist tradition for our contemporary reconstruction of the notion of the self.

Knowledge of God

An American religious perspective derived from Jonathan Edwards, Josiah Royce, John Dewey, and H. Richard Niebuhr concurs with Calvin that knowledge of the self and knowledge of the divine are mutually implicated. The two are related, however, not theoretically but practically. This perspective does not focus on the question of the existence of God or on an absolute ontological order that transcends experience. Instead, the discussion centers on a dimension within experience that orders and sustains its coherence. There is an irreducible religious dimension to experience which is a necessary ingredient in the constitution of the self as engaged and responsible in the world. Whether these philosophers attribute distinct ontological status to God or not, they portray the religious dimension as a pervasive ingredient of human living which enters into the constitution of the self. If this dimension is ignored, certain aspects of experience are obscured and action is frustrated.

These American thinkers expand Mead's social account of the self to include a religious dimension. When we attend to this dimension, we appreciate the microcosm of intimacy and the macrocosm of ultimacy which were neglected in Mead's social psychology.[5] Investigating the relations of trust and loyalty that establish intimate relations leads to ultimate questions about the trustworthiness of that on which the self depends and the value of the causes to which it commits itself. A "thicker," more adequate description of the self cannot be attained without probing the depths and comprehensive context of social relations.

Knowledge of the self and knowledge of the divine imply each other on a practical and affective level. God and the self are not known through introspection or abstraction. The two forms of knowledge imply each other because God and the self are intimately and ultimately related. The religious dimension has practical consequences for self-constitution because it: (a) organizes the self by relating it to an ordering environment, (b) orients the self by sustaining participation in the world, and (c) motivates the self by engendering dispositions to appreciate the world and to act constructively. Ironically, these benefits do not occur when the individual concentrates on developing the self but only when the person is captured by a reality and goodness beyond the self.

Organization of the Self: From Constriction to Expansion

The image of the constricted self and its expansion through authentic religious experience runs through this American discussion. Individuals are naturally plagued by a narrowness of affect and imagination. This constriction is remedied by locating their meaning in a more comprehensive framework than that offered by society alone. The social roles that help shape the emerging self tend to constrict its loyalties to certain groups and defend their interest against other groups. When properly engaged, the religious dimension counters the parochial identity of the self which is defined by social roles.

In late twentieth-century America, there is ample evidence of social fragmentation and the constriction of social sympathy. "Identity politics" encourages the self to find its meaning in the particularities of ethnic group, class, gender, or sexual orientation rather than in shared values and processes. As common ground shrinks, a pluralistic society can deteriorate into an angry crowd. Identity politics creates closed societies organized around group preservation. The religious dimension challenges members of these enclaves to expand their concerns and loyalties. Identity politics breeds a defensiveness, because others are valued only insofar as they resemble the self or can be enlisted as allies to the favored group. By contrast, expansive affections evoked by the religious dimension promote a community of universal intent that seeks the good of all. Persons, natural objects, the material world are valuable simply because they exist.

At the beginnings of American philosophical thought, Jonathan Edwards graphically portrayed the tension between the parochial self and the expansive transformation effected by genuine religion. One need not concur with his mythology of the Fall to recognize the centripetal force in human concerns:

Immediately upon the Fall the mind of man shrunk from its primitive greatness and extensiveness into an exceeding diminution and . . . as soon as he transgressed, those nobler principles were immediately lost and all this excellent enlargedness of his soul was gone and he thenceforward shrunk into a little point circumscribed and closely shut up within itself to the exclusion of all others.[6]

Natural moral dynamics contract to the narrowness of self-interest when divorced from the attractive comprehensive environment which religion appreciates. Genuine religious transformation has the opposite, centrifugal effect since it restores "an excellent enlargement and extensiveness to the soul."[7] Once people have been freed from obsessive concern over private interests, they can appreciate the goodness of God, nature, and other humans for what they are. The self can begin to interact with them in a new way marked by appreciation and respect.

From Edwards through the pragmatists, the American self seems capable of transformation, even reinvention. The self does not so much have experiences as it is constituted by experience, deeply felt and adequately interpreted. New experiences break open the confines of the old self and yield a new self, as when Edwards sensed the beauty of God, and William James, in the midst of depressive anomie, chose to act as if he were free. These transformations were not accomplished by self-determining, autonomous freedom. "Experience" is radically interactive in this American idiom. The self emerges in historical interaction that is shaped by the challenges of its environment and its practical responses. Openness to the possibilities of life's interactions depends on the self's predominant affective dispositions. A defensive agent will tend to interpret life's challenges as threats. The resulting actions may be more appropriate to a sense of precarious existence than to what is actually going on.

Affectivity feeds insight, since the more expansive the interpreter's affections are, the more comprehensive will be the framework in which possibilities are understood. Likewise, a more comprehensive framework of meaning will "put things in perspective" and encourage a more generous affective response. In these American thinkers, the extension of affective scope makes possible a larger perspective of understanding. The transformation of the self does not come from assuming the standpoint of universal rationality but expanding the scope of the heart by the attraction of a goodness larger than the individual.

This expansion for Edwards meant consenting to the beauty of finite realities in appreciation of their connection to the primary beauty of "Being itself." He contrasted a narrow self whose loyalties are limited to "private systems of being" with a self that endorses every value in relation to the full range of reality.[8] For James, when one believes that God exists and makes claims, "the more imperative ideals now begin to speak with an altogether new objectivity and significance, and to utter the penetrating, shattering, tragically challenging note of appeal."[9] John Dewey's commitment to egalitarian democracy was driven by the affection of socially inclusive sympathy and a sense of communion with the whole universe, realized particularly in aesthetic experience.

Openness to the religious dimension can prevent the self from constricting its sympathies and prematurely closing off challenges. By evoking an appreciation of a comprehensive community, it can prevent the agent from inflating finite goods into infinite importance.[10] The primary function of the "sense of the divine," therefore, is not to prove the existence of a transcendent object but to provide experience with an ordering general environment which keeps it open, expansive, and reconciling. The centrifugal pull of the religious dimensions can counteract the perennial human tendency to self-absorption and conferring ultimate devotion on causes that are limited.[11] This model of expansion of constricted experience through the recovery of the religious dimension recurs often in the subsequent American conversation from Edwards to H. Richard Niebuhr.

Orientation: Natural Piety and the Unity of the Self

The second feature of these American accounts is the role that "natural piety" plays in orienting the self to the world and unifying the self. Natural piety is an affective relation of dependence and purpose, of trust in and loyalty to the ultimate context of experience, which is variously described as nature, God, or "Being itself." These dispositions give the agent a sense of engagement in the world and orientation to worthwhile causes. When the self is viewed as an epistemological construct, as in Kant and idealism, the focus is on consciousness and universal rationality, which guide morality through universal truths. The individual is related to the ultimate context as finite self to the Absolute or as reasonable being to the universal structures of ahistorical reason. In contrast, when the self is morally and socially constructed, as in this American perspective, the focus is on character, commitments and affective dispositions.

This American approach portrays the self as engaged in the world, deriving integrity and meaning from interaction with others. These thinkers do not begin from an epistemological division between subject and object or between subject and world. Instead, Edwards's language of "consent" indicates an active engagement at the core of experience, a relation that is typical of American thinkers. It is an active agreement between the aspirations and projects of one portion of experience, the self, with other finite entities and with the most comprehensive, open context of experience. Later, John Dewey made experience the central term of his philosophy when he defined it as the process of transaction between the organism and its environment. For humans this transaction occurs principally through scientific reflection driven by practical aims and through democratic involvement in institutions motivated by social sympathy and justice.

Selves are not constituted by reflex awareness but by loyalties, commitments, and actions that define the self's character through engagement with others. The project of self-determination is disciplined by the potentials of the social and natural environment, unlike existentialism and deconstructionism, in which human decision and valuational engagement seem to occur in a vacuum. While Mead showed how social roles and standards construct the self, Edwards, Dewey, and Niebuhr argue that the religious dimension and the affective dispositions that it evokes are equally important in constituting the self.[12]

Even John Dewey, the most secular of these thinkers, recognized the importance of the religious dimension for pragmatic engagement in the world and providing a sense of unity and integrity to the self. For Dewey the self finds direction by meeting the challenges of the immediate environment. At a deeper level it finds unity through engagement with general ideals. One of these ideals is expressed in the term "the universe," namely, the holistic environment of all the conditions of action, the projected whole of which they are parts. The self requires some sense of a universal context of experience in order to achieve its own integrity. Dewey asserts that "the unification of the self through the ceaseless flux of what it does, suffers, and achieves, cannot be attained in terms of itself. The self is always directed toward something beyond itself, and so its unification depends upon the idea of integration of the shifting scenes of the world into that imaginative totality we call the Universe."[13] He was so convinced that the individual requires a sense of an extensive and unifying whole to demarcate personal experience that he believed a person would go insane without it.[14]

The integrity of the self depends on a unique relation to the whole context of experience, a relation that bears rich affective import. Although Dewey would not hypostatize the ideal of a unified environment into a supernatural divine entity, he explored the affective relation under the rubric of "natural piety." As we shall see below, H. Richard Niebuhr singles out the affections of trust and loyalty in relation to God as constitutive elements of selfhood. The traditional theist gains a sense of personal uniqueness from relating to the one God; the unity of the individual correlates with the presence and calling of the one God. For Dewey, the unity of the individual correlates with the unified attractive power of general ideals like truth and justice. Imagination naturally tends to unify these ideals into a single principle, just as it unifies personal experience into a whole and natural occurrences into a universe. The unity of ideals, their common power of attraction, forms the correlate for the unity of the individual self.

Dewey used the term "natural piety" to refer to particular moral dispositions which are evoked by the lure of this unity of ideal ends. Natural piety is "the sense of the permanent and inevitable implication of [humans] and nature in a common career and destiny."[15] Although the union of ideals is imaginary, it has real effects because it elicits dispositions that sustain human commitments.[16] Dewey believed that this naturalist conception of the divine would liberate the religious dimension inherent in all experience and perform all the practical functions that the concept of God formerly did.[17] It would harmonize the self with the universe in a sense of dependence and support as well as marshal moral sympathy and commitment to improve the conditions of life. These dispositions will anchor the self in nature and sustain it affectively. Dewey agreed with Santayana that *piety* is the "reverent attachment to the sources of [one's] being and the steadying of [one's] life by that attachment." Piety, which engenders a sense of gratitude and duty, is complemented by the more active dimension of "spirituality," which is more forward looking and includes "a devotion to ideal ends."[18] This piety is *natural* because it connects the self with nature, unlike militant atheism which depicts the individual as a Promethean character defying hostile nature.

The religious dimension of experience, therefore, provides a basic affective orientation to the world and contributes to the unity of the self. Dewey might ask contemporary proponents of virtue ethics whether character can be explained by moral traditions alone. Does a more pervasive natural piety locate moral selfhood in relation to a larger framework of meaning? Some versions of environmental ethics recently have revived naturalism. Concentrating on the unity of the ecosystem, they tend to overlook the human species' particular challenge of achieving moral selfhood and unique capacity for ultimate questions.[19] Although Dewey's naturalism acknowledged that the part depends on the natural whole, it refused to confer quasi-divine status on nature itself.

As an account of ultimacy, however, naturalism is problematic. If piety rests only on forces in nature and society that support human aspirations, they seem to lack the comprehensive character of the object of religious trust. If natural piety stems from a set of imagined ideals, it would leave the religious dimension without the natural grounding possessed by the moral and aesthetic dimensions of experience. In *Experience and Nature,* Dewey held that moral and aesthetic traits of experience have their roots in nature and reflect nature as surely as do the mathematical models used in physical sciences.[20] If these traits operate in experience, they cannot be subjective projections. To be consistent, Dewey should ask whether natural piety's trust and loyalty are also rooted in human experience in nature and not products of the imagination alone.

H. Richard Niebuhr pointed out the constricted range of Dewey's naturalism: "Being is greater in extent than nature as is indicated by the place naturalism must accord to ideals that attract and compel [humans], which, it believes, somehow emerge out of nature yet are not actual in it."[21] In effect, Niebuhr retrieves Calvin's more comprehensive notion of nature to challenge Dewey. Nature is not, finally, the context that serves human purposes but "the ultimate environment" which evokes a piety that challenges the tendency to make human aims central to the universe.[22]

Motivation: Trust, Loyalty, and the Emergence of the Self

H. Richard Niebuhr argued that trust and loyalty are the main affective components of the emergence of the self. Individuals are not automatically selves in this American perspective. They must consolidate their experience through a moral process of commitment and interpretation in order to attain the integrity of selfhood. Niebuhr found the dynamics of trust and loyalty operating from the microcosm of intimacy, through the midrange of sociality, to the macrocosm of ultimacy. Because the interactions that produce trust and loyalty extend beyond the human-centered natural world, the constitution of the self is necessarily a religious process as well as a moral one. Niebuhr provided a more adequate description of the religious dimension by grounding natural piety in a framework more comprehensive and more actual than the naturalists allowed. The self is constituted by social relations that are more intimate than the ties described by Mead and more ultimate than the bounds of nature on which Dewey relied.[23]

TRUST AND LOYALTY IN INTIMATE INTERACTION

Trust is the first component in constituting the integrity of the self. Trust poses the first challenge in infancy and possibly the final challenge provoked by death: On whom or what can I rely? Before we rely on the social roles that Mead described, we depend on significant others, as object relations theorists have discovered. Without these early bonds of trust, the self is crippled and disoriented. As life develops, we rely on others to be faithful to us—parents, friends, spouses, partners. Our social relations depend on the trustworthiness of others in speech, in making contracts, in being reliable colleagues.

We rely on these other persons in terms of some specific values. They are explicitly or implicitly committed to something we also value and which stands beyond our specific relation: fidelity in marriage, honesty in speech, or justice in society. Josiah Royce was accurate to describe the basic human relation as triadic. The self is related to the other in terms of some common interest or cause. Every "I-thou" relation requires an "it" beyond the two persons. Intimacy withers when it lacks some purpose beyond the immediate delight of the lovers. If they resist the common future to which love is drawing them, they undermine their present. Friends have certain aspirations and interests in common; they are responsible to each other in relation to common interests, from sports to politics to work.

Loyalty to some common interest shapes the trust of the I and thou. It makes them dependable and accountable to each other. The immature individual wants others to be dependable without the responsibilities of being loyal to them. Loyalty to a cause matures the individual into a self. Personal integrity is established over time by commitment to a cause larger than the individual, because devotion to a cause unifies disparate personal drives into a self. At the same time, this commitment brings accountability to others who share devotion to the same cause. Accountable to others, I become responsible to myself. Intimacy feeds sociality, and social bonds make intimacy substantial. They convey criteria that guide responsible choice and action. The self makes choices not only out of authenticity to itself but also out of responsibility to other persons and loyalty to shared values which it has deliberately embraced.

The individual attains a distinctive character by making and keeping promises. Promises coalesce the agent's transient experiences into the personal consistency of selfhood. They also forge the links to others which stabilize personal identity. The self is a moral construction because it comes into being by forging moral bonds of trust and loyalty, reliability and fidelity. Commitments to others extend personal consistency over time because they state that we will be reliable then as now. Niebuhr wrote that the self emerges from the exercise of human faith which underlies all social interaction. "Without interpersonal existence of which faith—as exercised in the reciprocities of believing, trusting, and being loyal—is the bond, there might indeed be experience from given moment to given moment but the continuity of the self in its experience would be hard to define, if such continuity would be thinkable."[24]

Loyalty and trust also undergird the process by which discrete experiences are integrated into the story of oneself over time. They unify the work of memory and interpretation. The attitude of trust arises from a positive relation to one's past and the attitude of loyalty and fidelity directs the self to a worthwhile future in continuity with who one has been pledged to be. Broken promises and betrayed causes attack the very integrity of the self and defy any piecemeal, pragmatic remedies. Unlike the naturalists, Niebuhr explored the existential crises of mistrust and betrayed faith to probe their religious depths.

TRUST AND LOYALTY IN ULTIMATE INTERACTION

The experience of finitude and the fragility of existence make us question whether reality itself is trustworthy. If neither nature nor society can account for my existence as a self, what can? I am not the cause of my own existence, since I neither willed myself into being nor can assure my survival indefinitely. Is the act by which I have been thrown into existence arbitrary or hostile? Mead's description of the social origins of the self did not resolve the question of the self for Niebuhr; it only posed it at a more comprehensive level.

"Why is there something rather than nothing?" is not a question that can be silenced by pointing to Darwin's account of evolution. While evolution and other natural processes can explain certain characteristics of the individual, they cannot account for the existence of the self, since selfhood arises from personal relations. "Why am I?" and "Why am I this I and not another?" pose the question of existential finitude on a more personal level.[25] Examining the self's relation to society, humanity, or nature cannot answer these questions; they point to a more comprehensive environment. Limiting the scope of meaning to anything less than the ultimate context of Being itself makes it impossible to answer these existential questions or to heal the anxiety and despair caused by ignoring them.

Loyalty, the second constituent of the self's integrity, also depends on a context that is more comprehensive than society or nature. If the self is constituted by its relations to other persons, groups, projects, and purposes, how can it be a single self? Multiple social roles and accountability to many diverse "others" tend to produce multiple selves, a different persona for each constituency. Niebuhr detected a fundamental human flaw in the pursuit of integrity from sources that cannot provide it. Although we seek a sense of identity from the nation, the scientific community, or democracy, they can provide only a provisional identity since they engage only part of the self. In addition, when we find our meaning exclusively in terms of a finite community, we become defensive about rival communities. This misplaced devotion leads to the constriction of heart described above.

Making any finite community the point of reference for value and meaning mistakes a limited scope of reality for reality itself. In Edwards's language, it is consenting to "a limited system of being" as if it were the whole of reality. Loyalty that fails to be sufficiently inclusive eventually becomes exclusive. Militant nationalism, racism, and a host of other "evil imaginations of the heart" proceed from defensive loyalties.[26] If human action and discourse are to be kept open, moral consent needs to extend beyond any finite community to a community that includes all that exists. The interpersonal dynamics of trust and loyalty which generate consistency in the self extend from finite relations to an ultimate Other, for whom all that exists is valuable simply because it exists.

Ultimacy here does not refer to an end-state, that terminal condition of resolution and rest which the naturalists considered a distraction to the practical efforts of humans. Ultimacy signifies for Niebuhr a regulative concept that prevents one from making the relative absolute or conferring infinite devotion on finite purposes. He criticized the naturalists for putting ultimate confidence in scientific progress and democracy as absolute arbiters of meaning and for making the human species the center of the universe.[27] When pragmatism construes the world anthropocentrically and human purposes are assumed to be final, this does violence to the organic balance of the natural environment.

Niebuhr's theology of "radical monotheism" reflects the Edwardsean vision of a sovereign God. Both insist that *the part*—events, agents, commitments, causes, institutions and societies—make sense only in respect to *the whole*—the comprehensive interaction of humans with all reality. When we confer ultimate loyalty on finite objects, it leads to the fatal parochialism which he described in a blend of Edwards and Henri Bergson: "Responsive and responsible to each other in our closed societies, we are irresponsible in the larger world that includes us all."[28] This moral parochialism lies at the root of the closed worlds of discourse which frustrate the search for meaning. Driven by a hermeneutics of suspicion about every position except their own, closed communities thrive on ideology. In order to prevent arbitrary cloture on the process of discourse, the self needs to locate itself in a community of universal intent. Such a community becomes possible when others are valued not in relation to private interest or group interest but to God, who is the source of both being and value. The value of all existents comes from their existence since they are all valuable to the ultimate Center of Value.

FROM HORIZON TO PRESENCE

The intimate and ultimate reaches of experience come together for Niebuhr in the religious dimension. The divine enters experience as a presence and not only as the universal horizon of action that Dewey described. Integrity rather than fragmentation becomes possible for us because God meets "us not as the one beyond the many but as the one who acts in and through all things, not as the unconditioned but as the conditioner."[29] The self can make an integrated response to the multiple interactions of experience because there is One to whom the self responds in all its responses to others. The purposes of this One are not transcendent in an otherworldly sense but pervade all relations in experience. What is demanded is "not the static unity of established order but the unity of life aspiring toward and impelled by an infinite purpose. This is not the one in whom we come to rest but the one through whom life comes to us."[30] God intends the universal reconciliation and flourishing of all and calls every agent to be loyal to this cause. It elicits an overall direction which resists the temptation to form closed systems of thought, allegiance, or institutions. Insofar as religious institutions defend their own interests, they are betraying the cause of the God, to whom they claim to be faithful.

How does this possibility of allegiance to a community of universal intent enter into experience? What invites us toward universal discourse and a comprehensive community? This American religious perspective points to the experience of *disclosure* to account for the attractive power of these ideals, an attraction that leads to participation and moral responsibility. We do not think our way into this presence; it occurs as the gift of an Other. The divided self cannot be healed by an idea of unity or a theory of faithfulness. What is needed is for an Other to disclose its covenant fidelity to the self. This renewal of faith does not come from logical inference but from an event of disclosure that enables the self to respond with radical trust and genuine loyalty. "We sought a good to love and were found by a good that loved us."[31] Knowledge of the self arises from being known and valued by the Other; knowledge of God arises in this gift through the self's dispositional response to this Other.

H. Richard Niebuhr, like Jonathan Edwards, believed that the attractive possibility of a "life aspiring toward and impelled by an infinite purpose" was disclosed in experience.[32] The religious dimension that opens up through an act of divine self-disclosure is called "revelation" because it unveils a pervasive presence that was obscurely realized before. The healing of fragmented faith comes from One who enters into interaction with selves by demonstrating its trustworthiness and disclosing its cause.[33] This event is a gift that evokes gratitude, confidence in the source of the self's existence, and fidelity to the cause of the One who has shown itself loyal to the self. Revelation of this Other decenters the self and revolutionizes morality.

This event of disclosure of One who values the self stands in marked contrast to the divine of Dewey's *Common Faith*. "God" is not a term for all that humans value, but for the One who values humans and all being. Because the divine in Dewey functions only to conserve human ideals, it is inevitably anthropocentric. Such an ideal would resist moral innovation since it canonizes the values of a given era as the ideals behind the universe. If the divine is an instrument, those values are the true absolutes. The divine in Niebuhr's thought does not principally function to support human values. Faith demands moral expression because loyalty is inseparable from trust. In responding to the Center of Value, we must also respond to all that is genuinely worthwhile. However, faith, like friendship, has value in itself which is undermined when it is made an instrument of something else.

Conclusion

This proposal for a reconstructed notion of the self drawn from American thinkers addresses some of the problems posed by contemporary philosophers of practical knowledge. It does not seek ahistorical universals as the ground of the self but seeks the One who conditions the many in experience. It identifies the tendencies that lead to closed societies and arbitrary limitations on the process of rational discourse. It indicates that the dynamics within experience that expand constricted discourse are the same ones that expand the constricted heart. With the existentialists, it recognizes that the most radical choices are not about what to do but about who we are to become. At the same time, it does not leave authenticity bereft of moral criteria. The self is constituted by specific social relations and guided morally by the affective behavioral dispositions that they engender.

Social roles, however, are not the only source of moral consistency for the self. The most crucial dispositions for self-constitution, trust and loyalty, point beyond society and a constricted notion of nature. The self is constituted by interaction with a more expansive social and natural environment. The intimate and ultimate reaches of experience converge in the engagement of God with the self. This American perspective holds that we cannot understand the microcosm of intimacy or the macrocosm of ultimacy without referring to the meaning disclosed in the religious dimension.

Notes

1. John Calvin, *Institutes of the Christian Religion*, ed. John T. McNeill (Philadelphia: Westminster Press, 1975), I, 35, 37.

2. Ibid., I, v, 58.

3. Ernst Tugendhat, *Self-Consciousness and Self-Determination,* trans. and with an introduction by Paul Stern (Cambridge, Mass.: MIT Press, 1986).

4. For other criticisms of the misleading character of these models in modern accounts of knowledge see Richard Rorty, *Philosophy and the Mirror of Nature* (Princeton, N.J.: Princeton University Press, 1979) and Richard Bernstein, *Beyond Objectivism and Relativism: Science, Hermeneutics and Praxis* (Philadelphia: University of Pennsylvania Press, 1983).

5. "Secular traditions are indispensable, yet they have had neither the time nor the maturity to bequeath to us potent cultural forms of ultimacy, intimacy and sociality comparable to older religious traditions" (Cornel West, *Keeping Faith: Philosophy and Race in America* [New York: Routledge: 1993], 132).

6. Jonathan Edwards, "Charity and Its Fruits," in *The Works of Jonathan Edwards* (New Haven: Yale University Press, 1989), vol. 8, ed. John E. Smith, 253.

7. Ibid., 253–54.

8. Jonathan Edwards, "The Nature of True Virtue," in *Works*, vol. 8, 550–60.

9. William James, *The Will to Believe and Other Essays in Popular Philosophy* (Cambridge: Harvard University Press, 1979), 160.

10. H. Richard Niebuhr described this perennial human tendency of the human heart. "It is always loyal to something and its problem is how to transfer its loyalty from the ephemeral, the partial, and the relative, which by assuming absoluteness becomes devilish, to the eternal, universal and truly absolute" (H. Richard Niebuhr, *Kingdom of God in America* [New York: Harper & Row, 1937], 103).

11. This approach is delineated in James M. Gustafson, *A Sense of the Divine: The Natural Environment from a Theocentric Perspective* (Cleveland: Pilgrim Press, 1994).

12. Dewey went beyond his colleague Mead in exploring the religious dimension and the affections it evokes. Mead died in 1931, three years before Dewey broke his decades-long silence on the topic of religion in *A Common Faith*, in vol. 9 of *Later Works* (Carbondale: Southern Illinois University Press, 1986).

13. Ibid., 14.

14. John Dewey, *Art as Experience*, in vol. 10 of *Later Works*, 198.

15. Dewey, vol. 4 of *Middle Works* (Carbondale: Southern Illinois University Press, 1977), 176.

16. "This unity signifies not a single Being, but the unity of loyalty and effort evoked by the fact that many ends are one in the power of their ideal, or imaginative, quality to stir and hold us" (Dewey, *A Common Faith*, 30).

17. Ibid., 9:35.

18. George Santayana, *The Life of Reason; or the Phases of Human Progress*, 5 vols. (New York: Scribner's, 1905), vol. 3, *Reason in Religion*, 179, 193–95.

19. See, for example, J. Baird Callicott, "Animal Liberation: A Triangular Affair," in *Ethics and the Environment*, ed. Donald Scherer and Thomas Attig (Englewood Cliffs, N.J.: Prentice-Hall, 1983), 61–65; also Holmes Ralston III, *Philosophy Gone Wild: Essays in Environmental Ethics* (Buffalo: Prometheus Books, 1986), and *Environmental Ethics: Duties to and Values in the Natural World* (Philadelphia: Temple University Press, 1988).

20. Dewey, *Art as Experience,* 13.

21. H. Richard Niebuhr, *Radical Monotheism and Western Culture* (New York: Harper & Row, 1970), 36.

22. Ibid., 47.

23. Niebuhr accepted Mead's account of the self as socially constituted but drew on Josiah Royce and Martin Buber to augment it. See Richard H. Niebuhr, *Faith on Earth* (New Haven: Yale University Press, 1989) and *Radical Monotheism*. See also H. Richard Niebuhr, *The Responsible Self: An Essay in Christian Moral Philosophy*, with an introduction by James M. Gustafson (New York: Harper & Row, 1963), 71–89.

24. Niebuhr, *Faith on Earth*, 83.

25. On the inadequacy of Dewey's treatment of questions about personal origins, see Douglas R. Anderson, "Smith and Dewey on the Religious Dimension of Experience: Dealing with Dewey's Half-God," *American Journal of Theology and Philosophy* 14, no. 2 (1993): 161–76.

26. H. Richard Niebuhr, *The Meaning of Revelation* (New York: Macmillan, 1960), 72–78.

27. James Gustafson identifies anthropocentrism as the bane of contemporary religion and morality in *Ethics from a Theocentric Perspective,* 2 vols. (Chicago: University of Chicago Press, 1981–1984), vol. 1. *Theology and Ethics.*

28. Niebuhr, *The Responsible Self,* 138. Niebuhr credited Edwards with making the same fundamental diagnosis of the human situation: "In all such offerings, something is virtually worshipped, and whatever it is, be it self, or [others], or the world, *that* is allowed to usurp the place given to God, and receive the offerings that should be made to [God]" (*Kingdom of God,* 103). The note reads "Jonathan Edwards, *Christian Love as Manifested in Heart and Life,* 6th ed. (Philadelphia), 87; cf. *Works* VII, 459 f."

29. Niebuhr, *Meaning of Revelation,* 133.

30. Ibid., 134.

31. Niebuhr, *Meaning of Revelation,* 138.

32. For Edwards, the disclosure has the character of a pervasive beauty which reorients the self to a more expansive appreciation and loyalty. See *Religious Affections,* vol. 2 of *Works of Jonathan Edwards,* ed. John E. Smith (New Haven: Yale University Press, 1959), 240–66.

33. Niebuhr states that the religious need is satisfied only insofar as human beings are able to recognize themselves as valued by something beyond themselves (H. Richard Niebuhr, "Value-Theory and Theology," in *The Nature of Religious Experience: Essays in Honor of Douglas Clyde Macintosh* [New York: Harper & Brothers, 1937], 115).

Chapter 8

The Role of Experience
in Moral Discernment

MARGARET A. FARLEY

"Deliberation is an aspect of discernment, but discernment is more than deliberation."[1] The distinction is a readily recognized one between deliberation primarily as a rational process (which may include, for example, clarifying empirical data, weighing reasons, calculating consequences, determining priorities in the application of ethical principles) and discernment as a more complex (imaginative, affective, perhaps aesthetic and even religious) process of searching, illuminating, sifting, recognizing, comprehending, and judging options for moral action against and within a wide horizon of relevant factors. Experience plays an important role in both deliberating and discerning. This essay, while not ignoring the importance of experience for deliberation, nonetheless aims beyond it to explore the implications of experience for moral discernment as a whole.

In its broadest sense, experience is essential for every form of knowledge. Whether one holds that "all knowledge comes through the senses" or that ideas can be innate to our minds, human knowledge consists in some grasping of what is known in the experience of knowing. When a narrower meaning is sought for "experience," however, a multitude of usages emerge.[2] Many of them are theory-dependent, as when "experiential" knowledge is contrasted with "objective" knowledge, or experience is contrasted with thought, or experience is limited to what is verifiable through the senses. Less theoretical or technical meanings of experience include the direct apprehension of an object, thought, or emotion, as in an "experience of a blizzard," or an "experience of hope"; the accumulation of knowledge or skills through repeated activities or encounters, as when one becomes "experienced with computers"; the development of an insight through participation in an event or the endurance of some influence, as when "experience teaches"; testing one's knowledge in some kind of experiment or trial, a meaning rooted in the Latin *experiri*, to test, confirm, find out.

The above meanings are familiar to most people, and they are not difficult to understand. When, however, we begin to ask about the role of experience in moral discernment and moral reasoning, its meaning becomes more elusive and its significance is frequently contested. Yet in theological ethics as in theology there has been a kind of "turn to experience" in the twentieth century. The turn has been sufficiently remarkable to generate overviews of its emergence as well as historical and analytical studies of the sorts of appeals it represents.[3] Readiness for such a turn may be accounted for in a number of ways. Western philosophical traditions consistently have found a role for experience in the development of anthropologies, in a search for epistemological groundings, and in a concern for practical guides to action. Contemporary examples abound in which historical attention to human experience is brought forward into constructive proposals for ethical theory. The twentieth century has brought a new interest in Aristotelian "spheres of human experience" and their corresponding virtues.[4] Even when the term "experience" is not used, those who draw on Thomas Aquinas's theory of moral action are depending on descriptive analyses of human experience of complex choices.[5] Varieties of British empiricism and American pragmatism continue to make claims on ethical methodology and moral epistemology.[6] Edmund Husserl, Jean-Paul Sartre, and Maurice Merleau-Ponty cast shadows (however drastically altered) on phenomenological descriptions of the experience of moral obligation and affective moral response.[7]

What I shall mean by "experience" in this essay is the actual living of events and relationships, along with the sensations, feelings, images, emotions, insights, and understandings that are part of this lived reality. Experience in this sense is a given, something providing data to be interpreted; but it is also something that is already interpreted, its content shaped by previous understandings in a context of multiple influences. Moreover, experience, as I shall address it, can belong both to the self and to others; it can be both personal and social. Experience is private, individual, unique to the one who experiences; but there are shared experiences, communicated as well as formed within communities and societies. Experience in each of these senses—given but not primitive, immediate but not innocent of interpretation, personal but not isolated, unique but not without a social matrix—plays an important role in moral discernment. It is a source of moral insight, a factor in moral judgment, a test of the rightness, goodness, and wisdom of moral decision.

There are, of course, other sources for moral discernment. In Christian ethics, for example, experience commonly is identified as a source along with scripture, tradition (theological, pedagogical, devotional, communal), and secular disciplines (philosophy, the physical and social sciences, literature, and any other of reason's disciplined approaches to morally relevant understandings of human life and the world). Within the many strands of the Christian tradition, individuals and communities have made varying decisions about the relative significance of the different sources. Depending on the nature of these decisions, each of the sources can shape the content of the others and provide a perspective for their interpretation. All of the sources together can be used dialectically in moral discernment. But whatever decisions are made about the use of sources, it seems fair to say that experience is never just one source among many. It is always an important part of the content of each of the other sources, and it is always a key factor in the interpretation of the others. Scripture, for example, is the record of some persons' experience of God; tradition represents a community's experience through time; humanistic and even scientific studies are shaped by the experience of those who engage in them.[8] Past experience, therefore, provides content for all of the sources, and present experience provides a necessary and inescapable vantage point for interpreting them.

Present experience also, in itself, offers a quasi-discrete (though not isolatable) source for knowledge, understanding, and moral discernment. It is experience in this sense—the contemporary actual living of events and relationships—whose role in moral deliberation and discernment is most frequently contested. It is beset by problems of access, authority, and the identification of criteria for governing its use. Deconstructive critiques have rendered knowledge of experience more and more unattainable and experience itself more and more suspect as a ground for self-knowledge or a guide for choice. Conflicts between appeals to experience and appeals to the Bible or to tradition have threatened to undermine the authority of experience or to place it over against the authority of at least other Christian sources for moral discernment. There are as yet no generally accepted criteria for determining what and whose experience counts as authoritative, especially when long-standing moral rules are challenged or when the experience of some is at odds with the experience of others.

It is not possible in an essay as limited as this one to address with any satisfaction all of the objections to a role for experience in moral discernment. Nonetheless, what I want to do is: (1) explore, however briefly, the positive uses of experience in Christian ethics; (2) take account of some of the most telling weaknesses in these uses; and (3) advance, however modestly, a discussion of the ethical importance of experience in spite of its problems.

An obvious way to examine the positive role of experience in moral discernment is to look to contemporary approaches to Christian ethics in which experience is given a central place. Two such approaches suggest themselves, unlikely in their overall pairing but alike in their insistence on a role for experience in more than one aspect of moral discernment. The two approaches are James M. Gustafson's in the development of his theocentric ethics and the approach taken by feminist theorists in their construction of a liberation ethics that is methodologically committed to beginning with the experience of women. In both of these efforts, experience has several significant roles. It is central for finding and establishing an overall framework for moral discernment; it is important for formulating and applying general ethical principles and specific ethical rules; and it plays a key role in developing theories of moral disposition.

Christian Ethics and Experience

Ethics and the Experience of God

No contemporary ethicist has addressed more consistently and systematically the question of the sources for Christian ethics than James Gustafson. For more than three decades he has provided the field of Christian ethics with careful considerations of the methodological roles of scripture, theology, tradition, the sciences, philosophy, human experience, and countless variations on these in the development of theological ethics.[9] Each source is important in itself, but Gustafson's position has been all along that no one source is sufficient without the others. None of them alone constitutes an adequate court of appeal in determining moral obligation in a particular situation; no one of them by itself can provide all that we need to know about moral dispositions and the moral requirements of relationships. This said, there always has been, nonetheless, at least an implicit recognition in Gustafson's work of what he explicitly identifies in *Ethics from a Theocentric Perspective* as the "priority of human experience."[10]

For Gustafson, experience is prior to other sources for Christian ethics at both the beginning and the end of moral discernment. It is chronologically and psychologically prior because it is what needs to be interpreted with the help of the other sources. And, in the end, it constitutes the final test of the accuracy and adequacy of the interpretation achieved.[11] There would be no Bible or any other form of revelation were there no human experience to be shaped and interpreted by it; there would be no work for practical reason were there no experience for reason to address and to employ; there would be no theology or ethics were there no religion and morality, aspects of experience whose meanings need to be understood and articulated. "Both revelation and reason are human reflections on human experiences."[12]

Criteria intrinsic to the formulations of both reason and revelation determine their general use in interpreting the moral significance of experience, and criteria governing the relationship between these resources and the experience to be interpreted determine their further usefulness for illuminating particular circumstances and events. In other words, there are tests to be met in the interpretive process, including the critical scrutiny of other interpreters.[13] But, in the end, the interpretation must "make sense" to the interpreter; it must make sense *of,* but also *to,* the interpreter's experience.[14]

The nature of experience insofar as it is relevant to Gustafson's moral theory is complex, and its content comes from multiple arenas, shaped by multiple forces. It is prior to reflection; yet like Aristotle's prime matter, it cannot exist without some form, some reflective elements that give it meaning from the start. Its arenas are nature, history, culture, society, the self, and the inevitable combinations of these. It involves more than one dimension of the self, for in it are commingled affectivity and cognition, imagination and the many forms of human activity. It can be predominantly aesthetic, intellectual, religious, or moral. It is profoundly social, rising out of the interaction between persons and events, generated in and by the historical and cultural matrix of meanings that make up the fabric of a community or society. "Its significance is explained and its meanings assessed in communities that share common objects of interest and attention and share some common concepts, symbols, and theories."[15] Socially conditioned, it also has universal human elements, as in the experience of "fault."[16]

If experience is always already structured (by previous experience previously interpreted), and if it is structured so that individually and socially we are predisposed to look for and find certain meanings, and if experience is itself the final judge of the interpretation it receives, then we appear to be faced, as Gustafson acknowledges, with an unavoidable circularity.[17] Moreover, insofar as moral theory depends on descriptive accounts importantly based in experience, "there is an inevitable circularity to moral theory."[18] But for Gustafson, the circles can be "large and nonvicious," drawn from different starting points, dependent not on naive intuition, subject to assessment and to change by the individual and the community. Perspective influences interpretation, but interpretations and their consequences can also influence perspective. Just as in modern science, a mutually corrective process can occur whereby "beliefs, metaphors, and theories presumed to be adequate to explain or interpret the meaning of what is experienced prove to be inadequate, and must be revised."[19] For Gustafson, then, there are "reality checks" for our interpretations of experience. These checks do not move us completely outside our experience but offer pragmatic tests within ongoing experience, social tests insofar as we share experiences, and even the tests endemic to experience itself because of its "objective pole": Grounded in experience of the self, it nonetheless has both content and sources that are "other than self."[20]

There are many ways in which James Gustafson appeals to experience, his own and others', in the development of his Christian ethic. Key to his theocentric ethic, however, is his initial description of the cultural and religious circumstances of the contemporary historical period. It is this description that both motivates and provides direction for Gustafson's ethic. In an age of unprecedented scientific and social progress, Gustafson finds a sharpened experience of human limitation. In an era of massive efforts and achievements in the control of nature and the alleviation of human suffering, he discovers relentless experiences of threat from powers we are helpless to tame. In this context, religion has become a utility value, a source of assurance that all shall be well, a promise of benefits in this world if not in another.[21] The result in our moral lives is the fueling of desires and of fears which turn us in upon ourselves. Everything is measured in terms of human needs; the human species becomes the center of the universe; and human well-being, individual and social, becomes the central ethical concern.[22] All of this, unfortunately, is counterproductive, for we remain limited and under threat, human well-being is not finally served, and we are not even genuinely religiously consoled.

But there is another way. The fundamental elements in contemporary cultural experience can yield a different meaning. Paradoxes of possibility and limitation, mastery and helplessness, dependence and threat, admit of radically different interpretations from the ones currently favored in the culture. If one takes the experiences with utter seriousness, tests them with the resources of scientific reason, and consents to the appropriateness of religious symbols in discerning their meaning, one can understand the experiences differently and even transform them as experiences. This is what James Gustafson proposes in his development of a theocentric perspective for theology and ethics.

It is possible (though not inevitable), Gustafson argues, to experience the reality of God in all of the arenas and forms of human experience. We do so insofar as our awareness of objects (in nature, culture, ourselves, etc.) evokes affections that have religious meaning. Affections have religious meaning when they are responses to objects that are perceived to be related to an Ultimate Power.[23] The Ultimate Power is the Power that bears down on us but also sustains us, that sets an ordering of relationships within the cosmos and provides conditions of possibilities and a sense of direction for human activity. The experience of such a Power is still accessible in a culture where new desires for progress and control bring with them a heightened sense of limitation and vulnerability. For God can be met in our experiences of contingency and powerlessness just as in our experiences of beauty and order. And a genuine experience of God, of an Ultimate Power, makes possible in and for us a decentering of ourselves and the human community in our understanding of the universe and even in our desires for its good. From this experience emerges the radical possibility of a Christian ethic that relativizes human well-being not only before God but before reality as a whole.

Critics of Gustafson largely have focused on his doctrine of God—its agnosticism about divine agency, the unrelenting *via negativa* that disallows concepts of personhood or intelligence to be attributed to God, and Gustafson's acknowledged ambivalence regarding God's "friendship" or "enmity" toward humans. Charges are made regarding the importance given to science as a source for theology and ethics, the selection of symbols inappropriate to the biblical traditions, and the practical denial of Christian beliefs about God's self-revelation. It may be that all of these criticisms are finally rejections of Gustafson's interpretation of the experience of God and his use of that interpretation as the keystone for a theocentric ethic.

Yet Gustafson's theory about the role of experience (and in particular the experience of God) in moral discernment is carefully nuanced. It cannot be rejected wholesale, at least not without taking account of its parts. First of all, Gustafson does not argue from a necessary and humanly innate experience of God, but from a human experience of the world which is open to theological construal. Secondly, he affirms the pluralism even in Christian accounts of the experience of God. It is an experience that admits of many aspects, and some particular experiences may be marked by the predominance of one aspect over others.[24] Thus, for example, while an argument may be made from experience and the biblical witness for a more personal, promising, providential God than Gustafson's Ultimate Power, the stark and ambiguous evidence of a deity who is "in the details" not a guarantor of individual temporal well-being is an important corrective to sentimental longings that reduce God to a safety net under life's mistakes and disasters. In addition, Gustafson has theoretical room for the selective retrieval of traditional concepts and symbols as interpreters of present experience. He acknowledges that there are strands in the biblical and Christian traditions suggesting purposes of God other than the ones he selects for his theocentric perspective.[25] Moreover, Gustafson's agnosticism regarding God's purposes and the well-being of humans does not rule out a divine intention for the genuine good of humans precisely as participants in the *telos* of the whole of creation.[26] To hold that the dignity of the human individual is within the order of nature rather than in the grandeur of freedom is not to deny both dignity and grandeur that are both natural and free.[27]

However one adjudicates Gustafson's position in relation to the problems raised by his critics, the point here is the centrality of experience for the basic framework of a Christian ethic. More specifically, the point here is the centrality of an experience of God which provides a framework for Christian ethics, a determinant of general principles and specific rules, and a source for understanding the dispositions necessary for moral discernment. As the shaper of a framework, this experience of God makes possible a radical conversion from the self to the other and from a part to the whole.[28] In our experience of dependence and interdependence, we understand what we *are*[29] and we know that we are obligated.[30] Our general obligation is to relate to all things as they are related to God.[31] Moral discernment becomes an act of piety as we probe our experience in all of its details, and as we explore (with every resource that we have) God's ordering of a world full of value.[32] Searching for God's purposes, for what is "fitting" in our relationships and activities, we are not often privileged with absolute clarity and certainty. Specific moral norms are at best "almost universal" or "almost absolute."[33] Nonetheless, whether we are discerning population policies, the morality of abortion in particular cases, or our obligation to those who choose suicide, we must examine the patterns of interdependence, hold ourselves accountable to one another and to the whole of which we are a part, and attempt to be faithful to the Power that is acting in it all. Dispositions of gratitude, of self-denial, of perseverance in attending to the objects of our experience, are to be nurtured alongside dispositions of epistemic humility and courage.

Ethics and the Experience of Injustice

It is difficult enough in a short essay to attempt to present fairly the uses of experience in the ethics of an individual theologian. It is more difficult to try to identify common features of a whole field within ethics. Contemporary feminist theological ethics has no one spokesperson and no one version upon which to draw. A shared enterprise, it has marked stages in its development and sharp disagreements among its participants. Still, some things can be said about it that will contribute to considerations of the role of experience in moral discernment.

Feminist uses of experience share much in common with James Gustafson's uses. In both there is a strong reliance on experience as a source of moral insight. Like Gustafson, feminists recognize the importance of other sources for Christian ethics, but the other sources can be tested by experience. Experience itself needs to be interpreted, but it also validates the interpretation it achieves. Experience is embedded in a social and cultural matrix, since "society is in us before we are in society."[34] A hermeneutical circle is unavoidable, but it need not be vicious. In fact, experience can "explode as a critical force,"[35] disrupting traditions even as it serves to sustain them.

If there are formal similarities between the role of experience in Gustafson's ethics and in feminist ethics, however, the content of the experience and the issues it raises are often different indeed. Contemporary feminist theory began with the experience of women, with the growing awareness among women of the dissonance between their interpretation of their own experience and the interpretations given to them by cultures and religious traditions whose experiential sources were almost solely those of men. Like other liberation theorists, feminists pressed the question of whose experience counts when a community discerns its goals and actions and when it distributes its goods and its roles. Attention turned to those whose voices of experience were largely absent from traditions, and the focus was on experiences of injustice and the efforts to change the systems and circumstances that caused the injustice. This is the experience that is necessary and primary, though not sufficient, for moral discernment.

Access to women's experience has been through individual reflection and group communication, but also through the gathering of new empirical data. The experiences of "ordinary people" as well as the "signs of the times" are raised up. Experiences of the past as well as of the present are retrieved and reinterpreted. What was hidden needs to be revealed, whether through biblical studies, literature, cultural analyses, or critical historical studies. In this process, the power of traditional religious symbols to explain women's experience has been weakened, so that reform efforts, reinterpretations of the symbols themselves, have become intrinsic to the task of feminist theology and ethics.

For women to claim their own interpretation of their experience is to claim a new identity. It is to claim gender equality, a capacity for mutuality, genuine agency, a right to bodily integrity, new valuations of sexuality, and gender justice in family and society. These claims are made as truth claims, the basis for ethical norms and for political strategies. To reach the beliefs that undergird such claims, feminists have not naively reflected on the experience of women but have engaged in a process of "unmasking" experience, deconstructing their own experience, resisting complicity in a generalized "false consciousness." This would not have been possible without some previous changes in experience, initiated by cultural shifts that allowed new possibilities for women. Access to experience has thus meant a dialectical process wherein the unthinkable becomes thinkable, experience influences experience, self-criticism yields cultural criticism, and a new consciousness develops.

Feminists who continue to stand in the Christian tradition have brought their experience to critical reformulations of doctrines of God and of creation, theological anthropology and ecclesiology. For many feminists, the problem with God has not been Gustafson's problem with utilitarian theological construals of a God too domesticated to be God; their problem has been whether God is an oppressor, one who uses women for men. For many feminists, the problem with traditional concepts of creation is not that women have been made the center of the universe, but that women, like nature, have been valued only instrumentally in relation to the human species and in relation to the goals of cosmic control. Feminist theologians have probed both experience and tradition, looking for intelligible and persuasive convergences, seeking theological meanings for the religious dimensions of experience. In doing so they have selected from the tradition symbols that they discerned to be appropriate to their experience. Through these symbols they can recognize the God of their tradition as both immanent and transcendent; they can expand on notions of *imago dei* and explore the possibilities of mutuality between God and the world; they can find theological models for justice and for judgment in human affairs; they are able to identify responsibility in relation to the universe; they find it possible to glimpse religious meaning even in human suffering.[36]

Critics of feminist theology frequently charge that the reformulation of symbols is unfaithful to the tradition. It offers a false god, the projection of selfish human desires. It gives human experience an unwarranted authority over God's self-revelation in the Bible and Christian tradition. Feminist ethics, it is said, imports both rationalism and romanticism into Christian understandings of relationship, eliminating rich concepts of gender complementarity and distorting the natural meaning of the human. Moreover, feminist theories of virtue trivialize traditional notions of self-sacrifice and miss the point of the sinfulness that pervades human nature. If liberation theologies generally are tempted to make of religion a utility value in the achievement of justice, feminist theologies go beyond even this when the justice they seek is distorted and false.

Yet feminists respond precisely that experience cannot be ignored and that religious traditions will be life giving insofar as they help to explain it. The biblical witness claims to present insights that are healing, "hard sayings" that are ultimately freeing. It cannot do so if it contradicts the fundamental convictions that make sense in and to human experience. These convictions, whether we like it or not, constitute a negative test for any revelation of knowledge and a positive key to the workings of reason and the fullness of revelation. As such they do not triumph over, nor are they formed apart from, the witness of the biblical tradition; rather they help to liberate its historically accessible meaning. As for the category of gender, it is socially constructed, and a genealogy of its interpretations shows the caution that must be exercised in claiming too much for its meaning in nature. And if self-sacrifice refers to the conversion of mind and heart required to see and see again, to find a center in what is beyond the self yet within it, to love and to reverence all that is for what it is, then feminist theology acclaims its importance. But if self-sacrificial love means a requirement whereby women are expected to sacrifice more than men, where some groups are intrinsically suited to sacrifice more than others, then it needs conceptual revision. Finally, the God who would only be useful for the fulfillment of human wishes could not be the God of feminist theologies, for in that construal lies a theoretical contradiction and a practical impossibility.[37]

In spite of the emphasis on the role of experience in feminist moral discernment, or because of it, feminist theories have also argued that experience itself must be seriously problematized. This leads us, along with other persistent difficulties, to some of the weaknesses attached to experience as a source for Christian ethics.

The Problems of Experience as an Ethical Source

Of all the problems that beset experience in terms of access, authority, and methodological criteria for its use, I will focus on three. If formulated into questions, they can look like these: (1) What sort of evidence does experience actually offer? (2) What sort of universalization from experience is possible? (3) How is the authority of experience to be reconciled with the authority of the Bible, tradition, and systematized disciplines of reason?

The first of these questions is closely related to the hermeneutical circle acknowledged by James Gustafson and pressed by many feminist philosophers and theologians. As theories of language, social location, and power are developed, they threaten to make any appeal to experience vacuous. For example, what can an appeal to women's experience mean if that experience is shaped completely and ineluctably by normative expectations of a culture? What are we to make of an ethics of care based on women's experience of caring if we suspect its construction is attributable to the social pressures on women to take care of men? Thus Catherine MacKinnon cautions that "Women are said to value care. Perhaps women value care because men have valued women according to the care they give. Women are said to think in relational terms. Perhaps women think in relational terms because women's social existence is defined in relation to men."[38] The supposed bedrock of evidence which experience provides disappears in the endless circles of construction that threaten to eliminate moral agency as well as genuine moral discernment.

The second question is also one we have already met, but its urgency has grown as feminists have faced it in their movement and in their theory. Everyone recognizes that experience is particular precisely because it is concrete, but is there sufficient overlapping in the content of one person's experience and another's so that generalizations can be warranted? Or again, is experience so particular that it cannot be shared, so concrete that it cannot be rendered intelligible to others? If individuals can share experiences, can they be shared between groups as well?

Thus, for example, when women began to claim their own self-understandings based importantly in their own experience, they did so not only as individuals but as a group. Herein lay the power of their insights and the inspiration for their action. Soon, however, women were brought up short by the challenge of the diversity among them. Just as they had argued that the experience of men cannot be universalized to stand for the experience of all humans, so they had to acknowledge that the experience of some women (in this case, white, middle-class, heterosexual, western women) cannot be universalized to stand for the experience of all women. Women of color, lesbians, working-class women, women from across the world rejected the adequacy of too-narrowly drawn a delineation of women's experience. This, then, forced the question of whether or not women as women have anything in common and whether their experience can constitute a genuine source for theology and ethics. Beyond this, it forces the question of whether differences in experience make impossible any common morality even within communities of faith if their social and cultural diversities run deep.

The third question follows from the first and the second, but it, too, has been with us from the start. How can experience—elusive, socially constructed, diverse—be authoritative in the process of moral discernment? It may have confirmatory power (or negatively, a veto power) at the end of a process, but it can do little work in the process itself. That is the point, so an argument may go, of our need not only for the disciplines of reason but for revelation. Experience is subject to the Bible and to faith traditions; if it helps us to understand them, it nonetheless does so only insofar as it does not at the same time usurp their authority. This is obviously not a problem for everyone, not even for everyone who does Christian ethics; but the question of how to relate the many sources for moral discernment is inescapable when experience is taken seriously as at least one of the sources.

Experience Revisited

To consider experience as a source for moral discernment probably gets closer to fundamental issues of moral epistemology than does a consideration of any other source. A major part of what is at stake is the nature of knowledge itself, its power and manner of access to reality, its cognitive and affective components, its communicability, and its consequences for those who come to know. These issues hover in the background of any responses to the questions I have raised regarding the validity, particularity, and authority of experience.

With this caution, let me nonetheless return to the first of my questions: What sort of evidence does experience actually offer? No one can argue that there is an uncontestable, foundational, direct and immediate "deposit" of moral insight in a fund of experience. Yet there are some things important for moral discernment that simply cannot be known without experience—things like the limitations and possibilities of ourselves as moral agents, the dimensions of suffering and diminishment, the ways to hope and to love, the parameters of intimacy, the multiple consequences of injury and injustice. Moreover, all of our morally relevant knowledge (from whatever source) is modified when it partakes of experience—whether this is our knowledge of disease or of the complexities of a moral situation or of God. And there are issues of specific moral rules (and their exceptions) that cannot be resolved without access to some persons' experience—for example, issues of sexuality, of discrimination, of fidelity to covenants. Finally, experience shapes who we are, our attitudes, our interests, and our capacities; "who we are" in turn influences our search for and appropriation of any of the knowledge that becomes part of our moral discernment.

This suggests that while the problems of learning from experience are serious, they are not intractable. Experience indeed may be socially constructed, lodged in a hermeneutical circle, layered with meanings never fully accessible, manipulated by forces never fully understood. But deconstructive methods yield more than an infinite regress. There *are* processes of discovery, of consciousness raising, of interpreting more accurately our experiences present and past, of making explicit what was previously implicit. Ambiguities in the evidence notwithstanding, critical uses of experience can be defended as both necessary and illuminating. James Gustafson's appeals to experiences of the divine and feminist theologians' appeals to experiences of injustice are cases in point.[39]

Yet my second question remains: How much can be generalized from experience as a source? Diversity in experiences does constitute a significant obstacle to their use as an ethical source. The obstacle, however, is real but not absolute. First of all, there is evidence of some commonalities in morally relevant experiences despite differences in meaning. Across diverse experiences of race and class, gender and culture, for example, feminists affirm some form of right to bodily integrity. The experience of aging differs vastly from one historical period to another and one culture to another, yet it can be argued that there is something similar going on, requiring interpretation, wherever people grow old. There are marked variations from one time and society to another in the meaning of experiences of sexual desire, yet as Michel Foucault discovered, some commonalities seem to persist.[40] Experiences of mortality, bodily limitation, human affiliation, humor, etc., are *in some ways* culturally invariant, as Martha Nussbaum argues in defense of Aristotle's theory of virtue.[41] And though the experiences highlighted by James Gustafson are not the same as those central to feminist theological ethics, they converge significantly in their developments of an ethics of the environment.[42]

More importantly, what is different—even profoundly different—in human experience is not thereby completely isolated and unsharable. Experience affords privileged access to some moral insights, but what is experientially perspectival can be rendered at least partially intelligible to others who lack the experience. There are all kinds of evidences of this—in the cross-cultural power of literary classics, the sheer possibility of truly vicarious experience; in the emergence of friendships across seemingly impossible divides; in the learning through second languages of what is translatable and what is not.

Feminists were once brought up short by the claims of diversity. They have since recognized that difference need not preclude community. It is not difference but the ignoring of difference that constitutes an insurmountable barrier between women with disparate experiences. Attention to diversity disallows false universalization from limited experience, but it allows new ways to common moral insight. From it emerges a requirement for the study of the causes of difference[43] and the development of skills for interacting between "different worlds."[44] Therefore, feminist theory is required to incorporate the experience of women not only as gendered but as differentiated by race, by class, and by culture; and it is finally required to include the experience of all those—women, children, and men—who suffer injustice.

Still, there remains in regard to "difference" a problem that has been less adequately addressed and resolved. What if the experiences of one person or one group lead to an ethical perspective and even specific moral rules that are not only different from another's but mutually exclusive? What if different ethical conclusions are warranted by diversity in moral experiences? Suppose, for example, that Gustafson's interpretation of experiences of human vulnerability and pain are read as contradictory to feminist theologians' interpretation of women's experiences of powerlessness and oppression? The former thus warrants, so it appears, consent to a divine being "bearing down," while the latter grounds a protest against the changeable forces of evil. This aspect of the problem of diversity leads back to my third question: How shall we discern the authority of experiences for moral discernment?

Throughout this essay's considerations of the role of experience in moral discernment has been threaded the question of authority, but some answers to the question have also been threaded throughout. From Gustafson's "priority of human experience" to feminist theologies' experientially based method and insights, from my articulation of the weaknesses of experience as a source for moral discernment yet defense of its role nonetheless, I have shown my own conviction that experience is authoritative. I do not thereby, any more than my conversation partners in this essay, maintain that only experience is authoritative or that it is ever sufficient for Christian moral discernment. I do not, any more than my conversation partners, adopt a fundamentalist view of the authority of experience. I am therefore not committed to agreeing with every conclusion that is drawn from experience—not committed, for example, to full agreement with Gustafson's understanding of God, or with every feminist theologian's interpretation of specific experiences of injustice, or even with all of my own interpretations from the past.

Decisions about whose experience and what interpretations of experience are to count in moral discernment are not without guiding criteria. Coherence of the conclusions of experience with general moral norms, intelligibility of accounts of experience in relation to fundamental beliefs, mutual illumination when measured with other sources of moral insight, manifest integrity in the testimony of the one who is experiencing, harmful or helpful consequences of interpretations of experience, confirmation in a community of discernment—all of these are tests for the validity and usefulness of given experiences in a process of moral discernment.[45] Yet experience may challenge its tests and assert an authority that modifies the prior norms that would order it. Something deeper is at stake.

Underlying all of these considerations is an understanding of authority itself. It is impossible, however, to separate the question of authority from the question of the intrinsic content or meaning of what is presented as authoritative. Hence, even if one accepts the authority of a source on some apparently extrinsic basis (e.g., that it is God's word, or that the voice of the community is determinative), this very acceptance must have meaning, must "make sense" to the one who gives it. The moral authority of any source is contingent on our recognition of the "truth" it offers and the "justice" of its aims.[46] No source has real and living authority in relation to our moral attitudes and choices unless it can elicit from us a responding "recognition." When Christian ethicists consider scripture, tradition, secular disciplines, and contemporary experience as sources, it is precisely because they find in and through these resources access to moral insight and motivation.

The reason, then, why experience may challenge other sources and the measures of its own validity is precisely because moral truth must "make sense" to us. Truth from whatever source presents itself, to use the words of Paul Ricoeur, as a "nonviolent appeal."[47] It asks for something less like a submission of will and more like an opening of the imagination and of the whole mind and heart. It can be believed only insofar as it rings true in our capacity for knowing, our moral sensibilities, our affective capacity for the good. When a deeply held conviction, grounded in our experience, appears to be contradicted by information from other sources, it must be tested against them. But if it continues to persuade us, continues to hold "true" so that to deny it would do violence to our very capacity for knowing, then it must function as the measure against which the other sources are tested. It becomes a hermeneutical key that may relativize the other sources or allow them to be interpreted anew.

This does not leave us without recourse when disagreements about experience run deep. In fact, the nature of the disagreement itself suggests at least two remedies. On the one hand, disagreement is often not about differences in experience but about whether or not some persons' experiences should be allowed at all as a source for social or communal discernment.[48] The initial requirement here is to acknowledge the importance of experience, to admit the particular experience into ethical consideration, to test it and weigh it at least as a source among sources. As a remedy, this may not resolve disagreement, but it makes more responsible the process of discernment.

On the other hand, disagreements actually lodged in contradictory interpretations of experience are not without some possibilities of adjudication. Here the requirement is communication, and the potential is for enlargement of experience and expansion of its sources for interpretation.[49] It would be naive in the extreme to suggest that all disagreements about experience are only apparent, and sufficient dialogue will in every case bring harmony. Nonetheless, what communication prevents is a premature acceptance of unbridgeable gaps. What it makes possible is the actual bringing together of diverse experiences in their concreteness and particularity. It prevents, for example, misleading interpretations of feminist ethics and of Gustafson's theocentric ethics that would conclude only to differences between dissent and consent, clarity of prophetic critique and ambiguities of moral experience, self-centered and other-centered grounds for moral obligation. It makes possible, for example, shared insights into systemic forces and individual responsibility, the relative value of particular social arrangements, the human part in a cosmic whole.[50]

But let me end where I began. Experience is essential to both moral discernment and deliberation. Its difficulties must be addressed because they cannot be allowed to vitiate its usefulness as a resource. Its significance is in its concreteness yet its potential for sharing. Its real fruitfulness depends not on the formal considerations I have offered but on its actual illumination of the matters for discernment and choice. Evidence of such illumination is available in the ongoing moral discernment of individuals and communities—and perhaps paradigmatically in the theocentric ethics of James Gustafson, the ethics of contemporary feminist theology, and the potential dialogue between them.

Notes

1. James M. Gustafson, Afterword, in *James M. Gustafson's Theocentric Ethics: Interpretations and Assessments*, ed. Harlan R. Beckley and Charles M. Swezey (Macon, Ga.: Mercer University Press, 1988), 243.

2. These meanings are selectively adapted from Karl Lehmann, "Experience," in *Sacramentum Mundi: An Encyclopedia of Theology*, ed. Karl Rahner et al. (New York: Herder & Herder, 1968), 2:307–9; F. W. Dillistone, "Religious Experience," in *The Westminster Dictionary of Christian Theology*, ed. Alan Richardson and John Bowden (Philadelphia: Westminster Press, 1983), 204–7; Antony Flew, ed., *A Dictionary of Philosophy*, rev. 2d ed. (New York: St. Martin's Press, 1984), 116–17; *The American Heritage Dictionary of the English Language*, 3d ed. (Boston: Houghton Mifflin, 1992), 644.

3. See, e.g., George P. Schner, "The Appeal to Experience," *Theological Studies* 53 (March 1992): 40–59; Donald L. Gelpi, *The Turn to Experience in Contemporary Theology* (New York: Paulist Press, 1994); Susan L. Secker, "Human Experience and Women's Experience: Resources for Catholic Ethics," *The Annual: Society of Christian Ethics* (1991): 133–50.

4. See Martha Nussbaum, "Non-Relative Virtues: An Aristotelian Approach," in *The Quality of Life*, ed. Martha C. Nussbaum and Amartya Sen (Oxford: Clarendon Press, 1993), 242–76.

5. See, e.g., Jean Porter, *Moral Action and Christian Ethics* (Cambridge: Cambridge University Press, 1995).

6. See, e.g., Gelpi, *The Turn to Experience*.

7. See, e.g., Maurice Mandelbaum, *The Phenomenology of Moral Experience* (Baltimore: Johns Hopkins Press, 1969); Jules J. Toner, *The Experience of Love* (Washington, D.C.: Corpus Books, 1968).

8. See, e.g., Sandra Harding, *Whose Science? Whose Knowledge? Thinking from Women's Lives* (Ithaca, N.Y.: Cornell University Press, 1991); Evelyn Fox Keller, *Reflections on Gender and Science* (New Haven: Yale University Press, 1985).

9. See, e.g., James M. Gustafson, *Christ and the Moral Life* (New York: Harper & Row, 1968), chap. 7; "The Place of Scripture in Christian Ethics: A Methodological Study," *Theology and Christian Ethics* (Philadelphia: Pilgrim Press, 1974), 121–45; "The Relationship of Empirical Science to Moral Thought," *Theology and Christian Ethics,* 215–28; "Theological Interpretation of the Significance of Circumstances," *Can Ethics Be Christian?* (Chicago: University of Chicago Press, 1975), 117–44.

10. James M. Gustafson, *Ethics from a Theocentric Perspective,* 2 vols. (Chicago: University of Chicago Press, 1981–1984), vol. 1, *Theology and Ethics*, 115.

11. The terminology here is mine, but I believe it is a faithful rendering of Gustafson's position—not only in *Ethics*, but earlier in, e.g., *Christ and the Moral Life*, 57; *Can Ethics Be Christian?*, 143, 176.

12. Gustafson, *Ethics*, 1:148.

13. See Gustafson, *Can Ethics Be Christian?*, 130–43.

14. See Gustafson, ibid., 176; *Christ and the Moral Life*, 57; *Ethics*, 2:144.

15. Gustafson, *Ethics*, 1:115.

16. See ibid., 1:194. The facets of "human fault" that Gustafson believes to be common to the experience of all human beings include misplaced trust, misplaced valuations of objects of desire, erroneous perceptions of the relations among things, unfulfilled obligations and duties.

17. Ibid., 1:234.

18. Ibid., 1:118.

19. Ibid., 1:3.

20. Ibid., 1:128.

21. Ibid., 1: chap. 1.

22. Ibid.

23. Ibid., 1:195–96, 225–35; 264.

24. Gustafson, *Can Ethics Be Christian?*, 138 ff.

25. Ibid., chap. 5; Gustafson, *Ethics*, 1:111.

26. Gustafson, *Ethics*, 1:91, 96, 112, 202, 271; *Can Ethics Be Christian?*, 159.

27. Gustafson, *Ethics*, 1:96, 99.

28. See summary profile of theocentric ethic in *Ethics*, 2: chap. 1.

29. James M. Gustafson, "A Response to Critics," *Journal of Religious Ethics* 13 (fall 1985): 191.

30. Gustafson, *Ethics,* 1:131–32; *Can Ethics Be Christian?*, 173.

31. Gustafson, *Ethics*, 1:131–32.

32. Gustafson, in *Gustafson's Theocentric Ethics,* ed. Beckley and Swezey, 243.

33. Gustafson, *Ethics,* 1:113, 244; *Can Ethics Be Christian?,* 158.

34. The phrase is Beverly Harrison's. See "The Older Person's Worth in the Eyes of Society," *Making the Connections: Essays in Feminist Social Ethics* (Boston: Beacon Press, 1985), 153.

35. Rosemary Radford Ruether, "Feminist Interpretation: A Method of Correlation," in *Feminist Interpretation of the Bible,* ed. Letty M. Russell (Philadelphia: Westminster, 1985), 113.

36. For examples of feminist theological and ethical efforts in these regards, see Rosemary Radford Ruether, *Sexism and God-Talk: Toward A Feminist Theology* (Boston: Beacon Press, 1983); Elizabeth A. Johnson, *She Who Is: The Mystery of God in Feminist Theological Discourse* (New York: Crossroad, 1992); Judith Plaskow, *Sex, Sin, and Grace: Women's Experience and the Theologies of Reinhold Niebuhr and Paul Tillich* (Washington, D.C.: University Press of America, 1980); Emilie M. Townes, ed., *A Troubling in My Soul: Womanist Perspectives on Evil and Suffering* (Maryknoll, N.Y.: Orbis, 1993).

37. This is an assertion of principle, not a generalization of the doctrine of a divine entity as it appears in all feminist theological writings or religious traditions. A conclusion about agreement on the principle would have to take account of the vast differences between, for example, the feminist theology of Elizabeth Johnson, on the one hand, and Mary Daly on the other. See Johnson, *She Who Is,* and Mary Daly, *Beyond God the Father* (Boston: Beacon Press, 1973), and her subsequent works.

38. Catherine A. MacKinnon, *Toward a Feminist Theory of the State* (Cambridge: Harvard University Press, 1989), 51.

39. There is not space here to provide other more specific cases in point. However, let me simply flag two issues regarding specific moral rules where experience appears to be an indispensable source. They are both issues in sexual ethics. The first is the issue of heterosexual marital intercourse when some form of "artificial contraception" is used. This issue is almost wholly unique today to the Roman Catholic tradition. One of the arguments currently offered in support of the continued official prohibition of artificial contraception is based on the supposed selfishness of married partners who use contraception. The claim is made that employing contraceptive technology to prevent pregnancy means that the love of the partners is intrinsically selfish, even exploitative (on the part of at least one of them). It takes little account, however, of the reported experience of married persons in this regard. The argument is difficult to sustain when this experience is taken seriously, for it offers the testimony of individuals who by their whole lives bear witness to unselfishness.

A second issue is that of same-sex relationships. Christian ethicists hold a number of positions on this issue, ranging from prohibition, to acceptance but as a lesser form of human relationship, to full acceptance as potentially conducive to human flourishing. Given the arguable inconclusiveness of testimony from scripture, tradition, and secular disciplines, experience appears to be a determining resource on this issue. This implies, of course, criteria for the inclusion of experience and its use in discerning this issue.

40. See Michel Foucault, *The History of Sexuality,* 3 vols., trans. Robert Hurley (New York: Pantheon Books, 1978; Vintage Books, 1988, 1990).

41. Nussbaum, "Non-Relative Virtues," 260 ff.

42. Compare, for example, the ecological ethical imperatives of Gustafson, *A Sense of the Divine: The Natural Environment from a Theocentric Perspective* (Cleveland: Pilgrim, 1994), and Rose-

mary Radford Ruether, *Gaia and God: An Ecofeminist Theology of Earth Healing* (San Francisco: HarperSanFrancisco, 1992).

43. See Mary McClintock Fulkerson, *Changing the Subject: Women's Discourses and Feminist Theology* (Minneapolis: Fortress Press, 1994). Fulkerson's analysis of the need for feminist theory to account for differences (not just to acknowledge them) is important, and it can be accepted without agreeing with her overall argument about the loss of the subject. For another analysis of difference and the possibilities of interpretation, see Joan W. Scott, "The Evidence of Experience," *Critical Inquiry* 17 (summer 1991): 773–97.

44. Maria Lugones proposes a skill that she calls " 'world'-traveling" in this regard. See Maria Lugones, "Playfulness, 'World'-Travelling, and Loving Perception," in *Making Face, Making Soul, Haciendo Caras: Creative and Critical Perspectives by Women of Color,* ed. Gloria Anzaldúa (San Francisco: Aunt Lute Foundation, 1990), 390–402. See also the discussion of this and other related matters in Janet R. Jakobsen, "Deconstructing the Paradox of Modernity: Feminism, Enlightenment, and Cross-Cultural Moral Interactions," *Journal of Religious Ethics* 23 (fall 1995): 333–63.

45. The usefulness of these tests can be illustrated effectively in relation to the experiences I have cited in note 39 above.

46. I use quotation marks for "truth" and "justice" to signal the complex issues surrounding their meaning. There is not the opportunity here to address these issues, nor, I think, the need.

47. See Paul Ricoeur, *Essays on Biblical Interpretation*, ed. Lewis S. Mudge (Philadelphia: Fortress Press, 1980), 95.

48. See again the relevance of the examples in note 39 above.

49. Proposals by feminist philosophers are particularly helpful in this regard. See, for example, Seyla Benhabib's case for a revised form of Jurgen Habermas's communicative ethics, in *Situating the Self: Gender, Community, and Postmodernism in Contemporary Ethics* (New York: Routledge, 1992). See also feminist debates on this and other proposals in Seyla Benhabib et al., *Feminist Contentions: A Philosophical Exchange* (New York: Routledge, 1995).

50. There is space here for me to be only suggestive and elliptical on these issues. Much of what I am pointing to refers comprehensively to whole theories, but interesting and less-usual places to begin dialogue might be Gustafson's analysis of problems of population and nutrition or his reflective interpretations of his experiences in World War II. See *Ethics*, 2: esp. 219–21; and "August Seventh, 1945," *Christian Century* 112 (August 16–23, 1995): 779–81.

Chapter 9

What Can Medical Science Contribute to Theological Ethics? Musings on Mortality

RICHARD B. GUNDERMAN

As a rogue medical student enrolled in James Gustafson's two-quarter seminar, "Theological Ethics: Aquinas and Barth," in the Divinity School and the Committee on Social Thought at the University of Chicago, I was occasionally asked by my more-senior and wiser fellow students what in the world I was doing taking a course in theological ethics. Knowing that the two avenues of study—biomedical science and theological ethics—are not typically pursued in tandem, they bore my eccentric presence with remarkable toleration, and kindly assumed that I had simply lost my way. My mentor and teacher, however, encouraged me to pursue the hunch that the two had something to do with each other, and, in addition to lighting the way, nudged me along to explore their common ground.

Since then, I have found myself devoting an increasing proportion of time to medical practice and research, and my opportunities for formal theological investigation have been limited. The geographic nidus at which my thoughts in this area began to take shape, Swift Hall, home to the Divinity School, alas, has become a building I rarely enter, but regularly scurry past on my way to the medical center. Far from diminishing my appreciation of the dynamic engagement possible between biomedical science and theological ethics, however, my deepening immersion in medicine, in fact, has enhanced it. In what follows, I aim to sketch out why I believe the potential for fruitful encounter between the two is, especially now, so great.

Specifically, I wish to address three broad questions, each stemming from my strengthening intuition that biomedical science has something important to say to theological ethics. First, what, broadly speaking, are the possible modes of interaction between contemporary biomedical science and theological ethics? Second, focusing on a particular and exemplary theme shared in common between the two, what sorts of material might biomedical science offer for theological reflection? Third, along what paths of investigation might this biomedical material orient the theologian? In this brief discussion, my goal is not to provide systematic answers to these questions, but to sketch out the terrain and provoke exploration.

Modes of Interaction

Beginning with the very first words of the Bible, natural science has influenced theological understanding. To say that the creation story of the book of Genesis has always seemed to readers to embody profound theological, cosmological, and anthropological truths is not necessarily to commit oneself to the proposition that our understanding of those truths has remained fixed and immutable since its earliest days. To be sure, some contemporary fundamentalists may maintain that the correct reading of the story has always been the literal one; for example, the literal interpretation that the world was made in six days, or that woman was fashioned from man as a divine afterthought, for the benefit of the male of the species. Yet most of us find that our contemporary scientific (and cultural) sensibilities render such literal interpretations of the creation account awkward and unsatisfying. Paleontology and evolutionary biology have taught us that the birth of the world required not days, but billions of years, and that the female is, by definition, coeval with the male in any sexually reproducing species.

Our understanding of the creation story has been shaped by the fruits of scientific progress. For example, our grasp of the very terms "universe" and "creation" has been altered profoundly over the centuries. At one time, the earth was regarded as the center of the universal cycle, and humankind seemed to shine forth from the pinnacle as the crowning glory of creation. Now we recognize that our planet orbits the sun; that in relation to the center of the Milky Way galaxy, our home lies in the dimly illuminated cosmic hinterlands; that even the mighty Milky Way constitutes but a small speck in an unimaginably vast expanse of intergalactic space comprising the known universe. Biologically speaking, humankind represents not the pinnacle of creation, but one of millions of species that have enjoyed a fleeting moment in the sun, destined, perhaps, to sink someday into evolutionary oblivion. To make creation subservient to human beings smacks of anthropocentrism, an outmoded point of view no longer tenable in a cosmos revolutionized by the likes of Copernicus and Darwin. edited to here

In some minds, the growth in our scientific understanding of the world, with a corresponding decline in our estimation of our own primacy within it, has resulted in a devaluation of theology. The story of creation, once framed in terms of divine grace, is now couched in the jargon of astrophysics and evolutionary biology. We write the history of the cosmos in terms of the behavior of subatomic particles and the distances between galaxies. We write the history of life on earth in terms of nucleic acids, the bearers of genetic information; random mutations, the wellsprings of variability; and selective environmental pressures, the engines of biological change. As scientists, we no longer feel the need to invoke an extramaterial animistic principle or divine agency in the processes of life. We can now offer scientific explanations not only for the history of the species down through the ages, but for the structure and expression of genetic characteristics in the growth and development of individual organisms in the present day. So successful are we in the latter sphere that we have even begun to put what we know into practice, undertaking to reconstruct the genetic endowments of a number of species, including our own.

From the vast expanse separating the cosmology of the ancient Hebrew poet(s) who composed the Genesis creation story and the authors of the contemporary scientific world view emerge many root metaphors for understanding the universal scheme—covenant, order, harmony, and adaptation among them.[1] From one point of view, the transition from covenant theology to evolutionary biology has lowered our estimation of human nature by according us a less privileged and exclusive status in the natural system. Yet during the same period, our role as actors on the natural stage has grown exponentially, affording us increasing latitude to bend nature to our own purposes.

One theological response to the winds of scientific change is that of the aforementioned fundamentalists—to cling ever more tightly to the world view implied by a literal interpretation of sacred texts. If we adopt as an article of faith the view that the world was created in six twenty-four-hour periods, then perhaps no amount of scientific evidence to the contrary need change our minds. An alternative response, favored by many in the scientific camp, is to abandon theological discourse altogether. The scientist's account may lack the human drama and moral scope of the sacred texts, but perhaps it makes up for these deficiencies in the degree of practical certainty and utility it seems to afford. On either of these opposing points of view, the choice between theology and natural science is taken to be one of mutual exclusivity—we must adopt one to the exclusion of the other, rendering us either antiscientific theists or atheistic scientists.

Between the two extremes of fundamentalism and scientism lies a middle ground, whose residents are willing to entertain the possibility that theology and natural science can engage each other in meaningful conversation.[2] On this view, theology and science are neither sworn enemies locked in mortal combat nor aliens trapped forever in idle incomprehension, and each may have something to learn from the other. In this era of unparalleled rapidity of change in our scientific understanding of the world, such a dialogue most often places theology in a responsive role. New scientific understanding of the physical laws governing the universe or the biological bases of human nature invites theology to reexamine and even revise its view of the world. Theologians will always tend to find God at work in creation, but their conception of precisely how God is at work may change, as new scientific insights into the nature of creation are achieved. From the point of view of such scientifically informed theology, natural science need not be regarded as the opponent of God's will. In fact, it may even be deemed its advocate, at least insofar as God's will is revealed by growth in our understanding of the natural order. The more deeply we understand creation, the better we understand the creator, whose imprint it bears.

To say that our theological understanding might be scientifically informed is not to say that theology is the puppet of science, or that all theological tenets are up for grabs. The idea that God intends the good of creation may, from the theologian's point of view, remain inviolable, even as scientific disciplines such as ecology stimulate revisions in our understanding of the meaning of that good. At one time, the welfare of creation seemed to consist in the unending expansion and proliferation of humankind over the face of the earth; "And you, be fruitful and multiply, abound on the earth and multiply in it" (Gen. 9:7). Uncharted oceans and continents seemed to beckon to human exploration. To such progenitors of modern science as Bacon and Descartes, Nature seemed literally to invite human conquest.

Today, by contrast, the once-inconceivable possibilities of terrestrial overpopulation and massive industrial pollution have become realities, and we recognize the potential harm that a myopic, anthropocentric perspective can wreak on the earth as a whole. In numerous cases, the recognition of such harms has spawned remarkably farsighted social and political action, as manifest in recent ecologically minded international treaties on chlorofluorocarbon (CFC) production and commercial fishing. More broadly speaking, science has helped us to realize what a complex and interdependent place the earth is, and to recognize that many apparently innocuous human actions can exert a profound and even deadly global impact, not only in the present day but for eons to come.

Science may also inform and enrich our sense of respect for life, particularly for the lives of nonhuman species. The better we appreciate the beauty and complexity of other forms of life—by gazing at them through a microscope, dissecting them at the laboratory bench, or interacting with them in the field—the more plausible it becomes that their existences embody values not wholly or strictly derivative from their instrumental value to human beings. From tiny bacteria such as E. coli to the mighty humpback whale, the more we know about other species, the more difficult it becomes to suppose that they exist merely to serve or amuse us. The more we know about their chemistry, behavior, and life cycles, the more plausible it becomes that their existences have ends or purposes of their own. Theologically, it might be said that advances in the natural sciences have helped us to better understand, and perhaps to take more seriously, our religiously grounded role as stewards of the earth.

The Contribution of Biomedical Science

In order to explore more fully the relationship between natural science and theology, let us consider in greater depth a biological problem drawn from relatively recent developments in the medical sciences. Medicine represents especially fertile ground for exploration, because it is one of the disciplines in which science most directly serves the welfare of humankind, and hence where the tension between human-centered and God-centered perspectives is most discernible. In medicine, one might say, we pursue scientific understanding in order to serve as better stewards of ourselves.

In particular, let us consider an age-old problem—one coeval with life itself, dealt with extensively in nearly all sacred texts, and a problem that constitutes one of the great existential tasks of any individual human life; namely, death. Although death has always been with us, biomedical science has of late offered deep insights into the origin, purpose, nature, and limits of death, with profound and potentially far-reaching theological implications which merit our careful consideration. What can our unfolding biomedical understanding of death teach us about the relationship between science and theology?

The Genesis creation story seems to ground death in the events leading up to humanity's expulsion from the Garden of Eden, as revealed in the words addressed to Adam: "By the sweat of your face you shall eat bread until you return to the ground, for out of it you were taken; you are dust, and to dust you shall return" (Gen. 3:19). Of course, in biological terms, mortality is not a distinctively human bane. So far as we know, death awaits every biological organism, from the simplest single-celled creatures, to complex multicellular plants and animals, to human beings themselves. From tiny airborne insects whose life spans are measured in hours to towering redwoods whose lives span hundreds of years, each species is marked by a finite term, beyond which its vital processes cannot extend. Death is coeval with life; everything that lives dies in its own time.

Consider the case of the longest-lived mammals, human beings. At first glance, we might appear to have made great strides in forestalling death. The average life expectancy in the United States has doubled since the turn of the century, now eighty-two years for women and seventy-six years for men. Yet during this time, human life's natural limits have not budged. The increase in life expectancy reflects not the fact that old people are living longer than they used to, but rather that more people are living to old age, and thereby encountering firsthand life's natural limit. The largest gains in life expectancy have resulted from reductions in infant and childhood mortality, due in large part to better living conditions and the control of communicable diseases. Even if we could cure every known disease and prevent every case of accidental death, nearly everyone would die before the 100-year mark. Tales of Methuselah's 969 years notwithstanding, the outer limits of the human life span are rigidly fixed at between 110 and 120 years. At most, only one in ten thousand persons in the United States lives beyond the age of 100.[3]

Why do we die? Aside from the myriad diseases and accidents (such as poisoning and trauma) that can cut short a human life, our understanding of the inevitability of death is currently grounded in two distinct and, to some degree, competing schools of thought. The first, which we might call the extrinsic school, holds that death results from the cumulative effects of countless insults suffered by our cells over the course of a lifetime. They die because something within or around them, including agents within our own bloodstreams, inflicts mortal damage on them.

These extrinsic agents include a variety of well-known environmental hazards. Ionizing radiation is one such hazard, which includes ultraviolet solar radiation, sources of background radiation in the earth's crust, and manufactured sources of radiation exposure, such as nuclear energy and medical X-rays. Chemical toxins may also be involved, including air and water pollutants, pesticides and herbicides ingested with food and water, and a variety of occupational and household chemical agents. Microbes may also play a role, especially the viruses, inasmuch as their infestation can produce permanent changes in cellular DNA.

Our cells are equipped with myriad mechanisms by which to repair radiation, chemical, and microbe-induced damage to our genetic material. Yet the process is not perfect, and it is possible that aging results from the gradual accumulation of extrinsically generated errors in DNA replication. One rationale for vitamin supplementation, especially such vitamins as A, C, and E, is the hope that their antioxidant properties may forestall the gradual "burning up" of our tissues, most notably DNA.

An additional extrinsic process that appears to be doing all of us in is the gradual accumulation of the by-products of cellular metabolism within and around our cells. As we age, for example, a yellowish pigment called lipofuscin slowly builds up in our tissues, including vital organs such as the brain, heart, liver, and kidneys. The longer we live, the more of this useless pigment we accumulate. As a result, more and more of our cellular living space is taken up by excess baggage, which at the very least displaces and crowds out the vital apparatus of life. This may not only interfere with such intracellular processes as the transport of nutrients and waste products, but it may also compromise the cell's function within the larger economy of the organism; for example, by causing a muscle cell to contract less effectively. It is even possible that such substances are directly toxic.

An additional line of thought on aging concerns the effects of changes in the endocrine (hormonal) and immune systems on the aging process. Could it be, for example, that aging results from a gradual breakdown in the immune system's ability to distinguish self from other, such that our bodies end up attacking their own tissues? Is the gradual "degeneration" taking place within the blood vessels, heart, brain, and joints of an elderly person in fact the result of years of "friendly fire" from the immune system's biological arsenal? Or is it possible that aging results from the progressively diminishing secretion of hormones, such as the sex steroids, growth hormone, and melatonin, by the hypothalamus, pituitary gland, and pineal gland? Recent evidence has begun to suggest that administering growth hormone to middle-aged and elderly individuals may not only halt the age-associated decline in a number of parameters of physical and biological fitness, but actually turn back the biological clock.

A second and perhaps even more intriguing school of thought on aging and death, which might be called the intrinsic school, suggests that aging and death are genetically predetermined processes. On this view, death is not the result of a gradual diminution in our powers due to years of damage and decay, but rather represents the active shutting down of vital processes. In fact, death is built into life in a particularly integral way, intertwined with the master molecule of life, DNA. On this view, the fact that every living thing eventually dies does not reflect the statistical aggregate of a lifetime of random potentially lethal events. We are not naturally immortal creatures eventually done in by accident. Rather, the very cells of which we are made appear to be programmed to fade away of their own accord, and in many cases, actively to self-destruct.

The intrinsic school is based in part on the observation made decades ago that human cell lines cultured in the laboratory can divide at most about fifty times before they grind to a halt. The older the individual from which the cells are taken, the fewer cell divisions remain. Even when protected to the maximum extent possible from all environmental insults, cells invariably seem to wear out and die.

One of the most important differences between normal human cells and cancer cells is the fact that cancer cells seem not to hear, or at least not to heed, the genetic death knell. Many types of cancer cells, grown in culture, will go on dividing indefinitely. The "immortal" cell lines used in the laboratory production of monoclonal antibodies are in fact derived from malignant lymphomas. Cancer cells exhibit a number of other aberrant biological properties as well, most notably a partial or total disregard for the normal limits on cell growth, with the result that cancerous rogue cells displace, divert nutrients from, and eventually destroy their "good citizen" neighbors. The cancer cell literally does not know when to quit. This observation seems to imply that one of the prime criteria of health among our cells is in fact knowing when to quit. The normal, healthy cell is distinguished from the cancerous cell in large part by the fact that it knows when to stop dividing and when to die.

Recently great scientific interest has been generated by the discovery of a form of programmed cell death called "apoptosis," from the Greek meaning "falling away." This process is related at least in part to a gene that seems to be shared by many species, called the myc gene. In some circumstances, such as nutrient deprivation, the myc gene is turned on, with the result that the cell appears rapidly to destroy itself. The phenomenon of apoptosis is of great interest to biomedical scientists because it may provide a genetic mechanism for the phenomenon of programmed cell death. We now know that we have genes not only for the growth, development, and maintenance of our cells and tissues, but for their destruction as well. Moreover, the myc gene may interact with other genes in such a way that the cell can perform additional functions, such as differentiation and division.

Differentiation refers to the process whereby a pluripotent cell takes on more or less irreversibly the specialized structure and function of a particular cell type. The B-lymphocyte, a type of white blood cell, may differentiate into either one of two types of cells once it has been stimulated by antigens (antibody-generating substances) in the form of the particular virus or bacterium against which it is equipped to respond. These two types are called plasma cells and memory cells. Once it is revved up, the plasma cell is a huge antibody factory, manufacturing up to thirty thousand copies per second of a particular type of immunoglobulin, although it takes about five days for this process to get fully underway. The memory cell, on the other hand, is a kind of guard cell, which remains quiescent, waiting for the organism's next exposure to that particular antigen, when it will divide, differentiate into plasma cells, and begin churning out antibodies at a furious rate almost immediately. After a time—a few days for the antibody-producing plasma cell, or perhaps decades for a memory cell—the cell will naturally die. Could it be that the same or similar genes that play an integral role in the programmed death of these cells are also necessary for their more primitive progenitors to take on their mature forms, and that a malfunction of these same genes plays a role in oncogenesis, the development of cancer?

This suggestion is especially intriguing in light of the overwhelming ubiquity of cell death in the normal biological processes of growth and development. Death is one of the most commonplace events in the biological biography of any human being. Without death, the life we enjoy would be utterly impossible. By this I do not refer to the death of the cells of other organisms, both plant and animal, which are necessary to fuel the metabolic processes of our own cells. Nor do I refer to the process of physiologic cellular attrition, whereby we shed the entire lining of our gastrointestinal tract every ten days or so and we naturally lose two million senescent red blood cells every second of our lives. I refer instead to the normal, programmed death of our own cells during the course of human development. To become what we are, untold legions of our own cells must be deliberately sacrificed.

In the process of embryogenesis, for example, we form countless cells that must be destroyed in order for normal development to occur. In the immune system, cells are produced that, if allowed to persist, would react against the antigens of our own cells, producing catastrophic autoimmune disease. One of the functions of the thymus, an organ in the upper chest that is prominent in size at birth but itself involutes by the time of adulthood, is to act as the theater in which these renegade cells are culled out. In the course of embryogenesis, we form a variety of structures, such as a primitive tail, which recapitulate our phylogeny but have no business in the mature human form. At least two separate forerunners of our mature kidneys are formed during the course of embryonic development, only to be destroyed. The brain forms a terrific excess of neurons during the first few years of life, many of which will never find a place in the integrated circuits of our mature nervous systems. In each of these cases, the redundant cells must be done away with, in a process best portrayed as wholesale slaughter.[4] In each case, the autonomous "falling away" of the redundant cells themselves seems to play a crucial role.

Let us move from the intimate theater of biomolecular and cellular development to the wider arena of evolution. In the view of many contemporary biomedical scientists, the utter necessity of death extends beyond the spheres of molecular biology and embryogenesis to permeate the evolutionary fabric of life. This elucidates one of the central paradoxes in contemporary theoretical biology. On the one hand, we attempt to understand biological structure and function in terms of their contribution to the survival of the organism. On the other hand, we recognize that the death of organisms is vital to the survival of the species.

From the point of view of Darwinian natural selection, immortality and eternal youth would constitute distinctly maladaptive traits. The key feature of the Darwinian universe, as distinct from the world view that preceded it, is the fact of change. To Darwin, and therefore to us, the universe is not a largely static system established more or less in its present form on the last day of creation, with an unmoving geological stage and a fixed cast of biological characters. Rather, the world is undergoing continual evolution, both geologically and biologically speaking. Given that survival involves effort on the part of the organism, every type of organism must be prepared to adapt to changing conditions in order to survive. Typically, this adaptation involves the development of new, better adapted species out of older, less-well-adapted ones. But adaptation is always relative to the conditions at hand, which are themselves changing. Hence the degree of adaptedness of any particular type of organism is both relative and continually subject to change.

Death is necessary because new forms of biological adaptation require reproduction. Any single organism's characteristics are largely fixed, and it is only through two processes, mutation and the reshuffling of the genetic deck of cards that occurs during reproduction, that new kinds of organisms can be produced. Yet in an immortal species, continuous reproduction could occur only for a short period of time before the increasing number of organisms would outstrip the resources available for the species' survival. Immortality would place very strict limits on the reproductive capacity of every species. Over the long haul of evolution, the resultant virtual cessation of reproduction would entail the obsolescence and extinction of an immortal species, stemming from its inevitable failure to adapt to ever-changing environmental conditions. Immortality, in short, would never evolve naturally, at least not in any long-lived form.

Interestingly, nature exhibits a close inverse relation between the differing rates of fecundity of animal species and their life spans. Human beings, who produce relatively few offspring, are among the longest-lived animals. Why? It seems reasonable to suggest that our relatively low fecundity is the necessary result of the relatively lengthy period of human gestation and the unparalleled period of nurturance and education required before a newborn human is able to live independently. Each new human life requires so much care that we cannot afford to produce many offspring, and adults must live long enough—but just long enough—to ensure that that process of rearing offspring to maturity is completed.

Interestingly, the increase in life expectancy in the United States and similar nations has been paralleled by an increase in the period of time that elapses between the birth of children and the time in life at which they become independent. In past times, when the majority of people earned their living by farming, children learned at home the skills necessary to provide for themselves, and married and had children at a relatively young age. Today the majority of adolescents not only complete twelve years of state-mandated education, but go to college as well, delaying marriage and childbearing into their third or fourth decade. In part, this may reflect the fact that young adults today feel less pressured by the prospect of their own death, and so can wait longer to have children. Moreover, thanks to lower infant and childhood mortality, fewer children need be produced to ensure that at least a few will survive into adulthood and produce children of their own. Such trends suggest that biology is not the only force at work in these matters, and that culture may play a role as well.

Theological Implications

These and other developments in our biomedical understanding of death provide provocative material for theological reflection. Whole volumes could be written on a number of the topics alluded to here. In the space remaining, however, I wish simply to begin to trace out what I regard as some of their more intriguing theological implications, albeit in somewhat tentative and incompletely developed form.

Lest the discussion seem too abstract and far-removed from the practical world of ethics, let us begin with one of the most practical problems arising from this research, that of the extension of the human life span. The pursuit of the fountain of youth is a very ancient endeavor, as can be discerned from prescriptions in ancient Egyptian hieroglyphic texts on how to restore youth to old people. In one sense, there is nothing new about the pursuit of eternal youth, and the millions of Americans who today gulp down antioxidant vitamin and mineral supplements, eschew all dietary animal protein, and slather on sun-protection lotions are doing nothing fundamentally different from their forebears, who eagerly consumed diets of human breast milk and submitted to injections of simian glandular extracts in hopes of forestalling the aging process.

What separates latter-day Ponce de Leóns from their predecessors is the remarkably high scientific likelihood that their efforts may finally meet with success. From the point of view of the extrinsic school's approach to aging and death, it may prove possible to remove many of the damaging agents to which we are exposed, or at least to counteract their effects. If aging is accelerated by air and water pollutants, food additives, and exposure to ionizing radiation, then we will devise technological means of removing the offending agents, or at least of shielding ourselves from them more effectively. If aging stems in part from a "deficiency" of growth hormone, then we will inject whatever quantity of the substance is required into our bodies to forestall or reverse the process. Most promisingly, if, as the intrinsic school of aging would suggest, aging is due to the switching on of an alarm of self-destruction in our genetic clock, then we will find some technological means of resetting the clock, preventing the alarm from sounding, or stopping our bodies from paying any heed to its call.

In many respects, aging and death have become biomedical problems awaiting biomedical solutions. One of the National Institutes of Health is the National Institute on Aging, symbolizing the fact that we are busily ferreting out the roots of aging at the laboratory bench. Aging has come to be regarded by many of us as a kind of disease. Death is an obstacle to be overcome, a problem to be solved, not a fact of life to be faced up to and meditated upon. In our noble pursuit of cures for all manner of disease, we have become scientific meliorists, expecting to find a technological fix even for our universal mortal affliction. The question is less "Do we want to live forever?" than "What do we have to do to achieve immortality?" The most urgent question is, "Will we find the cure for mortality in time; that is, within *my* lifetime?"

One obvious sense in which theology may have a role to play in the scientific endeavor to conquer death is in helping to trace out the ethical and more-broadly human implications of that endeavor. What does it say about us that we fear death so much? What implicit view of the human good does that endeavor entail? Were such technology to become available, who would receive it, and at what cost? What might be the effects of widespread extension of the human life span on the family and society? How would it impact future generations, or the lack thereof? Theology's unique contribution would be to consider such questions within an even larger framework— namely, their implications within the larger framework of God's plan for creation.

Although these ethical questions possess considerable intrinsic fascination and would require close attention in any complete exploration of the implications for theological ethics of our evolving biomedical understanding of death, an even more interesting line of inquiry for present purposes concerns the nature of the "life" we are attempting to preserve. Theology, too, has long concerned itself with the problem of death. The Bible contains many passages dealing with immortality. The Wisdom of Solomon counsels, "The love of wisdom means the keeping of her laws; to keep her laws is a warrant of immortality; and immortality brings a [person] near to God" (6:18). In the New Testament, the promise of eternal life seems to be one of the fundamental claims of Christianity. In John 3:16 we are reminded that God, in divine love, gave Christ to the world so that all who believe in God "may not perish but may have eternal life." Jesus Christ is portrayed as a life-giving figure, one who not only heals the bodies of the sick, but enjoys power over death itself, and even raises the dead back to life. Jesus' own resurrection from the dead can be regarded as the quintessential victory over death to which all Christians in some way aspire, and has served since its occurrence as the cardinal belief of the church.

Hearing a scientist talk of the technological realization of the biblical promise of immortality, a theologian might ask: In what respect(s) can the biomedical assault on aging and death be likened to the discussion of eternal life in the Bible? Do they represent competing means of achieving the same end? To what degree would the technological extension of the human life span represent a fulfillment of the biblically grounded thirst for eternal life? If the degree of overlap between the two is high, then are we perhaps on the verge of a virtual obviation of the need for religion, insofar as we soon may develop a technological surrogate through which to achieve its highest aspiration?

If the biblical and biomedical conceptions of eternal life are fundamentally distinct in some way, where do the roots of that distinction lie? What differentiates the supernaturally derived eternal life of which Jesus and his followers spoke from the quest for a scientifically based indefinite reprieve from our earthly death sentence? Most importantly, in what respects is the "risen life" of Christians essentially distinct from the lives many human beings are now leading, and therefore unattainable on the basis of a mere prolongation of their duration?

A second, less contentious topic for theological reflection growing out of our increasing scientific understanding of death is our sense of measure about creation, ourselves, and our place within the larger scheme of things. Biology can be a fascinating and illuminating area of study for the theologian. Through study and association with the anatomy, functions, and habits of life of various species of organisms, our appreciation for the beauty and complexity of other living creatures deepens. We acquire more knowledge of what these creatures do with their lives, and thereby come to an understanding of what their lives are about, and in what their good or flourishing might consist. Zoo exhibit designers, for example, have learned a great deal about how better to care for animals in captivity by virtue of having studied them more carefully in their native environments. As a result, barren and sterile cages have been replaced by complex and nurturing habitats.

These principles apply not just to individual animals, but more broadly to whole communities of organisms, ecosystems, and perhaps to the earth as a whole. Death is ubiquitous in nature; and everywhere we turn, we find the death of some organisms or perhaps even whole species playing a role in the larger biological economy. Every living thing must obtain raw materials and energy with which to fuel its activities, to rebuild itself, and to reproduce. Plants, through the process of photosynthesis, can obtain that energy without the sacrifice of other living forms. Human beings and other animals, however, can only live by tapping into the life substance of other creatures, meddling with their reproduction, harvesting the products of their bodies, and often bringing about their death in order to sustain our lives. Everything we consume—from seeds, to whole plants, to the products of other animals, such as milk and fur, to flesh itself—involves the appropriation of another creature's vital powers for our own. As the creatures at the very top of the food chain (at least until we expire), we are in some respects the greatest debtors of the living world. Death has been woven into the fabric of nature in part so that we may live.

As we have seen, the ubiquity of death extends in the opposite direction as well, into the inner life history of every human being. The "wholesale slaughter" of cells and tissues that comprises many chapters in the biography of our growth and development demonstrates that the death of some parts is often necessary for the larger whole. Not only cells and tissues but entire primitive organs are painstakingly manufactured, only to be completely discarded in the course of normal development. The entire linings of the gastrointestinal and integumentary systems are constantly being shed, and the immune system never ceases sending battalions of cells on suicide missions in order to protect the whole. Cells lining the respiratory tract that become commandeered by viruses during a bout of cold or flu cannot be cured and must be eliminated, their place in line being taken by reinforcements from the rear. So, too, precancerous and cancerous cells must be dispensed with quickly, before they gain a foothold and begin to undermine the life of the whole organism.

Evolutionarily speaking, death is positively vital to the well-being of any species. In anything but a completely static and therefore dead world, a community of immortals cannot long remain optimally adapted to its environment and will be replaced by an evolving and therefore mortal species. Of course, that very process of continual evolution presupposes not only the death of individuals, communities, and whole civilizations, but the death of species themselves. To survive, they must eventually give rise to organisms different from themselves, who, though descended from them, are so different in anatomical and functional respects that they merit designation as separate species. The life span of the members of a species must be long enough to ensure the success of the next generations but not so long that it begins to impede their progress. Each generation must eventually give way to the next.

In each of these respects, death is something we cannot live without. If we gaze on these biological principles intently enough, we may recognize that a certain circumspection is a natural lesson of life. Our time on this earth is limited, and necessarily so. Health, differentiation, and death are bound together. The healthy cell is the cell that gives up its immortality for the sake of taking on a particular identity within the larger organism, as a muscle cell, a glandular cell, a gamete, or neuron. With the exception of relatively small populations of stem cells, which are continually giving rise to cells that undertake the long process of growth and differentiation, the mutant cells that refuse to differentiate—or worse yet, cells that undergo dedifferentiation from the mature to the primitive, and thereby seem to achieve a certain measure of immortality—are in fact renegades, marauders, cancerous cells, which threaten to undo the delicate balance and order of the whole organism, and send the whole thing crashing down. They perform no useful function, leading a purely parasitic and destructive existence. The biology of the healthy organism teaches us the value of the natural limits on our regenerative and reproductive powers, and more broadly speaking, the value of respecting limits and knowing our place.

A third and final respect in which our growing biomedical understanding of death deserves theological attention is the nature of our sense of respect for life. This subject brings together all that we have discussed to this point. Yet there is an additional sense in which it beckons us to venture further still. It invites us to reflect more closely than ever before on the ways in which life is deserving of our respect.

A question posed in many great ancient texts, including the Old and New Testaments, Homer's *Iliad*, the Greek tragedies, and the dialogues of Plato, is the following: What in life remains of enduring value even in the face of unavoidable death? In spite of the sense of measure and deepened appreciation for the limits of life that biological study may afford the theologian, biology and cosmology also may seem to undermine the sense of meaning and transcendent purpose that many theologians find in life. One could argue, as does Job, that death is the great equalizer; that it comes to good and bad alike; and that all our earthly struggles for possessions, honor, goodness, and love eventually come to naught. In the end, the long-sighted biologist might say, possessions are distributed or crumble, the body itself becomes fodder for vermin, children forget who their grandparents and great-grandparents were, acts of goodness are ground to dust by the weight of succeeding events, the great songs of virtue are lost, and both lover and beloved sink into the uncaring sea of time.

One day, the whole species of humanity will fade into oblivion. Eventually, the cosmologist might add, the whole world will cease to exist, consumed in the expanding flames of our own sun as it begins to exhaust its atomic fuel and burn itself out. It appears likely that even the universe itself may eventually grind to a halt, as the second law of thermodynamics exacts its inevitable toll. Nothing endures forever.

Death, complete stasis and disorganization, will come, not only to each of us, but to our families, communities, nations, cultures and civilizations, to our species, to our phylum and kingdom, to life on earth, to the earth itself, our galaxy, and, perhaps, even to the whole universe. Viewed from such a perspective, all human life, no matter how prolonged its youth, would appear fleeting, and even our most heroic efforts at conquering death would seem futile, perhaps even vain and contemptible. Regarding the world from this ultimate scientific perspective—a point of view attempting to encompass both biomolecules and galaxies, both our own biographies and the history of the universe, enriched by innumerable marvelous and deeply revealing scientific discoveries—theologians may arrive not so far from where we started, face to face with mortality and the fearful sensation of the divine breath upon us. This, perhaps, is the surest foundation for the theologian's respect for life—the fear of God.

Notes

1. Stephen Toulmin, *The Return to Cosmology* (Berkeley: University of California Press, 1982).

2. James M. Gustafson, *The Contributions of Theology to Medical Ethics* (Milwaukee: Marquette University Press, 1975).

3. Sherwin Nuland, *How We Die: Reflections of Life's Final Chapter* (New York: Knopf, 1994).

4. Lewis Thomas, *The Youngest Science: Notes of a Medicine Watcher* (New York: Viking, 1983).

Chapter 10

Descriptive and Normative Uses
of Evolutionary Theory

STEPHEN J. POPE

According to evolutionary theory, selection pressures have broadly shaped basic human psychological dispositions and capacities which are manifested in a very broad range of behaviors across multiple contexts. While not directly theological, this claim and important implications that follow from it bear significantly on theological ethics, at least for those who believe that moral reflection must take into account the best available knowledge of human behavior. How this source is to be "taken into account" is, of course, disputed and will be the focus of this essay.

Can evolutionary theory be employed to provide justification for ethical claims? This essay examines various answers to the question by analyzing the writings of several prominent and representative "moralists" from various fields (law, psychology, and political theory) who reflect on morality from the point of view of evolutionary theory.[1] The great stir caused by the arrival of sociobiology in the mid-1970s reflected a strong reaction against the attempt to put evolution to ethical use. Sociobiology was most heavily criticized for failing to acknowledge the "fact-value" gap.[2] Repeated criticism of the presence of the "naturalistic fallacy" in sociobiology over the past twenty years has indeed made an impression, but has it notably improved the moral writings of sociobiology as a result? More aware of the dangers of the naturalistic fallacy, do sociobiologists now exhibit more careful interpretations of the relation between nature and morals? As I will argue below, unfortunately sociobiologists are not much more helpful now than they were twenty years ago, primarily because their scientific interpretations of human behavior are not balanced with complementary reflection in ethical theory. I will also claim, however, that analysis of current writings in sociobiology do provide some indications of what constitute more adequate ways of relating science and ethics, and, in particular, normative and descriptive uses of evolutionary theory.

The current spectrum of views on this topic in sociobiology ranges from the "normativists," who argue that science plays a crucial role in ethical justification, to the "instrumentalists," who reject this claim. Though authors along this spectrum differ strongly over whether ethics can in theory find ethical justification from science, in practice all of them operate with the assumption that the epistemological validity of ethics depends on finding a basis in scientific facts. For the most part, they have not been informed by or impressed with recent developments in the philosophy of science.[3] If ethics can be grounded in science, it is valid; if it cannot, ethics is reducible to private opinion. The use of ethics by science is in part a function of how ethics and morality are conceived. My view is that moral claims tend to be supported as part and parcel of a complex and interdependent "web of beliefs"[4] rather than as moral conclusions produced by a self-contained, logical system or by simple and straightforward procedures of deduction or induction. A wide variety of sources can and do function as forms of support for ethical positions. Science is one of these, to be sure, but it is only one from among a number of relevant sources. Though not sufficient for ethics, science can and often does shape operative views of human motivation, moral dangers, and moral possibilities.

Evolutionary Ethics

When sociobiology emerged two decades ago, its most distinctive feature was its intent to employ evolutionary views of human nature as the basis for a new scientifically based ethic. This general approach was not novel, of course, resembling as it did various nineteenth-century attempts to realign morality with the discoveries and theories of Darwin.[5] Herbert Spencer's *The Data of Ethics* was the most famous of such efforts because it featured prominently as the object of attack G. E. Moore's *Principia Ethica*, but there were many others.[6] Nineteenth-century efforts to base ethics on biology were the precedent for sociobiology in this regard, but the roots of the quest for an indubitable bedrock of scientific certainty on which ethics can be constructed reach back to Descartes. In our day many sociobiologists do not expect to find "certainty" in science. They recognize that scientific claims are provisional, acceptable for a time but always subject to possible falsification by further findings. Early sociobiolgists did, however, maintain that sociobiology provided objective knowledge of human nature, which they regarded as crucially significant for the renovation of ethics.

In his groundbreaking and highly controversial book, *Sociobiology*, E. O. Wilson predicted boldly that sociobiology increasingly would be able to explain human behavior and to understand the biological causation of "standards of good and evil."[7] If we were to ask the question, with James Gustafson, "What do we value about the human?"[8] Wilson's answer would be clear: Despite what people say, what they "really" value about the human is reproductive fitness. Sociobiology, he promised, would eventually provide "a precise account of the evolutionary origin of ethics and hence explain the reasons why we make certain moral choices instead of others at particular times."[9] His next effort, the Pulitzer Prize–winning *On Human Nature*, went even farther, claiming that sociobiology could not only explain the origin of moral values but also provide a solid basis from which "to elect a system of values on a more objective basis"[10] and to "make possible the selection of a more deeply understood and enduring code of moral values."[11] Science here was fundamental for providing the warrants upon which moral claims can be placed.

Science in this view was the basis for normative as well as purely descriptive inquiries into morality; indeed, for Wilson norm and description were fused together. He believed that his evolutionary understanding of human nature warranted the three central values that formed the core of his new moral code—the survival of the human gene pool, the preservation of diversity in the gene pool, and universal human rights. The last, justified by Wilson as the basic prerequisite for the "mammalian imperative" of reproduction, indicates Wilson's divergence from the social Darwinian endorsement of the "survival of the fittest" as social policy. A number of other secondary values also evolved as "enabling mechanisms for survival and reproductive success,"[12] for example, "exaltation from discovery . . . triumph in battle and competitive sports . . . the stirring of ethnic and national pride,"[13] etc. Why these kinds of behavior or goods "trump" others is never explained. Wilson moved quickly from "evolved" to "required" or "ethically justified" without recognizing the various complexities involved in so doing. James Gustafson has observed that Wilson's moral evaluation and normative prescriptions do not follow necessarily from his descriptions of human evolution,[14] and that he naively assumed that "the explanation of life serves as sufficient ground for interpreting its meaning."[15]

As every reader will know, Wilson and his followers received sharp and well-deserved criticism for its naive genetic determinism, simplistic reductionism, and "Panglossian adaptionism." Most important for our purposes, sociobiology was chastised repeatedly for committing the naturalistic fallacy, the illicit attempt to justify ethical prescriptions simply on the basis of purely descriptive claims about the evolutionary process. Wilson's "evolutionary ethics" wrongly assumed that behavioral "adaptiveness" is sufficient grounds for ethical justification.[16]

Instrumentalism

Recognizing the profound naiveté of Wilson's crude naturalism, chastened sociobiologists came to argue that ethics and biology are separate intellectual domains, each of which is required to follow the mandates of its own respective discipline. Even Wilson himself came to hold that "[t]he naturalistic fallacy has not been erased by improved biological knowledge, which still describes the 'is' of life but cannot prescribe the 'ought' of moral action."[17] In response to the charge of naive naturalism, the sociobiologists have attempted to account for the role of culture and socialization in human behavior.[18] Instrumentalists succeeded the advocates of evolutionary ethics. They accept the descriptive and explanatory account of human nature offered by sociobiology (though sometimes under different designations, like "behavioral ecology," "Darwinian anthropology," or "evolutionary psychology") but they are more reluctant regarding its moral application. They believe that knowledge of underlying psychological structures that constitute human nature can be used to modify and improve human behavior. What Wilson would unite, the instrumentalists would separate: means and ends, science and values, the "is" and the "ought." Instrumentalists thus repudiate all attempts to construct a "biology of ethics" and to use biology as the foundation for ethics.

One year after the publication of *On Human Nature*, evolutionary psychologist Donald Symons published a fascinating instrumentalist monograph entitled *The Evolution of Human Sexuality*, which examined in great detail psychological traits that the author believed were adaptive for Pleistocene human beings and that continue to influence human behavior in the present. Symons suggested that a degree of psychological malleability allows us to act in ways that run counter to our evolved propensities. Unlike Wilson, he both took into account degrees of human freedom and culture and avoided all discussion of normative ethics, save the suggestion at the end of his book that "Perhaps it is not excessively naive to hope that a creature capable of perceiving the plowshare in the sword is also capable of freeing itself from the nightmare of the past."[19]

A more recent book by Professor David Buss of the University of Michigan, *The Evolution of Desire*, elaborates on the line of "evolutionary psychology" initially developed by Symons. Its central point is that men and women are characterized by inherent psychological differences, particularly in patterns of "mate selection." Buss's book argues that male mate selection has evolved to be relatively more attracted to youth and physical beauty, and female mate selection to be relatively more attracted to social status and economic success. Psychological sex differences extend to a number of distinct tendencies—for example, male proclivities for casual sex, desire for sexual variety, and visual arousal (though both sexes, it should be noted, have a natural capacity for casual sex and "temporary mating" within their evolved repertoires).[20]

> Men and women face different forms of interference with their preferred sexual behavior and so differ in the kinds of events that trigger powerful emotions such as anger and jealousy. Men and women differ in their tactics to attract mates, to keep mates, and to replace mates. These differences between the sexes appear to be universal features of our evolved selves. They govern the relations between the sexes.[21]

Feminist critics have registered doubts about the scientific status of various behavioral patterns that are said to have been established by evolution and rooted in genes.[22]

There seems to be no reason why widely observed behavior patterns are necessarily genetically programmed. Buss does not intend, however, to argue that genes control behavior or that the tactics observed in social interaction between the sexes is really caused by genes. It is enough for him to hold that observable patterns of interaction reflect what would be, in fact, in the reproductive self-interest of their agents. He believes that a strong convergence of many different pieces of empirical evidence gathered in extensive surveys across a variety of cultures point to the evolutionary origins of some of the fundamental differences between the sexes. Buss does not attempt to examine the particular biochemical mediation of genotype to various aspects of human behavior. Feminists, of course, might find this a case of question-begging since many other kinds of behavior that never come to pass also would have promoted reproductive self-interest.

In any case, it should be noted that his account of sexual desire intends merely to describe human nature without presuming to prescribe moral norms for sexual activity or gender roles. From a scientific view, "there is no moral justification for placing a premium on a single strategy within the collective human repertoire."[23] Males and females have very different sexual strategies. These selfish mechanisms lead to frequent conflict among married couples over sexual accessibility, the allocation of money and other material resources, the investment of time and effort, and degrees of emotional commitment. They also lead to various forms of mutual deception and sometimes sexual infidelity, abuse, harassment, and abandonment. It certainly is not, as Buss puts it, "a pretty picture," but knowledge of these psychological mechanisms and of the "crucial contexts that activate" them brings both understanding and a basis for intervention and modification (and improvement) of behavior.[24]

One brief, if massively oversimplified, example suffices to illustrate this instrumentalist approach. Buss argues that, "A man's ability and willingness to provide a woman with resources are central to his mating value, central to her selection of him as a marriage partner, central to the tactics that men use in general to attract mates, and central to the tactics that men use to retain mates."[25] Male "provisioning failure" is a cause of marital dissolution worldwide, but female "provisioning failure" does not constitute legitimate grounds for divorce in a single known culture.[26] A man who is unable to supply resources to his wife and children fails to fulfill a standard by which he was initially selected as a mate, and his inability to do so contributes very significantly to the "defection" of his wife and to the dissolution of his marriage. Knowledge of the evolved psychological mechanisms underlying this pattern can alert those who decry marital dissolution to the need for social and economic policies that would promote employment, economic self-sufficiency, and other conditions that would increase males' ability to provide resources to their mates. Understanding the conditions that tend statistically to favor various "mating strategies" (like when it may "pay" a female to "defect" from one mate and become available for another) provides "the possibility of choosing which to activate and which to leave dormant."[27]

Knowledge of our evolved human psychological propensities brings with it a "powerful fulcrum for changing behavior," in that it helps to identify which environmental conditions will most likely discourage the kinds of behavior we judge to be undesirable and which will most likely facilitate the opposite. Buss's instrumentalism, however, is not as pure as it initially appears. He announces the separation of morality from science, but then proceeds to draw moral lessons from his descriptions of natural human proclivities. These lessons are both negative, as when he criticizes the monogamous norm for stifling sexual expression, and positive, as when he correlates an ethic of toleration with natural sexual diversity.

Instrumentalists who are more consistent than Buss disallow not only the "deduction" of ethics from science but also other positions which suggest that prescriptions are in any way dependent on scientific descriptions of the human. Normative ethics is independent of science, and the former is not in any way justified by appeals to the latter. Thus the question, "What do we value about the human?" needs to be divided into the empirical question, "What *do* we value, as a matter of fact?" and the moral question, "What *ought* we to value?" Science can provide some insight into the former but none into the latter.

John H. Beckstrom, emeritus professor of law at Northwestern University, strives to be an instrumentalist of the strict observance. He is acutely aware of the dangers of grounding ethics in biology, and he is especially concerned to appropriate the valid insights of sociobiology while avoiding the pernicious tendency of the "pop sociobiologists" to commit the naturalistic fallacy. To his credit, he is properly suspicious of attempts to use claims about human nature to give legitimacy to unjust social policies or narrow moralism, and he believes that the knowledge afforded by sociobiology provides information that can be used to resist external control and to support greater autonomy (an indication that his own position may be far from value free).

Rather than simply divorcing biology from ethics, however, his recent book, *Darwinism Applied: Evolutionary Paths to Social Goals*,[28] distinguishes proper from improper applications of neo-Darwinian biology to human affairs. Beckstrom aspires to convince his readers that evolutionary biology is relevant to human affairs, but not in the simplistic way that has been the appropriate target of so much trenchant criticism. Evolutionary biology is improperly used, Beckstrom argues, whenever it is employed to justify social goals or moral values, whether progressive or conservative in nature. He argues, for example, against Wilson, that one cannot infer the *value* of respect for genetic diversity from the *fact* of potential adaptation, because the former is premised on a silent assumption that survival is a moral value—a belief not justified by evolutionary biology alone.

Beckstrom's ambition for the instrumental value of sociobiology rivals Wilson's. "Large leaps forward in evolutionary learning in the last few decades," he writes, "have brought us to the beginning of an era where science may be able to offer social planners advice on how to reduce or even eliminate a large array of social problems."[29]

Evolutionary biology can reveal the best means to predetermined goals (i.e., which "behavioral mechanisms" can be "triggered" to obtain the goals we seek); it can act as a travel agent who provides the most efficient route for destinations that the traveler has chosen in advance.

For all its ambitious language, however, the actual content of what in evolutionary theory Beckstrom finds relevant to human behavior is disappointing. The practical solutions to social problems he proposes are not significantly enhanced by sociobiology. For example, he argues that one way to decrease the incidence of rape is to increase the severity (and the public perception) of the prescribed penalty paid for it,[30] that one way to reduce street crime is to place more police officers on the street,[31] and that one way to decrease the incidence of child abuse by emotionally immature parents is to encourage postponement of childbearing.[32]

Other proposals are less consonant with common sense—for example, his suggestion that one way to reduce child abuse by step-parents would be to encourage single parents to marry one of their in-laws (who, because of the genetic link, would have a significant incentive to care for these children). Still other proposals approach the bizarre—for example, that we might solve collective conflicts by attempting "to get everyone on both sides of a potential conflict speaking the same language with the same accent." Indeed, he writes, "One universal language is no longer farfetched."[33] Perhaps it is true that people are less likely to kill those whom they identify as close genetic kin, but "tricking" the "kin recognition mechanism" through lessons in Esperanto can hardly be the most effective means of attaining conflict resolution between contesting individuals or groups.

These serious flaws notwithstanding, Beckstrom's central claim, that it is improper to attempt to employ science to justify moral values and social goals, is representative of a broader tendency in recent sociobiology and ought to be examined in its own right.[34] Beckstrom takes what he assumes to be the definitive arguments of David Hume and G. E. Moore to establish the legitimacy of what amounts to a "sanitizing" principle—"No 'ought' from an 'is'"—that enables him to identify and then reject fallacious inferences from nature to ethics.[35] Science can provide reliable accounts of causal factors lying behind human behavior but, Beckstrom warns, its competence does not extend to rendering ethical justification for moral values.

Underlying this position are two undefended epistemological assumptions: that science is purely explanatory and that normative ethics simply cannot be justified at all, by any sources whatsoever. Both assumptions are questionable, to say the least. The former has been subject to vigorous criticism over the last fifty years.[36] The latter is based on the undefended assumption that if true knowledge is found in science, it cannot be found in any other sources. Rather than the kind of objective reference to truth or falsity that one finds in the natural sciences, he maintains, social morality is "largely a matter of personal values and tastes."[37] Science alone is regarded as competent to establish facts and to differentiate them from mere subjective opinions. This positivism is thus joined to ethical subjectivism, which regards morality as nothing more than the collection of purely subjective judgments.[38]

This subjectivist understanding of morality is odd even from a sociobiological perspective. Far from regarding moral conventions as a pooling of subjective preferences, sociobiology tends to view them as shaped by fitness considerations influenced by local ecological conditions (e.g., the impact of local demography on norms governing marriage, sex, and family).[39] Yet Beckstrom neither affirms nor denies that these preferences reflect fitness considerations. The status of moral conventions vis-à-vis fitness considerations is normatively irrelevant, and ignoring the adaptational advantages of various norms allows Beckstrom to avoid the impression that he believes nature can in any way be enlisted for normative purposes. The question of why anyone would care to apply sociobiology to human affairs in this nihilistic context is not addressed.

The weaknesses of the instrumentalist position are apparent. First, the instrumentalists contradict themselves in the most simplistic ways. They disavow morality and then proceed to advance moral pronouncements of various kinds from the virtue of tolerance to the need for human rights, a dangerous practice by which they attempt to appropriate the prestige of science for their own moral proposals. Second, their mechanistic language (e.g., we are "programmed to head toward a definite ultimate goal— optimum proliferation of our genetic package")[40] presents an exceedingly simple view of human motivation and behavior. Third, their mechanistic anthropology gives primacy of place to the "manipulation" of underlying "behavioral mechanisms," which is an ill-suited replacement of the traditional concerns of moral instruction, training, and exhortation—all of which have been premised on the nobility of human freedom, reason, and dignity, but are now regarded by instrumentalists as both ineffective and unnecessary. One need not deny that human nature is ordered to certain goods which include, among other things, survival and reproduction, to recognize the poverty of this highly simplistic and demeaning view of human nature.

The instrumentalist strategy advances the laudable goal of avoiding false inferences from the natural *is* to the ethical *ought,* but at the price of obscuring the ways in which normative and descriptive accounts of the human are intertwined. The image of "instrument" fails to capture the complexity of possible relations between descriptive and normative modes of reflection, and especially the ways in which they implicate one another. The moral observations and suggestions of the instrumentalists cannot be understood apart from their supporting descriptive premises, either assumed or explicit. They recognize that evolutionary biology cannot alone provide sufficient warrants for the most fundamental moral principles or values. But they fail to recognize that these principles and values cannot be established or understood without some wider interpretation of the human context from within which they emerge and take concrete form. The instrumentalist's avowed value-free stance obscures the extent to which its descriptions also include evaluative components.

Teleological Foundations

Professor Roger Masters regards the evolutionary approach to human behavior as an important source for establishing standards of social life. But, unlike Wilson, he recognizes that science alone is insufficient for accomplishing this task. His recent book, *Beyond Relativism: Science and Human Values*,[41] shares with our previous books an enthusiasm for the value of sociobiology (or "behavioral ecology," the term he prefers). Whereas evolutionary theorists like those examined above join a mechanistic view of nature with a naive naturalism in ethics, Masters connects a broadly teleological view of nature (in which mechanism is retained but complemented by finality and formality) with a eudaimonistic virtue theory. Evolved organisms, including human beings, are characterized by natural propensities, evolved species-typical tendencies to certain characteristic kinds of values. The natural teleology that is constituted by evolved organic functions points to what Roman Catholic moral theologians call fundamental "premoral values," knowledge of which is crucial to those who understand ethics in relation to human flourishing.[42]

The metaphor for understanding the relation between science and ethics that Masters prefers is that of "foundation." Masters holds that, "science and reason provide the foundation for standards of morality,"[43] that the evolutionary approach to human behavior offers a "reasonable basis for judging the rightness or justice of political institutions,"[44] and that evolutionary science "can help us to formulate more decent and humane standards of social life."[45] While he recognizes that, "moral obligations or values cannot be logically deduced from factual propositions," he also argues that, "factual or scientific propositions can and must inform the judgments about moral obligations."[46]

Philosophers have criticized extensively the use of the metaphor of "foundation" employed in modern philosophical foundationalism, which seeks an indubitable principle from which an ethical system can be logically derived.[47] The language of "foundation" is unhelpful in that it suggests a solid and irrefutable epistemological bedrock for ethics or if it is taken to imply that the foundation obviates the need for the supervening moral structure. Masters does not believe that nature acts as a foundation in either of these senses, however. Science can establish the foundations of moral values by examining the natural human ordering to certain standard goods which have proven adaptive over evolutionary history. It provides important data for moral reflection, but core disputes over the status of ethical values cannot be resolved simply by appealing to natural ends. Properly relating evolutionary theory and human life can be accomplished only through the exercise of wisdom and "reasoned dialogue among reasonable people."[48]

Science is central for Masters because he believes it can help to establish that certain ends are natural to human beings, a position contrasted with the relativistic claim that values are entirely the product of local custom. What people naturally desire reflects not simply custom but the long-term shaping of human nature by natural selection; evolution for Masters provides the key for distinguishing *physis* from *nomos*. Some of these values can be seen in what Masters calls "innate ideas," such as the inherent sense of justice which he believes is common to all human beings (though with some variation in content across cultures).

Beyond Relativism was written with the intent of using contemporary human sciences (particularly cognitive neuroscience, behavioral ecology, and mathematical theories of chaos) to demonstrate the untenability of the foundational anthropological assumptions underlying the "fact-value gap," particularly the modern mechanistic notion of nature and the complementary Lockean *"tabula rasa"* view of the mind.[49] According to Masters, modern "scientific value relativism" is based on two fundamental assumptions. First, following Locke, it holds that the variability of norms across cultures disproves the existence of a universal human morality. Second, it assumes with the positivists that truth is attained by science and that values are merely idiosyncratic "preferences." Masters responds to both claims. First, he argues that a proper philosophical understanding of nature, particularly that held by Aristotle rather than Bacon, acknowledges the variability of nature itself as well as of culture. The Aristotelian view of nature, Masters argues, supports universal values and virtues but not a set of unvarying universal norms binding on all people everywhere. (Aristotelian philosophy of nature, in other words, does not support the universality that is the goal of modern ethical theory.) Genuine diversity and relativity need not lead to moral relativism. Masters strives for a via media here, affirming the objectivity of moral values without promoting moral absolutism and dogmatism, and the need for tolerance and humility without endorsing relativism.

Evolutionary biology is regarded as the foundation for ethics in that it illumines innate behavioral predispositions toward certain core human values. Values are both grounded in our evolved natures as *Homo sapiens* and given varied expressions in different concrete cultural contexts. Human beings are construed teleologically, as moving toward desirable ends in ways suited to the varied circumstances of human lives. We naturally value family members, friends, and other reciprocators just as we naturally value security and comfort, food and drink, social approval and loyalty, etc. How natural values are exhibited varies tremendously with local conditions. The fact that we have an inherent predisposition to engage in parental care, for example, is not belied by the fact that in conditions of resource unpredictability or scarcity some human populations have engaged in infanticide. Nature itself is characterized by diversity, argues Masters, and therefore human values must be understood as both rooted in nature and manifested in diverse ways according to particular circumstances.

Abortion is a case in point. From an evolutionary standpoint, the practice of abortion can be said to be "according to nature" in cases where it promotes parental investment in other offspring. But it can also be said to "violate nature" when it contravenes parental care. How is nature a foundation for ethics here? According to Masters, nature provides guidance by indicating a ranking of preferences from more to less desirable alternatives for regulating birth in terms of their positive or negative effects on the health of women and the costs imposed on them and others. Artificial birth control is more desirable than abortion, abortion than infanticide, and so forth.[50] Values and their ranking, for Masters, are not arbitrary "preferences."

Beckstrom would argue, on the contrary, that science itself cannot provide ethical justification for valuing either the health of women or the control of social costs. For Beckstrom, one might speculate, health is a biological value but not necessarily a moral value—unless the relevant agents so choose. We have evolved to pursue these values because they favor the reproductive interests of individuals, but *knowledge of* this inherent predisposition and its evolutionary origins does not yield substantive ethical justification for *acting on* this predisposition. Science cannot prove that abortion is ethically inferior to artificial birth control; it can only show that it may be preferred on medical, biological, or other scientific grounds.

Thus while *Beyond Relativism* gives some preliminary indications of why we should not regard values as simply reducible to either arbitrary individual preferences or purely conventional mores, it does not make a satisfying case for the claim that science provides the central answer to relativism. The instrumentalists' major fault lies in not recognizing the connection between descriptions of human nature and moral prescriptions, an oversight which contributes to their failure to recognize that nonscientific sources might provide important avenues of moral wisdom. To his credit, and in contrast to the instrumentalists, Masters recognizes that science is one among a number of moral sources. He does not therefore simply dismiss the possibility that genuine moral wisdom can be attained by nonscientific circles—whether tradition, scripture, community, philosophy, or human experience. He recognizes that science alone is not definitive, but it can and often does shape operative views of human motivation, moral dangers, and moral possibilities.

Masters's flaw lies in his too easy identification of the natural and the moral. Though aware of the dangers of naive naturalism and the limitations of modern science, he strives to erect an ethical code on the basis of scientifically established "natural values." From the natural "sense of justice," he argues, we can conclude that "each of us is responsible for our moral choices," to which he adds, parenthetically, "if only because others will inevitably behave as if we were responsible."[51] The same leap is made from the "non linearity and chaos in natural phenomena [which] reminds us that many of our actions are certain to have unintended and unexpected results" to duties of toleration and forgiveness of others.[52] Finally, because the "conquest of nature" has proved to be futile, he argues, we ought to value natural justice: "[W]e are obligated, insofar as is humanly possible, to seek the just or fair resolution according to nature."[53] We have here Wilson *revividus,* though under a more sophisticated Aristotelian persona. Because the descriptive and normative are insufficiently differentiated, Masters glides back and forth from one to the other without pause. The result is less than satisfying—a return, in fact, to Wilson's projection of values onto nature.

Masters does not fulfill his agenda of using science to give foundations to moral value; nor does he demonstrate how knowledge of human nature might indicate "the proper way a person should live."[54] Perhaps science can provide interesting and significant insights into inherited human tendencies, but this is not to say that it can somehow determine for us which of these comprise the "perfection" of human nature (if, that is, by "perfection" we mean an inclusive fulfillment of moral character or something like Aristotelian *arete* rather than merely biological excellence). Even if values are somehow rooted in human nature, we are still left with the question of which values ought to be embraced and which ought to be spurned, or as Hume put it, to distinguish clearly, "the estimable qualities" and the "blamable" qualities of human beings.[55] Infanticide might be preferred by nature (our "inclusive fitness" or "reproductive interests") under certain circumstances, but the feature of being "according to nature" in these circumstances does not make it either ethically obligatory or even permissible. The same is true of adultery, lying, child abuse, theft, and a host of other vices. Even if clear agreement of natural teleology were reached, we would still have to engage in extensive ethical reflection on its moral significance. The connections between "natural ordering" and "normative" is thus more complicated than indicated by Masters.

Descriptive and Normative Uses of Evolutionary Theory

All of the recent representative efforts of sociobiology to relate descriptive and normative uses of evolutionary theory are unsatisfactory. What can we learn about appropriate uses of scientific material in moral reflection from these sources? I would like to conclude with five generalizations that can be gleaned from these writings in this regard.

First, these writings underscore the broadly accepted recognition that core disputes over ethical principles and values cannot be resolved simply by appealing to scientific description of human behavior, or even of natural ends. The instrumentalists are correct to argue that one cannot therefore "derive" ethics from nature in a direct way, that is, without any intervening ethical reflection or disciplined ethical theory. Science can provide assistance in determining the biological ends of human action, but religious and moral reflection bears the burden of discerning the morally proper ends of human action. Science cannot do the work of ethics any more than ethics can do the work of science. This is a point that continues to be insufficiently appreciated by many of those who are most impressed with the theoretical capabilities of science, including all of the evolutionary theorists discussed above.

The ethical significance attributed to science is in part a function of which wider philosophical or religious assumptions are brought to bear implicitly or explicitly on the subject matter. Despite the frequent interpenetration of normative and descriptive language in this literature, all of our authors recognize that science in and of itself does not lead to one ethical position. The same scientific description of human behavior can support quite different moral conclusions generated from different normative perspectives. A conservative Catholic or an evangelical Protestant, for example, might accept the validity of evolutionary claims about human behavior and interpret them as empirical confirmation of the depravity of postlapsarian human nature.

Second, these writings illustrate the pervasive way in which descriptive generalizations often lie behind judgments about what moral possibilities and moral expectations are appropriate to human behavior. They indicate which natural traits need to be corrected or restrained. By providing the range of values that can be regarded as viable, descriptive generalizations influence selection of ethical principles. According to Buss, for example, we ought to correct for evolved sexual strategies for dominance in males and complicity in females. We should not expect complete altruism of many people; but some people, under the right conditions, are capable of lifelong love. We should not expect unwavering monogamy and undying love in the presence of persistent male failure to provide resources or of female cuckoldry. Buss allows for the odd virtuous "high achiever," but he also expects a high frequency of vice. We may approve of honesty and fidelity, he argues, but should not be surprised when conditions encourage both ourselves and others to engage in deception and defection. In a similar vein, Masters's view of human nature as complex and variable under different ecological circumstances supports his moral principle of toleration.

Third, these writings indicate ways in which science can be used to confirm, disconfirm, or modify these background beliefs—at least to the extent to which they are subject to scientific investigation. Buss, for example, strives to correct what he thinks are descriptive errors implicit in the descriptive grounding of the monogamous norm, particularly what he takes to be the prevailing lack of awareness of the range of human sexual diversity. In so doing, Buss implicitly recognizes that moral claims often rest on implicit descriptive generalizations about human nature, which are themselves subject to scientific examination.

Fourth, these authors demonstrate the common desire for establishing a fundamental coherence between the descriptive views of human behavior based on science and the normative claims that are held in conjunction with them. Even Beckstrom, who adamantly disallows any dependence of normative discourse on science, displays a conviction that there is a fundamental coherence between his descriptive beliefs about human nature, taken from sociobiology, his moral subjectivism, and his skeptical beliefs about the nature and status of normative ethics. In some cases, the degree of coherence amounts to conceptual dependence. Buss's view of the nature of human sexuality, for example, influences not only his understanding of how prevailing mores do in fact function vis-à-vis natural sexual strategies, but it also supports his interpretation of what mores our society ought to encourage—toleration, respect, equality, openmindedness, and understanding—and which it ought to discourage—manipulation, abuse, failure of reciprocity, unjustified deception. It may also be the case that assumed moral values or disvalues also influence the development of scientific descriptions of human nature and the relative importance given to various features of human nature. In any case, both his descriptive claims about natural sexual diversity and his commitments to freedom of self-expression constitute important warrants for his appeal to loosen the traditional focus on monogamy.

Fifth, these authors exhibit the extreme difficulty inherent in attempts to establish ethical claims on the basis of scientific conclusions without explicit and more extensive ethical reflection. James M. Gustafson proposes that "we look to an ordering of nature as one basis, but not a sufficient one, for deciding what goods, for whom, and for what, ought to be pursued."[56] In this view, ethics can be informed by science but not in a way that eliminates the need for moral reflection proper.

It is interesting that though they disagree adamantly over whether ethics can in theory seek ethical justification in science, in practice all of the authors examined above assume as a matter of course that the epistemological validity of ethical judgments—or in Beckstrom's case, even the practical relevance of moral claims—ultimately rides on whether or not they can be given warrants in scientifically established facts. Masters regards science as the means for moving "beyond relativism," and presumably without science we are bereft of moral objectivity. For Beckstrom, on the other hand, ethics is relegated to the realm of the purely subjective precisely because it cannot meet the rigorous standards of scientific method. The suggestion in these authors, who are divided on so many other issues, is that ethics is significantly epistemologically dependent on science.

A more reasonable view, it seems to me, is that moral claims tend to be supported as part and parcel of a complex and interdependent "web of beliefs."[57] Rather than basing ethics in science, a more adequate approach recognizes the mutual interdependence of ethics and science and refuses either to oppose or to identify them. Evaluative positions do not stand in utter independence of descriptive positions. Descriptive and evaluative modes of reflection can be distinguished, but evaluative claims cannot be cleanly separated from any and all descriptive contexts. Our authors show that normative claims are in practice dependent on some kinds of descriptive claims. Evaluative or normative claims are always also claims about the human, and therefore we should expect to find that they implicitly rely on some descriptive assumptions about the human.

The kind of position suggested by these five generalizations is one that overlaps with important elements of the natural law tradition. This tradition places great importance on the empirical constituents of human behavior, and therefore, in principle at least, on whatever valid insights are forthcoming from science about human behavior or nature. The reversal of its teaching on the morality of usury, for example, came not from a change in ethical principles but from a development in its understanding of the empirical reality of the nature of money (i.e., that it is not simply a consumption good but also as an asset).[58]

Ethics can be grounded in knowledge of fundamental human goods, but we typically arrive at what are in fact the proper ends of human life through an intelligent grasp of the natural inclinations of human nature. Abstract knowledge of universal human goods is complemented in the concrete with the exercise of the classical virtue of prudence, or *phronesis*. The content of the more general kind of moral reflection no doubt includes various beliefs about which aspects of our natural human inclinations and our inherited behavioral repertoire ought to be approved of, acted upon, and promoted, and which ought to be inhibited, sublimated, or closely monitored. This is one important activity of what it means to be a "rational animal," constituted both by natural needs, wants, and capabilities and by intelligence, foresight, and freedom. This is one expression of the natural law as the "rational creature's participation in the eternal law."[59]

Notes

1. The scientific material examined here will be taken from sociobiology and its recent descendent, evolutionary psychology, both of which examine human behavior from the point of view of the contemporary evolutionary synthesis of Mendelian genetics and the Darwinian theory of natural selection. On evolutionary psychology, see Donald Symons, "A Critique of Darwinian Anthropology," *Ethology and Sociobiology* 10 (1989): 131–44.

2. See, *inter alia*, Gunther S. Stent, ed., *Morality as a Biological Phenomenon* (Berkeley: University of California Press, 1978).

3. For instance, an interesting treatment of these debates from a modified Lakatosian perspective is provided by Nancey Murphy, *Theology in the Age of Scientific Reasoning* (Ithaca and London: Cornell University Press, 1990). The one exception to this generalization is Roger Masters, who defends a realist position.

4. This image is used by Willard Quine, in "Two Dogmas of Empiricism," *Philosophical Review* 40 (1951): 20–43.

5. For a historical treatment, see James R. Moore, *The Post-Darwinian Controversies* (Cambridge: Cambridge University Press, 1979).

6. See Herbert Spencer, *The Data of Ethics* (New York: D. Appleton, 1895); G. E. Moore, *Principia Ethica* (London: Cambridge University Press, 1903).

7. E. O. Wilson, *Sociobiology: The New Synthesis* (Cambridge: Harvard University Press, 1975), 3.

8. James M. Gustafson, *Theology and Ethics* (Philadelphia: Pilgrim, 1974), 244.

9. Wilson, *Sociobiology*, 129.

10. E. O. Wilson, *On Human Nature* (Cambridge: Harvard University Press, 1978), 196.

11. Ibid., 208.

12. Ibid., 197.

13. Ibid., 199.

14. James M. Gustafson, "Explaining and Valuing: An Exchange between Theology and the Human Sciences," University Lecture in Religion at Arizona State University, 3.

15. James M. Gustafson, "Sociobiology: A Secular Theology," *Hastings Center Report* 9 (February 1979): 44.

16. The most systematic and comprehensive remains Philip Kitcher, *Vaulting Ambition: Sociobiology and the Quest for Human Nature* (Cambridge, Mass.: MIT Press, 1985).

17. E. O. Wilson, "The Relation of Science to Theology," *Zygon* 15 (1981): 430–31.

18. In what typified the second wave of sociobiology, Wilson collaborated with physicist Charles Lumsden to construct what they termed "gene-culture coevolution," which was one of several attempts to expand the role of culture in the evolutionary approach to human behavior. See Charles J. Lumsden and Edward O. Wilson, *Genes, Mind, and Culture* (Cambridge: Harvard University Press, 1981), and Lumsden and Wilson, *Promethean Fire: Reflections on the Origin of Mind* (Cambridge: Harvard University Press, 1983). Critics responded to this strategy by claiming that the sociobiologists continued to incorporate culture and various social factors in a merely superficial manner. For a particularly devastating critique of gene-culture theory, see Kitcher, *Vaulting Ambition*, chap. 10.

19. Donald Symons, *The Evolution of Human Sexuality* (New York: Oxford University Press, 1979), 313.

20. David Buss, *The Evolution of Desire* (New York: Basic, 1994), 215–16.

21. Ibid., 211.

22. See Ruth Bleier, ed., *Feminist Approaches to Science* (New York and London: Teachers College Press, 1986).

23. Buss, *The Evolution of Desire*, 216.

24. Ibid., 159.

25. Ibid., 177.

26. Ibid., 178.

27. Ibid., 209.

28. John H. Beckstrom, *Darwinism Applied: Evolutionary Paths to Social Goals* (Westport, Conn.: Praeger, 1993).

29. Ibid., 2.

30. Ibid., chap. 6.

31. Ibid., chap. 7.

32. Ibid., chap. 8.

33. Ibid., 94.

34. See, e.g., Mary Maxwell, *Human Evolution: A Philosophical Anthropology* (New York: Columbia University Press, 1984), 232–33.

35. Beckstrom cites Michael Ruse, *Taking Darwin Seriously: A Naturalistic Approach to Philosophy* (New York: Blackwell, 1986), 86–93, and Antony Flew, "From Is to Ought," in *The Sociobiology Debate*, ed. Arthur Caplan (San Francisco: Harper, 1978), 146–47.

36. See, *inter alia*, Richard J. Bernstein, *Beyond Objectivism and Relativism: Science, Hermeneutics, and Praxis* (Philadelphia: University of Pennsylvania Press, 1983).

37. Beckstrom, *Darwinism Applied*, 2.

38. For more adequate and interesting treatments of the relation between objectivity and subjectivity, see Michael Polanyi, *Personal Knowledge: Toward a Post-Critical Philosophy* (Chicago: University of Chicago Press, 1962), and Martin L. Cook, *The Open Circle: Confessional Method in Theology* (Minneapolis: Fortress Press, 1991).

39. See e.g., Vernon Reynolds, "The Socioecology of Religion," in *The Sociobiological Imagination*, ed. Mary Maxwell (Albany: State University of New York Press, 1991), 205–22.

40. Beckstrom, *Darwinism Applied*, 19.

41. Roger Masters, *Beyond Relativism: Science and Human Values* (Hanover and London: University Press of New England, 1993).

42. The status of teleology has of course been controverted throughout the modern period, but recently it has been undergoing a resurgence in some prominent circles in the philosophy of biology. See, for example, Ernst Mayer, *Toward a New Philosophy of Biology: Observations of an Evolutionist* (Cambridge, Mass., and London: Harvard University Press, 1988).

43. See Masters, *Beyond Relativism*, 10.

44. Roger Masters, "Evolutionary Biology and Political Theory," *American Political Science Review* 84 (1982): 204–5.

45. Masters, "Evolutionary Biology and Political Theory," 205. My emphasis.

46. Masters, *Beyond Relativism*, 45; original emphasis.

47. This notion of foundationalism is criticized ably by Jeffrey Stout, *The Flight from Authority: Religion, Morality, and the Quest for Autonomy* (Notre Dame, Ind.: University of Notre Dame, 1981).

48. Masters, *Beyond Relativism*, 152.

49. See ibid., chap. 7.

50. See ibid., 128.

51. Ibid., 155.

52. Ibid.

53. Ibid.

54. Ibid., 145

55. David Hume, "An Enquiry concerning the Principles of Morals," in *British Moralists 1650–1800*, 2 vols., ed. D. D. Raphael (Oxford: Oxford University Press, 1969), 2:60.

56. James M. Gustafson, *A Sense of the Divine: The Natural Environment from a Theocentric Perspective* (Cleveland: Pilgrim Press, 1994), 104. For an excellent discussion of this and related convictions in Gustafson's treatments of bioethics, see Gerald P. McKenny, "A Qualified Bioethic: James Gustafson and Stanley Hauerwas," *Journal of Medicine and Philosophy* 18 (1993): 511–29.

57. This image is used by Quine, in "Two Dogmas of Empiricism."

58. See John T. Noonan Jr., *The Scholastic Analysis of Usury* (Cambridge: Harvard University Press, 1957).

59. Thomas Aquinas, *Summa Theologiae*, I–II, 91, 2.

Part 2

The Moral Life

Chapter 11

Agency: Going Forward by Looking Back

STANLEY HAUERWAS

Why I Quit Worrying about Agency
and Learned to Love Stories

To be asked to think again about agency feels like an exercise in nostalgia. Nostalgia is not a bad thing, particularly in a book meant to honor James Gustafson. Of course Gustafson is anything but "in the past." He continues to write and think in a manner that rightly challenges his own students. He certainly is not in the past for me, though some might think that would be the case given what appear to be the considerable differences in how we do theology and ethics. Yet I should like to think I remain Gustafson's student at least to the extent that he has exemplified for all of us the necessity to rethink thoughts many assumed needed no rethinking.

The work of rethinking settled thoughts is not irrelevant to questions of agency or at least to the account of agency I will provide in this essay. The focus of agency often involves an attempt to suggest an understanding of the self that secures our ability to act freely or responsibly given the decisions facing us. Such a view of agency is correlative of a view of the moral life that assumes such a life is constituted by prospective decisions. In other words, the crucial task of ethics is to provide an account of reason to help the agent to make the right decision in a manner that the decision will not be determined by the agent's past decisions. In contrast I will suggest that agency names those skills necessary to make our past our own—our past often being constituted by decisions we thought at the time were "free" but which, from our current perspective, we can see were made without our knowing what we were doing when we made them. In other words I will argue that morally our lives are more properly constituted by retrospective rather than prospective judgments.

So nostalgia as a necessary component of memory is not irrelevant for any consideration of agency. Indeed, I remember vividly, in the introductory class in Christian ethics my second year in divinity school, Gustafson's lecture on H. Richard Niebuhr's account of responsiveness. He sympathetically criticized Niebuhr's account for failing to provide for our ability not only to respond but to act. I do not know if that was the beginning of my concern to develop an account of agency, but I have no doubt that Gustafson's general perspective was crucial for my attempt to recover the importance of the virtues and character. In short my own work has been made possible because of the gift and gifts of James Gustafson. Which is but a reminder that any account of agency that excludes the givens of our life, which so often come in the form of gifts, is insufficient.

Of course Gustafson would be the first to point out that his own work has in some ways been an attempt to develop the thought of H. Richard Niebuhr and in particular Niebuhr's account of the self. Many read and continue to read *The Responsible Self* as offering an alternative to other normative ethical theories. Accordingly they concentrate on the image of responsibility in the hope that such an image will produce a more adequate moral theory than deontological and teleological alternatives. Though obviously such readings of H. Richard Niebuhr are not incompatible with aspects of Niebuhr's work, Gustafson always rightly saw that insofar as Niebuhr's work can be said to have a center, that center is the "self."[1]

In his wonderful introduction to *The Responsible Self*, Gustafson observed that Niebuhr's "ethics" had as one of its purposes to aid us in our "struggle to achieve integrity. The personal situation of the moral [person] always involves an effort to come to wholeness and orderliness in life."[2] Such an ethic also is an attempt to provide us with "aid in accuracy in action" so that we might rightly describe that which we do and do not do. That was the agenda I tried to develop by employing the language of character, "vision and virtue," as I thought that might be a promising way to develop Niebuhr's and Gustafson's focus on the self.

That was how I was led to the language of agency. I thought such a language was required for giving an account of character. Accordingly I maintained, in *Character and the Christian Life,* that character is the qualification of our agency befitting our nature as creatures capable of self-determination. I was trying to have my cake and eat it to. That is, I was trying to find a way to sustain an account of moral continuity while not having our lives "determined" by our character. After all, it seemed that character had to qualify something, and I took that something to be our irreducible agency. I was trying to split the difference between Ryle's *Concept of the Mind* with its behaviorist implications and more-Kantian accounts of the self that assumed that some aspect of the self must remain free from its own determination.

In order to try to sustain such an account of agency, I was drawn to philosophical work in action theory. If actions had an irreducible character, then some account of agency was implied that could avoid dualistic and behavioristic understandings of the self. I remember that, at the time, Gustafson was quite skeptical about my attempt to develop a philosophical argument in support of agency that did not require an engagement with psychological and social factors that shape who we are. He was right to be skeptical, but my mistake was fundamentally philosophical.

I mistakenly had accepted the presumption of those who worked in action theory that a concept of agency could be derived from the notion of action *qua* action. Such analysis presupposes that "action" or "an action" is a coherent and conceptually primitive notion, but that was simply wrong. As I would later learn from MacIntyre:

> The concept of an intelligible action is a more fundamental concept than that of an action as such. Unintelligible actions are failed candidates for the status of intelligible actions; and to lump unintelligible actions and intelligible actions together in a single class of actions and then to characterize action in terms of what items of both sets have in common is to make the mistake of ignoring this. It is also to neglect the central importance of the concept of intelligibility.[3]

What MacIntyre helped me see is that we do not need an account of agency in itself to understand our ability to acquire character. Rather character is the source of our agency, that is, our ability to act with integrity. Interestingly enough, this puts me much closer to my other conversation partners in *Character and the Christian Life*, that is, Aristotle and Aquinas. We often forget that they had no account of agency or the self as such. Rather they discussed the kind of issues we associate with the language of agency in terms of the voluntary and the involuntary. They needed no account of agency or the self to insure our ability to act in a manner in which the virtues can be acquired. I began to understand that if the significance of habituation is appreciated, then questions of agency become secondary.[4]

This also helps to explain why I quit thinking about agency and began to think more about the narratives that constitute our lives. MacIntyre's account of intelligible action is a reminder that our ability to understand and identify what we are doing or what someone else is doing requires that we be able to place that episode in the context of a narrative. That such is the case is a reminder that action itself has a historical character. "It is because we all live out narratives in our lives and because we understand our own lives in terms of narratives that we live out that the form of narrative is appropriate for understanding the actions of others. Stories are lived before they are told—except in the case of fiction."[5] I have tried to exhibit MacIntyre's point by telling the story of how I mistakenly thought I needed an account of agency to develop lessons I thought I had learned from Niebuhr and Gustafson. The telling of the story entailed no agency more determinative than the skills the story itself makes possible.

The Postmodern Turn

The story I have just told occurred prior to what we now characterize as the "postmodern" turn. Yet the development of postmodern accounts of the self or, perhaps

more accurately, postmodern doubts about the self, helps me understand better why I
had quit worrying about questions of agency, particularly from a theological point of
view. For it is my own view that the doubts that postmodern thinkers have cast on
questions of agency are a great theological resource for those of us committed to providing accounts of the Christian moral life in terms of the virtues and character. I am
aware that such a suggestion will strike many as odd if not absurd given the antitheo-
logical stance of many postmodern thinkers, but I hope to show that the postmodern
turn was inevitable.

Put in quite general but, I believe, instructive terms, the antihumanism associated
with Nietzsche and Foucault is the only kind of atheism possible in modernity. Using
MacIntyre's terms, the encyclopedists—that is, those committed to the Enlightenment
project—could not help but produce the genealogist.[6] For if it was the project of the
encyclopedist to put the human in the place of God, it was the task of the genealogist
to be the thoroughgoing atheist, desiring no god including the human. If it is history
all the way down, it is equally the case in reference to the self that it is "masks" all the
way down. God, "the self," and agency are each in its own way metaphysical fictions
that we simply do not need.

The theological response to this kind of atheism in general has been one of horror.
It is one thing to deny God, but it is quite another to deny the self. If there is no "substantive self," then there can be no universal moral principles. If there are no universal
moral principles, then everything is relative. So the loss of the "self," the loss of our
agency, threatens the metaphysical presuppositions on which Christian ethics in
modernity has been built. As one of my feminist students observed in a seminar in
which we were reading Richard Rorty's *Contingency, Irony, and Solidarity*, "Just when
women were claiming the power to be selves they now tell us such a thing does not
exist. I suspect this is some kind of conspiracy to keep women in our place."[7]

For theologians to come to the defense of modernist conceptions of the self in the
interest of securing moral objectivity and moral agency strikes me as a deep irony.[8] As
I suggested above, the creation of such a self was but part of the Enlightenment attempt to construe the world as intelligible without any need for the "God hypothesis." Ann Hartle makes this wonderfully clear through her analysis of Rousseau's *Confessions*. Rousseau wrote his confessions inviting a comparison with Augustine and
Plutarch. Human beings, for Plutarch, are no more or less than who their cities tell
them they are. If they are noble, they are such because they are what others tell them
they are.

In contrast, Rousseau saw clearly that Augustine presupposed that he is what he is
for God. "Only God can say what Augustine is. God sees in Augustine what even Augustine cannot see in himself. Augustine has his being from and through another: he
is what God sees him to be."[9] In opposition to Plutarch and Augustine, Hartle suggests that Rousseau's enterprise in his *Confessions* is to expose himself as he is to himself. In short, he claims to be able to see himself as he is by *feeling* his own existence.

This feeling, moreover, is self-sufficient exactly because it is private and unshareable.[10] Accordingly Rousseau becomes one of the originators of the modern self, a self that migrates to become the noumenal self, a self that exists whether God exists or not.

The self that theologians now rush to save is the "sovereign self" which sought to be its own ground.[11] Of course Descartes, as is often pointed out, prepared the way for Rousseau. Descartes's "ego" is irrefutably present to itself as pure extensionless consciousness, requiring no acknowledgment or complicity with language or community. Another source of this view of the self, a source that in many ways is the opposite of the rationalist tradition, is Hobbes. In Hobbes the self is the center of assertion, by which one defines oneself over against other such centers. Yet, as Joseph Dunne observes, Descartes's and Hobbes's pictures of the self proved capable of being combined through incorporation by each into an ideal of knowledge which was becoming available at the same moment of their emergence: "Knowledge as explanatory and predictive with respect to its object and as residing in this newly masterful self as subject and knower—a subject, moreover, which could decisively extend its mastery by incorporating anything *in itself* which was not a pure faculty of knowing into the object-domain of knowledge."[12]

Postmodernism but names the vulnerabilities built into this view of the self and knowledge that were present from its inception. Descartes's account of the self's certitude could not help but create a corresponding unlimited doubt; and, in Hobbes, the omnivorousness of our fellow creatures means that we must live in a world in which we cannot trust even ourselves. The masters of suspicion, Marx and Freud, each in his own way, challenge the presumption of the self's transparency to itself, but do so within the humanism on which modernity is based. For again, as Dunne observes, neither Marx nor Freud is committed to the demise of the subject just to the extent that each remains committed to the possibility of attaining truth about the human condition by disciplines that make possible an undeceived subjectivity.[13]

Postmodernism represents a more radical questioning than that of Marx or Freud just to the extent that it denies subjectivity and correlative notions of agency altogether. Accordingly the postmodern thinker does not try to reconcile what he or she may say about the self or agency with anything that is implicit in his or her own act of propounding. The self, like language itself, is but a sign that gets its meaning from other signs that get their meaning through their relationships of similarity and difference with other signs. The self but names our attempt at agency to name the play of the languages that speak through us.

As I noted at the beginning of this section, I regard these developments as theologically hopeful. The self denied by the postmodernist is the self created by the displacement of God.[14] In some ways, such a self has surprising affinities with Christian accounts. As David Matzko has pointed out, who could be more "decentered" than the Christian saints, since they cannot know who they are until God through the church tells them who they are?[15] That does not mean, however, that the "decentered self" of the postmodernist is sufficient to sustain a practice as basic to the church as the naming of the saints. Indeed, I remain agnostic whether the genealogists can sustain their own project.[16] Yet there can be no question that the developments I have just sketched must be taken into account by those of us attempting to develop constructive accounts of Christian character.

Christian Character and Agency

Which brings me back to the story of how I learned to quit worrying about agency and love stories. For in some quite interesting ways the postmodernist challenges to substantive accounts of the self and correlative views of agency provide ways to help me spell out both what it means to say that character is our agency and why such a claim is crucial for helping us understand the kind of character we should hope should be characteristic of Christians. To be a Christian is to be a member of a community with practices that are meant to make us faithful to our baptism. We, therefore, have a stake in accounts of the moral life by which we can be made accountable to engagements and promises we have made in which we did not "know" what we were doing.

For example, consider this passage from a letter from a friend (I have his permission to share it):

> Over the past week or so, I have been working on a rough autobiography in order to help my spiritual director determine how the hell I got the way I am. What has struck me in reading my draft is the inexplicable, unpredictable hurricane of grace. How did a Baptist kid born in southern Kentucky ever wind up being incorporated into the Mystical Body at the font of Our Lady Mediatrix of All Graces Church in the Bronx? My free will was certainly involved, but chiefly in consenting to follow the unprovoked leads opening in front of me. I'm not sure I had anything more to do with the fact that I am baptized than someone baptized when only a few days old. Sacramental theology tells us that it is Christ who baptizes; well, Christ tracked me down, pinned me in, and baptized me whether I wanted it or not.

Note that the problem is never one of explaining how, within patterns of stability, change is possible. Rather the problem is explaining how, given the constant change that constitutes our lives, continuity is possible.[17] The answer, of course, is that not everything changes all the time, for if it did, then we would have no way of knowing that any change was happening. Yet that does not resolve the problem of the kind of continuity that should characterize our lives as Christians. What I believe is clear from the above is that such continuity is ill-conceived as a "core of selfhood, coated as it were with accumulated experiences but always capable of withdrawing itself from the latter into a transcendental point, an antecedent 'I.'"[18]

Put simply, story is a more determinative category than self. Indeed our very notion of self only makes sense as part of a more determinative narrative. We can only make sense of our lives—to the extent we can make sense of our lives at all—by telling stories about our lives. To be able to "make sense of our lives" is primarily an exercise, as I suggested above, of retrospective judgment. Such judgments are, by necessity, under constant negotiation just to the extent that we must live forward. We are able to go forward just to the extent that we can go back.

The reason my life's story can never be "set" is partly because I do not have a privileged perspective on my life.[19] Our lives as enacted narratives are too interconnected with other narratives for us to claim sole authorship. As MacIntyre has maintained, at most we are coauthors of our lives,[20] a point that helps us realize that the strong account of agency I originally thought necessary to sustain an account of character is equivalent to the fantasy that we can make our lives be anything that we want. This, of course, is a great terror—as nothing could be worse for us, at least as Christians, than to have such a fantasy fulfilled. At most, agency names the skills correlative of a truthful narrative that enable us to make our own the things that happen to us—which includes "decisions" we made when we thought we knew what we were doing but in retrospect seem more like something that happened to us.[21]

Examples are required if such obscure remarks are to be illuminated. Think, for example, of what it means for the church to witness the marriage of two people who make a promise to be faithful to each other for a lifetime. They allegedly know what they are doing when they make such a promise. In other words, they are supposed to have been tested to indicate that they have the "awareness" necessary for them to be held responsible for the "decision" they are making at the time. But surely no one can know what it would mean to promise another person lifelong fidelity at any time in one's life, much less when one is young. I take it that is why the church insists that marriages must be witnessed, since by having the marriage witnessed we can hold the couple to a promise that they made when they could not have known what they were doing. By witnessing the marriage, the church does not presume that the marriage partners know what they are doing, though of course we try to help them understand what it means to make a promise when they cannot know what they are promising. Rather, we trust that through the faithful lives they have exhibited among us to this point, they are the kind of people we can trust to live into a promise they made when they did not know what they were doing.

Marriage, of course, may be the unhappiest example for consideration of character given contemporary practice. But I take it that the "breakdown" of marriage in our society is partly due to an exaggerated sense of agency that underwrites the presumption that we should not be held responsible for decisions we made when we did not know what we were doing. The difficulty with such a view is that our lives are constituted by decisions we made when we did not know what we were doing. Such is the "stuff" of character. The crucial question is whether we are constituted by practices of good communities that provide narratives rich enough to make our lives our own with the appropriate regret and joy.

Sin and grace are among the skills the practice called Christianity gives for making our lives our own. Retrospectively we find our lives constituted by actions for which we now can feel only shame. For example my early life was constituted by practices that allowed me to treat African Americans in a manner that can only be called racist. The temptation is to relegate that part of my life to "what I did before I knew better." That was the "determined" part of my life, the "not me." But if it was "not me," then I cannot adequately account for the continuities of my life that now constitute my character. "Determinism" turns out to be a discourse necessary for people who no longer have the language of forgiveness of sin. My "racism" was, and continues to be, "me," but to make it part of my life, part of my memory, in a way that constitutes my character, I must accept forgiveness for it. So forgiveness of sin turns out to be an essential practice if I am to be capable of making my life my own.[22]

This is but a reminder that Christians believe that our lives are constituted by gifts that we learn to make our own through the gift of God's very life in the cross and resurrection instituted in baptism. Without participation in such a life, the postmodernist may well be right that our lives are but the infinite play of signifiers signifying nothing. Yet Christians are a people who believe that the many narratives that constitute our lives finally have the *telos* of making us God's friends and in the process making us friends with one another and even friends with our own life. As John MacMurray observed, "All meaningful knowledge is for the sake of action and all meaningful action is for the sake of friendship."[23]

Notes

1. Of course this generalization is quite misleading. God, not the self, is the center not only of H. Richard Niebuhr's work, but also of Gustafson's. By calling attention to the self, I am but emphasizing what might be called the phenomenological center of Niebuhr's thought.

2. James Gustafson, "Introduction," in H. Richard Niebuhr, *The Responsible Self: An Essay in Christian Moral Philosophy* (New York: Harper & Row, 1963), 16.

3. Alasdair MacIntyre, *After Virtue* (Notre Dame, Ind.: University of Notre Dame, 1984), 209. I discuss these mistakes more extensively in the introduction to the second edition of *Character and the Christian Life* (Notre Dame, Ind.: University of Notre Dame, 1989), xiii–xxxiii.

4. I am not suggesting that Aristotle and Aquinas have exactly the same views on these matters, but their similarities are certainly more striking than their differences when they are compared to more modern accounts of the self. Some might try to interpret Aquinas's account of the will as providing an analog to our sense of agency, but I think such an interpretation mistaken. The will requires determination by reason to will properly, just as reason requires movement of the will to do its work. Moreover will and reason alike are impotent without habituation.

MacIntyre contrasts an Aristotelian and post-Kantian view by noting that the latter assumes we are entitled to hold people responsible for their actions if it is true that they could have done other than they in fact did and could have chosen other than they chose. Such a view is the ultimate oddity for an Aristotelian. For the Aristotelian, the mark of the good person is that his or her character has been formed by training in the exercise of the virtues that he or she often could not do or be other than virtuous in his or her choices and actions. "We strive, if we aspire to be good, to be moved by the possession of good reasons to good actions. There is a causal chain stretching back from each good action far into our moral and psychological past. By contrast on the post-Kantian view there must be a decisive break in the chain of causes and reasons." The Kantian requires that our capacity for moral agency be detached from all other capacities in the interest of freeing us from the limits of our past so that we might be equal. According to MacIntyre, this results in an attenuated, if not ghostly, account of moral agency. "How Moral Agents Became Ghosts," *Synthese* 53 (1982): 295–312.

5. MacIntyre, *After Virtue*, 211–12.

6. I am, of course, referring to MacIntyre's Gifford Lectures, *Three Rival Versions of Moral Enquiry: Encyclopedia, Genealogy, and Tradition* (Notre Dame, Ind.: University of Notre Dame, 1990).

7. Of course such a response may not be fair to Rorty. His point is not that there is no self, but rather that any self we may achieve is contingent. Thus:

> To see one's life, of the life of one's community, as a dramatic narrative is to see it as a process of Nietzschean self-overcoming. The paradigm of such a narrative is the life of the genius who can say of the relevant portion of the past, "Thus I willed it," because she has found a way to describe the past which the past never knew, and thereby found a self to be which her precursors never knew was possible. (*Contingency, Irony, and Solidarity* [Cambridge: Cambridge University Press, 1989], 29)

Such a view of overcoming is one that might be quite congenial with some aspects of feminist thought, but not others. It would certainly not sustain some of the essentialist claims about the nature of women's experience.

8. I am aware, of course, that the self and agency are not equivalents, though they are often closely interrelated.

9. Ann Hartle, *The Modern Self in Rousseau's Confessions: A Reply to St. Augustine* (Notre Dame, Ind.: University of Notre Dame Press, 1983), 4.

10. I unfortunately cannot replicate the rich details Hartle uses to expose Rousseau's "method" for discovering himself on his own terms. His attitude toward his death is particularly interesting.

11. I borrow the language of the "sovereign self" from Joseph Dunne, "Beyond Sovereignty and Deconstruction: The Storied Self," *Philosophy and Social Criticism* 21, nos. 5–6 (1995): 137–57. As I hope will be clear I am indebted to Dunne's analysis for much of what follows.

12. Dunne, "Beyond Sovereignty," 138.

13. Ibid., 140.

14. I have obviously not done justice to the complexity of this story particularly as told by Charles Taylor in his *Sources of the Self: The Making of Modern Identity* (Cambridge: Harvard University Press, 1989). Taylor is certainly right that in many ways the sources of the self we now call modern were present in some aspects of Christianity. I am not at all convinced, however, by

his reading of Augustine as the source of "inwardness" that finds expression in Descartes. To be sure, given modern developments, it is easy to so read Augustine; but when Augustine looks "internally" he finds God, not self. I think such a reading is justified not only by *The Confessions*, but particularly in relation to Augustine's reflections on the Trinity. Aquinas, in many ways, remains the ablest Augustinian in his insistence that only God is capable of moving the will non-violently.

15. David Matzko, "Hazarding Theology: Theological Descriptions and Particular Lives" (Ph.D. diss., Duke University, 1992). Matzko argues that sainthood is displayed in a narrative of the saint's life because those who tell the story of the saint are the primary agents in that narrative practice.

16. See, for example, MacIntyre's suggestion that the genealogist's strategy of masking and unmasking may commit the genealogist to ascribing to the genealogical self a continuity of deliberate purpose and a "commitment to that purpose which can only be ascribed to a self not to be dissolved into masks and moments" (*Three Rival Versions of Moral Inquiry*, 54). MacIntyre's argument is not an attempt to show that Nietzsche's or Foucault's positions are self-refuting but whether their own lives can be displayed in their terms. The question must remain open whether their projects can be sustained, which is finally a question of whether they can be lived. For a compelling account of Nietzsche, see Alexander Nehamas, *Nietzsche: Life as Literature* (Cambridge: Harvard University Press, 1985). Equally interesting is James Miller's "biography" of Foucault, *The Passion of Michel Foucault* (New York: Simon & Schuster, 1997). See in particular the discussion Miller's book occasioned in *Salmagundi* 27 (winter 1993): 30–99. As usual, in his contribution to the symposium, MacIntyre puts the issue well:

> We have good reason to be suspicious of any contemporary ethics of free choice, according to which each individual makes of her or his life a work of art. For something very like this aesthetization of the moral, which places the choices of each individual at the core of her or his moral life and represents these choices as an expression of that individual's creativity, is characteristic of advanced capitalist modernity. It provides a reinforcing counterpart to the bureaucratized careers of its elites, one which enables individuals to think of themselves as independent of their socially assigned roles, while they live out what is in fact one more such normalizing role. We therefore need to be told by those who endorse Foucault's standpoint just how Foucault's conception of ethics of care for the self and his implementation of that conception in his own life avoided this normalizing function. ("Miller's Foucault, Foucault's Foucault," p. 60)

17. For a fascinating set of reflections on change, with which I am very sympathetic, see Stanley Fish, *Doing What Comes Naturally: Change, Rhetoric, and the Practice of Theory in Literary and Legal Studies* (Durham, N.C.: Duke University Press, 1989), 141–60.

18. Dunne, "Beyond Sovereignty," 143. This view of the self underwrites the presumption that any account of responsibility requires that we be able to "step back" from ourselves and decide whether we are the selves we want to be. This view is well defended in William Schweiker, *Responsibility and Christian Ethics* (Cambridge: Cambridge University Press, 1995), 163–67. Schweiker's position is complex as he argues that one's capacity for self-designation necessary to be an agent requires the linguistic resources of some moral community in which others identify one as a responsible agent. The temporal character of the self is thereby duly acknowledged. Yet Schweiker's ambition to develop a comprehensive account of responsibility means our tem-

porality is bounded by our ability to secure a standpoint outside our history. Thus he argues that, "We are responsible for our actions and to others because in some basic sense we possess, or own, our actions and our lives. An agent is self-directed or autonomous if she or he exercises some measure of control over her or his life" (Schweiker, *Responsibility and Christian Ethics,* 137). He thinks this to be equivalent to Aristotle's, Augustine's, and Aquinas's claim that the principle of voluntary action must be internal to the agent. That is the case only if one remembers that for Aristotle and Aquinas our ability to act depends on our being habituated by the virtues. Of course, habits can also be bad, or in Aquinas's language, vices. A bad action is still an action and thus habitual for Aristotle. Yet such habits result in bad character. Thus Aristotle observes one of the effects of being bad is that bad persons cannot even be constant in their badness. These are complex matters for Aristotle and Aquinas, which I cannot pretend to have thought through. Aquinas does not develop Aristotle's account of moral weakness precisely because he has the Christian concept of sin; this he develops through an account of the vices, which are disordered habits. On reflection it is clear that "badness" and the moral psychology attending to its description, is even harder to characterize than "goodness." I think it is such exactly because as Aquinas maintained, the vices are not connected in the manner of the virtues. I am indebted to Jim Childress for reminding me of these complex matters.

19. In *Character and the Christian Life,* I argued that the agent is privileged. But such a view I now think must be even more carefully qualified than the way I tried to put the matter there (see pp. 104–6).

20. Alasdair MacIntyre, *After Virtue,* 213.

21. I was struggling in my *The Peaceable Kingdom: A Primer in Christian Ethics* (Notre Dame, Ind.: University of Notre Dame Press, 1983) to say something like this. See, in particular, pp. 38 ff.

22. For an account of forgiveness along these lines, see L. Gregory Jones, *Embodying Forgiveness: A Theological Analysis* (Grand Rapids, Mich.: Eerdmans, 1995).

23. John MacMurray, *The Self as Agent* (London: Faber & Faber, 1957), 15. MacMurray's work remains a gold mine of analysis and insight for anyone who would pretend to think seriously about the matters discussed in this essay.

Chapter 12

Moral Norms in Practical Ethical Reflection

JAMES F. CHILDRESS

Thirty years ago, in what quickly became a classic essay in Christian ethics, James M. Gustafson argued that the vigorous debate about norm and context in Christian ethics was misplaced.[1] I will offer an analytical framework for some of the major methodological positions taken in that debate over the last thirty years and suggest, without developing, some ways out of the current impasse. My overall thesis is that we need to distinguish two aspects or dimensions of moral norms—what we might call their scope or range of applicability, on the one hand, and their weight, strength, or stringency, on the other. We also need to note how different metaphors and models for relating norms to concrete contexts tend to emphasize one or the other of these aspects or dimensions, even when attempting to attend to both and to relate them in various ways. I will show how this distinction can illuminate Henry Richardson's three metaphors and models for connecting moral norms to concrete cases: application, balancing, and specification.[2] Even though I affirm an important role for general moral norms (of action) in moral deliberation and justification, my main task in this essay is largely analytical. Nevertheless, I will indicate various strengths and weaknesses of different ways to connect such norms to concrete cases.

My approach is a methodological analysis, which is how Gustafson described his original essay "Context versus Principles. . . ." That essay contended that the debate about context and principles is no longer "fruitful": "The umbrella named 'contextualism' has become so large that it now covers persons whose views are as significantly different from each other as they are different from some of the defenders of 'principles.' The defenders of the ethics of principles make their cases on different grounds, and use moral principles in different ways."[3] Gustafson further argued that context and principles represent two of the four major base points in Christian moral discourse (the other two are theology and moral anthropology), and that, whatever a Christian ethicist's starting point, each of the other base points will appear, either implicitly or explicitly.

A few preliminary points, particularly about norm and context, will further indicate my own direction. First, Gustafson noted that the term "context" marks off no particular position because it covers so many different possibilities, ranging from the Christian community to the actual political situation. My own discussion will limit the term "context" to particular, concrete cases, while recognizing that part—frequently a hidden part—of the debate concerns what counts as a case, what its boundaries are, etc. Indeed, too often all the parties in the debate forget that cases are narratives, at least mini-narratives; and they thus neglect the way a narrator's own perspectives, norms, and the like will shape how cases are structured and presented. Such cases are not purely factual or descriptive, with moral judgments then based on either external norms or paradigm cases.

Second, I will use the broad language of moral norms, as well as the more precise language of moral principles and rules. Norms include both principles and rules as "general action guides specifying that some type of action is prohibited, required, or permitted in certain circumstances."[4] I will construe principles as more general norms, which often serve as the sources or foundations of rules, and rules as more concrete and detailed specifications of the type of prohibited, required, or permitted action. The difference appears in their degree of specificity, but both types of norms of action must be distinguished from particular judgments in concrete situations.

Third, since the late 1960s and early 1970s, the debate about the roles of general moral norms and particular case judgments has frequently emerged in "applied" or "practical" ethics (e.g., biomedical ethics and the ethics of war and peace), rather than in broader theological or philosophical ethics. It has largely addressed "what ought I/we to do?" and "how can I/we decide?" especially by reference to norms or to paradigm cases, without sufficient explicit attention to broader theological and philosophical issues. Nevertheless, the *methodological* debate about moral norms typically involves (frequently unacknowledged) *substantive* theological and philosophical convictions—for instance, about the possibility of moral dilemmas, about God's relation to human life, or about ecclesiology. And it often involves support for or opposition to certain material norms. Such support or opposition is then stated methodologically as support for or opposition to all norms of a certain kind or with a certain weight (e.g., absolutely binding or exceptionless). For example, many critics of the Roman Catholic hierarchy's absolute prohibition of the use of artificial means of contraception oppose exceptionless norms in order to oppose this prohibition (and other prohibitions), while the hierarchy supports exceptionless norms in order to avoid weakening this prohibition (and other prohibitions). These positions also reflect important disputes about fundamental theological-philosophical convictions, especially ecclesiology.

Fourth, several factors may well account for the relative lack of explicit attention to

the broader philosophical and theological perspectives that bear on methodological debates about norms. On the one hand, "applied" ethicists or "practical" ethicists often
stop with casuistic analyses, midlevel principles, or moral theories, believing that much
can be done, practically speaking, without resolving some of the larger anthropological and theological-philosophical issues. However, their formulations may actually presuppose answers to some questions they do not explicitly address. On the other hand,
several philosophers and theologians oppose both casuists and normists (i.e., those who
appeal to moral norms) on the grounds that they are only engaged in a "family quarrel" about "what ought I/we to do?" while neglecting the more fundamental question
"who ought I/we to be?"[5] Some philosophers and theologians also view appeals to
principles and rules as discredited foundationalist moves. In short, several virtue theorists, narrativists, and communitarians, among others (to use some overly broad labels)
dismiss this whole debate about norm and context as irrelevant. Even though I cannot
develop the point here, I believe that each of these critical approaches, all of which are
contextualist in a larger sense than casuistry, must in fact address the role and function
of general moral norms.

Such critics regularly charge that casuistic and normist approaches yield quandary
ethics, by focusing so much on moral perplexities, problems, and dilemmas that have
to be resolved. However, in concentrating on quandaries that various parties face, casuists and normists do not suppose that the moral life simply consists of various dis-
connected moral problems. Much of the moral life is a matter of doing what one recognizes to be right, obligatory, and good, without any direct appeal to norms or to
paradigm cases and without any perplexity about what one ought to do. Moral agents
can recognize that they ought to act as "good Samaritans" because of a neighbor's need,
without norm-based or casuistic deliberation. Only when novel situations and conflicts arise, as they sometimes do, must norms and paradigm cases be invoked. However common or uncommon, quandaries have to be faced when they arise. Preventing quandaries is desirable; but preventive ethics, just as preventive health care, is not
always successful, and then critical cases must be confronted.

A Current Misplaced Debate: Principlism versus Casuistry
in Biomedical Ethics

It has also become clear, Gustafson wrote in 1965, "that contextualists find some moral
principles or generalizations that give guidance to existential decisions, and that the
defenders of principles find some ways to proceed from generalizations to particular
situations."[6] A current example of such a misplaced debate involves some casuists and
principlists. In their excellent and important book, *The Abuse of Casuistry*, Albert Jonsen and Stephen Toulmin vigorously oppose "the tyranny of principles" (a formulation that appeared earlier in Toulmin's article by the same title), while supporting a

process of analogical reasoning in relation to paradigm cases.[7] However, as a careful reading of their book reveals, their target is not the inevitable tyranny of principles as such, but rather the tyranny of some conceptions of principles, particularly "eternal, invariable principles, the practical implications of which can be free of exceptions or qualifications."[8] Such principles commonly lead to problems, particularly to fruitless standoffs and deadlocks. By contrast, moral knowledge is essentially particular, and moral resolution and consensus can be reached by focusing on cases rather than on principles and rules.

Despite their language, modern casuists often recognize principles and rules. When, for example, Jonsen distinguishes ethically wrong, permissible, and obligatory actions, he focuses on relevant similarities and differences between what he calls paradigm cases and actual cases under consideration. In the process, he implicitly or indirectly appeals to what may be viewed as principles. What qualifies a particular case as a paradigm case can often be stated in terms of general moral norms. For example, in identifying the features and conditions that distinguish (justifiable) autopsy from (unjustifiable) vivisection of criminals, Jonsen focuses on cases of autopsy that do not involve harm or pain (because the subject is dead), or coercion, or unfairness, even if the prospect of benefit for others is limited. Several major moral principles are implicit in his argument: The noninfliction of pain expresses the principle of nonmaleficence; avoidance of coercion expresses the principle of respect for autonomy; and avoidance of unfairness expresses the principle of justice. In addition, the whole interest in autopsy stems from the principle of beneficence—that is, producing good.[9]

At points, Jonsen and Toulmin state that their aim is to argue for "good casuistry"— that is, casuistry that "applies general rules to particular cases with discernment [in contrast to] bad casuistry, which does the same thing sloppily."[10] And elsewhere Toulmin concedes that principles have special relevance in relations between strangers, even though not in relations between intimates.[11] Thus. one important question is how we can best characterize various relations, such as those in research, medicine, and health care. Only then can we determine the appropriate role for principles.

In short, Jonsen and Toulmin's casuistry-based attack on tyrannical principlism focuses on its absolutist versions, rather than on versions that view principles and rules as prima facie binding and require balancing and other modes of interpretation in situations of decision. And, I have suggested, they concede that casuistry may apply principles discerningly, allow principles in certain types of relations, and incorporate principles, at least implicitly, in their paradigm cases.

On the other side, Tom Beauchamp and I defend what critics label a "principlist" approach, which is allegedly opposed to casuistry.[12] Here, as is true of casuistry, it is necessary to distinguish formulas of basic positions from their fuller and more adequate interpretations. In fact, we are more receptive to particular cases than our language, metaphors, and diagrams sometimes suggest. Particularly problematic, for instance, is our use of the metaphor of "application," along with other metaphors such as hierarchical tiers, foundations, bases, and grounds, as well as our use of diagrams that depict the relations between theories, principles, rules, and particular judgments in ways that seem to reduce particular judgments to the mere application of general principles and rules.

Nevertheless, in the text we stress that particular moral judgments have relative independence and can lead us to modify our general principles. We note, for example, that it is a mistake to say that ethical theory and principles are "not *drawn* from cases but only *applied* to cases."[13] Furthermore, our several editions of *Principles of Biomedical Ethics* have all viewed the relation between principles and rules, on the one hand, and particular judgments about cases, on the other, as *dialectical,* with each thus potentially modifying the other.[14] And we have made actual cases central to our various editions.

A principlist approach need not hold that norms are chronologically, logically, or normatively prior to particular judgments. Let's suppose, for purposes of discussion, that particular judgments come first in time. Then the question arises: "First for whom?" Each of us participates in various communities with traditions of moral reflection that include both general moral norms and particular judgments about cases. Even if the particular judgments arose first historically (a claim that is difficult to establish), we do not encounter the moral wisdom of our communities and their traditions only through their particular judgments, for they usually present general moral norms as well. Indeed, it is hard to imagine effective communal moral education without general norms along with paradigm cases. Hence, the casuists' view of principles as "top down" holds only for a certain type of theoretical derivation; it does not fit a historical, communal conception of morality.

Furthermore, even if we assume, for purposes of argument, that particular moral judgments are primary, historically speaking, general moral norms logically arise as implications of those judgments. As R. M. Hare argues, "if we, as a result of reflection on something that has happened, have made a certain moral judgment, we have acquired a precept or principle which has application in all similar cases. We have, in some sense of that word, learnt something." And if we learn something useful from reflection on a particular case, Hare claims, the principle we gain must be somewhat general rather than having unlimited specificity. Since no two real cases are exactly alike, we have results of reflection that can be useful in the future only if we "have isolated certain broad features of the cases we were thinking about—features which may recur in other cases."[15] Hare's argument presupposes the formal principle of universalizability, which entails that relevantly similar cases should be treated similarly. This principle does not distinguish normist from casuistic approaches. Jonsen and Toulmin's casuistry also presupposes this formal principle since, after all, casuistry proceeds by identifying relevant similarities and differences between cases.

Hence, even on grounds that casuists accept, there are good reasons to affirm general moral norms: Particular case judgments generate such norms via the formal requirement of universalizability. In addition, they may be valuable and even indispensable because of human propensities to self-deception, bias, and other distortions in particular judgments, the need to coordinate activities in communities, and the like. Furthermore, within Christian (and Jewish and other) communities, moral norms appear in the tradition, whether based on scripture or on reason. They are part of the tradition's moral wisdom and cannot simply be ignored. Why they are there and how they can be defended theologically are important questions, which I cannot explore here. Instead, I will turn to debates about ways to connect those moral norms—however they arise and however they are defended—to particular judgments.

Connecting Moral Norms to Particular Cases

Norms rarely give unambiguous directions for particular cases. It is often unclear whether a particular case falls under a certain norm; the same norm may point in two different directions in the same situation; and norms may be in apparent or real conflict. In an important and influential essay, Henry Richardson identifies three metaphors and models for connecting general norms to concrete cases: (1) application, which involves the deductive application of principles and rules; (2) balancing, which depends on intuitive weighing; and (3) specification, which proceeds by "qualitatively tailoring our norms to cases."[16] Even though Richardson's constructive proposal of the primacy of specification to avoid the problems of (deductive) application and (intuitive, nondiscursive) balancing goes too far and itself encounters serious problems, his analysis is most instructive. I will use some of his categories in my own way (without always being faithful to his structure) to illuminate some debates, particularly in Christian ethics and moral theology, about moral norms and particular case judgments. It is possible, I believe, to make Richardson's framework even more illuminating and helpful by distinguishing two aspects or dimensions of moral norms: (a) their range and scope of application; and (b) their weight, strength, and stringency. These are not totally independent, but are rather closely related, even when a particular ethicist assumes one strategy rather than another as primary for dealing with conflict situations.

A study by Dennis Novak and colleagues suggests why it is necessary to distinguish but also to consider these two aspects or dimensions or moral norms. They attempted to determine physicians' attitudes toward the use of deception through a questionnaire involving hypothetical cases. One case concerns Mrs. Lewis, a fifty-two-year-old patient who is undergoing her annual examination.

> You tell her that everything looks normal and that you are going to order routine blood tests and her annual screening mammography, which you feel is important for women of her age. She is against the mammography, saying that the last time you ordered it, she had to pay for it herself. You know that she is of modest means and cannot easily afford it. You are surprised that her health insurance did not cover it.

Upon asking your secretary, you learn that the insurance covers the cost of mammography only if there is a breast mass or objective clinical evidence of the possibility of cancer. The secretary tells you that the way to get around this is to put down "rule out cancer" instead of "'screening mammography" on the form.[17]

The physicians surveyed were asked what they would do. Close to 70 percent indicated that they would write "rule out cancer," but 85 percent of those said that they would not be deceiving the insurance company by doing so. Now they could have conceded that they were deceiving the insurance company but then argued that their deception was justified in order to help the patient. However, most simply denied that putting "rule out cancer" would be deceptive. And they could thus consistently put "rule out cancer" while viewing deception as absolutely wrong. This case is less dramatic than such often-discussed cases as a would-be assassin asking the occupant of a house whether his friend is there (a case Kant discussed), or the Nazis asking the administrator of an orphanage whether any Jewish children reside there. Let's suppose that in both cases the answerer says "no" falsely in order to save someone's life.

How would we describe and evaluate the acts in all these cases? If, on the one hand, "lying" is viewed as any intentional falsehood, or any intentionally deceptive statement, or the like, then it is plausible to hold that putting "rule out cancer" is a lie. However, with this definition, it would be difficult for any moral theory, religious or secular, to consistently hold that lying is absolutely wrong—for example, in the cases of the assassin or the Nazis at the orphanage. And the moral debate would focus on whether the rule against lying could be overridden by some other principle or rule, such as saving a human life or benefiting a patient.

If, on the other hand, "lying" is defined as intentionally withholding information from or deceiving someone who has a right to the truth, the moral debate about these cases would focus on whether the parties seeking information had a right to the truth—for instance, whether the insurance company had a right to the truth in view of its (arguably) unjust policies. If this second definition of lying is accepted, it would be possible to hold that the rule against lying is absolute, because all the difficult moral questions would be answered by determining who has a right to the truth.

The debate about moral norms hinges, in part, on the description of acts, as well as on the weight or strength of such norms. Hence, it is not possible to determine whether an absolutist will agree with a nonabsolutist on what certain norms imply for particular cases of moral perplexity without knowing how they both understand the range and scope of those norms.

Opponents of absolute or exceptionless moral norms often contend that they are unclear either in their application or in their weight. To use the lying example, it is easy to determine, on the first definition, whether an act is a lie; but it may be difficult to determine the weight or strength of a rule against lying over against other conflicting rules. By contrast, it is easy to determine, on the second definition, whether a lie is right or wrong (it is wrong); but it may be difficult to determine whether any act is a lie, because of uncertainties about who has a right to the truth.

Applying Norms in a Process of Deduction

Many ethicists use the metaphor of *application*, as in *applied ethics*, but most concede that this metaphor is misleading if taken too literally. And they often use it very loosely—for example, for a variety of norms that often come into conflict and thus cannot all be applied, at least in the sense of rational deduction. Few normists actually take a deductive view of application, a mechanical view, as critics sometimes suggest.

Even though there may be some genuine applications of norms to concrete cases, the metaphor of application cannot helpfully cover all or even most significant relations between norms and particular judgments about cases. Not all such relations will involve rational deduction from norms to particular judgments. On the one hand, particular case judgments often proceed in relative independence of general moral norms. We *know* what we ought to do and do it, without reflecting on moral norms, which we might, however, articulate if someone asked us, "Why did you do X?" On the other hand, normists often recognize that particular case judgments may also modify our interpretation of general norms.

Where it might be relevant, the application/deduction framework can operate only if we assume: (a) that the norm's scope and range of applicability can be firmly set, (b) that its moral weight or strength can be set a priori, and (c) that it will never come into conflict with other equally significant moral norms. The eruption of conflicts between norms in concrete cases thus creates serious perplexities that lead communities and individual agents to adjust (a) or (b) for some norms in order to dissolve or resolve their conflicts with other norms. In short, they often end up specifying or balancing conflicting moral norms.

Specifying Norms

Specification is another model for connecting general norms to particular cases. It presupposes a distinction between general and specific, and between degrees of generality and specificity. There is, nonetheless, no hard and fast line between general and specific, since a moral species term may be a genus to some other term.[18] However general our moral norms, we interpret them in part by more specific formulations or by types of cases that we believe fall under them. Normists engage in specification in part because, as R. M. Hare notes, "any attempt to give content to a principle involves specifying the cases that are to fall under it. . . . Any principle, then, which has content goes some way down the path of specificity."[19]

Here the distinction between principles and rules (which Richardson neglects) is useful, because the latter are usually more specific than the former. Moral principles are frequently specified through rules that are more concrete and detailed. For example, rules that require physicians to seek voluntary informed consent before undertaking certain procedures on competent patients *specify* the requirements of the principle of respect for autonomy. And rules of confidentiality *specify* the requirements of several principles, including respect for autonomy and utility—the latter because of the value of confidential relations for the provision of effective health care.

The distinction between (a) the range or scope of applicability of a norm, and (b) the weight or strength of a norm helps to clarify the way specification works. Specification adjusts the circumstances of application of the relevant norm(s), its (or their) scope and range of applicability, rather than adjusting its (or their) weight or strength. As Richardson sketches this model of specification, it "proceeds by setting out substantive qualifications that add information about the scope of applicability of the norm or the nature of the act or end enjoined or proscribed." These substantive qualifications include clauses "indicating what, where, when, why, how, by what means, by whom, or to whom, the action is to be, is not to be, or may be done or the action is to be described, or the end is to be pursued or conceived."[20] Through such qualifications, which feature circumstances identified by the casuists, specification seeks "to rationalize away a given practical conflict"; it "yields a more coherent overall view by acceptably removing a given conflict."[21] It is often more "flexible, realistic, fruitful, and attainable" than application/deduction, but it maintains discursive rationality, which, he claims, balancing loses.[22]

The best work in applied or practical ethics, according to Richardson, already involves specification, even when its practitioners fail to recognize that what they are doing is distinct from application/deduction and from balancing. However, he fails to see just how widespread specification is and just how widely it is recognized as such, largely because philosophers tend not to read theologians as widely as theologians read philosophers. Specification is widespread and widely recognized as such in religious ethics. Furthermore, perhaps because of his own constructive position of specification, which appeals to pragmatism and to a coherence model of wide reflective equilibrium, he fails to see that many absolutists find specification not only attractive but even indispensable because it reduces conflicts between norms when their weights cannot be adjusted (because of claims of absoluteness).

Paul Ramsey is a good example of a recent Christian ethicist who employed the metaphor and model of specification. Distinguishing "specific" from "particular," Ramsey contends that "[s]uch specification of action is never a particular." Rather, moral reasoning "is always a matter of surrounding the particulars of action by increasingly specific general terms—i.e., increasing illumination—for the direction of concrete actions."[23] What is involved is "subsumption of cases," which for Ramsey is a work of prudence.

Rather than admitting exceptions, at least to certain moral norms, or overriding certain moral norms, Ramsey focuses on deepening or enlarging general moral wisdom or more correctly apprehending and understanding moral norms. So-called exceptions are really "feature-dependent," and they thus actually fall "under reformed or reformulated morally relevant principles of some sort."[24] Hence, rather than overriding the rule against lying in order to save a human life, Ramsey argues that we should more-adequately define or qualify the rule against lying by including "except to save a life," which is applicable to other cases as well.[25]

And instead of eliminating conflicts by taking moral norms as mere guidelines or rules of thumb, it is possible to develop (a) exempting conditions, or (b) qualifying, stipulating, or explanatory conditions. The former involve right-making qualifications *beside* or *beyond* the principle in question, while the latter involve right-making qualifications *within* the principle in question. We could, for instance, approach the rule against lying in terms of exempting conditions: "lying is wrong, except to save a life" states "the class or species of falsehoods that are right to tell," and there may well be others.[26]

Right-making qualifications *within* the principle itself are also important. They are not always "feature-dependent" (i.e., dependent on features of situations); they are often merely "feature-relevant" (i.e., relevant to the situation rather than actually drawn from our experience). Feature-dependence involves adjustment to the situation encountered, but in feature-relevance, experience brings to light "a further meaning of the defined-principle or rule" by providing the occasion for deeper reflection on what I have identified as the scope and range of applicability of principles.[27] Consider, for instance, forging documents to protect Jews in Nazi Germany: "This occasion," according to Ramsey, "only drew our attention to what was meant by forbidding forgery."[28]

Beyond exempting conditions and qualifying and stipulating conditions, we need "explaining-principles" or "explanatory-qualifications" to express the logic of movement along the spectrum from the most-general ethical principles to more-specific ones. Once we see the "breadth and depth and flexibility of good moral reason," we can find "creativity and sensitivity" in the moral life without a constant search for exceptions.[29] And the particular decision remains a matter of prudence.

In his multiplication of categories, Ramsey also distinguishes "definite-action rule" from "defined-action principle." For instance, we might have a definite-action rule that requires literal, verbal veracity; and, if we hold it firmly, then we might justify its breach to save a life by "the logic of feature-dependent exempting-conditions." However, within a "defined-action principle" that prohibits lying understood as "withholding the truth from someone to whom the truth is due," withholding the truth from a would-be assassin or Nazi troops would be an "implied species of acts within the meaning of truthtelling, not . . . an instance of 'lying.'"[30] Either way, Ramsey wants to avoid balancing norms, overriding norms, rebutting presumptions, and the like.

Even specification as a metaphor is subject to various interpretations. For instance, moral reasoning may be construed by analogy with reasoning by *genus* and *species* in the sense of classification or derivation, as long as we recognize that species-terms may be genus-terms to other species-terms. Specification may also be broader and looser, as in Hare's use, than classification or derivation. Or as Ramsey argues, "a better analogy [for specifying principles and rules] would be an evolutionary one, if biological *species* are thought to arise from some thrust forward or ahead."[31] This analogy suggests how, within the Christian context, "principles of faithfulness are unfolded from the elevating and directing power of divine charity," with various "intervening principles" producing "deeper meanings, clarifying explanations or stipulations" from within Christian morality. As an example, there are no good charitable reasons for holding that "mere verbal inaccuracies of speech to save life belongs [*sic*] among the meanings of 'lying.'"[32]

Ramsey is an absolutist, at least on certain moral norms, without using application and deduction for particular judgments. For him, specification and absolutism go hand in hand. However, only prudence can close the gap between the general moral norms, regardless of their degree of specification, and particular judgments: "However definitely a *rule* discriminates right from wrong, it cannot tell us '*This* is right or wrong.'"[33] The particular judgment cannot be certain in the same way as the norm, no matter how specific the norm.

Ironically, the pragmatist Richardson may try to close the gap to particular judgments more than the absolutist Ramsey. Whereas Ramsey relies on prudence for particular judgments, Richardson asserts, in both unqualified and qualified ways, that particular judgments will be clear and obvious once specification occurs: "The central assertion of the model of specification is that specifying our norms is the most important aspect of resolving concrete ethical problems, so that once our norms are adequately specified for a given context, it will be *sufficiently obvious* what ought to be done."[34] His next sentence offers a necessary qualification: "That is, without further deliberative work, simple inspection of the specified norms will *often* indicate which option should be chosen."[35] Nevertheless, Richardson still expects too much from specification for particular judgments.

Another complex use of specification appears in official Roman Catholic moral theology; it is complex because it is connected with application/deduction, with absolutism, and, perhaps, or so the proportionalists argue (and *Evangelium Vitae* and *Veritatis Splendor* suggest), with balancing on at least some level. Consider *Evangelium Vitae*'s discussion of the biblical precept "you shall not kill."[36] It uses the metaphor of depth to unpack the distinction between positive and negative implications of the precept "you shall not kill": "the *deepest element* of God's commandment to protect human life is the requirement to show reverence and love for every person and the life of every person."[37] Protestant thinkers such as John Calvin have made similar moves. While, negatively, this precept marks the "extreme limit," its deeper (positive) meaning becomes important in the tradition of interpretation.

Indeed, "as time passed, the church's tradition has always consistently taught the *absolute and unchanging value* of the commandment 'you shall not kill,' "[38] because killing a human being "in whom the image of God is present, is a particularly serious sin," and because "only God is the master of Life!"[39] Nevertheless, difficult situations emerged—situations "in which values proposed by God's law seem to involve a genuine paradox"—and the church had to think further, for example, about killing in self-defense, in warfare, and in capital punishment.[40] This reflection was a kind of specification, in Ramsey's sense of seeking the precept's deeper meaning: "Yet from the beginning, faced with the many and often tragic cases which occur in the life of individuals and society, Christian reflection has sought *a fuller and deeper understanding* of what God's commandment prohibits and prescribes."[41] It appears that this fuller and deeper understanding is consistent with absolute and unchanging value.

Hence, it became implausible to view the prohibition of killing in the Decalogue as absolute, unconditional, or exceptionless, in light of the sometimes conflicting fundamental values—others might say principles—behind this precept, such as the positive protection of life itself. Thus, the church over time sought to *specify* this precept in light of those values. And this specification further determined the precept's meaning by restricting its range and scope of application in at least two ways: first, to innocent persons, and, second, to direct actions (the second specification emerged later).

In short, "the commandment 'you shall not kill' has *absolute value* when it refers to the innocent person."[42] Thus, "the direct and voluntary killing of an innocent human being is always gravely immoral."[43] It can never be justified either as an end or as a means. Then by a process of rational deduction, not merely specification, the church applies this norm to the fetus in utero, and a particular judgment against abortion, even to save a pregnant woman's life, can be rationally deduced from these premises. The specification that produces the principle or rule against directly killing an innocent person proceeds in part by considering the principles or values that underlie it, and then rational deduction generates a more specific rule as well as a particular judgment.

Such a combination of specification and application is consistent with an absolutist position, once the initial norm ("Do not kill") is specified as "Do not directly kill innocent persons." Obviously the initial norm "Do not kill" would conflict with other important norms of agape and justice that provide for the positive protection of human life. However, the specified norm can be construed as absolute, unconditional, and exceptionless. When the potential conflict is specified away, the claim of absoluteness becomes more plausible. And once the specification occurs, then rational application/deduction also becomes more plausible.

Balancing may also play a role in specification. *Evangelium Vitae* appears to allow balancing into the process of determining the deeper meaning of the norm, when values come into conflict. But such balancing does not go as far as some proportionalists may want to go, at least as the Vatican interprets their position. One issue concerns "a specific kind of behavior," which *Veritatis Splendor* sees expressed in various precepts, for "the object of an act . . . specifies that act morally."[44] *Veritatis Splendor* rejects the opinion, which it attributes to the proportionalists, "that it is impossible to qualify as morally evil according to its species the deliberate choice of certain kinds of behavior or specific acts, without taking into account the intention for which the choice was made or the totality of the foreseeable consequences of that act for all persons concerned."[45]

However, despite such charges, proportionalists and traditionalists agree that certain acts are intrinsically evil—examples include murder, torture, slavery, and so forth—but they disagree about whether intentions, circumstances, and consequences went into those determinations or specifications. According to Lisa Cahill, terms and phrases such as "murder," "torture," and "slavery"

> do not . . . define acts in the abstract, but acts (like intercourse or homicide) *together with the conditions or circumstances* in which they become immoral. Such acts are indeed wrong, because immoral circumstances have already been specified in the examples given. A single term like "murder" or "genocide" makes it clear that what might have been a justifiable "act in itself" (homicide) was done in wrong circumstances; or a phrase like "killing an innocent person," which spells out exactly what circumstances of homicide are meant, results in an absolute moral norm. About this there is little disagreement.[46]

In short, these moral-offense terms go beyond neutral descriptions of physical acts to include various circumstances that specify the nature of the act and the range and scope of the precept.

The Vatican's discussion of killing represents a process of specification in the context of conflicting values, and it actually bears more similarity to what the proportionalists argue than the Vatican supposes. In fact, there is little disagreement about some specifications, such as the rule against murder, as distinct from disagreement about their application to particular cases; however, there is substantial disagreement about other rules. Indeed, the substantive debate about certain rules is central, even when it is couched in methodological terms. Thus, proportionalists and others challenge such rules as the prohibition of artificial means of contraception through their methodological arguments, while the hierarchy defends such rules through its own methodological arguments. Also behind this methodological dispute and connected with the substantive controversy about certain rules is a larger set of theological convictions, particularly concerning ecclesiology.[47]

In brief, specification is a very helpful metaphor, at least analytically. It can illuminate what is at work in some efforts to connect moral norms to concrete cases. However, it is less clear how well the process of specification succeeds, even in a combined model, which is how Richardson intends it to be used. Behind Richardson's move toward specification is a drive to coherence; he uses a coherentist method all the way down, general to specific to particular judgments. For Ramsey and Roman Catholic moral theology, however, there is also a substantive thrust: They believe that it is wrong to do (moral) evil so that good might result. Hence, it is usually not justifiable to override one moral principle or rule by another through balancing, compromise, sacrifice, or the like.

Richardson is also more comfortable than Ramsey and official Roman Catholic moral theology in describing the process of specification as one of "revision" of initial normative commitments "so as to make one of them more specific."[48] Richardson accepts the language of revision in part because of his pragmatist commitment and his coherence model as well as his nonabsolutist view of norms. By contrast, Ramsey, for instance, views specification as refining and deepening the meaning of initial rules rather than revising them. In general, Christian theologians have difficulty describing the process of specifying the divine commandment, "Do not kill," as one of *revision*, in contrast to refinement or deepening.

Specifying norms is often helpful for ethical guidance, especially but not exclusively, in conflict situations; and it always merits a trial effort to see if a conflict can be avoided or eliminated. I am not convinced, however, that specification can serve as the exclusive or perhaps even the dominant metaphor in a model for connecting norms and concrete cases. My skepticism stems in part from my belief that moral conflict is inescapable, in the moral universe as well as among people. Hence, we will have to engage in balancing at times, because we cannot specify principles fully enough to avoid or eliminate all moral conflicts.

Specification has been offered as a way to reduce the role of intuition in concrete decisions, but there is debate about how far it actually succeeds in this regard. Some critics charge that it falls prey to the same problems as balancing. John Arras asks, "what motivates and guides the modification and specification of abstract principles, what compels one to lard them with qualifying clauses, if not precisely the sort of countervailing values and principles encountered by the principlist?"[49] Specification thus may be as arbitrary as intuitive balancing allegedly is, especially in the absence of controls over the interpretation of the meaning of key moral categories. An example appeared above in my discussion of the moral category of lying in physicians' willingness to enter "rule out cancer" on the insurance form because the company would not pay for annual screening mammography. Without some controls on how lying is defined, and on how the conditions of the norm's applicability are specified, agents may deceive themselves by supposing that the statement "rule out cancer" requires no moral justification because it infringes no moral rule in that particular context, even though it in fact misleads the insurance company about the actual reason for the mammography.[50]

Finally, it is plausible to argue, as the proportionalists do, that some balancing—at least of values if not moral norms—occurs in the very process of specification. In specifying several moral norms, we are balancing, for instance, whether saving a life is more important than verbal accuracy, or whether protecting the innocent is more important than killing the guilty, and so forth.

Balancing Norms

In situations of moral conflict, both specifying and balancing norms qualify the initial norms. While specification adjusts the conditions of application by attention to range and scope, balancing adjusts the weight or strength of competing moral norms so that one can outweigh or override another. Balancing is often connected with a view of norms as prima facie binding or as presumptive. However, this is only one possible approach to the assignment of weights to moral norms. Arrayed from the most stringent to the least stringent, norms may be construed as: (a) absolute, (b) lexically ordered (i.e., some are absolute relative to some but not all others), (c) prima facie binding, and (d) illuminative rules of thumb. Much of the debate concerns which norms have which degree of prescriptivity.

Rules of thumb pose no serious problems in conflict situations, because they are at most only illuminative, not prescriptive.[51] They are expendable, because they only summarize the wisdom of the past. For some case-oriented approaches, such as act-deontology or act-utilitarianism (with Joseph Fletcher as a proponent of the latter), moral rules resemble the rule of thumb in baseball: "Don't bunt on third strike."[52] Rules of thumb are often attractive because they avoid absolutism. However, they do so at a heavy price—by sacrificing prescriptivity and bindingness.

Although some moral norms may resemble rules of thumb, others are arguably more binding and perhaps even absolutely so. Some plausible candidates for absolute status include norms that refer to traits of character or general directions of action, such as agape and justice; even Fletcher held that agape, which he equated with the principle of utility, is absolute. Other plausible candidates for absolute rules include prohibitions of murder and cruelty. For instance, the prohibition of cruelty is absolute if "cruelty" refers to the infliction of suffering for the sake of suffering (with no end or beyond any end such as punishment and the like).

As noted earlier, specification of material norms often combines with absolutism. Material norms with a limited range or scope (e.g., the prohibition of murder) are more plausibly considered absolute than broader norms (e.g., the prohibition of killing). Specified norms, with exceptions built into them, could also be absolute. An example might be: "Always obtain the informed consent of your competent patients except in emergency or low-risk situations." Now, there would be debate about "competence," "emergency," "low-risk," "informed," and "consent." But such matters determine when the rule applies, not whether it is absolute. Similar points hold for some of the other norms that Ramsey identified.

Some rule deontologists (i.e., those who recognize various independent principles and rules of intrinsically right and wrong action) have explored priority rules—for example, contending that the principle of respect for autonomy always trumps or overrides the principle of beneficence, when the only beneficiary is the competent person whose wishes, choices, or actions are overridden. A major effort to find a lexical or serial ordering of principles appears in Robert Veatch's *A Theory of Medical Ethics*, where all the deontological or nonconsequentialist principles "are given lexical priority over the principle of beneficence." However, in cases of conflict, the deontological or nonconsequentialist principles are themselves balanced against each other in what Veatch labels a "balancing strategy." He thus finds "a solution to the inevitable unacceptable tension between Hippocratic individualism and the utilitarian drive toward aggregate net benefit." This solution "comes from the articulation of other nonconsequentialist principles that will necessarily have a bearing on medical ethical decisions: contract keeping, autonomy, honesty, avoiding killing, and justice" and from assigning them collective priority over the production of good consequences for individuals (Hippocratic individualism) or for society (utilitarianism). Nonconsequentialist principles are thus given "coequal ranking" in relation to each other and "lexical ranking" over the principle of beneficence.[53] Richardson claims that lexical ordering is actually a form of application/deduction and is problematic on that score: The priority rule runs into conflicts, too. However, lexical ordering is also an example of specification in setting the weights of norms, even though specification usually operates in setting the range and scope of norms.

One way to hold onto prescriptivity or bindingness, against mere maxims or rules of thumb, but without either absolutism or lexical ordering, appears in W. D. Ross's distinction between prima facie and actual duties. Ross used the phrase "prima facie duty" to indicate that duties of certain kinds are on all occasions binding unless they conflict with stronger duties. One's actual duty in a situation is determined by examining the weight of all the conflicting prima facie duties. Prima facie duties such as not lying (defined as making an intentionally deceptive statement) and keeping promises can sometimes be overridden. Yet they are more than rules of thumb. They are always morally relevant and provide strong moral reasons for performing (or not performing) the acts in question. However, they may not always prevail over all other prima facie duties. They always count morally even when they do not win. Except for a very modest ranking—the principle of nonmaleficence (not inflicting harm) takes precedence over the principle of beneficence (producing benefit) when the two come into conflict—Ross assigned no priority among the other principles. And since these principles are all independent, he lacked the kind of grounding principle (utility) that (some) rule-utilitarians use to adjudicate conflicts among other norms. In cases of conflict, Ross affirmed with Aristotle: "the decision rests with the perception."[54]

Richardson suggests that this approach to norms is a "hybrid," in that it combines—or at least may combine—application and balancing. If only one prima facie principle is relevant in a particular case, then it is binding; it determines what ought to be done. (However, it is not clear that Ross is as much of a deductivist as this line of interpretation supposes—the role of perception is too strong.) In general, as Richardson notes, the prima facie hybrid model tends not to worry too much about the "exact contours" of the principles. However, many who follow much of Ross's model of balancing also employ specification; prima facie principles are specified in prima facie rules.[55]

The process of *balancing* is common in several recent normist approaches—for example, it appears in Beauchamp and Childress, *Principles of Biomedical Ethics* (PBE) (1994 and earlier editions), and significantly (but within limits as noted above) in Veatch, *A Theory of Medical Ethics*. It also appears in the language of setting and rebutting presumptions favored by Sissela Bok and Philip Wogaman.[56] All these writers develop a conception of several moral principles as prima facie or presumptively binding but potentially in conflict in particular cases. For example, *PBE* features several prima facie binding principles—respect for autonomy, nonmaleficence, beneficence (including utility or proportionality), and justice, along with various derivative or specified principles and rules including veracity, fidelity, privacy, and confidentiality—all of which have to be balanced in conflict situations.

At first glance, this perspective might appear to be very close to one that recognizes only maxims or rules of thumb, but, as already suggested, there is an important difference. For instance, *PBE* recognizes principles as prima facie binding and thus prescriptive, whereas for Fletcher they only illuminate the application of the one ultimate principle of neighbor-love (or utility). Hence for *PBE*, the moral agent has to justify departures from principles by showing that in the situation some other principles have more weight. However, the assignment of weight or priority depends on the situation rather than on an abstract, a priori ranking. This approach suffers from the limitations of any pluralistic approach that does not assign weights or priorities to various principles in advance. A great deal rests on what has been variously called prudence, practical moral reasoning, or discernment in the situation within the framework of prima facie principles.

Some trends in recent Catholic moral theology have some affinities with approaches that recognize prima facie norms. Without going into some important differences, Richard McCormick notes that some Catholic "proportionalists" who have been suspicious of the language of "intrinsic evil" have adopted arguments that resemble Ross's use of prima facie right and wrong. Such proportionalists do not hold that actions have no meaning in themselves but "only that no final assessment of rightness and wrongness can be made until more has been said of the action than that it is [for example] 'breaking a promise.'"[57] Proportionalists also hold that nonmoral evils—the language varies: premoral, ontic, etc.—such as killings are to be avoided as far as possible, but admit that such evils may be justified in conflicts of values and disvalues. Choosing in such a conflict may give rise to regret but not to moral remorse. Many proportionalists find the language of "intrinsic evil" unsatisfactory because of the way it has been used in some recent theological and magisterial literature (e.g., to hold that direct sterilization is wrong regardless of the circumstances), because it seems more at home in a deontological than in a teleological setting, and because it is confusing.

However, as I construe the debate, the prima facie approach is not as close to the position taken by many of the proportionalists, such as McCormick, Bruno Schuller, Louis Janssens, and Josef Fuchs, as it is to the position developed by Albert R. Dilanni, S.M., who distinguishes nonmoral evil (e.g., death) from the free causation of that evil (e.g., killing/homicide). The latter has "at least minimal *moral* meaning in itself prior to consideration of intention and circumstances." Thus, he construes concepts such as homicide as "bearers of negative *moral* meaning (as intrinsically evil in a weak sense) and not merely as bearers of negative ontic or pre-moral meaning." This weak sense of "intrinsically evil" (which he also calls the prima facie moral meaning of negative acts in the tradition of Ross) implies that the negative moral ought is always relevant even though it is not always decisive. Even when an action that is prima facie or intrinsically evil, in the weak sense, is justified in particular circumstances, it should engender "creative regret" though not guilt.[58]

The main criticism of the process of balancing is its intuitive assignment of weights to conflicting principles or rules, since an a priori assignment would involve something like application, specification, or both. Richardson believes that it dismisses discursive reasoning. Insofar as balancing is truly distinct from application, Richardson claims, "it affords no claim to rationality, for to that extent its weightings are purely intuitive, and therefore lack discursively expressible justification."[59]

Perhaps Richardson presses the metaphor of balancing too far in his interpretation and critique of balancing moral norms that are prima facie binding. For balancing may not only be combined with specification, as we have seen, but it may incorporate discursive rationality in other ways, too. While there is a ineliminable role for intuitive judgments in actual situations of conflicting prima facie norms, it is also possible to develop and use a decision procedure to reduce and constrain the reliance on intuition. Indeed, "the logic of prima facie duties does contain moral conditions that prevent just any judgment based on a grounding principle from being acceptable in a moral conflict."[60] Thus, it is plausible to identify several "requirements for justified infringements of a prima facie principle or rule": There must be a realistic prospect of realizing the moral objective that appears to justify the infringement; the infringement of a prima facie principle must be necessary in the circumstances; the infringement should be the least possible, commensurate with achieving the primary goal of the action; and the agent must seek to minimize the negative effects of the infringement. Neither moral experience nor moral theory warrants a stronger decision procedure for resolution of conflicts between prima facie principles in concrete cases.

Such conditions of rational constraint on intuition are not new. Indeed, similar (though more expansive) conditions have been elaborated in the just-war tradition, which I have argued can plausibly be reconstructed in terms of prima facie principles.[61] And they also appear in different areas of biomedical ethics, such as research involving human subjects, abortion, and the use of human fetal tissue in transplantation research, as well as in other conflict situations.[62]

214 JAMES F. CHILDRESS

Conclusion

In the final analysis, it is important, I believe, to recognize the value of all three approaches—application, balancing, and specification—to connecting norms to concrete cases, rather than viewing them as alternative models. Sometimes a norm can be directly applied. Sometimes potentially conflicting norms can be specified to reduce or eliminate the conflict. And sometimes conflicts can be resolved only by balancing, within the constraints and directions of a decision procedure, such as operates in the just-war tradition.

Attention to the two aspects or dimensions of norms I identified—range or scope, on the one hand, and weight or strength, on the other—and to the various ways of adjusting those aspects or dimensions in relation to concrete cases will enable to us identify exactly where positions differ and whether those differences are really relevant. It is also a substantive, and not merely a formal, moral debate about which approach works where and how they may be combined in moral decision making. And that debate presupposes answers to some broad questions, such as the possibility of genuine moral dilemmas, order and coherence in the universe, and the like. Much of the debate is misplaced, as it was thirty years ago. But through the categories and approaches I have proposed we can perhaps see more clearly where the real methodological and substantive differences arise between various positions, understand what is at stake, and find ways to overcome the differences.

Notes

1. James M. Gustafson, "Context versus Principles: A Misplaced Debate in Christian Ethics," *Harvard Theological Review* 58 (1965): 171–202; reprinted in James M. Gustafson, *Christian Ethics and the Community* (Philadelphia: Pilgrim Press, 1971), 101–26. All references will be to the latter.

2. Henry S. Richardson, "Specifying Norms as a Way to Resolve Concrete Ethical Problems," *Philosophy and Public Affairs* 19 (1990): 279–320.

3. Gustafson, "Context versus Principles," 102.

4. William David Solomon, "Rules and Principles," in *Encyclopedia of Bioethics*, ed. Warren T. Reich (New York: Free Press, 1978), 1:407–13.

5. This theme appears in the various writings of Stanley Hauerwas, among others.

6. Gustafson, "Context versus Principles," 117.

7. Albert R. Jonsen and Stephen Toulmin, *The Abuse of Casuistry* (Berkeley: University of California Press, 1988). See also Stephen Toulmin, "The Tyranny of Principles," *Hastings Center Report* 11 (December 1981): 31–39.

8. Jonsen and Toulmin, *The Abuse of Casuistry*, 2.

9. See Albert R. Jonsen, "Transplantation of Fetal Tissue: An Ethicist's Viewpoint," *Clinical Research* 36 (1988): 215–19. See also Albert R. Jonsen, Mark Siegler, and William J. Winslade, *Clinical Ethics*, 2d ed. (New York: Macmillan, 1986).

10. Jonsen and Toulmin, *The Abuse of Casuistry*, 16. See also Jonsen's contribution to this volume, as well as his "Casuistry: An Alternative or Complement to Principles?" *Kennedy Institute of Ethics Journal* 5 (September 1995): 237–51, in which he notes that "no sound casuistry can dispense with principles" (p. 248).

11. Toulmin, "The Tyranny of Principles."

12. See Tom L. Beauchamp and James F. Childress, *Principles of Biomedical Ethics* (New York: Oxford University Press, 1st ed., 1979; 2d ed., 1983; 3d ed., 1989; 4th ed., 1994). The label "principlism" was applied to this position by K. Danner Clouser and Bernard Gert in "A Critique of Principlism," *Journal of Medicine and Philosophy* 15 (1990): 219–36.

13. Beauchamp and Childress, *Principles of Biomedical Ethics*, 3d ed., 16.

14. Beauchamp and Childress, *Principles of Biomedical Ethics*, 1st ed., 13; 2d ed., 13; 3d ed., 16; 4th ed., 23.

15. R. M. Hare, "Principles," *Essays in Ethical Theory* (Oxford: Clarendon Press, 1989), 49–65.

16. Richardson, "Specifying Norms," 283.

17. Dennis Novack et al., "Physicians' Attitudes toward Using Deception to Resolve Difficult Ethical Problems," *Journal of the American Medical Association* 261 (26 May 1989): 2980–85.

18. Paul Ramsey, "The Case of the Curious Exception," in *Norm and Context in Christian Ethics*, ed. Gene H. Outka and Paul Ramsey (New York: Charles Scribner's Sons, 1968), 67–135.

19. Hare, "Principles."

20. Richardson, "Specifying Norms," 296.

21. Ibid., 302.

22. Ibid., 283.

23. Ramsey, "Curious Exception," 76. For a good discussion of Ramsey's position, see Donald Evans, "Paul Ramsey on Exceptionless Moral Rules," *American Journal of Jurisprudence* 16 (1971): 184–214.

24. Ramsey, "Curious Exception," 77.

25. Ibid., 80–81.

26. Ibid., 222.

27. Ibid., 91.

28. Ibid., 101.

29. Ibid., 92.

30. Ibid., 89.

31. Ibid., 91.

32. Ibid., 91–92.

33. Ibid., 94.

34. Richardson, "Specifying Norms," 294, my italics.

35. Ibid., my italics.

36. Pope John Paul II, *Evangelium Vitae*, Origins 24 (6 April 1995). For a fuller methodological statement, see John Paul II, *Veritatis Splendor*, Origins 23, no. 18 (14 October 1993).

37. John Paul II, *Evangelium Vitae*, par. 41, my italics.

38. Ibid., par. 54.

39. Ibid., par. 55.

40. Ibid.

41. Ibid., my italics.

42. Ibid., par. 57, my italics.

43. Ibid.

44. *Veritatis Splendor*, par. 78.

45. Ibid., par. 82; see par. 79.

46. Lisa Sowle Cahill, "Accent on the Masculine," in *Considering Veritatis Splendor*, ed. John Wilkins (Cleveland: Pilgrim Press, 1994), 57–58. For earlier debates about norms, see Charles E. Curran and Richard A. McCormick, S.J., eds., *Readings in Moral Theology, No. 1: Moral Norms and Catholic Tradition* (New York: Paulist Press, 1979).

47. Richard A. McCormick, S.J., "Some Early Reactions to *Veritatis Splendor*," *Theological Studies* 55 (1994): 481–506. Some issues about the physical act, such as falsehood (in contrast to lying) and homicide (in contrast to murder), will emerge in my discussion of balancing.

48. Richardson, "Specifying Norms," 283, 297.

49. John Arras, "Principles and Particularity: The Role of Cases in Bioethics," *Indiana Law Journal* 69 (1994): 983–1014.

50. In this connection, it might also be possible to construe this case in terms of the notion of "mental reservation," which has often been used in Roman Catholic moral theology. The doctor's written statement, "rule out cancer," might be accompanied by the mental reservation, "because a *screening* mammography is designed to *rule out* cancer." However, this strategy fails, I believe, because the insurance company specifies that the designation "rule out cancer" is to be used only when there is a breast mass or objective clinical evidence of the possibility of cancer. Hence, putting "rule out cancer" rather than "screening mammography" in this context is a deliberate falsification, which is selected because it will mislead the insurance company.

51. Gustafson drew this helpful distinction between illuminative and prescriptive construals of norms in "Christian Ethics and Social Policy," in *Faith and Ethics*, ed. Paul Ramsey (New York: Harper & Bros., 1957), 119–39. In "Context versus Principles," he writes: "In the illuminative use of principles the center of gravity is on the newness, the openness, the freedom that is present, in which the conscientious [person] seeks to achieve the good and do the right. In the prescriptive use of principles the center of gravity is on the reliability of traditional moral propositions and their reasonable application in a relatively open contemporary situation" (pp. 116–17).

52. See Joseph Fletcher, *Situation Ethics* (Philadelphia: Westminster, 1966).

53. See Robert M. Veatch, *A Theory of Medical Ethics* (New York: Basic Books, 1981). See also Veatch, "Resolving Conflicts among Principles: Ranking, Balancing, and Specifying," *Kennedy Institute of Ethics Journal* 5 (1995): 199–218.

54. W. D. Ross, *The Right and the Good* (Oxford: Clarendon Press, 1930), and *Foundations of Ethics* (Oxford: Clarendon Press, 1939).

55. See Beauchamp and Childress, *Principles of Biomedical Ethics*, 4th ed., for a clear statement of a process that also appeared in earlier editions.

56. See Sissela Bok, *Lying: Moral Choice in Public and Private Life* (New York: Pantheon Books, 1978). See also J. Philip Wogaman, *Christian Moral Judgment* (Louisville, Ky.: Westminster John Knox, 1989).

57. Richard McCormick, S.J., "Notes on Moral Theology 1977: The Church in Dispute," *Theological Studies* 38 (1978): 103.

58. Albert R. Dilanni, S.M., "The Direct/Indirect Distinction in Morals," *Thomist* 41 (1977): 350–80.

59. Richardson, "Specifying Norms," 282–83.

60. Beauchamp and Childress, *Principles of Biomedical Ethics*, 3d ed. (1989), 32.

61. See Childress, *Moral Responsibility in Conflicts: Essays on Nonviolence, War, and Conscience* (Baton Rouge: Louisiana State University Press, 1982).

62. See, for example, Richard Miller, *Interpretations of Conflict: Ethics, Pacifism, and the Just-War Tradition* (Chicago: University of Chicago Press, 1991); LeRoy Walters, "Some Ethical Issues in Research Involving Human Subjects," *Perspectives in Biology and Medicine* (1977): 193–211; James F. Childress, *Priorities in Biomedical Ethics* (Philadelphia: Westminster, 1981), chap. 3; Lloyd Steffen, *Life/Choice: The Theory of Just Abortion* (Cleveland: Pilgrim Press, 1994).

Chapter 13

The Ethicist as Improvisationist

ALBERT R. JONSEN

The word "ethicist" is now ensconced in the English language. It appears even in the headlines. An article in the *New York Times*, in late November 1994, appeared under the banner "Ethicists Wary over New Gene Technique's Consequences." It began, "Ethicists said new work on sperm stem cells could have a variety of consequences, ranging from the potentially beneficial to the deeply troubling." Four professors, all described as "ethicists" (although one is a theologian, another a philosopher, and the others lawyers), are quoted, their one-liners showing the spectrum from "extraordinary wariness" to the claim that it would be "morally wrong" not to pursue the research.[1] Similar appearances, with similar spreads of opinion can be found almost daily on television and the press. *Ethicist* is now a category that must be filled on government panels and conference agendas. Yet it still is not quite clear to many folks (including some who call themselves ethicists) what ethicists do for a living. Are they like preachers? Are they something like police? This essay is an attempt to describe the ethicist's work and, in so doing, distinguish the working ethicist from two close relations, the moral philosopher and the moral theologian.

James Gustafson once wrote, "in response to a query from a friend (who is a distinguished philosopher) about how the term 'ethicist' has come about, I responded in a pejorative way, 'an ethicist is a former theologian, who does not have the professional credentials of a moral philosopher.'"[2] Professor Gustafson is rarely given to such sarcasm. I can only assume that he was disappointed that theological ethicists, many of whom had been his students, let their theology slip away as they forged into the ethical complexities posed by technology and the life sciences. He went on to say "the relation of the moral discourse (of many theologically trained persons) to any specific theological principles, or even to a definable religious outlook is opaque."

Gustafson and the distinguished philosopher were conversing "about how the term 'ethicist' has come about." At that time, the term had arrived but recently in common parlance. It is my impression that the word "ethicist" was not commonly used in those days as a collective noun for people who studied ethics, whether philosophical or religious. I have not done a scientific survey, but in recent months I have been reading books and articles from the 1950s and 60s by philosophers and theologians on the topic of ethics, and, trying to be alert to its appearance, have rarely found the word. The first edition of the *Oxford English Dictionary* (1928) defined "ethician" as "one versed in ethics," and supplied an 1886 citation; but "ethicist" is, rather disdainfully, given a mere "ethic" + "ist" with nary a cite. However, the 1989 edition is much more generous. "Ethician" is now designated "rare" while "Ethicist" is given a full, if rather odd, definition: "one who supports ethics or morality in opposition to religion," and is decorated with six citations, the earliest from 1891 ("the scientific ethicist must proceed like any other naturalist") and the most recent, a somewhat less-than-lucid comment from 1964 ("among the ethicists . . . the new technological age was seen as the function of an immanent axiological model").

I recall how the word "ethicist" came into my consciousness. In the mid 1960s, Professor Gustafson's graduate students lunched together in the Yale Divinity School refectory at least once a week. Stanley Hauerwas, James Childress, Gene Outka, James Laney, and I were the regulars; Professor Gustafson sometimes joined us. Our conversation, if not always of High Table quality, was vivacious, due usually to Hauerwas's colorful discourse. On a certain day, probably in 1966, we debated what title we students of theology interested in ethics ought to bear. I came from the Roman Catholic tradition, where such persons were called "moral theologians," or more commonly "moralists." My companions were Protestants, among whom no specific designation was used for those who studied and taught "Christian ethics." They preferred, I believe, to be called simply theologians. "Moral philosophers" was the common title of the rather rare breed of academics who followed in the footsteps of Kant and Mill. Our table talk reviewed the possibilities. I said I was uncomfortable being called a "moralist"; it sounded so censorious. We joked that "moral theologian" might be taken by the irreverent as the antonym for "immoral theologian." We tried "ethician" for size and rejected it as too much like "physician," or as someone added, like "mortician." "Ethicist," even though like "dentist," pleased us, for one could, if necessary, qualify it nicely with "theological," "religious," "Christian," or "philosophical." Ecumenical as we were, we thought a nondenominational moniker might be suitable, one that would designate Roman Catholics and Protestants, philosophers, and theologians alike. Behind this light luncheon chatter was, I suppose, the hope that soon we would be invited to speak to the wide world, not just to our own churches, about momentous moral issues. We needed a respectable professional label.

Between our table talk of 1966 and the turn of the decade, the term seems to have been domesticated. Paul Ramsey's 1970 *Patient as Person* opens with the affirmation, "This is a book about ethics, written by a Christian ethicist,"[3] and James Gustafson addressed the audience at the 1970 Society for Christian Ethics meeting as "ethicists."[4]

The word spread rapidly and soon became the preferred title of those who, as they say, "do" ethics. Whatever its provenance and definition, "ethicist" is certainly now in the common parlance.

Recently, Professor Gustafson told me that he first noticed the word "ethicist" in the 1955 English translation of Dietrich Bonhoeffer's *Ethics*, published in German in 1949.[5] I imagine the word in the German edition might have been *"ethiker,"* a word that is not in my *Brockhaus German Dictionary*, but I do not have the German Bonhoeffer to verify this surmise. At any rate, the heading of the first section of the chapter titled "Ethics as Formation" does read, "The Theoretical Ethicist and Reality." The word does not appear anywhere else in that chapter, but "theoretical moralist" appears as a synonym in one other place. Bonhoeffer is commenting on his generation's lack of interest in "any sort of theoretical or systematic ethics . . . the academic question of a system of ethics seems to be of all questions the most superfluous." It appears that by "ethicist" he means those who expound such systems. He says of them, "with the concepts [they have] in mind [they are] unable to grasp what is real and still less able to come seriously to grips with that of which the essence and power are entirely unknown to [them]." There follows one of the most eloquent passages in that martyred theologian's writings.

> One is distressed by the failure of reasonable people to perceive either the depths of evil or the depths of the holy. With the best of intentions they believe that a little reason will suffice them to clamp together the parting timbers of the building. They are so blind that in their desire to see justice done to both sides they are crushed between the clashing forces. Bitterly disappointed at the unreasonableness of the world, they see that their efforts must remain fruitless and they withdraw resignedly from the scene or yield unresistingly to the stronger party.[6]

In those words, Bonhoeffer sketches the *traison des clercs* of German academics in the 1930s and 1940s. Too many "theoretical ethicists" confided in little reason and in nothing else. Bonhoeffer's passage, with what may be the signature appearance of "ethicist," provides me with a theme that will serve a dual purpose: First, I reflect on what it is that "ethicists" do; and second, I replay Bonhoeffer to suggest how "ethicists" and the work they do differ from "moral philosophers" and "moral theologians," with their respective tasks.

What Ethicists Are

Those of us who are called ethicists know, of course, that ethicists are a strange species, with so many variations that species may not be the right word. While ethics has, once more, become a legitimate topic of conversation and even of serious study, we know that the study we profess is amorphous. We know that while there are fads and fashions, there is no canon in either philosophical or theological ethics. No one theory holds sway; no method is considered standard. Some moral philosophers are able to rehearse the history of moral arguments from Socrates to Rawls; others bring the sharp conceptual tools of language analysis in its old and newer forms to dissect the arguments. Some theologians bring the depth and breadth of the scriptural and theological traditions. Most ethicists, however, are eclectic. It is noteworthy that almost none of the early philosophers who became interested in bioethics had studied ethics as graduate students. Almost all had read "philosophy of science" or "philosophy of mind." Most of them, in the fashion of the 1960s, considered moral philosophy a dead field, having been given the *coup de grâce* by the assassins of the Vienna Circle. Other ethicists are graduates from fields far from ethics: law, psychology, sociology. Thus, when two stranger ethicists are introduced, neither knows, as two particle physicists certainly do, what the other thinks his or her discipline is or what its methods are. The physicists can get right down to solving a problem; the ethicists will have to circle each other for a bit. Some conversation may tease out their intellectual genotype, but even then, how they go about being ethicists and "doing" ethics may remain obscure.

Still, the ethicists are here and ethics is being done. It is a matter of perpetual interest, to the ethicists and to those who observe them, to figure out how they do what they do. What gives them the right, say some observers, to pronounce on moral matters? Where do we get the principles that we use to pronounce on moral matters, say the ethicists? I take Professor Gustafson's "pejorative" comment of some years ago as the theme for these reflections. In saying that "ethicists" were former theologians without the credentials of philosophers, he was assuming that theological ethics and/or moral philosophy were, in some way, credentials for doing ethics. This assumption requires, I think, some qualification. Unquestionably, both of those venerable disciplines bear on the moral life of humankind. Perhaps one or the other or both are even necessary to competently study moral problems in depth, but neither is sufficient for doing ethics, at the point where moral conceptions, theories and doctrines must move toward decision and action, policy and practice. Now, anyone familiar with the literature of religious ethics and moral philosophy will recognize that I am on the edge of a massive platitude. Aristotle broke fresh ground on the question of how generalizations meet particulars, and many a fine philosopher has plowed that ground. By now, it is difficult to say anything new about universals and particulars, particularly without showing, by an exhaustive review of the literature, that your "new" opinion has not been turned up many times before. I am not about to engage in an exhaustive review and I am not even going to claim that I am about to unearth some treasure. Nevertheless, I will venture to offer a different, if not new, view of how the disciplines of moral philosophy and theological ethics bear on the activities of the contemporary ethicists, particularly the bioethicists.

I now believe that our table talk of years ago was misguided. We were seeking a synonym for "moral theologian" and we chose "ethicist." That word is not, in my present view, a synonym; rather it is a specification. It designates a special function or activity of persons who have some academic background in philosophical or theological ethics. Such persons may perform that special activity regularly—or from time to time or never—but when they do, they can be called "ethicists." Those who do it regularly deserve the title as a matter of course; those who do it occasionally or never are best called moral philosophers or moral theologians. What is the special function or activity that deserves the appellation "ethicist"? What do ethicists do when they do ethics?

My thesis about what ethicists do when they are being ethicists is this: They invent and improvise arguments. Some will relish that statement because they have always believed that ethicists did just that: They made it all up! However, I use "invent" and "improvise," not in their common sense of "originate" or "concoct," but in a special, technical sense. Both words are terms of art, the first in classical rhetoric and the second in classical music. Classical rhetoric provided the model and methods for classical casuistry. The invention that I will describe is an essential element of casuistry, as Stephen Toulmin and I attempted to show.[7] We did not, however, explore deeply enough the way in which the rhetorical technique of invention functions within casuistic reasoning. I hope my reflections in this essay will intrigue someone to a deeper exploration. As for the musical term of art, "improvisation," it has no intrinsic connection with casuistry, even though Toulmin and I have suggested that casuistry had many of the characteristics of the Baroque era in which casuistry thrived, and the great music of that time provides the most exquisite examples of improvisation. Rhetorical and casuistic invention, I claim, is an actual feature of the ethicist's art and improvisation is a simile to elucidate rhetorical and casuistic invention.

Invention

"Invention" was a central concept of classical rhetoric. Cicero, most eloquent of the classical rhetoricians, wrote, "Invention is the primary and most important part of rhetoric," and defined it as "the thinking out (*excogitatio*) of valid or seemingly valid arguments to render one's cause plausible (*probabilem*).[8] A modern philosophical rhetorician defines invention as "the art of discovering new arguments and uncovering new things by argument . . . [it] extends from the construction of formal arguments to all modes of enlarging experience by reason as manifested in awareness, emotion, interest, and appreciation."[9] All classical rhetoricians devoted lengthy treatises to invention, explaining the ways in which an orator, usually in a forensic or political case, might "discover" the arguments that will "make the case." The classical rhetoricians offer a plethora of rules and methods to guide invention.

These rules and methods were based on the "topics," literally, the "places" where arguments are found. These "topics" of classical rhetoric are resources for invention of argument. The rhetoricians distinguished topics into common and special. Common topics are the constant, intrinsic features of all reasonable discourse regardless of the subject matter. These are: stating definitions; making distinctions; reasoning by induction or deduction; offering examples; proposing analogies, comparisons, and contrasts by similarity, difference, and degree; stating relationships of cause/effect, of antecedent and consequent; describing circumstances as possible and impossible, past and future. These are developed as ways of arguing about any issue. They have no content or matter on their own, but receive all content and matter from the subject under discussion. The special topics applied only to discourse about certain subject matter. Thus, in a judicial case about a crime, causation, occasion, and motive, would be central topics; in a discourse on foreign policy the national interest, feasibility, and effects on other nations would be essential elements. These, in contrast to the common topics, have a subject matter that derives from the kind of issue under discussion. For this reason Aristotle said that one who "would invent arguments must know some, if not all, the facts about the subject under discussion." Again, this does not mean the "data" of the case but the nature of the contingent activity, practice, or institution under analysis. Thus, one cannot invent arguments about medicine without knowing what medicine is and how it proceeds in its application to the care of patients; one cannot invent arguments about banking without knowing what banks are and how they work. The information contained in these understandings is not only empirical—what, for example, a surgical operation is as distinguished from a medical intervention or what a rate of interest is. It is also valuational—under what circumstances of risk would medicine be preferred to surgery, or a line of credit to an equity loan. Within the factual and valued realm of these practices and institutions, arguments are invented. They are invented, in the sense of discovered or found, because they lie within the practices of those institutions (and not of others); but they are invented, in the sense of improvised, by being formulated, justified, and criticized by the methods of rhetorical argument. The arguments become regulated reflections or methodic considerations in the context of the subject under scrutiny.

The common and special topics provided frames, already constructed by the nature of reasonable discourse and the subject under debate, within which the particular circumstances of persons, times, and places posed by the case at hand could be set. The orator had the freedom to select, order, and emphasize those particulars within the frame of appropriate topics. In this way orators invented arguments whereby they moved from the statement of the case to confirmation or proof which, as Cicero wrote, "marshals arguments to lend credibility, authority and support to our case."[10]

Improvisation

The word "invention" or "discovery," even in this technical sense, can be somewhat misleading. Although a review of its treatment in the classical rhetoricians reveals it bound in conventions and rules, it suggests to the modern mind an exercise of unfettered imagination. In order to render clearer my contention about what ethicists do, permit a simile between invention and musical improvisation. Again, we begin with a broad definition. "Improvisation," says a dictionary of music, "is the invention of music at the time it is being performed . . . on the spot, without being written down."[11] This is, of course, the way most music has been made through human history and it is the way much of the best jazz is made today. In the seventeenth and eighteenth centuries, as composers perfected the concerto form for orchestra and solo instrument, they allowed the soloist an opportunity to show technical skill by departing from the composer's notation and playing freely for some time. These "cadenzas" came just before the end of the first movement, following the statement of themes and their recapitulation, so that the player might pick up the melodies already established in the notated score and modify them in harmony, rhythm, modulation of key, and phrasing. The player now becomes an improvisationist, allowed to depart from the notation of the composer's score, but still restrained within certain limits as he or she creates music extemporaneously. Melodies, while varied, are still heard; keys are modulated but not forgotten. The sounds of the improvisation must, in some definite way, echo the sounds of the score. Haydn, it is said, was once so dismayed by a soloist's liberties that he loudly remarked at the end of the cadenza, "welcome home, Mr. Dubourg." Improvisation allows the virtuoso to stray, wander, explore, but not too far from home. It departs from the composition and must return to it; and, indeed, even as it flows from the artist's virtuosity, it must remain at least remotely true to the composer's inspiration. Improvisation is, I am told, a difficult art. While Mozart and the other great composers left cadenzas to their performers, they also wrote them themselves. Today most players play the composer's cadenza rather than improvise.

Improvisation is like invention in that both take definite material as the base and frame for creative interpretation. Rhetorical invention finds the common and special topics suited to the case and allows the orator to work creatively with the actual circumstances of persons, times, and places. The orator invents with the standard materials and with the unique elements that a particular case presents. Musical improvisation provides musicians with melodies and key and lets them display notes, harmonies, and rhythms that expand, emphasize, and reorder the original set composition. The simile is not, of course, perfect but it begins, I think, to reveal how ethicists work with their materials, which are the general concepts of morality and the particulars of issues, questions, and cases.

Ethics as Improvisation

Contemporary ethicists do ethics the way a classical pianist improvised a cadenza in a Mozart concerto. Banish any thought that this simile is intended to lend the genius of Mozart or of Horowitz, Rubenstein, Brendel, de la Rocha, et al. to the humble work of the ethicists! Rather, I suggest that the nature of classical improvisation is similar to the task of practical ethics. The classical rhetoricians proposed that rhetoric was, as Aristotle said, "a combination of logic and ethics."[12] It had, among its functions, persuasion to live "the good life" by reason, emotion, example, and argument. Thus, its prime and principal part, invention, must also be the prime and principal part of doing ethics. However, the invention of arguments in practical ethics is properly improvisation because, like the classical soloist, the ethicist must improvise by moving from themes already laid down.

Ethicists must improvise. The very nature of ethical discourse and reflection demands it. Improvisation consists in the movement of mind as it seeks to understand concepts and arguments as they appear in particular issues and cases. Aristotle, writing about rhetoric, said, "whether our argument concerns public affairs or base and noble deeds, or justice and injustice, we must know some, if not all, of the facts about the subject about which we argue. Otherwise we can have no materials out of which to construct arguments."[13] Note that the material of the argument comes from "the facts about the subject." This might seem peculiar to those who are committed to ethical theory and/or to theological premises as the source of ethical arguments. Aristotle certainly does not mean to deny that those constructions are relevant. After all, his *Ethics* and *Politics* are landmark attempts to formulate similar universal truths about life and society. Even *Rhetoric*, in which he makes this statement, contains a minitreatise on ethics and politics. Still, the "facts of the subject" are, in his view, an indispensable source of the material of argument. The argument is invented and improvised out of these facts; the facts are brought into contact with the broader considerations by the rational ingenuity appropriate to that sort of argument.

Some clarifications are in order. First, the phrase "facts of the subject" is a poor translation of Aristotle's Greek, which comes closer to "the way things are." He is not thinking of facts, as we do today, namely, the supposedly hard-edged bits of the material world that one offers in evidence as judicial proof or scientific data. Rather, "the way things are" refers to events in time, institutional structures, cultural conventions, professional practices, and many other features of the world of personal and social experience. Even the "real facts about justice and goodness" (hardly empirical data) must be known and, says the philosopher, "This is the only way in which anyone ever proves anything . . . by trying to think out arguments for special needs as they arise." This invention, however, does not ignore the broader considerations, as the improvisationist does not ignore the themes established by the composer. Aristotle, Cicero, and the other rhetoricians give large place to general understandings and appreciations of human nature and the human condition. But never do they pretend that the arguments about the goodness and justice of this or that action, this or that event, can be ascertained by reference only to those general considerations.

The activity of invention and improvisation is essentially an exercise of rational ingenuity. One aspect of that rational ingenuity is the drawing of the broader consider-

ations into the particular issue under scrutiny—that is, the relating of theory to decision. I shall say more about this much-discussed matter in a moment. For the time being, suffice it to say that, in this rhetorical invention of argument, theory and decision
are not drawn together by the deductive syllogisms of formal logic. Aristotle takes great
pains to distinguish the syllogism of dialectic from that of rhetoric, to which he gives
the name "enthymeme." Modern logic texts define an ethymeme as a truncated syllogism in which one of the premises is implied rather than expressed. The classical
rhetoricians used the term to describe arguments that led from probable premises to
tentative conclusions as distinguished from scientific syllogisms which moved from
universal truths to necessary conclusions. This is the kind of reasoning suited to contingent, human affairs. The word "enthymeme" itself suggests this: It comes from the
Greek, "to take to heart, to consider, to reflect," and thus is properly Englished as "reflections" or "considerations," a far cry from the "linking of concepts" which constitutes the categorical, hypothetical, and disjunctive syllogisms of formal logic. On the
other hand, those English words are very lax and loose. As we shall see, the rhetorical
notion of enthymemic argument has some structure and some rules, even though not
precisely those of formal logic. Perhaps some expression such as "regulated reflection"
or "methodic consideration" might strike a mean. Nevertheless, Aristotle asserts,
"everyone who effects persuasion through proof does in fact use either enthymemes
or examples: there is no other way."[14]

An Ethicist Improvising

It is time to turn from this vague and probably obscure exposition to an example. We
could find examples on many pages of contemporary bioethics. The authors of the
best examples will probably be unaware that they are inventing and improvising by using Aristotle's examples and enthymemes. They may not consciously be employing the
topics of classical rhetoric. Yet close examination of many essays will show just that.
The literature on forgoing life support, informed consent, confidentiality, truth telling,
genetic screening, and all the other standard subjects of bioethics will bear witness. A
good article in bioethics is a cadenza of ethical improvisation.

I choose one such good article, written many years ago: Professor Gustafson's
"Mongolism, Parental Desires, and the Right to Life."[15] Jim Gustafson is not often an
ethicist, in my sense of the word. He prefers to remain a theologian, working to articulate the "Theocentric Perspectives" for ethics.[16] However, in this essay he becomes
an exemplary ethicist. The essay was written as commentary on a short film that dra-
matized the decision to allow a newborn infant to die. The film was produced by the
Joseph Kennedy Jr. Foundation and was shown at a conference, "Choices on Our Conscience," held in Washington, D.C., on October 16, 1971. The infant in the film was
affected by the genetic disorder Down's syndrome, which causes severe to moderate

mental retardation. (In 1971, that condition was commonly called by the now discarded term "mongolism," which was used in the film and in Gustafson's article.) Within hours of its birth, the baby was discovered to have esophageal atresia, a blockage of his intestines that could be easily corrected by surgery. His parents elected not to have the life-saving surgery and the child died of malnutrition several days later. This film, based on two similar cases at the Johns Hopkins University Hospital, was shown in many settings, particularly in medical schools, and aroused vigorous debate about the morality of the parent's choice.

Gustafson begins his article by relating the facts of the case. He then acknowledges that the case will appear differently to various participants and observers, depending on the "picture we draw of its salient features." He sets out to represent those "salient features for each of the participants: features that are value laden and in part determinative of their decisions . . . and indicate the reasons that might justify their decisions." Working from the dialogue of the film, other materials, and interviews with doctors and nurses, he attempts to construct the way in which the principals viewed the dilemma. The mother's view is captured in her remarks that she had "negative feelings," did not want a retarded child, and that raising a child with Down's syndrome would not be fair to the other children in the family. These remarks allow the ethicist to invent arguments that follow the first steps in rhetorical invention: definition, distinction, and analogy. He asks, "what moral weight can negative feeling have?" To this, he responds with a distinction that moral weight could be granted on "two quite different grounds": first, the view that in all moral decisions there are emotional elements that defy rational justification and yet must be given some weight; and second, the possibility that the negative feelings reflect the mother's apprehension that she would be unable to love such a child in the future. The ethicist then turns to the terms, "wants" and "desires," and attempts to clarify their ethical relevance by two analogies, one with a person not wanting to give money for a charitable cause, the other with a woman not wanting to accept an offer of marriage. The ethicist then notes the similarities and differences between the pertinent points of the analogies and the case at hand. Both analogies shed light on what is a difficult point to make when considered only in the abstract—namely, the distinction between the moral force of an obligation and of a desire. Analogy, with precise designation of the relevant similarities and differences, is a classical technique of invention.

The use of the analogies allows the ethicist to introduce "the ethical question to the mother. . . . Does the infant's physical life lay an unconditioned moral claim on the mother (who does not want to acknowledge it)?" Gustafson then proposes the strongest argument that could justify her negative answer: There are no unconditioned moral claims on a person when those presumed claims go against one's desires; one's personal wishes and desires are sufficient moral grounds to reject any claim from another. The ethicist then notes that one trend in our culture, strong individualism, supports such a proposition; however, another, arising from a repudiation of discrimination, goes against it. Thus, cultural backing is ambiguous and doubt is thrown on the strength of the proposition. Finally, the ethicist uses the classical technique of definition: What does it mean to say that raising a child with Down's syndrome would be "unfair" to the other children? Recourse to the tradition of moral philosophy shows that fairness and justice have several different meanings with quite different implications for this case. However, all these meanings point to a basic issue: Is the child with Down's syndrome "unequal" to other children, such that he or she can justly be treated differently? If so, in what does that difference consist? This leads the ethicist to another exercise in distinction: What are the qualities that are deficient in this child and how might they justify different treatment?

Thus far the ethicist has invented several important arguments, uncovered by the techniques of definition, distinction, and analogy. Each technique, which could be used in any sort of ethical discourse, becomes concrete and specific in the setting of the facts about medicine, Down's syndrome, and the presumed stance taken by the mother. The resolution of this first section is tentative, but the invented arguments have at least cast some doubt on the soundness of the claim that preferences are sufficient to deny all moral claims.

The ethicist then examines the physicians' contributions in the case that "enable us to formulate a constellation of values that determined their actions. . . . The physicians felt no moral or legal obligation to save the life of a[n] . . . infant [with Down's syndrome] by an ordinary surgical procedure when the parents did not desire that it should live." He then distinguishes this into two points, the obligation of the physicians to acquiesce to the parents' desires and the fact that the infant had Down's syndrome. The first of these presumably rests on the principle that parents have the right to determine whether an infant shall live. The classical rhetoricians would call this principle a "maxim," for it is a moral affirmation more tailored to the matter at hand (i.e., the parent-infant relationship) than are the more universally phrased principles about autonomy. This maxim is then examined, first by noting its similarities and differences with the widely accepted practice of allowing family to chose termination of life support for a dying patient. The analogy is more different than similar to the case at hand. The second probe asks how far parental discretion might extend. If one admits it in abortion, does one admit it after birth? and, if one admits it after birth, does one admit it for active killing? and, if so, for any reason or only for certain ones? The ethicist is asking whether the maxim can be consistently applied to various apparently similar situations and, if not, why not.

This line of argument leads to an examination of the reason that was central to this case, namely, the deficiency in intelligence predictable in children with Down's syndrome. The ethicist now attempts "to find as precisely as possible what principles or values might be invoked to claim that the 'defectiveness' was sufficient to warrant not sustaining the life of this infant." One general principle or maxim is invoked, "an infant with any empirically verifiable deficit has no right to life." The ethicist immediately dismisses this: "no one would apply such a principle." This is a rhetorical *reductio ad absurdum*. A more limited maxim is tried, namely, "carriers of a genetic defect that would have potentially bad consequences for future generations have no right to life." The ethicist knows that this does not apply to Down's syndrome, which is not an inheritable genetic defect, but he offers as a more pertinent example hemophilia. He then says that he "finds no evidence" that physicians would accept so broad a principle. They would wish to have a more specific designation of the kind and degree of abnormality. This argument appeals to an important element of rhetoric, which philosophers often disdain: How likely is it that persons in general or of a certain sort will entertain the claim seriously?

The ethicist then refines the maxim down to whether the right to life depends on "the capacity for normal intelligence." He tests that maxim by suggesting that it is "simplistic"—that is, its simple statement hides many confounding variables. For example, many intelligent persons are not commendable, and many persons of limited intelligence do commendable things. Therefore, why should intelligence be selected as the overriding feature among all features of human life? To come closer to the case, why should "the potential of a [person with Down's syndrome] for satisfaction in life, for fulfilling his [or her] limited capacities, for happiness, for providing the occasions of meaningful (sometimes distressing and sometimes joyful) experience for others" not also count? These confounding variables suggest that the maxim about limited intelligence is less than adequate for moral guidance.

Ethicists, Theologians, and Philosophers

Gustafson reviews a variety of other arguments in the rest of his essay. In all of this invention, he has made no notable reference to moral theory or to theological principle. His allusions to moral philosophy are glancing at best. Someone who has read moral philosophy might recognize the problem of making moral obligation contingent on desires. Even without that background, the ethicist's use of definition, distinction, and analogy suffices to make the point clear to any thinking person. Again, the philosophical tradition provides the ethicist with classical definitions of "fairness and justice," but the passage in which these appear can be understood (and probably could have been crafted) by any thinking and morally sensitive person. Finally, an excursus on the meaning of "ordinary" and "extraordinary" means of treatment presupposes some knowledge of Roman Catholic moral theology which originated those terms. Nonetheless, the excursus, while illuminating, is not an essential part of the case, since no reference was made to it by the participants, nor is it an essential part of the argument invented by the ethicist. Thus, for most of its text, Gustafson's article does ethics by invention and improvisation. It offers maxims that any person might offer (and some of the participants did offer). These maxims were largely situational—that is, they state values relevant to the situation of parents deciding about the medical treatment of a child with a known genetic defect leading to impaired mental development. Those maxims are examined by testing the definition of the terms within them, by inquiring whether they can be consistently applied to analogous cases, by suggesting that they are too broad or too limited or too simplistic to be useful moral guides. These are classic techniques of invention. They are improvised by the author to suit the case.

In the very last pages of the essay, the improvisation becomes manifest. Gustafson concludes by stating a point of view, which he espouses as his own, from which the case might be evaluated differently from the way the parents and physicians actually evaluated it. This requires replaying the two major themes of the case, namely "(1) whether what one ought to do is determined by what one desires to do and (2) whether a[n] . . . infant [with Down's syndrome] has a right to life." The ethicist now states that "one can recast the moral dilemma by giving a different weight" to these two themes. In the musical analogy, the themes are transposed into a different key. The tonalities of the new key come more directly from moral philosophy and moral theology than did the inventions of the first part of the essay. Even then, they are subtle. The ethicist reexamines the relation between desires and obligations. In the first part, he had cast doubt on the proposal that obligations are contingent on desires; now he firmly asserts that they are not—first by an analogy with common experience, then by a dissertation on an unequivocally stated principle: "I would argue that the fact that we brought our children into being lays a moral obligation on my wife and me to sustain and care for them to the best of our ability." This principle is not merely stipulated; it is defended by arguments, and again the arguments are invented. The relationship of dependence initiates the obligation; it is not conditioned by the qualities of the child or by the child's future (which may be relevant only in certain extreme cases). The features of a humane society are invoked to support this principle, and the negative consequences of ignoring it are noted. The suffering that fulfilling these obligations might entail is assessed for its moral relevance, again by analogies, with the conclusion that suffering, if not unbearable, is often a consequence of moral obligation.

In the last two paragraphs, the improvisation returns to the tonality of theology, just as a pianist ends an improvisation in the tonic key that brings his invention back to the keynote of the score. In actuality, Gustafson had not stated these themes at the beginning of the essay. He could have exposed this theological doctrines at the beginning of the essay, as do many philosophers and theologians. However, he has stated them powerfully in other writings, which might be thought of, within our metaphorical analysis, as the opening chords for this particular ethical concerto. His theological premises for the moral life are: God intends the well-being of the creation; God is both the ordering power that preserves and sustains the well-being of creation and the power that creates new possibilities for well-being in nature and history; humans are finite and "sinful" agents whose actions have a large measure of power to determine whether the well-being of the creation is sustained and fulfilled.[17] These theological themes were not announced in the opening pages of Gustafson's essay. When they are heard in the last paragraphs, they come in muted tones. "My view, grounded ultimately in religious convictions as well as moral beliefs, is that to be human is to have a vocation, a calling and the calling of each of us is 'to be for others' as least as much as 'to be for ourselves.'" Even then, Gustafson suggests, this view is not a recourse to "dogmatic religious authority," but indicates a "central thrust in Judaism and Christianity which has nourished and sustained a fundamental moral outlook." In so qualifying his theological affirmations, he suggests that anyone sensitive to that fundamental moral outlook, regardless of his or her commitment to its theological sources, could understand and appreciate his arguments. The theological perspective, however, "shapes a bias, gives a weight, toward the well-being of the other against the inconvenience or cost to oneself. In this case, I believe that all the rational inferences drawn from it and all the emotive power that this calling evokes, lead to the conclusion that the ordinary surgical procedure should have been done, and the . . . infant's life saved."

Gustafson's coda, then, announces his theological premises. When he says, "all the rational inferences drawn from" those premises, he commits a slight slip, for which Aristotle might have chided him. The philosopher says, "there is an important distinction between two sorts of enthymemes that has been wholly overlooked by almost everybody."[18] The overlooked distinction is that between the lines of argument proper to a special discipline, say politics or theology, and those lines that can be applied "equally to questions of right conduct, natural science, politics and many other things that have nothing to do with one another.," that is, the "common topics of classical rhetoric." Professor Gustafson can be chided because the words "rational inferences that can be drawn" suggest that his arguments concluding in favor of the child's life are syllogistically deduced from his theological premises. I would contend, however, that rather than being so inferred, they have been invented and improvised. He has done in his article on Down's syndrome what he described elsewhere as the work of ethical analysis "in circumstances of great novelty," and which I believe is the work of ethical analysis in general. "Analogies must be explored; general rules or principles applied insofar as possible and exceptions to them thought through carefully, probabilities of consequences must be weighed."[19] This is the work of invention and improvisation.

He goes on to say, "I believe it is coherent with the three theological principles stated above to act in such circumstances if there appears to be a significant series of good reasons to do so. . . . Absolute moral certitude is impossible." In these words, he returns to the good graces of Aristotle and Cicero. Both of these ancients strongly endorse the view that ethical deliberation is about probabilities and contingencies and hence that absolute certitude is out of the question. Moreover, Gustafson's "series of good reasons" echoes Cicero's call for a *"copia argumentorum,"* an abundance of argument, to make a case.[20] Indeed, that is what he has done in "Mongolism, Parental Desires, and the Right to Life"; a multitude of arguments of different sorts, but all pertinent to the case, are summoned, scrutinized, and assessed for their utility as guides toward a moral decision. Finally, "coherent" is the word to be preferred to the phrase "inferences drawn from," for his own selection of regulated reflection and methodic considerations (i.e., enthymemes) is not dictated by the theological premises but is suggested by them, in the way that the melodies of an improvisation are suggested by the melodic materials and tonalities of the noted composition. They are coherent with each other.

Practical Ethics and the Depths of Good and Evil

I have tried to suggest that ethicists do something different than, but compatible with, the activities of philosophers and theologians. Ethicists invent arguments following the general patterns of reasoning proper to deliberation and persuasion in practical matters that were first sketched by the classical rhetoricians. In McKeon's words, "they discover new arguments and uncover new things by argument."[21] The discoveries are made in the matter of the issue at hand, and drawn out of the facts that constitute that matter. They are articulated by the rational ingenuity of argument. In making these discoveries, they need not draw in any explicit way on moral theory or theological doctrine. However, because ethicists usually are philosophers and theologians, those theories and doctrines will be present somehow as they invent argument. I have suggested that the improvisation of the classical sonata might be a useful metaphor to aid in understanding how that presence manifests itself. Arguments are improvised, not only by the techniques of invention, but under the influence of the themes and tonalities of the larger composition. It is possible, then, for a theologian or philosopher to write a compelling essay in bioethics with hardly a word of explicit theology or philosophy. Indeed, Stanley Hauerwas has admitted that he "kidded Paul Ramsey that all the theology in *The Patient as Person* was in the Preface. He did not find the remark humorous."[22] I do not know quite why Ramsey was not amused, but I believe it is possible for the themes of Christian ethics or of moral philosophy to preface a series of ethical arguments and to influence them in ways that do not require explicit reference or constant restatement. Ramsey's arguments about experimentation on children, on organ transplantation, and on caring only for the dying are invented ones that carry their own plausibility; his preference everywhere evident for the sanctity of the individual is the constant echo of the Christian theme of the preface.

In the end, Dietrich Bonhoeffer's eloquent denunciation of the "theoretical ethicists" serves as a context for my interpretation of how ethicists work and how they differ from theologians and philosophers (which they may, of course, often be). Recall that Bonhoeffer said, "One is distressed by the failure of reasonable people to perceive either the depths of evil or the depths of the holy." It is my belief that contemporary practical ethics, at least bioethics, is rather remote from the depths of evil or the depths of the holy. These depths lie beneath many aspects of modern life. War—with its potential for total destruction of the earth, on the one hand, and gruesome, hateful savagery on the other—clearly hangs above those depths. Tyranny, with its extinction of human liberty and its raw exploitation of people, also hangs there. Many forms of political power that are not quite tyrannical but live off corruption are close by. Hatred fostered by religious belief collapses the depth of the holy into the depth of evil. Sexuality that destroys innocence or tramples freedom does the same. In these matters, no ethics need be done. There is no room for "little reason" before these horrors. Religious and philosophical ethics may consider these issues, but not in order to explicate arguments for their justification or even condemnation. They must be condemned outright. The chain of argument leading to that condemnation is not long. These disciplines may consider these subjects in order to unmask them. As Bonhoeffer says in the same passage, "If evil appears in the form of light, beneficence, loyalty and renewal, if it conforms to historical necessity and social justice, then this is clear additional proof of its abysmal wickedness, but the moral theorist is blinded by it."[23] Should such evil disguise itself, moralists must tear off the disguise. Bonhoeffer's "theoretical ethicist" failed to do that, and monstrous evil triumphed for a while.

Condemnation of evil and tearing off the disguises under which evil masquerades as good require a vision of the good. In this sense, the Platonic insight into the good still serves us well: There must be a vision *(theoria)* of what the good human life must be. Theologians articulate that vision by the way in which they read the documents of their faith and interpret the experiences of the people, past and present, who have lived that faith. Philosophers articulate it by reflection on the human condition as it appears not simply in its contingencies, but in the conditions that make those contingencies possible. Since theologians' and philosophers' visions may encompass many aspects of human life, it is legitimate to focus on the moral aspect and thus make moral philosophy and theology. Both of these disciplines should present visions that reveal the depths of evil and the depths of the holy or of the good life.

None of this is the work of ethics, as I understand it. Ethics is at work in a quite different setting. It works where persons of decency and integrity attempt to understand how they can live humanly and humanely in a complex world of competing forces and enticements. They live on a plateau between the twin abysses of evil and the holy and rarely venture up to the brink of either. The plateau itself is not an entirely peaceful place. It is built up with many enterprises that are themselves positive contributions to human life, but most of which are, at least in our times, very complex. They offer benefits and burdens (rather than holiness and evil), and the relation of the benefits to the burdens is often obscure. Benefits rarely come without burdens, and even when they do, they may turn burdensome by time, abuse, neglect, or exploitation. The distribution of benefits and burdens is a particularly vexing problem, for the people who inhabit the plateau are of diverse power and talent. The enterprises are many: Family, education, government, business, religion, and medicine are among them. Each of these has many conventions and rules which often conflict, and each has features that can be corrupted and exploited. This is the place where the practical ethicist must work, inventing arguments with "the little reason" that may not "clamp together the parting timbers of the building," but will shed some light into the obscurity that besets the enterprises of decent but confused persons.

Notes

1. Gina Kolata, "Ethicists Wary over New Gene Technique's Consequences," *New York Times,* 22 November 1994, B9.

2. James Gustafson, "Theology Confronts Technology and the Life Sciences," *Commonweal* 105 (16 June 1978): 386.

3. Paul Ramsey, *The Patient as Person* (New Haven: Yale University Press, 1970), ix.

4. James Gustafson, "The Burden of the Ethical: Reflections on Disinterestedness and Involvement," in *Theology and Christian Ethics* (Philadelphia: Pilgrim Press, 1974), 33.

5. Dietrich Bonhoeffer, *Ethics,* trans. N. H. Smith (New York: Macmillan, 1955), 64.

6. Ibid., 65–66.

7. Albert Jonsen and Stephen Toulmin, *The Abuse of Casuistry: A History of Moral Reasoning* (Berkeley and Los Angeles: University of California Press, 1988), 83–88, 145, 257–58.

8. Marcus Tullius Cicero, "On Invention," in *Cicero,* trans. H. M. Hubbell (Cambridge: Harvard University Press, 1976), 2: 178; 1: 9.

9. Richard McKeon, *Rhetoric* (Woodbridge, Conn.: Ox Bow Press, 1987), 58.

10. Cicero, "On Invention," 1: xxiv.

11. *HarperCollins Dictionary of Music* (New York: HarperCollins, 1995), 194.

12. Aristotle, "Rhetoric," in *The Basic Works of Aristotle,* ed. R. McKeon (New York: Random House, 1941), I, 4, 1359b10.

13. Ibid., II, 22, 1396a5.

14. Ibid., I, 2, 1356b5.

15. James Gustafson, "Mongolism, Parental Desires, and the Right to Life," *Perspectives in Biology and Medicine* 16 (summer 1973): 529–57.

16. James Gustafson, *Ethics from a Theocentric Perspective,* 2 vols. (Chicago: University of Chicago Press, 1981–1984).

17. James Gustafson, *Contributions of Theology to Medical Ethics* (Milwaukee: Marquette University Press, 1975), 18–22.

18. Aristotle, "Rhetoric," 1358a3.

19. Gustafson, *Contributions of Theology to Medical Ethics,* 90.

20. Cicero, "On Invention," 1: xii.

21. McKeon, *Rhetoric,* 58.

22. Stanley Hauerwas, "How Christian Ethics Became Medical Ethics: The Case of Paul Ramsey," *Christian Bioethics* 1 (1995): 15.

23. Bonhoeffer, *Ethics,* 65.

Chapter 14

Human Genetic Intervention and the Theologians: Cosmic Theology and Casuistic Analysis

LEROY WALTERS

The central thesis of this essay is that, from 1965 to the present, theologians have employed two distinct and quite different modes of thought in discussing the question of human genetic intervention. The first mode is what I will call cosmic theology. This mode takes the long view in examining the question of genetic intervention: It sees such intervention in the context of evolution, the divine role in creating and sustaining the world, and human responsibility vis-à-vis the entire creation. In the 1960s cosmic theology was represented by thinkers like Paul Ramsey, Karl Rahner, and James Gustafson. The second mode of thought is what might best be called casuistic analysis. This mode looks at near-term technological possibilities and attempts to draw lines among potential applications of new genetic knowledge. The second mode of analysis was initially represented by such theologians as James Gustafson and Paul Ramsey and was later embodied in the writings of John Fletcher.

A subsidiary thesis of this essay is that James Gustafson has made important contributions to both modes of thought about human genetic intervention. However, as his thinking has evolved, he has tended more in the direction of cosmic theology and has been less engaged in casuistic analysis. This trend is especially clear in his magnum opus, *Ethics from a Theocentric Perspective*.

Cosmic Theology: The Early Years

In the beginning there were the geneticists and a paleontologist. The early writings that most closely parallel cosmic theology were authored by geneticists J. B. S. Haldane,

Hermann J. Muller, and Theodosius Dobzhansky. Their works bore titles like *Daedalus, or Science and the Future* (1924),[1] *Out of the Night: A Biologist's View of the Future* (1935),[2] and *Mankind Evolving: The Evolution of the Human Species* (1962).[3] Independently, a French Jesuit who was also a paleontologist, Pierre Teilhard de Chardin, mused about human evolution in an essay about "The Directions and Conditions of the Future" (1948)[4] and in a book about *The Human Phenomenon* (1955).[5]

Between 1965 and 1967 three theologians based on two continents laid the foundations for the cosmic-theological approach to genetic intervention: Paul Ramsey, Karl Rahner, and James Gustafson. Two of the theologians were Protestants; the other was a Catholic. Because the theological presuppositions and methods of the three theologians were so diverse, they reached quite different conclusions about the appropriateness of human genetic intervention.

There is a direct link between one of the geneticists mentioned above, H. J. Muller, and the first U.S. essay written in the mode of cosmic theology. In January 1965 Paul Ramsey launched a vigorous attack on Muller's voluntary-eugenic proposals. His essay, which was part of the First Nobel Conference at Gustavus Adolphus College, was entitled "Moral and Religious Aspects of Genetic Control."[6] The essay is best known to most of us through its republication as the first chapter in *Fabricated Man*, which appeared in 1970.[7] What is less well known is that Paul Ramsey had corresponded with H. J. Muller in October of 1964 and that Muller in his reply had provided Ramsey with an extensive reading list on the topics of genetic intervention and eugenics.[8] In his usual thorough fashion, Ramsey had devoured the literature suggested by Muller, and much of that literature appears in the footnotes of Ramsey's essay.

The subtlety and complexity of Ramsey's pioneering essay cannot be rehearsed here. The principal themes of his cosmic theology are that God is in control of history and that human beings have no strong moral obligation to prevent the gradual, inexorable deterioration of the human gene pool which Muller had so graphically described. In fact, Ramsey argued, "God means to kill us all in the end, and in the end [God] is going to succeed."[9] Because of this lack of a strong obligation to save the human race, humans are free, in Ramsey's view, to opt for an ethic of means rather than an ethic of ends.[10] Specifically, Christian and Jewish theologians are empowered to reject artificial insemination with donor sperm (AID) and the improvement of the human gene pool as illegitimate means to a seemingly worthy end.

Eight months after Paul Ramsey had delivered his lecture at Gustavus Adolphus College, Catholic theologian Karl Rahner spoke to the Dutch Society of St. Adelbert in the Hague in a lecture entitled "Experiment Human Being: Theological Remarks on the Self-Manipulation of Human Beings.[11] In his September 1965 essay Rahner explicitly declined to discuss the moral-theological dimensions of his topic.[12] Instead, he sought to develop a theological anthropology, a general perspective on human nature. The contrast in tone between Ramsey's view and Rahner's could hardly have been more pronounced. Here is the core of Rahner's anthropology.

No longer does man create himself merely as a moral and theoretical being under God, but as an earthly, corporeal and historical being. Passive biological evolution is being extended, at least to an initial degree, by an active evolution of civilisation. But the latter is not only external and supplementary: it is actually continuing its own biological evolution. This self-manipulation is not only carried out unconsciously, as was the case almost exclusively in the past, but deliberately planned, programmed and controlled. Man no longer makes himself merely with reference to eternity but with reference to history itself as such.

In this way, however, what he has always been now comes to light. What he has always been at the root of his transcendental spiritual and intellectual essence as a free being now extends its influence to his psyche and his physical and social existence, and is made manifest expressly in these dimensions. To a certain degree his ultimate essence has broken through to the outer regions of his existence. To a larger, more comprehensive, radical and tangible extent man has become what, according to the Christian understanding, he *is*: the free being who has been handed over to himself.[13]

In his 1965 essay Rahner gave little indication of the sources that he had been reading, in either theology or biology, that had given rise to his choice of genetic intervention as a topic. The only two sources he explicitly cited were "Huxley" (presumably Julian) and "Elisabeth Mann Borghese," whom he identified, respectively, as "Anglo-Saxon and Communist prophets of this future self-manipulation."[14] However, Rahner had been engaged in an ongoing conversation with the natural sciences, and especially with his confrere Paul Overhage, since at least 1959. In that year, Rahner included Overhage's book, *On the Appearance [or Phenotype] of the First Human Beings,* in the *Quaestiones Disputatae* series that he was coediting.[15] He also wrote an introduction to Overhage's work. Two years later, Rahner and Overhage collaborated in writing a book entitled *The Problem of Hominization.*[16]

Both of these works were cited in Rahner's 1967 essay entitled "The Problem of Genetic Manipulation,"[17] in which he further developed his thought on human self-manipulation. Though Rahner reaffirmed his anthropological point in the early part of this second essay, the general tone of the 1967 essay was much more cautious, particularly when Rahner considered the use of artificial insemination by donor (AID) as a means by which human genetic intervention might be attempted. Rahner also expressed opposition to the "neurotic" attempt to control all the characteristics of one's progeny by genetic means.[18]

James Gustafson's first discussion of human genetic intervention followed the publication of Rahner's first essay on the subject (in German) by a few months. At the third Nobel Conference sponsored by Gustavus Adolphus College, in January 1967, Gustafson presented a paper entitled "Christian Humanism and the Human Mind."[19] In that paper, he discovered a theme that would remain central to his work for the remainder of his academic career: human responsibility for "human nature" and for the future evolution of the human race. The most relevant sciences were molecular biology and neurobiology. The problematic had been set by Teilhard de Chardin when he wrote, "We are evolution," and "We have become aware that, in the great game that is being played, we are the players as well as being the cards and the stakes."[20] In the essay, Gustafson acknowledged his indebtedness to thinkers as diverse as Henri Bergson, Alfred North Whitehead, Charles Hartshorne, Teilhard, and H. Richard Niebuhr. In his own constructive proposal, Gustafson opted for a position that he acknowledged "sounds terribly like a 'middle way'"—a way that opts "for realism without despair, for hope without illusions, for avoiding the attitudes of apocalypticism on the one hand and utopianism on the other."[21]

Gustafson returned to the theme of human genetic intervention in a paper entitled "Genetic Engineering and the Normative View of the Human,"[22] which he prepared for a December 1969 interdisciplinary symposium. By 1969 Gustafson could cite not only Teilhard de Chardin but also Rahner's essay, "Experiment: Human Being," in his musings on this topic. For Gustafson, the new genetic possibilities meshed neatly with the process philosophy of Bergson, Whitehead, and Hartshorne and the interactive model of Christian ethics developed by his mentor, H. Richard Niebuhr.[23] The history of human evolution and the prospect of directed genetic change in the future seemed most compatible with—in fact, seemed to call for—a dynamic rather than a static view of human nature. While stopping far short of H. J. Muller's technological optimism, Gustafson joined the Karl Rahner of "Experiment: Human Being" in affirming a human obligation to develop inherited capacities in every realm, including the realm of the human body and mind. In Gustafson's words,

> The procedure for thinking ethically about human [genetic] experimentation ought not to begin with a fixed image of what was, is, and always ought to be, from which are derived authoritative and unalterable rules which govern experimentation. Rather, the weight is on human initiative, human freedom (if you choose) to explore, develop, expand, alter, initiate, intervene in the course of life in the world, including [one's] own life.[24]

It may be worthwhile to pause at the end of this section to consider the language employed by the early commentators who wrote in the mode of cosmic theology. Paul Ramsey used the language of "genetic control" in the title of his pioneering essay. Within the text of his essay, he freely referred to eugenics, seeming to affirm efforts at "negative" or "preventive" eugenics while opposing any proposed "program of 'progressive' eugenics or 'positive' genetic improvement."[25] In the same context, Ramsey echoed H. J. Muller's metaphors of "genetic surgery," "microsurgery," and "nanosurgery."[26] However, these images from clinical medicine played only a subsidiary role in Ramsey's essay. Karl Rahner employed the language of "manipulation" or "self-manipulation" and of an "experiment" being conducted by human beings on human beings. While both the metaphors of manipulation and experimentation often carried negative connotations in the late 1960s, Rahner seemed to use both images in a neutral or even a positive way, viewing these types of human activity as legitimate exercises of human freedom. James Gustafson chose the phrase "genetic engineering" for the title of his 1969 symposium paper, perhaps following the lead of Bernard Davis, whose paper in the same symposium was originally entitled "Threat and Promise in Genetic Engineering."[27] However, this phrase did not carry pejorative connotations in Gustafson's thought: Gustafson affirmed the moral legitimacy of at least some types of human genetic engineering.

In summary, by the end of 1969, the foundations for the cosmic-theological approach to human genetic intervention had been laid. Three distinct positions on the effort to change human beings by genetic means can be identified. Paul Ramsey was critical of both the effort to intervene in human evolution and the means proposed by Muller to achieve such an intervention. Karl Rahner and James Gustafson adopted mediating positions that affirmed the general goal of changing human beings while expressing caution about the potential risks of the enterprise. And H. J. Muller, later to be joined by Joseph Fletcher,[28] vigorously supported the exercise of rational control over the human genetic future.

Casuistic Analysis

The casuistic analysis of gene therapy (or "genetic therapy" or "genetic surgery" as the technique was sometimes called) began in the year 1969. Theologians were briefly involved in the early stages of the ethical discussion, usually in conjunction with technical discussions by scientists or physicians. However, after 1971 the attention of the theologians drifted primarily to other topics that were only tangentially related to gene therapy: genetic testing and screening, in vitro fertilization, cloning, and recombinant DNA research. Only in the 1980s and 1990s did theologians and religious bodies begin to devote more sustained attention to gene therapy as an ethical issue.

Bernard Davis, a microbiologist from Harvard University, and James Gustafson participated in the first symposium to confront the nearer-term issue of human gene therapy. The symposium was held in Boston on December 28–30, 1969, and was cosponsored by the Boston University School of Theology and the American Association for the Advancement of Science.[29] In his symposium paper, Bernard Davis used a few deft distinctions to move the discussion of human genetic intervention away from the global, evolutionary sphere and closer to the everyday practice of medicine. Davis noted the difference between somatic-cell interventions, which would affect only an individual patient, and germ-line interventions, which would be passed on to future generations. He also observed that, while certain genetic diseases were caused by mutations in a single gene and thus potentially amenable to gene therapy, most human be-

havioral traits were based on the complex interaction of multiple genes. Genetic al-
terations of these distinctively human characteristics were technically infeasible, at least
in the foreseeable future.[30]

In his response to the Davis paper, James Gustafson modified in a most interesting
and instructive way an earlier essay on "Basic Ethical Issues in the Bio-Medical Fields."[31]
He added a new proposition to his discussion of whether scientists have a right to "intervene in the natural processes of human life":

> A scientist has the right to intervene in the course of human development in such a
> way that the uses of his [or her] knowledge foster growth of those distinctive qual-
> ities of life that humans value most highly, and remove those qualities that are dele-
> terious to what is valued.
>
> Various reasons might be given in support of this proposition. a: The basic moti-
> vating reason for any investigation is to achieve some control over the processes to
> which [humans] have in the past passively consented. This has been the case with the
> development of surgery, drug therapy, means of birth control, chemical fertilizers,
> etc. There is an implicit intention in all research to enlarge the human capacities for
> self-determination. It has been assumed that these capacities are directed toward the
> goal of the improvement of the conditions of human life, for examples, relief from
> suffering, and prolongation of life.[32]

Gustafson's comments are highly significant in two respects. First, he seems to accept the notion that genetic intervention might be (or at least become) a conventional
therapy like surgery and the use of medications or a customary practice like the use of
contraception. Second, insofar as genetic intervention increases human freedom and
decreases human suffering, it should be affirmed as a good. In other words, this new
biomedical technology at least has the potential to be beneficial both in an obvious and
in a more profound way.

The next well-documented encounter of theology with the emergent possibility of
human gene therapy occurred at a May 1971 symposium convened by Canon Michael
Hamilton of the National Cathedral in Washington, D.C. The interlocutors were
physician W. French Anderson of the National Institute of Health and Paul Ramsey.
Anderson began his presentation by defining "gene therapy" as "the attempt to treat
hereditary diseases by influencing the genes directly."[33] He noted that an attempt to
perform gene therapy was already in progress, in Germany, with two girls suffering
from an enzyme-deficiency disease called argininemia. No results were yet available
from that experiment. Anderson went on to reiterate the distinction between somatic
and germ-line interventions and to draw a new distinction of his own, between therapeutic uses and enhancements like giving one's son "a double dose of the gene for
size so that [he] will have a better chance to be a professional football player."[34] According to Anderson, a national advisory commission like the one being proposed by

Senator Walter Mondale might helpfully accompany the early years of gene therapy. However, the early years of cardiac transplantation had shown clearly that existing social structures could exert control over a new biomedical technology that had perhaps been introduced too quickly.

Paul Ramsey's response to Anderson's presentation was divided into two parts. In the first part, Ramsey sought to wrestle casuistically with Anderson's distinctions and theses. Ramsey protested the use of the term "gene therapy" to describe either germ-line intervention or genetic enhancement. In Ramsey's view, those practices should be branded with the name "genetic engineering" rather than smuggled into the medical sphere.[35] Ramsey clearly struggled to find the best analogy for the new technology of gene therapy. The case of the German experiment did not reassure him; he was concerned that, at least in the case of the older girl, the intervention might hold out no possibility of benefit.[36] Anderson's citing of cardiac transplantation as a precedent worried Ramsey even more; as we know from his *The Patient as Person*, Ramsey viewed the first heart transplants as foolhardy and premature.[37] Even the most innocuous metaphor, that of genetic surgery, was problematic: Ramsey noted that somatic cell gene therapy would have deleterious effects on the gene pool.[38] At the same time, however, Ramsey acknowledged that genetic surgery, even in utero genetic surgery, could in principle be viewed as a good.[39]

The concluding section of Ramsey's response to Anderson was entitled "Beyond Morality: Fundamental Questions." In this section, Ramsey sharply criticized the dualism and perfectionism that he saw implicit in the entire notion of healing genetic diseases or repairing genetic defects:

> The underlying anthropology [of geneticists], the additive view of [the human being] is this: Each of us is a package of normal abnormalities or abnormal normalities, combinations of more or less weak genetic strengths and more or less strong genetic weaknesses, plus a number of defects that have arisen with us to be passed on in the species' gene pool. This scientific anthropology claims to have replaced Augustine's theological insight that ours is a "dying life" and a "living death"—but "explained" is the word, not "replaced," since the cellular secrets of aging and dying are now said to be open to us and subject to fundamental change. The creation in us, now known, is to be altered into something that never was.

In short, geneticists are engaged in a Promethean effort to defy the Creator by eliminating disease and death from human existence.

The promising dialogue between theology and the biomedical fields that begin with Gustafson and Ramsey was unfortunately not sustained in the 1970s. A study of "Genetics and the Quality of Life," initiated in 1971 by the World Council of Churches, led to a 1973 conference in Zurich and a 1975 publication, but gene therapy was not a central concern of the participants.[40] In 1978 theologian Roger Shinn's article on ethical issues in gene therapy was published in the first edition of the *Encyclopedia of Bioethics.*[41]

In the 1980s the interdisciplinary discussion that had been initiated in the years 1969 to 1971 was renewed. The central figure in this renewal was theologian John Fletcher, who was Chief of the Bioethics Program at the NIH Clinical Center during most of the decade. Again a partnership with a person in the biomedical fields was important. In Fletcher's case, once again, it was W. French Anderson. In late 1980, as in 1971, a recent case was on everyone's mind: Martin Cline of UCLA had performed unauthorized gene therapy on patients in Israel and Italy. Anderson and Fletcher collaborated in writing a response to the Cline case, "Gene Therapy in Human Beings: When Is It Ethical to Begin?"[42] In November 1982, Fletcher testified at Congressional hearings on "Human Genetic Engineering";[43] his testimony was published in the *Virginia Law Review* in April of the following year.[44] Two years later, Fletcher published a critique of Jeremy Rifkin's perspective on human genetic intervention in the *Journal of Medicine and Philosophy.*[45]

What is striking in Fletcher's writings on the ethics of human gene therapy is that, even though he had been trained as a theologian, virtually all of his analysis was carried out with secular philosophical arguments. Nor was Fletcher alone in this regard: Other theologically trained ethicists—among them Albert Jonsen, James Childress, and Robert Veatch—were also employing philosophical categories in most of their work. The reasons for this trend toward nontheological casuistry are undoubtedly complex. All of the theologians mentioned were deeply involved in the public-policy debates of the 1970s and 1980s. Further, somatic-cell gene therapy began to look more and more like a simple *extension* of traditional medical practice. It was difficult to find profound theological questions in such an incremental step.

Religious leaders were centrally involved in the U.S. debate about human genetic intervention at two points in the 1980s. In June of 1980, leaders of three major U.S. religious groups—Jews, Catholics, and Protestants—wrote then-President Carter, warning of potential perils in genetic engineering. The proximate cause of this letter seems to have been the U.S. Supreme Court decision that allowed genetically altered bacteria to be patented. However, a sense of unease about the prospects for human genetic engineering also comes through quite clearly in the letter.[46] The President's Commission on Bioethics agreed to take on the issue of genetic engineering in addition to its mandated topics. The result of the commission's study process was a report entitled *Splicing Life,*[47] released at the November 1982 Congressional hearings. The central message of the report was that somatic-cell gene therapy raised no qualitatively new issues and that even germ-line genetic intervention, if employed to prevent disease, could fit comfortably within the biomedical model.

An important theme in *Splicing Life* was whether "genetic engineering with human beings" was tantamount to "playing God."[48] This way of construing the debate about human genetic intervention had first been put forward by Paul Ramsey in his 1970 book *Fabricated Man*, when he asserted that human beings "ought not to play God before they learn to be [humans], and after they have learned to be [humans] they will not play God."[49] Seven years later, the same image was given wide circulation by Ted Howard and Jeremy Rifkin in their popular book, *Who Should Play God?*[50] The metaphor of "playing God" had also been employed by the leaders of major U.S. religious bodies in their 1980 letter:

> Control of such [new] life forms by any individual or group poses a potential threat to all of humanity. History has shown us that there will always be those who believe it appropriate to "correct" our mental and social structures by genetic means, so as to fit their vision of humanity. This becomes more dangerous when the basic tools to do so are finally at hand. Those who would play God will be tempted as never before.[51]

In its response to "Concerns about 'Playing God'" the President's Commission was at pains to explain that neither a fuller understanding of the machinery of life, nor an interference with nature, nor the creation of new life forms is incompatible, in principle, with religious belief or traditional theological principles.[52]

Religious leaders and theologians in the U.S. again made the news in June 1983 when many of them signed a letter drafted by Jeremy Rifkin, requesting a moratorium on the genetic modification of human germ-line cells.[53] However, no proposals to perform genetic alteration of human germ cells were being planned at the time, and public policymakers seemed reluctant to ban hypothetical experiments.

Other modes of involvement in the genetic-intervention debate of the 1980s by ecumenical bodies, theologians, and religious leaders have been nicely summarized by J. Robert Nelson[54] and Ronald Cole-Turner.[55] In my view, the following picture emerges from this decade of renewed interest in genetic intervention by theologians and religious leaders. Somatic-cell gene therapy was viewed as an extension of current medical techniques, and little explicitly theological analysis was applied to the technique. Theologians and religious leaders were divided on germ-line genetic intervention, with some proposing to fit the technique within a biomedical model of disease prevention while others expressed alarm about human beings arrogating too much power to themselves. Again there was little explicit theological analysis. The possible use of genetic means to enhance human capabilities was usually labeled "eugenics" and rejected as ethically unacceptable—without sustained theological discussion.

Again, at the conclusion of this section, it is worthwhile to consider the language and metaphors employed in the ethical debate. Jeremy Rifkin and the religious leaders who wrote President Carter in 1980 sought to portray a variety of developments in science and technology as human attempts to play God. Their opponents and critics sought to draw distinctions among such diverse issues as programs of involuntary eugenics, the crossing of lines between species in laboratory research, and efforts to treat patients suffering from life-threatening diseases. Proponents of human genetic intervention reached almost instinctively for phrases like "gene therapy" in an effort to accentuate the continuities between traditional and innovative approaches to treatment. Phrases like "genetic engineering" and "genetic manipulation" gradually fell into disuse, at least among proponents of the new technologies.

It is perhaps worth noting that other phrases or metaphors would have been available for use in casuistic analysis. For example, the phrase "human gene transfer," would have carried with it less optimistic connotations than the eventually predominant phrase "human gene therapy." While the word "therapy" is accurate in the sense that recipients of gene transfer are patients and in the sense that the intent of the intervention is therapeutic, the word may also carry with it the misleading overtones of "standard and accepted therapy." In fact, even in the late 1990s all attempts to transfer genes into human beings are both innovative and experimental, and few of the first one hundred clinical trials of "gene therapy" in the United States have produced tangible benefits for patients.[56]

The Renaissance of Cosmic Theology and the Possibility of a New Synthesis

An essay first presented by James Gustafson[57] at a 1992 conference organized by J. Robert Nelson,[58] a 1993 book by Ronald Cole-Turner,[59] and Nelson's own 1994 book[60] helpfully remind us that cosmic theology did not end with the writings of the late 1960s. In fact, on a track that has paralleled the bioethics field, seldom touching it, theologians have been engaged in another kind of dialogue with the natural sciences.

To mention the names of any contributors to the renaissance of cosmic theology is to risk omitting important scholars. Here are some of the authors and titles mentioned or alluded to by Gustafson, Nelson, and Cole-Turner (in alphabetical order by author):

Barbour, Ian G. *Issues in Science and Religion*, 1966; *Religion in an Age of Science*, 1990.
Barrow, John D., and Frank J. Tipler. *The Anthropic Cosmological Principle* (1986).
Birch, Charles, and John B. Cobb Jr. *The Liberation of Life: From the Cell to the Community*, 1981.
Burhoe, Ralph W. *Toward a Scientific Theology*, 1981.
Farley, Edward. *Good and Evil: Interpreting a Human Condition,* 1990.
Hefner, Philip. *The Human Factor: Evolution, Culture and Religion*, 1993.
Kaufman, Gordon D. *In Face of Mystery: A Constructive Theology*, 1993.
Midgley, Mary. *Beast and Man*, 1978, 1995; *Evolution as a Religion*, 1985.
Peacocke, Arthur R. *Creation and the World of Science,* 1979; *God and the New Biology*, 1986.

Peters, Ted, ed. *Cosmos as Creation*, 1989.
Polkinghorne, John. *Science and Providence*, 1989.
Wilson, E. O. *On Human Nature*, 1978.

Gustafson understands his own theological approach in *Ethics from a Theocentric Perspective* to be more akin to the work of the writers listed above than to the analyses of the casuists. In a pregnant footnote he writes:

> Over the past twenty years I have, in a lay person's way, attempted to grasp the main lines of genetic and neurological research because I believe that in biology these have the deepest and widest implications for future human participation. [The human being], in my judgment, will come closer to being the ultimate orderer of life through the uses of these investigations than through the matters that preoccupy so much of the attention in clinical medical ethics. Of course in practice it will not be ["humanity"] but those persons and institutions that have the power to control the use of such investigations.[61]

In a similar but slightly different fashion, Ronald Cole-Turner seeks to integrate casuistic "bioethical" writings on ethics and genetic intervention with the new approaches to the question of human nature proposed by the cosmic theologians. This integration allows him to take seriously the work of sociobiologists and behavioral geneticists and places his theological work within a global and evolutionary context that casuists sometimes fail to see.

The integration of casuistic thinking and cosmic theology may point the way toward a new synthesis that helps to resolve some difficult problems for the biomedical model. For example, most casuistic analyses have rejected genetic enhancement because it seems unrelated to human health and disease.[62] Perhaps an exception would be made by the casuists for health-related enhancements, such as stimulating the normal immune system and helping it to retain its youthful vigor.[63] A broader approach to human nature could look at human characteristics in the light of millennia of evolution, as well as in the light of the best-established findings of behavioral genetics, and ask questions like "How did human beings come to have such violently aggressive tendencies?" and "To what extent are personality traits and cognitive abilities influenced by the genes that we inherit from our parents?"

A second possible contribution of the new synthesis may be a healing of the traditional divide between the two fields that Van Rensselaer Potter has aptly called "medical bioethics" and "global bioethics."[64] The escape from a narrowly biomedical focus allows ethics to look at human responsibility for world population and nutrition (à la James Gustafson in an important chapter of his magnum opus),[65] at our general moral obligations to nonhuman animals, and at our duty to use natural resources wisely and to protect the environment from irreversible harm.

The integration of cosmic theology and casuistic analysis may also lead to the transformation, or at least reinterpretation, of traditional metaphors. As we noted earlier, according to Paul Ramsey and Jeremy Rifkin, scientists, clinicians, and human beings in general should avoid engaging in activities that could be characterized as "playing God." Several recent commentators on theology and genetics (including Gustafson, Cole-Turner, and Nelson) have addressed this theme in a new way. Drawing their inspiration in part from Rahner and Teilhard, they have depicted human beings as cocreators, or at least created cocreators, with God when they attempt to conquer disease and otherwise improve the human future. Alternatively, the commentators have employed the venerable image of stewardship to depict the relationship of human beings to the world and its many resources, including human genes.[66]

Exploration into the possible intersections between cosmic theology and casuistic analysis in the realm of human genetics has barely begun. If a creative synthesis does emerge from the interaction of these two modes of inquiry, it will be deeply indebted to James Gustafson's efforts to include both modes in his comprehensive approach to religious ethics. The implications of Gustafson's work for scholarship will be quite immediate and visible. The benefits, for the human future, of his resolute refusal to oversimplify will become apparent only in the longer term.

Notes

1. J. B. S. Haldane, *Daedalus, or Science and the Future* (New York: E. P. Dutton, 1924).

2. H. J. Muller, *Out of the Night: A Biologist's View of the Future* (New York: Vanguard Press, 1935).

3. Theodosius Dobzhansky, *Mankind Evolving: The Evolution of the Human Species* (New Haven: Yale University Press, 1962).

4. Pierre Teilhard de Chardin, "Les Directions et les Conditions de l'Avenir," *Psyché*, October 1948; reprinted as essay 15 in *L'Avenir de l'Homme* (Paris: Editions du Seuil, 1959), 291–305.

5. Pierre Teilhard de Chardin, *Le Phenomene Humain* (Paris: Editions du Seuil, 1955).

6. Paul Ramsey, "Moral and Religious Aspects of Genetic Control," in *Genetics and the Future of Man*, ed. John D. Roslansky (Amsterdam: North-Holland, 1966), 108–69.

7. Paul Ramsey, *Fabricated Man: The Ethics of Genetic Control* (New Haven, Conn.: Yale University Press, 1970).

8. Letter dated October 2, 1964, from Paul Ramsey to H. J. Muller; letter of reply dated October 20, 1964, from H. J. Muller to Paul Ramsey. Copies of both letters are included in the Muller archive at the University of Indiana in Bloomington.

9. Ramsey, *Fabricated Man*, 27.

10. Ibid., 29.

11. The German version of this essay was originally published in Heinrich Rombach, ed., *Die Frage nach dem Menschen: Aufriss einer philosophischen Anthropologie* (Freiburg: Verlag Karl Al-

ber, 1966), 45–69. See Karl Rahner, *Schriften zur Theologie* (Einsiedeln: Benziger Verlag, 1967) 8:260–85. See also Karl Rahner, *Theological Investigations*, trans. Graham Harrison (New York: Herder & Herder, 1972), 9:205–24. The first English translation of Rahner's essay, by William V. Dych, appeared in *Theology Digest* 16, no. 5 (February 1968): 57–69.

12. Rahner, *Theological Investigations*, 9:210.

13. Ibid., 9:213–14.

14. Ibid., 9:211.

15. Paul Overhage, *Um das Erscheinungsbild der ersten Menschen* (Freiburg: Herder, 1959).

16. Paul Overhage and Karl Rahner, *Das Problem der Hominisation: über den biologischen Ursprung des Menschen* (Freiburg: Herder, 1961).

17. Rahner, *Theological Investigations*, 9:225–52.

18. Ibid., 9:243–48.

19. James M. Gustafson, "Christian Humanism and the Human Mind," in *The Human Mind,* ed. John D. Roslansky (Amsterdam: North-Holland, 1967), 83–109.

20. Ibid., 85; citing Pierre Teilhard de Chardin, *The Phenomenon of Man,* trans. Bernard Wall (New York: Harper & Brothers, 1959), 231, 229.

21. Gustafson, "Christian Humanism," 97–98.

22. James M. Gustafson, "Genetic Engineering and the Normative View of the Human," in *Ethical Issues in Biology and Medicine,* ed. Preston N. Williams (Cambridge, Mass.: Schenkman), 46–58.

23. See especially H. Richard Niebuhr, *The Responsible Self* (New York: Harper & Row, 1963).

24. Gustafson, "Genetic Engineering," 57.

25. Ramsey, "Moral and Religious Aspects of Genetic Control," 118; cf. *Fabricated Man,* 9–10.

26. Ramsey, "Moral and Religious Aspects of Genetic Control," 118.

27. Interestingly, the title of Davis's essay was toned down to "Prospects for Genetic Intervention in Man" when it was published in *Science* in December 1970. In this change, Davis may have been influenced by Joshua Lederberg, who had argued in a September 26, 1970, letter to the *New York Times* that the overtones of the phrase "genetic engineering" were undesirable. See note 2 in Bernard D. Davis, *Science* 170, no. 3964 (18 December 1970): 1283.

28. Joseph Fletcher, "Ethical Aspects of Genetic Controls," *New England Journal of Medicine* 285, no. 14 (30 September 1971): 776–83.

29. Preston N. Williams, Introduction to *Ethical Issues in Biology and Medicine,* ed. Williams, 1.

30. Bernard D. Davis, "Threat and Promise in Genetic Engineering," in *Ethical Issues in Biology and Medicine,* ed. Williams, 17–32. A slightly modified version of this essay appeared in *Science* 170, no. 3964 (18 December 1970): 1279–83.

31. This essay was published in *Soundings* 53, no. 2 (summer 1970): 151–80. A footnote on p. 162 of the *Soundings* essay notes that the section that begins on that page "has been refined and expanded in a subsequent paper, 'Genetic Engineering and the Normative View of the Human.'"

32. Gustafson, "Genetic Engineering," 48–49.

33. W. French Anderson, "Genetic Therapy," in *The New Genetics and the Future of Man,* ed. Michael P. Hamilton (Grand Rapids, Mich.: Eerdmans, 1972), 109.

34. Ibid., 119.

35. Paul Ramsey, "Genetic Therapy: A Theologian's Response," in *The New Genetics*, ed. Hamilton, 159.

36. Ibid., 162–64.

37. Ibid., 165.

38. Ibid., 169–71.

39. Ibid., 160–61.

40. Charles Birch and Paul Abrecht, eds., *Genetics and the Quality of Life* (Elmsford, N.Y.: Pergamon Press, 1975).

41. Roger Shinn, "Gene Therapy: Ethical Issues," in *Encyclopedia of Bioethics*, ed. Warren T. Reich (New York: Free Press, 1978), 2:521–27.

42. W. French Anderson and John C. Fletcher, "Gene Therapy in Human Beings: When Is It Ethical to Begin?" *New England Journal of Medicine* 303, no. 22 (27 November 1980): 1293–97.

43. U.S. Congress, House Committee on Science and Technology, Subcommittee on Investigations and Oversight, *Human Genetic Engineering*, Hearings, 97th Congress, 2d Session, 16–18 November 1982 (Washington, D.C.: U.S. Government Printing Office, 1983), 342–87.

44. John C. Fletcher, "Moral Problems and Ethical Issues in Prospective Human Gene Therapy," *Virginia Law Review* 69, no. 3 (April 1983): 515–46.

45. John C. Fletcher, "Ethical Issues in and beyond Prospective Clinical Trials of Human Gene Therapy," *Journal of Medicine and Philosophy* 10, no. 3 (August 1985): 293–309.

46. U.S. President's Commission for the Study of Ethical Problems in Medicine and Biomedical and Behavioral Research, *Splicing Life: A Report on the Social and Ethical Issues of Genetic Engineering with Human Beings* (Washington, D.C.: The Commission, November 1982), 95–96.

47. Ibid., entire report.

48. Ibid., esp. 53–60.

49. Ramsey, *Fabricated Man*, 138.

50. Ted Howard and Jeremy Rifkin, *Who Should Play God?* (New York: Dell, 1977).

51. U.S. President's Commission, *Splicing Life*, 95–96.

52. Ibid., 53–60.

53. See Colin Norman, "Clerics Urge Ban on Altering Germline Cells," *Science* 220, no. 4604 (24 June 1983): 1360–61.

54. J. Robert Nelson, "The Role of Religions in the Analysis of the Ethical Issues of Human Gene Therapy," *Human Gene Therapy* 1, no. 1 (spring 1990): 43–48.

55. Ronald Cole-Turner, *The New Genesis: Theology and the Genetic Revolution* (Louisville, Ky.: Westminster John Knox, 1993), 66–78.

56. On this point, see LeRoy Walters and Julie Gage Palmer, *The Ethics of Human Gene Therapy* (New York: Oxford University Press, 1997), esp. chap. 2.

57. James M. Gustafson, "Where Theologians and Geneticists Meet," *Dialog* 33, no. 1 (winter 1994): 7–16.

58. J. Robert Nelson, *On the New Frontiers of Genetics and Religion* (Grand Rapids, Mich.: Eerdmans, 1994).

59. Cole-Turner, *The New Genesis*.

60. Nelson, *On the New Frontiers*.

61. James M. Gustafson, *Ethics from a Theocentric Perspective*, 2 vols. (Chicago: University of Chicago Press, 1981–1984), vol. 2, *Ethics and Theology,* 282.

62. See, for example, W. French Anderson, "Human Gene Therapy: Why Draw a Line?" *Journal of Medicine and Philosophy* 14, no. 6 (December 1989): 681–93.

63. See the summary of my remarks at the March 1992 Houston conference on "Genetics, Religion, and Ethics," in Nelson, *On the New Frontiers*, 115.

64. Van Rensselaer Potter, "Aldo Leopold's Land Ethic Revisited: Two Kinds of Bioethics," *Perspectives in Biology and Medicine* 30, no. 2 (winter 1987): 157–69; Potter, "Getting to the Year 2000: Can Global Bioethics Overcome Evolution's Fatal Flaw?" *Perspectives in Biology and Medicine* 34, no. 1 (autumn 1990): 89–98.

65. Gustafson, *Ethics*, 2: chap. 7.

66. On these metaphors, see Nelson, *On the New Frontiers*, 110–14.

Chapter 15

Creating a Global Discourse in a Pluralist World: Strategies from Environmental Ethics

CRISTINA L. H. TRAINA

Postmodernism has enriched ethics in many ways. It has uncovered oppressive ideologies and recognized the authority of the moral experience and reflections of people outside of the academy and other powerful institutions, widening the scope of both the considerations and the practice of moral discourse.

Yet ironically it has also fragmented that discourse. The tools that have identified and dismantled systematic injustices cannot be used credibly to construct alternative ethics or institutions. For postmodernism forbids us to assume the existence of any common ground, based in nature or experience, among cultures or even among persons.[1] In its method, if not always in all of its concrete conclusions, a consistent postmodern ethic is utterly relativistic. This relativism undermines ethics, both as a discipline and as a guide for action, by demanding a sort of perspectivalism which prohibits reaching any binding agreement—even within a culture—and so leaves us with an ethic of unassailable, individually generated values and preferences.

The paralyzing consequences are palpable in everyday human decisions but devastating when we must address practical problems of global proportions. How can we make international policy on human rights, armed intervention, or economics if we share neither a common foundation nor a guiding vision? Arguably the most urgent global problem today is the condition of the globe itself. We have the sense that every moment spent in deliberation moves us deeper into possibly irreversible ecological devastation. Simply slowing the process requires a common practical effort. The high stakes and the pressure of time press the question even more: How can we quickly develop global ecological strategies if there are and can be no legitimately global foundations, norms, or visions?

The solution is to articulate claims and methods of reasoning that take the postmodern critique of cultural imperialism seriously and yet are able to argue credibly and successfully for a common moral discourse yielding some shared norms and even shared practical strategies. Unsurprisingly, environmental ethicists are among the pioneers in this wilderness. In this essay I describe and assess the work of three such pioneers: J. Baird Callicott,[2] James M. Gustafson,[3] and Rosemary Radford Ruether.[4]

A collection of mutually reinforcing stands binds these authors together. First, the experience of nature—filtered through science and immediately encountered by individuals—figures centrally in the development of their moral norms, their ethics, and even their fundamental philosophical and theological commitments. They grapple in particular with the place of scientific knowledge in moral reflection, concluding that the hard sciences are sources of morally significant experiential knowledge. For instance, the sciences tell us that the earth and all its inhabitants are caught up in a single, dynamic, and interdependent ecosystem, fixed in a common substrate of matter and energy. This de facto common ground supplies a monistic counterweight to cultural pluralism by rooting human cultures in a common physical order of being. They agree, for example, that ecosystematic interdependence provides important (if not conclusive) arguments for rejecting moral anthropocentrism; ethics concerns the whole ecosystem, of which humans are only one part (albeit an influential one). It also supplies an alternative to romanticism, pointing out that the physical and biological structures of life as we know it limit the possibilities of individuals, species, and the finite global system as a whole (for example, entirely apart from moral evil, change, conflict, senescence, and death are inevitable).

Two concerns, then, guide the analyses below: How does each author navigate between the pluralist claims of contemporary philosophy and the monism of contemporary science? And what role does science-as-experience-of-the-world play in their moral reflections? In particular, is commonly held scientific knowledge an adequate basis for global moral reflection on shared environmental problems?

J. Baird Callicott

Environmental philosopher J. Baird Callicott begins his most recent book, *Earth's Insights*, with a genuine regard for cultural pluralism. The bulk of the book explores the ecological practices and moral tenets of over a dozen religious and cultural systems. But rather than stand helpless before their variety, he demonstrates that no matter how different our cultures may be, our existence within and experiences of the global ecosystem yield values that are recognizable—if differently explained and realized—across cultures. This "reconstructive" approach qualifies as postmodern, Callicott thinks, because it is not based in a priori claims about the structure of the natural order. Rather, it relies on thorough a posteriori scientific observation of the ecosystem, including humanity, and its evolutionary history.[5]

How can such a descriptive project yield the univocal, global prescriptions for which the global environmental crisis calls? Callicott realizes that he cannot articulate an ethic without a worldview. Although he insists that the diversity of human culture be preserved, he denies that any existing particular cultural or religious viewpoint can function as this authoritative standpoint. His solution is a worldview, "an emerging global environmental consciousness," compatible with all the world's cultures but identical with none of them—a moral Esperanto[6] "expressed in the cognitive lingua franca of contemporary science" that describes the physical world all cultures inhabit. The result would be "a single cross-cultural environmental ethics based on ecology and the new physics," and "corresponding to the contemporary reality that we inhabit one planet, that we are one species and that our deepening environmental crisis is worldwide and common."[7]

Among science's universally acceptable lessons are that we are parts of a radically interdependent global ecosystem which has evolved in Darwinian ways, favoring species and lines which instinctively, intentionally, or accidentally both respect their natural surroundings and privilege kin. Callicott's distinctive move is to convert these seemingly unbiased descriptions of states of affairs into prescriptive claims, to transform the *is* of an apparently neutral account of the status quo into the *ought* of a moral ideal.[8] The first transformation evolves from his nodal understanding of identity. Consciously echoing the philosophical doctrine of internal relations, he describes organisms as "knots in the web of life," their essences "exhaustively determined by" their relationships.[9] Humanity, too, is "plain member and citizen"[10] of the interdependent biotic community, integrally connected with it and in no way privileged over it. *Is* implies *ought:* Our actions should respect these connections.

Second, evolution has favored human beings who reason morally and behave accordingly. Once again, *is* implies *ought*; moral reflection—an unselfconscious evolutionary heritage—is now a moral dictum.[11]

Third, Callicott's description of the functioning of the biotic community privileges species over individuals. The moral point is to preserve evolutionary niches. Thus no individual has a right to life;[12] and it is not clear whether there is any reason, beyond natural affinity, for human beings to respect one another. The harmonious coexistence that we are to pursue is not the coexistence of individuals but the balance among species: the net births and deaths of each.

Finally, by examining the beliefs and practices of cultures we can develop, inductively, a list of de facto universal human values. Of particular importance are the habits of tending to those who are near and dear—both human and animal—and of caring for (or at least not pillaging) one's surroundings.[13] Here again, *is* implies *ought:* Successful human lines act in these ways, and so ought we. This yields not only the content but the concern of ethics: to do good rather than to be good.[14]

In each case, scientific description becomes ethical prescription. Yet science is to have been a lingua franca—a language—not a source of meaning. In order legitimately to base prescription (ought) on description (is) one must either insert statements about value between the descriptive and prescriptive terms or articulate and defend the values implicit in the description. One could do both; Callicott does neither.

His less satisfying means of moving from premise to conclusion is to slip values in without making cogent arguments for them. For example, Callicott holds that we have a practical, morally obliging goal: to "preserve the integrity, stability, and beauty of the biotic community."[15] However, this obligation not only is not self-evident but also is problematic in a number of directions. It is not clear why the biotic community should be preserved or stabilized. Callicott himself has near-contempt for grand teleological schemes of evolution[16] and therefore for the claim that we know toward what end the ecosystem should be steered. The relentlessness of evolution and the apparent capriciousness of the development of organic life in the universe would seem to be scientific arguments against trying to preserve anything. If the history of evolution is the measure, dynamism and instability are far more logical goals. Certainly preservation encourages diversity by maintaining old species as new ones evolve, but then one must ask why diversity is a value. Diversity does sustain humanity, but again, why this is a moral obligation and not just an inclination is unclear.[17]

The origins of moral obligation itself are cloudy as well. One could counter that although most human beings exhibit a concern to behave morally, they frequently fail, and some are antinomian. In addition, neither a global moral justification for preserving beauty and integrity nor even a global standard for recognizing them follows easily from the scientific worldview. For although science is aesthetically pleasing, it does not contain an aesthetic. In short, Callicott fails to explain why we should care about the ecosystem in the first place, or even that we do.

The mistake here is neither the attempt at developing a universal environmental language nor the project of unearthing implicit universal norms. It is the failure to explain why a descriptive language is adequate to the task of constructing an ethic, why de facto shared values are necessarily universally binding, and why one can support simultaneously two ethical worldviews, the universal and the local.[18] Science can describe a possible object of value; anthropology and sociology can confirm that we value it. But none can say why we should value it or whether, even valuing it, we should preserve it.

James M. Gustafson

If Baird Callicott views the world through a fish-eye lens, James Gustafson approaches it with a magnifying glass. What Callicott explores on a global scale, Gustafson examines in a single tradition; what Callicott seeks in panhuman experience, Gustafson probes in his own tradition and even his own life. Callicott begins with the need to coordinate plural cultural viewpoints with a common moral standpoint on environmental ethics; James Gustafson asks how one of these viewpoints can understand its own participation in such a global conversation and what sort of concrete difference that viewpoint can make in people's thoughts and actions.[19] In keeping with this approach, he also provides explicit theological warrants for his use of scientific descriptions in moral arguments.

Like Callicott, Gustafson sees human attitudes toward the environment as keys to de facto human values. Unlike Callicott, however, he passes over articulated religious beliefs and established cultural practices to feelings. In particular, feelings of revulsion are clues to deeply held values.[20] Gustafson illustrates this universal pattern by recounting his own aesthetic disgust at pollution and cookie-cutter commercial development. But instead of claiming, as Callicott does, that beauty is simply a criterion of proper environmental *practice* (necessitating cross-cultural agreement on the content of beauty), Gustafson makes the experience of beauty's destruction the experiential doorway to the correct moral *attitude* toward the natural world (eliminating the need for cross-cultural agreement on content). The moral subject's proper initial response to beauty is wonder and respect.[21] Contemplating this response to beauty in light of the discoveries of the contemporary physical sciences, Gustafson reflects:

> What is finally indisputable . . . is that human and other forms of life are dependent upon forces we do not create and cannot fully control, forces that bring into being and sustain us and life around us, but forces that also limit and destroy us and determine the destiny of the cosmos. This dependence—a matter of fact, no matter how it is interpreted—evokes a sense of the sublime, or for some of us a sense of the divine.[22]

But this is a disturbing sublimity. It encompasses unpreferential destruction and supersession and supports an ecosystem which is not only dynamic but out of equilibrium. It reminds human beings that they have created neither themselves nor the limits within which they operate. Although they can modify their surroundings to a degree, the cosmic order does not privilege their needs:[23] "The purposes of nature, relative to 'anything that exists' and to the interdependence of all, are conflictual relative to the human good and even various 'goods' of the nonhuman world."[24]

Yet, as Gustafson is fond of noting, if one believes in God then one may say reverently that nature is God, the place where human beings sense God's presence, "the theater of the power and glory of the Divine."[25] This is the move Callicott cannot make. It permits Gustafson to surmise that this nature, which seems particularly unconcerned with human welfare and unimpressed by human accomplishments, is not merely the product of chance. Humans can read in nature, if not God's ends and intentions, at least some of God's activity. And that activity does not privilege human beings absolutely. God and God's doings are at the center of Gustafson's worldview; hence his insistence on theocentrism. Human beings must try to understand nature not in order to dismantle or control it, but to live respectful of the limits and boundaries that it imposes on all of life.[26] Only in this way can they also respect its creator.

The implications for ethics are mixed. Goods and values, and even the project of being moral, are not arbitrary. For in the descriptive-prescriptive gap left by Callicott, Gustafson inserts the following justifications: We must behave with care and humility within the limits that nature sets because we must love and honor God; and to love God is to act in concert with the divine activities we see reflected in the order of the universe. Yet as Gustafson admits, this position is of limited substantive help in concrete deliberations.[27] Nature's guidance is sketchy, for divine intentions are present in nature in hints and traces rather than in clear directives. Although we can discern a certain sort of benevolence (i.e., nature provides the grounds for human and other flourishing), nature also provides us no evidence that God intends the ultimate survival of humanity, for instance, or even global ecological equilibrium. Likewise, it provides no vision of human participation in the divine liberation of the earth from death and conflict.[28] It instills humility before God's power rather than infusing that power in people. It is a source of inspiration for respectful human behavior in the world, of limits and criteria, not of a utopian vision of future cosmic transformation.[29] It prohibits wanton destruction but provides no single clear criterion—or even a permanent hierarchy of criteria—with which to sort out the genuine conflicts that arise in practical deliberation about concrete problems.[30]

> If we could say that there is one supreme human good which even ideally would be in harmony with one good of the natural world, then our thinking, if not our acting, would be easier. The multidimensionality of value, or values, that I spoke of, casts us into ambiguities of choices that are unavoidable. We may be able to define limits beyond which our interventions ought not to go, though agreement on these is difficult because different persons or groups value different things in relation to themselves or to the natural world.[31]

Gustafson's articulation of the role of science within his environmental ethic is clearer than Callicott's. We read divine activity in nature with the aid of scientific glasses: Physics, astronomy, and biology all point to the profound dynamism and interdependence of the natural world. Science then both forms our moral sensibility and is one source of knowledge about God.[32] Scientific knowledge of systematic interdependence also increases our moral accountability for the results of our actions.[33] Science, one key to the ordering of nature, may also discover potential objects of esteem or explain relationships among them. But although scientific facts ground values, science is an insufficient basis "for deciding what goods for whom, and for what, ought to be pursued."[34] Values from other sources—affective, theological, philosophical—are significant here, but no comprehensive, determinative ranking exists. Decisions must be made in context.[35]

From this point of view, what is the relationship between a particular religious tradition and the global discourse on environmental ethics? Like Callicott, Gustafson believes that each moral and religious tradition should contribute its own insights to the debate. Common acceptance of those insights that are helpful to the larger conversation would not imply endorsement of the theological foundations of the traditions from which they came. But the phrase "helpful to the larger conversation" conjures the need for an elaboration of values and criteria specific to the global conversation.[36] A practical focus on concrete problems seems in order.

Through this same global conversation, science informs theology by describing God's ordering activity and so setting some of the boundaries for theologically and spiritually informed human action in the world.[37] Science, Gustafson hints, can be a tool of ideology critique, deconstructing traditional anthropocentric theology to reveal its unfounded confidence in God's special benevolence toward humanity.[38]

Gustafson's greater care in identifying the sources of moral value makes for a more satisfying and rigorous account of the relationship among science, environmental ethics, and religion. Yet this intentional grounding of values outside science does not eradicate ambiguity, for two reasons. To begin with, Gustafson's process of juggling multiple sources, always letting God be God,[39] precludes the establishment of permanent practical guidelines or even hierarchies of value. Gustafson stands in the Reformed theological tradition, traced through John Calvin, Jonathan Edwards, and H. Richard Niebuhr. This approach evokes a profound sense of humility, of near powerlessness, of decisions and actions severely constrained by concern for both their possible effects on earthly others and divine prerogative; for the latter is only partially evident even in explicitly Christian revelation.[40]

Adding to this complexity is a second factor: Slightly different theological choices would have yielded distinct arrangements of authorities and different estimates of the possibilities for human transformation of the ecosystem. For instance, Christian scriptures also contain prophetic accounts of the reign of God, a nascent but unrealized reign of harmony, justice, peace, and (in Gustafson's words) equilibrium. From the point of view of these texts, God's intentions for humanity and the ecosystem seem more perspicuous, and moral reasoning becomes a less tentative, if still self-critical, process. Related choices about the scope of one's scientific vision—theologically backed or not—can make critical differences in one's moral outlook as well, even before one introduces the concept of sin. Callicott's focus on evolution and the earth places humanity at the capstone of creation and holds humanity and its capabilities in high esteem. In Gustafson's spatially and temporally cosmic view, humanity seems a random, fragile, and temporary development, hardly significant in the divine plan for the cosmos. These options are significant in the work of Rosemary Radford Ruether, whose commitments are arrayed differently from either Gustafson's or Callicott's.

Rosemary Radford Ruether

Callicott begins with a global tour of environmental beliefs and practices, and Gustafson begins with the individual's experience of revulsion and awe. Rosemary

Radford Ruether adds another dimension to experience: time. Like all feminist liberation theologians, she attends carefully to the experiences of women and other victims of oppression in all periods; unlike many, she is concerned less with their concrete, individual reflections than with their collective welfare in different cultures and periods. Among these victims is the earth itself. Thus she grounds *Gaia and God: An Ecofeminist Theology of Earth Healing* in the collective history of humanity, the global ecosystem, and human reflection on both.

Ruether's liberationist vision of history makes a telling difference in her ethic. History evolves toward an end far different from its origins. There is no golden age of justice or ecological balance to which we can return. Creation was never paradise; nature writ large is neither originally benign for human life nor "capable of completely fulfilling human hopes for the good, in the sense of benign regard for individual and communal life, which is the human ideal."[41] Nor has any tradition, religious or secular, produced a normative blueprint for human and ecosystematic flourishing.

Ruether's response to this assertion is the reverse of Gustafson's. She takes this lack of concrete moral guidance in the ecosystem and the theological tradition as the divine cue that humans are to construct and pursue a heretofore unarticulated and unrealized ideal. To construct a version of the vision which makes sense to Western audiences, Ruether employs liberating elements of the Western Christian covenantal and sacramental traditions: criteria of "consciousness and kindness" gleaned from both Christian theology and contemporary cosmological and evolutionary reflection, and "the laws of Gaia," which impose practical limits on the transformations that humans can work in the global ecosystem.[42] Ruether's vision is not a finished portrait but a work in progress, in places characterized more aptly by negative space than by positive images.[43]

The challenge for Ruether is to coordinate contributions from a number of sources. Science, culture, and religion, she argues, are practically and ideologically interdependent.[44] Like Gustafson and Callicott, Ruether makes use of contemporary scientific observations about the structure of reality: the interrelation of all beings; the "coevolution of plants, air, water, soil, and animals"; "food chains and the cycle of production, consumption, and decomposition"; balance and diversity among species as conditions for sustaining interdependence.[45] Her insight is that the scientific lesson of ecosystematic interdependence coheres with feminist observations that human institutions and systems are interdependent and mutually reinforcing. The combination of claims yields the ecofeminist insight that the same patterns of attitudes and actions tend to characterize human treatment of both humanity and the natural world.[46] A third Christian theological element specifies the connection: Within this interdependent system, sin (i.e., wrong or unjust relationship of any sort) sends shock waves far beyond its immediate surroundings into both human and nonhuman systems.[47]

Ruether is particularly interested in the Western Christian dualistic array of humanity, spirit, masculinity, infinitude, moral goodness, and life against nonhumanity,

CRISTINA L. H. TRAINA

matter, femininity, finitude, moral evil, and death. Observation of the ecosystem—combined with the assumption that basic patterns of generation, sustenance, and senescence are good—falsifies these connections.[48] Finitude is the condition of the ecosystem's existence; death, decay, and gender differentiation are the prerequisites for life. Sin, on other hand, undermines all of these. It is "the misuse of freedom to exploit other humans and the earth and thus to violate the basic relations that sustain life."[49]

Science is thus a necessary but not sufficient or independent interpreter of the world; it must never appear in environmental reflections without history and theology. Science needs historical and theological chaperons because it tends—as Callicott seems in places to do—to forget that its descriptions of the world are not "objective" or "value free."[50] Ruether believes that the contemporary erosion of the traditional distinctions between matter and energy, fact and value, and subject and object has not inspired parallel reflection on the valuative powers of the metaphors that science traditionally uses in these descriptions.[51] What sort of value transformation would occur, Ruether asks, if scientists replaced "Big Bang" theory with hypotheses about the cosmic egg?[52]

Because Ruether recognizes the particular, value-laden character of scientific language, she can legitimately do what Callicott cannot: evaluate science on moral terms and ask it to contribute to liberating descriptions for use in ethical reflection. If science has its own values, we can—provided we subject them to careful ideological critiques—properly speak of new, *scientific* myths of creation and destruction,[53] and we can legitimately find in scientific descriptions of nature's systems "echoes of our ethical and spiritual aspirations."[54] In a plea that resonates with Brian Swimme's and (to a degree) James Gustafson's work, Ruether asks for scientists who can tell "the story of the cosmos and the earth's history, in a way that can call us to wonder, to reverence for life, and to the vision of humanity living in community with all its sister and brother beings."[55]

Ruether joins both Callicott and Gustafson in refusing to discount the technical usefulness of science. Certainly *metanoia* (i.e., the conversion from exploitation and sin to right relationship) can bear no fruit unless we understand the intricacies of the global ecosystem. Only then will we know which strings to pull, how to "rearrange patterns in nature to suit human demands" without exacerbating existing imbalances.[56] Here the hard sciences play much the same role that sociology, political science, and economics play in nonecological liberation theologies: They describe the functioning of structures as a practical prelude to their liberative transformation.[57] And as in liberation theology, such description often reveals systematic beliefs and habits that protect one group at the unjust expense of others.

What is the significance of ecofeminist Christian reflection for global discussion of environmental ethics? Ruether approaches this question slightly differently: Why examine Christianity at all if it contains so much that is destructive? Ruether acknowledges that Christianity is her own tradition, the background from which she can speak most honestly and knowledgeably. It is also the dominant religious tradition of the

Western powers, which hold sway internationally. More importantly (and here Ruether betrays a systematic commitment to cultural and religious pluralism), she hints that the prerequisite for genuinely constructive global dialogue is careful internal study and criticism of each tradition by its own adherents in light of contemporary science.[58] Finally, she believes that Christian culture contains discrete elements that are helpful to the global task of defining and building just human and ecological relations.[59] Here Ruether's language is very like Callicott's, but her method is radically different. Callicott recounts and analyzes multiple existing traditions himself; Ruether examines and criticizes her own tradition, in preparation for anticipated conversations with representatives of other traditions. Callicott's approach risks reductionism; like Gustafson's, Ruether's facilitates genuine dialogue, both within her tradition and outside it.

Coordinating scientific descriptions with religious worldviews does not end the conversation, however. Both Ruether and Gustafson insist that we exercise our capacity for transformation within the limits of the natural order, but they do not agree precisely on where these boundaries lie. Ruether—whose position echoes in different ways process, liberation, and natural law theologies—holds that we have been granted both the capacity and the responsibility to construct a just and sustainable new order. She envisions the possibilities of profound change in theology, the ecosystem, and even God.[60] Gustafson, who draws primarily on the Reformed tradition, proposes a more obscure and sovereign God, who orders the cosmos of which our planet is a painfully insignificant part. Although Gustafson holds that we must and do alter our surroundings and formulate tentative understandings of divine purposes, he is less willing than Ruether for human beings to attempt to transform the ecosystem in extreme or irreversible ways; for to do so would be prideful and anyway probably futile.

Conclusion

Callicott, Gustafson, and Ruether concur that the natural sciences provide us with an indispensable fund of common knowledge which reflects a common foundation for human experience: We inhabit an interdependent global ecosystem, and human beings are an integral part of this ecosystem. All three authors respond to this knowledge with profound awe and with moral approbation: All of this is good. And all three combine their knowledge and awe with a further moral claim that some version of human and ecosystematic flourishing ought to be pursued.

Yet awe and moral conviction do not follow necessarily on scientific analysis. Affective responses and judgments about ends are statements about values, and these must include foundations beyond the hard sciences. So what role can these sciences play in the global ethical dialogue? They help us first simply to develop precise *descriptions* of our experiences of shared residence on a finite planet, to *understand* our commonly held world and our ecological place in it.[61]

No such description—no matter how detailed and how widely accepted—is also universally or comprehensively prescriptive, telling us which moral ideals to pursue or what moral rules to follow. After all, on the basis of the same sorts of scientific knowledge, Callicott and Gustafson push for the maintenance of the environmental status quo, Ruether argues for its transformation, and others make equally plausible cases for its destruction.[62] Nonetheless, scientific knowledge is indispensable here. It systematically marshals inductive, experiential evidence about which ideals the existing ecosystem's structures and processes may be able to support (foundation),[63] what seems to comprise human and global flourishing (end), and how we may be able to accomplish it (technical means).[64] Negatively put, science sets limits. For instance, visions of future edenic harmony can seem to ignore the fact that in the existing order interdependence involves death and killing. Ethics must account for this.

Here the old connection between theological natural law (human rational participation in divine providence) and the laws of nature (the systems of the cosmos) might be dusted off and employed from a new perspective. Practical rationality, guided by concrete ends, must operate within the limits of the possible as we understand them. In Thomas Aquinas's day, these were the limits of Aristotelian physics and biology. Today, they are the materiality, finitude, and interdependence of concrete creatures and systems. In this sense we can truly say that to operate according to the natural law, according to reason, is to respect fully the limits and possibilities imposed by the laws of nature and requires an ever-clearer scientific understanding of their content.[65]

Callicott is correct to a point: Science can be the "cognitive lingua franca" of pluralist global environmental ethical discourse. The hard sciences organize the common grounds and possibilities of existence upon which ethics reflects. Yet these contributions, while necessary, are not sufficient. For science does not generate values beyond those it assumes. Only particular philosophies and theologies can attribute meaning and moral status to the world that science describes; provide the content of the ends humans are to pursue within the limits that the natural order imposes; decide on the size of the gap between these ends and the status quo; and supply motivations and justifications for acting to close it (for example, the claim that being good entails doing good). The prerequisites for participation in global ethical discourse on the environment are a carefully organized description of the ecosystem we share *and* a particular philosophical or religious argument for pursuing its welfare.[66]

Notes

My thanks to Lisa Sowle Cahill, Carol Robb, Martin Cook, Harlan Beckley, Stephen J. Pope, William French, and two anonymous reviewers for the Society of Christian Ethics *Annual* for their helpful comments on earlier versions of this essay.

1. For an extreme form of this claim, see Jeffrey Stout, *Ethics after Babel: The Languages of*

Morals and Their Discontents (Boston: Beacon Press, 1988): We cannot construct even a personal comprehensive moral outlook but must use different norms and methods in different portions of our lives.

2. J. Baird Callicott, *In Defense of the Land Ethic: Essays in Environmental Philosophy* (Albany: State University of New York Press, 1989); J. Baird Callicott, *Earth's Insights: A Multicultural Survey of Ecological Ethics from the Mediterranean Basin to the Australian Outback*, with a foreword by Tom Hayden (Berkeley: University of California Press, 1994).

3. James M. Gustafson, *A Sense of the Divine: The Natural Environment from a Theocentric Perspective* (Cleveland: Pilgrim Press, 1994); James M. Gustafson, *Ethics from a Theocentric Perspective*, 2 vols. (Chicago: University of Chicago Press, 1981–1984). The emphasis will be on the former as an explication of the importance of the latter for environmental ethics.

4. Rosemary Radford Ruether, *Gaia and God: An Ecofeminist Theology of Earth Healing* (San Francisco: HarperSanFrancisco, 1992); Rosemary Radford Ruether, *New Woman/New Earth: Sexist Ideologies and Human Liberation* (New York: Seabury Press, 1975). The emphasis will be on the former, in which the ideas nascent in the latter are more fully developed.

5. Callicott, *Earth's Insights*, 185–87; J. Baird Callicott, "The Case against Moral Pluralism," *Environmental Ethics* 12 (1990): 117.

6. Amy J. Rosenbaum coined this term. Callicott argues that although the "new science" has Western historical roots, its substance more closely resembles important traditions of non-Western thought and does not perpetuate cultural imperialism. See Callicott, *Earth's Insights*, 192.

7. Callicott, *Earth's Insights*, 12.

8. The claim that arguing directly from a morally neutral description to a morally prescriptive conclusion is fallacious is generally traced to David Hume, *A Treatise of Human Nature*, ed. P. H. Nidditch (New York: Oxford University Press, 1978), III, i, 1: 469–70. Contemporary philosophers counter that descriptions generally have moral valences, because descriptive knowledge and moral approbation tend to arise simultaneously. See, e.g., Basil Mitchell, *Morality: Religious and Secular: The Dilemma of the Traditional Conscience* (Oxford: Clarendon Press, 1980), 118–20. In different ways others have argued that in order to bridge the "is-ought" gap legitimately, one must either build valuative "bridges" between states of affairs and moral prescriptions or explicate the values that are implicit in the descriptions of states of affairs. See David O. Brink, *Moral Realism and the Foundations of Ethics*, Cambridge Studies in Philosophy (Cambridge: Cambridge University Press, 1989), 144–70; Kai Nielsen, "The Myth of Natural Law," in Sidney Hook, ed., *Philosophy: A Symposium* (New York: New York University Press, 1964), 134–36; Morton White, *What Is and What Ought to Be Done: An Essay on Ethics and Epistemology* (New York: Oxford University Press, 1981); and Hans Jonas, *The Imperative of Responsibility: In Search of an Ethics for the Technological Age*, trans. Hans Jonas with David Herr (Chicago: University of Chicago Press, 1984), 25–50.

9. Callicott, *Land Ethic*, 110; see also Callicott, *Earth's Insights*, 206–7.

10. Aldo Leopold, *A Sand County Almanac* (New York: Oxford University Press, 1949), 204, quoted in Callicott, *Earth's Insights*, 130. Callicott reads the Genesis story of the fall as an account of the origins of anthropocentrism, of the human habit of organizing the world around the human self and its needs. See J. Baird Callicott, "Genesis and John Muir," in *Covenant for a New Creation: Ethics, Religion, and Public Policy*, ed. Carol S. Robb and Carl J. Casebolt (Maryknoll, N.Y.: Orbis Books, 1991), 123–26.

11. See for example Callicott, *Earth's Insights*, 1–3, 200; Callicott, *Land Ethic*, 54, 122.

12. Callicott, *Land Ethic*, 57.

13. Ibid, 58; this inner circle may include animals (pp. 55–59). See also Callicott, *Earth's Insights*, 204.

14. See *Earth's Insights,*169.

15. Leopold, *A Sand County Almanac*, 224–25, quoted in Callicott, *Land Ethic*, 21.

16. Callicott, *Earth's Insights*, 40. He denies that human life or global processes have a transcending end; based on our scientific reflections, we cannot properly see ourselves or the world as being on the way to an ideal state envisioned or enabled by God (see p. 22; there is no God to fill the "axiological void").

17. "Hence a nonanthropocentric environmental ethic, fully ecologized, so to speak, turns out to be a form of enlightened—or, better, embedded—collective human self-interest, after all" (Callicott, *Earth's Insights*, 208). William French might criticize this as "back door" anthropocentrism. See William French, "Catholicism and the Common Good of the Biosphere," in *An Ecology of the Spirit: Religious Reflection and Environmental Consciousness*, ed. Michael Barnes, Annual Publication of the College Theology Society (Lanham, Md.: University Press of America, 1994), 36:177–94.

18. Callicott could have argued that universal norms are generated by a convergence of the common *and morally laudable* instinct for self-preservation and the practical prerequisites for survival: adequate food, security from murder, etc. See Nielsen, "Myth," 136–38; and Lisa Sowle Cahill, *Sex, Gender, and Christian Ethics* (Cambridge: Cambridge University Press, 1996).

19. Gustafson, *Sense of the Divine*, xiv.

20. Ibid., 23–29. Note the connections to the negative contrast experience in liberationist thought. See Patricia McAuliffe, *Fundamental Ethics: A Liberationist Approach* (Washington, D.C.: Georgetown University Press, 1993), 1–38.

21. Gustafson, *Sense of the Divine*, 29–31. The experience of beauty contributes necessary but insufficient building blocks for the development of a standard for behavior as well. Even instrumentalist, anthropocentric justifications for attending to the ecosystem tend to express a sense of the sublimity of nature (pp. 36–41).

22. Ibid., 44; see also 101. Unstated is an assumption that part of the divine wisdom is to create human beings to be receptive to the divine through affectivity.

23. Ibid., 67–68, 96; the key phrase is "interdependence without equilibrium" (p. 67).

24. Ibid., 49.

25. Ibid., 45. This "favorite sentence" comes from John Calvin, *The Institutes of the Christian Religion*, ed. John T. McNeill (Philadelphia: Westminster Press, 1955), 1: 58. See Gustafson's caveats in *Sense of the Divine*, 97.

26. See, e.g., Gustafson, *Sense of the Divine*, 70.

27. It both evokes and explains, but the affective/evocative function is stronger than the relational/explanatory one (Gustafson, *Sense of the Divine*, 44–46).

28. See, e.g., ibid., 72–74, 106.

29. Gustafson can think of no visions which both take the structure of reality seriously and eliminate both conflict and destruction (ibid., 96).

30. Ibid., xiv, 48–49, 62, 69, 106.

31. Ibid., 68–69.

32. Because one can speak of God only as God-known-to-us, theology is reflection on hu-

man experience. These reflections encompass revelation, the developed theological tradition, and the reasoned explorations of the sciences, among other modes of thought. See Gustafson, *Ethics*, 1:115–54.

33. Gustafson, *Sense of the Divine*, 68.

34. Ibid., 104; Gustafson, *Ethics*, 2:295.

35. Gustafson, *Sense of the Divine*, 104.

36. The immediate concerns which inspire discussion at this level are generally practical: for example, affective reactions to environmental degradation and utilitarian or anthropocentric arguments for preservation (ibid., 29–44).

37. Ibid., 105.

38. See ibid., 121–22, 145. For a full treatment of Gustafson's use of science in theology and ethics, see Robert Audi, "Theology, Science, and Ethics in Gustafson's Theocentric Vision," in *James M. Gustafson's Theocentric Ethics: Interpretations and Assessments*, ed. Harlan R. Beckley and Charles M. Swezey (Macon, Ga.: Mercer University Press, 1988), 159–85, esp. 164–68. Thanks to the relationship between God and creation, science remains clearly in the service of theology even when it criticizes theology. For a demonstration of the converse argument, see Frank J. Tipler, *The Physics of Immortality: Modern Cosmology, God, and the Resurrection of the Dead* (New York: Anchor Books, 1994).

39. Gustafson, *Ethics*, 2:319–22.

40. This by no means exhausts the Reformed heritage. See ibid., 1:157–93.

41. Ruether, *Gaia and God*, 31.

42. Ibid.

43. See, e.g., ibid. 258–68.

44. Ruether, *New Woman*, 186–214.

45. Ruether, *Gaia and God*, 48–54.

46. Ruether, *New Woman*, 186–218. Lois Daly has described this move as "taking the feminist critique of dualism another step." See Lois Daly, "Ecofeminism, Reverence for Life, and Feminist Theological Ethics," in *Feminist Theological Ethics: A Reader*, ed. Lois Daly (Louisville, Ky.: Westminster John Knox Press, 1994), 299–314. Daly criticizes ecofeminists in general for passing too lightly over the sorts of concrete conflicts to which Gustafson alludes.

47. Ruether, *Gaia and God*, 141, 256.

48. Ibid., 53. Yet human-being-as-it-should-be is not equivalent to human-being-as-it-is, either; a phenomenological description of women's being, here and now, is not yet a description of women's "nature," in either the biological or the normative sense. See Ruether, *New Woman*, 148–49.

49. Ruether, *Gaia and God*, 141.

50. Scientific use of mechanistic language, intended to be neutral, conveys instrumentalist assumptions (ibid., 57).

51. Ibid., 36–40.

52. Ibid., 57.

53. Ibid., 57–58, chap. 4.

54. Ibid., 48. Note the divergence from Gustafson, in which such descriptions tell us a little about *God*. The project of theological anthropology can bridge this gap from either direction, but the difference in starting points is significant.

55. Ibid., 58.

56. Ibid., 86; "the biblical picture is one of keen awareness of the limits of human power" (p. 210).

57. Gustavo Gutiérrez, "Theology and the Social Sciences," in *The Truth Shall Make You Free: Confrontations*, trans. Matthew J. O'Connell (Maryknoll, N.Y.: Orbis Books, 1990), 53–84.

58. Ruether, *Gaia and God*, 10–11, 206.

59. Ibid., 201.

60. On Ruether's connections to the natural law tradition of ethics see Cristina L. H. Traina, "An Argument for Christian Ecofeminism," *Christian Century* 10, no. 18 (2–9 June 1993): 600–603.

61. I am not claiming that scientific description is value free. Rather, I am arguing that scientific description alone is not an adequate explicit foundation for moral values, no matter how value laden that description may be implicitly.

62. See Ruether on traditional apocalyptic literature, *Gaia and God*, 61–84.

63. A mismatch between ideal and practical possibility does not dictate that the ideal be discarded. For instance, perhaps God fulfills the ideal at the eschaton, and until then humanity can only approximate it.

64. Guarded language comes from the fact that the ecosystem is not a machine and that all human action in the ecosystem is an experiment with uncertain results.

65. See also Nielsen, "Myth," n. 8, and Cahill, *Sex, Gender, and Christian Ethics*, n. 18.

66. Any of a number of worldviews can generate similar action guides. Combined with a good technical understanding of ecosystematic interdependence, for example, the norms "sustain human life justly" and "maintain order and balance in the global environment" produce nearly identical practical guidelines.

Chapter 16

Marriage and Family

STEPHEN G. POST

Marriage and family are important in the history of Christian social thought. However, as James M. Gustafson indicates, neither is highlighted in current Christian ethics: "Even the casual reader of literature produced by Christian ethicians, for example, knows that far more attention has been given to homosexuality, abortion, and pre- and extramarital sexual relationships than to marriage and families as communities and institutions."[1] Courses in Christian social ethics reliably take up the state, war, and property as key topics, perhaps assuming that in a just society the family will naturally prosper and does not need much discussion. But in fact economic well-being does not ensure that children will have the benefits of both a mother and father.

This essay begins with a summary of empirical assessments of the problem of fatherlessness. It then turns to current Christian ethics against this background and offers an interpretation of the historical tradition of Christian ethics, suggesting a theological meaning for the two-parent family—our last remnant of the extended family.

Much of my analysis deals with liberal Protestant thought, where Gustafson's claims about inattentiveness to marriage and family are most pertinent. The Roman Catholic tradition has concentrated more on this area due to encyclicals affirming the religious and social importance of the two-parent family (e.g., John Paul II's 1980 *Familiaris Consortio* [*On the Family*]). Yet, as Stephen J. Pope documents, recent Catholic ethicists, both personalists and liberation theologians, have not discussed the family.[2] Edward C. Vacek states that this omission contrasts with a classical Catholic approach to agape that "tends to begin with special relationships" and to "lead through them to the dignity of all human beings," since without these relations "most people, including the poorest, would be worse off."[3] The contributions of Pope and Vacek retrieve Catholic interest in parental inclinations as part of a created *ordo caritatis* (order of love).

One qualification is needed from the outset: My approach centers on the theological meaning of marriage and family and is therefore somewhat idealized. A different sort of essay in Christian ethics would focus instead on economic contexts—dual careers, attitudes toward property, patterns of saving and consumption, class factors, issues of welfare and family policy, and the like. My purpose is to discuss the importance of love in marriage and in familial ties on the parent-child axis. I acknowledge, however, that the social dynamic of poverty and joblessness is a devastating injustice that far too many families must struggle to overcome.

Setting a Contemporary Context:
The Costs of Fatherlessness

The deletion of the family from Christian social ethics, a major concern of Pope and Vacek, does not pertain to Gabriel Marcel, whose 1943 essay titled "The Creative Vow as Essence of Fatherhood" is an important benchmark.[4] Marcel attends to the responsibility that defines fatherhood, in contrast to "the man who gives free rein to his progenitive instinct—a Restif, for instance, boasting that he has peopled the whole of France with his bastards."[5] Feelings of paternal tenderness can give way to "a growing irritation in the presence of a mewling, unclean creature who demands ceaseless attention and exercises a veritable tyranny over its relations."[6] Fatherhood, a "hazardous conquest," is "achieved step by step" consistent with "an unfathomable order, divine in its principle."[7] In his earlier essay, "The Mystery of the Family," Marcel had sketched a metaphysic conferring on the family a "sacred character" as a reflection of divine nature. Without such theological consecration, the family "decomposes and dies."[8] My own recent study of theology and the family is an effort to further this line of analysis.[9]

Whatever one's conclusions about the need for a sacred canopy over the family, David Blankenhorn's summary of the social cost of "the flight of males from their children's lives" raises issues of universal concern.[10] He observes: "Over the past three decades, many religious leaders—especially in the mainline Protestant denominations—have largely abandoned marriage as a vital area of religious attention, essentially handing the entire matter over to opinion leaders and divorce lawyers in the secular society."[11] Blankenhorn writes that a culture of fatherlessness threatens the well-being of today's children, and that fatherhood is "less the inelastic result of sexual embodiment than the fragile creation of cultural norms."[12] The rate of fatherlessness is higher than ever—in 1994 40 percent of the nation's children did not live with their fathers. Driven by divorce and out-of-wedlock childbearing, we have "split the nucleus of the nuclear family."

Youth violence, especially among males, is due in some measure to the absence of a father-mentor, which results in undisciplined lives and deep resentment. Blankenhorn asserts that "Prisons cannot replace fathers."[13] While economic injustice is surely an equally relevant cause of violence and of fatherlessness itself, I agree with Blankenhorn that "we must fashion a new cultural story of fatherhood." We must "change from a divorce culture to a marriage culture," and affirm that "being a real man means being a good father."[14] Many, though obviously not all, children damaged by fatherlessness will be unable to take their rightful places in society.

According to Princeton sociologist Sara McLanahan, longitudinal research over two decades establishes that the two-parent family promotes children's success through enhanced economic security and greater parental involvement and supervision.[15] This is not just because two parents can share responsibility and cooperate with each other; rather, it is because single-parent and stepfamilies are "less stable in terms of personnel (grandmothers, mothers' boyfriends, and stepfathers are more likely to move in and out), which creates uncertainty about household rules and parental responsibility."[16] Further, psychiatric studies show that single mothers in general experience more stress and depression because they lack the economic and emotional support of another committed parent, and children suffer the consequences.[17] Children without fathers suffer from residential instability and loss of community: "In order to take full advantage of whatever a community offers, a child must know and trust his [or her] neighbors and teachers, and they must know and care about him [or her]."[18]

The necessary revolt against patriarchal family structures will hopefully allow for the emergence of a gender-egalitarian family model in which mothers and fathers together can provide and care for their children. Across the spectrum of race, gender, and class, children whose parents live apart are twice as likely to drop out of high school, one and a half times more likely to be idle in young adulthood, and twice as likely to become single parents themselves.[19]

Against the background of the above problem, I will now turn to some selected contemporary responses to the family in Christian ethics. My sources are largely Protestant ones in which the current debate over the family converges in a pointed manner. In a later section on the historical tradition, as well as in a concluding section of the essay, I will consider Roman Catholic sources.

Selected Contemporary Theological Ethicists

In the following discussion, a nonpatriarchal evangelical perspective is treated first to underscore the fact that Protestant conservatives can move beyond the patriarchal "headship" model of the family which derives from Pauline writings; this approach does not pretend that patriarchy is no longer a severe problem. Discussion then turns to two more-liberal views which vary in their affirmation of the two-parent family.

Nonpatriarchal Evangelical

Among the most influential statements of an evangelical familial ethics is Gary R. Collins's *Family Shock: Keeping Families Strong in the Midst of Earthshaking Change.*[20]

Collins summarizes the end-of-the-century cultural forces which he believes threaten the stability of marriage and family, and he calls on the churches to give direction. His embracing of "Christian feminism" as an alternative to antifamily feminism is significant:

> These moderates reject the caricature that a woman's place is solely in the home, waiting on her husband and forced to squelch her gifts, abilities, interests, and calling so she can stick around the house and do her husband's bidding. But these women—their numbers include many Christians—value motherhood, support strong family ties, applaud both those who work in the marketplace and those who work at home, believe in the sanctity of marriage, and are committed to sexual purity and faithfulness.[21]

Christian feminists, argues Collins, are prepared to acknowledge that radical feminism has helped to "improve the lot of women" and "bring healthy balance to many marriages."[22] This transition—probably not as pervasive as Collins suggests—opens the possibility for Christian (or good) feminism, described thus: "In its more balanced, biblically sensitive forms, feminism brings honor to the Creator and strengthens families."[23]

If Collins's rejection of patriarchal "headship" is taken at face value, then some of evangelical Christian thought has moved in a direction outlined by the late Paul K. Jewett in *Man as Male and Female*, published in 1975 while Jewett was on the faculty at Fuller Theological Seminary.[24] Jewett states that while the classical notion of *imago Dei* refers to "unique powers of self-transcendence" of the individual, it can also be asserted that "creation in the divine image is so related to creation as male and female that the latter may be looked upon as an exposition of the former."[25] Thus, the relationship of wife and husband hints at certain features of God—although Judeo-Christian theism obviously contrasts with any Asian images of the female and male in some form of embrace. Jewett reaches this conclusion:

> Since God created [humans] male and female, both must acknowledge the call of God to live creatively in a relationship of mutual trust and confidence, learning through experiment in relationship what God has ordained that they should learn no other way. This calls for integrity on the part of the man to renounce the prerogatives, privileges, and powers which tradition has given him in the name of male headship.[26]

Jewett's key insight, informed by Genesis 1:27, is that the image of God includes maleness and femaleness, and that the human completion of this image includes both marriage and Pauline (Gal. 3:26–28) equality. The love of parents for children reflects within human nature a central aspect of God's love for each human person. There could hardly be a stronger sacred canopy for marriage and family.

Liberal Departures

While some evangelicals—most notably Jewett—have attempted to strengthen by way of constructive theology a nonpatriarchal marriage and family consistent with fidelity, some liberal Protestant thinkers have departed from tradition in significant ways.

The highly influential James B. Nelson published his *Embodiment* in 1978.[27] The present essay does not address the literature on sex and embodiment, but rather concentrates on the fate of the family; nonetheless, Nelson's accomplishments in asserting the goodness of the body and of sex must be lauded as a contribution to marital fullness. He affirms the goodness of creation, body, and *eros*; he is properly critical of male images that result in violence and abuse of women instead of affective intimacy. His Freudian framework can be questioned on empirical grounds, as can some derivative assertions about absence of sexual expression inviting "self-destruction." Nevertheless, his analysis of the relationship of sex to human well-being is helpful—for Christianity, in contrast to Judaism, has frequently been unduly suspicious of sexual intimacy.

Yet, relevant to my subject matter, Nelson departs from the moral signposts of Christian ethics when he indicates that in some cases marital fidelity is fully consistent with nonexclusive sexual intimacies.[28] This "open marriage" departure from the sexual exclusivity associated with Christian monogamy represents a serious criticism of the tradition. Nelson argues for personal relativism (i.e., the form of marriage ought to be "congruent with the authentic needs of persons," and further, we ought never to "absolutize" a particular institutional form).

However, Christian tradition teaches an exclusive monogamy, as indicated by the New Testament, even if it allows for divorce in compelling cases. Christian thinkers have attached great importance to fidelity in marriage: Biblical warrants require it; marriage is considered a one-flesh union for the duration of lives (an increasingly lengthy commitment in our aging society); the pattern of Christ's own faithfulness is considered an ideal for marriage.[29] Critics indicate that this emphasis on fidelity is too great and that it presents an ideal view inconsistent with real human needs.

On the matter of fidelity, a position such as Nelson's will stir response from even moderately conservative Christian ethicists. Gilbert Meilaender, for example, summarizes Nelson's position to mean "I promise . . . unless and until new possibilities for growth and self-realization lead me to a new partner."[30] While Nelson has not responded to this criticism, Meilaender does raise an important point.

Drawing on Nelson's work, Christine E. Gudorf repudiates spirit-body dualism, the purely procreational justification of sex, and the practice of patriarchy. Again, relevant to this essay, she does not affirm monogamous marriage and the two-parent family.[31] In a brief discussion of marriage, Gudorf cites Jessie Bernard's 1971 essay indicating that married women are "more phobic, passive, and depressed" than single women.[32] This claim is questionable. No doubt some women have been and are oppressed by marital patriarchy through control of property and the potentially stifling role of full-time mother. But Bernard's analysis reflects a form of antifamily feminism that eventually was to be moderated through the later writings of Betty Friedan and others.

Gudorf contemplates alternatives to the two-parent family with statements such as: "Families need not be based on marriage. Families can be collections of persons who are committed to the physical, moral, spiritual, social, and intellectual development of other members of the collective unit in an ongoing way."[33] Further, "Marriage can take many shapes and forms."[34] While I laud Gudorf for attacking inequalities in marriage, I am concerned with the suggestion for alternatives to the ideal of an egalitarian marriage form. Further, it is troubling that Gudorf lets the following query dangle without response: "Is there a purpose and content to marriage once it is no longer about the ownership and control of woman and children, once both entering and remaining within marriage are voluntary?"[35] For the sake of providing children with the love of both a mother and a father, there clearly is a reason for marriage. On Gudorf's behalf, she does indicate that the best solution to the problem of marriage and family is to abolish patriarchal inequalities, rather than the husband-wife form itself.

Theologians such as Gudorf and Nelson are among many who have helped Christian women to establish patterns of liberation from marriages that are tantamount to enslavement. The Exodus narrative can be applied to marriage. As social-scientific data mount indicating that, in general, children benefit considerably from having two parents and that the quality of society is deeply affected by the breakdown of this family form, Christian thinkers who address the harms of patriarchy may wish to reflect on the facts. Surely the final answer to the fate of our children at risk cannot be that the fatherly role is inessential and that fathers do not matter.

Liberal Affirmations

At the outset of this essay, Gustafson was quoted for his concern with inattention to marriage and family in recent Christian ethics. He intimates that inattention may be "a reaction to the highly idealized portrayals of the 'Christian family' that churches propagated in their family literature for several decades."[36] This idealization explains in part the emergence of views such as those of Nelson and Gudorf. In his own survey of Christian literature on the family in the 1950s, Gustafson found little appreciation for the ways in which the family is affected by other institutions and dependent on them.

Rejecting the model of family that draws on male hierarchy, Gustafson attempts to portray a different image. This alternative does not depend on "order of creation" theology. Indeed, Gustafson states that "There is no immutable order of marriage and family that can be traced from an order of nature or from an order of creation that is itself imprinted in the mind of God."[37] Given the normal ratio of males to females, he adds that monogamy would be the first candidate. Gustafson asserts that "The divine empowering and ordering of life takes place in and through 'nature': through human biological relationships first of all."[38] Given the normal balance between male and female, monogamy remains normative. Further, Gustafson affords marriage and family a theological dignity and a central role in "the order of human love."[39]

Gustafson emphasizes stewardship, mutual commitment, and "vocation" in marriage. He stresses the rewards of marriage and family in the responsiveness of others with love and gratitude. But "There is pain and suffering in our stewardship: the anxiety and sufferings of others become our own; our intentions for the well-being of others are sometimes misunderstood, and sometimes are misguided."[40]

Because of the potential burden of stewardship, the "human fault" of egocentrism can destroy marriage and family. Drawing on Marcel's writings, Gustafson views "fidelity" and loyalty as imperative for good stewardship in this and any context. Fidelity allows the family to become a school for piety and morality. In the family, people develop the senses of "dependence, gratitude, obligation, remorse and repentance, possibility, and direction that ground piety and ultimately theology, and morality and ultimately ethical thought."[41]

Gustafson's students have found in him a supportive mentor for studies on marriage and family. For example, Lisa Sowle Cahill, a Roman Catholic thinker, provides a hermeneutics of retrieval for the two-parent family. She finds in Genesis 1–3 a higher critical locus from which to critique patriarchy and subordination in marriage, concluding that "supremacy and subordination, as distinct from difference and cooperation, are not part of the original creation but of the condition of sin. God's creation of humanity in the divine image, as male and female, and as companions who become 'one flesh,' functions as a standard by which to evaluate and criticize the male and female dialogue and struggle in history."[42] She accepts the tradition insofar as "woman and man are ordained normatively to community," and in its view of the communal significance of sexual differentiation, complementarity (not in the sense of opposites), and partnership.[43] The Genesis texts indicate that the two sexes are equally good and "designed for a harmonious and productive existence."[44]

As Cahill asserts, "liberal individualism and relativism in sexual ethics stand to be corrected by the traditional service-oriented and communal ideals against which contemporary personalism arose as modification."[45] Cahill finds that both Testaments "favor the institutionalization of sexuality in heterosexual, monogamous, permanent, and procreative, marriage that furthers the cohesiveness and continuity of family, church, and body politic, and that respects and nurtures the affective commitments to which spouses give sexual expression."[46] Such marriage includes pleasurable, reciprocal, affective, and unitive sex, but does not condone "sexual trivialization, glorification, manipulation, narcissism, and infidelity," or the sexual hierarchy that underlies these.[47]

In the following section, I indicate a suggestive trajectory of Christian thought on the sanctity of the family that begins with the New Testament and the early church and then, for reasons of limited space, arches over into American theology. Attention to this line reflects my own intuitions and preferences, and is not meant to provide a systematic history. However, I intend this historical backdrop to provide a strong contrast to the omission of the family in much current theological ethics.

A Constructive Interpretation of Christian Tradition

My purpose in this section is to suggest profound theological meaning behind the often trivialized assertion that marriage and family have a sacred value. This suggestion cannot be proven true; the most one can offer is the claim that such meaning is a significant element in Christian tradition.

The New Testament

Few passages have been more influential on the history of Western civilization and the order of marriage than Genesis 2:24, which decrees that a man shall leave father and mother to cleave to his wife, that they might become "one flesh." In the New Testament, the appeal to this passage is definitive (see Matt. 19:3–9; Mark 10:3–9; Eph. 5:31). Jesus appears to have found in Genesis 2:24 an authoritative basis for monogamous marriage. Thus marriage circumscribes the command to procreate in Genesis 1:28.

The firmness of Jesus' appeal suggests significance consistent with his concern for the well-being of children, so evident in his blessing of them despite the protest of his adult followers (Mark 10:14–16), and with his concern for women, long subjected to the patriarchal double standard and arbitrary divorce.

New Testament exegete E. P. Sanders writes that marriage was especially significant to Jesus and that "the long form of the tradition about divorce, which includes the appeal to Gen. 1:27 and 2:24 (Matt. 19:3; Mark 10:2–12), or something very like it, represents Jesus' original saying."[48] Jesus' prohibition against divorce is part of a dominion worldview, not to be understood "as an interim ethic nor as an ideal goal which will never be reached, but as a serious decree for a new age and a new order."[49]

But what of Jesus' criticisms of familial ties? These only occur when the ties prevent people from following him (e.g., Matt. 10), and therefore hinder the coming dominion of God. The hard sayings, including the warning that the follower "will find enemies under his [or her] own roof" (Matt. 10:35–36), do not negate an exceptional reverence for familial ties (Mark 10) and parental love (e.g., Matt. 7:9–11). The hard sayings occur in an atmosphere of tension between a controversial and demanding new religious movement and a society that opposes it. In ancient cultures, even more than today, the familial control of family members (especially under legal patriarchy) was onerous. This tension is perennial. For example, the establishment called the youthful medieval converts to the Dominicans and Franciscans *dementes* (insane). Both Saint Francis and Saint Thomas Aquinas were kidnapped and imprisoned for lengthy periods by their parents and relatives, who tried to "deprogram" them (to make an analogy with modern practice) away from their beliefs. Saint Thomas wrote a brief treatise based on his experience, *Contra pestiferam doctrinam retrahentium homines a religionis ingressu*, or "Against the Pernicious Teaching of Those Dragging Youth Away from Entering the Religious Life." But the struggle with families endured by Jesus and early Christians does not mean that Jesus did not place high value on marriage and family.

Paul drew on the same passages that Jesus did (Gen. 1:27, 2:24) when he called the unity of marriage a divine "mystery" (Eph. 5:31). Paul is consistent with Jesus when he seems to reject hierarchy in marriage (Gal. 3:28) and dignifies marriage by analogy to the union of church and Christ (2 Cor. 11:2; Eph. 5). His teachings emphasize the benevolence that should be mutually manifest (1 Cor. 7:3). Paul's reason for ambivalence about marriage, misunderstood by later church ascetics, is that "the present world is passing away" (1 Cor. 7:29–31). Otherwise, contra gnosticism, he views marriage as a good. Even when he endorses marriage not as a good but as a remedy for lust, he is addressing a specific Christian community verging on antinomianism. His personal singleness, which he did not require of others, is grounded in his historical perspective (i.e., because the end time is near, Christians might wisely forgo marriage if able).

Nothing Paul wrote departs from the idea that marriage between man and woman with the intention of forming a family is filled with divine intentionality and meaning. The seriousness of this meaning was sometimes compromised in the long course of ancient Hebrew history: Polygamy surfaces among rulers (resulting in God's displeasure with Solomon), murderous adultery appears (Yahweh punishes King David for his affair with Bathsheba), and concubinage occurs (note that in the story of Abraham and Hagar, it is ultimately Abraham's only wife, Sarah, who bears Isaac). The ideal remains monogamy, even though polygamy was not outlawed in Judaism until the medieval period. It was the Jewish Jesus, who claimed to come to fulfill the law and the prophets, who strongly condemned men who looked outside of marriage with even the attitude of lust (Matt. 5:28).

The Christian biblical ethics of marriage and family has been summarized within the Reformed tradition to include the following five elements:

1. Only within marriage does the procreative demand have relevance.
2. The marital structure is that of monogamy.
3. Marriage and family, because formed by the creator, are rightly governed by the principle of piety.
4. Marriage within certain degrees of consanguinity is forbidden.
5. Marriage is a calling of God that is not without exceptions, for some people are called to singleness.[50]

This summary reflects a conviction that the New Testament builds on the Old. But even if the New and Old Testaments are separated, I hope that the above discussion of the teachings of Jesus and Paul indicates continuities (and discontinuities) between the Testaments. One clear discontinuity is that Pauline Christianity endorses singleness (Paul spoke of his own "special gift" in 1 Cor. 7), allowing a meaningful freedom from marriage and family which does not present itself in Judaism.

The line of exegesis I have focused on is recently represented by Eduard Lohse, a Lutheran New Testament exegete, who points out that in the preaching of Jesus, men and women were "addressed in the same way." Jesus went against the custom of his times in speaking with women in public and in having close associations with them, even though his disciples were men. Thus, the patriarchal conditions of society and marriage are conclusively set aside.[51] The will of God is "set forth in creation for the good of humanity," Jesus reliably taught, drawing on the creation story that "God had created humanity as a unity of male and female in order that they might live together in partnership their whole life long (Mark 10:6–7)."[52] Further, "By conceiving marriage as a unity of husband and wife that in the intention of the creator is indissoluble, Jesus attributes a dignity to marriage that it received neither among the Jews nor the Greeks."[53] Jesus clarified the unity of man and woman according to "the original intent of the creator."[54]

In a nonconfessional and impartial summary of the trajectory sketched here, historian of religions Geoffrey Parrinder has written that "Every religion has some distinctive characteristics and Christianity is the only major religion which from the outset has seemed to insist upon monogamy."[55] He points out that Jesus' teachings on marriage, relying on Genesis, provide a "high but difficult morality, and much has been made of these verses in the later Church's rigorous attitudes toward divorce."[56] This rigor is demanding, "but in this instance Jesus seems to have been looking to the purpose of creation, and he took the divine pattern of the creation of man and woman in singleness and unity. In such a context, for a married man or woman to take another partner would be against the unity of their creation."[57] To deter the violation of this unity, even the wayward imagination must be controlled. Parrinder concludes, "The unity of man and wife in "one flesh," commanded by Jesus and referred back to the original action of God at creation, seems to require a single lifelong union. Paul repeated this doctrine."[58] While this was true of Judaism as well, argues Parrinder, polygamy was nevertheless tolerated until the eleventh century C.E.

The Early Church

Paul's eschatological ambivalence about the responsibilities of marriage and family was misinterpreted by the early church. As David G. Hunter writes, it was "read by later Christians in a context no longer troubled by the impending eschaton. Shorn of their apocalyptic significance, Paul's views took on a rather different meaning: Marriage itself came to be regarded as a state inferior to that of celibacy."[59] This misinterpretation of Paul is surprising because later New Testament writings continued Paul's resistance to the demands of ascetic Christians by providing a detailed marriage ethic modeled after patriarchal Roman household codes (Col. 3:18–4:1; 1 Pet. 2:17–3:9; 1 Tim. 2:8–15, 6:1–10; Titus 2:1–10).

Increasingly, early Christianity formed a bridge with the family morality of Roman stoicism. Many early Christian writers read and cited the stoic philosopher Musonius Rufus (first century C.E.) for his ideal of a marriage based on companionship and a mutual affection that endures sickness and other adverse conditions.[60] Christianity, then, spread an ethics of marriage and family rooted in Judaism, Jesus, Paul, and the stoics. Only Jesus and Paul, however, challenged the patriarchal and oppressive nature of the ancient family.

Some Christians did not wish to appropriate stoicism, relying instead on Judeo-Christian scriptural sources alone. For example, Tertullian, in his elegant treatise titled "To His Wife" (c. 200 C.E.), wrote:

> What words can describe the happiness of that marriage which the church unites, the offering strengthens, the blessing seals, the angels proclaim, and the Father declares valid? For even on earth children do not rightly and lawfully wed without their fathers' consent.
>
> What a bond is this: Two believers who share one hope, one desire, one discipline, the same service! The two are brother and sister, fellow servants. There is no distinction of spirit or flesh, but truly they are two in one flesh (Gen. 2:24; Mark 10:8). Where there is one flesh, there is also one spirit. Together they pray, together they prostrate themselves, together they fast, teaching each other, supporting each other.[61]

Tertullian emphasized the inner spiritual unity possible within marriage.

Consistent with Tertullian, the writings of Clement of Alexandria (*Miscellanies*), John Chrysostom ("Homily 20 on Ephesians"), and Jovinian indicate that marriage is as high, and in some respects a higher, form of Christian life as ascetic singleness. Clement indicates that the care of one's family is a human analog to God's own providential care. In his treatise titled "On Marriage," Clement wrote that, "Both celibacy and marriage have their own different forms of service and ministry to the Lord; I have in mind the caring for one's [spouse] and children." Clement adds (citing 1 Tim. 3:4) that those who succeed in family responsibilities should be appointed as bishops, for "by their oversight over their own house" they "have learned to be in charge of the whole church."[62]

Occasionally a former ascetic would embrace the ideal of marriage in enthusiastic terms. In 390 C.E. Jovinian, for example, argued against the exaltation of virginity. He drew on Genesis 1–3 and the statements of Jesus confirming these passages. The opposition from Jerome was fierce and immediate. But even Jerome's *Against Jovinian*, for all its exaltation of virginity and negative images of married women, does not condemn marriage. Using the metaphors of gold and silver for the virgin and married states, Jerome asks, "Will silver cease to be silver, if gold is more precious than silver?"[63] He urges marriage to be "honored" even if virginity is "preferred."

The late historian John Boswell ignores many of the above-mentioned sources when he describes early Christianity as "overwhelmingly ambivalent" about marriage.[64] He states that, "Honest modern biblical analysis, not pursuing any other agenda, is generally struck by Jesus' disregard for the family (as in Matt. 8:22, Mark 3:33–34, Luke 8:21 and especially 14:26)."[65] Yet E. P. Sanders is struck by Jesus' affirmation of the family, and I have argued that criticism of the family arises only in a context of tension between sect and society. Still, Boswell does succeed in highlighting the theologians' ambivalence about the family, since it had so much control over loyalties, conflicted often with religious commitments, and overly favored one's own kin group at the expense of the poor and of outsiders.

Many scholars have provided overviews of Christian social thought on marriage and family through the medieval period and the Reformation, where Luther made family life a religious vocation and denounced the monasteries. Since I have nothing new to contribute to that scholarship, I will leap forward to the American context, where I am able to highlight several sources that are insufficiently considered and that pertain to the current debate over two-parent family structure.

American Puritanism: Familial-Social Ethics

Partly through the influence of John Milton, the Puritans combined romantic love with the Reformation retrieval of marriage as a vocation, creating the institution of romantic marriage. Calvinism's imprint is apparent, for it placed emphasis on the social and companionate value of marriage. Contrary to negative stereotypes, the American Puritans appreciated the romantic love possible within marriage and emphasized the good of sexual pleasure within marriage.

Edmund S. Morgan's study on the Puritan family is a classic that is relevant to the current American debate over fatherlessness.[66] As Morgan describes, Puritans encouraged warm affections and love between spouses, although they warned against spouses loving each other so much that they descend into idolatry in violation of the "order of being." Parental responsibilities were taken with utmost seriousness and enforced by law: "The laws obliged all parents to perform this duty: no New England father could loaf away his time while the cupboard was bare."[67] The neglectful father could be indicted for idleness, although these problems were generally averted with the help of the churches, which insisted on high parental standards of duty.

A principal parental duty was to assist the child in the solemn effort to find his or her "particular calling," since God gives each person gifts that can be discovered with effort, and that serve both the individual and the commonweal: "It was not so much a choice as a discerning of what occupation God called one into."[68] Often, the gift would be discovered by apprenticeship.

Puritan children could change apprenticeships in their search for the fitting use of their energies. Morgan writes that, where "children's material welfare was concerned, a Puritan parent could call his [or her] duty done when he [or she] saw them established in their callings with good husbands and wives."[69] Parents, especially fathers, were responsible for teaching their children to read and to study the principles of Christianity. Literacy was important as a means to understand scripture and thereby to bring the child "into the covenant" of conversion, and to find one's vocation.

Three principles informed parental duties: the divine ordinance or sanction of marriage and family; the presence of a vocation in every soul; and the importance of extending the covenant to the next generation. The Puritans understood familial duties to be the keystone of social ethics and political order. Consistent with Aristotle's *Politics*, which the Puritan theologians read, society was considered an association of families. Morgan describes a familial-social ethics:

> This was the first premise of Puritan political and social thought. In the Garden of Eden, which was the world as God had originally planned it, [humans] lived innocently and happily with no need for any social organization apart from that provided by the family. It was only after Adam and Eve had tasted the forbidden fruit that need arose for stronger organizations.[70]

As Cotton Mather argued in his classic *Family Religion Urged*, God could have produced millions of people all at once; instead, God produced Adam and Eve, who were to form a family united with God. Because of the Fall, however, the congregation of worshipers was formed to strengthen worship. The Puritans took God's covenant with Abraham's family as a model.[71] As John Cotton wrote, "Abraham brought his household of old under the same covenant."[72] In Morgan's phrase, "The Puritans, in other words, thought of their church as an organization made up of families rather than individuals."[73]

Puritan families conducted regular devotions in the home, including prayer, scriptural reading, singing, and grace. They believed, argues Morgan, that if the family failed to inculcate religion and morality, neither the church nor the state could succeed. The family was prior to and served by the church. Had there been no Fall, there would have been no need for churches. Similarly, the state only existed because the family needed help in enforcing virtue in a degenerate world. Eleazer Mather wrote that families are "the root whence church and Commonwealth cometh."[74] All the Puritan theologians argued that the good ordering of society was only possible if families instructed in virtue.

Puritan theologians believed that while "a Christian should exclude no one from his [or her] love, he [or she] should pay the amount expended on each person according to the intimacy of the connection."[75] The balance of love between those near and dear, and those who are distant or strangers, is classically considered as the problem of the "order of love."[76]

Morgan's justly famous thesis is that the Puritan experiment failed because covenant theology placed so much weight on the redemption of one's children or lineage that the evangelical impulse was paralyzed. "Love thy neighbor" became "Love thy family." In Morgan's final phrase, "When theology became the handmaid of genealogy, Puritanism no longer deserved its name."

The Puritan failure teaches that the Christian family cannot be hermetically sealed, but must actively turn its attention to the needs of strangers.

Rauschenbusch

The Puritan emphasis on the family was not lost. Throughout the great awakenings and the social gospel period, familial love retained its importance (e.g., in the writings of Horace Bushnell). Because it is relatively unknown, I focus here on Walter Rauschenbusch's text, *Dare We Be Christians?* Like all Christian thinkers, Rauschenbusch values love for persons as such, even if they are strangers. Love for the stranger evolves from the experience and lessons of more intimate ties of "solidarity," like a pebble cast into a smooth pond from which ripples then flow outward in all directions. Eloquently put by this journalist-theologian, "The love of fatherhood and motherhood is a divine revelation and a miracle. It is a creative act of God in us."[77] Rauschenbusch continues:

Last year it was not; this year it is, and all things are changed. The dry rock of our selfishness has been struck and the water of sacrificial love pours forth. The thornbush is aflame with a beautiful fire that does not consume. The springing up of this new force of love is essential for the very existence of human society. Unless it were promptly forthcoming, children would die like the flies of late summer and the race would perish.[78]

In the family, God works through nature to develop the capacities in us for concrete love and sacrifice which can then be given fruitfully to the world.

A Modest Hope

The trajectory suggested here from the New Testament to the social gospel emphasizes the moral meaning of parental and familial love, even as this love is rightly haunted by the requirements of pure equal regard. Discussions of familial relations have been lacking in American Protestant writings on love, due in part to the writings of Anders Nygren, who omits the family in his analysis of agape and eros.[79] Gene Outka, in his magisterial work, *Agape: An Ethical Analysis*, does not take up the family. His theory of agape as "equal regard" is, however, by no means antifamily and may provide special relations with the protective foundation of equal respect.[80] The value of the "equal regard" approach to agape is not to be underestimated; special relations such as marriage and family are prone to moral myopia unless shaped by narratives such as the story of the good Samaritan.

It is hoped that leading American liberal Protestant theologians of all ethnicities will be able to recover the moral and theological significance of the family. Don S. Browning, who is contributing to this recovery, is concerned that mainline Protestant churches and theologians have left middle-class families and their struggles for the conservative Christian Coalition—as if the poor will ever have hope if the middle class disappears.[81]

There is much to be gained from the example of Catholicism, which balances concern for the oppressed with papal encyclicals on the family. Starting in 1930 with Pius XI's *Casti Connubii*, restrictions on contraception diverted attention from the larger Christian meaning of marriage and family which these modern encyclicals so skillfully articulate. John Paul II's *Familiaris Consortio*, referred to in my introductory paragraphs, indicates that the future of society and the church "passes through the family."[82] Marriage and family are affirmed as gifts of creation and as holy opportunities to raise children toward faith, creativity, and fulfillment. The principle of subsidiarity is based on the notion that the family is the "first and vital cell of society." The humanizing and personalizing of society occurs first and most profoundly on the parent-child axis, taking us all "out of anonymity" and into love. Setting aside important debates over natural law, contraception, and gender roles, *Familiaris Consortio* provides a profound familial theology.

Envoi: Function and Form

Over the last two decades, many Christian theologians have set aside any concern with the form of the family. Among these are John Patton and Brian H. Childs, who in their study of theology of the family and pastoral care state, "There is no ideal form for the Christian family toward which we should strive. There is, however, a normative function: care."[83] While there is much value in their definition of care as a combination of appreciation, respect, compassion, and solicitude, they refuse to "argue for or against any particular form of the family or for who ought to be living together and for how long."[84] For Patton and Childs, liberal Protestants both, any form is acceptable if redemptive "care" is present, for however long. No formative order or *nomos* shapes their ideal of marriage and family.

The compelling studies on the advantages of the two-parent family discussed at the outset of this essay suggest that this formlessness may not be good for children, a sensitivity that underlies the Judeo-Christian tradition. Formlessness is one response to a tradition of marriage and family that is plagued by patriarchy and injustice. While it is possible to reject the two-parent family altogether for the freedom of uncommitted relationships created for adult self-fulfillment, our children will suffer. The teachings of Jesus on monogamous marriage and parental love (including the forgiving father of the prodigal son) are still useful.

The Christian family cannot be a haven of private separation from outsiders. Rodney Clapp rejects the public-private split typical of the modern bourgeois family, described as a "haven in a heartless world." Clapp is concerned that among evangelicals, Jesus has become a "domestic mascot," and Yahweh a "household god."[85] He recovers the notion of the Christian home as a mission base open to all sorts of public comings and goings, consistent with the pattern of housechurches so important in the formation of early Christianity. It is this public purpose that drives family activities, not the privatized ideal of intimacy. Clapp believes that the family, in order to avoid the problem of insularity, must be "decentered" by the church.[86]

A socially responsive Christianity must, in my view, construct a new ethics of marriage and family that, informed by gender equality, thinks deeply about what spouses owe each other, their children, and outsiders near and far. In such a Christianity, family becomes a central concern of the church, but never so as to exclude or burden those who are called to singleness, or to tolerate patriarchal abuses. Practically, the church cannot succeed unless families support its beliefs and values. By the same token, families need the support of the community of believers lest they become insular and exclusionary. Christianity points to love in family and the church as looking outward in the spirit of the good Samaritan.

Notes

1. James M. Gustafson, *Ethics from a Theocentric Perspective*, 2 vols. (Chicago: University of Chicago Press, 1981–1984), vol. 2, *Ethics and Theology*, 165.

2. Stephen J. Pope, *The Evolution of Altruism and the Ordering of Love* (Washington, D.C.: Georgetown University Press, 1994). See esp. chap. 1, "Recent Catholic Ethics of Love."

3. Edward Collins Vacek, S.J., *Love, Human and Divine: The Heart of Christian Ethics* (Washington, D.C.: Georgetown University Press, 1994), 306.

4. Gabriel Marcel, *Homo Viator: Introduction to a Metaphysic of Hope*, trans. Emma Craufurd (1951; reprint, Gloucester, Mass.: Peter Smith, 1978), 98–124.

5. Ibid., 107.

6. Ibid., 108.

7. Ibid., 121.

8. Ibid., 96.

9. Stephen G. Post, *Spheres of Love: Toward a New Ethics of the Family* (Dallas: Southern Methodist University Press, 1994).

10. David Blankenhorn, *Fatherless America: Confronting Our Most Urgent Social Problem* (New York: Basic Books, 1995).

11. Ibid., 223.

12. Ibid., 65.

13. Ibid., 32.

14. Ibid., 223.

15. Sara McLanahan and Gary Sandefur, *Growing Up with a Single Parent: What Hurts, What Helps* (Cambridge: Harvard University Press, 1994).

16. Ibid., 96.

17. Ibid., 135.

18. Ibid., 116.

19. Sylvia Ann Hewlett, *When the Bough Breaks: The Cost of Neglecting Our Children* (New York: HarperCollins, 1992).

20. Gary R. Collins, *Family Shock: Keeping Families Strong in the Midst of Earthshaking Change* (Wheaton, Ill.: Tyndale House, 1995).

21. Ibid., 302.

22. Ibid.

23. Ibid., 303.

24. Paul K. Jewett, *Man as Male and Female: A Study in Sexual Relationship from a Theological Point of View* (Grand Rapids, Mich.: Eerdmans, 1975).

25. Ibid., 13.

26. Ibid., 149.

27. James B. Nelson, *Embodiment: An Approach to Sexuality and Christian Theology* (Minneapolis: Augsburg, 1979).

28. Ibid., 149.

29. Gilbert Meilaender, *The Limits of Love* (University Park: Penn State University Press, 1987), 124.

30. Ibid., 126.

31. Christine E. Gudorf, *Body, Sex, and Pleasure: Reconstructing Christian Sexual Ethics* (Cleveland: Pilgrim Press, 1994).

32. Ibid., 74.

33. Ibid., 79.

34. Ibid.

35. Ibid., 80.

36. Gustafson, *Ethics,* 1:155.

37. Ibid., 1:158.

38. Ibid.

39. Ibid., 1:164.

40. Ibid., 1:166.

41. Ibid., 1:173.

42. Lisa Sowle Cahill, *Between the Sexes: Foundations for a Christian Ethics of Sexuality* (Philadelphia: Fortress/Paulist, 1985), 56.

43. Ibid., 70.

44. Ibid., 55.

45. Ibid., 141.

46. Ibid., 143.

47. Ibid., 144.

48. E. P. Sanders, *Jesus and Judaism* (Philadelphia: Fortress Press, 1985), 257.

49. Ibid., 233–34.

50. John Murray, *Principles of Conduct: Aspects of Biblical Ethics* (Grand Rapids, Mich.: Eerdmans, 1957), chap. 3, "The Marriage Ordinance and Procreation."

51. Eduard Lohse, *Theological Ethics of the New Testament*, trans. M. Boring (Minneapolis: Fortress Press, 1991), 99.

52. Ibid., 100.

53. Ibid., 101.

54. Ibid.

55. Geoffrey Parrinder, *Sex in the World's Religions* (New York: Oxford University Press, 1980), 202.

56. Ibid., 208.

57. Ibid.

58. Ibid., 215.

59. David G. Hunter, "Introduction," in *Marriage in the Early Church*, ed. and trans. David G. Hunter (Minneapolis: Fortress Press, 1992), 5.

60. Ibid., 8.

61. Tertullian, "To His Wife," in *Marriage in the Early Church*, 33–39.

62. Clement of Alexandria, "On Marriage," in *Women and Religion: A Feminist Sourcebook of Christian Thought*, ed. Elizabeth Clark and Herbert Richardson (New York: Harper & Row, 1977), 48.

63. Jerome, "Against Jovinian," in *Women and Religion*, 61.

64. John Boswell, *Same-Sex Unions in Premodern Europe* (New York: Vintage Books, 1994), 111.

65. Ibid., 112, n. 13.

66. Edmund S. Morgan, *The Puritan Family: Religion and Domestic Relations in Seventeenth-Century New England* (New York: Harper & Row, 1944).

67. Ibid., 65.

68. Ibid., 171.

69. Ibid., 87.

70. Ibid., 133.

71. Ibid., 135.

72. Ibid.

73. Ibid., 136.

74. Ibid., 143.

75. Ibid., 153.

76. Post, *Spheres of Love*.

77. Walter Rauschenbusch, *Dare We Be Christians?* (Cleveland: Pilgrim Press, 1993 [original 1914]), 21.

78. Ibid., 22.

79. Anders Nygren, *Agape and Eros*, trans. Philip S. Watson (1932; reprint, Chicago: University of Chicago Press, 1982).

80. Gene Outka, *Agape: An Ethical Analysis* (New Haven: Yale University Press, 1972).

81. Don S. Browning, "Contractual Problems," *Christian Century* 112, no. 16 (7–14 June 1995): 596–97.

82. Pope John Paul II, *Familiaris Consortio* (Washington, D.C.: U.S. Catholic Conference, 1981).

83. John Patton and Brian H. Childs, *Christian Marriage and Family: Caring for Our Generations* (Nashville: Abingdon Press, 1988), 12.

84. Ibid.

85. Rodney Clapp, *Families at the Crossroad: Beyond Traditional and Modern Options* (Downers Grove, Ill.: InterVarsity Press, 1993), 154.

86. Ibid., 166.

Chapter 17

Love, Power, and Justice in Sexual Ethics

JAMES B. NELSON

Though Christian sexual ethics has received a great deal of attention ever since the 1960s, the vigorous debates are alive and well. Our culture is still enormously ambivalent about sexuality, and so are the churches. In a time of cultural and economic insecurity, numerous other fears are easily attached to sexual issues—perhaps because the human body so readily symbolizes the body politic. Thus, discussions about the rights of women and sexual minorities, abortion, new reproductive technologies, sex education and contraception in public schools, teen pregnancy, population control, commercial sex, pornography and censorship, HIV-AIDS prevention, and "family values" often have become occasions for strident rhetoric.

Though there are some happy exceptions, the churches generally have not handled sexuality well. Still deeply suspicious of the human body and its sexuality, still struggling with the legacies of sexism and heterosexism, still preoccupied with the evaluation of specific sexual acts, still embarrassed into silence by sexual misconduct and abuse in their midst, still divided over issues of ethical sources and authority, and still fearful of the divisiveness of sexual issues in a time of membership attrition, many church bodies have been virtually paralyzed about sexuality. Indeed, recent sexual debates in mainline churches have taken on extraordinary proportions in symbolic weight and emotional intensity.

To ethicists working on these sexual issues, at least one thing is clear: Many if not most of the basic assumptions long taken for granted in traditional Christian sexual ethics are now under serious question. These challenged assumptions include body-spirit dualism, the genitalization of sexual meanings, gender complementarity, dominant/submissive patterns of sexuality, penile-vaginal intercourse as the only "real" sexual act, procreation as a primary sexual norm, the inevitability of male sexual violence, the exclusion of eros and self-love from the Christian life, and the belief that sexual ethics is reducible to an ethics of marriage. Though most of these beliefs have been seriously questioned by ethicists for several decades, their staying power is strong in the churches.

In surveying what I believe to be critical and problematic issues in current Christian sexual ethics, I am drawing particularly on several ethicists who have especially addressed these things: Lisa Sowle Cahill, Marvin Ellison, Christine Gudorf, Beverly W. Harrison, Carter Heyward, Carol Robb, Adrian Thatcher, and my own work.[1] Others could and perhaps should be mentioned as well. However, the ethicists I have named, while not in uniform agreement, are united in their desire to move beneath particular questions of sexual morality to the underlying assumptions of sexual theology and ethics. Unlike many secular liberals, they refuse to confine sexual ethics to the "private" sphere, and, unlike many religious conservatives, they are unwilling to reduce virtually all morality to the sexual. They are convinced that there is urgent need for a continuing and searching ethical discourse about sexuality.

Methods and Sources

In his careful and richly nuanced methodological work, James M. Gustafson argues that how we construe God and how we construe the world in light of our convictions about God remains the most fundamental issue in theological ethics. The practical question then follows: "What is God enabling and requiring us to be and to do?"[2] I believe that a sexual formulation of that critical question is useful: "What is God enabling and requiring us, *as sexual persons,* to be and to do?" While I will not here attempt a thorough, systematic answer to that question, my framework sketches at least the outline of a response: God is enabling and requiring us to be sexually loving and just, claiming and exercising our sexual powers responsibly.

Gustafson's sources for testing Christian theological ethics (formulated only slightly differently from the familiar "Wesleyan quadrilateral") are the Bible and Christian tradition, philosophical methods and principles, science and other sources of knowledge about the world, and human experience.[3] Some comments about the use of these sources in sexual ethics are in order.

First, as Gustafson says, "The insights of the biblical people are more complex and varied" than many ethicists assume.[4] For our purposes, taking seriously the historicity of scripture and its varied cultural sexual biases simply will not allow us to discover any single coherent or defensible biblical sexual ethics. What we *can* find, however, are ample revelations of God's intentions for humanity and for the community of faith, and we can attempt to discern these meanings for our sexuality.

As with scripture, we must avoid any "selective literalism" in working with the Christian sexual tradition. Regarding specific sexual matters, tradition (like scripture) is a mix of good news and bad news. However, it is also replete with broad theological-ethical insights, and (also like scripture) with specific, often jarring ways of reshaping our current sexual perceptions.

Like Gustafson, many of us working in sexual ethics often have "relied more heavily on scientific and other sources of our knowledge of the world, and on human experience (e.g., piety) than traditional Christian ethics has."[5] While current scientific knowledge of sexuality possesses no infallibility, it has dramatically changed our understandings of reproductive processes, sexual orientation, the nature of gender, and a host of other sexual matters—understandings that have sizable ethical relevance.

Just as the voice of science looms larger in sexual ethics now, so also does the voice of experience. At this point, I think it important to distinguish between *theologies of sexuality* and *sexual theologies*. Theologies of sexuality have dominated in Christian history. They have proceeded in a one-directional way, beginning first with "religious" sources (scripture, tradition, or sometimes philosophy) and only later applying these understandings to human sexual experience. The movement has been overwhelmingly one-way: from religious truth to sexual experience.

Recent articulations of *sexual theology* are much more dialogical. Indeed, they are intentional about the interaction of experience with every other source.[6] After the manner of various liberation theologies, we inquire about the ways in which our sexual experience reveals God's action and how that experience affects understandings of scripture, tradition, and reason. Body knowledge is important moral knowledge, and when body awareness is dimmed because of disconnection, shame, or violence, our capacities for both moral understanding and action are diminished.

Though in some significant measure people have always perceived the world and its moral meanings through their sexual and body experiences, consciousness of this is relatively recent. Body psychology now has demonstrated that bodies are active sources of meanings and worldviews, not simply photographic receptors. More important for Christian sexual ethics, feminist and gay/lesbian liberationists have amply demonstrated how unexamined sexual assumptions have been always present in theology, and often oppressively so. In patriarchy, we who are men predictably have been much less conscious of these things, but we too have paid a price. Taking heterosexual male experience as normative has made such men invisible to themselves. (We seldom measure the ruler—in either sense of that word.)

Sexual theology, then, is an ongoing conversation moving back and forth in both directions between bodily/sexual experience and religious meanings. How we go about defining our sexuality can serve as an illustration. Experience tells us that it involves far more than our genital expressions. We experience our sexuality as including our feelings about our own embodiment and that of others, as our appropriation of our varied gender meanings and of our varied sexual orientations, as our participation in sexually determined social power or in its absence, as our capacity for sensuous communion with others and with the world. We experience our sexuality as the source of great joy and often great suffering. While these insights are largely experiential and not limited to any particular religious perspective, they are highly relevant theologically and ethically.

Yet we also bring specifically religious meanings to our sexual bodies. Thus, some of us perceive our sexuality as part of the radical goodness of God's creation. Incarnationally, we see our flesh as a major vehicle for revelation of the sacred. Our sexuality expresses the mystery of our creation as bodyselves who need communion with others, with the natural world, and with God. It is one of the great arenas for celebrating the source of life. Beverly W. Harrison captures its significance: "Our sexuality is the deepest, most intense dimension of our interaction with the world and because it is, it really is a key to the quality and integrity of our over-all spirituality . . . the deepest paradigm for our moral relations to the world."[7]

A critically important source for sexual ethics is the experience of the sexually marginalized, the sexually oppressed and dispossessed.[8] They know most keenly the evils of sexual oppression and see most clearly how our scriptures and traditions have often been used as instruments of injustice. William Sloane Coffin puts it well: "Just as someone coming in from outside is better able to tell those inside how stuffy a room has become, so women and minorities are better able to gauge the injustices of our society."[9]

Finally, in our sexual experience we participate with others in constructing sexual meanings. Speaking of the family, Gustafson aptly says, "The institution is grounded in nature, but it is not determined by nature."[10] Indeed. Not only the family but all of human sexuality, while grounded in nature, is subject to an enormous range of socially constructed meanings. The counterpart to the social constructionism position is essentialism, which emphasizes the given, intrinsic, and unchanging meanings inherent in human sexuality quite apart from culture and history.

In reaction to the oppressiveness of many essentialist claims (for example, about gender), some constructionists veer perilously close to denying any biological influence and seem to argue the infinite plasticity of sexual realities. Neither extreme serves us well. For example, while there is much we do not understand about sexual orientations, current scientific evidence indicates that there is *something* biologically "given" about them. The moral meanings of our particular orientations, however, are not fixed once and for all. They are dependent on processes of social discourse and construction in which we are active participants, and that is profoundly hopeful. If sexual meanings are significantly socially constructed, they can also be reconstructed to be less oppressive and more life-giving.[11]

Love

What is God enabling and requiring us as sexual persons to be and to do? God is enabling and requiring us to be sexually loving and just, claiming and exercising our sexual powers responsibly. One way, then, of approaching the central substantive issues in current Christian sexual ethics is through the norms of love, power, and justice—in their distinguishable features and in their final unity.[12]

Attempts to construct sexual ethics around the centrality of love have been fairly common, and with mixed results. Dangers in those efforts have included certain tendencies toward individualism, subjectivism, and romanticism. Successes in those efforts have depended in no small measure on the interpretation of love as inseparable from its components of power and justice. At this point, my intent is simply to ask what needed contributions a love focus can make to contemporary sexual ethics.

One contribution is a strong challenge to the norm of procreation in Christian sexual ethics, a norm that has functioned covertly as well as overtly. Love's challenge to procreationism is not new. It has been with us at least since the seventeenth century, when Reformed, Anglican, and Quaker folk elevated the unitive purpose of marital sex to centrality. Nor is the current struggle about procreationism limited to Roman Catholics; nor is artificial contraception the singular issue. The covert persistence of the procreative norm even among Protestants who long have affirmed the responsible use of contraception seems evident in several ways.[13]

Procreationism is present in the ethically privileged status commonly assumed for penile-vaginal coitus as the "real" sexual act. It is a status that makes every other sexual expression either foreplay or perversion. Lesbian and gay sex is judged abnormal. Countless persons with physical disabilities are desexualized. The sexuality of many of the elderly is trivialized. All sexual self-pleasuring is judged perverse.

Further, the persistence of procreationism makes difficult an adequate Christian ethics for nonmarital sexuality. For many single heterosexuals, contraception has effectively undercut this traditional reason for the ban on nonmarital sex; but a different, effective guiding norm has not taken its place. Hence, the churches have had little success giving persuasive guidance to the unmarried. An additional problem results when the procreationist emphasis encourages unprotected sexual activity because it seems to bless noncontraceptive sex as more "natural."

Finally, the world's urgent overpopulation problem has not been well served by the persistence of both overt and covert procreationism in Christian ethics. Admittedly, population control issues are ethically highly complex. They call for both environmental sustainability and distributive justice in resources. However, the urgency of the situation demands that a much clearer distinction between sex and reproduction be made and that the ethics of reproduction be rethought altogether.

Further, a reexamination of love in sexual ethics raises a whole cluster of issues around eros, including self-love, bodily integrity, and pleasure—issues to which many feminist ethicists have given important emphasis. Regarding eros, several questions deserve attention: What is it? Why has it been so difficult to incorporate into Christian sexual ethics, and what is the importance of doing so?

We mistakenly reduce eros to genital sexual urge. It is that dimension of our love born of desire. It is the yearning for fulfillment and deep connection. It is sensual and bodily in its energy, open to feeling and passion. It is a divine-human energy, a drive toward union with that to which we belong. Eros seeks the integration of body and spirit, of human and divine. As Augustine taught us, the problem is not to uproot or transcend desire (which is an essential mark of our humanity and of our belonging to God), but rather to order all objects of our desire in accord with their true relation to God, in whom alone our restless hearts will find satisfaction and fulfillment.[14]

While the theological debate over agape and eros is familiar, less explored is the sexual experience lying behind much in that debate. A major factor has been men's erotic anxiety. Eros still runs deeply counter to the basic notion of manhood that boys learn early in life. In separating from the erotic bonding with their mothers and in the absence of effective images of masculinity from fathers, boys learn largely negative foundations for masculinity: the rejection of all things feminine (and gay), including the erotic. Eros contradicts a manhood that prizes self-sufficiency and the rational control of all things bodily.

For men of church and synagogue there is another cause for anxiety. Eros questions the basic structure of the theologies that men have written and believed to be true. Men project onto God the separation they learned as essential to manhood, and God is imaged having exaggerated qualities of otherness and self-sufficiency. Moreover, men's phallic genitalization of sexual feeling and value accents those same phallic values in the holy. That which is most valuable (in sex, in culture, or in faith) is big, hard, and up. God is sovereign in power, righteous in judgment, wholly other in transcendence.

We have had a long masculine legacy of imaging God as unilateral, nonrelational power, glorified by the weakness and dependency of humanity, and deficient in mutuality. But it is threatening to relate to such a deity. Thus, male-dominated theology has compensated by attributing to the divine a one-sided and unilateral type of love: sheer agape, utter self-giving. Of course there is profound truth in the revelation of divine agape, but half-truth taken as the whole picture becomes distorted. So, our theologies cheapened, devalued, even vilified the erotic. We confused self-love with selfishness. Hunger, sensuous desire, passion, and yearning for fulfillment were banished as inappropriate to Christian spirituality.

Serious theological and ethical problems have flowed in the wake of the denigration of eros. The integration of sexuality and spirituality becomes forever problematic, for sexual energy participates deeply in the erotic. Self-love continues to be confused with egoistic narcissism, and self-effacing behavior is baptized (especially for the marginalized). In spite of an incarnationalist faith, the body remains theologically suspect, and hence so does passion. Important elements of power and justice are diminished, for the erotic is passionate and powerful, and justice inevitably is about bodily things.

Furthermore, those persons who appear to symbolize the body most fully—women, gay men and lesbians, persons of color—are especially stigmatized by the rejection of the erotic. A case in point: Many current denominational sexuality statements still suggest that eros is dangerous and must be controlled, and those same statements identify lesbians and gay men as symbols of sexuality out of control.[15]

Bodily integrity and self-determination are issues of positive self-love. Regrettably, these concerns have not been strong in straight male sexual ethics. They have been pressed "from below"—by those whose bodily freedom has been denied and whose bodies have been violated.[16] Our bodies *are* ourselves—the selves we are enabled and required to love; and the integrity of the bodyself is fundamental to moral freedom and responsibility. Sexual responsibility requires freedom from bodily manipulation or control, freedom from unwanted touch, and freedom to direct one's own body use. To be sure, individual body rights are always experienced within community and are always in tension with others' body rights. But those whose bodies have not been taken from them need to listen carefully to those whose bodies have.

The denial of the erotic also is linked closely to the confused state of sexual pleasure in Christian ethics.[17] The two dominant historic positions, the Augustinian and the Thomistic, are still most common. Augustine found sexual pleasure dangerous because it is virtually irresistible and it threatens grave sin. Aquinas argued, typically more moderately, that sexual pleasure is not evil. Neither, however, is it truly a human good, hence not a proper end for human activity. Rather, sexual pleasure is justified insofar as it is a means to higher human ends, particularly procreation.

Much of contemporary Christian ethics harbors a strong suspicion of sexual pleasure as a good in its own right, a premoral good. The doubts linger hand in hand with suspicion of eros and self-love. Fearing rampant hedonism and individualism (which our sexual culture has in abundance), ethicists are still inclined to bless pleasure only as a means to a "higher" end—primarily that of strengthening the relational bond. It is parallel to common arguments about self-love: Self-love is justified derivatively, as a means to neighbor love but not as a good in itself. However, I find Christine Gudorf's argument more persuasive: Sexual pleasure "is perhaps one of the best life arenas for demonstrating that self and other are not naturally hostile. Their relationship is much more complex . . . [and] the interests of the self and the interests of the partner are largely linked."[18]

In a variety of ways, then, the recovery of eros constitutes a major issue in Christian sexual ethics. Marvin Ellison's strong words are justified: "And Christian spirituality *without* erotic passion is lifeless and cold. It is also boring. More tellingly, the pervasive fear of sex and of strong passion, so rampant in our churches, is deeply implicated in the difficulty many religious people have in sustaining their passion for justice."[19]

If a reexamination of love in sexual ethics raises such critical issues as these, it must also be admitted that much Christian love-centered sexual discourse has been idealized, almost rhapsodic, and has failed to deal realistically with power, conflict, sexual injustice, and oppression.[20] Such is the inadequacy of any understanding of love deficient in power and justice. So, to these elements we turn.

Power

Sexuality is always about power. It is about the power or powerlessness of gendered bodyselves. It is about relationships of shared or coercive power. It is about the ways in which communities exercise powers of inclusion or exclusion on sexual grounds. By no accident, the early church increasingly turned to sexual matters in order to exercise power in enforcing doctrinal orthodoxy and clerical authority. The Council of Elvira in 309 C.E. is a memorable illustration. In recent decades, building on their own experience of exclusion, women and sexual minorities have pressed Christian sexual ethics toward power issues with new intensity.

Among many sexual power issues, two will serve as illustration here: sexual power as mutuality, and sexual power in communal inclusion.

To be effective moral agents we must be subjects more than objects of history. We must be subjects who can be reflective about ourselves, our actions, and our relationships, and who have some ability and willingness to accept responsibility for our actions. To be such a moral agent, however, requires power, including sexual power.

Persons can be disempowered racially, economically, politically, and in a host of other ways. When they are disempowered because of their sexuality, however, there is typically an added element of significance—the eroticization of the power pattern. Because the usual experience of our sexuality is so directly erotic, sexuality more than other arenas of life seems to invite the eroticization of patterns of dominance and submission. The rapist provides the extreme example. Abundant evidence demonstrates that genital pleasure is neither the primary motivation for rape nor do most rapists experience much genital pleasure in the act. Although the rapist's real turn-on is in control over the victim, he still experiences sexual pleasure. Though seldom genital pleasure, it is a pleasure he finds in demeaning, violating, and controlling another as a sexual object. The power he experiences in the act—however distorted and vicious that power may be—is to him a pleasurable, eroticized power which seems to fulfill his own self-understanding as a sexual person.

An important part of contemporary sexual culture in this society is the general eroticization of patterns of dominance and submission. It is a constant theme of mass entertainment and the constant source of our alarming rates of sexual harassment, abuse, and violence. It is always destructive to mutuality. Whenever sex is imagined as an unequal relationship between a superior partner and an inferior one, neither justice nor mutuality but rather coercive power is expressed.

The direction of contemporary ethicists in this matter is twofold. First, those who have been unjustly deprived of their sexual, erotic power must be allowed to claim it and celebrate it. Carter Heyward describes the experience: "Mutuality is the process of loving and is a way of speaking of love. It is the experience of being in right relation. Mutuality is sharing power in such a way that each participant in the relationship is called forth more fully into becoming who she is—a whole person, with integrity."[21]

Second, those who have feared mutuality and instead have clung to the sexual pleasure of dominating others must be both confronted and transformed. In our still-sexist society, this typically means heterosexual men. Recall my earlier observations about male gender formation. Our current patterns of child rearing maximize ways in which boys acquire a largely negative basis for their sense of masculinity. Unsure of what it *is*, they are sure of what masculinity is *not*. Since they have learned their early sense of gender through separation from women and all things feminine, they identify themselves over against women and also gay men (who, they are taught, represent the feminized male). Thus both sexism and homophobia become foundational, and this in turn links masculinity psychically to a deep suspicion of both mutuality with women and intimacy with men. Indeed, the anger of straight-identified men at gay men suggests a profound fear that masculinity is quite fragile and that rigid controls are necessary to establish and keep true male power and identity.

Thus, a strong profeminist, gay-affirming men's movement that will provide support and direction for the transformation of men's images of masculinity is of moral urgency for both church and society. Men are not by nature or essence more violent or less capable of affect and intimacy than women. Masculinities are socially constructed and, as such, can be reconstructed and transformed. The challenge to men is not to become less powerful, but more authentically so. The invitation to men is to reclaim an erotic power that has been feared as dangerous, to reclaim feelings that have been feared as feminine, and to let go of the need to control. The challenge in such a movement is also to become faithful and strong allies of women and gay men, to break the silence about male violence, and to join with other men in the hard but promising work of transforming male lives. It is all about the sexual power of mutuality.[22]

Another power issue in current Christian sexual ethics involves the church's power to include or exclude persons for reasons of their sexuality, and one of its obvious manifestations is heterosexist exclusion. Heterosexism is the socially sanctioned, institutionally enforced belief that male-female relationships are both superior and normative. Indeed, because of the power of this norm, traditional Christian sexual ethics often has been reduced to an ethics of marriage.

The reframing of theological-ethical arguments in scripture and the Christian tradition can effectively challenge the exclusion of lesbian and gay Christians. So much of the biblical discussion has been centered around a small handful of texts of questionable application to the central question. However, reframing the biblical discussion around the scripture's fundamental vision shifts the argument significantly.

For example, there is Isaiah's inclusive welcome to those considered sexually irregular, a radical word from Yahweh that overturned both the Levitical and Deuteronomic traditions: "To the eunuchs . . . I will give, in my house and within my walls, a monument and a name better than sons and daughters . . . an everlasting name that shall not be cut off" (Isa. 56:4–7).[23]

So also the Christian scriptures depict Jesus setting aside every barrier of prejudice or fear, every false tradition that violates the inclusiveness of God's community. While his vision of all-embracing compassion was deeply rooted in the Jewish tradition, it was not the dominant worldview of that day. Paramount was the holiness-purity vision, and its reigning interpretations emphasized classifications and boundaries, contrasts between pure and impure. And the impure and untouchable included those considered to be sexually irregular. Marcus Borg argues that central to Jesus' self-understanding was being a prophet of the politics of compassion in a social world dominated by the politics of holiness and purity. The parallels to the current debates about inclusiveness are striking.[24]

There are plenty of other textual sources—Philip's baptism of the Ethiopian eunuch, Peter's vision of "clean" food, Paul's arguments about circumcision. These examples and others are not peripheral to the scripture's central testimony. Shifting the grounds of the biblical debate away from a handful of texts about homosexual acts— texts of questionable application to our present situation—and moving that debate to the fundamental question of the community's inclusiveness is an empowering act.

Likewise, a careful look at the Christian tradition can reveal specific, often surprising challenges to the exclusionary assumptions often made in the current debates. Tradition will tell us that no single form of "family" has been considered normative throughout the centuries of the church. It will show us that heterosexual marriage and family have not always been expected or desired for all Christians. Tradition will teach us that biological procreation has not always been looked upon as central to God's design for human sexuality.

Furthermore, tradition will instruct us that openly gay and lesbian Christians have not always been judged adversely by the churches. It will reveal an uneven pattern of toleration—and even, in some times and places, affirmation—followed by periods of intolerance and persecution. But it will also show that the church's most vigorous persecution of gays and lesbians arose at the same time as the persecution of witches and heretics, and for similar reasons. In addition, tradition will reveal that same-sex unions were blessed and celebrated in parts of the Christian church a thousand years ago. Whether or not such unions were genitally sexual cannot be proven, but that they were unions of deep, emotionally felt love and commitment seems clear.[25]

In light of tradition's revelations, G. K. Chesterton's advice is warranted: We might yet take out membership in "the democracy of the dead," knowing that the best insights and experiences of our forebears have much to teach us.

Sexuality's power is highly symbolic. In its procreative meanings, sex long has symbolized the power of life over death. Now when the human community requires lower birth rates for sustainable life, we must find ways of moving the power of sexuality to symbolize the sustaining of life. One of the most sustaining of all powers is that of full inclusion in community. The current challenge of gay, lesbian, bisexual, and transgendered people to the churches for their full inclusion constitutes a major example of the recognition of sexual power. It is a call to move from dominant/submissive sexuality to mutuality.

The complementarity gender theory that underlies so many churchly documents on sexuality is also an instrument of the power of exclusion and oppression. Complementarity is the notion that there is a divinely ordained feminine nature and similarly an essential masculine nature. Complementarity can imply that a person of one gender is incomplete without a partner of the other, that heterosexuality is compulsory, and that any sexual expression outside of a male-female marriage is sinful, unnatural, or both. Complementarity makes the gay man a traitor, because he has broken ranks with men's cause by refusing to invest his own energy in controlling the sexuality of women. And the lesbian threatens a straight man's manhood by testifying that at least some women do not need men to complete them (and maybe no woman really does). Complementarity teachings of compulsory heterosexuality have contributed to the terrible AIDS epidemic that is killing many in the prime of their lives. Indeed, the church statements that exclusively speak of one man and one woman in one flesh, whatever their intent, have the effect of punishing all those who refuse to conform to compulsory heterosexuality. And, whatever their intent, these church statements do feed the fires of violence against lesbians and gay men.[26]

But, note well, dismantling the framework of compulsory heterosexuality will require us to do new and hard work on our Christian sexual ethics, for we are challenging a foundational assumption of most traditional approaches. Issues we once thought central must be set aside and issues we have not really addressed loom large. The issue of what causes sexual orientation loses relevance, but our moral culpability for forcing a sexual minority to live with the corrosive power of concealment looms large. The distinction between orientation and practice fades, but the question of what makes sexual relationships life-giving or life-denying looms large.[27]

The question of inclusion or exclusion is, of course, a justice question as well as a power question. It is also a question of love. Once more the ultimate inseparability of these central norms is evident.

Justice

For most of its history, Christian sexual ethics has focused more on form than on substance. Thus, marriage has been the primary justifying criterion for coitus, while such issues as respect, mutual power, consent, commitment, and tenderness have been neglected. Similarly, the typical disapproval of same-sex relations has focused on the gender of the partner rather than on the moral substance of the relationship. Now, though the results are still uneven, the movement in sexual ethics from an act-focus to a focus on the meaning and quality of relationships has been underway for several decades. It is a change inspired in no small measure by the recognition of the injustice done to persons by an ethical preoccupation with external form rather than with relational quality.

Newer on the justice agenda is the development of a Christian sexual ethics that is truly social. If one of the problems with some of the love-centered sexual ethics has been a privatization of sexuality, we clearly need a sexual ethic that demonstrates the inseparability of love and justice, of the personal and the social, of the relational and the structural.[28]

To be sure, the public dimensions of many sexuality issues are well recognized in ethical discourse and churchly social-action programs. Equal justice regardless of gender or orientation, family planning, population control, abortion, sexual abuse and violence, pornography, prostitution, reproductive technologies, varied family forms, sexually transmitted diseases, teenage pregnancy—the list could go on.

However, there are major social-justice issues that do not, in the first instance, appear to be sexual ones, yet are fueled by critical sexual dynamics. Social violence, racism, and environmental abuse are examples. True, we should be cautious about treating sex as if it were, in Foucault's term, "the master key" to all things. Sexual distortions are never a singular explanation for any complex social problem. Nevertheless, the sex factor does have significance in these problems far beyond that recognized in most Christian sexual ethics.[29]

Consider our pervasive social violence. Is there any doubt that its dynamics are heavily sexualized? That the vast majority of acts of violence—military, criminal, interpersonal—are done by males is, indeed, a sexual phenomenon. Our dominant cultural model of masculinity encourages competitiveness, the cult of winning, the armoring of emotions, an abstraction from bodily concreteness, the tendency to dichotomize reality into good versus evil, and high mortality anxiety coupled with a fascination with violent death. Regarding the military in particular, dissociation from bodily emotions and contempt for all things "feminine" are central to the socialization of the soldier, and the masculine virtues of invulnerability and controlling power are writ large in the military state. Surely, social violence has sexual dynamics that demand ethical attention.

What of racism? As James Weldon Johnson observed years ago, the sex factor is so deeply rooted in the race problem that it is often not recognized. Historically, white males' categorization of women ("either virgins or whores") proceeded along racial lines: White women were symbols of delicacy and purity, whereas African American women symbolized an animality that could be sexually and economically exploited. White men projected their guilt onto the black male, fantasizing him as a dark, sexual beast who must be punished and from whom white women must be protected. To defend their sons against white male vengeance, black mothers nurtured docility in them, a factor that later complicated black marriages and led to overcompensating attempts to recover black manhood.

White racism has taken an enormous toll on African American sexual self-esteem. As Cornel West observes, "Much of black self-hatred and self-contempt has to do with the refusal of many black Americans to love their own bodies—especially their black noses, hips, lips, and hair."[30] Further, the HIV-AIDS epidemic has been complicated by sexual racism. The black community has been reluctant to deal forthrightly with AIDS prevention in black gay and bisexual males because openly gay men and lesbians still symbolize the weak male and strong female produced by slavery and Jim Crow.[31] We are the heirs of a distorted racial history in which such sexual dynamics as these have been a major force.

The sexual factor is powerful, likewise, in our current and critical ecological situation. We are heirs of a hierarchical spirit-body dualism that has largely shaped our relation to nature. The hierarchy begins with God as nonmaterial spirit on top and continues downward to nonspiritual matter at the bottom. Below God are men, followed by women and children, animals, plants, and finally inorganic matter. That which is lower (more bodily) is of value only as it serves that which is above it. It is a clear chain of both value and command.

The earth alienation is explicitly gender-related as well. Men, who have learned that their bodies are machines, treat the earth accordingly. And the earth is feminized—Mother Nature, never Father Nature—the feminine over against which masculinity is defined. Dominion of the earth becomes domination, even rape.

With an environmental movement now, we are beginning to see more ecological sanity emerging from enlightened human self-interest. Yet, a deeply transformed ecological consciousness will not come through self-interest alone, however enlightened that may be. It must involve a new erotic sensibility, a hunger to realize our deep human connection to every other part of creation. The Hebrew word *yada*, "to know," also means "to make love sexually." When more of us know creation with an erotic knowing, we shall have better reasons to hope for the environmental future.

James Gustafson observes, "As intentional participants we have responsibility, and the destiny of the natural environment and our parts in it is heavily in our hands, but the ultimate destiny of all that exists is beyond our human control."[32] Indeed, and we will do greater justice to the environment when we can love it with passion, through our love for the One in whose hands our common destiny rests.

Conclusion

James Gustafson's theocentric ethics is a legacy of enormous importance. He has not developed its implications in detail for sexual ethics, and hence it is difficult to know how congenial he would find the perspectives and agenda sketched in these pages. Undoubtedly, he would warn us against the anthropocentric tendencies common to much in sexual ethics. Undoubtedly, he would test all sexual norms in the widest context of social and natural interdependence. Undoubtedly, he would warn us against the self-deception to which we are unfailingly subject—in our sexuality at least as much as elsewhere in our lives. Each warning would be well taken.

The perspectives in these pages emerge from a sexual theology with a more strongly incarnational center than Gustafson would claim, and the ethicists upon whom I have drawn identify more closely with feminist and gay/lesbian liberationist perspectives than he might. Nevertheless, I believe there is strong common ground in the convictions that all life is centered in God, that all life stands in need of transformation, and that power and justice are characteristic of God's love and must be of ours, too.

There is considerable irony in the fact that a religion named after the one perceived as incarnate love should have such a theological vacuum concerning our human sexual embodiment and desire. Perhaps that is a call for us to explore more fully the marriage of theocentric and incarnational ethics. Thomas Traherne, a seventeenth-century Anglican, saw the Godly vision of a transfigured world in incarnational terms: "By the very right of your senses, you enjoy the world. . . . [But] you never enjoy the world aright, till the sea itself floweth in your veins, till you are clothed with the heavens and crowned with the stars, and perceive yourself to be the sole heir of the whole world, and more than so, because others are in it who are everyone sole heirs as well as you."[33]

Notes

1. See Lisa Sowle Cahill, *Between the Sexes* (Philadelphia: Fortress and Paulist, 1985); Marvin Ellison, *Sexual Justice* (Louisville: Westminster John Knox, 1996); Christine Gudorf, *Body, Sex, and Pleasure* (Cleveland: Pilgrim Press, 1994); Beverly W. Harrison, *Making the Connections* (Boston: Beacon, 1985); Carter Heyward, *Touching Our Strength* (San Francisco: Harper & Row, 1989); James B. Nelson, *Embodiment* (Minneapolis: Augsburg, 1978), and *Body Theology* (Louisville, Ky.: Westminster John Knox, 1992); Carol S. Robb, *Equal Value* (Boston: Beacon, 1995); and Adrian Thatcher, *Liberating Sex* (London: SPCK, 1993).

2. James M. Gustafson, *Ethics from a Theocentric Perspective*, 2 vols. (Chicago: University of Chicago Press, 1981–1984), vol. 2, *Ethics and Theology*, 143f.

3. Ibid., 2:1.

4. Ibid., 2:144.

5. Ibid.

6. For a fuller discussion, see Nelson, *Body Theology*, and James B. Nelson, "Epilogue," in *Men's Bodies, Men's Gods*, ed. Bjorn Krondorfer (New York and London: New York University, 1995).

7. Harrison, *Making the Connections*, 149.

8. Gustafson argues, citing Hans Jonas, that "the perception of the *malum* (evil) is infinitely easier to us than the perception of the *bonum* (good)." And, there is "a revulsion of feeling which acts ahead of knowledge." *A Sense of the Divine* (Cleveland: Pilgrim Press, 1994), 24.

9. William Sloane Coffin, *A Passion for the Possible* (Louisville, Ky.: Westminster John Knox, 1993), 59.

10. Gustafson, *Ethics*, 2: 160.

11. This tension between social constructionism and essentialism seems to have connections with a holistic perception of the bodyself. Essentialism alone implies body without spirit (the body alone carries a fixed sexual reality), while extreme constructionism suggests spirit without body (sexual meanings are infinitely plastic regardless of bodily realities). I also find a parallel with Niebuhr's relational value theory in which he eschews both pure objectivism and pure subjectivism. See H. Richard Niebuhr, *Radical Monotheism and Western Culture* (New York: Harper & Bros., 1960), 102 ff.; also Nelson, *Body Theology*, 46 ff.

12. See Paul Tillich, *Love, Power, and Justice* (New York: Oxford, 1960), esp. chap. 1. One need not embrace all of Tillich's ontological analysis to profit from his insights about the differentiations and yet ultimate unity of these three.

13. See Gudorf, *Body, Sex, and Pleasure*, chap. 2, to which I am particularly indebted here.

14. See Tillich, *Love, Power, and Justice*, 30.

15. See Anne Bathurst Gilson, *Eros Breaking Free* (Cleveland: Pilgrim Press, 1995), 57.

16. See Robb, *Equal Value*, 116 ff.

17. Gudorf (*Body, Sex, and Pleasure*, esp. chap. 4) develops pleasure more thoroughly than any other contemporary Christian ethicist.

18. Ibid., 94.

19. Marvin M. Ellison, "Common Decency: A New Christian Sexual Ethics," in *Sexuality and the Sacred*, ed. James B. Nelson and Sandra P. Longfellow (Louisville, Ky.: Westminster John Knox, 1994), 241.

20. See Ellison, *Sexual Justice*, chap. 1.

21. Heyward, *Touching Our Strength, 191.*

22. See Marvin M. Ellison, "Refusing to Be 'Good Soldiers': An Agenda for Men," in *Sexuality and the Sacred*, ed. Nelson and Longfellow; also, see James B. Nelson, *The Intimate Connection* (Philadelphia: Westminster, 1988), 71 ff.

23. See Frederick J. Gaiser, "A New Word on Homosexuality? Isaiah 56:1–8 as Case Study," *Word & World* 14, no. 3 (summer 1994).

24. See Marcus J. Borg, *Meeting Jesus Again for the First Time* (San Francisco: HarperCollins, 1995), 49.

25. This paragraph relies on the research in John Boswell, *Christianity, Social Tolerance, and Homosexuality* (Chicago and London: University of Chicago Press, 1980), and John Boswell, *Same-Sex Unions in Premodern Europe* (New York: Villard Books, 1994). While some scholars have challenged Boswell's research, particularly on the nature of gay unions, I believe that he has convincingly demonstrated at least what I have described here and that this much constitutes a significant challenge to certain assumptions frequently made in current churchly discussions.

26. See Gilson, *Eros Breaking Free,* 104.

27. Here I am indebted to Patricia Beattie Jung, "Moving beyond Heterosexism: Making a Case for Sexual Authenticity," unpublished paper presented at Society of Christian Ethics, Savannah, Ga., January 1993.

28. The committee that prepared the most vigorously debated denominational sexuality report in recent history, the Presbyterian Church (U.S.A.), chose the wording "justice-love" to describe its key norm. In the ensuing debate over the report, many church members objected to the term as unbiblical.

29. I have expressed these concerns more fully elsewhere. See esp. James B. Nelson, *Humanly Speaking* (Cleveland: United Church Board for Homeland Ministries, 1995), and James B. Nelson "Male Sexuality and the Fragile Planet: A Theological Reflection," in *Redeeming Men: Religion and Masculine Identity*, ed. Stephen B. Boyd, W. Merle Longwood, and Mark W. Muesse (Louisville, Ky.: Westminster John Knox, 1996).

30. Cornel West, *Race Matters* (Boston: Beacon, 1993), 85.

31. See Harlan Dalton, "AIDS in Blackface," *Daedalus* (summer 1989): 217.

32. Gustafson, *A Sense of the Divine*, 149.

33. Quoted in A. M. Alchin, *The World Is a Wedding* (New York: Crossroad, 1982), 41.

Chapter 18

Recent Theological Discussions of Democracy

JOSEPH L. ALLEN

This essay analyzes recent discussions of democracy in theological ethics. Here as in many other ways theologians enter into interdisciplinary conversation between theology, on the one hand, and philosophy and the empirical sciences, on the other, an endeavor in which James Gustafson has frequently participated. Only occasionally has he written on political topics, theoretical or empirical.[1] When he has, however, he has shown that he believes it necessary for moral theologians to draw on the expertise of specialists in political studies, as they would in other similar interdisciplinary inquiries.[2]

My aim here is to trace the development and show some of the range of topics and viewpoints in recent Protestant and Catholic theological treatments of democracy, to offer some generalizations about this literature, and to point to issues needing further attention. I have limited the topic in three ways. First, it is democracy rather than political life and thought more broadly. Yet what theologians have said about democracy in recent years reveals much about their views on other political issues. Second, the topic is limited mainly to theologians whose understandings of democracy have been shaped primarily by the United States experience and who usually have U.S. democracy mainly in mind. Although much recent theological work has been devoted to democracy and its prospects in other countries,[3] reasons of time and space lead me not to consider that literature here. Third, I am considering only the period from around the beginning of World War II to the present. Significant theological rethinking of democracy occurred in the 1940s and soon thereafter, and, as we shall see, it strongly shaped subsequent consideration of the subject.

Because the theologians to be discussed sometimes differ over details of how they understand the term "democracy," I am using the term in a broad sense. One of Robert A. Dahl's definitions includes all the viewpoints discussed here and is still sufficiently restrictive for present purposes: "A democracy is a political system in which the opportunity to participate in decisions is widely shared among all adult citizens."[4] That general idea leaves open such questions as whether to understand democracy as involving citizens' participation directly or through representatives, whether as majority rule or protection of minorities or both, and whether as parliamentary or presidential or some mixture.

The subject is divided here into two time periods. In the first, from around 1940 to the late 1960s, attention is limited to a few major thinkers whose work has provided a framework for subsequent discussions. In the second period, the most recent quarter-century, I consider a wider array of theologians and issues. The conclusion sums up the discussion and identifies two issues about U.S. democracy that warrant further attention.

Midcentury Influences on the Direction of Recent Discussions

Events of the 1930s and 1940s, and Christians' responses to them, have heavily influenced the direction and content of later theological discussions of democracy. Modern totalitarianism, especially Naziism and Stalinist communism, became the occasion for Protestant and Catholic thinkers from the 1940s to the 1960s to voice new interpretations of democracy and a strong preference for it as a form of government.

The most influential Protestant commentator on democracy in that period was Reinhold Niebuhr. His view of democracy was a rejoinder, both to a liberal culture's undue confidence in human rationality and goodness, and to an equally undue political pessimism that saw anarchy as the paramount danger and maintaining order as the chief function of government. This two-front argument is reflected in his well-known aphorism stating that the human "capacity for justice makes democracy possible; but [the human] inclination to injustice makes democracy necessary."[5] The second half of the sentence reflects Niebuhr's belief that all are sinful—rulers and ruled alike—and that sin's primary expression is pride, the inclination to dominate others, with its resultant injustices. Democracy restricts but cannot eliminate pride's destructiveness. It restrains rulers by making them subject to the electorate; it restrains the ruled by requiring them to compete with one another, as through political parties, in their efforts to elect and influence the rulers.

For Niebuhr, the first half of the aphorism was equally important. Freedom, the capacity for some degree of transcendence over existing arrangements—ways of life, ideas, institutions—is from creation and thus is also universal. Because human possibilities are indeterminate, it is impossible to design an ideal state. Democracy as a form of governance allows for peaceful change to respond continually to the new in life—new needs, new dangers, new preferences and social patterns.

This double rationale for democracy underlies Niebuhr's argument for democratic toleration. Negatively, toleration is a way of restraining that intellectual, moral, and spiritual pride that "possesses the truth" and wills not to hear contrary opinions. Positively, in its recognition of our limits it affirms the possibility of learning from others, of being enriched by diversity.

While he preferred democracy, Niebuhr maintained a critical stance toward it. In an earlier time, Walter Rauschenbusch, though aware of democracy's failings, linked it more closely with Christian faith and life: "Democracy is not equivalent to Christianity," he wrote, "but in politics democracy is the expression and method of the Christian spirit"; "our political system has really entered on a decisive moral change"; "politics has been christianized."[6] For Niebuhr, political life was continuous moral ambiguity, not "decisive moral change." No human arrangement conforms to the demands of the dominion of God. All efforts at justice both approximate (at best) and contradict what love demands. For him that very truth was an argument for democracy: "It is the highest achievement of democratic societies that they embody the principle of resistance to government within the principle of government itself," so that "criticism of the ruler becomes an instrument of better government."[7] Yet democracy is bound up with serious failings, as when its advocates make undue claims for it, indeed worship it, even while they distort and misuse it.[8]

The enduring influence of Niebuhr's interpretation of democracy followed, not from any one of these ideas alone, but from the combination, and especially his understandings of sin and of indeterminate freedom. Many American Protestant ethicists writing on the subject in the next few years (and more recently as well) presupposed his perspective and often cited his aphorism—or if not the words, still its substance.[9]

Unlike most American Protestants, Roman Catholics' official teaching was strongly negative toward democracy in the nineteenth century, as reflected especially in encyclicals of Popes Gregory XVI and Pius IX and in the Syllabus of Errors in 1864.[10] They associated democracy with opposition to the church unleashed by the French Revolution, support for moral relativism, and an attack on any special relation between the church and the state. Although in the 1880s Leo XIII eased the opposition to democracy somewhat, Catholics in the United States worked within a largely negative papal stance well into the twentieth century. During and after World War II, however, Pope Pius XII clearly affirmed democracy. In his Christmas message of 1944, he sided with the people when they "oppose . . . the monopolistic reaches of a power that is dictatorial, uncontrollable, and intangible" and when they "demand a system of government that will be more in accord with the dignity and freedom of the citizenry."[11] In a 1953 address, he spoke of "circumstances in which human authority has neither mandate nor duty nor right to use its coercive power against error and evil." John Courtney Murray later interpreted that address as opening the way to a revision in official Catholic teaching on the relation of church and state.[12]

American Catholics also found support for a positive stance toward democracy in the work of the French Catholic philosopher Jacques Maritain, who lived and taught in Canada and the United States for a number of years.[13] His argument for personalist democracy, over against both totalitarianism and individualistic democracy, provided a valuable resource for Catholics and others in the United States, in addition to its impact in Western Europe and Latin America.

Among American Catholic theologians in the years following World War II, John Courtney Murray's series of learned and nuanced essays on the relation of church and state was a major influence, both in the United States and eventually in the deliberations of the Second Vatican Council.[14] Parallel to a distinction between civil society and the state, he distinguished between the common good, which includes all the social goods in accord with human nature, and the narrower concept of public order, which includes the public peace, commonly accepted moral standards, and justice. Whereas government has the limited role, he argued, of maintaining the public order in those three dimensions, it is the role of civil society to seek the complete common good. Catholic teaching should then support civil freedoms, including religious freedom. Government should not favor one religion over another; it is not qualified to pass judgment on what some take to be religious error.[15] "The Church demands, in principle and in all situations," Murray declared, "religious freedom for herself and religious freedom for all."[16]

In the judgment of J. Bryan Hehir, "The first authoritative indication that the Murray thesis could succeed was the 1963 encyclical of John XXIII, *Pacem in Terris*."[17] There Pope John took a major step beyond earlier papal statements about democracy. Discussing the relation of person, states, and the world community, he declared that Catholic teaching "is consonant with any genuinely democratic form of government," that people have a right to participate actively in government, and that each state should declare these and other fundamental human rights in a public constitution. Among the rights he listed was "that of being able to worship God in accordance with the right dictates of [one's] own conscience, and to profess [one's] religion both in private and in public."[18]

Two documents of the Second Vatican Council, *The Pastoral Constitution on the Church in the Modern World* (*Gaudium et Spes*) and *The Declaration on Religious Liberty* (*Dignitatis Humanae*),[19] further strengthened authoritative Catholic support for democracy. The former called on states to provide citizens the opportunity to participate in establishing and governing (par. 75). The latter supported Murray's thesis when it declared "that the human person has a right to religious freedom"—i.e., "to be immune from coercion" by any individual or group, so that "no one is to be forced to act in a manner contrary to his [or her] own beliefs," or "restrained from acting in accordance with [them]," except as necessary for public order (pars. 2, 7). These documents were the culmination of a twenty-five-year process of Catholic reassessment of democracy.

Interpretations of Democracy in the Past
Quarter-Century

Since the late 1960s, many Roman Catholic and Protestant theologians in the United States have worked within a theological framework heavily shaped by the thinking of such figures as Niebuhr and Murray. One can use that framework in different and even conflicting ways, of course. The discussion of the following quarter-century examines how theologians of this later generation have interpreted democracy in light of the United States experience. The exposition here takes up three topics: first, the idea of "limited government"; second, conflicting assessments of the U.S. brand of "liberal democracy"; and third, the responses of some nonmainstream theologians.

Democracy as Limited Government

Many recent theological interpreters of democracy characterize it, implicitly and explicitly, as limited government—with constitutional restraints, internal checks and balances, and recognition of citizens' rights, including the right to dissent by religious and other groups.[20] In so doing they carry forward Niebuhr's argument that "irresponsible and uncontrolled power is the greatest source of injustice," and that democratic governments are those that limit the power of rulers so as to balance freedom and order.[21]

This emphasis on limited government often carries with it a two-sided judgment toward democracy: approval of major aspects of its theory along with suspicion of (especially) its practice. An articulate example is Glenn Tinder's *The Political Meaning of Christianity*. Though by Christian principles no state is fully justifiable, he argues, still Christianity is not neutral toward forms of government. Because God's agape exalts every individual, "Christianity . . . implies democracy," which "is the only political form based on the idea of equality." Yet governmental leaders must pursue equality with prudence, leaving room for minorities and small groups, observing constitutional limits, and realizing that government cannot produce true community.[22]

Recent theologians have devoted special attention to three topics concerning democracy as limited government. We will examine each of these topics in the paragraphs that follow.

First, some have focused on the relation of independent associations to democratic governance. In midcentury and after, James Luther Adams devoted much thought to what he called "voluntary associations"—business, religious, union, educational, political, recreational, and other kinds of nongovernmental groups. These can promote discussion from various perspectives, encourage criticism and revision of accepted views and practices, help existing structures adapt to meet new needs, disperse power, and train people in the skills needed in a democracy. They are, he said, "a distinctive and indispensable institution of democratic society."[23] So identified was Adams with this subject that a volume of essays written in his honor had voluntary associations as its theme.[24]

In 1977 Peter Berger and Richard John Neuhaus invited further attention to the subject with their brief book, *To Empower People: The Role of Mediating Structures in Public Policy*. They argued that mediating structures—"those institutions [e.g., the neighborhood, family, and church] standing between the individual in his [or her] private life and the large institutions of public life"—"are essential for a vital democratic state," because they can balance the demands of the public and private spheres and help to legitimate the political order.[25] Their work evoked further theological attention, as in a collection including essays by Michael Novak, James Luther Adams, and J. Philip Wogaman. Novak defined "mediating structures" broadly to include "all private, nongovernmental structures, including corporations, unions, and universities."[26]

The most systematic treatment of the topic and its relation to democracy is Franklin I. Gamwell's *Beyond Preference: Liberal Theories of Independent Associations*. He examines the significance of political theory for independent associations (not including commercial associations), and vice versa. On the basis of a metaphysical grounding of the comprehensive moral principle, "so act as to maximize unity-in-diversity," he argues that "governmental activity is, in principle, teleologically subservient to voluntary associations which maximize the public world" and that democratic government provides for discussion and debate that cultivates people's individuality.[27] That these various works do not agree on the name or scope of their category does not diminish their contribution to the study of this dimension of democratic political life.

Second, in recent years theological concern with the relation of church and state has turned to what role religious groups should play in the discussion of public issues in a democracy. The range of viewpoints is immense. On the one hand, Stanley Hauerwas argues that the primary effort of Christians should be to become "a truthful society," rather than to seek to influence policy decisions. He argues that the church *is* a social ethic, rather than *has* one.[28] In contrast, Dana Wilbanks voices the opinions of many when he asserts that the churches should seek not only to be signs of transformation, but also agents of transformation in the public order.[29]

Within the public arena, however, there is disagreement over whether religious groups should play any role at all. Richard John Neuhaus poses the issue as that of "the naked public square," a "political doctrine and practice that would exclude religion and religiously grounded values from the conduct of public business." The central issue, he asserts, is not political or legal, but theological—the capacity of religious groups "to make theological truth-claims in public that challenge prevailing cultural assumptions." Neuhaus argues that the doctrine is false, that no such practice is possible, and that religious groups must enter actively into the public dialogue. They must do so, however, on the basis, not of "private truths," but truths publicly examinable; and they must refuse to restrict the discussion to those sharing a particular religious covenant.[30] Critics of Neuhaus, however, point to a different kind of doctrinal exclusivity in his "litmus test" for participation in the public dialogue—agreement that "On balance and considering the alternatives, the influence of the United States is a force for good in the world."[31]

In his book, *Love and Power*, the Catholic legal philosopher Michael J. Perry has analyzed the place of religious-moral discourse in political discourse. Like Neuhaus, he denies the possibility of neutral or nonreligious political discussion. He identifies prerequisites and principles of what he calls "ecumenical political dialogue" and in the process explores the ideas of tolerance and rationality, what it means to participate in a political community and its dialogue, and the "existential prerequisites" for that dialogue.[32] Critics find in his argument a different litmus test from Neuhaus's—exclusion of those lacking the right kind of tolerance, such as some conservative religious groups—though he denies that this is his intent or implication.[33]

Third, a disputed question is what legislation Christians should seek in the democratic dialogue, especially when their moral convictions conflict with those of others. As we have seen, *Dignitatis Humanae* stated that all people have a right not to be coerced to act (or refrain from acting) contrary to their own beliefs, except as necessary for public order. There continues to be dispute among Catholics, however, about this issue, about how to interpret that statement, and about how to apply it to abortion. Logically there are three positions. One can accept the position of *Dignitatis Humanae* and argue, as Charles Curran does, that because personal morality and civil law are different, "one can truly be convinced abortion is morally wrong but still support legislation that allows for abortion." Given the existing pluralism in society, he holds, civil law must give the benefit of the doubt to the civil freedom of the individual.[34] Or one can accept the position of *Dignitatis Humanae* and argue that the right to life of the fetus is a matter of public order which civil law must protect at the cost of individual freedom. Or finally, one can continue to assert the pre–Vatican II position—as some thinkers do, not without support from the Vatican—and argue that the fundamental natural law, which is understood to prohibit intentional abortion, transcends social pluralism.[35] The disagreements among these three positions are most immediately over (a) how important individual freedom is vis-à-vis the state and (b) whether or to what extent decisions about abortion are matters of public order.

"Liberal Democracy" in the United States

Much theological discussion has revolved around how to interpret and assess the mixture of political democracy and economic policy to be found in the United States, sometimes referred to as "liberal democracy" or "democratic capitalism." On the one hand are theologians who offer a justification for what they call "democratic capitalism." The most widely known work of this kind may be Michael Novak's *The Spirit of Democratic Capitalism*,[36] though critics have found in it more a celebration of its subject than a careful or critical examination.[37] Robert Benne's *The Ethic of Democratic*

Capitalism is more an inquiry.[38] Relying for purposes of evaluation on Reinhold Niebuhr and John Rawls, Benne finds both virtues and vices in democratic capitalism. The United States combination of democracy and a market economy, he argues, encourages economic efficiency and growth, decentralizes power so as to restrain destructive effects of pride, and has a role for government in seeking justice for the weak. Yet problems accompany those virtues: damage to the environment, depletion of energy resources, exploitation of weaker countries, and serious injustice to the poor. Even so, democratic capitalism has many resources for responding to those problems. On balance he finds in it "a morally defensible arrangement."

In sharp contrast are theologians who find affinity between democracy and some form of socialism rather than capitalism. Many of them write from the experience of some other political context, e.g., Latin American or European.[39] Among those with the United States mainly in mind, Douglas Sturm provides a critique of democratic capitalism and a justification for "social democracy."[40] There is, he says, a built-in tension between democracy and capitalism, the one a process of public governance, the other a system of private control over economic questions that affect the quality of life of the entire community. Social democracy would subordinate questions of economic growth and distribution to the good of the community.

Still other theologians see the issue, not as a choice between economic systems, but as how to reform liberal democracy while continuing to rely on a market economy. Franklin Gamwell argues that, given the goal of "optimal public freedom," it is desirable for the economic order to be subservient to the good of the public order. The state can and should supervise a decentralized economic order so as to prevent serious harms to the environment, social diversity and belongingness, cultural activities, and the democratic process itself.[41] Jon Gunnemann sees "the single most distinctive feature of liberal democracy" as its "commitment to a plurality of human ends and consequently to political toleration and liberty." Yet our market society may be displacing social relations and creating a crisis in personal identity. The alternative is not to reject a market economy, but to make the common good central to democratic governance.[42] And Richard John Neuhaus, responding to the collapse of communism in Eastern Europe, points to Pope John Paul II's distinction between two possible meanings of "capitalism": either an economic system that simply gives the market and private property a central role, or one that is not willing to serve "human freedom in its totality." Capitalism can and should be affirmed in the first sense, not the second.[43]

The same issue arises in theological discussions of human rights. Many recent Catholic and Protestant theologians hold that the array of human rights includes both civil-political and social-economic rights. David Hollenbach, John Langan, and Max Stackhouse, among others, have argued for this view.[44] Supportive of this outlook is the argument advanced by Hollenbach, Stackhouse, and Arthur Dyck,[45] that the concept of rights must be grounded in ideas of responsibility and community and of the moral bonds that underlie them. In contrast, Michael Novak maintains that so-called social-economic rights are not properly rights at all—that while food, clothing, shelter, and the like are needs for which everyone has a claim upon others for support, government is not obligated to provide them to the needy.[46] Differing with both positions, Dennis McCann holds that anyone can claim both types as a matter of right, but that the state must avoid paternalism. Instead of formulating a substantive content of the common good, he argues that it is procedural—"the good to be pursued in common" through a process of continual inquiry and discourse.[47]

Nonmainstream Appraisals of Democracy

One would expect mainstream Protestants and Catholics today to prefer democracy to other forms of government, whatever their reservations about its theory or problems with its practice. But what about nonmainstream theologians, and especially those shaped by the Anabaptist tradition, with its refusal to join in the state's coercive or violent maintenance of order? There is more variation in their response to democracy than one might expect.

With certain qualifications, John Howard Yoder expresses a definite preference for democracy. We should not misinterpret it, he cautions: Democracy is not rule by the people, but a kind of oligarchy. It is not "a fundamentally new kind of social order," for here, too, some use power oppressively over others, and much of democratic governance is coercive and violent.[48] But "of all the forms of oligarchy, democracy is the least oppressive."[49] Its own structures and language of justification provide means for its subjects to mitigate its oppressiveness. And because a welfare state—democratic or not—is not all coercion, it can "provide usable structures of mutual service."[50] In many societies, then, "democracy is preferable to any other form of government."[51] What Yoder prefers is not majority rule, with its dangers of demagoguery and conformity, but protection of the right to dissent, with room for minorities to speak and be heard and for faith communities and other groups to pursue their own purposes. Dissent itself is witness to the oppressiveness of even a democratic state and the need to call it repeatedly to account.[52]

In contrast, Stanley Hauerwas interprets democracy in almost purely negative terms. Democracies "after all can be just as tyrannical in their claims on the loyalties of their citizens as totalitarian alternatives." There is, certainly, a linkage between Christian faith and human freedom, but freedom is different from what exists in a democracy. The "only true polity we can know in this life" is the church.[53] Hauerwas claims that there has been "a long history of Protestant Christians who have assumed that Christianity means democracy."[54] He points to Rauschenbusch, Jerry Falwell, and Reinhold Niebuhr, the latter two of whom, he says, "assume wrongly that the American church's primary social task is to underwrite American democracy."[55] This judgment is unmoved by Niebuhr's views of the universality of sin, the inadequacies of all "structures of justice," and the idea that Niebuhr and Yoder alike express—that democracies make provision for resistance to government. Some of Hauerwas's antagonism is to liberal democracy, its individualism, and its inability to account for a common good; but he does not point to any preferable kind of democracy, nor does he mention recent mainline theologians' criticisms of democracy. This may be because he rejects what he believes they presume, "that the church has a . . . theological stake . . . in making American democracy a success."[56]

Concluding Observations

From the above we can identify several salient features of the past half-century of discussion of democracy. First, the rise of totalitarian regimes in Europe, culminating in World War II, moved both Protestants and Catholics to rethink their stances toward democracy. Reinhold Niebuhr's reflections shaped the framework within which most Protestant—and some Catholic—thinking about democracy of the subsequent half-century has proceeded. Catholics from Maritain and Pope Pius XII to Murray, Pope John XXIII, and the Second Vatican Council brought the church from earlier antagonism and suspicion to a strongly positive stance toward democracy. These changes have been more formative than any subsequent theological reflections on democracy.

Second, following on that midcentury experience, recent Roman Catholic and Protestant theologians with near-unanimity prefer democracy to other forms of government, at least in the U.S. context. Even so, they refuse to identify democracy with an ideal community and find many faults in its practice.

Third, many theologians characterize democracy as limited government, approving of one or another kind of limit while often also saying that government should promote the common or public good.

Fourth, significant disagreement continues over how to assess the kind of democracy they perceive in the contemporary United States, with some approving what they call democratic capitalism, some preferring some kind or degree of democratic socialism, and some looking for ways to reform liberal democracy so that the economic system can more fully serve the common good.

The latter two features point to an unresolved—and perhaps insufficiently recognized—tension within recent theological reflection on democracy. That tension is between two dimensions of the common good. The emphasis on limited government points to one of these dimensions: the goods of the individual members and groups that are protected by government's limits. This emphasis tends, however, to neglect the other dimension: a good overall pattern of relationships among the many members and groups. Given that there is no natural harmony of interests, that goal requires positive government action.

There are always conflicts within the common good. Limiting government's capacity to act allows some members greater freedom of choice while restricting that of others. Similarly, limiting a government's capacity to act can hinder efforts to encourage just and peaceful relationships among the members. At midcentury, David Riesman observed that there has evolved in the United States an array of groups, which he called "veto groups," with the power to stop things from happening that might be inimical to their interests.[57] That is all the more true today.[58] In the U.S. government (more than in parliamentary democracies, where it is easier to mobilize a majority), veto power is much more prominent than what someone has called initiating power—the capacity to put forward initiatives which are subsequently adopted as policy. Since World War II, "gridlock" has been more the rule than the exception. When most groups are defending their (short-term) supposed interests and there is little incentive for leaders to seek a good over-all program, it is difficult to develop a national policy, whether for medical care, welfare, taxes, or whatever.

In an earlier day, some political theorists argued that United States democracy would benefit from a greater capacity to mobilize a majority and take positive action, and not only from further limits on government's capacity to act. The issue they posed, though, has received little attention from political theorists in recent years.[59] Theologians have given it similarly little attention.[60] Yet the present arrangement threatens that dimension of the common good that is the pattern of just and enhancing relationships among the members. It is important not only to commend the common good, but to reexamine the two dimensions in our context. Perhaps theologians can help to identify ways for government to take positive action on behalf of the commonweal without exceeding its appropriate limits. The growing concern in theology and political theory for the community would be well served by greater examination of this question.

Theologians have given more attention to a related but distinguishable issue: the problem of neglected minorities. In a democracy, those who are in an economically or socially favored condition sometimes constitute a substantial majority of the populace and thus also of its legislative bodies. If many among that majority are indifferent to the plight of the poor, for example, there is little that the poor—inadequately represented as they are—can do through established democratic procedures to change government policies that reinforce their disadvantages. This is, I believe, precisely the situation in the United States today.

If so, and given the continuing need to emphasize the limits on democratic government, the theological-ethical issue might be posed this way: In U.S. democracy, how can the political power of the advantaged be limited on behalf of greater justice for the disadvantaged? Although theological ethicists are constantly pursuing issues of justice for the disadvantaged, they need to give further attention to how the workings of democracy aggravate the problem or might alleviate it. It is a perennial problem for democracies, and an especially pressing one in the United States today.

Here then are two of the problems of United States democracy that call for special attention. They are closely related and might be pursued together. In a time of increased strain and conflict within the national political community, there is much reason for theologians to continue to give attention to the subject of democracy.

Notes

1. Uses of political studies in Gustafson's theological work occur in James M. Gustafson, "The Church: A Political Community," in *Treasure in Earthen Vessels: The Church as a Human Community* (New York: Harper & Bros., 1961), 28–42; James M. Gustafson, "Authority in a Pluralistic Society," in *The Church as Moral Decision-Maker* (Philadelphia: Pilgrim Press, 1970), 47–61; and James M. Gustafson, "The Relationship of Empirical Science to Moral Thought," in *Theology and Christian Ethics* (Philadelphia: United Church Press, 1974), 215–28.

2. Cf. "The Relationship of Empirical Science to Moral Thought," 215.

3. To mention only one work, John Witte Jr., ed., *Christianity and Democracy in Global Context* (Boulder, Colo.: Westview Press, 1993), includes a valuable array of essays on Christianity and democracy in various parts of the world.

4. Robert A. Dahl, *Modern Political Analysis*, 3d ed. (Englewood Cliffs, N.J.: Prentice-Hall, 1976), 6.

5. Reinhold Niebuhr, *The Children of Light and the Children of Darkness* (New York: Scribner's, 1944), xi.

6. Walter Rauschenbusch, *Christianizing the Social Order* (Boston: Pilgrim Press, 1912), 150–53.

7. Reinhold Niebuhr, *The Nature and Destiny of Man* (New York: Scribner's, 1943), 2:268.

8. Cf. Reinhold Niebuhr, "Democracy as a Religion," *Christianity and Crisis* 7 (4 August 1947), 1–2, as quoted in *Reinhold Niebuhr on Politics,* ed. Harry R. Davis and Robert C. Good (New York: Scribner's, 1960), 191–92.

9. From the 1950s, cf. Paul Ramsey, *Basic Christian Ethics* (New York: Scribner's, 1950), 330–37; George F. Thomas, *Christian Ethics and Moral Philosophy* (New York: Scribner's, 1955), 291, 299; John C. Bennett, *Christians and the State* (New York: Scribner's, 1958), 151–56; and Walter G. Muelder, *Foundations of the Responsible Society* (Nashville: Abingdon, 1959), 115–19.

10. For works on the history of Roman Catholic views toward democracy see J. Bryan Hehir, "Catholicism and Democracy: Conflict, Change, and Collaboration," in *Christianity and Democracy*, 15–30; John Courtney Murray, "The Problem of Religious Freedom," in *Religious Liberty: Catholic Struggles with Pluralism*, ed. J. Leon Hooper, S.J. (Louisville, Ky.: Westminster John Knox Press, 1993), 128–97 (originally published in *Theological Studies* 25 [1964]: 503–75; Paul E. Sigmund, "The Catholic Tradition and Modern Democracy," *Review of Politics* 49, no. 4 (fall 1987): 530–48; and Paul E. Sigmund, "Catholicism and Liberal Democracy," in *Catholicism and Liberalism: Contributions to American Public Philosophy*, ed. R. Bruce Douglass and David Hollenbach (Cambridge: Cambridge University Press, 1994), 217–41.

11. Quoted in Murray, "The Problem of Religious Freedom," 165.

12. Quoted in Murray, "Leo XIII and Pius XII: Government and the Order of Religion," in *Religious Liberty*, 107.

13. Works of Maritain bearing on democracy include *Integral Humanism*, trans. Joseph W. Evans (Notre Dame, Ind.: University of Notre Dame Press, 1973; orig. French ed., 1936; first Engl. trans., 1938); *The Rights of Man and Natural Law* (New York: Scribner's, 1943); *Christianity and Democracy* (New York: Scribner's, 1944); and *Man and the State* (Chicago: University of Chicago Press, 1951).

14. Among Murray's numerous articles on the subject see especially those included in *We Hold These Truths* (New York: Sheed & Ward, 1960) and in *Religious Liberty*. Of others' commentary on Murray's work, I am especially indebted to Hehir's "Catholicism and Democracy," and J. Leon Hooper's "General Introduction" to *Religious Liberty*, 11–48.

15. Cf. Hooper, "General Introduction," 24; the approving interpretation of Pius XII's statement in Murray's "Leo XIII and Pius XII," and "The Problem of Religious Freedom," both in *Religious Liberty*, 106 and 145, respectively.

16. Murray, "The Problem of Religious Freedom," 147.

17. Hehir, "Catholicism and Democracy," 20.

18. Quotations from and references to *Pacem in Terris* are from the translation published in *The Pope Speaks* 9 (1963), no. 1, pars. 52, 73, 75, and 14.

19. Quotations are from *The Documents of Vatican II*, ed. Walter M. Abbott, S.J. (New York: America Press, 1966).

20. Such themes are voiced by writers with widely different theological outlooks, as, e.g., Stephen Charles Mott, in *A Christian Perspective on Political Thought* (New York: Oxford University Press, 1993), 160; James W. Skillen, "Toward a Contemporary Christian Democratic Politics in the United States," in *Christianity and Democracy*, 85–99 ; J. Philip Wogaman, in *Christian Perspectives on Politics* (Philadelphia: Fortress Press, 1988), 153–54; and John Howard Yoder, "The Christian Case for Democracy," in *The Priestly Kingdom* (Notre Dame, Ind.: University of Notre Dame Press, 1984), 168.

21. Niebuhr, *Children of Light*, xi–xii, 1–3; cf. Niebuhr, *Nature and Destiny*, 2:268.

22. Glenn Tinder, *The Political Meaning of Christianity* (San Francisco: Harper, 1991), 141, 178, 189–92. Tinder is by specialization a political theorist; in this work he is clearly also dealing with his topic theologically.

23. James Luther Adams, "The Indispensable Discipline of Social Responsibility: Voluntary Associations," in *The Prophethood of All Believers*, ed. George K. Beach (Boston: Beacon Press, 1986), 257–58.

24. D. B. Robertson, ed., *Voluntary Associations: A Study of Groups in Free Societies* (Richmond, Va.: John Knox Press, 1966).

25. Peter L. Berger and Richard John Neuhaus, *To Empower People: The Role of Mediating Structures in Public Policy* (Washington, D.C.: American Enterprise Institute for Public Policy Research, 1977), 2–6. Cf. also Richard John Neuhaus, "Christianity and Democracy: A Statement of the Institute on Religion and Democracy," *Center Journal* 1, no. 3 (summer 1982): 13–15.

26. Michael Novak, "Editor's Preface," in *Democracy and Mediating Structures: A Theological Inquiry*, ed. Michael Novak (Washington, D.C.: American Enterprise Institute, 1980).

27. Franklin I. Gamwell, *Beyond Preference: Liberal Theories of Independent Associations* (Chicago: University of Chicago Press, 1984), 2, 5, 136, 144, 145. See also Franklin I. Gamwell, *The Divine Good: Modern Moral Theory and the Necessity of God* (San Francisco: HarperCollins, 1990), esp. chap. 7.

28. Stanley Hauerwas, *A Community of Character* (Notre Dame, Ind.: University of Notre Dame Press, 1981), 3, 11; and other of his works.

29. Dana Wilbanks, "The Church as Sign and Agent of Transformation," in *The Church's Public Role: Retrospect and Prospect*, ed. Dieter T. Hessel (Grand Rapids, Mich.: Eerdmans, 1993), 27–38. Among many who share that view are Hessel, Peter Paris, and Max Stackhouse, in their

articles in the same volume, and James Skillen, in "Toward a Contemporary Christian Democratic Politics in the United States," in *Christianity and Democracy,* 85–99, however much they may differ over the details of efforts at transformation.

30. Richard John Neuhaus, *The Naked Public Square: Religion and Democracy in America* (Grand Rapids, Mich.: Eerdmans, 1984), ix, xii, 36, 52.

31. Ibid., 72; cf. Arthur J. Moore, "Dressing Up the Public Square," *Christianity and Crisis* 44 (29 December 1984): 406–7; and Dean K. Thompson, in a review, *Theology Today* 42 (July 1985): 225–27, 230.

32. Michael J. Perry, *Love and Power: The Role of Religion and Morality in American Politics* (New York: Oxford University Press, 1991).

33. Cf. John Francis Burke, *Cross Currents* 43 (fall 1993): 425–26; and Robert F. Drinan, S.J., *Journal of Church and State* 35 (summer 1993): 613–14; Perry replies to similar arguments in *Love and Power,* 139–45. For other discussions of the role of religion in public discourse see John A. Coleman, *An American Strategic Theology* (New York: Paulist Press, 1982), 209–34; and Gerrit G. de Kruijf, "The Christian in the Crowded Public Square: The Hidden Tension between Prophecy and Democracy," *Annual of the Society of Christian Ethics,* 1991, 21–42.

34. Charles E. Curran, "Civil Law and Christian Morality: Abortion and the Churches," in *Ongoing Revision in Moral Theology* (Notre Dame, Ind.: Fides Publishers, 1975), 136–37.

35. Cf. Brendan F. Brown, "Individual Liberty and the Common Good—The Balance: Prayer, Capital Punishment, Abortion," *Catholic Lawyer* 20 (1974): 215, 218, 219; and "Declaration on Procured Abortion," Sacred Congregation for the Doctrine of the Faith (Vatican City: Vatican Polyglot Press, 1974), as cited in Curran, "Civil Law and Christian Morality," 136–37.

36. Michael Novak, *The Spirit of Democratic Capitalism* (New York: Simon & Schuster, 1982).

37. See, e.g., Tom Blackburn, "Novak's Capitalism with a Human Face," *Christianity and Crisis* 42, no. 9 (24 May 1982): 143–48; Daniel A. Dombrowski, "Benne and Novak on Capitalism," *Theology Today* 42 (April 1984): 61–65; Andrew Greeley, *Journal of Religion* 65 (October 1985): 557–58.

38. Robert Benne, *The Ethic of Democratic Capitalism: A Moral Reassessment* (Philadelphia: Fortress Press, 1981).

39. For a study of several recent Latin American and European Christian socialist theologians—Tillich, Moltmann, Gutiérrez, and Miguez Bonino—see Gary J. Dorrien, *Reconstructing the Common Good: Theology and the Social Order* (Maryknoll, N.Y.: Orbis, 1990); also see Gary J. Dorrien, *Soul in Society: The Making and Renewal of Social Christianity* (Minneapolis: Fortress Press, 1995).

40. Douglas Sturm, *Community and Alienation: Essays on Process Thought and Public Life* (Notre Dame, Ind.: University of Notre Dame Press, 1988), 164–86. Among other recent visions of this connection, see Rosemary Radford Ruether, *Sexism and God-Talk* (Boston: Beacon Press, 1983), 232–34; and Cornel West, *Prophesy Deliverance! An Afro-American Revolutionary Christianity* (Philadelphia: Westminster Press, 1982), 18–19, 131–47.

41. Franklin I. Gamwell, "Democracy, Capitalism, and Economic Growth," in *Economic Life: Process Interpretations and Critical Responses,* ed. W. Widick Schroeder and Franklin I. Gamwell (Chicago: Center for the Scientific Study of Religion, 1988), 223–50.

42. Jon P. Gunnemann, "The Promise of Democracy: Theological Reflections on Universality and Liminality," in *Christianity and Democracy,* 131–50. Cf. James Childress's critique of "re-

alist-pluralist" interpretations of democracy, that they tend to support the pursuit of private interests rather than the common good, in James Childress, *Civil Disobedience and Political Obligation* (New Haven: Yale University Press, 1971), 152.

43. Richard John Neuhaus, *Doing Well and Doing Good: The Challenge to the Christian Capitalist* (New York: Doubleday, 1992), 55–59; the pertinent passage is par. 42 of Pope John Paul II's *Centesimus Annus* (1991).

44. See David Hollenbach, S.J., *Claims in Conflict: Retrieving and Renewing the Catholic Human Rights Tradition* (New York: Paulist Press, 1979); John Langan, S.J., "Defining Human Rights: A Revision of the Liberal Tradition," in *Human Rights in the Americas: The Struggle for Consensus*, ed. Alfred Hennelly, S.J., and John Langan, S.J. (Washington, D.C.: Georgetown University Press, 1982), 69–101; Max L. Stackhouse, *Creeds, Society, and Human Rights: A Study in Three Cultures* (Grand Rapids, Mich.: Eerdmans, 1984); and the National Conference of Catholic Bishops, *Economic Justice for All: Pastoral Letter on Catholic Social Teaching and the U.S. Economy* (Washington, D.C.: United States Catholic Conference, 1986), pars. 79–84.

45. Arthur J. Dyck, *Rights and Responsibilities: The Moral Bonds of Community* (Cleveland: Pilgrim Press, 1994).

46. Cf. Michael Novak, "The Future of 'Economic Rights," in *Private Virtue and Public Policy: Catholic Thought and National Life*, ed. James Finn (New Brunswick, N.J.: Transaction Publishers, 1990), 69–81.

47. Dennis P. McCann, "The Good to Be Pursued in Common," in *The Common Good and United States Capitalism*, ed. Oliver F. Williams and John W. Houck (Lanham, Md.: University Press of America, 1987), 158–78.

48. John Howard Yoder, *The Christian Witness to the State* (Newton, Kans.: Faith and Life Press, 1964), 26.

49. Yoder, "Christian Case for Democracy," 158–59.

50. Ibid., 165.

51. Yoder, *Christian Witness to the State*, 26.

52. For another Anabaptist preference for democracy, see Ronald J. Sider, "An Evangelical Vision for American Democracy: An Anabaptist Perspective," in *The Bible, Politics, and Democracy*, ed. Richard Neuhaus (Grand Rapids, Mich.: Eerdmans, 1987), 40–43.

53. Stanley Hauerwas, *Against the Nations: War and Survival in a Liberal Society* (San Francisco: Harper & Row, 1985), 126, 130.

54. Hauerwas, "The Democratic Policing of Christianity," *Pro Ecclesia* 3, no. 2 (spring 1994): 216.

55. Stanley Hauerwas and William H. Willimon, *Resident Aliens: Life in the Christian Colony* (Nashville: Abingdon, 1989), 32.

56. Hauerwas, *Against the Nations*, 122.

57. David Riesman, *The Lonely Crowd* (New Haven: Yale University Press, 1950), 244–48.

58. Paul Kennedy (*Preparing for the Twenty-first Century* [New York: Random House, 1993], 310) has recently observed that "the American political structure in particular offers the most marvelous opportunities to *obstruct* changes."

59. Cf. Robert A. Dahl and Charles E. Lindblom, *Politics, Economics, and Welfare* (New York: Harper & Brothers, 1953), 335–48; Austin Ranney, *The Doctrine of Responsible Party Government: Its Origin and Present State* (Urbana: University of Illinois Press, 1962). Elaine Spitz (*Majority Rule*

[Chatham, N.J.: Chatham House, 1984]), surveys the literature and a variety of issues having to do with majority rule, but mostly in other senses of the term than that which I have identified here.

60. Cf. David Alan Bard, "Political Majorities, Political Minorities, and the Common Good: An Analysis of Understandings of Democracy in Recent Christian Political Ethics" (Ph.D. diss., Southern Methodist University, 1994), 347–413.

Chapter 19

Thinking Theologically
about the Economic

JON P. GUNNEMANN

Introduction

[What is] the significance of Christianity for the solution of the social problem of
the present day? This social problem is vast and complicated. It includes the problem
of the capitalist economic period and of the industrial proletariat created by it; and
of the growth of militaristic and bureaucratic giant states; of the enormous increase
in population, which affects colonial and world policy, of the mechanical technique,
which produces enormous masses of material and links up and mobilizes the whole
world for purposes of trade, but which also treats men and labour like machines.[1]

This is Ernst Troeltsch in 1911. Several turns of phrase and omissions betray its context: The reference to "colonial" and the "proletariat" place it before the great wars and
revolutions of this century; the appeal to "Christianity" and the "social problem" in
the singular—not to mention "the solution"—rings anachronistically to our pluralist
and skeptical ears; the perception is innocent of worry about environmental issues
alongside population growth, and about issues of ethnicity, race, and gender; the modern corporation had not yet developed as the master instrument of world mobiliza-
tion and trade. But these important differences should not obscure the extent of the
profound commonality with our situation at the end of the century: the fact that the
most important forces at work in the world are economic (with political and military
dimensions) and seem to outstrip our capacity to give them ethical direction. Indeed,
Troeltsch's own answer to the question he poses is gloomy, his book concluding that
the two major sources the churches had for addressing social issues, medieval Catholi-

cism and ascetic Protestantism, "have now spent their force" and seeing nothing to replace them.[2]

Some might still try to find Christian principles for directing the whole, or an alternative to the philosophy of history embraced in Troeltsch's perspective,[3] although the optimism implied in such efforts surely must be tempered by the intervening events of the century. Others might argue, and have argued, that Troeltsch's own interpretation was misguided insofar as he tried to grasp his time with the help of "discourses" outside the Christian tradition, and that his dark prognosis simply demonstrates that it is *this* approach that is spent, not the resources of the Christian tradition itself.[4] The very desire to articulate a problem using non-Christian sources and then to offer a Christian solution misunderstands Christian ethics.

In this essay, I argue for a third position—one that neither frames the economic in a Christian philosophy of history nor abandons deep engagement with the economic and its specialized discourse. Economics is an important part of Christian ethics, because theology has to do with the economic (the family of terms derived from the Greek for household, *oikos*, displays the unity: economics, ecology, ecumenics; and "stewardship" translating *oikonomos*). At the same time, economic inquiry cannot do its work without theology, the discourse about the whole. In making the argument, I draw on the economic implications of James Gustafson's theocentric ethics. I do not discuss his ethics directly nor attempt to defend his perspective, and certainly do not claim that he would agree with my analysis. Some points I make could be, and have been, developed from other theological positions. But I find his ethics theologically congenial and deeply provocative in both its Reformed and Troeltschian aspects. And while Gustafson's work on economics is not large, his theocentric ethics is economically fertile—perhaps more than that of any other major figure of the last half-century, owing to several of its central themes.[5] These can be briefly stated.

First and perhaps most important is that scarcity, the generative problem of all economic activity and theory, is deeply connected to *finitude*, a theme central to Gustafson's theocentrism: We live and have our being in a finite world in which scarcity and tragedy are neither accidents nor the consequences of sin but are woven into the fabric of human destiny. This perspective holds the promise of offering "a continuous realm of discourse"[6] between the theological and the economic. Closely related to the emphasis on finitude is Gustafson's "ontological *realism*" (my phrase, not his, but I think accurate): He believes that there is a world to be known and that a major portion of the theological and ethical task is to come to know that world, our place of habitation.[7] Even though this knowledge is necessarily incomplete, and even though descriptions of the world by various disciplines such as theology, natural science, social science, and others may differ, and differ importantly, these differing descriptions have a great deal to say to one another. Our knowledge is won through continual interpretation and reinterpretation, and the knowledge is better when it comes through genuine engagement between and among differing descriptions: All benefit from serious mutual engagement. Thus, what the economist has to say is of importance for the theologian, and vice versa. Following closely on the realism is the central importance of the *empirical* in Gustafson's ethics, of knowing and interpreting "what is going on" and using all the sciences, social and natural—indeed all human inquiry—to help us to know. Moreover, all such description and interpretation reveals the *interdependence* of the world and of human life, and this in turn leads to a strong appreciation for the complexity of *social processes and institutions* as the arena in which ethical life is played out. These processes and institutions are ambiguous, being both bearers of genuine value and humanly flawed.[8] Finally, Gustafson's distinctive understanding of *piety*, its connection to a religious tradition, and its concomitant teleology and view of sin, informs and qualifies all these themes with specific implications for economics.

I work with these themes, in varying degrees of specificity, under three headings: the natural, the social, and the religious.

The Natural: Finitude and Scarcity

The common view has it that capitalism and socialism have been the chief alternatives, indeed, antagonists, for modern (which is to say, post-eighteenth-century) economies. This perception is deeply misleading, for capitalism in its most common form and socialism in its Marxist form are of a piece in their underlying view of scarcity and their commitment to the production of abundance as the solution to human problems. Their common antagonist ideationally is Thomas Robert Malthus, whose thought has been obscured because of the immense productive success of capitalism in the last two centuries.

Marx believed that scarcity could be overcome through the development of human productive and social powers, and saw in the extraordinary productive energies of capitalism, if yet in need of some significant rearrangement of power, confirmation of that belief. Scarcity is a contrived problem—or, admitting that it is rooted in nature, contrived in its continuance once human historical development has reached a certain stage. If scarcity is seen as *the* fundamental human problem, with all human social energies aimed at its solution, then economic activity has a salvific dimension, and economists a priestly role: Produce abundance, distribute it broadly, and human discord and misery will cease. The seeds for this historical optimism were already in Adam Smith and are nurtured by at least a large portion of his capitalist followers. Transformed by Hegel's and Marx's (both had learned deeply from Smith) historical eschatology, the salvific roots grow to full maturity. The human problem is *nature*, and human historical energy can finally triumph over it. In Marx's language, real human history will begin once the battle with nature is won.[9]

Malthus, whom Marx scorned, believed that scarcity was a permanent condition of life, and that however much human productive powers increased, they could not keep up with the exponential growth of population. Scarcity did indeed cause conflict and misery, and was "solved" through famines, illness, and war—which is to say that it was solved on the population side of the equation through further misery rather than on the production side. The only relief from misery comes from a clear assessment of the consequences of unbridled reproduction, an educated willingness to live a sober life of sexual continence if not abstinence, and the cultivation of economic prudence, i.e., through an increased utilitarian rationality combined with a certain stoic acceptance of limits, institutionalized in private property, an eighteenth-century translation of Malthus's Calvinist (Presbyterian) heritage.[10] The relief afforded by rational self-control, sexual continence, and economic prudence was not itself salvific, even if part of divine intention, although when Malthusian arguments are used to justify some forms of capitalist property arrangements as the end of history, they, too, are not free from an eschatologically inspired philosophy of history.

The theological core of each of these visions is a theodicy. Hegel was explicit about the theodicy, the background being Jewish-Christian eschatology and also Joachim of Fiore's version of it—a tripartite division of history, based on the Trinity, promising the triumph of history over nature in the third age of the Spirit. In Marx's inversion of Hegel, the justification of the ways of God become the justification of the struggles of history understood as the process of anthropogenesis, the vehicle of eventual human emancipation.[11] Malthus's theodicy was also explicit, developed in the last two chapters of the first edition of the *Essay on Population,* where he argued that God created scarcity in order that mind would be developed.[12] Forced by necessity to attend to the consequences of one's actions, human reason (utilitarian calculation) is drawn forth and up from the torpor of the material, finite world.

The Marxist version of the drama of scarcity and abundance continues to wield imaginative power in some circles, but the political failure of Marxist regimes at the end of this century has permitted the deeper divide within modern economies to emerge. On the one side, the salvific drama is now played out by the supporters of capitalism who put primary faith in economic abundance, in increasing production, as the solution to human problems. This faith may be found in a variety of guises—for example, in champions of economic growth, in celebrations of liberal democracy (in which capitalism has had a central role) as the end of history,[13] and in the linking of Christianity with capitalism and its central institutions such as the modern business corporation.[14] The engine driving all these is a conviction not much different from Marx's: that history can triumph over nature, that economic and technical history is salvation history.[15] That the champions of capitalism are now in alliance with the peoples of post-Communist nations because the latter yearn for the material abundance of the West is an irony without Hegelian redemptive possibility.

On the other side, Malthusians, a minority over the last two centuries, have received new life not only from the collapse of Communist regimes but also from increasing alarm about population growth and the fragility of the biosphere. Malthusian themes are often heard as parts of larger melodies: in resurgent nationalism aimed at protecting scarce resources (economic and cultural) from external threats; in metaphors of triage and the claim that the boat is full;[16] in moral criticism of the habits and character of the poor in this country and of Third World populations;[17] and, above all, in the sense that capitalist property arrangements are part of the natural order of a scarce (divine) economy. Emphases on individual self-reliance and self-control, and the central role of private property in promoting these and other civic virtues, with the not-so-thinly implied criticism of the lack of virtue on the part of the poor, could come directly from the pages of Malthus's *Essay.*[18] In all these, the theodicy continues to do its work, justifying hard decisions and existing social arrangements.[19]

One perduring task of theology, theocentric or otherwise,[20] is to critique the not-so-cryptic theology (its role is often so large that calling it "theological residue" is misleading) of such social theory. From a theocentric perspective, both theodicies are anthropocentric, interpreting scarcity in relation to the special role of human beings in creation. More generally, the deepest human problem is not scarcity, or our always difficult relationship with nature, but rather our relationship with God. In either case, economic problems are, *at their base,* problems of finitude, not sin. The problems are, of course, exacerbated by sin; and the disentangling of the scarcity and burden of production presented by nature from those imposed by human ingenuity and deformity is no easier than disentangling culture from nature, or the evil caused by sin from the evil caused by finitude. Nonetheless, the central point should be clear: Economic problems and their associated evils cannot be reduced to sin; nor can they be overcome through the human effort to achieve freedom from nature. The history of economic production is not salvation history; nor is it destined by providence or nature to produce capitalist property arrangements (or socialist freedom) as its end.

Having done the theological critique does not, however, make the problem of scarcity go away. If finitude and scarcity are permanent aspects of human existence, interpreted by the doctrine of Creation as well as by Fall, several critical points follow.

First, any solutions to problems of scarcity will have coercive aspects because scarcity is by definition coercive: It constrains our choices. The theory of abundance, whether in its capitalist or Marxist forms, has always connected economic growth to the expansion of human freedom. In the capitalist version, economic growth expands the domain of individual liberty and choice; in the Marxist version, it ushers in the domain of socialist freedom, where human beings are the free creators of their own history. The rejection of a theodicy of scarcity and a salvation of abundance means that the ethical domain always will be marked by elements of coercion and even of tragedy. Whatever salvation entails for our temporal life, it cannot remove these marks of our creatureliness. And this means, quite specifically, a permanent and central role for the *political*, not simply to constrain sin but as a natural and necessary part of the human requirement to make the necessary choices among goods and to justify the coercion entailed in the choices.[21]

Second, if abundance is not salvation, neither does scarcity dictate a particular outcome. The history of modern economies and technology suggests the impossibility of specifying a "natural" limit or a "natural" set of social arrangements dictated by finitude itself, and there is no ground for assuming, for example, that liberal democratic capitalism is the end of history, the best we can do given certain permanent "realities." Constraints are not foreordination, and human freedom in this understanding is the freedom to discover, to choose, and to will emergent possibilities under continuing conditions of limited over-all possibility.[22]

Third, as permanent aspects of our finite existence, finitude and scarcity are proper areas of human inquiry and of the development of methods and of a specialized language to study them. In short, the empirical tools of economic inquiry—to which Smith, Malthus, and Marx all contributed immensely—remain critical, indeed central, to ethics because they can help us identify and more clearly understand the nature of the possibilities that do emerge and the choices that have to be made. They are, in a very real sense, part of the science of human constraints.

I do not mean to suggest that economic inquiry is a "value-free" tool to be used by any normative framework like a hired gun. It is unlikely that any economist, as a human being, can function without a social theory that is deeply normative; and we know that economic language and analysis is inevitably shot through with metaphors and value judgments.[23] Nor do I think that theology and ethics can first operate free of specialized economic language and then turn to it as convenient. If our understanding of finitude is first and foremost a theological understanding, then economic language is present from the beginning—as it abundantly is, for example, in scripture. What I mean is that economic language and inquiry is—as scripture, Aristotle, and most economists have known—a part of the ethical. There is no clean divide between the ethical and the economic. The *foundational* task is ethical and theological, but the remarkable growth of economic understanding as a field of human science marks genuine learning, a genuine increase in the human capacity to order a critical part of our social life as it increases in scale and complexity. Here, aspects of capitalism and of the liberal democratic forms that sometimes accompany it can be understood as genuine human moral achievements under specific historical conditions. So also are their criticism by socialism. But this learning is not itself salvific, and there is more and other to learn.

What ethics and theology do, in part, is to define the wholes (the scale) about which the economist inquires, attending to omissions and exclusions and thereby also adding to the complexity. In doing so, theology and ethics transform the way we look at the economic, changing deep metaphors and frames of thought. At the same time, economic inquiry calls attention to the interrelatedness of our social life, an interrelatedness we already know on ethical and theological grounds but for which we require constantly new and specialized articulation as we are faced with new situations. There is no way of avoiding this dialectic, which is, finally, the basis of *phronesis* in reaching ethical judgment. I am willing to argue that a good economist must be a good theologian, and a good theologian a good economist.

Since such a combination in one person is rare,[24] a distinguished example of creative collaboration deserves special attention: Herman Daly and John Cobb's book, *For the Common Good*, sets out to change those "habits of the mind" that keep us on a collision course with ecological disaster.[25] It does so by offering numerous alternative metaphors and ways of thinking about everything from income to energy to the meaning of land—seeing earth and land, for example, as *active* rather than as a passive and empty resource waiting to be developed. Such metaphorical transformations alter dramatically the balance sheets with which economists work, particularly in assessing costs. The alternative balance sheet implied in the metaphorical transformations is the centerpiece of the book: an index of sustainable economic welfare offered as a replacement for the GNP as a measurement of economic well-being. However one may quarrel with specific recommendations,[26] this signal effort presses economists to look at a larger whole, defined ethically and theologically, and it presses religious people to think in terms of economics.

The Social: Membership and Its Institutions

During my preparation for writing this essay, a widowed aunt of mine, suffering from cancer and the slow and irreversible effects of the dementia often associated with aging, collapsed in her apartment in Estes Park, Colorado. She had been living with the help of Meals on Wheels, weekly public nursing visits, and the support of friends and neighbors. Neighbors bringing food discovered her and took her to the nearby hospital. Because she has no children, it fell to me and my sisters to take over her life for her and, in consultation with doctors and nurses, to commit her to a nursing home. She had worked until the last year of her life cleaning the homes of others in order to eke out a living, and the only resource for paying for the nursing home was Medicaid. Under the guidance of the state social-services agent we "spent down" her meager bank account below the Medicaid-required threshold, paying off a pile of bills. We cleaned out her apartment (which contained in three rooms the accumulations of a lifetime), donating much to charity and to the nursing home itself. We were immensely fortunate that small-town mores were still in place: There were many neighbors who looked after one another; church members and others loaned pickup trucks and willing hands for the physical work; the nursing home was uncommonly clean and cheerful, attended by a caring and immensely helpful staff. We are comforted to know that my aunt has a steady stream of visitors.

These circumstances epitomize, I think, what many of us might regard as the characteristics of a just society. Someone at the end of life, with meager means and without a primary family to care for her, is nevertheless cared for in a decent and dignified setting. Something of an eccentric, she was nevertheless known by everyone and was fully a *member* of her community. That membership entitled her to a range of human goods when she could no longer take care of herself, goods provided by a remarkably variegated and complex web of personal relationships, institutions, and social processes that make up the circumstances of her full membership.

Alter any element in this complex situation and you alter the justice and the care. Take away the culture of the small town where an ethos of independence and hard work is combined with a commitment to mutual care and support—where everyone knows almost everyone else—and my aunt might not have been found on her apartment floor; and dealing with the banks and institutions to which she owed money might have been even more difficult. Put the nursing home in Denver or Manhattan, and there would likely be less cheerfulness, more smells, a less-personally committed staff. Take away persons shaped by active church life and small community mores, and there would be fewer visitors. Remove Social Security, Medicare, and Medicaid—a partial social-welfare system in which income from myriad strangers flows through the "numberless capillaries of the state," first to her pockets, now to the nursing home—and you would have a human disaster.[27] Take away market relations, and you would remove the efficient transportation and communication that permit care at long distances, not to mention the source of income for those who supply care, paid and nonpaid. Take away a committed extended family with means to travel and the ability to negotiate the complex transactions of the many institutions, and then an even larger burden would fall on the state.

We know, of course, that millions of persons in our society—not to mention the world—live in circumstances where one or more of these elements is not in place, and where the almost symbiotic workings of the elements are seriously impaired if not dysfunctional. Nor do we have to look simply at the end of life to see the consequent human damage: Narratives of the beginning of life for some of the millions of poor children in our society could offer even more poignant portraits of injustice. The fundamental point in either case is that economic institutions, whether private or public, are *situated* in a complex web of other social institutions and of culture and persons, all profoundly moral in nature; and changes in one affect the others, profoundly transforming the way members are treated, effectively rendering some or many "nonmembers."

Michael Walzer has rightly underscored recognition and membership as the chief social goods that societies distribute—the distribution of all other social goods either helps to secure membership, or renders membership tenuous.[28] The range of possible social and institutional patterns for securing membership is historically and culturally immense. In a society where free markets play a central role, private property is the central institution for securing membership, the basis of political franchise and other rights. But as Marx and many others have pointed out, private property has historically excluded as many or more than it has included. It would be possible, of course, to "unbundle" the various rights actually packaged in a given understanding of private property, determine which are essential to membership in a market society, and then universalize them (this is what Marx tried to do). For example, in America the right to income, dwelling, use for production, alteration, and transfer are all packaged confusedly in the right to private property. If income is considered a necessary if not sufficient condition for membership in a market society, then there would have to be something like a guaranteed annual income, a proposal that in fact originated with Milton Friedman, an economist who favors free markets.[29]

While such a policy might secure the minimal resources for participation in market exchange,[30] it would not come close to providing the range of protection, participation, and meaning, not to mention care, essential to social membership and personal identity. Historically, membership has come from belonging to larger bodies: tribes, families, the *polis*, estates, the body of Christ.[31] In the modern world, we typically establish membership through participation in multiple "social bodies," whether these be relatively stable towns and neighborhoods like my aunt's, or churches, political organizations and parties, and the like. One of these may be primary, but our membership and our identities tend to be complex rather than simple.

Increasingly in modern societies, membership is achieved by participation in the "artificial body" of the business *corp*oration,[32] the distinctive invention of modern market economies and—as the chief source of capital and employment, as well as the vehicle for the vast bulk of technological development—their dominant institution. In the United States, close to 90 percent of all employed persons are employed by large organizations, either corporations or government, and we may assume that this trend will be true of other nations as their economies develop.

The range of possible forms of corporation—how they are structured and governed internally and how they relate to other institutions—is wide, varying historically and cross-culturally;[33] and the specifics of these forms determine whether the corporation can be understood as the chief way in which people achieve social membership. In the well-known example of Japan, the corporation's close ties with government policies, together with a culture that values and rewards solidarity and loyalty in personal relationships, combined even with the practice of religious rites within corporate structures, permit a "cradle-to-grave" standing virtually indistinguishable from one's full social standing.

In the United States, with a far larger role played by the market and with less protectionism in relation to international markets, it is extremely doubtful that the corporation ever could be the basic securer of membership. Some theologians have celebrated the covenantal basis of the modern corporation, seeing it as an important place in which Christian stewardship can be exercised; as a vehicle for extending the realm of covenantal relations in, for example, traditional or authoritarian cultures; and as creating new patterns of global interdependence.[34] Others are convinced that the corporation is the major obstacle to economic justice. Our national confusion on the issue is neatly displayed by the recent debate on health care: The Clinton administration's proposal for health care was less distinctive ethically for its "managed care" approach than it was for specifying that the chief conduit for the provision of health care resources should be businesses themselves. If health care is understood as something we typically want to provide to all who are members (for example, families would never deny a member health care, nor would close communities of any kind), then attaching health to one's place of work means that, for the purposes of this policy, being engaged in paid work counts as the chief qualification for membership in our society.[35] The plan drew the wrath of persons who worried about those who were not employed in large business (alternative sourcing was provided for these, but they were likely to be "second class") and of businesses who believed they would be made noncompetitive.

Apart from the values a corporation may or may not realize internally, the unambiguous empirical point is that the more a corporation is accountable chiefly to the market (rather than to other social institutions), the less suited it is to be the chief body for social membership. And the accountability of the corporation is the fundamental issue. In the developing global economy, it is the corporation that crosses the traditional membership boundaries of neighborhood, city, and state, transferring capital, jobs, knowledge, and essential services from one region to another. It may create new patterns of global and regional interdependence, but often at serious costs to local communities, both those from which capital leaves and those to which it relocates. This is the pattern Schumpeter long ago called "creative destruction";[36] just how creative and how destructive it is depends on the strength of other social institutions, including government, and the way the market is situated within them. Any assessment of the larger "social balance sheet" must be done on something like a case-to-case basis.

Moreover, the freer the move of corporation and capital, the freer must be the movement of peoples in order to leave places of diminished possibilities (if not desolation) and to find places of increased opportunity. The ideal of a "world without borders," the dream of some free market utopians,[37] would entail a constantly shifting pattern of population, undercutting precisely those institutions, whether governmental or socially organic, essential to securing membership and making the corporation accountable. A "world without borders" would be a world of formally universal membership, which is to say a membership that provides *nothing* in the way of meaning, security, or identity. These would be secured only through "local projects"—something like "clubs" of meaning. But there would be nothing to legitimate the whole and nothing other than money to connect those inside to those outside each local project. It is no accident that Marx characterized the socialist person as one who goes fishing in the morning, hunts in the afternoon, and is a critic at night, without ever becoming any one of these (Hannah Arendt calls them "hobbies"); and that champions of the free market think of utterly voluntary associations as the source of all meaning and identity. The idea that we can freely adopt different personae ("lifestyles" in the contemporary idiom) is a common theme in any salvation of abundance. When we achieve freedom from nature and necessity, establishing a fixed identity is no longer necessary.[38]

Because of the mobility of capital and people and the fluid social relationships that such mobility facilitates, the primary ethical task in a modern economy is, again as Walzer has argued, the care and maintenance of boundaries.[39] But where should the boundaries be? Walzer's unimpeachable answer is: That depends on the goods we create and value, and want to protect. But are some goods more important than others, and do some kinds of human community or institutional forms deserve more protection than others? When we ask these questions—questions about good—we are in the realm of the religious.

The Religious: Love and Money

In order to understand the religious (the spiritual), we do well to begin with money. Abstractly, money is a system of signs, based on numbers, representing value and permitting rational calculation. But using Tillich's distinction, money functions in society not simply as a sign but also as a symbol: It does not simply "stand in for," or "point beyond," but participates in the reality to which it points. Removed from precious metals—and the ancients knew that even gold was barren and could not *produce* anything out of itself (hence the prohibition against usury)—money represents value which is not inherent in its own material. But where does the value lie? Marx thought money was reified labor: True value lay in human labor, and money was simply an objectified representation of this, an abstraction from its human basis. Others have thought that money could represent the natural value of things, but this has long been abandoned for exchange value. For two persons, money can be created on any piece of paper to state a claim of the one on the other—an I.O.U. But to represent claims in general—to have social currency—it must be more than paper with numbers; it must also represent authority. Therefore, money has portraits of kings, queens, presidents, national heroes, and engravings of national monuments. On American money, God is invoked.

This admixture of God and mammon, of the spiritual and the material, goes to the heart of the ambiguity of the economic. On the one side, economics is the study of the production of goods (and services) under conditions of finitude and modest scarcity; it deals with the material world. On the other side it is the study of the allocation, exchange, and circulation of goods in society, all dependent on meaning or the spiritual world. Money represents the material; but it and its associated institution, the market, are primarily instruments of exchange and allocation embedded in the realm of social meaning. Because money facilitates exchange and immensely extends the market's reach, the market in a modern economy is not simply a place where material goods are exchanged but becomes a principle of social organization and a transformative *power*.

Jean-Christophe Agnew has brilliantly interpreted the historical transformation of the role of market and money in his book on market and theater.[40] The medieval market was local, a *place* situated among and bounded by other social institutions—including especially the church, whose cross towered over the market, sanctioning the exchanges and protecting the transactors. As it grew in power, it moved to the outskirts of towns, becoming an important part of a transactional *process* uniting one town with another, providing new contacts among strangers, eventually connecting and coordinating whole regions according to a principle that transcended the effective reach of religion and politics. The *principle* was the principle of exchange value, the utter liquidity and commensurability of anything given the universality of money. From this it was only a small step to being a *power*, unbounded by other institutions and capable of transforming everything. No longer institutionally situated, everything else is situated in the market.[41]

The transformative power of money and market is exercised at every level of human existence. On the *social* level, it is capable of transforming every human institution, as noted in the preceding section. On the *personal* level, it creates a new kind of person, a new social psychology, in commercial societies transforming the meaning of human action and freedom (here the classic work of Georg Simmel is especially pertinent[42]); giving birth to what some have called "economic man";[43] and giving human identity a fluidity it had never had before. Here is the connection to the masks and personae of drama: Agnew traces the origin of Elizabethan and Jacobean theater, with their blurring of identity and often of gender, to market and carnival, arguing that theater "brought forth 'another nature'—a new world of 'artificial persons,'" bestowing "an intelligible albeit Protean human shape on the very *form*lessness that money values were introducing into exchange."[44] No longer established by virtue of membership in relatively permanent "natural" social bodies, identity increasingly is something to be negotiated through a history of transactions with other agents/actors whose personae are achieved through "the exhibition and commercialization of the self . . . [requiring] an audience."[45]

Thus, on the cultural level, meaning itself becomes a commodity, the meanings of historical and religious traditions replaced by commercial fantasies and an explosion of narrative entertainment.[46] It is not just that religious beliefs come to be considered, as often noted, "preferences" and "individual goods"; rather the very understanding of our temporal existence is utterly transvalued so that past, present, and future are not interpreted in light of religious tradition but in the light of the "hope" of economic abundance, institutionalized in pension funds, Social Security, financial speculation (bets on the future), the official commitment of all governments to economic growth and a future cornucopia, and perhaps above all the "normalization" of debt as a way of being in the world.

In all these transformations, money does the work that is, in religious language, the domain of "spirit," a point expressed nicely in Marx's ironic characterization of money as "the real mind of all things." (The German "*Geist*" captures this in a way that English does not.) Spirit and love transgress boundaries and create new human institutional forms with a universal *telos*. Baptism renames, and persons are reborn through spirit and forgiving love, their identities and memberships profoundly altered. The meaning of life is found in love itself. Both money and love lay claim to represent ultimate reality, the way things ultimately are;[47] both claim to be the ultimate coordinating principle of human life and the basis of hope.

Marc Shell has argued that money, being both a physical reality and an ideal, is similar to the Christian idea of incarnation, where Jesus is both human and divine, so that "money [is] disturbingly close to Christ as a competing architectonic principle."[48] From a theological perspective, we can say that money, absent a moral frame, is "counterfeit spirit." The difference is critical: while love *reveals* reality, money *conceals* reality, hiding its representations including patterns of power and injustice. Money's *universality*, its capacity to translate the value of anything, means that the reality it symbolizes is ultimately empty: We fill in its meaning imaginatively while at the same time being blind to the social deformities it also represents. The money in a savings account can represent a new car, a college education, a comfortable retirement; saved money can also be used to exploit others or to distort political processes. The twenty-dollar bill put in the church plate for refugees may have been used for a drug transaction two nights earlier. The money left in a bequest may represent the labor, frugality, and love of parents, or the rapacity of a "robber baron." By looking at money, you cannot tell what it represents or what it has represented; but when we get it, hold it, and pay it out, our imaginations fill in symbolic meanings. In this curious capacity of being able to represent anything, money as a symbol *conceals* what it represents; and in so doing, it continually calls attention to itself, giving the illusion that money itself has value, is itself the end and meaning of action, is itself the sufficient coordinator of our social life. When this happens, money as a symbol becomes identical to itself.

If Tillich is right, that the Christian cross, one of the symbols of love, is a "broken symbol," emptying itself for the sake of the divine reality in which it participates, money does just the opposite: It pulls reality into itself, reducing all to itself, claiming to *be* reality. Love, by contrast, does not conceal but *reveals*. In the theocentric tradition, with roots in Augustine (and Plato), progressing through Jonathan Edwards and Gustafson, love reveals in two ways. On the one hand, love *attends* to the reality of the other, the object of love. Iris Murdoch cites Simone Weil's characterization of love as "attention," expressing "the idea of a just and loving gaze directed upon an individual reality."[49] Love as attention is just because its intention is to permit the individual reality—the object of love—to exist, to come to know it in its singularity rather than pulling it into the lover's own orbit, frames of reference, and uses. In so doing, love as attention "unselfs" (i.e., causes one to be astonished, delighted, pulled out of oneself; to see differently), and it can also be costly.[50] On the other hand, love in the theocentric tradition, because its *telos* is God, widens the field of attention so that love properly directed is the "love of all being."[51] These two aspects of love—attention to the otherness of individual realities and to the whole of being—might seem to be competing vectors for an individual person, but not if love is a social and communal reality where the different abilities, personal characteristics, education, and immense variety of circumstances of its members, sharing a common tradition, permit attention complexly to a larger whole.

From a theological perspective, money and economics—to use the language of economics itself—live on religious capital. Choices cannot be made in the marketplace without love of *some* kind (economists long ago translated Augustine's love as "interest");[52] and the "wholes" to which human beings attend in the balance sheets of their choices depend on the quality and scope of their love. Remove the religious motivation to love larger wholes, remove the *telos* of the whole of being, and the balance sheets are disastrously wrong. The person's vision is constricted, the human spirit "contracted,"[53] and people, traditions of meaning, the earth and its resources, are reduced to their exchange value. The human unity achieved and the directions taken by market decisions are blind, led only by human fantasy and the obscured underlying structures of power. Money marches on when the spirit flags, but only for a time. When the spiritual capital is spent, the collapse of political economy is inevitable.

Formally, the theological and ethical task is to *resituate* money and the market so that they serve the whole of the created order, the entire household of God in all its economic and ecological complexity. Because this household remains finite, attention to it and to the individual realities within it will not undo the fact that things come to an end, species die out, whole ways of human life are lost, and difficult choices must of necessity be made: Love cannot do without justice. The substance of these choices and the justice achieved will, as I suggested in the preceding sections, differ from context to context and be political in nature. But their quality will depend on the human spiritual capacity to think in terms of larger and larger frames and on the technical, empirical knowledge we bring to bear on those wholes.

If what I have argued here is correct (i.e., that the love of all being is the *telos* of human life), it follows that an essential part of theological and ethical study must include the study of the material basis of life as a central component, not simply an interesting area of inquiry. The fact that this virtually never happens, that neither a theological education nor a liberal education necessarily requires the study of economics, and that economic inquiry usually proceeds independently of explicit theological and ethical grounding, is perhaps the most alarming aspect of this time at the end of Troeltsch's century. The absence of education about the most powerful engine driving human decisions reflects, of course, the popular belief that spirit and material life are opposites; and the educated belief, part of secularization theory, concerning the "differentiation" of various spheres of human activity, effectively seals off the economic from ethics, confirming the popular view. Together, these virtually guarantee that the unities and directions achieved by money, market, and fantasy will go on "over our heads" or "behind our backs," independent of human intention and detached from reality. The task before us in this situation is not so much the articulation of Christian principles to guide the whole as it is a recovery of the capacity to love the whole, and to live responsibly within it. This means, on the one hand, the rediscovery of the material dimension of being: an awareness that the care of souls, of spirit, requires disciplined and educated attention to the material aspects of our place of habitation. On the other hand, it means a renewed awareness of the spiritual basis of the whole of material and human reality. Such awareness offers no salvific economic agenda. At most it places human history within the larger history of creation itself, offering a more modest appraisal of our destiny, a more realistic basis for responsible judgments and choices in that frame, and perhaps the hope that we may do less damage.

Notes

1. Ernst Troeltsch, *The Social Teaching of the Christian Churches* (New York: Harper Torchbooks, 1960), 1010.

2. Ibid., 1012. Brent Sockness has offered a fine discussion of this and other issues in Troeltsch's ethics in "Looking behind the *Social Teachings*: Troeltsch's Methodological Reflections in 'Fundamental Problems of Ethics' (1902)," paper presented at the 1995 Annual Meeting of the Society of Christian Ethics. Published in *The Annual* (Society of Christian Ethics, 1995), 221–46.

3. Theologies of hope and liberation theologies connected to dialectical interpretations of history would be examples of alternatives to Troeltsch's more linear philosophy of history.

4. See John Milbank, *Theology and Social Theory: Beyond Secular Reason* (Oxford: Blackwell, 1990), for an extraordinarily ambitious statement of this theme. Stanley Hauerwas's narrative ethics (which Milbank cites approvingly) offers a similar perspective.

5. The themes are all developed most fully in James M. Gustafson, *Ethics from a Theocentric Perspective*, 2 vols. (Chicago: University of Chicago Press, 1981–1984). His most important explicit writings on economic issues include "Population and Nutrition" in *Ethics,* 2: chap. 7; "Interdependence, Finitude and Sin: Reflections on Scarcity," *Journal of Religion* 57, no. 2 (April 1977), 156–68; (with Elmer W. Johnson) "Resolving Income and Wealth Differences in a Market Economy: A Dialogue," in Thomas Donaldson and Patricia H. Werhane, eds., *Ethical Issues in Business: A Philosophical Approach* (Englewood Cliffs, N.J.: Prentice-Hall, 1983), 382–92; and three essays in the volume he edited with John R. Meyer, *The U.S. Business Corporation: An Institution in Transition* (Cambridge, Mass.: Ballinger Publishing, 1988): with Elmer W. Johnson, "Efficiency, Morality, and Managerial Effectiveness," 194–209; with John R. Meyer, "Introduction," xiii–xv; and "Epilogue: For Whom Does the Corporation Toil?," 211–34.

6. The phrase is Sheldon Wolin's, characterizing the seamless relation between political and religious thought in Calvin. See Sheldon Wolin, *Politics and Vision* (Boston: Little, Brown, 1960), 179.

7. The metaphor is Gary Hauk's, from his fine study of the ethics of James Gustafson and Iris Murdoch, "Habitations of Goodness: Selfhood, Reality, and Language in the Work of Iris Murdoch and James M. Gustafson" (Ph.D. diss., Emory University, 1991).

8. See Gustafson's first book, *Treasure in Earthen Vessels: The Church as a Human Community* (New York: Harper & Row, 1961), on the ambiguity of the church, displaying the deep influence especially of James Luther Adams and Troeltsch.

9. Perhaps the most astonishing statement of this point is in Marx's newspaper article, "The British Rule in India," in which he argues that British colonialism has served to introduce history into a culture which, because it worshiped nature, had no "historical energy" and was therefore incapable on its own of realizing human destiny. The article, written in 1853, is reprinted in numerous collections of Marx's works.

10. Malthus's thesis was a backhanded argument for utilitarianism, but his pessimism about limits set him aside from most of his utilitarian contemporaries, whose optimism about the possibilities for maximizing good fit well with the nascent industrial capitalism of the time and remains a part of the dominant capitalist ethos to this day.

11. See my discussion of Marx and theodicy in Jon P. Gunnemann, *The Moral Meaning of Revolution* (New Haven: Yale University Press, 1979), chap. 4.

12. For an important discussion of Malthus's theodicy, see Edmund Santurri, "Theodicy and Social Policy in Malthus' Thought," *Journal of the History of Ideas* 43 (1982): 315–20. Milbank, *Theology and Social Theory*, argues that all social theory is theodicy, with which I agree. For an earlier treatment of the theological underpinnings of eighteenth-century social thought, see Jacob Viner, *The Role of Providence in the Social Order: An Essay in Intellectual History* (Philadelphia: American Philosophical Society, 1966).

13. See Francis Fukuyama, *The End of History and the Last Man* (New York: Free Press, 1992), which argues that liberal democracy is the end of history, but that this is not necessarily cause for celebration.

14. See, e.g., Max Stackhouse, "Spirituality and the Corporation," *Public Theology and Political Economy* (Grand Rapids, Mich.: Eerdmans, 1987), chap. 7. Reprinted in Max L. Stackhouse, Dennis McCann, and Shirley J. Roels, eds. (with Preston N. Williams), *On Moral Business: Classical and Contemporary Resources for Ethics in Economic Life* (Grand Rapids, Mich.: Eerdmans, 1995), 501–7. The whole of chapter 11 of the latter volume contains critical essays pertinent to the topic of the changing business corporation.

15. I have taken up these themes in Jon P. Gunnemann, "Alchemic Temptations" (The Presidential Address), *Annual of the Society of Christian Ethics* (1995): 3–18.

16. Cf. Gustafson's discussion of this in *Ethics*, 2:224–50.

17. Cf., e.g., George Gilder, *Wealth and Poverty* (New York: Basic Books, 1982). See Robert N. Bellah, Richard Madsen, William M. Sullivan, Ann Swidler, and Steven M. Tipton, *Habits of the Heart: Individualism and Commitment in American Life* (Berkeley: University of California Press, 1985), 262–66, for an analysis of these themes during the Reagan years.

18. See A. M. C. Waterman, *Revolution, Economics and Religion* (New York and Cambridge: Cambridge University Press, 1991), for a fascinating discussion of these themes among the political economists of Malthus's time. I am indebted to Ed Santurri for calling my attention to this book.

19. For a book that raises Malthusian themes, but absent the moralism and with great attention to empirical realities and possibilities, see Paul Kennedy, *Preparing for the Twenty-first Century* (New York: Random House, 1993).

20. For an extraordinary example of an "otherwise," see Milbank, *Theology and Social The-*

ory. There is much in Milbank with which I agree. One fundamental point of disagreement is that I do not think that theology can be done, or has ever been done, without the language of existing social philosophy and theory.

21. Understanding both politics and economics as natural rather than as concessions to sin clearly places theocentric ethics in close relation to the natural-law tradition of Roman Catholicism.

22. Cf. Gustafson, *Ethics*, 2:239.

23. On metaphor and rhetoric in economics, see Donald N. McClosky, *The Rhetoric of Economics* (Madison: University of Wisconsin Press, 1985).

24. But I think of the careful contributions of Daniel Rush Finn to the Society of Christian Ethics over the years.

25. Herman E. Daly and John B. Cobb Jr., with contributions by Clifford W. Cobb, *For the Common Good: Redirecting the Economy toward Community, the Environment, and a Sustainable Future* (Boston: Beacon Press, 1989). Gustafson frequently notes the affinity between his theocentrism and the process theology that underlies Daly and Cobb's work.

26. Daly and Cobb choose to make nations and small, local, sustainable communities the primary units for the development of a sustainable society. Achieving such a social and political pattern is likely to require far more coercion than they wish to admit. This is more of a problem given some of their other ethical commitments than it is for theocentric ethics, per se.

27. The metaphor is Michael Ignatieff's, *The Needs of Strangers* (New York: Viking Penguin, 1984), 10.

28. Michael Walzer, *Spheres of Justice* (New York: Basic Books, 1983).

29. See Daniel Patrick Moynihan, *The Politics of a Guaranteed Income: The Nixon Administration and the Family Assistance Plan* (New York: Random House, 1973), for the classic analysis of how American political will can fail for a policy that should appeal to both left and right.

30. It is an essential feature in a market society, because for the market to be just—to protect person and liberty—a person must be able not only to say "yes" to an exchange but also "no," to walk away from the exchange if it is not just and to avoid "desperate exchanges." See C. E. Lindblom, *Politics and Markets* (New York: Basic Books, 1977), 49, for discussion of the profound injury caused by termination of a job; see Walzer, *Spheres of Justice*, 102, on "desperate exchanges"; see Jon P. Gunnemann, "Capitalism and Commutative Justice," *The Annual of the Society of Christian Ethics* (1985), 101–22 for a discussion of these issues more generally in relation to the requirements of membership in a market society.

31. The whole of the gospel can be understood as being about property, about who we are and to whom we, and everything else, belong. One example is "The earth is [God's] and the fullness thereof" (Ps. 24:1). Another is to be found in the Heidelberg catechism's first question and answer: *Question:* "What is your only comfort in life and in death?" *Answer:* "That I belong—body and soul, in life and in death—not to myself but to my faithful Savior Jesus Christ, who at the cost of his own blood has fully freed me from the dominium of the devil." "Dominium" is the Latin for "property; depending on who has "made payment," one *belongs* (is the property of, hence a member) either to the "body" of the devil or the "body of Christ."

32. Thomas Hobbes's *Leviathan* stands as one of the earliest recognitions that human beings create artificial social bodies (e.g., the state) and with this also, artificial persons. The standing of the corporation in law is as an "artificial person."

33. Many of these issues are addressed in the essays in Meyer and Gustafson, *The U.S. Business Corporation*.

34. See note 14 above.

35. William Johnson Everett first pointed this out to me. He will recognize other debts in this essay.

36. Joseph A. Schumpeter, *Capitalism, Socialism, and Democracy*, 2d ed. (New York: Harper & Bros., 1947), esp. chaps. 7 and 12.

37. It is important to note that, from the standpoint of capital, a borderless world is to a large extent already a reality. It is not so with the free movement of peoples. These issues are central to Kennedy, *Preparing for the Twenty-first Century*.

38. Arendt's reference to Marx's "hobbies" is in Hannah Arendt, *The Human Condition* (Garden City, N.Y.: Doubleday Anchor, 1959), 101. The idea that people can change fundamental identity and membership is, of course, at the center of what is meant by religious conversion and by baptism. But in these cases it happens only once, and the body or community into which one is baptized, the church, takes responsibility for the re-formation of the individual whose persona is changed.

39. The characterization is Walzer's, *Spheres of Justice*.

40. Jean-Christophe Agnew, *Worlds Apart: The Market and the Theater in Anglo-American Thought, 1550–1750* (Cambridge: Cambridge University Press, 1986).

41. Ibid., 17–56.

42. Georg Simmel, *The Philosophy of Money*, trans. Tom Bottomore and David Frisby (London: Routledge & Kegan Paul, 1978). See esp. chaps. 4–6.

43. See the comparison of "economic man" and "psychological man" in Philip Rieff, *Freud: The Mind of the Moralist*, 3d ed. (Chicago: University of Chicago Press, 1979), 356–57. The masculine form is important to keep here because the subject of these historical types is overwhelmingly male. Agnew, *Worlds Apart*, 187, discusses Ann Douglas's notion of the "commercialization of the inner life." Many of these themes were already taken up in Simmel, *The Philosophy of Money*, and Schumpeter, *Capitalism, Socialism, and Democracy*.

44. Agnew, *Worlds Apart,* xi.

45. Ann Douglas, quoted in ibid., 187.

46. In addition to Agnew's discussion of theater and drama, see Frank Kermode's discussion of the rise of the novel in *The Sense of an Ending* (Oxford and New York: Oxford University Press, 1967), as providing narrative endings when the canonical endings of Western culture have lost their power. We would need also to look at the extraordinary importance of the mass media, including especially movies and videos, for providing surrogate narrative "endings" in the face of the increasing impotence of traditional symbolizations of the end.

47. Gustafson says, "To say something theological is to say something about *how things really and ultimately are.*" See James M. Gustafson, "A Response to Critics," *Journal of Religious Ethics* 13 (1985), 185.

48. Marc Shell, *Art and Money* (Chicago: University of Chicago Press, 1995), 8.

49. Iris Murdoch, *The Sovereignty of Good* (London: Routledge & Kegan Paul, 1970), 34.

50. Ibid., 84. Murdoch's understanding has a strong aesthetic component (as in Plato), referring to our aesthetic response to the variety of persons and the variety and beauty of nature, thereby underestimating the *cost* that love can exact.

51. Jonathan Edwards's phrase is "love to being in general." See *The Nature of True Virtue* (Ann Arbor: University of Michigan Press, 1960), 3–5.

52. Cf. Albert Hirschman, *The Passions and the Interests* (Princeton, N.J.: Princeton University Press, 1977). Hirschman traces the path by which "interest" came to replace "passion" as the spring of human action and the mechanism of social cooperation in the writing of the early political economists. Augustine's "love" embraces both ideas.

53. Cf. Gustafson, *Ethics*, 1:304; 2:247.

Chapter 20

Just-War Criteria and Theocentric Ethics

RICHARD B. MILLER

Circumstances and Ethics

Changing circumstances in international affairs have produced a new cluster of problems and cases for the ethics of war. Emergent nationalism in central Asia; internecine conflict in Somalia; the Gulf War; human-rights violations in China and Tibet; war between ethnic and religious factions in Bosnia, the Sudan, and Rwanda; and the reality of state-sponsored terrorism have generated a fresh set of questions about the proper use of force. In the United States, these events seem more complicated, and their just resolution more elusive, than conflicts framed by a vision of the world divided between two superpowers and their client states. For American policymakers, the dissolution of the Warsaw Bloc means that deterring war or defending against an enemy nation are now less obvious rationales for maintaining (and financing) a military force. *Economic embargoes* and *interventions* into other nations' conflicts have moved to the center of debate for social critics, U.S. policymakers, and UN officials. As a result, it has become increasingly necessary for ethicists and policy analysts to evaluate uses of force by some nations to protect other communities (interventions),[1] as well as methods of coercion that eschew military force (sanctions).[2]

The overall effect of these changes is to force pacifists and nonpacifists to engage in political-philosophical reflection and to clarify some basic terms. Nonpacifists must articulate more clearly the justification for using force to protect others in need, thereby shifting their center of focus from *self-defense* to *rescue* as a basis for entering war.[3] But such clarification is not without its challenges. As several commentators have noted, if we assign greater weight to rescuing innocent life or protecting human rights as a *causa belli*, we must assign less value to what has hitherto been the cardinal principle in the modern ethics of war: state sovereignty.[4]

In order to avoid violating state sovereignty as a means of settling international disputes or protecting human rights, policymakers often recommend sanctions as a way of nonviolently coercing a nation's leadership to abide by principles of international law or common morality. But on this point, pacifists and nonpacifists have yet to address definitional issues that surround such forms of coercion as an alternative to war. In particular, they must address the question: Are measures that impose socioeconomic hardships on a nation's citizenry as a way of coercing its leaders to comply with certain directives truly "nonviolent"?

In this essay, I will not pursue these issues directly. I mention them to highlight the importance of context and circumstances in ethics. Parts of the world are changing dramatically, and such changes cut across economic, cultural, religious, national, ethnic, and regional lines. Slowly and unpredictably, often violently, new configurations of power are emerging across the globe. As James M. Gustafson argues throughout *Ethics from a Theocentric Perspective*, how we describe parts, wholes, and their interrelation bears directly on how we conceive and apply normative ideals.[5] In the present context, changes in the distribution of power between and within nations are forcing ethicists to reconsider normative principles about entering war or using various methods of coercion to settle international disputes. When parts and wholes are reconfigured, ethical norms may need to be adjusted, or at least refined.

My aim in calling attention to parts, wholes, and their changing configurations in global affairs is also a prelude to a more ambitious goal. I wish to embark on a thought experiment about the morality of using force and coercion in a world of growing economic interdependence, nationalist aspirations, changing regional alliances, and increased awareness of ecological issues. In particular, my questions are:

How might interpretations and responses to international conflict be qualified when situated within the broad contours of ethics from a theocentric perspective?

What kinds of values and principles might receive greater emphasis, or a more pronounced profile, when placed within the parameters of Gustafson's theocentric ethics?

What traditional values might decrease in importance when qualified by an ethics of theocentrism?

What parts, wholes, and relations does a theocentric ethic emphasize, and how might they affect the way we construe international relations and occasions for conflict?

To keep this experiment within manageable limits, I will focus on the just-war tradition, the dominant approach in Western culture for evaluating the ethics of war. The overall goal will be to imagine the values that might receive greater or lesser prominence when qualified by ethics from a theocentric perspective, and to consider some methodological questions about how we might apply just-war tenets to real-life circumstances.[6] Accordingly, I will concentrate on the general values involved in just-war reasoning as well as the specific criteria. But before beginning, several qualifications are in order.

Five Caveats

First, while this experiment will focus on the just-war tradition, it is not without relevance to pacifists. Although pacifists forbid war, they can refer to just-war criteria to identify incongruities between political discourse and events in a particular war, especially when that discourse invokes just-war categories. As social critics, pacifists can use just-war tenets to accuse political leaders of moral hypocrisy.[7]

Pacifists also can appeal to the just-war tradition to reveal discrepancies between the principles of limited war and actual practices in a specific war, hoping to keep international conflict from becoming total war. Using just-war criteria in this way enables pacifists to follow the general mandate to make the world less violent.[8] For these reasons, pacifists have a vital interest not only in using just-war tenets, but also in ensuring that the just-war tradition is not co-opted by those who may wish to pitch political interests in moral terms. When co-optation occurs, just-war criteria can conceal the practice of total war, which is premised on values contrary to those of just-war theorists and pacifists alike.

Second, I do not wish to suggest that just-war criteria would exhaust the terms according to which a theocentric ethicist would evaluate a particular war. This point holds regardless of the extent to which the doctrine must be qualified by theocentrism. The just-war tradition enshrines what Gustafson calls presumptions, boundary terms, general rules, and "points to be considered" in an assessment of war.[9] These would contribute to the process of moral discernment, providing a set of terms that ought to inform a discriminating judgment.

Third, and in a related vein, an evaluation of a particular war would require a more elaborate method than is often associated with just-war reasoning. Calling for an expansive understanding of the time and space coordinates of moral conduct, Gustafson's theocentrism would require a careful interpretation of the relevant historical, sociological, economic, and political factors involved in any particular conflict. As he remarks, "Any explanation of a particularly nettlesome international situation, such as the perennial eruptions of violence in the Middle East, must take into account historical factors of political, economic, and religious sorts, as well as the sequence of particular crises such as the Holocaust and the 1948 War."[10] The same would be true for ethical assessments of such nettlesome situations. No deductive application of the just-war tradition to the circumstances of war would be sufficient.[11] In all likelihood, moreover, conclusions from a more expansive analysis would be qualified and cautious, seeking to provide counsel for responsible participation (or nonparticipation). They would not aim at making apodictic pronouncements from a detached vantage point.[12]

Fourth, while just-war tenets have wide currency in philosophical ethics today, they are not foreign to theology. With their roots in the writings of Augustine, Aquinas, and the Spanish scholastics, just-war criteria enshrine the attempt to craft a religious ethic responsive to problems in political life. Given that Gustafson's work represents one of the most significant and original contributions to theology in the United States, it behooves us to consider some of its implications for traditional Western ethics of war.

Fifth, the interpretation that follows is suggested but not entailed by ethics from a theocentric perspective. I do not expect Gustafson or others persuaded by his account to agree with what follows. But I am confident that a theocentric reconstruction of just-war criteria, with the caveats mentioned above, is possible. Careful consideration of this possibility can offer insights into the practical implications of ethics from a theocentric perspective; it may also shed light on some of the political problems facing us as we approach a new century.[13]

The Theocentric Presumption against War

The practical moral question from a theocentric perspective is: What is God enabling and requiring us, as participants in the interdependent patterns and processes of life, to be and to do? The general answer is: We are to relate ourselves and all things in a manner appropriate to their relations to God.[14] Gustafson adds that this theology is not meant to back an ethical theory that is already in place. Theology is not in the service of ethics; rather, ethics must follow from theology.

At the same time, Gustafson does not avow that ethics follows from theological principles in a strict, logical sense. Theological ideas provide the basis for ethics in that they accentuate certain values and principles, but the specific implications of theology for ethics are not derived deductively from obvious or self-evident first principles. In the process of moral reasoning, interpretation is necessary from beginning to end.

Gustafson is tireless in insisting that a theocentric perspective ought to widen the compass of what is typically conceived as a value (or set of values) in Western ethics. In particular, we are to relativize the importance of the human good and relocate our conception of that good in terms of the divine governance, God's ordering purposes. In theocentric ethics "there are fundamental requisites that can be perceived and must be taken into account not only for individual and interpersonal life but also for social institutional life and the life of the species; and not only for these but also for the proper relationships of human activity to the ordering of the natural world."[15] God's purposes, insofar as they might be divined from natural purposes and processes, do not necessarily include human flourishing as an end. "God is the source of human good," Gustafson remarks, "but does not guarantee it."[16] When we must ascertain how we ought to relate ourselves and all things in a manner that is appropriate to their relations with God, we are to look to the good of the natural order and heed the indicators that nature might provide in understanding the wider, ecological good. Hence a general imperative: "Act so that you consider all things never *only* as a means to your ends, or even to collective human ends."[17]

Methodologically, such an approach is unable to produce exceptionless moral rules, a morality of absolutes. This is so for two reasons.

First, according to Gustafson the natural order is not static and immutable; it is a dynamic ordering system. Directives that are inferred from patterns and processes in nature are tentative and subject to revision.[18] A view of nature as fixed and unchanging, characteristic of medieval natural-law theology, can produce action guides that are apodictic. But if we view nature as an ongoing process, our inferences about what is appropriate in relation to its patterns and processes cannot but be mutable.

Second, the ordering of the cosmos is not only dynamic, it lacks complete harmony. Although there is interdependence among things in the realm of nature (and society), "there is no guarantee that the service of one another issues in a desired outcome of each, or in the well-being of each. . . . The common good of the whole is never in perfect harmony with justifiable goods of its parts."[19] As a result, serving one good may require sacrificing another. Theocentrism includes a theory of moral tragedy; we cannot harmonize all of our pursuits of the good. Some conflicts are inevitable and irreconcilable.[20]

Instead of relying on absolute rules and the expectation of moral harmony, practical reasoning ought to be mindful of moral presumptions. Presumptions enshrine general rules and articulate values or principles that have great weight in their favor.[21] They cannot be overridden without strong justification. Which presumptions we invoke depends in large measure on how we interpret the relevant parts and wholes of a practical problem. Moral reasoning should maintain a sober recognition that some presumptions will compete with others for our allegiance; as I have said, for Gustafson the goal of harmony is elusive. Since the goods of parts and wholes do not necessarily harmonize, our presumptions are bound to clash.

These views cohere with and qualify one important approach to just-war reasoning, which begins with a presumption *against* war and injuring others.[22] Without further description, acts of suffering are typically associated with wrongful injury. At the very least, we feel compassion for those who suffer, and we feel alarm about their pain. This presumption designates a moral bias against war and injury. All else being equal, it is wrong to injure another person.

For the just-war theorist, however, this presumption against harm is not necessarily the last word about the ethics of war. Rather, in war a moral conflict arises between the duty not to harm and the duty to protect those who would otherwise be victims of harm.[23] The idea is that when someone needs protection against aggression, the duty not to harm may conflict with other duties, such as the duty to defend oneself or to assist others in need. The duty not to harm may be overridden by the obligation to protect oneself or third parties from aggression.[24]

Ethics from a theocentric perspective coheres with this general approach insofar as theocentrism views the loss of life, even for just purposes, as tragic. The basic idea is that killing to protect values like justice or innocent life involves us in trading off one value against another. Gustafson remarks, "The tragic character of many actions resides precisely in the fact that the legitimate pursuit of legitimate ends, or action in accordance with reasonable moral principles, entails severe losses to others—not only persons but other living things—and even sometimes diminishes the possibilities for development of future life and future generations of human beings."[25] Given the fact of interdependence, we must view such a loss as unfortunate, a sacrifice of some good on behalf of another. Abiding by one set of values requires losing others; the use of force is morally conflictual and complex. It can never be ethically tidy or without anguish.

Yet the presumption against war in a theocentric ethic would go further than these last comments imply. Given the damage to social sources of interdependence that frequently occurs in war—damage to socioeconomic infrastructures, cultural resources, family ties, and ethnic solidarity—the presumption against war would seem to be stronger than standard approaches have hitherto suggested. As we shall see, ethics from a theocentric perspective provides strong grounds for censuring acts of wanton destruction in war, especially when those acts are aimed at undermining sources of interdependence that are necessary for normal social life.

Moreover, and more important, given the importance of nonhuman goods (i.e., the environment) in a theocentric ethic, the destruction characteristically wrought by war would generate added presumptions against recourse to lethal force. Central to ethics from a theocentric perspective is a bias in favor of life, of the sources of natural interdependence, and perhaps biodiversity.[26] As a result, the "lethal" in "lethal force" would now have to be viewed within the wider compass. A theocentric perspective would deepen the importance of goods that are inevitably sacrificed in war. It accentuates goods—natural goods—that are intrinsically valuable, apart from their impact on human flourishing. Evaluative descriptions of war must thereby take into account the good of the patterns and processes of the natural world and social life. Stated differently, goods that are inevitably sacrificed in war would now stand within a new discursive configuration. In this way, ethics from a theocentric perspective qualifies our standard presumptions, placing them within a wider horizon.

At the same time, and cutting in the opposite direction, the good of protecting the interdependence, patterns, and processes of nature might create reasons for employing military force or methods of coercion. The good of nature can generate both a presumption against war *and* a set of reasons for considering coercive measures. For example, it is not inconceivable that, from a theocentric perspective, the use of force or coercion in response to ecological terrorism or the profligate destruction of natural resources is warranted. Nature, like nations and people, deserves protection from oppression. In order to see how this might be so, it will be instructive to turn to the criteria themselves, now situated within a new horizon of value. Before we do, however, let us consider an important case.

The Rain Forest

The case involves the ecological consequences of rain forest destruction. Covering 2 percent of the earth's surface, or 6 percent of the earth's land mass, rain forests house one-half of all plant and animal species. They are home to 40–50 percent of all life forms and as many as thirty million species of plants, animals, and insects.[27] Rain forests provide a warehouse of foods, genetic materials for agriculture, and a cornucopia of resources for pharmaceutical drugs: analgesics, antibiotics, cardiac drugs, enzymes, hormones, dysentery treatments, and diuretics, among others. Materials for rubber products, latex, resins, glues, natural oils, and gum are extracted from rain forest plants. Tropical forests provide a home to migratory birds in addition to indigenous wildlife throughout the year. Rain forests play a crucial role in the atmosphere because they hold vast reserves of carbon in their vegetation. When forests are burned, or when trees are felled and left to decay, the carbon is released as carbon dioxide into the atmosphere. This is the second-largest factor contributing to the greenhouse effect.[28]

Rain forests are being destroyed at an alarming rate, largely through farming, commercial logging, cattle raising, population resettlement, mineral excavation, dam construction, and oil production. The National Academy of Sciences claims that at least fifty million acres of rain forest are lost each year, an area equal to England, Scotland, and Wales combined. As a result, over fifty thousand species are driven to extinction annually. Scientists estimate that if current rates of deforestation continue, nearly all tropical forest ecosystems will be destroyed by the year 2030.[29]

Consider, more specifically, the devastating effects of oil production near the waters of the upper Ecuadorian Amazon, known as the *Oriente*. The *Oriente* is an especially lush rain forest, with a high level of biodiversity and with flora and fauna found nowhere else in the world. It is home to Yasuni National Park, a World Biosphere Area, with four to five thousand species of flowering plants, five hundred species of fish, six hundred species of birds, and 120 species of mammals. The *Oriente* also includes Cuyabeno Wildlife Reserve, where record levels of biodiversity have been registered. But this area is increasingly vulnerable to pollution as a result of oil extraction. In 1992 a 275,000-gallon oil spill gushed into the *Oriente*, and thirty ruptures of the pipeline have spilled 16.8 million gallons of crude oil into Ecuador's river systems during the last twenty years—50 percent more than spilled by the Exxon *Valdez*. Also, 4.5 million gallons of drilling by-products and toxic chemicals are dumped into Amazon tributaries weekly from oil producers. Because the *Oriente* lies at the headwaters of the Amazon system, spillage from oil fields contaminates waterways that flow into the main branch of the river and eventually into the Atlantic. Ecuador's record of rain forest destruction is abysmal: It has the highest rate of deforestation in South America, losing 2.3 percent of its forests annually, largely as the result of an expanding oil frontier. At the current rate, Ecuador's deforestation will be complete in fifteen years.

Working with the state oil company, Texaco is responsible for 88 percent of the region's oil production. Most of the oil pumped in Ecuador is shipped to the United States. Ecuadorian President Duran Ballen has shown no sign of concern. In 1994 he withdrew his country from OPEC to enable Ecuador to exceed OPEC's production restrictions, and he has awarded new oil licenses. Five areas of the *Oriente*, encompassing approximately three million acres, have been awarded to twelve companies, including Mobil and Amoco.[30]

In Central America, rain forests are victims of widespread cattle farming and beef production. About two-thirds of Central American farmland is devoted to cattle, largely in order for Americans to increase their consumption of low-cost hamburgers. The United States purchases three-fourths of all Central American beef exports, much of which goes to fast-food restaurants. In 1980 Peter Raven testified before a U.S. congressional subcommittee that since 1960 more than 25 percent of all Central American forests have been destroyed to produce beef. In Costa Rica, one-third of the country has been converted to pasture land since 1961. Ironically, beef consumption among the citizens of Nicaragua, El Salvador, Guatemala, and Costa Rica has dropped precipitously since 1961, even though beef production in those countries has tripled.[31] Typically, cattle ranchers in Central America clear out virgin timber with slash-and-burn techniques, raise cattle for a brief period, and then abandon the land. Such methods leave the landscape permanently degraded. (Nearly all cattle ranches created in the Amazon before 1978 have been abandoned.)[32]

On the other side of the globe, Japan has been involved in the rapacious destruction of Southeast Asian rain forests. The largest importer of tropical hardwoods in the world, Japan has involved itself in the construction of roads, dams, bridges, and plantations that degrade and deplete tropical forests. Particularly vulnerable are Sarawak and Sabah in Malaysian Borneo, from which Japan imports 90 percent of its timber. Mitsubishi Corporation owns 25 percent of Agusan Wood industries in the Philippines, which manufactures plywood, and 30 percent of Dalya Malaysia Sdn. Bhd. in Malaysia. The target of boycotts spearheaded by the Rainforest Action Network, Mitsubishi is considered "the world's worst corporate destroyer of tropical, temperate, and boreal forests."[33]

In North America, perhaps the most noteworthy incident involving rain forest degradation occurred in British Columbia. Almost 50 percent of the trees cut from the ancient rain forest of Clayoquot Sound on Vancouver Island's western coast are used to make phone books and newspapers. Pacific Bell, GTE, and the *New York Times* are the three chief purchasers of pulp from this area. MacMillan Bloedel, the supplier of pulp, was fined thirty-three times by the British Columbia Ministry of Forests between 1992 and 1994 for violating environmental regulations. GTE and Pacific Bell claim that they buy only sawmill byproducts and inferior wood from MacMillan Bloedel, but the firm estimates that about 20–25 percent of the trees it cuts go directly to paper.[34]

These incidents raise serious ethical questions about the claims of nature on the rest of humanity and political questions about the appropriate response from the rest of the world. At the very least, they raise questions about whether and how the exploitation of the world's rain forests can be brought to a halt and, in particular, whether coercion of some sort might be justified as a means of protecting environmental interests. With these questions in mind, let us turn to just-war criteria, situated within the broad contours of ethics from a theocentric perspective.

Just-War Criteria and Theocentrism

The just-war tradition is premised on the distinction between killing and murder. It presumes that some forms of killing are justified, namely, to defend individuals and communities from aggression. The human good is its center of value: Killing may be warranted if it is ordered toward protecting human life and the conditions in which human life is sustained and nurtured. But this justification implies some restrictions as well: Intentionally killing individuals who are not contributing to aggression goes beyond the prohibitions implied by the justification. In the effort to refine the ethics of war, theorists have labored since the time of Augustine to coordinate just-war tenets underneath two general categories, the *jus ad bellum* and the *jus in bello*.

Jus ad Bellum

The *jus ad bellum* is designed to answer the "when" or "whether" question: When, if ever, is resort to war ethically justified? Under what conditions may nations or communities have recourse to lethal force? The components within this category consist of several tenets, explained below.

The *jus in bello* is designed to answer the "how" or "methods" question: What methods are morally acceptable once recourse to war has been justified? Who (or what) are legitimate and illegitimate targets in war? How does one keep the killing in war from becoming murderous?

In its broadest outlines, *ad bellum* criteria provide the basis for justifying war, while *in bello* criteria articulate the morally acceptable methods that may be employed in war. Both sets of terms are necessary for an adequate understanding of the just-war tradition. Let us consider how they might be reconfigured within the broad contours of Gustafson's theocentric ethic, with an eye to the case of global rain forest deforestation and degradation.

Ad bellum criteria include the following: just cause, right intention, legitimate authority, last resort, proportionality, relative justice, and reasonable hope for success. We will examine these criteria in the paragraphs that follow.

JUST CAUSE

In its standard form, this condition justifies war in response to attacks against national sovereignty and human dignity. In these circumstances, the presumption against harm may be overridden—but only if we keep in mind additional *ad bellum* conditions (to be discussed below). War is not justifiable as an exercise of revenge, imperialist ambition, or domination.

In the ethical and policy literature, just cause generally turns on two values: state sovereignty and human rights. War may be used to protect a nation's right to govern itself; the just-war tradition distills a presumption against interference and intervention from without. War also may be used to protect human rights; just-war tenets may justify the use of force to keep vulnerable individuals or groups from being oppressed.

As I have noted, these two values stand in some tension with each other. The former principle allows nations to enter war when international boundaries have been trespassed by an aggressor. When it is viewed as the sole basis for justifying war, this principle creates a strong, perhaps absolute ban against intervention, even at the expense of protecting human rights that may be violated under a despotic regime. It would thereby prohibit intervening in another nation's affairs unless that nation has been attacked from without. The latter principle justifies war to protect or promote human dignity and conditions of human flourishing. When it is viewed as the sole basis for justifying war, this principle can lead to a strong ethic of interventionism, at the expense of national sovereignty. It would thereby allow intervening in another nation's affairs regardless of whether that nation has been attacked from without. The problem with the first principle is that it may encourage isolationism and excessive tolerance of tyrannies elsewhere; the problem with the second principle is that it may allow nations to assume the prerogative of policing the internal affairs of other regimes.

Attempts to develop a modern account of just cause seek to hold these two principles in balance and to mitigate the extremes toward which they could tend.[35] Perhaps the best known effort is Michael Walzer's work, *Just and Unjust Wars: A Moral Argument with Historical Illustrations*.[36] Walzer develops an account of just cause that places a strong, but not absolute, presumption against intervention, given the (almost absolute) value of state sovereignty. He calls this account the legalist paradigm. Stated briefly, this paradigm justifies recourse to lethal force in two cases: in wars of self-defense, and in wars of law enforcement by victims of aggression and by any other members of the international community.[37] By his account, Britain's use of force against Germany and the Allied cause in the Gulf War both stand within the legalist paradigm.[38] In each case, nations responded to the crime of violating political sovereignty—by Germany and Iraq, respectively.

According to Walzer, this paradigm is subject to four revisions, the last of which provides a muted affirmation of human rights.

First are *anticipations*: States may resort to military force "in the face of threats of war, whenever the failure to do so would seriously risk their territorial integrity or political independence."[39] In such circumstances, states may attack preemptively if they are able to do so.

Second are *secessions*: A group with territorial integrity within a nation secedes and establishes clear evidence of the existence of a community whose members are committed to independence. Moreover, they are able to show that they have a reasonable hope for establishing an autonomous state so long as their efforts are not impeded by the prior regime. In this case, interventions may be warranted to protect the fledgling community from the tyranny of what is in effect foreign rule; interventions are justified to protect nascent political processes.[40]

Third are *counterinterventions*: A nation may intervene in a civil war after a foreign party has intervened to lend support to one side, thereby shifting the balance of power. "As soon as one outside power violates the norms of neutrality and nonintervention," Walzer writes, "the way is open for other powers to do so."[41] Counterinterventions are justified not to win the conflict, but to equalize the effects of another nation's prior intervention, thereby "making it possible once again for the local forces to win or lose on their own."[42]

Fourth are *humanitarian interventions*: In this case, one nation enters another to rescue victims of ongoing, systematic oppression. In effect, those who oppress their own people "lose their right to participate in the normal (even in the normally violent) processes of domestic self-determination."[43] A humanitarian intervention is justified when it is a response to acts that shock "the conscience of [hu]mankind." But here, too, the justification implies a limitation: The intervening nation must enter into the causes of the oppressed and may not seek to promote its own interests. Humanitarian interventions ought to enshrine the same kind of respect for local autonomy that shapes the justification for intervening in secessions and cases of counterintervention.[44]

Theocentric ethics would have some quarrel with this account of just cause in its paradigmatic version and its four revisions; it would have some sympathies as well. As I have noted, an ethic of theocentrism may impose a heavier burden of proof on entering war, given the kind of presumption against war that follows from Gustafson's concern for social and ecological well-being. The prospective damages to patterns of social and natural interdependence wrought by battle may make war, on balance, unwarranted. The common goods of society or nature may require nations or communities to deny themselves recourse to lethal force to protect themselves or others from aggression.[45]

That is not to suggest that the human good is always to be subordinated to the good of preserving the processes of interdependence and nonhuman life. Circumstances matter in theocentrism, and no certain verdict is possible in theocentric ethics without reference to context. Moreover, Gustafson is clear that acts of (human) self-preservation can occupy an important place in an ethic of theocentrism. But the reasons for such acts differ notably from those found in much ethical literature.

Rather than concluding that the duty of self-defense is implied by the value of self-determination or human dignity, Gustafson suggests that self-preservation is a function of our duties to others. We have duties to ourselves, in other words, as a condition for participating in and serving the common good of others and the natural world as a whole. This argument might be understood as a derivative warrant for self-defense: The duty to defend the self derives from an understanding of what is necessary to participate in the ordering processes of nature and society.[46] As Gustafson remarks, "Our capacities to meet the needs of others are dependent upon our own strength; our first duties are to ourselves."[47]

This rationale applies to institutions no less than to individuals. Gustafson recurrently stresses the importance of social, political, and cultural institutions and our dependence on them for human well-being.[48] The institution of the state can be one of those institutions. Indeed, one searches in vain throughout *Ethics from a Theocentric Perspective* to find a remark critical of the modern nation-state or the international state security system. Institutions like the nation-state provide conditions for our participation in society and nature.[49] As Gustafson remarks, communities and institutions "are also, in Luther's term, 'masks of God' in the sense that their functions are necessary for the ordering of life in the world. To do what they should properly do they must be; they must have the means to exercise their functions."[50] Institutions cannot avoid the requirement "to develop the conditions needed for their participation. To be participants, institutions, like individual persons, have duties to themselves."[51] Taken together, these ideas about justified self-defense, political institutions, and the value of participation enable us to (re)conceive the duty of collective self-preservation within a theocentric framework.

But for Gustafson emphasis on the social conditions and interdependencies of existence means that "theocentric ethics will be weighted . . . more readily . . . on claims for the common good of a whole."[52] Such a view would relativize the value of state sovereignty and human dignity, placing them within a wider center of value: patterns of international cooperation, stability, and harmony. Theocentrism might thereby ask us to look not to the individual person or the nation-state as the principal unit of value, but to relations between nations, patterns of interdependence, cultural and economic exchanges, and historic alliances. These concerns would be relevant to judgments about just cause and decisions about whether entering war is warranted. In this way, subordinating the goods of human dignity or state sovereignty to concerns about international comity coheres with theocentrism's desire to situate the good of human flourishing within wider spheres of value.[53]

The case of the rain forest is meant to call attention to patterns of natural dependence, the value of which Gustafson affirms when distinguishing his views from most accounts of Western ethics. These patterns are relevant, he might add, to the occasions of conflict, and no account of war would be complete without properly considering the impact of natural events on human affairs. Given the fact that conflicts are often nourished by famine, drought, or lack of arable land, regard for environmental factors might enable policymakers to understand some occasions of conflict and to find remedies before outbreaks occur. Ethics from a theocentric perspective would thus welcome the "greening" of foreign affairs, in which policymakers seek to ascertain how soil erosion, rapid population growth, harvest patterns, water-table levels, or the expansion of deserts might destabilize regions around the world.[54]

Indeed, from a theocentric perspective, changes in natural and related cultural forces merit our attention independently of their impact on human beings. In theocentric ethics, it is not possible to say that human flourishing, the nation-state, or patterns of human interdependence are the obvious or only goods to be included in interpretations of conflict. We must also attend to the good of the ecological whole, and not simply for humanistic or self-interested reasons. The good of the environment in its own right places demands on us.

I have already noted how considering this good of the natural whole deepens a presumption against war. But it is also true that the good of nature enables us to add another category to Walzer's revisions of the legalist paradigm: *ecological intervention*, in which one nation enters another in order to rescue natural goods from ongoing, systematic tyranny or undue exploitation. Those who rule despotically over their natural heritage lose their right (or some of their right) to participate in the normal processes of domestic self-determination. A crude utilitarian approach to natural resources—an exploitative, opportunistic, selfish dominion over natural resources—receives some of the strongest negative remarks that one can find in Gustafson's *oeuvre*. Indeed, Gustafson labels such despotism idolatrous.[55] Ecological interventions might be justified, then, as a response to acts that shock "the conscience of humanity," especially as we become more ecologically sensitive. Here, as with humanitarian intervention, the intervening nation must enter into the causes of the oppressed (in this case, natural wholes). An ecological intervention would find sanction in terms that are analogous to the justification for humanitarian intervention. Nations may interfere with the internal affairs of other nations because the good of the political whole (the nation-state) must be subordinated to wider nonhuman, environmental wholes.

These remarks leave unanswered the practical question of how an ecological intervention might be carried out. Considerations of proportionality (to be discussed below) would suggest extreme caution about military action. The intervening nation(s) must first pursue alternatives to intervention, as I shall soon make clear. Intervening nations should use methods that avoid ecological damage; after all, it would make no sense to destroy a rain forest in order to save it. Theocentrism's affirmation of social and natural interdependence would suggest intervening first through diplomatic channels and then through well-targeted sanctions. In either case, theocentrism would counsel active diplomacy and engagement.

RIGHT INTENTION

This condition requires us to evaluate the purposes in pursuit of which war is being waged. *Intention* here denotes the aims or goals of war. Having a just cause, in other words, is not enough in the just-war tradition: We must also be intending peace as the goal of war. As G. E. M. Anscombe once argued, it is not enough to say that we are fighting against an unjust cause; we must also be fighting for justice and peace.[56]

Typically *peace* is understood in two different senses in the just-war literature: "military peace" and "political peace." The first category reflects a thin notion of right intention, interpreting *intention* to refer to the military goal of thwarting aggression and returning the situation to the *status quo ante bellum*. The advantage of this view is that it adopts a relatively modest set of purposes, in keeping with the politics and ethics of limited war. A robust notion of right intention, in contrast, involves more than removing aggressors from foreign territory or ending hostilities. It also requires nations to consider how to reduce the occasions of future hostility and establish genuinely peaceful conditions between nations and communities.

A thick rendition of right intention, in other words, includes the political as well as the military dimensions of war and peace. Seen in this way, a robust understanding of right intention requires us to ask: What political arrangements will emerge in the wake of war, and to what extent will such arrangements mark an improvement in justice and peace? Here *peace* is understood in terms of just and harmonious relations, habits of trust and good will, and the equitable sharing of power.

Given its emphasis on patterns of interdependence and social relations, ethics from a theocentric perspective would find good reasons to endorse a robust interpretation of peace. This latter notion, echoing theocentrism, expresses a concern for establishing rightly ordered relationships. The purposes of war ought to include efforts to produce cooperative arrangements and social ties with an eye to the good of future generations and the environment as a whole. Merely ending military confrontation would be insufficient in pursuing the goal of peace.

Yet it should be added that, from the vantage point of theocentric ethics, neither military nor political peace seems wholly adequate. In both cases, the center of value is the human good. A theocentric perspective enjoins us to order our purposes toward maintaining or constructing "the proper relations of things to each other, of parts to various wholes, in the light of what we understand the divine governance to be in the various conditions set by human finitude."[57] At the very least, theocentrism suggests that the aims of war, and of political activity in general, would do well to heed human and nonhuman goods. Peace and justice would thereby include consideration of the justice owed to the patterns and processes of interdependence, including those patterns within the realm of nature.

Seen in this way, theocentrism frames right intention within a wider discursive configuration when compared with conventional approaches. It thereby adds merit to the idea that ecological interventions may be warranted under well-defined circumstances insofar as such interventions can be ordered toward proper relations of human and nonhuman goods in light of our understanding of the divine governance. Moreover, as we shall see, right intention construed within a theocentric framework suggests that acts of wanton destruction in war, especially those with ecological implications, deserve special censure.[58]

LEGITIMATE AUTHORITY

This criterion forbids resort to war by private individuals or paramilitary groups acting on their own initiative. It permits only those who are responsible for the public order to declare war and marshal a defense. But given the kinds of causes I have mentioned, those who are responsible for the public order may vary.

In the legalist paradigm, legitimate authority would fall to representatives of those nations defending themselves or participating in the enforcement of international law. But amendments to the paradigm might shift responsibility away from leaders of sovereign states to international agencies like the United Nations. One's sense of membership might likewise shift from the nation-state to environmental groups who can appeal to UN agencies to take action, or who might coordinate grassroots action against nations or firms implicated in environmental destruction. When causes become international in scope, cutting across sovereign boundaries or national interests, the need for international authority increases. Causes that reflect global interests might do well to rely on international agencies first.

LAST RESORT

Perhaps more than any other just-war criterion, this condition crisply articulates the presumption against war and injury. It holds that public authorities must exhaust all peaceable means of settling disputes within their reasonable reach before they can justifiably resort to war. If successful defense of a just cause is reasonably possible according to nonviolent methods, then there is a duty to use them.

I have already mentioned how theocentrism could articulate a presumption against war. It is a corollary of this presumption to articulate the general caution about entering war expressed in the criterion of last resort. Once again, theocentrism would call attention to the prospective dangers to our social and natural surroundings.

Recently this condition has been the focus of considerable discussion. For example, before the outbreak of the Gulf War, the U.S. Catholic bishops urged U.S. policymakers to continue the course of "peaceful pressure" in the form of economic sanctions as an alternative to war.[59] They argued against going to war in light of a strong presumption against force and emphasized the criterion of last resort. Their remarks bring us to a central problem surrounding last resort: whether sanctions constitute a nonviolent alternative to war.

On this point, it is by no means clear that sanctions find warrant from a theocentric perspective. Sanctions are meant to place pressure on a country's infrastructure, subverting the conditions of interdependence on which ordinary people rely. The kinds of suffering wrought in countries subject to sanctions are clear and tangible; otherwise sanctions would not be used. Sanctions are designed to cripple the "externalities" of human existence, which Gustafson recurrently calls to our attention as vital for understanding the full parameters of moral agency. Lacking fuel (or revenue acquired from selling fuel), tools, technological hardware, natural resources, construction materials, or communication equipment seriously impairs a society's ability to function. Sanctions harm individuals by attacking the backbone of their common good. Given the emphasis that theocentrism places on the conditions of interdependence for human life, it would be easy to label the use of sanctions "violent." If so, then ethics from a theocentric perspective could be strongly critical of sanctions as a "nonviolent" alternative to war.

Yet theocentrism might not rule out all forms of sanctions, especially those that target companies or organizations responsible for heinous activity. Boycotting trade with corporations involved in or directly profiting from rain forest destruction, for example, would not harm nations or communities indiscriminately. The goal would be to place pressure on those agencies responsible for widespread ecological problems, seeking to call attention to their activities and to cripple their capacity to function.

PROPORTIONALITY

As an *ad bellum* criterion, proportionality requires one to ascertain whether the prospective suffering, the costs incurred in war, will be balanced by the values that are being defended. When we think in proportionate terms, we ask: Is the war morally worth the risk? What losses to a nation or to the world can be sustained given the values war is seeking to defend?

In theocentrism, this condition is arguably the most important when determining whether to enter war. It is certainly the condition that is most tangibly qualified by the values to which Gustafson appeals. Given the wider horizon of value in theocentric ethics, proportionality would require us to weigh more than losses of human goods when considering the risks of war. Instead, we must make prospective judgments about the loss of social and natural wholes, and whether such risks are worth incurring in pursuit of a just cause. Central to a theocentric concern would be whether a nation (or group of nations) would be risking a disproportionate amount of natural and social goods by embarking on war.

RELATIVE JUSTICE

This criterion holds that no state may act as if it possesses "absolute justice," that neither side in war may claim to be the sole possessor of justice. Rather, justice is relative: On balance, one side is able to claim greater justice in defense of its cause.

In many ways this criterion is less a rule to constrain action than a virtue-term, aimed to qualify our dispositions and affections. The main idea is to limit the kinds of self-righteous language that can motivate soldiers and citizens, to humanize war by reminding us that the other side should not be demonized during the course of battle.

Both sides carry out acts of valor and virtue, and both sides make moral (and other) errors. Demonizing the enemy makes it easier to develop a sanctimonious attitude, the idea that "God is on our side." Relative justice is meant to underwrite the notion that neither side is wholly righteous—or, for that matter, unrighteous. In this way, the just-war tradition enshrines attitudes that distinguish it from holy war.

Echoing these ideas, theocentric ethics enjoins a view of moral ambiguity and complexity. From a theocentric perspective, killing another involves moral trade-offs, sacrificing the good of another for the sake of justice or care.[60] Such a loss illustrates our conditions of finitude and the tragic outcomes of our moral choices. For this reason, sanctimonious rhetoric about killing in war is inadmissible from a theocentric perspective. Killing is a sacrifice, a loss to the total matrix of being. The destruction in war to social and natural conditions of life, moreover, ought to occasion mournful regret.

REASONABLE HOPE FOR SUCCESS

A practical criterion, this condition forbids futile fighting. Although it may permit a defense of very noble values against tremendous odds, it is meant to prevent irrational uses of force. Upon entering and throughout war, we are to assess the relative effectiveness of using force.

Several issues arise about how to view this condition in relation to other criteria. For example, how one approaches the condition of reasonable hope for success depends on how one defines right intention. Intentions to remove an army from one's sovereign boundaries (military peace) generate different expectations about what will count as "success" than do intentions to produce right relations and conditions for harmony (political peace). If we increase our goals or purposes, in other words, we inflate the burdens of successful action.

Theocentric ethics would reconfigure this criterion with two ideas in mind. First, as I have indicated, Gustafson's account of duties to the self would support the general caution against futile fighting. The fact that we have a general obligation to keep ourselves in being as a condition of serving others would counsel against entering wars that look to be suicidal.

Second, the thicker rendition of right intention implied by theocentrism suggests that we consider reasonable hope for success in correlative terms. That is, given the importance of producing right relations as the overriding intention of war, we ought to ask whether such goals are reasonably possible before we enter war.

Jus in Bello

In bello criteria, establishing the moral limits to the use of force, are discrimination and proportionality. They are typically applied according to the rule of double effect.

DISCRIMINATION

This criterion forbids the intentional attacking of civilians (noncombatants). In its conventional form, it has two distinctions. First is the distinction between combatants and noncombatants. Combatants are those who materially cooperate with the war effort—for example, soldiers and those working for war-related industries (e.g., bomb factories). Noncombatants are those who are not contributing materially to the war—healthcare workers, teachers, farmers, telecommunications workers, shopkeepers, clothing manufacturers, children, the disabled, and the sick, for example. They are "innocent" in the sense that they are not implicated in the material efforts to prosecute the war.

Second is the distinction between intentional (i.e., purposeful) and foreseen, but unintentional, effects of an act.

Taken together, these distinctions produce the verdict that intentional attacks against noncombatants are murderous. Such attacks are directed against people against whom defense is unnecessary and therefore unwarranted. The foreseen, unintentional loss of innocent life passes the test of discrimination, but it is subject to scrutiny required by the other *in bello* criterion, proportionality.

PROPORTIONALITY

As an *in bello* criterion, proportionality typically requires us to balance the foreseen, unintended losses against the values that are defended in a particular act of war. Is the good that is being pursued outweighed by the unintended losses that may reasonably be expected? Tactics are immoral when the foreseen, unintended loss of life outweighs the defended values, even if those tactics are discriminate.

Ethics from a theocentric perspective would insist that these tenets function as "boundary conditions." Such conditions identify proscriptions of conduct, limits beyond which we may not proceed. They follow from what is perceived to be our proper ends. "If one first establishes ends," Gustafson writes, "then boundary conditions are indications of limits within which the ends ought to be pursued."[61] What is valued, or the ends that are sought, affect which boundaries are established and how they are drawn.[62] Accordingly, theocentrism's attention to social and natural interdependence—and the intention in war to preserve and protect such interdependence—suggest that boundary conditions (discrimination and proportionality) would take social and natural wholes into account.

By way of contrast, consider some of the damaging effects of the Allied bombing of Iraq during the Gulf War. Within a month of the onset of war, Baghdad was without water and electricity. For those who failed to stockpile food early, nourishment was scarce. The sewage system overflowed, creating the danger of widespread disease. Citizens were forced to cut down trees for fuel; reports indicate that the city's infrastruc-

ture as a whole was virtually destroyed.[63] The 300,000 barrel-a-day oil refinery in Be-
jii in northern Iraq, far from the war's chief theater of operations, was not bombed until the final days of the air war.[64] This fact raises questions about whether late bombing missions over Iraq were undertaken to defend legitimate Allied interests. The UN
report after the war described the landscape of Iraq as "post-apocalyptic" and warned
that it threatened to reduce "a rather highly urbanized and mechanized society to a
pre-industrial age."[65] After the war, a Harvard public health team reported that the lack
of electricity, fuel, and transportation links in Iraq led to acute malnutrition and epidemic levels of cholera and typhoid. It was predicted that at least 170,000 children
under five years of age would die in 1992 from the delayed effects of the Allied
bombing.[66]

These data raise moral concerns about the damage to Iraq's infrastructure—in particular, whether water supplies and electrical sources, vital for ordinary human life, are
proper targets in war. Those who construe the "delayed" loss of civilian life as an indirect effect of military targeting might nonetheless wonder if such effects are sufficiently foreseeable as to be morally dubious. Such events require us to assess morally
the damage to "externalities" of existence, the material conditions for livelihood, in
the war against Iraq.

The Allies were not alone in committing acts that would be questioned from a theocentric perspective. Iraqi soldiers carried out direct attacks aimed at ruining the natural
environment, a campaign of ecological terrorism. In one instance, Hussein's troops created an oil spill in the Persian Gulf that was reported to be one hundred miles long and
ten to twenty miles wide. In another, retreating Iraqi soldiers set hundreds of Kuwaiti
oil wells ablaze, producing thick clouds of smoke that stretched from Turkey to Iran.

Acts of profligate destruction find no sanction among just-war theorists.[67] But
given its conventional emphasis on the human good, the just-war tradition has few resources for censuring acts aimed at poisoning the environment *as an intrinsic wrong*.
Theocentric ethics, in contrast, would deem such acts a violation of basic boundary
conditions. Its emphasis on social sources of interdependence would raise serious questions about the morality of these acts by the Allies and Iraqis. Theocentrism suggests
that we view indiscriminate acts not merely in terms of their direct effects on persons,
but also in terms of the social and natural sources of human life. Moreover, viewing
nature as a good in itself, theocentrism would censure ecological terrorism as a woe-
ful act in its own right, apart from its effects on human flourishing.

These examples are meant to illustrate how *in bello* criteria, theocentrically recon-
strued, would incorporate a broader set of values than is conventionally the case. Those
values would include sources of interdependence and the nonhuman good. The principle of discrimination would forbid acts that attack human life by intentionally injuring the externalities of existence. The principle of proportionality would ask us to
weigh the value of nonhuman goods in calculations about what may be foreseeably
risked in pursuit of specific tactics.

Conclusion

A nettlesome question in just-war ethics turns on the question of sufficiency: How many conditions must be satisfied for participation in war to be justified? What happens when some criteria are satisfied and others are not? For example, how do we assess a war that has satisfied just cause, right intention, and legitimate authority, but was entered into hastily, rashly, and without due regard for proper means?

On this point, Gustafson would advise against expecting our terms and conditions to harmonize. Moral experience does not admit of tidy ethical judgments. Instead we must pay careful attention to circumstances and rely on our intuitions, properly disciplined by the relevant criteria and data. No less than other moral problems, war is an arena of moral ambiguity, trade-offs, and tragedy. We ought to attend to the good of various wholes, and their possible relations, with fear and trembling.

Such an approach does not counsel timidity in the task of practical reasoning, but a sober recognition of the wider purposes to which human action should be ordered and how those purposes ought to affect our construal of the morally relevant features of a problem. I have sought here to indicate how those purposes would qualify just-war tenets, conventionally understood. In some areas, a theocentric perspective broadens what is normally considered obligatory in just-war reasoning, as the case of ecological intervention illustrates. In others areas, theocentrism deepens what is normally viewed as the proper limits of war, as we see in a reconstructed account of *in bello* principles. In either case, our duties and limits are placed within a theocentric horizon of value.

Gustafson's theology qualifies our ethical conventions, putting some values in a more prominent profile. A just war is not inconceivable, at least in principle, from within a theocentric framework. But just-war criteria would be reconfigured and the verdicts they might help produce would be nuanced and contextually bound. Such are the requirements of moral discernment informed by theocentrism's understanding of God, the patterns of natural and social interdependence, and the conditions of finitude for human agency.

Notes

I wish to thank Judy Granbois and David H. Smith for their comments on an earlier draft of this essay, Jenny Girod for an instructive conversation about Gustafson's ethics, and Lisa Sideris for research assistance.

1. I say *communities* rather than *nations*, given the fact that defining state sovereignty is difficult in some regions in which conflict has occurred (e.g., Chechnya). See Barbara Crossette, "What Is a Nation?" *New York Times*, 26 December 1994, 5.

2. I have commented on the implications of such changes for pacifists and just-war theorists in Richard B. Miller, "Casuistry, Pacifism, and the Just-War Tradition in the Post-Cold War

Era," in *Peacemaking: Moral and Policy Challenges for a New World*, ed. Gerard F. Powers, Drew Christiansen, S.J., and Robert T. Hennemeyer (Washington, D.C.: United States Catholic Conference, 1994): 199–213.

3. One exception to this pattern is the work of Paul Ramsey, who placed rescue, or selfless care, at the center of his account of just-war ethics. See Paul Ramsey, *The Just War: Force and Political Responsibility* (New York: Charles Scribner's Sons, 1968).

4. For discussions, see Russell Sizemore, "Just Cause and New World Order: Sovereignty, Rights, and International Comity," *Annual*, Society of Christian Ethics (1992): 173–99; Stanley Hoffmann, "A New World and Its Troubles," in *Sea Changes: American Foreign Policy in a World Transformed*, ed. Nicholas X. Rizopoulos (New York: Council on Foreign Relations, 1990), 274–92; J. Bryan Hehir, "Just-War Theory in a Post-Cold War World," *Journal of Religious Ethics* 20 (fall 1992): 237–57.

5. James M. Gustafson, *Ethics from a Theocentric Perspective*, 2 vols. (Chicago: University of Chicago Press, 1981–1984).

6. My language of "profiling" and "qualifying" ethics is meant to echo Gustafson's own account of how theocentrism relates to conventional principles or values. See Gustafson, *Ethics*, 2:1–22 and passim.

7. One recent example of a pacifist drawing on just-war criteria is Stanley Hauerwas, "Pacifism, Just War, and the Gulf," *First Things* (May 1991): 40.

8. Yet many pacifists do not adopt pacifism on the basis of this mandate, as Hauerwas argues. See ibid., 39 and passim.

9. These terms shape Gustafson's understanding of the components of practical reasoning or moral discernment. I shall show their relevance to the just-war tradition below. For a discussion of these terms, see Gustafson, *Ethics*, 2:302–15.

10. Ibid., 2:14.

11. Gustafson describes the various features of moral discernment within a theocentric ethic in ibid., 1:333–42.

12. Ibid., 2:315: "The function of the ethician is to broaden and deepen the capacities of others to make morally responsible choices."

13. Gustafson remarks on war as a historical event and describes the kinds of responses to which it often gives rise in ibid., 1:211–12.

14. Ibid., 1:327; 2:279.

15. Ibid., 1:339; see also 1:88, 95, 96, 99, 113, 240, 308, 317. As this citation makes plain, at times Gustafson speaks as if reference to social and institutional wholes qualifies the notions of moral agency typically assumed in standard accounts of ethics. At other times, he calls attention to natural or environmental wholes as defining the proper horizon for human activity. But these two appeals are distinct, and only the latter, strictly speaking, serves as a principle for criticizing anthropocentrism. *Appeals to the social and institutional wholes qualify individualism, not anthropocentrism.*

16. James M. Gustafson, *A Sense of the Divine: The Natural Environment from a Theocentric Perspective* (Cleveland: Pilgrim Press, 1994), 48.

17. Ibid., 106 (emphasis in original).

18. Gustafson, *Ethics*, 1:316; 2:302.

19. Ibid., 2:302; see also Gustafson, *A Sense of the Divine*, passim.

20. Gustafson, *Ethics*, 2:19.

21. Ibid., 2:307. It should be added that Gustafson equivocates about the relationship between presumptions and general rules. In places he conflates the two and at times he speaks of them as distinct. Cf. ibid., 2:303, 311.

22. See Ralph Potter, "The Moral Logic of War," in *War in the Twentieth Century: Sources in Theological Ethics*, ed. Richard B. Miller (Louisville, Ky.: Westminster John Knox, 1992), 198–214; James F. Childress, "Just-War Criteria," in *War in the Twentieth Century*, 351–72; U.S. Catholic Bishops, *The Challenge of Peace: God's Promise and Our Response* (Washington, D.C.: U.S. Catholic Conference, 1983), pars. 71–80; Richard B. Miller, *Interpretations of Conflict: Ethics, Pacifism, and the Just-War Tradition* (Chicago: University of Chicago Press, 1991), 16–18, 39–46, 161–63.

23. For an alternative interpretation of the logic of just-war tenets, see Paul Ramsey, *Speak Up for Just War or Pacifism: A Critique of the United Methodist Bishops' Pastoral Letter, "In Defense of Creation,"* with an epilogue by Stanley Hauerwas (State Park: Pennsylvania State University Press, 1988), 109–10.

24. See Childress, "Just-War Criteria," 352–54, 358.

25. Gustafson, *Ethics,* 2:21.

26. See, ibid., chap. 1.

27. For these and other data, see Catharine Caufield, *In the Rainforest: Report from a Strange, Beautiful, Imperiled World* (Chicago: University of Chicago Press, 1991), 59–60.

28. Ibid., 71; Norman Myers, *The Primary Source: Tropical Forests and Our Future* (New York: Norton, 1992), chaps. 3, 4 and passim. The leading factor is fossil fuel consumption.

29. Caufield, *In the Rainforest*, 37–38 and passim.

30. See *Rainforest Action Network Factsheet* 10A (June 1994).

31. Caufield, *In the Rainforest*, 108–9; see also Myers, *The Primary Source*, chap. 7.

32. Caufield, *In the Rainforest*, 112.

33. *Rainforest Action Network Factsheet* 1B (1995).

34. *Rainforest Action Network Action Alert* 107 (April 1995).

35. For a discussion, see Sizemore, "Just Cause and New World Order."

36. Michael Walzer, *Just and Unjust Wars: A Moral Argument with Historical Illustrations*, 2d ed. (New York: Basic Books, 1992).

37. Ibid., 58–63.

38. Walzer is more reserved about this second judgment. See ibid., xi–xxiii.

39. Ibid., 85.

40. Ibid., 91–95.

41. Ibid., 97.

42. Ibid., 101.

43. Ibid., 106.

44. Ibid., 104, 107.

45. Something like this presumption is developed by the U.S. Catholic bishops in their discussion of the prospective effects of war in *The Challenge of Peace*. The bishops develop their caution about war within an expansive understanding of the "whole" to be considered in social ethics, although they eschew explicit attention to the common good of nature. Nonetheless, those concerns are implied in their cautions about recourse to nuclear war. I unpack the developments in Catholic teaching that help shape the bishops' presumption against war in Miller, *Interpretations of Conflict*, chap. 2.

46. Ramsey develops a similar argument, but without reference to the common good of nature. See Paul Ramsey, *Basic Christian Ethics* (New York: Charles Scribner's Sons, 1950), 177.

47. Gustafson, *Ethics,* 2:231.

48. See, ibid., 1:209–22; 2:292–98.

49. Ibid., 2:297.

50. Ibid., 2:287.

51. Ibid., 2:289.

52. Ibid., 2:19.

53. See Sizemore, "Just Cause and New World Order," 190–99 for a discussion of international comity as an alternative to state sovereignty and human rights in considerations of just cause.

54. For a discussion, see Steven Greenhouse, "The Greening of American Diplomacy," *New York Times,* 9 October 1995, A6.

55. Gustafson, *Sense of the Divine,* 85.

56. See G. E. M. Anscombe, "The Justice of the Present War Examined," in *War in the Twentieth Century,* 129.

57. Gustafson, *Ethics,* 2:2.

58. In the just-war tradition, *right intention* is an expansive category, since intentions of policymakers will set the overall framework within which specific plans will be conceived and carried out. With that in mind, it is important to note Gustafson's remark that "it is with reference to purposes that a theocentric perspective makes the greatest difference to moral activity." I say this to call attention to the fact that, given the importance of purposes to theocentric ethics *and* to just-war criteria, the implications of theocentrism for my thought experiment are considerable indeed. For Gustafson on purposes, see *Ethics,* 2: 2–3.

59. U.S. Catholic Bishops, "Letter to President Bush: The Persian Gulf Crisis," in *War in the Twentiety Century,* 445–48.

60. Gustafson, *Ethics,* 2:21.

61. Ibid., 2:305; Gustafson uses the principle of discrimination to illustrate boundary conditions (ibid. 2:306).

62. Ibid., 2:306.

63. Dilip Ganguly, "Baghdadis More and More Demoralized by Raids," *New York Times,* 22 February 1991, 6A.

64. Barton Gellman, "Allied Air War Struck Broadly in Iraq," *Washington Post,* 23 June 1991, 1A, 16A.

65. *New York Times,* 23 March 1991, cited in Theodore Draper, "The True History of The Gulf War," *New York Review of Books,* 23 January 1992, 40.

66. Gellman, "Allied Air War," 16A; see also George Lopez, "Not So Clean," *Bulletin of the Atomic Scientists* 47 (September 1991): 30–35.

67. Among just-war theorists, mention of ecological issues and the effects on the Allies' bombing on the infrastructure of Iraq was scant during and after the Gulf War. For two exceptions, see James Turner Johnson, "Just War Tradition and the War in the Gulf," in *War in the Twentieth Century,* 451–62, and John Langan, "An Imperfectly Just War," in *War in the Twentieth Century,* 463–65.

Chapter 21

Comparative Ethics and Intercultural Human-Rights Dialogues: A Programmatic Inquiry

SUMNER B. TWISS

Introduction

A colleague and I recently proposed a new intercultural venue for comparative religious ethics, illustrating our vision with reference to contemporary controversy about the status and role of international human rights in relation to cultural moral traditions.[1] In this essay I intend to extend and deepen this illustration by first characterizing a class of intercultural human-rights dialogues, and then developing further a constructive framework that may mitigate some of their tensions. For the purposes of this discussion and governed by my own experience, I am confining my attention to nongovernmental dialogues designed to bring together scholars and representatives of cultural moral traditions with scholars of human rights and human-rights activists from various parts of the world.[2] While international and intercultural in content, these dialogues, as contrasted with, for example, the UN-sponsored variety, are much smaller in scope, much less public and world-historical in character, and, I believe, more revealing of how and why human rights may or may not "fit" with diverse cultural traditions.

Three broad issues have consistently arisen in these dialogues. The first issue is whether international human rights are relative only to particular cultural traditions (e.g., Western liberal traditions), or whether they are properly conceived as universal and interculturally applicable. An especially significant aspect of this issue as I have encountered it is whether the perception of some scholars about an incompatibility between universal human rights and particular cultural traditions is sound. The second issue is how international human rights and their justification ought to be construed within intercultural human-rights dialogues. A particularly salient aspect of this issue is whether it is possible and helpful to distinguish between levels or arenas of justification—e.g., pragmatic consensus at the international level versus forms of internal justification at the cultural level. The third issue is how one ought to respond to and manage the difficult hermeneutical and moral problems that arise when different cultural visions and idioms encounter one another in dialogue. And a large element of this issue is how to adjudicate tensions among seemingly divergent understandings of the nature of person and community. I will be addressing all of these issues in what follows.

Characterizing Intercultural Human-Rights Dialogues

The dialogues under consideration present a range of aims falling between and including at one pole the practical aim of encouraging the uptake of international human rights into the social ethos of cultural traditions, and at the other the scholarly aim of analyzing and comparing cultural moral traditions with international human rights. The practical and scholarly poles often interact to produce a variety of intermediate hybrid goals with both practical and scholarly dimensions, for example: the revitalization or reform of one or more cultural traditions based on scholarly analysis of their moral idioms and assessment of their conceptual resources for the inclusion or strengthening of human rights; the prompting of self-criticism of human-rights thinking and practice by comparing these with the visions of and paths to a good society represented by certain cultural moral traditions; and with human rights as a touchstone, attempting to combine aspects of two or more cultural traditions (e.g., Eastern and Western) into a new moral and social vision that constructively addresses how people should live together in society. Needless to say, these illustrative aims are neither exhaustive of the possibilities nor mutually exclusive, but they are typical and should whet our collective moral imagination.

Two broad methodological programs often appear to be at work in intercultural human-rights dialogues. These programs are ideal types that are frequently mixed in practice. One program is what I call the hermeneutic-constructive, involving the use of empathetic understanding and appreciation of cultural moral traditions to pursue in a disciplined way one or another of the aims identified above. The discipline conforms to a respectful dialogue of equals, representing different cultural traditions (or alternative perspectives on one tradition), where the assumptions of one tradition (or perspective) are critically exposed to the standpoint of others in the attempt to solve the shared sociomoral problems identified by the subject matters of international human rights. The other program is what I call the social-critical, which overlaps with the hermeneutical-constructive but focuses particular attention on the social-historical forces and institutional factors that shape and constrain cultural moral traditions. This program keeps real-world factors at the forefront in trying to identify elements of viable social visions and humane forms of life that are consistent with international human rights. Participants working within these two programs employ various over-lapping tools of analysis and argument, though the first tends to emphasize textual criticism and interpretation, intellectual history, and philosophy, while the second tends to emphasize sociological and political analysis.

Participants working within both methodological programs employ a range of typical strategies of inquiry, three of which appear particularly important.[3] One strategy involves the systematic identification of convergences and/or analogues between cultural moral traditions and international human rights. This sort of strategy can take a number of specific forms depending on what sorts of analogues are regarded as important or fruitful. Examples include basic moral principles (e.g., principle of reciprocity); fundamental moral intuitions about the dignity and equality of persons; practice-correlates to specific human rights (e.g., systemic priority of satisfying basic social and economic needs); apparent entailments of a tradition's normative moral theory (e.g., strong correlativity of virtues and duties, on the one hand, and prerequisite freedoms to express or fulfill these, on the other); apparent "liberal" elements of cultural traditions as resources for developing an internal human-rights subtradition (e.g., notions of autonomy, communal self-governance); and moral limits on law and state (e.g., notions of due process, justified rebellion). Often the variants of this sort of strategy involve what Abdullahi An-Naᶜim has called the retrospective enlightened interpretation of traditional cultural norms: that is, from a perspective informed by international human rights, trying to highlight and recast certain traditional norms and categories as conforming with, converging on, or implicitly "intending" certain human concepts and norms as currently understood in the international context.

A second strategy of inquiry involves the systematic analysis of the moral, social, and philosophical matrix of a given tradition—in terms of, for example, its conceptions of self, community, the good, and their interrelation—and then comparing this matrix point by point with other cultural traditions (e.g., forms of liberalism and communitarianism) as well as with the international human-rights regime (often perceived as a Western moral construct and recommendation to the rest of the world). Such comparison is then followed by assessments, guided largely by the philosophical and political leanings of particular participants, of both the traditional matrix of interest and the other traditions used in the comparison, as to whether and how far both sides of the comparison measure up to the content and "spirit" of international human rights.

A third strategy involves systematically comparing elements of normative cultural traditions against the historical record and social reality of the societies in which they are embedded. Discerned similarities and discrepancies are diagnosed in the light of international human-rights norms, guided by the following sorts of questions: What in the normative tradition is similar to human-rights norms, and what is different in

this regard? If similarities are found, did these shape social and legal practices and institutions, and to what extent? If not, what causal factors were/are at work in preventing this (e.g., countervailing cultural traditions, economic constraints, realities of
political power)? The answers to such questions are then followed by practical recommendations encouraging those aspects of the tradition and those social practices and
institutions that conform, whether explicitly or implicitly, to the recognition of international human rights.

Crucial to the successful use of these methodological programs and strategies of inquiry in intercultural human-rights dialogue is a reasonable degree of consistency or
coherence in participants' assumptions about, for example, the nature of cultural moral
traditions, and ground rules for how such dialogue ought to be conducted. Other presuppositions are also at work, but these two are sufficient to illustrate what I mean.

Participants in such dialogues, regardless of their disciplinary backgrounds, display
a remarkable agreement about the nature of cultural moral traditions.[4] A cultural moral
tradition appears to be understood as a worldview expressed through a set of values or
way of life that provides its members with a reasonably coherent and comprehensive
understanding of the world and the place and role of human beings (and often other
sentient beings) within that world. In addition, a moral tradition is understood as a historically extended accumulation of practical wisdom that provides its members with
prescriptions and recommendations about how best to live good personal and social
lives within the world approached from its comprehensive understanding and set of
values. In this way a moral tradition shapes its members' personal and social identity
and contextually guides their experience, behavior, and reasoning.

At the same time participants in human-rights dialogues also assume that moral traditions have the capacities to be self-critical and to change in response not only to internal problems and incoherencies that may emerge over time but also to new problems and situations that may be externally encountered, including interaction with
other cultural traditions. Thus, it is assumed that moral traditions, while perhaps having a degree of conservative inertia, are neither static nor totally closed on themselves.
Moreover, participants in the dialogues appear also to assume that traditions and communities share similar sorts of practical moral and social problems and tasks as well as
similarities of thought and experience sufficient to gain access to one another across
cultural boundaries. Examples of these practical similarities range from communal
moral traditions' functionally regulating in some effective way internal issues of, for example, violence, deception, dispute-settlement, satisfaction of basic material needs, and
protection of important "natural" interpersonal relations (systemic problems needing
to be addressed if a tradition is to fulfill its function and maintain itself over time), to
their also addressing in some effective manner external issues commonly imposed on
them by an increasingly complex and interdependent world—e.g., environmental
problems and international violence.

Another type of assumption—about how intercultural dialogues ought to be conducted—is specified by a reasonably stable set of ground rules that guides in a deeply implicit way the diological process. Examples of such ground rules include: provisional acceptance of the existing standards of international human rights as a primary frame of reference; affirmation of the relevance of cultural, moral, religious, and philosophical factors to the dialogue; commitment to open-mindedness and a willingness to be persuaded by reasoned argument from other points of view; and acceptance of the value of self-criticism of one's own tradition and society at a variety of levels (e.g., domestic policy, foreign policy, history of one's tradition). Although these ground rules are rarely discussed or justified in the dialogues themselves, it is possible to project rationales for their operative presence. For example, some sort of shared understanding of human rights seems necessary—at least provisionally—for a working dialogue. That is not to say that all human rights are uncontested or uncontestable, but rather that the dialogue must start somewhere on this matter, and what better place than a hard-won and long-standing, even if dynamic and changing, international consensus.

During the course of intercultural human-rights dialogues, certain problems emerge that for convenience I classify into four principal types. One type involves problems concerning the meaning of cultural moral categories and idioms, particularly those that are relatively rare and central to the traditions in question and that may be intraculturally contestable—e.g., "li" (rite) in Confucianism; nonself and emptiness in Buddhism. A second type involves problems of intercultural comparison about such central notions as self/person, community, and transcendence, understandings of which are interculturally divergent and contestable, being embedded as they are in different worldviews and social practices. A third type involves problems of how to interpret properly the complexities of the historical record and sociological data of given societies, cultures, and traditions, particularly when broad generalizations are offered about social and historical tendencies that may be insufficiently sensitive to internal cultural variation and change. A fourth type involves problems concerning the interpretation and justification of human rights and related notions of human dignity, person, and community—even given the provisionally assumed framework of international human rights.

Of these four problem areas, the first three types are often successfully addressed in the dialogues, but the fourth is often not. Issues regarding the interpretation and justification of human rights are in fact the most contentious, generating the greatest heat and uncertainty and frequently leaving participants dissatisfied and in a state of anomie. It may be somewhat surprising that tensions about the interpretation and justification of human rights recur in intercultural human-rights dialogues without satisfactory solutions. After all, is not the very aim of these dialogues to advance in one way or another the cause of human rights? Moreover, have I not suggested that the acceptance of international human rights constitutes one of the important ground rules for such dialogues? In response to these rhetorical questions, however, I wish to emphasize that one operative aim of these dialogues involves critical assessment of human-rights thinking and practice from cultural moral perspectives, and, further, that the acceptance of a human-rights framework as a dialogical ground rule is provisional and does not preclude either criticisms of specific contestable human rights or criticism of theories about how the subject matter of human rights ought to be formulated and justified. Thus, there is considerable room left for contentious debate about human rights.

I hypothesize that many of the tensions and problems over the interpretation and justification of human rights may be largely the result of the ideological "baggage" brought especially by Western participants. In my view this baggage is not so much carried by, for example, their methods of inquiry as it is by their unexamined assumptions about how international human rights are shaped and justified as viewed through the lenses of their own moral and political commitments and leanings. If this is true, whether wholly or in part, then I further hypothesize that it might help these dialogues if I were to sketch an understanding of international human rights that addresses head-on the issues of their status, history, and justification as well as introducing my perception that they are relatively "theory thin" as opposed to being culturally loaded. In effect, I wish to propose a constructive framework for intercultural human-rights dialogues that I believe avoids, or at least mitigates, one central type of problem often encountered.

Revisiting and Revisioning International Human Rights

In developing this constructive framework or counterportrait of international human rights, it will be useful to keep in mind three interrelated concerns about international human rights that arise in the dialogues. The first is the worry that international human rights represent a distinctively Western moral ideology intended to supplant the moral perspectives of diverse cultural traditions. The second is the perception that human rights are principally or exclusively civil-political liberties (associated with liberal individualism) that are incompatible with communitarian cultural traditions. The third is the perception that international human rights embody or are otherwise grounded in problematic metaphysical-moral assumptions about human nature, personhood, and community (e.g., radical autonomy, social atomism), as well as problematic moral epistemologies (e.g., foundationalism). I believe that these concerns betray a serious misunderstanding of the nature, function, and source of international human rights and that it is important to set the record straight in this regard, beginning with the history of human rights over the last fifty years.[5]

History

Despite the common perception that international human rights are simply an outgrowth and entailment of Western assumptions about human nature and moral rationality, it is a fact that the Universal Declaration of Human Rights (1948) was reached through a pragmatic process of negotiation among representatives of different nations and cultural traditions.[6] While it may be true that Western representatives had the upper hand in this process, the simple fact remains that pragmatic negotiation between differing views about the subject matter was the process of choice, not theorizing about matters of moral knowledge, political philosophy, or even jurisprudence. Moreover, this pragmatic approach has continued to characterize the drafting and adoption of subsequent human-rights covenants, conventions, and treaties. In light of these facts, we need to ask, therefore, what this process implies or otherwise suggests about the nature and status of international human rights.

The framers of human-rights declarations, conventions, and treaties explicitly take a pragmatic approach to the relationship between human-rights norms and particular cultural traditions. This approach starts with the facts of moral plurality and cultural particularity and finds that in situations of crisis peoples of quite different traditions are able to agree upon and acknowledge their mutual respect for certain basic values. The Universal Declaration was, for example, in large part the historical and social product of a very particular crisis brought about by the genocide and brutalization of persons and communities during the Second World War. In the face of this crisis, representatives from a variety of cultural traditions were able to recognize their mutual agreement in the judgment that such acts are antithetical to each and all of their traditions, and through a process of pragmatic negotiation, they were able to agree on incorporating this judgment in the language of specific human rights. The fact that rights language was employed was doubtless due to the dominance of the Western legal tradition in the international arena, but the mutually agreed upon judgment about the proscription of certain acts was not exclusively a Western moral judgment.

Similarly, the subsequent human-rights covenants of the 1970s were born from the mutual recognition that oppression and material disadvantages suffered especially by peoples in developing countries were incompatible with moral sensibilities contained in many cultural traditions. Significantly, the influence of non-Western (or at least non–First World) cultural representatives was more prominent here, accounting in part for negotiated agreement to give greater emphasis to social and economic rights as well as collective rights of self-determination and development, in response to the historical crisis of colonialism and its long-term effects. And functionally similar crises and processes have characterized other international human-rights conventions and treaties. The point is that far from preempting or replacing the moral teachings of various cultural traditions, specific expressions of human-rights concerns have arisen from the mutual recognitions by adherents of these traditions that they have a shared interest in the protection of certain important substantive moral values as well as a shared capacity to suffer at the hands of those who would violate the dignity and well-being of persons and communities.

On pragmatic moral grounds, then, adherents of particular cultural traditions might consider specific expressions of human rights as the products of successive recognitions by diverse peoples of a set of values embraced by their own distinctive cultural moral traditions. No one cultural tradition is the sole source of human-rights concepts and norms. Human rights are, from this point of view, the expression of a set of important overlapping moral expectations to which differing cultures hold themselves and others accountable.[7] In effect, international human rights constitute a grand social practice embodying intercultural moral recognitions of and agreements about crucial conditions for human flourishing. This reading of the record is a far cry indeed from the overly simplistic and, I believe, false belief that international human rights represent nothing more than a Western and hegemonic moral ideology.

An important implication of this reading of the record is that it is most appropriate to take a historical perspective on the emergence and formulation of human-rights norms. The international and intercultural recognition of human rights has a history, and, as pointed out by Burns Weston and others, that history is marked by at least three distinctive generations or types of human rights, with each successive generation not supplanting the earlier one(s) but rather adding to as well as nuancing the earlier.[8] The first generation, emerging most definitively in the aftermath of World War II, is generally comprised of civil-political rights and liberties, although also touching on certain social and economic rights, as influenced by the background of Franklin Roosevelt's "Four Freedoms" and the identification of "freedom from want."[9] The second generation, emerging most definitively in the human-rights covenants of the 1970s, adds a new emphasis on the importance of social and economic rights to certain crucial goods and services and their just allocation, though this generation is also clearly linked with the first and looks forward to the third (by identifying the right of peoples to self-determination and their cultural rights). The third generation, which is now most definitively emerging amid Third and Fourth World claims for global redistribution of power, wealth, and the common welfare of humankind (e.g., ecosystem, peace), adds yet another new emphasis on developmental-collective rights of peoples' self-determination and development (e.g., political, economic, cultural) as well as a more generalized just distribution of material and nonmaterial goods on a local and planetary scale. This generation also is linked with the preceding ones, inasmuch as it is concerned not only with the collective rights of peoples but also the liberties and material welfare of their individual members. The international human-rights community recognizes all three generations or types of human rights as important and interrelated and needing to be pursued in a constructive balance or harmony, though in a given situation or context one or another generation may merit temporary emphasis.

On its face, then, the fact of the international recognition of these three generations of human rights challenges quite directly the perception that human rights are principally or exclusively civil-political liberties, for they include also the social and economic rights of persons as well as the developmental-collective rights of peoples. Simply noting this fact of a more extensive range, however, does not dispose of the further perception and claim that civil-political human rights may be incompatible in some way with communitarian cultural traditions. This is the deeper problem that consistently arises in intercultural human-rights dialogues, and it deserves systematic attention in its own right.

Questions of Incompatibility and Incoherence

In addressing this concern, I begin by noting that in some quarters of the human-rights community there appears to be a tendency to correlate strongly the three generations of human rights with distinctive assumptions about human nature, persons, and community, in such a way as to seemingly undermine the contention (or aspiration) that all three generations are coherently interrelated.[10] This tendency, of course, raises a deeper issue about whether international human rights presuppose or are otherwise grounded in metaphysical-moral assumptions that may be internally incoherent. Weston himself, though a sensitive interpreter who resists the charge of internal incoherence, associates civil-political human rights with the philosophy of liberal individualism, social-economic rights with socialist traditions, and developmental-collective rights with the philosophies of holistic community. Inasmuch as different cultures and traditions have made their own distinctive contributions to international human rights, there is something to these correlations, speaking historically, but they could also be misleading as well, for, as argued by Weston, they deflect attention away from the fact that successive generations not only add new human-rights emphases to the earlier generations but also modify our understanding of the nature and import of those earlier generations. There is, in effect, a recursive and spiraling hermeneutical process at work here that needs to be taken into account—recursive in the sense of returning to and interpreting the earlier generations in light of the succeeding, and spiraling in the sense of interpreting the later generations in the light of the recursive move. International human rights constitute, in short, a dynamic tradition in their own right that may mitigate the effects of perceived internal incoherence.

In baldly characterizing, for example, civil-political human rights as the "negative" freedoms from government intrusion advanced by liberal individualism, one might run the risk of deflecting attention away from the fact that these liberties are also properly understood as "enablements" or "enpowerments" for persons to function as flourishing members of a polity or community where they work with others to advance their lives together in their society.[11] That is to say, the civil-political liberties of first-generation human rights are not simply (or even mainly) the negative "freedoms from" associated with a caricatured liberal individualism concerned with protecting the privacy of radically autonomous, isolated, self-interested, ahistorical, and acultural selves, but rather are positive enpowerments to persons' involvement in a flourishing community that are compatible with, for example, many communitarian traditions of moral and political thought and practice. The subsequent generations of social-economic and developmental-collective human rights, with their concerns about the exploitation of, respectively, certain social classes and colonial peoples, help to highlight and focus this positive function of civil-political rights, by driving home the point that certain minimal social-economic conditions as well as collective enpowerments are necessary for people, individually and collectively, to flourish fully as politically involved members of their societies. By the same token, however, we can also appreciate the wisdom behind the thesis that civil-political rights may be crucially important to the enhancement of peoples' social and economic situation: e.g., exercising civil-political liberties may result in pressures necessary for change in social and economic conditions as well as for the more just distribution of material goods.[12] Thus do these generations interact and affect our understanding of both, beyond the traditional philosophies and assumptions that may have once been historically associated with them, enabling us to appreciate their interdependence and mutual effects. A similar case could be made regarding the effects of the third generation (developmental-collective) on the other two.

My major point is that all three generations of human rights in fact identify a wide range of enpowerments, both individual and collective, that are crucial to individual and community flourishing on a local and wider scale. And, insofar as they do this, they are intended to be interdependent, mutually influential, and compatible all the way down, so to speak. Within this understanding, human rights in general are intended to be compatible in principle not only with cultural traditions and societies that emphasize the importance of individuals within community (a more apt characterization of Western liberalism) but also with cultural traditions and societies that may emphasize the primacy of community and the way that individuals contribute to it—that is, *both* more liberal individualist *and* more communitarian traditions and societies.[13] Rigid dichotomies as well as static understandings of the historical sources of international human rights may be quite misleading with regard to their conceptual flexibility and interactive development.

I suspect that some may think I am glossing over some major difficulties regarding human rights—especially civil-political liberties—in relation to communitarian traditions. One difficulty devolves upon the frequently encountered claim that virtue-based or duty-based communitarian cultural moral traditions lack the conceptual resources for recognizing and appreciating rights, human or otherwise. A second difficulty is that, even granting that such traditions may be able to recognize and acknowledge human rights in some of their generations (e.g., social-economic, developmental-collective), nonetheless they may be quite resistant to first-generation civil-political rights. Yet a third difficulty is that, even granting that such traditions may be able to acknowledge civil-political rights, they would nonetheless subject them to significant constraints, so that there will be necessarily large differences between, for example, liberal and communitarian interpretations of civil-political liberties. These three difficulties may account for a large share of the tensions at intercultural human-rights dialogues.

The perception or claim that virtue-based or duty-based communitarian cultural traditions lack the conceptual resources for acknowledging rights, human or otherwise, can be addressed by three lines of counterresponse. One is to show that such traditions do not, simply by virtue of their orientations to community, virtues, and duties, lack the conceptual resources at issue. A second is to show examples of particular communitarian traditions that in fact acknowledge rights and human rights. Yet a third is to show that even if a tradition lacked rights-conceptuality per se it could nonetheless use its resources to justify its agreement to participate in international human-rights consensus, apart from developing an internal human-rights tradition of its own.

With regard to the first line of counterresponse, there appears to be no logical reason for contending that rights discourse is necessarily incompatible with communitarian traditions, so long as we resist asseverations that such discourse must presuppose strong assumptions about the radical autonomy of persons abstracted from communal bonds, social roles, and historical and cultural traditions. As I have suggested, such assumptions seem manifestly inapplicable when considering the meaning and history of human rights. Moreover, as a number of philosophers have pointed out, referring, for instance, to the work of Joel Feinberg, it is difficult to conceive of any cultural tradition that incorporates social practices of property, promises, contracts, loans, partnerships, marriages, etc., as utterly devoid of conceptual counterparts (to duties or virtues) that have the function of rights.[14] As Seung Hwan Lee has said, "In this sense, the concept of rights is indispensable for our moral life, regardless of social ideals (whether communitarianism or liberalism) and regardless of types of morality (whether virtue-based or rights-based) we adopt." Indeed, I know of no cultural moral tradition that lacks at least an implicit sense of strong claims that can be made against others in the context of cooperative social practices relying upon interpersonal or intergroup expectancies produced by the behavior they regulate.

The second line of counterresponse is to produce examples of communitarian traditions that acknowledge human rights. Here I might instance the UN Draft Declaration of the Rights of Indigenous Peoples, which speaks for the views of over 120 indigenous traditions that are largely communitarian and that clearly acknowledge all three generations of human rights, as well as the Dalai Lama's government-in-exile, which authoritatively represents the similarly extensive human-rights commitments of contemporary Tibetan Buddhism.[15] For an example closer to home, I might mention Catholic social teachings, which simultaneously reject radical individualism, advance a thoroughly social understanding of the person and the importance of the community as well as duties and virtues oriented to the common good, and yet accept human rights in their three generations. I think that these three examples are sufficiently suggestive to make the point that communitarian traditions do exist that are compatible with international human rights.

The third line of counterresponse involves showing that even if a communitarian tradition lacked the conceptuality of rights, it could nonetheless use its resources to justify its agreement to participate in international human-rights consensus apart from developing an internal human-rights tradition of its own. Since I have recently argued this point with respect to the Confucian tradition, which is often interpreted as incompatible with rights and human rights, I will use this tradition as my example. It is acknowledged by all scholars of Confucianism that this tradition is thoroughly communitarian in outlook. It is further argued by some scholars that, conceptually and historically speaking, rights and human rights have no place within this tradition.[16] I myself have serious doubts about this claim, but let us assume for the sake of argument that it is true. Nevertheless the following facts about this tradition are regarded as indisputable. First, from its classical phase to the present, Confucianism has historically emphasized the responsibility of the ruler and the state to ensure the material welfare of the people (e.g., nutrition, clothing, shelter, employment, education) to the degree of allowing that the people are justified in rebelling against a ruler or government that manifestly fails in this task.[17] Second, the Neo-Confucian phase of this tradition, which includes many of its most distinguished and revered figures, has emphasized such notions as autonomy of the moral mind and individual conscience (even while construing the "true person" as a thoroughly social being), self-governing communities and voluntarism at the local level, a reformed conception of the law as a crucial check on internal political abuse, and the important role of public education in enhancing people's political participation.[18] Third, the highest Confucian ideal is its moral and metaphysical vision of one-bodiedness with Heaven and Earth and the myriad things, which extends the Confucian sense of moral responsibility to a planetary or even universal scale, emphasizing the importance of the welfare of the entire holistic community of interdependent beings.

Now, apart from the fact that these resources of the tradition seem but short steps from, respectively, social-economic, civil-political, and developmental-collective rights, it seems to me that they are sufficient to contend that the Confucian tradition has the resources to at least recognize and appreciate the subject matters addressed by the three generations of human rights. The tradition clearly supports, for example, the importance of meeting people's social and economic needs as well as the importance of the idea of civil and political enpowerments being needed for personal self-cultivation and local communal self-governance, not to mention the importance of more broadly collective considerations pertaining to the welfare of the whole biosphere. Thus, even if the tradition itself preferred not to use the language of human rights, its internal resources seem more than adequate to support its agreement to participate in, and abide by, international human-rights consensus for reasons pertaining to its own vision of human moral nature and human welfare. It could do this entirely apart from forging its own internal human-rights categories. I will have more to say about the underpinnings of this justification strategy later.

Let us now return to the remaining perceived difficulties regarding communitarian traditions in relation to human rights—namely, their possible resistance to, or placement of significant constraints on, civil-political rights. Here it is important to be aware that the international human-rights conventions themselves permit some restrictions on civil-political liberties: e.g., the freedom to manifest one's religion and to associate with others can be subject to legal limitations necessary "to protect public safety, order, health, or morals"; the freedom of expression is stipulated to carry with it "special duties and responsibilities" and "may therefore be subject to certain restrictions . . . such as are provided by law and are necessary."[19] That is to say, the international human-rights conventions make some room for differing societal and cultural judgments about the exercise of these rights, while at the same time enjoining a relatively high standard for their limitation.

With this clarification in the background, we need now to consider more directly the question of whether there are necessarily large differences between liberal and communitarian interpretations of civil-political liberties. In particular, the claim is often pressed that in liberal traditions such rights are held by individuals against the state, whereas in communitarian traditions they are granted by the state only so long as they are exercised in the interests of the state. While such a contention may be applicable in some cases, it is not true for all, and may not necessarily be true for any, pending analysis of the social ideals of the traditions in question. Insisting on the general applicability of this supposed gap between liberal and communitarian traditions runs the risk of identifying traditions with states. It also overlooks those cases in which civil-political liberties are regarded as constitutive and defining elements of both liberal and communitarian ideals of a flourishing community that can be used to critique deviations of respective states from those ideals. There may indeed be a large difference between, on the one hand, liberal and communitarian social ideals incorporating civil-political liberties in their respective traditions, and, on the other, the actual constitutions and practices of states in measuring up to those ideals. This is an unfortunate fact of our less-than-ideal world, but in itself it does not undermine the possibility that both liberal and communitarian traditions can recognize and value the importance of civil-political liberties in their respective ideals of communal flourishing. The differences between liberal and communitarian traditions would then devolve on differences in the content of their respective ideals of communal flourishing apart from their shared commitment to civil-political liberties and perhaps on differences regarding the priority of and degree of limitation placed on those liberties. It is, of course, this understanding of a shared, even if somewhat different, commitment to the role of civil-political liberties in diverse social ideals that is forwarded by international human rights. And, although international conventions place limits on how far these liberties may be constrained by societies, there appears to be some recognition and toleration about how exactly they are balanced against other social goods in diverse settings.

If the further question is posed—how *can* communitarian traditions in particular recognize civil-political liberties—I can only say, drawing on my preceding discussion and examples, that emphasis on the primacy of community is no conceptual bar to ascribing such liberties to members of communitarian traditions when these are interpreted as enpowerments to make political contributions to community flourishing. Of course, one could conceive of cases where the exercise of such liberties might present prospects of changing a society's practices and institutions, but the possibility of such cases is no bar to a tradition's maintaining its own commitment to a concept of communal flourishing that incorporates civil-political liberties. The more difficult case would come in situations where the members of a communitarian tradition chose to exercise their liberties in such a way as to change radically the tradition's own understanding of communal flourishing. One could, of course, imagine such a situation occurring within liberal traditions as well, but I would agree that the problems presented for communitarian traditions would be greater in such a situation. Ought such problems, from a communitarian tradition's point of view, to be addressed by revoking its commitment to civil-political liberties? I doubt it, since such a revocation would itself most assuredly undermine its own understanding and commitment to a communal flourishing that constitutively incorporates such liberties. A more reasonable solution would be to use civil-political liberties as a framework for public argument, debate, suasion, and countersuasion about the sort of ideal the community wishes to advance in the future, in light of its deepest values and traditional sources and the circumstances of its people.

What I have said thus far leaves unresolved the question of how exactly communitarian traditions will balance civil-political liberties against other social goods, without disruption to the integrity of their own social visions of the good. This is a difficult question to which there is no easy solution, but I can offer some relevant observations. First, it must be observed that there is no algorithm or easy formula for balancing civil-political liberties against other social goods. One needs instead to consider particular cases and examine the arguments for alternative balancings in light of a given tradition's moral and social vision and in light of international human-rights standards as well as historical experience. Second, given what I have said about the in-principle compatibility of civil-political liberties and communitarian traditions, I think the burden of proof is shifted onto a tradition that wishes to limit severely such liberties. If a tradition wishes to argue that the attainment of other social goods (e.g., better material and economic conditions) requires severely constraining civil-political liberties, then it must take into account the considerable empirical data that attainment of social and economic goods is historically correlated with the effective recognition of relatively unconstrained civil-political liberties, and the further data that such recognition seems pragmatically necessary for the just allocation of such goods.[20] It may be that some traditions in some social circumstances would be able to argue an effective case for the temporary severe restraint of civil-political liberties, but the historical and empirical record weighs rather decisively against this being a justifiable permanent condition.

In offering these observations, I am attempting to reiterate the fact that international human rights incorporate intercultural agreement on the importance of a sort of "homeostatic balancing" (in the words of Erich Loewy) of communal and individual interests for both liberal and communitarian societies and traditions.[21] Loewy maintains, for example, that at one extreme those liberal societies that emphasize only freedom of individual goal-pursuit at the expense of the welfare of radically disadvantaged persons and groups run the risk of pathological disorganization and eventual demise of the community, while at the other extreme those communitarian societies ignoring or repressing individual interests in personal flourishing, self-expression, and political participation run the risk of eventually undercutting their communal solidarity. Suggests Loewy, both extremes in effect deny people's interests in both individual and communal flourishing, failing to recognize that individuals and their communities are deeply interdependent and require a balancing of interests in both freedom and solidarity. And I am suggesting that international human rights in their three generations attempt to forward a homeostatic balance that avoids these extremes, enjoining for all traditions and societies the need to assure basic social and economic material goods as well as a modicum of the civil and political freedom for enhancing personal development and communal involvement and flourishing.

Justification

The final element of my pragmatic and historical revisioning of international human rights is how to understand properly their status and justification. Human rights identify and specify conditions that are crucially important for a life worthy of human persons and communities as negotiated and agreed upon by representatives from diverse cultural moral traditions from their varying points of view. In effect, human rights represent a common vision of central moral and social values that are compatible with a variety of cultural moral anthropologies—a unity within moral diversity. Clearly, at one level their justification depends on a practical moral consensus among diverse traditions that have openly acknowledged their mutual recognition of the human importance of these values. This recognition is grounded in shared historical experiences of what life can be like without these conditions as well as in a negotiated agreement and commitment to see these conditions herewith fulfilled. Moreover, this negotiation, consensus, and commitment are open and public: made by, to, and before the peoples of the world.

At a second level of justification, each of these traditions may justify its own acknowledgment of, and participation in, the consensus by appealing to its own set of moral categories as appropriate to its particular philosophical or religious vision of human nature, person and community, and moral epistemology. Thus, internal to a cultural moral tradition, the subject matter of particular human rights (what they are about or what they address) may be justified as, e.g., divinely ordained precepts, implications of natural law or natural reason, self-evident moral truisms, systemic moral assumptions about appropriate relations between state and citizen, entailments of certain

SUMNER B. TWISS

virtues, etc. (the list is open-ended precisely because of the rich variety of cultural moral traditions). This distinction between levels or arenas of human-rights justification makes possible the justification I mentioned earlier in connection with a communitarian tradition's having the resources to justify its agreement to participate in and abide by international human rights without necessarily being compelled to forge its own internal human-rights categories. My point here is that even lacking the internal conceptuality of rights and human rights, most (if not all) traditions have the internal moral resources at least to recognize the importance of the subject matters being addressed by international human rights and to justify on internal cultural moral grounds, pertaining to their own visions of human nature and welfare, their agreement to abide by the pragmatic international consensus on human rights. This may constitute a different and possibly more attainable burden of justification for some traditions than that of having to develop their own internal human-rights subtraditions. While these traditions would presumably develop internal understandings of how their moral visions and idioms relate to the subject matters addressed by international human rights (i.e., a "theory" of relationship), they are not compelled to adopt or develop an internal human-rights subtradition in any stronger sense (e.g., the active internal deployment of the language and discourse of human rights).[22]

Recognition of a two-level approach to the source and justification of human rights has a number of advantages, not the least of which is that it appears to capture the actual state of affairs about how human rights are justified. Moreover, it permits us to acknowledge in a reasonably sophisticated manner both commonalities and differences among cultural moral traditions—they share a set of important values while at the same time articulating and living by the richer and more variegated moral visions appropriate to their historical circumstances and cultural settings. Furthermore, it allows us to acknowledge that while human rights may be justified on grounds of pragmatic agreement at the point where moral traditions may overlap in their shared insights and commitments, they may also be justified and even construed within different moral idioms as appropriate to cultural moral diversity. Additionally, this approach permits us to appreciate the historical specificity and development of human-rights norms at the international level as the result of reciprocal interactions among diverse traditions, while still being able to respect internal variations among different conceptions of human nature and corresponding moral conceptualities, languages, and epistemologies. Moreover, inasmuch as this approach is founded on a historical and pragmatic vision of the source of human rights, it allows us to appreciate more thoroughly the specific contributions that different moral cultures might make to the recognition and formulation of human-rights norms. Finally, the two-level approach permits us to handle some of the epistemological controversies about human rights by resisting the imposition of one culture's moral epistemology on all the rest. Human rights need not be justified monolithically by one particular epistemology, entailing the rejection of all other epistemic approaches, precisely because we can distinguish between levels of appeal—

pragmatic and negotiated consensus for all at the international level, but tolerance for a variety of approaches at the cultural level. I would be the first to admit that this two-level approach will not resolve all problems about the moral epistemology of human rights, much less all tensions between the universality of human rights and the particularity of cultural moral traditions, but it may mitigate these problems and tensions for the purposes of intercultural human-rights dialogues.

I conclude this revisioning of international human rights by returning to those concerns mentioned at the outset of this section and summarizing how this view addresses them. The facts, as I have represented them, of an international pragmatic moral consensus regarding human rights and of the history of their three successive generations, inspired by the sociomoral visions of diverse cultural traditions, clearly contradict the simplistic claim that human rights represent a hegemonic Western moral ideology. Furthermore, the fact of three generations of human rights, together with their recursive and spiraling hermeneutical interaction, contradicts also the myopic perception that human rights are exclusively civil-political liberties. Moreover, I believe that I have provided some strong reasons for rejecting the claim that civil-political liberties are in any necessary way incompatible with communitarian cultural traditions. In addition, the two-level approach to human-rights justification, together with the historical and pragmatic perspective I have provided on the background of international human rights, clearly implies that these rights are not strongly associated with or grounded in problematic metaphysical and epistemological assumptions. Quite the contrary, they are in a significant sense "theory thin" at the international level, permitting wide diversity at the internal cultural level and mitigating the temptation to locate human rights within any one moral or political theory. Finally, I might observe that while it is an open question as to whether certain cultural traditions may lack, either explicitly or even implicitly, their own internal human-rights subtraditions, it seems more than likely that all cultural traditions have the resources necessary to justify on internal grounds and in their own moral idioms, their agreement to abide by international human-rights consensus, for this constitutes a lesser burden of justification that does not require cultural traditions to employ the conceptuality of human rights at the cultural level.

Conclusion: A Program for Intercultural Human-Rights Dialogues

I wish to conclude by sketching how the preceding constructive framework might be translated into a program for intercultural human-rights dialogue. In so doing, I want briefly to introduce and take issue with two other dominant frameworks for the cross-cultural study of human rights that some might see as alternatives to the "middle way" that I have perceived as being operative in actual dialogues. For convenience, I will call these two alternative frameworks, respectively, "the universalist" and "the particularist." Universalists tend to emphasize the universality of human rights as legal and moral norms that they see grounded in some sort of foundationalist epistemology.[23] They also tend to impose this framework and understanding on cultural moral traditions in order to make judgments about how the traditions measure up to universal human rights and to make recommendations for cultural and social change. Particularists, by contrast, tend either to deemphasize the legal status of human-rights norms or to stress their roots in Western moral ideology (e.g., liberal individualism), as well as resisting the supposed legitimacy and persuasiveness of a moral epistemology (e.g., foundationalism) traced to and linked with the Enlightenment period in the West.[24] They tend also to stress the differences between cultural moral traditions and the regime of international human rights, emphasizing, in order to resist, the ideological individualism supposedly associated with human rights, and contrasting especially the communitarian moral visions of non-Western societies and cultures with this ideological individualism.

In my view there are problems with both of these frameworks. With respect to the universalist framework, as I suggested in connection with the two-level justificatory approach developed above, there are dangers implicit in trying to justify *tout court* human rights by appealing to a contestable moral epistemology within the international arena. Such a move deflects attention away from the power and function of justification through negotiated pragmatic consensus as well as enmeshing human rights in what promises to be endless epistemic uncertainty and debate. Moreover, this framework seems insufficiently sensitive to the dynamic history and hermeneutical interaction among types of human rights. For in imposing human rights as a static framework on cultural traditions, it seems somewhat closed to the possibility that those traditions may have something new to offer, as they have in the past, to our understanding of international human rights: e.g., new emphases, new understandings of their interaction, even perhaps new generations (such as the nascently emerging "green" rights).

With respect to the particularist framework, there also appears to be a significant myopia about the complexity and historical development of human rights. Much of this myopia stems from the failure to take account of the fact that there are three generations (not just one) of human rights and the further fact that the latter two generations (social-economic, developmental-collective) significantly modify the ideological individualism with which this framework seems preoccupied. As a consequence, this framework appears ill-positioned to explore the possible—indeed, I would say likely—compatibilities between communitarian cultural traditions and social-economic, developmental-collective, and even civil-political human rights (under our revised understanding).

In contrast to these two frameworks, the actual human-rights dialogues in which I have been involved employ methodological programs and strategies that appear to be aimed at avoiding both sets of problems. And one way of interpreting the role of my revised understanding of international human rights is an attempt to strengthen this avoidance, by providing a middle-way framework that constructively combines aspirations to universality with the realities of cultural particularity, in a manner intended to benefit both human-rights and cultural moral traditions. This framework can be deployed in seven steps that are intentionally designed to accommodate the plurality of aims, methodological programs, and strategies of inquiry identified in the first section of this essay. In articulating these steps, I do not mean that they must be followed in some rigid succession, but only that they represent nodal points that it would be helpful to keep in mind during the course of dialogue.

The first step is to adopt an understanding of international human rights informed by the history of their three generations, the features of their conceptual and hermeneutical flexibility, the two levels of their justification, and the considerations regarding liberal and communitarian traditions that I have outlined, in addition to the explication of the largely implicit assumptions I specified earlier (e.g., regarding moral traditions, dialogical ground rules). The second step is to identify the parameters of the cultural traditions which are being focused on that may have a particular bearing on human-rights concepts and norms—e.g., conceptions of person, community, and their relationship; notions of the common good and their specific content; notions of and grounds for the dignity and equality of persons; moral and metaphysical visions of the world; distinctive emphases within their political thought and practice; etc. The third step is to explore, within these parameters and with one or more of the strategies of inquiry identified earlier, the range of historical materials available, in order to develop systematic hypotheses about the traditions' openness to the subject matter addressed by the three generations of human rights, noting carefully whether possible openness and compatibility are expressed or expressible in the conceptuality of rights.

The fourth step is to test these hypotheses against the range of material available— e.g., historical, sociological, political, philosophical—and in light of alternative perspectives on these materials articulated in the dialogue. The fifth step is to ascertain, keeping in mind the two-level approach to human-rights justification, (1) whether the traditions have the moral resources and idioms necessary to form their own internal human-rights subtraditions, and (2) whether the traditions have the resources to at least justify to themselves (internally) their agreement to participate in international human-rights consensus. The sixth step is to ascertain, in light of all the above, (1) what distinctive contributions the traditions might be in a position to make to international human-rights negotiations (in the form of hypotheses), and (2) how their involvement in the international human-rights community might affect their own commitments, whether explicit or implicit, to the subject matters addressed by human rights (again, in the form of hypotheses). And the seventh step—which is not part of the dialogue per se—is the communication of the results of the dialogue to other scholars and cultural representatives, including those located within the societies in which the traditions are embedded, as well as to relevant government officials and international human-rights officials and activists.

I believe that with our increasing awareness of a global community it becomes ever more important that the world's cultural moral traditions be heard at the highest level of participation on the subject of international human rights. The more extensive and intensive this participation, the greater the opportunity of not only gaining a more subtle view of human rights but also seeing them become more effective in the alleviation of human suffering and oppression. I hope that this essay may serve as one small contribution to this process.[25]

Notes

1. Sumner B. Twiss and Bruce Grelle, "Human Rights and Comparative Religious Ethics: A New Venue," *Annual of the Society of Christian Ethics, 1995,* 21–48. Much of the content of the present essay is drawn from and extends my contributions to the aforementioned article as well as other papers and materials written in the past few years. For the section on characterizing intercultural human-rights dialogues, see Sumner B. Twiss, "Curricular Perspectives in Comparative Religious Ethics: A Critical Examination of Four Paradigms," *Annual of the Society of Christian Ethics, 1993,* 249–69 (esp. 254–58, 262–66), and Sumner B. Twiss, with Abdullahi An-Na'im, Ann Mayer, and William Wipfler, "Universality vs. Relativism in Human Rights," in *Religion and Human Rights,* ed. John Kelsay and Sumner B. Twiss (New York: Project on Religion and Human Rights, 1994), 30–59 (esp. 42–48; see also introductory editorial material on p. iv). For the section on revisiting and revisioning international human rights, see Twiss and Grelle, "Human Rights," 29–35, 39–48, Twiss et al., "Universality," 56–58 (see also editorial material on 118–20), and Twiss, "A Constructive Framework for Discussing Confucianism and Human Rights," a paper forthcoming in a volume of conference proceedings edited by Wm. Theodore de Bary. For the concluding section on a program for intercultural human-rights dialogues, see Twiss and Grelle, "Human Rights," 36–38, and Twiss, "A Constructive Framework."

2. Dialogues in which I have been involved include, e.g., Conference on Religion and Human Rights Columbia University, 1982; Conference on Human Rights in the Modern State, Ditchley Park, Oxfordshire, England, February 1984; Conference on Religion and Human Rights, General Theological Seminary, New York, May 1994; selected sessions of the Seventh East-West Philosophers' Conference on Justice and Democracy: A Philosophical Exploration, University of Hawaii, January 1995; Conference on Confucianism and Human Rights, University of Hawaii, August 1995. I am enormously indebted to these conferences and their participants.

3. The inspiration for distinguishing these three strategies is provided by, respectively, Abdullahi A. An-Na'im, ed., *Human Rights in Cross-Cultural Perspectives: A Quest for Consensus* (Philadelphia: University of Pennsylvania Press, 1992), 1–15, 19–43, 427–35; Harvey Cox and Arvind Sharma, "Positive Resources of Religion for Human Rights," in *Religion and Human Rights,* 61–79; and oral remarks by Randle Edwards (Columbia University) at the Conference on Confucianism and Human Rights. For the subsequent reference to An-Na'im's views, see An-Na'im, ed., *Human Rights in Cross-Cultural Perspectives,* esp. 5–6, 21.

4. See Alasdair MacIntyre, *After Virtue* (Notre Dame, Ind.: University of Notre Dame Press,

1981), chap. 15, and Garrett Bardin, *After Principles* (Notre Dame, Ind.: University of Notre Dame Press, 1994), 1–19.

5. These reflections were inspired in part by Michael Walzer, *Thick and Thin: Moral Argument at Home and Abroad* (Notre Dame, Ind.: University of Notre Dame Press, 1994), 1–19.

6. See John P. Humphrey, *Human Rights and the United Nations: A Great Adventure* (Dobbs Ferry, N.Y.: Transnational Publishers, 1984).

7. See Walzer, *Thick and Thin,* 17–18. For the following point about international human rights as a social practice, see Donnelly, *The Concept of Human Rights* (New York: St. Martin's Press, 1985), chap. 2, and William O'Neill, "Ethics and Inculturation: The Scope and Limits of Rights' Discourse," *Annual of the Society of Christian Ethics, 1993,* 73–92.

8. Burns H. Weston, "Human Rights," in *Human Rights in the World Community: Issues and Action,* 2d ed., ed. Richard Pierre Claude and Burns H. Weston (Philadelphia: University of Pennsylvania Press, 1992), 14–30 (esp. 14–21).

9. I am indebted to Louis Henkin (Columbia University) for reminding me of this background influence of FDR's "Four Freedoms" speech. See also Louis Henkin, *The Age of Rights* (New York: Columbia University Press, 1990), 16, 18.

10. See, e.g., Adamantia Pollis, "Human Rights in Liberal, Socialist, and Third World Perspective," in *Human Rights in the World Community,* 146–56. For the subsequent reference to Weston's views, see Weston, "Human Rights," 18–20.

11. See David Hollenbach, "A Communitarian Reconstruction of Human Rights: Contributions from Catholic Tradition," in *Catholicism and Liberalism: Contributions to American Public Policy,* ed. R. Bruce Douglas and David Hollenbach (Cambridge: Cambridge University Press, 1994), 127–50, and Weston, "Human Rights," 18.

12. See, e.g., Han S. Park, "Correlates of Human Rights: Global Tendencies," *Human Rights Quarterly* 9 (1987): 405–13.

13. See Weston, "Human Rights," 21.

14. See Joel Feinberg, *Rights, Justice, and the Bounds of Liberty: Essays in Social Philosophy* (Princeton, N.J.: Princeton University Press, 1980), 143–55. Lee makes excellent use of Feinberg in Sueng-Hwan Lee, "Was There a Concept of Rights in Confucian Virtue-based Morality?" *Journal of Chinese Philosophy* 19, no. 3 (September 1992): 241–61 (esp. 241–45). The following quotation is from p. 245.

15. The Draft Declaration of the Rights of Indigenous Peoples is reprinted in Alexander Ewen, ed., *Voice of Indigenous Peoples: Native People Address the United Nations* (Santa Fe: Clear Light Publishers, 1994), Appendix B. The following point about Catholic social teachings is drawn from Hollenbach, "A Communitarian Reconstruction."

16. See e.g., Henry Rosemont, "Why Take Rights Seriously? A Confucian Critique," and Roger T. Ames, "Rites as Rights: The Confucian Alternative," in *Human Rights and the World's Religions,* ed. Leroy Rouner (South Bend, Ind.: University of Notre Dame Press, 1988), 167–82 and 199–216, respectively; and Tu Wei-ming, *Way, Learning, and Politics: Essays on the Confucian Intellectual* (Albany: SUNY Press, 1993), 30–31.

17. See. e.g., *Mencius,* trans. D. C. Lau (London: Penguin Books, 1970), I.B.8 and 12, I.A.7, IV.A.1., VII.B.14.

18. For these points I am indebted to Wm. Theodore de Bary, *The Liberal Tradition in China* (Hong Kong and New York: Chinese University Press and Columbia University Press, 1983),

esp. 12, 20, 27, 32–33, 40–50, 85–86, as well as his "Neo-Confucianism and Human Rights," in *Human Rights and the World's Religions,* 183–98. The following point about the Confucian metaphysical vision is influenced in part by Tu Wei-ming, *Confucian Thought: Selfhood as Creative Transformation* (Albany: SUNY Press, 1985), 171–81.

19. *The International Bill of Human Rights* (New York: United Nations, 1993), 27–29 (Articles 18, 19, 21, and 22 from the Covenant on Civil and Political Rights).

20. Again, see, e.g., Park, "Correlates," and its references.

21. "Homeostatic balance" is the major theme in Erich H. Loewy, *Freedom and Community: The Ethics of Interdependence* (Albany: SUNY Press, 1993); for the following points drawn from his work, see, e.g., 124–25 and 139–40.

22. For a similar approach but with important differences, see Tore Lindholm, "Prospects for Research on the Cultural Legitimacy of Human Rights: The Cases of Liberalism and Marxism," in An-Naᶜim, ed., *Human Rights in Cross-Cultural Perspectives,* 387–426 (esp. 395–401).

23. See, e.g., Alan Gewirth, *Human Rights: Essays on Justification and Applications* (Chicago: University of Chicago Press, 1982), and his "Common Morality and the Community of Rights," in *Prospects for a Common Morality,* ed. Gene Outka and John P. Reeder Jr. (Princeton: Princeton University Press, 1993), 29–52, as well as the critique of foundationalist approaches in Michael Freeman, "The Philosophical Foundations of Human Rights," *Human Rights Quarterly* 16, no. 3 (August 1994): 491–514.

24. See, e.g., Adamantia Pollis and Peter Schwab, "Human Rights: A Western Construct with Limited Applicability," in *Human Rights: Cultural and Ideological Perspectives,* ed. Pollis and Schwab (New York: Praeger, 1979), 3–8, and Alison Dundes Rentelen, *International Human Rights: Universalism versus Relativism* (Newbury Park, Calif.: Sage Publications, 1990).

25. I wish to thank a number of colleagues for their critical comments and suggestions in preparing this essay, notably Aaron Stalnaker, Andrew Flescher, and Jung Lee, doctoral students in a current seminar on comparative ethics and human rights, and Mark Unno, Post-Doctoral Fellow (all at Brown University). In addition, this essay has benefited from critical feedback from other colleagues on earlier and concurrent papers, notably Jock Reeder, Hal Roth, Giles Milhaven (Brown University), and Ann Mayer (University of Pennsylvania). A special debt of gratitude is owed to my coauthor, Bruce Grelle (California State University, Chico), and my coeditor, John Kelsay (Florida State University), for our work together on previous related material. Finally, I wish to acknowledge certain colleagues at the Conference on Confucianism and Human Rights whose critical comments on my essay there forced me to develop my reflections further in this work, notably Henry Rosemont (St. Mary's College of Maryland), Irene Bloom, and Louis Henkin (both of Columbia University).

A Brief, Unscholarly Afterword

JAMES M. GUSTAFSON

The achievements of women and men who were members of my seminars and whose dissertations I directed, or advised, or stimulated in some way, have always been a source of great satisfaction to me. The breadth of the interests they have pursued both during their formal studies and in their scholarly writing is also a matter of great satisfaction. This volume honors me by demonstrating the contributions of some of those who have passed through my seminar rooms and studies at Yale University and the University of Chicago. Even the chapters that address the same basic subject are quite different, and the agenda of Christian and religious ethics is quite well covered by the variety.

I would like to honor the contributors to this volume and others who are not included for their contributions to scholarship in religious ethics generally and in Christian ethics particularly. The best I can do, however, apart from writing scores of pages, is offer a general thanksgiving for my good fortune to the places I have been employed, for the resources those universities have provided, for the colleagues in ethics and other fields whose stimulation both I and my students have enjoyed, and especially for the high quality of students I have taught.

I continue to state what is simplistic in the eyes of many who evaluate educational processes: If one has a significant agenda of issues, literature that grapples with those issues at their deepest and most interesting points, and good students and colleagues, the instructor's primary role is as a conductor and not a teacher. I am certain that the persons represented in this volume, and many more who are not, would agree with my own observation about my graduate studies: At both Chicago and Yale I had great teachers, but I probably learned as much in interaction with my peers and in solitary reflection on what I read as I did from my instructors. When one is honest, one can take little credit for the achievements of one's students.

Each chapter in this volume surpasses anything I could write on the same subject. To respond to each is a task I need and cannot attempt. "The Idea of Christian Ethics,"[1] presents my most recent and probably final analysis of the field. For the efforts of the two editors, and each of the authors, I hope that the reward will be attention to this volume as a whole and to its separate parts in further writing about Christian and religious ethics.

The chapters are quite representative of various aspects of religious ethical research, and the comments I here record about the field are made to emphasize some features present in this book and some that, for practical reasons at least, are not.

First, the chapters represent more of the analytical agenda of theological ethics than they do substantive issues of the relations of religion to morality and theology to ethics. A conviction that is central to *Ethics from a Theocentric Perspective*[2] is that the Deity is the primary object of concern for theological ethics, and that what one experiences, believes, and expresses about God and God's relations to the world, structure and order the issues of theological ethics. Analytically, this involves studies of how different conceptions of God and human knowledge of God correlate with different views of morality and ethics, how different interpretations of the work of Christ stress different aspects of Christian morality and ethics; how different interpretations of sin and redemption lead to different moral anthropologies, and so on.

Synthetically, I attempted to develop my own views in a self-consciously critical way in *Ethics from a Theocentric Perspective,* a book quite accurately referred to by Edward Farley as being praised with loud damns. I hope that proper concerns for methodological issues, for issues that are basically philosophical (e.g. agency) and practical issues, do not eliminate matters about which I continue to have deep passion—for example: How can the relations between piety or faith and moral life be articulated? And if Calvin is correct, that it is with God "whom" we have to deal, should theology, rather than moral philosophy, and practical moral issues, be more prominent in setting the agenda for the teaching and writing of theological ethics? This concern is by no means absent from certain chapters in this book; I hope my minor legacy to my main field of scholarship includes its importance.

Second, studies focused on the theological ethics of historical and contemporary authors and actors need to be continued and developed, both for historical and constructive interests. The qualifications to do such work sometimes are contested; how much history and how much historical method are required for a scholar in ethics to write acceptable work? Or, how much knowledge of ethics is required of a historian? As has been done with Augustine's ethics, so also symposia drawing from various subspecialties might be written about the work of other major contributors. Also, however, we need historical scholars whose agendas focus on the ethical aspects of various thinkers, as well as ethical scholars who gain historical competence. Happily, some such writing, not represented in this volume, has been affected by my seminars.

Third, among the various areas to which theological ethics is related in this volume (e.g., sexuality and democracy), the introduction of theological ethics as an approach to creative literature is omitted for practical reasons. This kind of work has been done both in dissertations and in published work by persons who have gained sufficient competence in literary criticism, primary literary works, and ethics and theology. The effect, on me, is twofold. First, theological, religious, and ethical questions and concepts can be used to interpret novels, drama, and other art forms to draw attention to features which are underdisclosed from other perspectives. The second effect, particularly of novels and dramas, is to complicate any excessive reductions of human motives, intentions, ends, actions and circumstances that more generalized ethical writing necessarily commits. Many of us who use literature in our teaching perhaps feel incompetent to publish in this area, but happily there are persons with the training and confidence to do so.

Fourth, some of the chapters directly or indirectly address what I have called my primary location of intellectual life at Emory University—namely, the intersections between disciplines, as different ones describe and analyze the same or similar phenomena. Most work in theology and theological ethics addresses, from a standpoint of their autonomy, issues addressed by other disciplines. Other disciplines (e.g. medicine or economics) help interpret the circumstances of action. The traffic tends to flow in one direction from theology and ethics to other disciplines, applying them to the information in order to render a judgment. Clearly, in *Ethics from a Theocentric Perspective* and in subsequent writing, I have been concerned to have traffic move both ways across the intersection when it is relevant to do so. If theology and ethics include descriptive premises about how various things really are, and other disciplines interpret the same things that theology and ethics speak about, can those other disciplines simply be ignored? Or do changes at least have to be considered, if not made, in how we articulate the theological and ethical premises?

Finally, this volume is by scholars writing for students and other scholars in the field of religious ethics—most appropriate for its intention. In my professional lifetime, the field represented by this volume has gone from one primarily found in theological seminaries, where one of its purposes is to educate clergy and other professional persons, to one that now includes many persons in Religious Studies. An achievement over the more than forty years of my career has been increased rigor in many aspects of what was taught and published by, particularly, some Protestant writers. That this has improved the intellectual and academic level of publication is evident, and the improvement is laudable.

There are contributors to this volume, and others, whose vocation includes writing and speaking to participants in particular religious communities, clergy and lay persons alike. There are also those who address the practical moral issues of the medical and other professions. Awareness of such readerships, participation with them in various ways, and writing for them should be part of the activity of at least some scholars. For some, at least, there continues to be a vocation to ministry, understanding their work to be in the service of God and of a religious community; for others, the role is more aptly named moral counselor. Those vocations need to continue, bringing intellectual sophistication in method and content to the religious and moral lives of persons whose social roles bear responsibility for the well-being of the human and all things in ways our academic roles do not.

With these comments, meant more for emphases than criticism, I need to say clearly and explicitly that my own thinking has been extended and challenged by each of the articles. I have always learned a great deal from students; they have always been among my teachers. At the end of a career, there might be signs of role reversal: One becomes more the student of one's former students since they surpass you in each of their special endeavors. The fact that they chose to honor me by moving forward each of the topics in this book makes me profoundly grateful. I, like the editors and each of the authors, hope that these chapters further research, teaching, and writing that will surpass the contributions of this book.

I am deeply honored by these friends, and others. But: *soli Deo gloria!*

Notes

1. James M. Gustafson, "The Idea of Christian Ethics," in *Companion Encyclopedia of Theology,* ed. Peter Byrne and Leslie Houldon (London: Routledge, 1995).

2. James M. Gustafson, *Ethics from a Theocentric Perspective,* 2 vols. (Chicago: University of Chicago Press, 1981–1984).

Contributors

Joseph L. Allen is professor of ethics in the Perkins School of Theology at Southern Methodist University. Among his publications are *Love and Conflict: A Covenantal Model of Christian Ethics* (1984) and *War: A Primer for Christians* (1991).

Thomas A. Byrnes is professor of religious studies at Benedictine University. He has published articles and presented papers on American empirical philosophy.

Lisa Sowle Cahill is J. Donald Monan Professor at Boston College, teaching Christian ethics in the Department of Theology. Her several books include *"Love Your Enemies": Discipleship, Pacifism, and Just War Theory* (1994) and *Sex, Gender, and Christian Ethics* (1996).

James F. Childress is Edwin B. Kyle Professor of Religious Studies and professor of medical education at the University of Virginia. He is the coauthor with Tom L. Beauchamp of *Principles of Biomedical Ethics*, 4th ed. (1994), and *Practical Reasoning in Bioethics* (1997).

Margaret A. Farley is Gilbert L. Stark Professor of Christian Ethics at the Yale University Divinity School. Her publications include *Personal Commitments: Beginning, Keeping, Changing* (1986), and, as coeditor, *Readings in Moral Theology No. 9: Feminist Ethics and the Catholic Moral Tradition* (1996).

Richard B. Gunderman is Spencer Fellow for Medical Education at the University of Chicago. A physician, he has published articles on medical education and medical ethics.

Jon P. Gunnemann is professor of social ethics at Candler School of Theology and director of the graduate division of religion at Emory University. His publications include *The Ethical Investor*, with John G. Simon and Charles W. Powers (1972), and *The Moral Meaning of Revolution* (1979).

James M. Gustafson is Henry R. Luce Professor of Humanities and Comparative Studies at Emory University. Among his numerous books are *Ethics from a Theocentric Perspective*, 2 vols. (1981, 1984), and *A Sense of the Divine: The Natural Environment from a Theocentric Perspective* (1994).

Stanley Hauerwas is the Gilbert T. Rowe Professor of Theological Ethics, Duke University. His most recent books are *In Good Company: The Church as Polis* (1996) and *Christians among the Virtues: Theological Conversations* (forthcoming).

David Hollenbach, S.J., is the Margaret O'Brien Flatley Professor of Catholic Theology at Boston College. He is the author of *Justice, Peace, and Human Rights* (1988) and the coeditor with R. Bruce Douglass of *Catholicism and Liberalism: Contributions to American Public Philosophy* (1994).

Albert R. Jonsen is professor and chairman of the Department of Medical History and Ethics, School of Medicine, University of Washington. He is the author of *The New Medicine and the Old Ethics* (1990), and, with Stephen Toulmin, *The Abuse of Casuistry: A History of Moral Reasoning* (1988).

Richard B. Miller is professor of religious studies at Indiana University. His publications include *Interpretations of Conflict: Ethics, Pacifism, and the Just-War Tradition* (1991) and *Casuistry and Modern Ethics: A Poetics of Practical Reasoning* (1996).

James B. Nelson is professor emeritus of Christian ethics at United Theological Seminary of the Twin Cities. His several books include *Body Theology* (1992) and, as coeditor with Sandra P. Longfellow, *Sexuality and the Sacred: Sources for Theological Reflection* (1994).

Douglas F. Ottati is professor of theology and ethics at Union Theological Seminary in Virginia. His most recent books are *Reforming Protestantism: Christian Commitment in Today's World* (1995) and *Jesus Christ and Christian Vision* (1995).

Gene Outka is Dwight Professor of Philosophy and Christian Ethics at Yale University. He is the author of *Agape: An Ethical Analysis*, and most recently, coeditor of and contributor to *Prospects for a Common Morality*.

Stephen J. Pope is associate professor of theology at Boston College. His publications include *The Evolution of Altruism and the Ordering of Love* (1994).

Stephen G. Post is associate director of the Center for Biomedical Ethics in the School of Medicine at Case Western Reserve University and associate professor in the Department of Religion. He is the author of *Spheres of Love: Toward a New Ethics of the Family* (1994) and *The Moral Challenge of Alzheimer Disease* (1995).

William Schweiker is associate professor of theological ethics in the Divinity School at the University of Chicago. He is the author of *Mimetic Reflections: A Study in Hermeneutics, Theology, and Ethics* (1990) and *Responsibility and Christian Ethics* (1995).

William C. Spohn is the John Nobili, S.J., University Professor at Santa Clara University. His publications include *What Are They Saying about Scripture and Ethics?* (rev. ed., 1995).

Cristina L. H. Traina is an assistant professor in the Department of Religion at Northwestern University. She has published articles on sexual and environmental ethics.

Sumner B. Twiss is a professor and chair of the Department of Religious Studies at Brown University. He is coeditor of the *Annual of the Society of Christian Ethics*, a co-chair of Religion and Human Rights Consultation in the American Academy of Religion, and an Elected Fellow in the Institute of Society, Ethics, and the Life Sciences (The Hastings Center). His recent publications include *Religion and Human Rights* (coeditor and contributor, 1994).

Allen Verhey is the Evert J. and Mattie E. Blekkink Professor of Religion at Hope College. He edited *Religion and Medical Ethics: Looking Back, Looking Forward* (1996) and coedited, with Wayne Boulton and Tom Kennedy, *From Christ to the World: Introductory Readings in Christian Ethics* (1994).

LeRoy Walters is the director and Joseph P. Kennedy, Sr., Professor of Christian Ethics, Kennedy Institute of Ethics, and professor of philosophy at Georgetown University. He is the coeditor with Tom L. Beauchamp of *Contemporary Issues in Bioethics*, 4th ed. (1994), and the coeditor with Tamar Joy Kahn of *Bibliography of Bioethics* (22 vols. to date; 1975–1996).

Index

387

context, 196–98; and deduction process, 203; historical development of, 65–66; language of, 197; lexically ordered, 210–11; material norms, 210; and moral absolutes, 61–65; prima facie binding, 211–13; principlism versus casuistry, 198–201; rules of thumb, 210; specification of, 203–9. *See also* normative ethics
moral realism, 84–87
moral rules, Bible as direct source of, 4
Morgan, Edmund S., 276–78
Mornay, Phillippe du Plessis, 47
mortality. *See* death
Mulhall, Stephen, 100–101
Muller, Hermann J., 236, 239
murder. *See* killing
Murdoch, Iris, 327
Murray, John Courtney, 70, 301, 302
myc gene, 158
"Mystery of the Family, The" (Marcel), 266

narratives, 105, 187, 191–92
National Institute on Aging, 162
natural law ethics, 84–85
natural piety, 124–26
naturalism, 126, 174–77
Nelson, J. Robert, 243
Nelson, James B., 269
Neuhaus, Richard John, 304–5, 306
New York Times, 341
Newman, John Henry, 66, 69
Niebuhr, H. Richard, ix; on Christian moral philosophy, 90; credited by Gustafson, 238; on God, 54, 55–56; Gustafson on, 186; on naturalism, 126; on radical faith, 53; on reflexive thinking, 82; on responsiveness, 186; on revelation in Jesus, 51; on self, 121, 125, 186; on trust and loyalty, 126–30
Niebuhr, Reinhold, 52, 300–301, 303, 307
Nietzsche, Friedrich, 76, 106
nominalism, 61
Noonan, John, 65–68
normative ethics, 172–73, 177–80; material norms and absolutism, 210. *See also* moral norms
Novak, Dennis, 201–2
Novak, Michael, 304, 305, 306–7

Nussbaum, Martha, 145
Nygren, Anders, 278

Oecolampadius, John, 47
Ogletree, Thomas, 85
oil production, and rain forest destruction, 340–41
Olevianus, Caspar, 47
On Human Nature (Wilson), 168, 245
"On Marriage" (Clement), 275
On the Appearance of the First Human Beings (Overhage), 237
ontological realism, 316
Oriente, 340–41
Out of the Night: A Biologist's View of the Future (Muller), 236
Outka, Gene, 219, 278–79
Overhage, Paul, 237
Overton, Richard, 48

Pacem in Terris, 302
Pacific Bell, 341
pacifism, 336
paradigm cases, 198–99
Parrinder, Geoffrey, 274
particularism, 94–96; and cultural contingency, 100–108; and Enlightenment, 96–99; fallibilism and, 96–97, 102–3, 108; framework for human rights, 373–74; historical viewpoint, 97–100; and philosophical ethics, 93–96; and sin, 109–10; sites of, 95–96; social identity and, 98; and theological virtues, 110–11; and tradition-dependence, 100–108; and universal relevance, 108–15; and vindication of moral insights, 111–15
Pastoral Constitution on the Church in the Modern World, The (*Gaudium et Spes*), 302
Patient as Person, The (Ramsey), 219, 232, 241
Patton, John, 279
Paul: on early churches and ministry of Jesus, 11–14; Jewish background of, 12–13; on marriage and family, 273–75; on moral discourse, 34; on morality, 14; views on women, 4–5